ORIGINS OF THE JUST WAR

Origins of the Just War

MILITARY ETHICS
AND CULTURE IN THE
ANCIENT NEAR EAST

Rory Cox

PRINCETON UNIVERSITY PRESS
PRINCETON & OXFORD

Copyright © 2023 by Princeton University Press

Princeton University Press is committed to the protection of copyright and the intellectual property our authors entrust to us. Copyright promotes the progress and integrity of knowledge created by humans. By engaging with an authorized copy of this work, you are supporting creators and the global exchange of ideas. As this work is protected by copyright, any reproduction or distribution of it in any form for any purpose requires permission; permission requests should be sent to permissions@press.princeton.edu. Ingestion of any IP for any AI purposes is strictly prohibited.

Published by Princeton University Press
41 William Street, Princeton, New Jersey 08540
99 Banbury Road, Oxford OX2 6JX

press.princeton.edu

GPSR Authorized Representative: Easy Access System Europe - Mustamäe tee 50, 10621 Tallinn, Estonia, gpsr.requests@easproject.com

All Rights Reserved

First paperback printing, 2026
Paperback ISBN 9780691253626

The Library of Congress has cataloged the cloth edition as follows:

Names: Cox, Rory, 1982– author.
Title: Origins of the just war : military culture in the ancient world / Rory Cox.
Description: Princeton : Princeton University Press, [2023] | Includes bibliographical references and index.
Identifiers: LCCN 2022060320 (print) | LCCN 2022060321 (ebook) | ISBN 9780691171890 (hardcover) | ISBN 9780691253619 (ebook)
Subjects: LCSH: Military history, Ancient. | Middle East—History, Military. | Just war doctrine—History. | War (International law)—History. | War—Moral and ethical aspects. | BISAC: HISTORY / Wars & Conflicts / General | PHILOSOPHY / Ethics & Moral Philosophy
Classification: LCC U31 .C69 2023 (print) | LCC U31 (ebook) | DDC 355.0093—dc23/eng/20230504
LC record available at https://lccn.loc.gov/2022060320
LC ebook record available at https://lccn.loc.gov/2022060321

British Library Cataloging-in-Publication Data is available

Editorial: Ben Tate and Josh Drake
Production Editorial: Kathleen Cioffi
Jacket/Cover Design: Drohan DiSanto
Production: Danielle Amatucci
Publicity: William Pagdatoon and Charlotte Coyne

Jacket/Cover image: The Palette of Narmer, circa 3200–3000 BCE.

This book has been composed in Miller

To my light, Melati

CONTENTS

List of Illustrations · ix
Acknowledgements · xiii
List of Abbreviations · xvii
A Note on Names and Places · xix
Maps · xxi

	Introduction	1
CHAPTER 1	The Art of War in the Ancient Near East	32
PART I	EGYPT, C. 3150–C. 1069 BCE	
CHAPTER 2	Egypt: Historical Introduction	59
CHAPTER 3	Egypt: *Ius ad bellum*; Conceptualising Justice and War	85
CHAPTER 4	Egypt: *Ius in bello*; Concepts and Practices	118
PART II	HATTI, C. 1650–C. 1200 BCE	
CHAPTER 5	The Hittites: Historical Introduction	165
CHAPTER 6	Hatti: *Ius ad bellum*; Conceptualising Justice and War	185
CHAPTER 7	Hatti: *Ius in bello*; Concepts and Practices	234
PART III	THE ISRAELITES, C. 1000–C. 450 BCE	
CHAPTER 8	The Israelites: Historical Introduction	269
CHAPTER 9	The Israelites: *Ius ad bellum*; Conceptualising Justice and War	295

CHAPTER 10	The Israelites: *Ius in bello*; Concepts and Practices	343
	Conclusion: The Characteristics of Ancient Just War Thought	413

Appendix 1: Periodic Chronology of Ancient Egypt with Primary Centres of Power · 457

Appendix 2: Internal Narrative Chronology of the Tanakh · 459

Reference Bibliography · 461

Index · 493

ILLUSTRATIONS

Maps

1. Map of Ancient Egypt.	xxi
2. Geography of the Hittite Empire, c. 1350–c. 1300 BCE.	xxii
3. Kingdoms of Samaria/Israel and Judah, c. ninth century BCE.	xxiii

Figures

1. King Narmer/Menes smiting a prisoner of war under the gaze of the gods: Narmer Palette (recto), c. 3100 BCE.	34
2. King Narmer/Menes inspecting rows of bound and decapitated prisoners of war, and a pair of entwined lions, symbolising the unification of Upper and Lower Egypt: Narmer Palette (verso), c. 3100 BCE.	35
3. Egyptian soldiers carrying the regimental standards of the gods: Narmer Palette (verso), c. 3100 BCE.	36
4. Vultures carrying away enemy body parts after a battle: Stele of the Vultures, Sumeria, c. 2500 BCE.	36
5. Ramses II fighting at the battle of Kadesh (c. 1274 BCE): Ramesseum, Egypt, mid-thirteenth century BCE.	39
6. Ramses II fighting from chariots, shooting a bow and arrow, and spearing an enemy chief: Temple at Abu Simbel, Egypt, thirteenth century BCE.	46–47
7. Ramses III depicted as a great archer fighting the Sea Peoples: Temple of Medinet Habu, Eygpt, mid-twelfth century BCE.	48
8. Egyptian model spearmen: grave goods from the tomb of Mesehti at Asyut, Middle Kingdom, c. 2000 BCE.	49
9. Egyptian model spearmen: grave goods from the tomb of Mesehti at Asyut, Middle Kingdom, c. 2000 BCE.	49
10. Seti I (r. c. 1305–c. 1290/c. 1294–c. 1279 BCE) fighting Libyans: Great Hypostyle Hall, Karnak Temple, Egypt, early thirteenth century BCE.	50
11. The massive fortified mud-brick walls of the Fortress of Buhen, Upper Egypt, Middle Kingdom, early second millennium BCE.	53

12. Defensive rampart, Hattuša, mid-second millennium BCE. 54
13. A modern reconstruction of part of Hattuša's fortified ring wall. 54
14. Relief of the goddess Ma'at, with feather crown: Temple of Edfu, Egypt. 67
15. Sheshonq I (r. c. 943–c. 922 BCE) with triumphal list of conquered cities: Bubastite Portal, Karnak Temple, Egypt. 72
16. Egyptian–Hittite Peace Treaty (c. 1259 BCE), Egyptian version: Karnak Temple, Egypt. 82
17. Hittite–Egyptian Peace Treaty (c. 1259 BCE), Hittite version: clay tablet. 83
18. The weighing of a heart (soul) against Ma'at, as symbolised by a feather: Egyptian Book of the Dead. 93
19. Annals of Thutmose III (r. c. 1479–c. 1425 BCE): Karnak Temple, Egypt. 108
20. Piling enemy hands after battle: Temple of Medinet Habu, Egypt, twelfth century BCE. 115
21. Counting enemy hands after battle: Temple of Medinet Habu, Egypt, twelfth century BCE. 115
22. Piling enemy phalli after battle: Temple of Medinet Habu, Egypt, twelfth century BCE. 116
23. Captured Shasu spies being tortured (beaten) and interrogated by Egyptians prior to the battle of Kadesh: Temple at Abu Simbel, Egypt, thirteenth century BCE. 122
24. Thutmose III (c. 1479–c. 1425 BCE) smiting captured enemies: Karnak Temple, Egypt. 126
25. Seti I leads Libyan prisoners of war back to Egypt: Great Hypostyle Hall, Karnak Temple, Egypt, early thirteenth century BCE. 126
26. Bound African prisoners of war: Temple of Abu Simbel, Egypt, thirteenth century BCE. 127
27. Bound Asiatic prisoners of war: Temple of Abu Simbel, Egypt, thirteenth century BCE. 128–129
28. Bound prisoners of war and enemy dead: Battlefield Palette, Egypt, Naqada III period (c. 3300–c. 3100 BCE). 130
29. Impalement: Egyptian hieroglyphic determinative for impalement, Amada stele of Pharaoh Merneptah, late thirteenth century BCE. 137
30. Earliest smiting scene, showing a chief smiting three bound prisoners: wall painting (reproduction) from Tomb 100, Nekhen (Hierakonpolis), c. 3500–c. 3300 BCE. 143

LIST OF ILLUSTRATIONS [xi]

31. Seti I forces enemy chiefs to cut down cedar trees in
    Lebanon: Great Hypostyle Hall, Karnak Temple, Egypt,
    early thirteenth century BCE.   152
32. Bronze tablet recording a treaty between the Hittite king
    Tudhaliya IV and Karunta of Tarhuntašša, c. 1235 BCE.   176
33. Hittite rock shrine of Yazilikaya, above the royal capital of Hattuša.   178
34. Procession of twelve deities carrying weapons: Hittite rock
    shrine of Yazilikaya.   179
35. Tudhaliya IV (r. c. 1237–c. 1228/c. 1227–c. 1209 BCE) before
    the god Šarruma (son of the storm-god Teššub), wearing a
    long sword: Hittite rock shrine of Yazilikaya.   194
36. The 'Apology' of Hattušili III (r. c. 1267–c. 1237 BCE): clay tablet.   217
37. One of the 'Plague Prayers' of Muršili II (r. c. 1321–c. 1295 BCE):
    clay tablet.   226
38. The sky-god killing the dragon Illuyanka: Neo-Hittite, from
    the Lions Gate at Malitiya, c. 850–c. 800 BCE.   242
39. King Jehu of Samaria (r. c. 842–c 815 BCE) pays tribute to
    the Assyrian king Shalmaneser III: the 'Black Obelisk' of
    Shalmaneser III, mid-ninth century BCE.   276
40. The 'Isaiah Wall', New York City.   340
41. Aramean warriors duelling: Palace of Kapara, Tell Halaf,
    c. tenth–ninth century BCE.   354
42. Assyrian soldiers carrying decapitated heads: Palace of
    Nimrud, Assyria, c. 865–c. 860 BCE.   355
43. Assyrian attack on the Egyptian city of Memphis (c. 667 BCE),
    with soldiers carrying decapitated heads: Palace of Nineveh,
    Assyria, c. 645–c. 635 BCE.   356
44. Perseus decapitating Medusa: terracotta pithos, Greek,
    c. 670 BCE.   356
45. Transportation of Lebanese cedar: Palace of the Assyrian
    king Sargon II, at Dur Sharrukin, Assyria, late eighth
    century BCE.   369
46. Assyrian soldiers impaling Judahites outside the city of
    Lachish: Palace of Nineveh, Assyria, c. 700–c. 692 BCE.   375
47. Assyrian soldiers flaying Elamites: Palace of Nineveh,
    Assyria, c. 700–c. 692 BCE.   376
48. Assyrian soldiers amputating prisoners of war, with
    severed heads hanging from city walls: embossed bronze
    band from the Balawat gates, reign of Shalmaneser III
    (r. c. 858–c. 824 BCE), Assyria.   388

ACKNOWLEDGEMENTS

I BEGAN RESEARCH for this book in earnest in late 2014. In any project stretching over such a considerable period of time, one will inevitably incur many debts of gratitude, and not all of them can be listed here. I have benefited from the overwhelming generosity of friends and colleagues, who, despite increasingly busy lives, have willingly given their time to help my work. A huge thank you goes to each and every one of them.

There are a number of people to whom I am especially indebted: people who have provided essential help in shaping and improving my arguments, as well as encouraging me to continue the project over many years of development and gestation. Special thanks go to Cian O'Driscoll, who throughout the course of this project has been an enthusiastic advocate and valued critic. Anyone who knows Cian will be aware that his insights are always thoughtful and incisive, and I have benefited greatly from them. Equally, Tony Lang (whom I'm lucky to count as a colleague at the University of St Andrews) has been unfailingly supportive, reading much of the draft material and offering me his wizardly wisdom. Cian and Tony are not only excellent scholars, they are thoroughly decent human beings and good friends. Thanks to you both.

I am exceedingly grateful to Theo van den Hout of the University of Chicago's renowned Institute for the Study of Ancient Cultures. Professor van den Hout generously agreed to read the entire section on the Hittites and provided detailed feedback and encouragement. To my regret, I have not actually had the opportunity to meet Professor van den Hout in person, yet his actions are testament to the kind of intellectual generosity mentioned above. I am greatly indebted to him.

Nick Rengger, sadly no longer with us, read an early proposal for the book and I always found his eclectic yet detailed knowledge of the ancient and modern worlds to be deeply inspirational. I only wish our conversations could have continued to this day. Throughout my career, meanwhile, I have benefited from the published work and, later, the personal feedback of James Turner Johnson. As ever, his learning and intellectual generosity have aided me throughout my work. Thank you, Jim. A big thank you also to Anthony Black, with whom I have enjoyed many discussions about ancient and medieval political thought and theology, and who also provided me with access to his personal library.

I was fortunate to be able to complete important research and writing during the course of two fellowships. The first was a Wallenberg Fellowship at the University of Stockholm's Centre for the Ethics of War and Peace (June 2016). I am grateful to all the wonderful fellows and guests that I met at the Centre, whose challenging questions (they being for the most part analytical moral philosophers) much improved the way I thought about and presented the ancient material. My special thanks go to the Centre's director, Helen Frowe, with whom it is always great fun to wrangle and whose arguments are always frustratingly persuasive.

The second fellowship was a Caltech-Huntington Humanities Collaboration Fellowship, held at the California Institute for Technology and the Huntington Library, Los Angeles (September 2017–August 2018). I would like to say a huge thank you to Warren Brown, Jennifer Jahner, Leah Klement, Keith Pluymers, Benjamin Saltzman, and Fran Tise for many stimulating conversations and workshops, but most of all for making myself and my family feel so welcome in California. I would like in particular to thank Steve Hindle at the Huntington, and each of the many fellows in residence there over the 2017–18 academic year, as well as the amazing administrative staff. Their personal support to myself and my family during an unexpectedly painful period (following a serious cycling accident) was simply breathtaking, and a true example of human decency. Thank you all from the bottom of my heart, and David and Gobnait O'Shaughnessy especially.

The initial 'test piece' for this book was an article published in *International Studies Quarterly* in 2017, on ancient Egyptian ethics of war. I would like to thank the then-editor of the journal, Daniel Nexon, as well as the anonymous reviewers for supporting an admittedly unusual submission to one of the world's leading international relations journals, and for providing extremely useful feedback. It helped shape how I approached the project going forward.

There are many others who have similarly expanded and inspired my thought about the nature of the just war tradition and the ethics of violence more broadly. Chief among these, I would like to thank William Bain, Daniel Brunstetter, John Emory, John Kelsay, Valerie Morkevičius, Brent Steele, and Hans van Wees. Thanks also to Peter J. Brand at the University of Memphis for kindly allowing me to reproduce some of the images from the excellent Karnak Hypostyle Hall Project.

I am lucky enough to participate in a collegiate culture at the University of St Andrews, across several academic schools. Thank you to Frances Andrews for suggesting Princeton University Press in the first place and for commenting on my initial proposal; also to Ali Ansari, Robert Bartlett, Caroline Humfress, Alice König, Richard Whatmore, Nicholas Wiater, Tim Wilson, and Alex Woolf, for numerous interesting discussions.

Thank you, too, to the whole editorial team at Princeton, including Josh Drake and Kathleen Cioffi, and especially Ben Tate. Not only has Ben been incredibly patient, but he has consistently supported the project even as it evolved into something quite different from that initially proposed. Thanks also to Francis Eaves for his careful copyediting of the manuscript, and to Derek Gottlieb for preparing the index.

Having benefited from so much wisdom and kindness, it goes without saying that any errors in this text are entirely my own.

Most importantly, I want to thank my family. My wonderful children, Elsa and Kaspar, soon figured out a winning strategy for delaying bedtime by posing the question, 'Can you tell us something interesting about history, Dad?' Of course, this challenge is easy to fulfil and difficult to resist. I can only hope that one day, when they are a bit older, they may think it is worthwhile to take this book down from the shelf and read it . . . if only to delay bedtime a little longer. Finally, my deepest expression of gratitude is reserved for my wife, Melati, who is beautiful in so many ways. She is an insightful and honest critic, yet always knows the right thing to say to lift me up when my enthusiasm is waning. She's the love of my life, and it is to her that this book is dedicated.

ABBREVIATIONS

AEL   *Ancient Egyptian Literature: A Book of Readings*, compiled and translated by Miriam Lichtheim, 3 vols (Berkeley: University of California Press, 1973–1980).

ANEA   *The Ancient Near East: An Anthology of Texts and Pictures*, edited by James B. Pritchard, 2 vols (Princeton, NJ: Princeton University Press, 1958–1975).

ANET   *Ancient Near Eastern Texts relating to the Old Testament*, edited by James B. Pritchard, 3rd edn (Princeton, NJ: Princeton University Press, 1969).

AoH   P.H.J. Houwink ten Cate, 'The History of Warfare according to Hittite Sources: The Annals of Hattusilis I (Part II)', *Anatolica* 11 (1984): 47–83.

ARE   *Ancient Records of Egypt: Historical Documents from the Earliest Times to the Persian Conquest*, edited and translated, with commentary, by James Henry Breasted, 5 vols (Chicago: University of Chicago Press, 1906–1907).

CANE   *The Civilizations of the Ancient Near East*, edited by Jack M. Sasson, John Baines, Gary Beckman, and Karen S. Rubinson, 4 vols (Peabody, MA: Hendrickson, 2000).

ERCIL   Amnon Altman, *Tracing the Earliest Recorded Concepts of International Law: The Ancient Near East (2500–330 BCE)* (Leiden: Martinus Nijhoff, 2012).

HDT   Gary Beckman, *Hittite Diplomatic Texts*, edited by Harry A. Hoffner Jr., 2nd edn (Atlanta, GA: Scholars Press, 1999).

HitM   Harry A. Hoffner Jr., *Hittite Myths*, edited by Gary M. Beckman (Atlanta, GA: Scholars Press, 1990).

HitP   Itamar Singer, *Hittite Prayers*, edited by Harry A. Hoffner Jr. (Atlanta, GA: Society of Biblical Literature, 2002).

HST   *The Ancient Near East: Historical Sources in Translation*, edited by Mark W. Chavalas (Malden, MA: Blackwell, 2006).

ILA   David J. Bederman, *International Law in Antiquity* (Cambridge: Cambridge University Press, 2001).

JSB   *The Jewish Study Bible* [Tanakh], edited by Adele Berlin and Marc Zvi Brettler, consulting editor Michael Fishbane, 2nd edn (New York: Oxford University Press/Jewish Publication Society, 2004).

KANE   Amélie Kuhrt, *The Ancient Near East c. 3000–330 BC*, 2 vols (London: Routledge, 1995).

LawH   *The Laws of the Hittites: A Critical Edition*, edited by Harry A. Hoffner Jr. (Leiden: Brill, 1997).

LCMAM   *Law Collections from Mesopotamia and Asia Minor*, edited by Martha T. Roth, with a contribution from Harry A. Hoffner Jr. (Atlanta, GA: Scholars Press, 1995).

LettGK   Trevor Bryce, *Letters of the Great Kings of the Ancient Near East: The Royal Correspondence of the Late Bronze Age* (Abingdon: Routledge, 2003).

LettH   Harry A. Hoffner Jr., *Letters from the Hittite Kingdom*, edited by Gary M. Beckman (Atlanta, GA: Society of Biblical Literature, 2009).

LIR   Mario Liverani, *International Relations in the Ancient Near East, 1600–1100 BC* (Basingstoke: Palgrave Macmillan, 2001).

MHTH   *The Major Historical Texts of Early Hittite History*, edited by Trevor R. Bryce (Brisbane: University of Queensland, 1983).

ToS   *The Tale of Sinuhe and Other Ancient Egyptian Poems 1940–1640 BC*, translated by Robert B. Parkinson (Oxford: Oxford University Press, 2009).

WANE   William J. Hamblin, *Warfare in the Ancient Near East to 1600 BC: Holy Warriors at the Dawn of History* (Abingdon: Routledge, 2006).

WHB   Susan Niditch, *War in the Hebrew Bible: A Study in the Ethics of Violence* (New York: Oxford University Press, 1993).

A NOTE ON NAMES AND PLACES

KEEPING TRACK OF proper nouns can be confusing when dealing with the personages and places of the ancient Near East. Many Egyptian names, for example, have Greek equivalents and also have varying anglicised transliterations. So, a pharaonic name such as Senusret might also appear in the literature as Sesostris or Senwosret, just as Thutmose can appear as Tuthmose, Thuthmosis, Thothmes, or other variants. I have adhered to current scholarly convention, which is to render anglicised transliterations guided by the Egyptian rather than the Greek equivalents: Sunusret and Thutmose rather than Sesostris and Tuthmosis, for example. However, when quoting directly from a scholarly work, I have followed the original author's preference.

For other ancient Near Eastern proper nouns, again, I have adhered to current scholarly conventions as far as possible. So, Hattuša rather than Hattusha, Hattušili rather than Hattushili, and Aššurbanipal rather than Ashurbanipal, and so on. Again, when quoting directly from a scholarly work, I have followed the original author's preference. Finally, all dates are approximate, and all should be read as BCE except where stated otherwise.

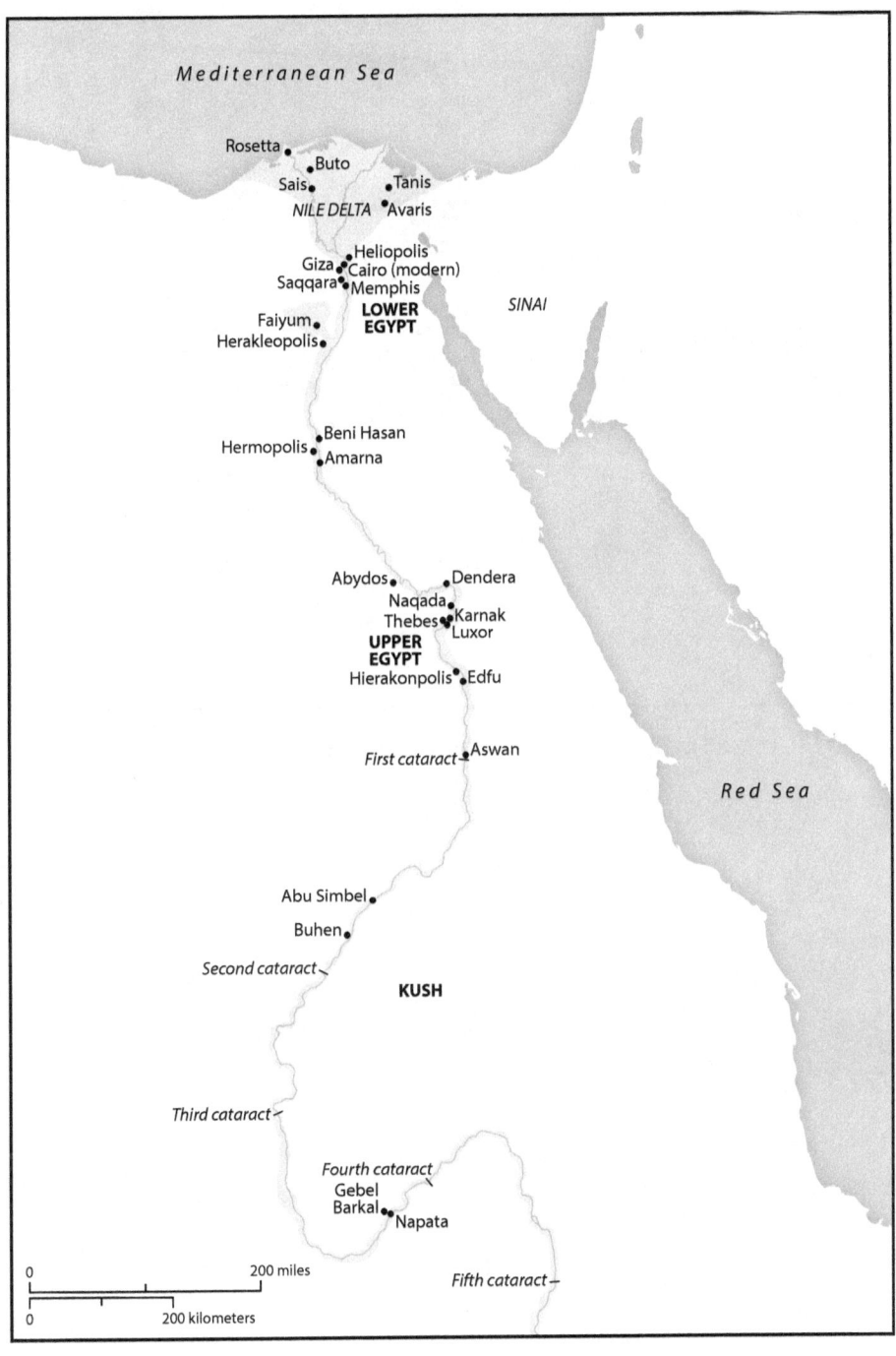

MAP 1. Map of Ancient Egypt

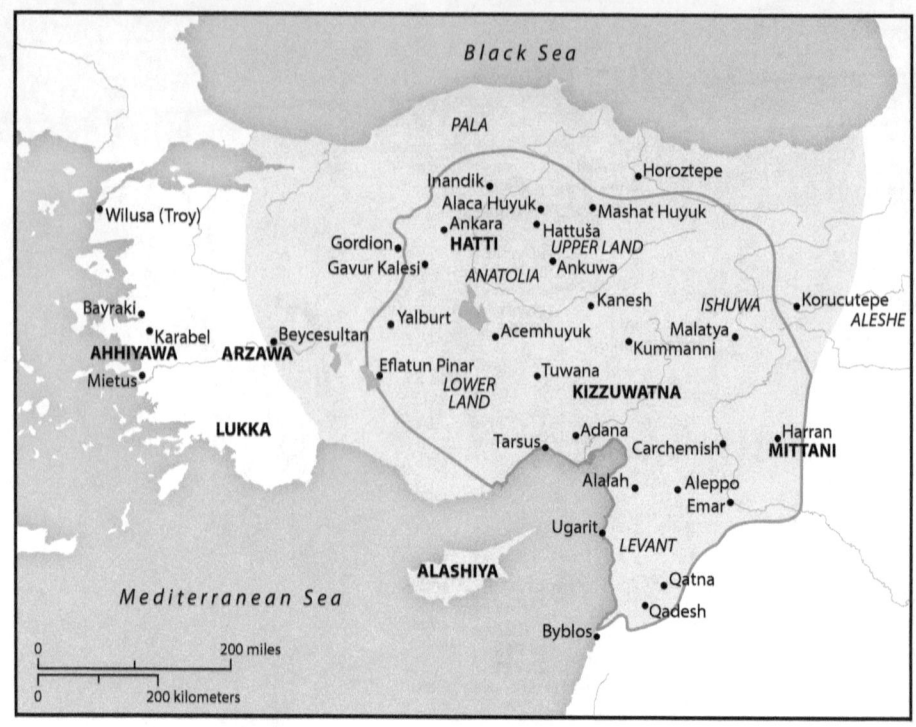

MAP 2. Geography of the Hittite Empire, c. 1350–1300 BCE

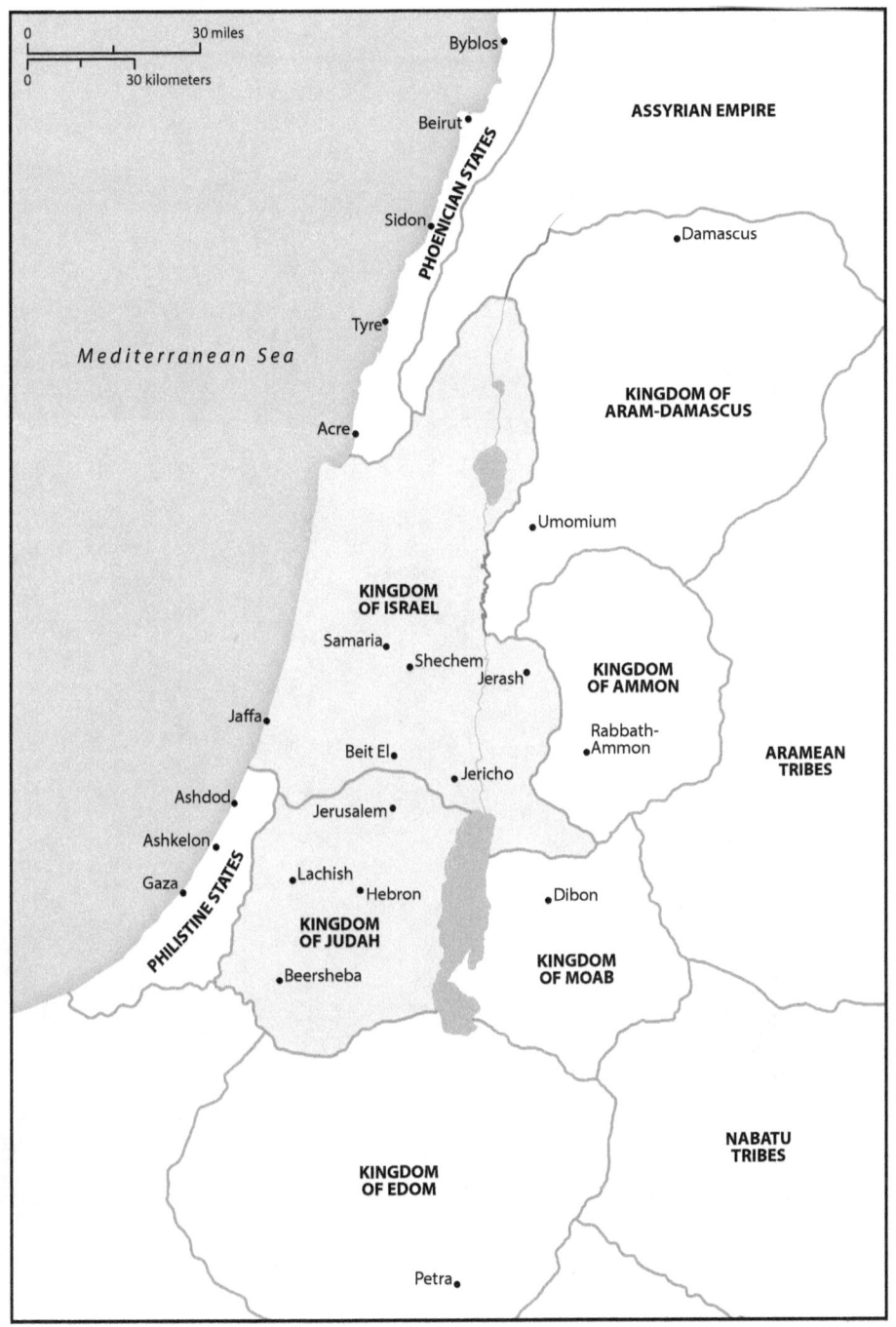

MAP 3. Kingdoms of Samaria/Israel and Judah, c. ninth century BCE

ORIGINS OF THE JUST WAR

INTRODUCTION

THIS BOOK ATTEMPTS to trace the very earliest emergence of ideas concerning the complex, often fraught, relationship between war and ethics. It looks back to more than five thousand years before our modern era, utilising some of the earliest textual evidence that human civilisations have produced, as well as a good deal of material evidence. In it, I push the history of just war thought back into the deep past, revealing the incredible richness and complexity of ethical reflections on war in the three millennia preceding the Greco-Roman period. In doing so, I strive to show that the history of the just war is more geographically diffused and far more ancient than has previously been assumed.

This study is entitled *Origins of the Just War* (rather than, for instance, *The Origin of the Just War*) because I wish to make clear that the ideas examined within it represent a number of *different* origins of ethical thought about war, albeit some of them interconnected and all of them of considerable antiquity. The investigation focuses principally on three ancient martial cultures: Egyptian, Hittite, and Israelite. These cultures flourished between the third and the first millennium BCE, within a single relatively coherent geographical unit referred to as the 'Near East'. This unit composed those lands fringing the eastern Mediterranean seaboard: Egypt, Sinai, Syria-Palestine, and Anatolia.

As will become clear, each of these three ancient Near Eastern societies developed sophisticated ethics of war and distinctive doctrines of just war. However, as will be discussed in depth, the development of just war thought in each society was almost entirely concentrated on what we now term *ius ad bellum* (i.e., justice/right to wage war) criteria, especially considerations of proper authority and just cause. I argue that these ancient *ius ad bellum* doctrines were built on political theologies that were at once both universalising and (to our minds perhaps incongruously) highly chauvinistic. Moreover, these political theologies did not recognise the status of the individual person in the same way that modern societies have come to recognise individual 'rights'.[1] These universalising yet chauvinistic *ius ad bellum* doctrines, which possessed no concern for the welfare of individual enemy persons, were so prepotent that they almost completely inhibited the development of so-called *ius in bello* (i.e., justice/right in the conduct of war) norms. Each of these ancient just war doctrines was grounded in a desire to rationalise, sacralise and, ultimately, to legitimise the act of war, not to restrain it or condemn it. I argue in the Conclusion that, in its presumption in favour of war, ancient just war thought is best described as *ius pro bello*. Further, I posit that a more accurate understanding of the ancient origins of just war thought provides lessons about how we should think about and apply just war theory in a modern context.

Michael Walzer's seminal *Just and Unjust Wars* opens with the remark that '[f]or as long as men and women have talked about war, they have talked about it in terms of right and wrong'.[2] Quite so; and though the chronological starting point for this study is roughly the year 3100,[3] even this deep history is unlikely to represent *the* origin of ethical thought about war. It is highly likely that ethical thought about war significantly predates the late fourth millennium. Indeed, it is likely that ethical thought about war is almost as old as warfare itself. We would do well to remember that non-literate societies are perfectly capable of developing normative ethical systems, and that oral traditions usually contain powerful ideas about right and wrong action. When written texts did begin to emerge in the ancient Near East, the patterns of thought expressed within them did not erupt *ex nihilo*, as if thinking was dependent upon writing. Rather, such texts began to record ideas that had been brewing in oral traditions for centuries, and possibly millennia, beforehand. Such oral traditions continued to contribute to evolving cultural norms as literature gradually evolved.[4] Nor is there any reason to assume that ethical thought about war, when it did emerge, sprouted from a single source, like some gently civilising Hippocrene spring. Thus it is not fitting to speak of *the* origin of the just war. It should rather be recognised that, as various human communities gradually became more complex and increasingly competed for

---

1. One of the best examinations of the early emergence of 'rights' in medieval and early-modern Europe remains Brian Tierney, *The Idea of Natural Rights: Studies on Natural Rights, Natural Law and Church Law 1150–1625* (Atlanta, GA: Scholars Press, 1997).

2. Michael Walzer, *Just and Unjust Wars: A Moral Argument with Historical Illustrations*, 4th edn (New York: Basic Books, 2006), 3.

3. All dates and references to centuries and millennia should be read as BCE unless stated otherwise.

4. As Moses Finley observes of Greco-Roman history: 'the epoch-making invention of literacy was followed for centuries by the survival of a fundamentally oral non-literate society. Man can function reasonably well in a pre-industrial society with little or no use of the written word.' Moses Finley, *Ancient History: Evidence and Models* (1985; repr. London: Pimlico, 2000), 16.

resources, they undoubtedly began thinking about the ramifications of killing and perhaps dying in the service of their community.

While ethical thought about war probably predates the late fourth millennium, the problem for us is one of available evidence, and availability of evidence ultimately constrains all historians. When examining pre-literate societies, or societies which have left no traces of literature (which amounts to much the same thing for modern researchers), it is almost impossible to reconstruct complex religious, ethical, legal, or political thought. Material and iconographic evidence—including sometimes intricate images and carvings of deities, animals, and more—can offer us a glimpse of the nature of ancient beliefs: a sense of what these people valued, perhaps even a sense of what they hoped or feared. But as to the true richness of the cultures and belief systems which produced these artefacts—what Clifford Geertz famously referred to as the 'webs of significance'—we can only really guess.[5] So, while ethical thought and norms concerning violence and warfare may date back to Neolithic, Mesolithic, or even Palaeolithic human communities, the form and content of those traditions and ethics must inevitably remain a mystery. Lacking textual evidence, we are severely constrained as to what we can say about the 'ethics' of such cultures, or what they thought about the myriad cultural, religious, social, and psychological challenges created by large-scale acts of violence.

Principally, this book is intended for just war scholars of all stripes, although it is also for anyone with an interest in the ancient world and its cultures of thought, as well as for those interested in historical international relations or military history more broadly. It engages with the long-standing and extensive debates regarding the history, evolution, purpose, and efficacy of the just war tradition. In demonstrating that sophisticated ethics of war were developed in the ancient world, long before the emergence of Greek philosophers, Roman jurists, or Christian theologians, it hopes to encourage just war scholars to see their subject in deeper chronological terms, as something that is truly ancient, and not a novel creation of the medieval or early modern world. The value of this, I believe, is that by observing just war thought in its infancy—in seeing it emerge inchoate and half-formed—we are better able to analyse its essential objectives and the motivations for its creation. We can do so unemcumbered by the accretion and obfuscation of centuries of polemical moral and legal exposition. If this is correct, then all just war theorists—even philosophers of the moral analytical school—should take note, for arguably we are observing the creation of just war thought from first principles; seeing in 'real time' how it was developed in response to immediate social, cultural, religious, and military exigencies.

5. Clifford Geertz, *The Interpretation of Cultures: Selected Essays* (New York: Basic Books, 1973), 5.

More fundamentally, this study suggests that ethical thought about war is intrinsic to human society and that where complex societies develop, we should also expect complex thought about the ethical qualities of warfare to emerge. In almost every case, I would argue, this ethical reflection will, in some way, seek to legitimise and justify warfare for the sake of preserving or enhancing the existing socio-political order. Thus this book is also intended for anyone interested in the anthropology, sociology, or politics of war, for it shows how the intellectualisation of war is a peculiarity of humans as political animals.

Ultimately, for those interested in the ethics and the social functions of war, this book is intended as a starting point. It reveals where springs of ethical thought about war and violence bubbled to the surface, where they ran off in similar or divergent directions, and where, occasionally, they converged. Although this is a historical study, then, it is written as much for international relations scholars, ethicists, and anthropologists as it is for historians. Just war studies is a lively field of contemporary scholarship, and my hope is that this book will make a substantial contribution by revising a number of conventional assumptions about the origin, purpose, and nature of just war thought.

What I do not offer is a genealogy in simple terms of just war thought.[6] I make no claim for a single source of just war thought or a single 'Ur-concept' of war or justice, to which all other just war doctrines can be traced back. I do not claim to have recovered a single just war tradition which regulated and restrained ancient warfare across cultural, political, or epochal boundaries. Rather, the principal question is whether individual societies of the ancient Near East conceived of such things as 'good' and 'bad' wars in moral or legal terms. In other words, did they think in terms of 'just' and 'unjust' wars? Did they think that war was an activity that was or should be governed by certain ethical or behavioural norms?

First and foremost, I argue that ancient societies did indeed think about war in relation to ethics and justice, and that just war traditions did indeed emerge in the ancient Near East, and can be identified in Egyptian, Hittite, and Israelite culture. In each case, just war traditions were closely tied to claims of political authority, mediated through theological conceptions of how divine power was exercised in the terrestrial world. In each of the societies examined, there are numerous elements of just war thought that bear direct comparison to modern just war traditions: a concern for authority, the conceptualisation of various 'just causes' for war, the importance of punitive and retributive justice, and a recognition that war and peace constitute different legal relationships between states, to name but a few. The possibility that certain elements of these ancient just war traditions influenced the gradual development of

---

6. I use the term 'genealogy' here in the simple sense of a line of descent, not in the sense of a Foucauldian genealogy.

more modern just war thought seems highly plausible; however, as will be discussed, direct connections remain extremely difficult to prove empirically.

Yet the discussion of ancient just war traditions throughout this volume also brings into sharp relief the danger inherent in making absolute distinctions between 'right' and 'wrong' in the international arena. These traditions contain a warning, perhaps, of the potential ramifications of overly confident claims regarding morality or justice in war, and the impact that such claims may have on the conduct of war itself. Ancient Near Eastern warfare was a realm of activity which recognised almost no protections for combatants or non-combatants and witnessed shocking cruelties, and this was unequivocally connected to how violence, justice, and enemy culpability were conceived at a fundamental level. Nonetheless, pragmatism and prudence remained at work in the prosecution of ancient wars. At times, such considerations could even act as a brake on some of the worst ideologically justified excesses.

Structure and Terminology

Beyond the Introduction, chapter 1, and Conclusion, this book is organised into three main parts, each tackling one of the historical case studies in question: Egyptian, Hittite, and Israelite just war thought. As readers will see, each part is made up of three chapters, consisting of a general historical introduction followed by analytical chapters pertaining to thought on war, which I discuss under the broad categories of *ius ad bellum* and *ius in bello*. Complementing chapter 1, which offers a brief overview of the art of war in the ancient Near East, the introductory chapters of each section are intended to provide historical context for the analytical chapters that follow. They offer a concise outline of the key historiographical, geopolitical, and cultural histories of each society, as well as an introduction to the types of sources available to the historian. Needless to say, the introductory discussions of such vast topics are far from exhaustive. Readers already well versed in ancient Near Eastern history, or primarily interested in the conceptual frameworks of just war thought from a modern comparative perspective, may wish to proceed directly to the analytical chapters of each section.

Readers will notice that throughout the volume I have included many quotations from the primary sources (some quite lengthy) as well as a number of images of the outstanding material evidence. In doing so, I wanted to provide the reader with a direct experience of the original sources, and to allow those sources to speak for themselves as much as possible. I hope it will become apparent that the sophisticated ethical concepts discussed throughout the book are not an artificial creation of this author, but rather a faithful rendering of the historical material. All quotations of the Near Eastern material are taken from published translations of the originals. A number of quotations are taken from translations of fragmentary sources, which in the original editions can often include editorial insertions or contested translations. As a rule, I have excised editorial insertions from quotations so as to make the primary sources more readable. If readers are interested in any specific text, I would always refer them to the original scholarly edition, details of which are to be found in the footnotes.

Defining war has proven consistently troublesome, and there remains no real consensus among scholars as to what war *is*. Needless to say, the conceptual challenges become greater still when attempting to define violence more broadly.[7] The problem of definition is exacerbated when thinking across cultures or across large expanses of time, for a definition that may appear capable of describing ancient warfare may fail to describe industrialised modern warfare.[8] A satisfactory universal definition becomes yet more elusive when thinking across academic disciplines, for the assumptions and interests of various disciplinary approaches will inevitably focus on differing elements that constitute the complex phenomenon of war, thereby generating contrasting definitions.

I understand war to be *organised armed conflict between distinct and exogenously and/or endogenously recognised groups*. This definition is broad enough to encompass most disciplinary interests in war as well as encompassing forms of warfare that have traditionally been termed 'primitive'.[9] It accepts the possibility that some feuds can attain the status of war, *if* such violence is sufficiently organised and the opposing groups are recognised as distinctive communities. It also encompasses civil war, which involves the creation of two (or more) competing communities within a single polity, with such groups achieving some

---

7. The literature on violence is vast, but some attempts across disciplines to trace a history of violence include: Philip L. Walker, 'A Bioarchaeological Perspective on the History of Violence', *Annual Review of Anthropology* 30 (2001): 573–96; Warren C. Brown, *Violence in Medieval Europe* (New York: Longman, 2011); Steven Pinker, *The Better Angels of Our Nature: A History of Violence and Humanity* (London: Penguin, 2011); Robert Muchembled, *A History of Violence: From the End of the Middle Ages to the Present* (Cambridge: Polity, 2012); Andrew Linklater, *Violence and Civilization in the Western States Systems* (Cambridge: Cambridge University Press, 2017); Philip Dwyer, 'Violence and Its Histories: Meanings, Methods, Problems', *History and Theory* 56 (4) (2017): 7–22.

8. For definitions of ancient warfare, see James A. Aho, *Religious Mythology and the Art of War: Comparative Religious Symbolisms of Military Violence* (Westport, CT: Greenwood Press, 1981), 3–4; *LIR*, 108; Ronald Cohen, 'Warfare and State Formation: Wars Make States and States Make Wars', in *Warfare, Culture, and Environment*, ed. R. Brian Ferguson (Orlando, FL: Academic Press, 1984), 329–58 at 330. See also Wright's 'dual' definitions of war: Quincy Wright, *A Study of War*, 2nd edn, 2 vols (1942; repr. Chicago: University of Chicago Press, 1965), 1:8.

9. For example, Joseph Schneider argues that primitive warfare is a form 'of crime and punishment within populations where systems of public justice are undeveloped. That is not war.' Joseph Schneider, 'Primitive Warfare: A Methodological Note', *American Sociological Review* 15 (6) (1950): 772–77 at 777. However, Schneider's characterisation of primitive warfare would undeniably include much armed conflict up to the early modern period (and indeed beyond it), and thus appears overly restrictive and too greatly influenced by twentieth-century Western assumptions about the role of the state.

degree of endogenous and/or exogenous recognition.[10] The definition is also flexible enough to include different scales of conflict. It may take only two to tango, as they say, but it takes considerably more than two people to wage war. War is a social activity and takes place on a grand scale. However, scale is relative. We should not dismiss the potential trauma of what might appear to us as 'small' conflicts when, in fact, such conflicts represented a major commitment and risk of human resources for the communities involved. Finally, the definition is intended to be narrow enough to preclude elements such as propaganda or other forms of psychological warfare as *independently* meriting the identification of 'war'.[11] By the definition offered above, a propaganda campaign alone is not sufficient to be defined as war; it fully comprehends, however, that such aspects of hostility usually accompany armed conflict. Indeed, for the purposes of investigating the ethics of war, sources that could easily be described as propagandistic—monumental architecture, royal annals, campaign reports, poems and prayers—provide much of the historical evidence.

As I use the term, 'just war thought' refers broadly to ideas that posit or assume a relationship between war and ethics—in the simplest sense, that war can be either 'good' or 'bad' under certain circumstances. (Of course, many different things could constitute what was thought of as 'good' or 'bad'.) As just war thought became more sophisticated, the sense of war being 'good' or 'bad' increasingly implied a working relationship between war and justice, in that war could be both an expression of and a tool for justice or injustice.[12] Just war thought also refers to customs, obligations, or laws pertaining to normative behaviour in the conduct of warfare: that is, the expectation that fighting wars be a rule-bound activity and not simply an exercise in unrestrained violence.[13]

---

10. Stathis Kalyvas, who provides a particularly thorough analysis of civil war, defines it as 'armed combat within the boundaries of a recognized sovereign entity between parties subject to a common authority at the outset of the hostilities'. Stathis N. Kalyvas, *The Logic of Violence in Civil War* (New York: Cambridge University Press, 2006), 5.

11. In a contemporary context, this could also include 'cyber warfare'.

12. Just war thought thus excludes notions of pacifism, which posit that there can be no working relationship between war and justice, with absolute pacifism holding that war is manifestly immoral and universally antithetical to justice. The literature on pacifism is extensive, but an excellent comparison between historical and contemporary pacifism and just war thought can be found in Jenny Teichman, *Pacifism and the Just War: A Study in Applied Philosophy* (Oxford: Blackwell, 1986). See also Peter Brock, *A Brief History of Pacifism, from Jesus to Tolstoy* (Toronto: Syracuse University Press, 1992).

13. Of course, we should not necessarily assume that the existence of 'rules' in an international system actually reduces violence, and even a rule-based system can encourage violence. See, inter alia, Anthony F. Lang Jr., 'Rules and International Security: Dilemmas of a New World Order', in *War, Torture and Terrorism: Rethinking the Rules of International Security*, ed. Anthony F. Lang Jr. and Amanda Russell Beattie (Abingdon: Routledge, 2009), 1–22. Equally, Maja Zehfuss has argued that a commitment to 'ethical war' in modern international relations has actually enhanced international violence: Maja Zehfuss, *War and the Politics of Ethics* (Oxford: Oxford University Press, 2018).

Throughout this volume I generally prefer the term 'just war thought' to 'just war tradition'. This is because it remains to be seen, as the chapters that follow examine, whether we can reasonably describe ancient Near Eastern just war thought as constituting a 'tradition' (or multiple 'traditions'). The most influential modern commentator on the character and composition of the historical just war tradition being James Turner Johnson, it makes sense to refer to his concept of what is meant by the *tradition* of just war. Johnson conceives moral values and traditions in the following manner:

> My own understanding of the nature of moral values is that they are known through identification with historical communities, while moral traditions represent the continuity through time of such communal identification.[14]

While noting that there is much elision between the terms 'just war theory' and 'just war tradition', Johnson prefers the latter, because a *theory* implies a level of singularity which masks the varied contexts, languages, and interpretations of just war thought as a whole. Despite these divergences, 'what is remarkable is how much agreement exists among theorists who have written on the restraint of war, operating out of their own creativity at sometimes widely separated moments in time. Such agreement makes it meaningful to speak of a just war *tradition*, if not a just war *theory*.'[15] Since the Middle Ages, this tradition has included areas of thought and practices that can be loosely grouped into the dual categories of *ius ad bellum* (justice/right to wage war) and *ius in bello* (justice/right in the conduct of war). It should be noted, however, that the relationship between these *ad bellum* and *in bello* categories is far from unproblematic, and throughout the medieval period and later, elements from each were conflated with one another or entirely disregarded.

At the heart of Johnson's conceptualisation of the tradition is the notion of a continuous 'historical stream of moral reflection on war', into which the historically informed ethicist can enter.[16] Johnson has defended the merits of approaching the just war as a historically embedded tradition which continues to have relevance for contemporary just war studies precisely *because of*

---

14. James Turner Johnson, *Just War Tradition and the Restraint of War: A Moral and Historical Inquiry* (Princeton, NJ: Princeton University Press, 1981), x.

15. Ibid., xxi, xxii–xxiii. For an insightful overview and critique of Johnson's concept of tradition and just war, see Anthony F. Lang Jr., 'The Just War Tradition and the Question of Authority', *Journal of Military Ethics* 8 (3) (2008): 202–16.

16. James Turner Johnson, 'Thinking Morally about War in the Middle Ages and Today', in *Ethics, Nationalism, and Just War: Medieval and Contemporary Perspectives*, ed. Henrik Syse and Gregory M. Reichberg (Washington, DC: Catholic University of America Press, 2007), 1–10 at 4. Johnson's approach has been described as 'an historical hermeneutics of just war'. Cian O'Driscoll, 'Hedgehog or Fox? An Essay on James Turner Johnson's View of History', *Journal of Military Ethics* 8 (3) (2009): 165–78 at 167.

its historical character. He maintains that to comprehend the language of just war and the concepts underlying it, theorists must enter 'into a stream of reflection, debate, and dialogue as it has developed over history'.[17] Only then can it usefully be applied to contemporary problems. I support Johnson's insistence on the importance of approaching just war thought from a historical perspective. I am also inclined to agree on the continuing value of historical just war thought to contemporary debate.

Nevertheless, I am uncomfortable with the notion that thinkers within a tradition of thought enter into a 'dialogue' with one another. The problem with this image is that it bestows agency on *both* speakers. In reality, when we read and interpret the works of dead (or possibly even living) authors we are engaged not in a dialogue but in a monologue. Our interpretation of their thoughts is one-sided, and being dead they do not have the luxury to respond, refute, correct, or agree. So, whilst commentators have clearly engaged with the thought of their historical predecessors, it is perhaps better to think of this in terms of 'acts of translation of past concepts into contemporary theoretical languages', as Ian Hall describes it, rather than an active 'dialogue' in which both parties contribute equally.[18] As a general rule, Patrick Curry's assertion that '[t]raditions only exist in so far as they are continually re-invented and reconstructed by the historical participants', strikes me as correct.[19]

Historiography and Methodology

In a stimulating interdisciplinary work, Vilho Harle argues that 'to contribute to the current needs of intercivilizational communication and understanding, peace and international studies must break out of the jail of conventional academic borders and pay more attention to ancient and non-European worlds'.[20] This study is rooted in a similar conviction, that a move away from canonical texts is a necessary and fruitful enterprise when thinking about the history of ethics and war.

Arguably, just war studies has been hindered by a tendency to indulge in two prejudices. The first is a tendency to ignore historical evidence prior to (at best) classical Athens or (at worst) the rise of Christianity. Ancient states have typically been viewed as primitive and living in a constantly warlike condition, thus incapable of sophisticated ethical or legal thought about war or

17. Johnson, 'Thinking Morally about War', 9.
18. Ian Hall, 'The History of International Thought and International Relations Theory: From Context to Interpretation', *International Relations* 31 (3) (2017): 241–60 at 254–55.
19. Patrick Curry, 'Introduction', in *Astrology, Science and Society: Historical Essays*, ed. Patrick Curry (Woodbridge: Boydell, 1987), 1–4 at 4.
20. Vilho Harle, *Ideas of Social Order in the Ancient World* (Westport, CT: Greenwood Press, 1998), xiv.

international relations.[21] So we read that while the 'modern world considers the natural condition of life in our society to be the state of peace [...] in the ancient world, generally, the natural attitude of one state towards another was that of potential and actual enmity. Hence, war, not peace, was the foundation of international relations'.[22] This narrative has been reinforced by the influential (albeit historically problematic) sociological and psychological studies of Norbert Elias and Steven Pinker, both of whom convey a theory of the gradual pacification of society and the 'human condition' over time.[23]

Fortunately, however, there has been an increasing appetite to consider the just war tradition in a longer diachronic view. The contributions of pre-Christian authors such as Thucydides, Plato, Aristotle, Xenophon, and Cicero have become more commonly acknowledged, although sustained analysis of pre-Christian just war thought remains limited.[24] This recognition is nevertheless

21. For a summary of these attitudes, see *ILA*, 11–13; *ERCIL*, xxiii–xxiv.

22. Michael I. Rostovtseff, 'International Relations in the Ancient World', in *The History and Nature of International Relations*, ed. Edmund A. Walsh (New York: Macmillan, 1922; repr. Miami: HardPress Publishing, 2013), 31–65 at 35; cf. J. L. Holzgrefe, 'The Origins of Modern International Relations Theory', *Review of International Studies* 15 (1) (1989): 11–26. See also Wright, *Study of War*, 1:155; *ILA*, 12–17, 52; *LIR*, 1; Harle, *Ideas of Social Order*, xvi–xvii.

23. Norbert Elias, *The Civilising Process: Sociogenetic and Psychogenetic Investigations*, trans. Edmund Jephcott, revised edn, ed. Eric Dunning, Johan Goudsblom, and Stephen Mennell (Malden, MA: Blackwell, 2000); Pinker, *Better Angels*. For a recent powerful critique of the 'pacification thesis', see Philip G. Dwyer and Marc S. Micale (eds), *The Darker Angels of Our Nature: Refuting the Pinker Theory of History and Violence* (London: Bloomsbury, 2021).

24. See Josiah Ober, 'Classical Greek Times', in *The Laws of War: Constraints on Warfare in the Western World*, ed. Michael Howard, George J. Andreopoulos, and Mark R. Shulman (New Haven, CT: Yale University Press, 1994), 12–26; Ober, 'The Rules of War in Classical Greece', in Josiah Ober, *The Athenian Revolution: Essays on Ancient Greek Democracy and Political Theory* (Princeton, NJ: Princeton University Press, 1996), 53–71; Stephen Neff, *War and the Law of Nations: A General History* (Cambridge: Cambridge University Press, 2005), 13–38; Alex Bellamy, *Just Wars: From Cicero to Iraq* (Cambridge: Polity, 2006): 15–114; Gregory M. Reichberg, Henrik Syse, and Endre Begby (eds), *The Ethics of War: Classic and Contemporary Readings* (Oxford: Blackwell, 2006), 3–59; Richard Sorabji, 'Just War from Ancient Origins to the Conquistadors Debate and its Modern Relevance', in *The Ethics of War: Shared Problems in Different Traditions*, ed. Richard Sorabji and David Rodin (Aldershot: Ashgate, 2006), 13–29 at 13–15; Adriaan Lanni, 'The Laws of War in Ancient Greece', *Law and History Review* 26 (3) (2008): 469–89; Gregory A. Raymond, 'The Greco-Roman Roots of the Just War Tradition', in *The Prism of Just War: Asian and Western Perspectives on the Legitimate Use of Military Force*, ed. Howard M. Hensel (Farnham: Ashgate, 2010), 7–28; Henrik Syse, 'The Platonic Roots of Just War Doctrine: A Reading of Plato's *Republic*', *Diametros* 23 (2010): 104–23; Hans van Wees, 'Defeat and Destruction: The Ethics of Ancient Greek Warfare', in *'Böser Krieg': Exzessive Gewalt in der antiken Kriegsführung und Strategien zu deren Vermeidung*, ed. Margit Linder and Sabine Tausend (Graz: Grazer Universitätsverlag, 2011), 69–110; Josiah Ober and Tomer Perry, 'Thucydides as a Prospect Theorist', *Polis: Journal for Ancient Greek Political Thought* 31

a good starting point for a more holistic understanding of the constitutive elements and deeper history of just war thought.[25] Yet there has been little appetite to look further abroad—chronology or geographically—than classical Rome or Greece, the latter of which is seen as something of a *terminus post quem*. Thus even those studies which give attention to Greco-Roman culture, or think about the common roots of the Western and Islamic just war traditions, do nothing to crack the facade of the just war as a distinctly post-classical and predominantly Western system of thought. Happily, there has been some excellent comparative work in the fields of ancient international relations and legal history, of which studies by David Bederman, Mario Liverani, Amnon Altman, and Iver Neumann and Einar Wigen are particularly valuable.[26]

The second predjudicial tendency is an undeniable streak of Eurocentrism, bolstered by the close relationship between academic just war studies and political theory. In the West, the tradition of political theory has long assumed the superiority of Greco-Roman and Christian philosophy, theology, and jurisprudence. As a result, the just war is 'widely regarded as an artifact of Christian political theology' and thus 'the alleged property of Christians'.[27] The heroising of the classical Western tradition of political philosophy by thinkers such as Leo Strauss, Eric Voegelin, and Hannah Arendt (among others) proved itself so persuasive and pervasive because in many ways it simply built upon assumptions that were already ingrained within the Western intellectual consciousness.[28] It is surely no coincidence that the accepted genealogy of the

---

(2014): 206–32; Cian O'Driscoll, 'Rewriting the Just War Tradition: Just War in Classical Greek Political Thought and Practice', *International Studies Quarterly* 59 (1) (2015): 1–10; O'Driscoll, 'Keeping Tradition Alive: Just War and Historical Imagination', *Journal of Global Security Studies* 3 (2) (2018): 234–47; Rory Cox, 'The Ethics of War up to Thomas Aquinas', in *The Oxford Handbook of Ethics of War*, ed. Seth Lazar and Helen Frowe (New York: Oxford University Press, 2018), 99–108.

25. See, for example: Frederick H. Russell, *The Just War in the Middle Ages* (Cambridge: Cambridge University Press, 1975), 3–15; Nicholas Rengger, 'On the Just War Tradition in the Twenty-First Century', *International Affairs* 78 (2) (2002): 353–63 at 353–54; Mark Evans, 'Moral Theory and the Idea of a Just War', in *Just War Theory: A Reappraisal*, ed. Mark Evans (Edinburgh: Edinburgh University Press, 2005), 1–21 at 1–6; Charles Guthrie and Michael Quinlan, *Just War: The Just War Tradition: Ethics in Modern Warfare* (London: Bloomsbury, 2007), 5–9; Nicholas Fotion, *War and Ethics: A New Just War Theory* (London: Continuum, 2007), 9; Bellamy, *Just Wars*, 15–114.

26. *LIR*; *ILA*; *ERCIL*; Iver B. Neumann and Einar Wigen, *The Steppe Tradition in International Relations: Russians, Turks and European State Building 4000 BCE–2018 CE* (Cambridge: Cambridge University Press, 2018).

27. Anthony F. Lang Jr. and Cian O'Driscoll, 'Introduction: The Just War Tradition and the Practice of Political Authority', in *Just War: Authority, Tradition, and Practice*, ed. Anthony F. Lang Jr., Cian O'Driscoll, and John Williams (Washington, DC: Georgetown University Press, 2013), 1–16 at 6.

28. For an outline of this paradigmatic 'tradition', see John G. Gunnell, *Political Theory: Tradition and Interpretation* (Lanham, MD: University Press of America, 1987);

just war tradition could appear, Janus-like, as a genealogy of political thought. Take John Gunnell's description of the hallmarks of this 'tradition' of political theory:

> Most important is the assumption that the conventional chronology of classic works (including at least those of Plato, Aristotle, St. Augustine, St. Thomas Aquinas, Machiavelli, Hobbes, Locke, Rousseau, and Marx) is the product of a distinct activity and constitutes a definite tradition of inquiry extending well over two millennia.[29]

With the exception of Marx, this list of authorities reads like a list of celebrities within the just war tradition. While we should not be surprised that thinkers interested in political theory should also be interested in the relationship between states, justice, and war, this intimate association between the dual traditions of political theory and just war has encouraged a dependence on a relatively restricted canon of sources. Moreover, just war scholars do not have to strive to persuade those working outside their field that thinkers such as Plato, Augustine, Aquinas, Hobbes, or Rousseau are worth taking seriously, because such *auctores* are already taken seriously: they are *authorities*.[30] As one colleague eloquently put it in response to the aforementioned 'accusations', just war scholars have been guilty of the 'hermeneutic fallacy of availability [. . .]. That is to say, we have written histories of the just war tradition based only on the bookshelf that we have easiest access to.'[31]

Since the work of Alfred Vanderpol in the early twentieth century, and cemented by the highly influential contributions of Paul Ramsey a generation later, modern academic studies of just war have often sought to address the subject from the perspective of Catholic or Protestant Christian ethics, even when not explicity acknowledged in such terms.[32] Even as the literature on the ethics of war became increasingly secularised—most notably with the

---

R.B.J. Walker, *Inside/Outside: International Relations as Political Theory* (Cambridge: Cambridge University Press, 1993), 26ff.

29. Gunnell, *Political Theory*, 34.

30. On the lasting importance of authority within modern just war thought, see the collected essays in Anthony F. Lang Jr., Cian O'Driscoll, and John Williams (eds), *Just War: Authority, Tradition, and Practice* (Washington, DC: Georgetown University Press, 2013).

31. This particular colleague thought it safer to remain anonymous.

32. Vanderpol bemoaned the ignorance of his contemporaries regarding the historical Christian just war tradition and fervently believed in its continuing relevance for modern international relations: 'Généralement ils l'ignorent complètement; ils ne se doutent même pas qu'elle existe, et qu'un retour à cette doctrine constituerait un immense progrès sur l'état actuel des relations internationales.' Alfred Vanderpol, *La Doctrine scolastique du droit de guerre* (Paris: A. Pedone, 1919), 2. See also P. Batiffol, P. Monceaux, E. Chénon, A. Vanderpol, L. Rolland, F. Duval, and A. Tanquerey, *L'Église et le droit de guerre* (Paris: Bloud and Gay, 1920); Paul Ramsey, *War and the Christian Conscience: How Shall Modern War Be Conducted Justly?* (Durham, NC: Duke University Press, 1961); Ramsey, *The*

philosophical revitalisation of the field sparked by Walzer's *Just and Unjust Wars* (1977) and the emergence of the determinedly anti-historical 'revisionist school' of just war theory—such discussions are arguably embedded in essentially Eurocentric and Judeo-Christian cultural assumptions.[33]

No other scholar has done more to stress the importance of the *history* of just war thought than James Turner Johnson, who has repeatedly—and influentially—argued for the necessity of understanding the just war as a historical tradition. Only by contextualising the conceptual categories and language of the just war, maintains Johnson, can we fully grapple with its meaning and its possible relevance to real-world politics.[34] He has acknowledged the pre-Christian roots of just war thought (by which he means the Greco-Roman and/or Hebrew tradition), but maintains that 'just war doctrine proper owes its early development to Christian theologians and canonists'.[35] More specifically, Johnson associates this genesis with the medieval and early modern interpretation of excerpts from the writings of authorities such as Augustine, alongside the roughly contemporaneous emergence of a secular law of arms associated with the nebulous ethos of chivalry. It was the coalescence of these religious and secular strains of thought and practice around 1400–1500 CE that gave birth to what Johnson recognises as a mature just war doctrine.[36]

The Eurocentric and Christian-centric analysis of just war thought and norms has created a narrative of the just war in which non-Western histories

---

Just War: Force and Political Responsibility (1968; repr. Lanham, MD: University Press of America, 1983).

33. For further discussion of revisionist literature, see Conclusion below, 'Lessons from the Earliest Just War Traditions'. For major contributions to revisionist just war theory, see David Rodin, *War and Self-Defense* (Oxford: Oxford University Press, 2002); Jeff McMahan, *Killing in War* (Oxford: Oxford University Press, 2009); Seth Lazar, 'Responsibility, Risk, and Killing in Self-Defense', *Ethics* 119 (4) (2009): 699–728; Cécile Fabre, *Cosmopolitan War* (Oxford: Oxford University Press, 2011); Helen Frowe, *Defensive Killing* (Oxford: Oxford University Press, 2011).

34. James Turner Johnson's *oeuvre* on the ethics of war is extensive, but for the major contributions, see: *Ideology, Reason, and the Limitation of War: Religious and Secular Concepts 1200–1740* (Princeton, NJ: Princeton University Press, 1975); *Just War Tradition; Can Modern War be Just?* (New Haven, CT: Yale University Press, 1984); *The Quest for Peace: Three Moral Traditions in Western Cultural History* (Princeton, NJ: Princeton University Press, 1987); *Morality and Contemporary Warfare* (New Haven, CT: Yale University Press, 1999); *Ethics and the Use of Force: Just War in Historical Perspective* (Farnham: Ashgate, 2011). See also the articles in Cian O'Driscoll (ed.), *James Turner Johnson and the Recovery of the Just War Tradition*, special issue of *Journal of Military Ethics* 8 (3) (2008): 163–262.

35. Johnson, *Just War Tradition*, xxiv.

36. See, inter alia, Johnson, *Ideology, Reason, and the Limitation of War*; Johnson, 'Thinking Morally about War', 10; Johnson, 'St. Augustine (354–430 CE)', in *Just War Thinkers: From Cicero to the 21st Century*, ed. Daniel R. Brunstetter and Cian O'Driscoll (Abingdon: Routledge, 2018), 21–33.

have little part to play. This has funnelled just war studies down a relatively narrow channel. One can refer to a huge number of publications devoted to analysing a reasonably small canon of works within the so-called Western just war tradition, while other non-canonical works and cultures of just war thought have lingered in comparative obscurity. So Gunnell's critique of the 'myth of the tradition' of political theory and an over-reliance on 'a basic repertoire of works' might equally apply to contemporary assumptions about the just war tradition.[37]

This Eurocentric and Christian-centric tendency is revealed as all the more inadequate when one thinks about the intellectual foundations of Christian thought itself. When Augustine searched for intellectual and spiritual authorities for legitimising warfare, he not only depended on Cicero (via Saint Ambrose) but on the Vulgate Old Testament. This, of course, was derived directly from the Greek Septuagint and ultimately from the Hebrew Bible or, to give it its Hebrew name, the Tanakh. This rich and complicated compilation of texts, which will be the subject of Part III below, was already coalescing into a recognisable whole well before Plato had even been born; and, as we shall see, sophisticated ethical thought about justice and war had been developing in the Near East for at least two thousand years prior to that. Equally puzzling is that, while most just war scholars identify Saint Augustine as the 'father of the just war tradition', the north African origins and context of Augustine himself are rarely acknowledged.[38]

---

37. Gunnell, *Political Theory*, 68; cf. ibid., 85–90. In a similar vein, Robert Walker has cautioned against the prescriptive and constrictive effects of academically dominant intellectual traditions: 'References to a tradition of international relations theory are by no means innocent [. . .]. [A]ccounts of a tradition serve to legitimise and circumscribe what counts as proper scholarship.' Walker, *Inside/Outside*, 29.

38. Augustine was born in Thagaste, modern Souk Ahras, in Algeria; he later became bishop of Hippo Regius, modern Annaba, Algeria. The superlative biography remains Peter Brown, *Augustine of Hippo: A Biography* (Berkeley: University of California Press, 1969). For Augustine as the 'father' of the just war tradition, see Arthur Nussbaum, 'Just War: A Legal Concept?', *Michigan Law Review* 42 (1943) (3): 453–79 at 455; Georges Hubrecht, 'La "Juste Guerre" dans le Décret de Gratien', in *Studia Gratiani, Volume 3*, ed. Jos Forschielli and Alph M. Stickler (Bologna: Institutum Gratianum, 1955), 160–77 at 163, 166–67; Johnson, *Just War Tradition*, xxiv; Russell, *Just War*, 16; William V. O'Brien, *The Conduct of Just and Limited War* (New York: Praeger, 1981), 4; Jonathan Barnes, 'The Just War', in *The Cambridge History of Later Medieval Philosophy: From the Rediscovery of Aristotle to the Disintegration of Scholasticism 1100–1600*, ed. Norman Kretzmann, Anthony Kenny, and Jan Pinborg (Cambridge: Cambridge University Press, 1982), 771–84 at 771; Jean Bethke Elshtain, *Just War Against Terror: The Burden of American Power in a Violent World* (New York: Basic Books, 2004), 49–50; John Mark Mattox, *Saint Augustine and the Theory of Just War* (London: Continuum, 2006), 14; Lang, 'Just War Tradition', 202–3; Gregory M. Reichberg, 'Jus ad bellum', in *War: Essays in Political Philosophy*, ed. Larry May (New York: Cambridge University Press, 2008), 11–29 at 12–13; David D. Corey and J. Daryl Charles, *The Just War Tradition: An Introduction* (Wilmington, DE:

An exception to this trend is the considerable body of work devoted to the ancient Israelite military tradition, albeit the bulk of this work has been undertaken as an extension of Christian hermeneutics by scholars working in the fields of theology and biblical history. This literature will be discussed at length in Part III, but it is worth noting here that a good deal of biblical scholarship on the topic of war has been steered by theological hermeneutics and doctrinal commitments. Whether such treatments proceed by seeking to identify a holistically consistent ethic of war that is in fact difficult to detect in the primary sources, or by seeking to 'reveal' biblical norms palatable to modern theological or evangelical requirements and sensibilities, they must be approached with caution.[39] These treatments typically conceive ancient Israelite attitudes to warfare—particularly the depiction of Yahweh as an uncompromising and frequently savage god of war—as a hermeneutical problem to be overcome by modern believers who find such attitudes incompatible with their own faith.[40]

The unwelcome upshot of all this is that the presentation of the just war as an intrinsically Christian doctrine 'curtails its appeal in parts of the world that historically have no affinity with Christianity', as Cian O'Driscoll has shrewdly observed.[41] Given the central influence of just war thought on modern international law generally, and the laws of armed conflict specifically, the negative effects of mischaracterising the history of the just war tradition, although difficult to gauge, should not be underestimated. It is perhaps not too outlandish to suggest that such mischaracterisations potentially hinder attempts to forge a global consensus pertaining to the limitation of war. Establishing that

---

ISI Books, 2012), 10. I have argued elsewhere that Saint Augustine does not really deserve the title of 'father of the just war tradition' that most scholars are happy to bestow upon him. I believe that the present study further strengthens this claim. See Rory Cox, 'Gratian (circa 12th century)', in *Just War Thinkers: From Cicero to the 21st Century*, ed. Daniel R. Brunstetter and Cian O'Driscoll (Abingdon: Routledge, 2018), 34–49.

39. A typical example of this approach is that of Tremper Longman and Daniel Reid, who state, '[W]e approach the Bible as an organic whole [. . .]. [I]n the final analysis we treat the Old Testament, even the Bible as a whole, as a single writing that presents an internally consistent message, including an internally consistent, yet unfolding picture of God as a warrior. [. . .] [F]or us the basic ground is a theological one based on the self-attestation of Scripture that leads us to an evangelical hermeneutic.' Tremper Longman III and Daniel G. Reid, *God is a Warrior* (Grand Rapids, MI: Zondervan, 1995), 26–27. The authors are thus willing to prioritise doctrinal 'internal consistency' over the evidence of the text itself, for example: ibid., 33.

40. For example: A. Gelston, 'The Wars of Israel', *Scottish Journal of Theology* 17 (3) (1964): 325–31 at 325; Peter C. Craigie, 'Yahweh is a Man of Wars', *Scottish Journal of Theology* 22 (2) (1969): 183–88 at 183; Craigie, *The Problem of War in the Old Testament* (Eugene, OR: Wipf and Stock, 1978); Paul D. Hanson, 'War, Peace, and Justice in Early Israel', *Bible Review* 3 (3) (1987): 32–45. See also the historiographical summary in *WHB*, 5–9.

41. O'Driscoll, 'Rewriting the Just War Tradition', 1–2.

just war thought is neither uniquely Christian nor exclusively Western may broaden its appeal in the realms of international relations policy and military practice.[42] By recognising that efforts to reconcile war with justice are not purely Western or Christian, this study seeks to make the debate about the just war tradition, as well as its ongoing relevance to international relations, more culturally inclusive than it sometimes appears.

A shift of focus is therefore required, away from the history of Christianity and away from the geographical frontiers of Europe and those historical societies traditionally claimed as Western antecedents.[43] Some effort has already been made in this direction, with a number of scholars drawing attention to the rich veins of ethical thought on war in the Chinese, Hindu, and especially Islamic traditions. Indeed, though Johnson's work is principally associated with the Western tradition, he himself has played a notable role in this comparative movement.[44] As a result, there has been a growing awareness and appreciation that comparative studies of global traditions can be remarkably fruitful. Thus we see that in China, writings touching upon the relationship of justice and war date back to at least the Warring States period (481–221), with the writings of Confucius (c. 551–c. 479) slightly predating this. The Confucian, Daoist, and Legalist traditions all considered the possible licit and illicit uses of war, with licit war generally conceptualised as defensive or the highest form of judicial punishment, to be used by state rulers alone.[45] The ancient Hindu tradition also

---

42. Again, also noted by Lang and O'Driscoll, 'Introduction: The Just War Tradition', 1, 6–7; O'Driscoll, 'Rewriting the Just War Tradition', 1–2; Rory Cox, 'Expanding the History of the Just War: The Ethics of War in Ancient Egypt', *International Studies Quarterly* 61 (2) (2017): 371–84 at 371.

43. For an initial attempt at this approach, see Cox, 'Expanding the History'.

44. James Turner Johnson, *The Holy War Idea in Western and Islamic Traditions* (University Park: Pennsylvania State University Press, 1997); James Turner Johnson and John Kelsay (eds), *Cross, Crescent, and Sword: The Justification and Limitation of War in Western and Islamic Tradition* (New York: Greenwood, 1990); John Kelsay and James Turner Johnson (eds), *Just War and Jihad: Historical and Theoretical Perspectives on War and Peace in Western and Islamic Traditions* (New York: Greenwood, 1991).

45. An excellent collection of essays is available in Ping-cheung Lo and Sumner B. Twiss (eds), *Chinese Just War Ethics: Origin, Development, and Dissent* (Abingdon: Routledge, 2015). See also Mark E. Lewis, 'The Just War in Early China', in *The Ethics of War in Asian Civilizations: A Comparative Perspective*, ed. Torkel Brekke (Abingdon: Routledge, 2006), 185–200; Daniel A. Bell, 'Just War and Confucianism: Implications for the Contemporary World', in *Confucian Political Ethics*, ed. Daniel A. Bell (Princeton, NJ: Princeton University Press, 2008), 226–56; Ni Lexiong, 'The Implications of Ancient Chinese Military Culture for World Peace', in *Confucian Political Ethics*, ed. Daniel A. Bell (Princeton, NJ: Princeton University Press, 2008), 201–25; Ping-cheung Lo, 'The *Art of War* Corpus and Chinese Just War Ethics Past and Present', *Journal of Religious Ethics* 40 (3) (2012): 404–46; Vladimir Tikhonov, 'Chinese and Korean Religious Traditions', in *Religion, War and Ethics: A Sourcebook of Textual Traditions*, ed. Gregory Reichberg and Henrik Syse (Cambridge: Cambridge University Press, 2014), 597–630.

contained critical thought about the ethics of war, with concerns for just cause, right intention, last resort, and proper conduct identifiable in the *Rāmāyaṇa* and the *Māhabhārata*. Significantly, parts of these classic texts date back to the sixth and fourth centuries BCE respectively.[46] While the fields of early Chinese and Hindu just war studies remain limited within anglophone literature, the later Islamic tradition has received much greater attention. Beginning with Majid Khadurri and continued by scholars such as John Kelsay, there is now a significant corpus of work exploring all aspects of Islamic thought on war, from its early medieval origins through to the present day.[47]

The study of just war thought in the Chinese, Hindu, and Islamic traditions is obviously valuable and much to be encouraged, but they are excluded from the remit of this study for two reasons. The first is that the earliest evidence from China and the Indian subcontinent is roughly contemporaneous with the intellectual flowering of classical Athens: that is, from around the sixth to the third century BCE. Therefore, even these venerable Asiatic traditions are significantly predated by the Egyptian and Hittite evidence, and only catch the tail-end of the Israelite material. Islam, emerging as it did in the seventh century CE, is separated from the fall of the kingdoms of Samaria and Judah by over a thousand years, and from the height of the Hittite and Egyptian kingdoms by two thousand. Put simply, these alternative global traditions appear too late for a study which focuses on the *earliest* origins of just

---

46. Robert E. Hume, 'Hinduism and War', *The American Journal of Theology* 20 (1) (1916): 31–44; Roderick Hindery, 'Hindu Ethics in the *Rāmāyana*', *The Journal of Religious Ethics* 4 (2) (1976): 287–322; Francis Xavier Clooney, 'Pain but not Harm: Some Classical Resources toward a Hindu Just War Theory', in *Just War in Comparative Perspective*, ed. Paul Robinson (Aldershot: Ashgate, 2003), 109–26; Surya P. Subedi, 'The Concept in Hinduism of "Just War"', *Journal of Conflict and Security Law* 8 (2) (2003): 339–61; Nick Allen, 'Just War in the *Māhabhārata*', in *The Ethics of War*, ed. Richard Sorabji and David Rodin, 138–49; Raj Balkaran and A. Walter Dorn, 'Violence in the *Vālmīki Rāmāyaṇa*: Just War Criteria in an Ancient Indian Epic', *Journal of the American Academy of Religion* 80 (3) (2012): 659–90; Kaushik Roy, 'Hinduism', in *Religion, War and Ethics: A Sourcebook of Textual Traditions*, ed. Gregory Reichberg and Henrik Syse (Cambridge: Cambridge University Press, 2014), 471–543; Valerie Morkevičius, *Realist Ethics: Just War Traditions as Power Politics* (Cambridge: Cambridge University Press, 2018), 159–93.

47. An indicative list of the anglophone literature on Islamic just war thought includes: Majid Khadduri, *War and Peace in the Law of Islam* (Baltimore: Johns Hopkins University Press, 1955); Rudolph Peters (ed. and trans.), *Jihad in Medieval and Modern Islam* (Leiden: Brill, 1977); Kelsay and Johnson, *Just War and Jihad*; Bassam Tibi, 'War and Peace in Islam', in *The Ethics of War and Peace: Religious and Secular Perspectives*, ed. Terry Nardin (Princeton, NJ: Princeton University Press, 1996), 128–45; Sohail H. Hashmi, 'Interpreting the Islamic Ethics of War and Peace', in ibid., 146–68; Johnson, *Holy War Idea*; John Esposito, *Unholy War: Terror in the Name of Islam* (Oxford: Oxford Uinversity Press, 2002); Ahmad Atif Ahmad, 'The Evolution of Just War Theory in Islamic Law: Texts, History, and the Purpose of "Reading"', *American Foreign Policy Interests* 28 (2) (2006): 107–15; Alia Brahimi, *Jihad and Just War in the War on Terror* (Oxford: Oxford

war thought. Secondly, while a good case can be made for the cultural interaction and influence of Mediterannean and Near Eastern peoples during the Bronze Age and early Iron Age, there is little evidence of significant interaction between the Near East and eastern or southern Asia during the same period.

In sum, though this study does not position itself specifically as a contribution to post-colonial literature, one of its central aims is to encourage a move away from the academic and popular idea of the just war as an exclusively Western or Christian ethical tradition. In showing that the earliest evidence of just war thought is to be found among the ancient Egyptians, Hittites, and Israelites, this work does, to some degree, attempt to 'decolonise' its history. While not wishing to detract from the remarkable contributions of the Greek, Roman, or Christian traditions, we must recognise that these were neither the first nor the only philosophical, theological, legal, or practical attempts to interrogate the relationship between justice and war.

The Value of Comparison

Discussions of scholarly method tend to represent it as something far more grandiose and systematic than the realities of scholarly research and writing usually permit. Nevertheless, I think there is some value in explaining to readers the key intellectual assumptions underpinning my approach to the historical sources and subject more generally. It will also help to elucidate what I take to be the main objectives of this study, as well as its limitations.[48]

The methodological approach at the heart of this study is that of comparison, and the comparative method is especially effective when testing a hypothesis.[49] The primary hypothesis tested in this book is that ancient Near Eastern societies prior to c. 500 BCE thought of war in ethical terms, distinguished

---

University Press, 2010); Ahmed Al-Dawoody, *The Islamic Law of War: Justifications and Regulations* (New York: Palgrave Macmillan, 2011); Makram Abbès, 'Can We Speak of Just War in Islam?', *History of Political Thought* 35 (2) (2014): 234–61; Nesrine Badawi and John Kelsay, 'Sunni Islam', in *Religion, War and Ethics: A Sourcebook of Textual Traditions*, ed. Gregory Reichberg and Henrik Syse (Cambridge: Cambridge University Press, 2014), 301–82; Mohammad H. Faghfoory, 'Shi'ite Islam', in ibid., 389–470; Morkevičius, *Realist Ethics*, 109–58. For John Kelsay's work, see, inter alia, *Islam and War: A Study in Comparative Ethics* (Louisville, KT: Westminster John Knox Press, 1993); 'Al-Shaybani and the Islamic Law of War', *Journal of Military Ethics* 2 (1) (2003): 63–75; 'Islamic Tradition and the Justice of War', in *The Ethics of War in Asian Civilizations: A Comparative Perspective*, ed. Torkel Brekke (Abingdon: Routledge, 2006), 81–110; and *Arguing the Just War in Islam* (Cambridge, MA: Harvard University Press, 2007).

48. The discussion that follows is partly adapted from a broader discussion of methodological approaches in Rory Cox, 'Approaches to Pre-Modern War and Ethics: Some Comparative and Multi-disciplinary Perspectives', *Global Intellectual History* 6 (5) (2018): 592–613.

49. William H. Sewell Jr., 'Marc Bloch and the Logic of Comparative History', *History and Theory* 6 (2) (1967): 208–18 at 208–9, 214, 217.

between morally 'good' and 'bad' wars, and developed what might accurately be termed 'just war thought'. In addition, I posit two ancillary claims: firstly, that ancient just war thought is analogous to, perhaps even homologous with, that body of later thought associated with the Greco-Roman and Christian just war tradition; and secondly, that societies engage in ethical reflection on war as a self-legitimating and self-justifying process resulting directly from the necessity or desire to wage war.

There are good grounds for selecting the ancient Egyptian, Hittite, and Israelite cultures as units of comparison. The history of the kingdom of Egypt (in one form or another) spans the entire period of antiquity, but we will focus on the expanse of time from the Early Dynastic period to the late New Kingdom (c. 3150–1069). The kingdom of Hatti, meanwhile, flourished from c. 1650 and had attained the status of a superpower by c. 1450, until finally crashing into obscurity around 1180. The political history of the Israelites is more obscure, although we know that the Israelite kingdoms of Samaria (also referred to as the northern kingdom of Israel) and Judah were flourishing by the early ninth century. Both kingdoms eventually succumbed to external conquest: Samaria in 721/0 and Judah in 587/6. The cultural history of the Israelites, however, was significantly shaped by these experiences, and subsequently played a major role in influencing how Israelite scribes constructed their own histories. It is these histories, preserved in the books of the Tanakh, on which we are almost entirely dependent.

Each of these three societies represents a distinct type of political, social, and religious organisation and character. From the highly centralised semi-divine monarchy of Egypt, with its official pantheon and richly endowed royal cults, we transition to what has been characterised as a federated empire of the Hittite priest-kings and the 'thousand gods' of Hatti. Both Egypt and Hatti became mighty empires during the second millennium, covering vast tracts of land throughout the eastern Mediterranean, north Africa, the Levant, Syria-Palestine, and Anatolia. Their political make-up and experience was notably different from that of the territorially and demographically minor kingdoms of Samaria and Judah. According to the Tanakh, these Israelite kingdoms had emerged from earlier tribal units and developed an idiosyncratic cult of Yahwist monotheism, probably from around the mid-first millennium.

Taken together, Egyptians, Hittites, and Israelites flourished over a period of roughly two-and-a-half thousand years, from c. 3000 to c. 500. This represents a period prior to the domination of the Mediterranean and Near Eastern worlds by first Hellenic and then Roman armies and culture. If we are serious about pushing back the history of just war thought, then we must investigate societies and sources as 'pristine' as possible in terms of Hellenising and/or Romanising influences. It is for this reason that I have not carried the investigation of Egypt into the Ptolemaic or Roman period, for example. Likewise, I have not included First or Second Maccabees in the main discussion of

Israelite thought, because these books, whilst having much to say about violence and war, are not part of the Tanakh and appear only in the later Greek Septuagint. Dating from the second and first centuries, they are clearly products of Hellenistic Judaism. Similarly, the rabbinical texts of the Mishnah and Talmud are products of late antiquity rather than ancient history, and continued to be composed and redacted up until the sixth century CE and beyond.

In exploring whether these societies of the ancient Near East developed ideas or traditions of war as an activity bounded by ethical norms, there is no assumption that each society will have produced identical just war thought. Just as we would not expect any given individuals or communities to experience war in identical ways, so there is no reason to expect distinct societies to produce identical just war doctrines. Yet we should not discount the possibility of similarity, nor the possibility of transmission and influence from one society to another. After all, these societies were in contact with one another through various channels (albeit sometimes that communication was one-way, such as between Hatti and Israel), and such contact included forms of 'higher culture' as well as demographic movement and warfare.[50] More than any other state activity, warfare necessitates some degree of cross-border interaction. Armed conflict may therefore have created opportunities for sharing practices and ideas. The Egyptian state waged war with both Hatti and the Israelite kingdoms at various periods of its history, while the Hittites had an active military presence and lasting cultural influence in the area of the Levant in which Samaria and Judah were later to emerge.

Comparative methodology within historical studies is nowhere better described than by the French historian Marc Bloch:

> [The historian] selects two or more phenomena which appear at first sight to be analogous and which occur in one or more social milieus. He finds out how these phenomena resemble or differ from one another, traces their evolution, and, as far as possible, explains the similarities and differences.[51]

Bloch, along with his fellow *Annalistes*, was keen to promote a comparative approach to history that utilised a range of interdisciplinary methods, considering socio-cultural developments across the *longue durée*.[52] If we lack

---

50. William F. Albright, *From the Stone Age to Christianity: Monotheism and the Historical Process*, 2nd edn (Baltimore: Johns Hopkins University Press, 1957), 209–12.

51. Marc Bloch, 'Toward a Comparative History of European Societies', in *Enterprise and Secular Change: Readings in Economic History*, ed. Frederic C. Lane and Jelle C. Riemersma (Homewood, IL: Richard D. Irwin, 1953), 494–521 at 496 [originally published as 'Pour une histoire comparée es sociétiés européennes', *Revue de synthèse historique* 46 (1928): 15–50].

52. Others have utilised this methodology in the history of international law: 'The ultimate aim of all conceivable comparative work in the area of the history of international law

a comparative perspective, arguably we are unable to appreciate the true uniqueness or generality of phenomena, or to judge their importance in either relative or absolute terms.[53] The reality of human experience is that different cultures interact in myriad ways and 'are not hermetically sealed from each other'.[54] I believe that just war studies has concentrated too much on the modern, so that hallmarks of the tradition claimed as special and unique may well begin to appear as ordinary and common when viewed comparatively over the *longue durée*.

Bloch stipulated that the comparative method required two conditions: 'a certain similarity or analogy between observed phenomena [...] and a certain dissimilarity between the environments in which they occur'.[55] The ethics of war seem particularly well suited to such a comparative project. The core phenomena of war remain relatively consistent: communities deliberately inflict various harms upon one another in order to achieve their ends (whatever those may be). Yet the *environments* in which war occurs, including the intellectual environment in which the relationship between ethics and war is thrashed out, vary considerably.

The three historical societies examined throughout this book were geographically proximate, and though the evidence spans two millennia, there was also a good deal of temporal overlap between them.[56] War, of course, frequently breaks down old geographical borders and throws up new ones in its wake. And yet military conquest rarely constitutes the simple expansion of one victorious society and the complete removal or eradication of another. Populations could be forcibly moved (for example, the Israelites' exile in Babylon), or conquerors might impose a governor and a garrison to ensure regular tribute payments. But pre-existing social structures and cultures were frequently left

---

is not the comparison of individual phenomena, whatever their intrinsic importance, but the comparison of entire epochs [...]. [W]hat is here at issue is a comparative examination of independently developed, functional international legal orders which helped influence the legal character of their respective eras.' Wolfgang Preiser, 'History of the Law of Nations: Basic Questions and Principles', in *Encyclopedia of Public International Law*, vol. 7: *History of International Law, Foundations of International Law, Sources of International Law, Law of Treaties*, ed. Rudolph Bernhardt (Amsterdam: North Holland Publishing, 1984), 128–29, cited in *ILA*, 5.

53. Chris Wickham, 'Problems in Doing Comparative History', in *Challenging the Boundaries of Medieval History: The Legacy of Timothy Reuter*, ed. Patricia Skinner (Turnhout: Brepols, 2009), 5–28 at 6.

54. Richard Sorabji and David Rodin, 'Introduction', in *The Ethics of War: Shared Problems in Different Traditions*, ed. Richard Sorabji and David Rodin (Ashgate: Aldershot, 2006), 1–10 at 2.

55. Bloch, 'Toward a Comparative History', 496.

56. Sewell points out that 'temporal and spatial proximity [...] does not assure similarity', just as temporal and spatial distance does not assure dissimilarity. Sewell, 'Marc Bloch', 215. Cf. Bloch, 'Toward a Comparative History', 496–98.

intact, and acculturation can be seen to have occurred. Political borders were not (and are not) the same as socio-cultural borders, and all borders in the ancient world were in a state of flux. The blurring and intermixing of political, social, and material culture is witnessed in the archaeological record, testifying that frontiers were 'zones of cross-cutting social networks'.[57]

Of equal import is whether we are utilising 'appropriate units of comparison'.[58] Are we comparing like with like, or are we wilfully misinterpreting the phenomena of one society in order to mould them into something they are not? Ethics of war are complex cultural products. The organisation of the chapters according to the categories of *ius ad bellum* and *ius in bello* concepts and practices is one way to simplify and organise the analysis. These categories are conceived as ideal types and are primarily an analytical tool rather than an exact rendering of how ancient peoples distinguished between different areas of military ethics.[59] Indeed, notwithstanding the Latin formulation, the terminological distinction between *ius ad bellum* and *ius in bello* was not an ancient Roman innovation.[60] Even medieval European jurists and theologians did not explicitly bifurcate the *ius ad bellum* and *ius in bello* categories. They certainly debated *ad bellum* issues such as *auctoritas* (authority), *iusta causa* (just cause), and *recta intentio* (correct intention); they also understood such issues as related to, but distinct from, *in bello* questions touching upon the *ius armorum* (law of arms), concerning how wars should be fought according to certain behavioural norms. But the modern usage of *ius ad bellum* and *ius in bello* as organising terms (and certainly the increasing prominence of *ius post bellum* as an independent category) can effectively be traced to the mid-twentieth century CE.[61] Employing these Latinate categories and criteria to discuss ancient Near Eastern thought thus requires a degree of translation,

---

57. Kent G. Lightfoot and Antoinette Martinez, 'Frontiers and Boundaries in Archaeological Perspective', *Annual Review of Anthropology* 24 (1995): 471–92 at 471. See also Claudia Glatz and Roger Matthews, 'Anthropology of a Frontier Zone: Hittite–Kaska Relations in Late Bronze Age North-Central Anatolia', *Bulletin of the American Schools of Oriental Research* 339 (2005): 47–65 at 49.

58. Sewell, 'Marc Bloch', 215.

59. 'The ideal typical concept [. . .] is not a *description* of reality but it aims to give unambiguous means of expression to such a description.' Max Weber, *The Methodology of the Social Sciences*, trans. and ed. Edward A. Shils and Henry A. Finch (New York: The Free Press, 1949), 90. Gottwald adopts a similar approach to his analysis of ancient Israelite political order: Norman K. Gottwald, *The Politics of Ancient Israel* (Louisville, KY: Westminster John Knox Press, 2001), 10–12.

60. See also Nathalie Barrandon, 'La Transgression dans la guerre au temps de Cicéron: Droit et crauté', in *La Transgression en temps de guerre: De l'Antiquité à nos jours*, ed. Nathalie Barrandon and Isabelle Pimouguet-Pedarros (Rennes: Presses Universitaires de Rennes, 2021): 97–123 at 98, 101.

61. See Robert Kolb, 'Origin of the Twin Terms *jus ad bellum/jus in bello*', *International Review of the Red Cross* 37 (320) (1997): 553–62.

anachronism, and abstraction. Nonetheless, when used as a tool for organisation and analysis, these heuristic categories are extremely useful. After all, as Quincy Wright noted in his study of war, fictions 'are the essence of the social sciences', and interpretation always requires some degree of historical imagination.[62] And while our ancient Near Eastern sources never used the direct equivalents of technical terms such as *ius ad bellum, iusta causa*, or *recta intentio*, they undoubtedly possessed ideas very close to the concepts these express. My intention is not to force the evidence to conform to a debate or discourse, but to approach the sources as *indicative* of dominant norms and assumptions, which can be organised together like the pieces of a jigsaw puzzle. I will leave it to the reader to judge whether these 'fictions' are effective and thus justified.

Encountering Obstacles When Reconstructing Ancient Ethics of War

There are numerous reasons why any description of ancient ethics cannot faithfully reflect the reality of an entire culture, and I will not go into all of them here. Among the most important, however, is that we are largely reliant upon a selection of texts and other forms of evidence that represent the lives of a small, albeit highly influential, cadre of society. Any impression of the lives and values of the less privileged and illiterate majority is much harder to gain. Archaeology might reveal elements of their social and economic lives: urban structures, the remains of quotidian household items, human remains. It might even provide glimpses of their religious and ritualistic lives, in the form of religious artefacts or murals. But we cannot be sure that the masses shared the same ethical and political ideals as those articulated by the social elites. Undoubtedly there must have been significant overlap between elite and non-elite beliefs and social norms, but where, how, and why these overlaps occurred must remain hidden. As a result, it is difficult to say how representative our image of any historical society truly is.[63] Most obviously, we might think of the marked disregard of women's experiences and opinions in most societies prior to the late modern era.[64] The grossly skewed representation of economic elites is, again, typical of the pre-modern era. Given the overt reliance of intellectual historians on texts, produced in societies in which the

---

62. Wright, *Study of War*, 2:683. See also Finley, *Ancient History*, 17; Harle, *Ideas of Social Order*, 32.

63. Also noted by Carly L. Crouch, *War and Ethics in the Ancient Near East: Military Violence in Light of Cosmology and History* (Berlin: Walter de Gruyter, 2009), 5.

64. Regarding the experience of women in war specifically, see the important treatment by Jean Bethke Elshtain, *Women and War* (Chicago: University of Chicago Press, 1995).

vast majority were illiterate, this bias is especially notable. We might also think of marginalised minorities within a social system, such as slaves, or those marginalised on the basis of ethnicity or religion (though it should be noted that our modern understanding of racism or religious intolerance is very different from ancient attitudes).

Ethics of war can also be difficult to situate temporally. Our evidence for ethical thought about war is often the product of authors looking to the past and writing about military events that possibly took place years, decades, or even centuries earlier. In some cases, these 'historical' events probably did not take place at all, being merely literary inventions of a scribe to serve an ideological, didactic, or rhetorical purpose. We must be aware, therefore, that the ethical standards of the scribes who wrote about such events do not necessarily represent those of the time in which the military events supposedly took place. Nor should we assume that ancient scribes—who themselves usually comprised non-military elites—shared the same values or codes of conduct as soldiers.[65] Even scribes and soldiers living contemporaneously to one another could have possessed quite different world-views, especially concerning the meaning and purpose of war, or how wars should be fought. (This remains as true today as in the past.) Yet, as vicarious modern observers, our view of the ancient scene is more often through the eyes of a literate scribe than of an illiterate soldier.

Just as ethical thought about war is often characterised by elements of retrospection, so too can it be characterised by prospection—judging or justifying the past to provide guidance for the future. As a result, claiming that this or that ethical standard pertained exactly to this or that military event (a single battle, for example) becomes very difficult indeed. Instead, we must extrapolate dominant patterns of thought and behaviour that emerge from the textual and material evidence, and apply them broadly to relatively long periods of military activity. This is not an exact science. Any attempt to describe an ancient ethics of war will require a degree of generalisation and speculation that undoubtedly goes beyond the ancient 'reality' of that system of thought; there is no way of knowing whether our descriptions of a culture would ring true to the historical persons who constituted it.[66] However, for all that the processes of millennia have ravaged the remains of the ancient world, there remains a truly enormous wealth of material for the historian to pore over. As Walter Burkert notes, the challenge for any individual historian 'is not so much the limits of our knowledge as the superabundance of what can be

---

65. Charlie Trimm, *Fighting for the King and the Gods: A Survey of Warfare in the Ancient Near East* (Atlanta, GA: SBL Press, 2017), 7–8.

66. Geertz, for example, stresses the need to distinguish between culture as a reality and culture as an object of analysis; it is only the latter that scholars can describe: Geertz, *Interpretation of Cultures*, 15.

known'.⁶⁷ By utilising well-tested historiographical methods, we can therefore proceed with our analysis at the same time as accepting the speculative elements of our endeavour.⁶⁸

At its heart, the comparative approach is as much about discovering idiosyncrasies as it is about highlighting commonalities.⁶⁹ But whether universalising or relativising, such comparative insights potentially prove unsettling to contemporary society. By comparing ethics and norms, groups open themselves up to the possibility that 'their own morals and customs may not be right, sacred, or universal'.⁷⁰ Such threatening ideas are frequently stigmatised or trivialised as a result. Yet, concerning something as horrible as war, I believe it is incumbent upon scholars of the subject to challenge prevailing social norms, or perhaps merely social apathy, and to encourage a constant reassessment of our moral principles.

Moving beyond the Just War Canon

I have spoken above about a desire to move beyond the traditional canon of sources used to the describe the development of just war thought. Fortunately, when exploring Egyptian, Hittite, and Israelite history we are blessed with a plethora of sources, which vary considerably in form and character. These include sources not typically considered relevant to just war studies. Prayers, poetry, literary tales, and material evidence are often overlooked, yet can tell us much about ethical norms and attitudes towards war and death. Such sources might even provide a more realistic—or at least more emotionally informed—rendering of societal attitudes than, for example, abstract treatises on jurisprudence.

Myth in the ancient world combined history, theology, and entertainment. Susan Niditch suggests that '[m]yths and metaphors if properly read may be the truest indicators of essential perceptions of existence'.⁷¹ Myth certainly provided a guide to both personal and communal identity, and as such carried considerable weight. 'Myth was tradition, and tradition was authority,' as Ken

---

67. Walter Burkert, *Homo necans: The Anthropology of Ancient Greek Sacrificial Ritual and Myth*, trans. Peter Bing (Berkeley: University of California Press, 1983), xix. It should also be stressed that while I have endeavoured to utilise as wide a range of primary material as possible, my investigation is constricted by my reliance on translations of the original ancient Near Eastern languages and is thus not exhaustive.

68. As Bederman also insists: *ILA*, 11.

69. Bloch, 'Toward a Comparative History', 507; Geertz, *Interpretation of Cultures*, 43; Émile Durkheim, *The Division of Labor in Society*, trans. George Simpson, cited in Neil J. Smelser, *Comparative Methods in the Social Sciences* (Eaglewood Cliffs, NJ: Prentice Hall, 1976), 2.

70. Smelser, *Comparative Methods*, 1.

71. *WHB*, 37.

Dowden and Niall Livingston astutely observe.[72] Referring to ancient Greek examples, which may be more familiar to readers, we can illustrate the importance of myth by asking which had a greater influence on ancient Hellenistic culture and attitudes to war: Homer's *Iliad*, Plato's *Laws*, or Aristotle's *Politics*? Merely in terms of sheer audience numbers (as well as virtually any other metric), few would dispute that the *Iliad* would win hands-down. The same comparison could be made between Homer and Thucydides, or Hesiod and Xenophon, with the same result, that the poets and myth-tellers had the greatest impact on Hellenic martial culture. As Paul Veyne so eloquently elucidates in his classic study, for ancient Greeks 'myth was a subject of serious reflection', and myth and *logos* (reason) were not thought of as antithetical.[73] When thinking about the Greek ethics of war, why, therefore, has our attention been drawn principally to Thucydides, Plato, and Aristotle, rather than the Greek mythic cycles? Part of the answer, surely, is because *we* take Thucydides, Plato, and Aristotle more seriously than we do the tales of Athene, Herakles, or Odysseus. In other words, when discussing so serious a subject as the ethics of war, we allow our modern qualitative judgements to determine the sources we deem relevant. Yet the fantastical can also contain truth. Indeed, Veyne posits that mythology is important precisely because '[l]egend has its origin in the popular genius, which makes up stories to tell what is really true. That which is most true in legends is precisely the marvellous.'[74] This is not to say that ancient Greeks understood myths as ethical blueprints for real-life action (although Greek scholars such as Plato and Strabo could think of them as instructional and educational);[75] it is rather to urge that just war scholars should maintain a catholic (stressing the lower-case 'c'!) attitude towards the types of sources they use. Put simply, we should look past the canonical and extraordinary, and pay more attention to the quotidian and ordinary.[76]

---

72. Ken Dowden and Niall Livingstone, 'Thinking Through Myth, Thinking Myth Through', in *A Companion to Greek Mythology*, ed. Ken Dowden and Niall Livingstone (Malden, MA: Wiley-Blackwell, 2011), 3–23 at 16; cf. Ken Dowden, *The Uses of Greek Mythology* (London: Routledge, 1992), 39.

73. Paul Veyne, *Did the Greeks Believe in their Myths? An Essay on the Constitutive Imagination*, trans. Paula Wissing (Chicago: University of Chicago Press, 1988), 1; cf. ibid., 62.

74. Veyne, *Did the Greeks Believe in their Myths?*, 60.

75. Or, as Dowden says, 'Greeks did not turn to mythology for guidance on what to believe and how to live. They did not turn to their religion for morals and creeds, either. [. . .] Myth is not there to state what must be believed: myth is not dogmatic.' Dowden, *Uses of Greek Mythology*, 22. See also Veyne, *Did the Greeks Believe in their Myths?*, 62.

76. As in an anthropological superstructural approach, we might track down the minutiae or *spie* (clues) in order to enable a thick description or to reveal 'a deeper reality'. See Carlo Ginzburg, 'Morelli, Freud and Sherlock Holmes: Clues and Scientific Method', *History Workshop Journal* 9 (1) (1980): 5–36 at 11.

The literary, documentary, and material evidence offered by each society under investigation varies significantly. The mass of literature across different genres and the abundant archaeological record from ancient Egypt contrasts with the rich legalistic and diplomatic corpus that survives from Hatti. Both of these bodies of evidence contrast again with the source material of the Israelites, which, to a study such as this, is effectively limited to the Tanakh—better known as the Hebrew Bible or Old Testament. Yet this 'single' source is in fact no such thing: it is, rather, a composite of texts drawn from different genres and periods, conglomerated and redacted over a span of several centuries to give us the lengthy and complex document we now possess. Thus the Egyptian, Hittite, and Israelite sources evince a variety of features, both similar and distinct, making comparison both more interesting and ultimately more rewarding. If we are seeking to test the hypothesis that there were concepts of just war in the ancient Near East over two thousand years before the birth of Plato, then it is important to look for evidence in both similar *and* dissimilar contexts.

Adjacent cultures such as those of Babylon and Assyria will occasionally be discussed. These kingdoms, which experienced a number of turbulent political peaks and troughs, partook in the cultural and politico-military milieu of the ancient Near East, and each displayed some interest in the ethical dimensions of war. However, these Mesopotamian cultures are not the focus of this book, for several reasons. The bulk of the evidence for military and ethical matters derives from the 'new kingdom' periods of both Assyria and Babylon—that is, considerably later than the Egyptian and Hittite periods examined herein. The Neo-Assyrians (c. 911–c. 610) and Neo-Babylonians (c. 626–c. 539) were indeed contemporaneous to the Israelite kingdoms, but there already exists a handful of excellent studies on Assyrian martial culture and ethics.[77] Some shorter comparative surveys have also been undertaken by biblical scholars, albeit with a firm focus on the biblical history of Israel.[78] Finally, reasons of economy dictated against a detailed analysis of Assyria, Babylon, or the Medes (Persians). To have given adequate space to these cultures would have created an unwieldy and even longer volume.

---

77. See especially Bustenay Oded, *War, Peace and Empire: Justifications for War in Assyrian Royal Inscriptions* (Wiesbaden: Reichert, 1992); Crouch, *War and Ethics*; Frederick M. Fales, *Guerre et paix en Assyrie: Religion et impérialisme* (Paris: Publications de l'École pratique des hautes études, 2010); Mario Liverani, 'The King and His Army', in *At the Dawn of History: Ancient Near Eastern Studies in Honor of J. N. Postgate*, ed. Yağmur Heffron, Adam Stone, and Martin Worthington (University Park: Penn State University Press, 2021), 301–12.

78. See Sa-Moon Kang, *Divine War in the Old Testament and in the Ancient Near East* (Berlin: Walter de Gruyter, 1989); K. Lawson Younger Jr., *Ancient Conquest Accounts: A Study of Ancient Near Eastern and Biblical History Writing* (Sheffield: Sheffield Academic Press, 1990).

The Value of Investigating Ancient Just War Thought

War and justice are arguably the two social forces which do most to shape political communities. If we discount forces of nature, then war poses the greatest existential threat to communities. And yet war may also provide the means by which communities can seek to expand their resources, power, and influence. Moreover, war has the potential to unite otherwise fractious communities in the face of a common enemy.[79] It is hard to deny that war has been central to both the evolution of cultural systems and the emergence of complex states.[80] 'War made the state, and the state made war,' as Charles Tilly memorably put it.[81]

Justice, by contrast, is the principle that makes complex communal life possible in the first place. Without some principle of justice to govern human relationships, it is difficult to imagine how any community could long survive, let alone prosper. The Roman orator Cicero believed that '[j]ustice is necessary [. . .]. Its effect is so great that not even those who win their bread from evil-doing and crime are able to live without any particle of justice. [. . .] Indeed they say that there are even laws among bandits which they obey and respect.'[82] Exactly what this principle of justice entails is, of course, subject to significant variation, contingent upon the norms and requirements of specific groups.[83] But it seems reasonable to assume that stable political communities

---

79. The function of war to enhance social cohesion has been recognised from fourth-century Athens up to and including modern security studies: Aristotle, *The Politics*, trans. Stephen Everson (Cambridge: Cambridge University Press, 1998), bk 5.1308a25–30 (p. 125); Martin Wight, *Systems of States*, ed. Hedley Bull (Leicester: Leicester University Press, 1977), 85–86; Jeff Huysmans, 'Security! What Do You Mean?: From Concept to Thick Signifier', *European Journal of International Relations* 4 (2) (1998): 226–55 at 238–39.

80. Jonathan Haas (ed.), *The Anthropology of War* (Cambridge: Cambridge University Press, 1990), xiii; Morton H. Fried, 'Warfare, Military Organization, and the Evolution of Society', *Anthropologica* 3 (2) (1961): 134–47 at 134–35. For a useful overview of the major streams of debate concerning the 'origin' of human warfare, see Doyne Dawson, 'The Origins of War: Biological and Anthropological Theories', *History and Theory* 35 (1) (1996): 1–28.

81. Charles Tilly, 'Reflections on the History of European State-Making', in *The Formation of National States in Western Europe*, ed. Charles Tilly (Princeton, NJ: Princeton University Press, 1975), 3–83 at 42. See also: David Webster, 'Warfare and the Evolution of the State: A Reconsideation', *American Antiquity* 40 (4) (1975): 464–70; Samuel E. Finer, 'State- and Nation-Building in Europe: The Role of the Military', in *The Formation of National States in Western Europe*, ed. Charles Tilly (Princeton, NJ: Princeton University Press, 1975), 84–163; Cohen, 'Warfare and State Formation'.

82. Marcus Tullius Cicero, *On Duties (De officiis)*, ed. M. T. Griffin and E. M. Atkins (Cambridge: Cambridge University Press, 1991), bk 2, § 40 (pp. 77–78).

83. David Lyons, 'Ethical Relativism and the Problem of Incoherence', *Ethics* 86 (2) (1976): 107–21 at 108.

could simply not exist if a majority of individuals indulged in unrestrained violence. It is hardly surprising, therefore, that a social force as important as justice should have a long and complex relationship with the violence of war.

We learn much about a society from its conception of war because war is an intrinsically social phenomenon. War is deeply affected by all manner of socio-cultural norms and beliefs which shape its conceptualisation and experience, from justifying it to condemning it, from formulating grand strategy to engaging in individual hand-to-hand combat, and from understanding what it means to achieve victory, or likewise what it is to suffer defeat. Thinking about ethics is one way of ordering the experience of war, and tells us something powerful about how societies view themselves and others. Sigmund Freud insisted that the extreme and traumatic experience of warfare 'strips us of the later accretions of civilization, and lays bare the primal man in each of us'.[84] Under the stress of fear and perhaps existential threat, what are the values that a society clings to? What is jettisoned as superfluous? These are fundamental questions and may provide fundamental insights.[85] One might even think of the ethics of war as a communal coping mechanism: bestowing a deeper moral or religious meaning on an otherwise horrific and troubling activity.

Alas, there is no tract from the ancient world conveniently entitled *Just and Unjust Wars*; but this does not mean that ancient people did not conceive of wars in this way. In attempting to reconstruct ancient just war thought, we are concentrating on the values by which warfare was conceived, recorded, and judged. Such work is vital before we can properly understand ancient warfare in terms of its strategy, tactics, and logistics. For good or ill, the majority of our evidence for ancient military history comes via texts, and this textual record was mediated through the dominant cultural values of the specific society in which it was produced. Before we can understand politico-military events, we must learn the 'webs of significance' through which military deeds were filtered.[86] We must 'reconstruct a "grammar" in order to read a text', as Liverani describes it.[87]

The mass of ancient evidence has allowed scholars to push back the history of international relations to the mid-third millennium. Interstate relations in

---

84. Sigmund Freud, 'Thoughts for the Times on War and Death (1915)', in *The Standard Edition of the Complete Psychological Works of Sigmund Freud*, vol. 14: *1914–1916*, trans. and ed. James Strachey et al. (London: Hogarth Press and the Institute of Psycho-Analysis, 1957), 273–302 at 299. For a useful discussion of Freud's thought on war, see Anthony Simpson, 'Freud on the State, Violence, and War', *Diacritics* 35 (3) (2005): 78–91.

85. See also G. Scott Davis, 'Introduction: Comparative Ethics and the Crucible of War', in *The Ethics of War in Asian Civilizations: A Comparative Perspective*, ed. Torkel Brekke (Abingdon: Routledge, 2006), 1–36 at 1, 15. Cf. John Dewey, *The Middle Works, 1899–1924*, ed. J. A. Boydston, 15 vols (Carbondale: Southern Illinois University Press, 1976–1983), 15:134–204.

86. As Finley reminds us, '[t]he ability of the ancients to invent and their capacity to believe are persistently underestimated.' Finley, *Ancient History*, 9.

87. *LIR*, 11, 201.

the ancient Near East were formalised and governed by norms which intersected different cultures, creating an international system which reached the peak of its refinement during the Late Bronze Age (c. 1550–c. 1200) and was adopted by the successive polities of the Iron Age.[88] Thus we see an 'essential unity in the nature of State behaviour' that stretched from the earliest Sumerian city-states all the way through to the Roman empire.[89] Studying ancient ethical thought on war adds to our understanding of ancient political ideology as well as to our understanding of ancient concepts of international relations in their most dangerous and dynamic form: war between independent states.

For those interested in more modern issues, ancient ethical thought is worthy of our attention because of its influence in shaping numerous aspects of modern intellectual, religious, and political life. Our modern cultures are melting pots with many and varied ingredients—some of them very ancient indeed. To better understand the ancient is, therefore, to better comprehend the modern. Moreover, if one accepts (as one must) that contemporary international society has yet to untie the Gordian knot of ethical military violence, then there is value in investigating how our forebears struggled with analogous problems. In seeing the results of their efforts, we may choose to revise some of our own assumptions and reshape some of our approaches.

I did not set out to discover, through exploring ancient just war thought, a monolithic ancient doctrine of just war, or a doctrine that could be 'recovered' to lend legitimacy to the modern just war tradition.[90] The lines of thought and practice connecting the ancient to the modern are almost infinitely complex, and the forms of transmission are myriad. If certain elements of just war thought appear very similar across different cultures, this by no means implies that they are conceptually identical. As Shabtai Rosenne cautions, societies facing similar problems may produce similar solutions, but still 'start from different underlying premises and different general philosophies'.[91] To construct

---

88. Ibid., 1–2, 197.

89. *ILA*, 3; *LIR*, 2; Jonathan Rosner Ziskind, 'Aspects of International Law in the Ancient Near East' (PhD dissertation, Columbia University, 1967); Harle, *Ideas of Social Order*, 10. Martin Wight also saw an international system of sorts in the ancient Near East, although not meeting the same criteria as the later Greco-Romano system: Martin Wight, 'De systematibus civitatum', in Martin Wight, *Systems of States*, ed. Hedley Bull (Leicester: Leicester University Press, 1977), 21–45.

90. See also discussions in *ILA*, 4; *ERCIL*, xxiv–xxvi; Carlo Focarelli, 'The Early Doctrine of International Law as a Bridge from Antiquity to Modernity and Diplomatic Inviolability in 16th- and 17th-Century European Practice', in *The Twelve Years Truce (1609–1621): Peace, Truce, War and Law in the Low Countries at the Turn of the 17th Century*, ed. Randall Lesaffer (Leiden: Brill/Nijhoff, 2014), 210–32.

91. Shabtai Rosenne, 'The Influence of Judaism on the Development of International Law', *Netherlands International Law Review* 5 (2) (1958): 119–49 at 121. See also *ILA*, 6; Jared L. Miller, *Studies in the Origins, Development and Interpretation of the Kizzuwatna Rituals* (Wiesbaden: Harrassowitz, 2004), 458–59.

a history of ideas, one need not indulge in ahistoricism or anachronism. And attempting to give voice to ancient ideas is not the same as seeking a 'false essentialism' between ancient and modern concepts.[92] It would be absurd to claim that an ancient Egyptian pharaoh's concept of justice was exactly the same as that held by Saint Augustine, or Hugo Grotius, or John Rawls. But it is equally absurd to deny that ideational affinities and even continuities can exist through time and across communities. There would simply be no cultural traditions if that were not the case.

I hope to emphasise that if we want to understand the history of just war thought and *why* it emerged, then we must excavate and investigate it in its entirety. Sixteen hundred years separate Saint Augustine from our current era, but the span of time between Augustine and Old Kingdom Egypt was *three thousand* years. Even Plato and Confucius were born two thousand years after the Great Pyramid of Giza was built. If scholars continue to cling to the idea of 'proper' just war thought beginning in the classical or post-Christian period, then in a very real sense we are not seeing even half of the historical picture. It is akin to gazing at an iceberg and ignoring what lies beneath the water. By thinking more expansively and more holistically about the history of just war thought, we may come to a more coherent understanding of the claims it makes, and why it makes such claims. In sum, we may come to a deeper understanding of its nature and purpose.

92. As noted by Bederman in *ILA*, 14.

CHAPTER ONE

The Art of War in the Ancient Near East

THIS IS NOT a book of military history in the traditional mould, in as far as it does not focus on topics such as strategy, tactics, military technology, recruitment, or logistics. For those interested in these aspects of ancient Near Eastern warfare, there are a number of resources already available.[1] Nonetheless, a summary of the key features of Bronze Age and early Iron Age warfare will be useful in providing a historical context for the discussions which follow. The intellectual

---

1. The most extensive recent treatment is Trimm, *Fighting for the King*, which introduces readers to a wide selection of primary sources. See also Albrecht Goetze, 'Warfare in Asia Minor', *Iraq* 25 (2) (1963): 124–30; H.W.F. Saggs, 'Assyrian Warfare in the Sargonid Period', *Iraq* 25 (1963): 145–54; Yigael Yadin, *The Art of Warfare in Biblical Lands in the Light of Archaeological Discovery* (London: Weidenfeld & Nicolson, 1963); Jacob Liver (ed.), *The Military History of the Land of Israel in Biblical Times* (Jerusalem: Israel Defence Forces Publishing House, 1964); Chaim Herzog and Mordechai Gishon, *Battles of the Bible: A Modern Military Evaluation of the Old Testament* (New York: Random House, 1978); Florence Malbran-Labat, *L'Armée et l'organisation militaire de l'Assyrie à l'époque des Sargonides* (Geneva: Droz, 1982); T. Raymond Hobbs, *A Time for War: A Study of Warfare in the Old Testament* (Wilmington, DE: Michael Glazier, 1989); Ian Shaw, *Egyptian Warfare and Weapons* (Princes Risborough: Shire, 1991); JoAnn Scurlock, 'Neo-Assyrian Battle Tactics', in *Crossing Boundaries and Linking Horizons: Studies in Honor of Michael C. Astour on His 80th Birthday*, ed. Gordon D. Young, Mark W. Chavalas, and Richard E. Averbeck (Bethesda, MD: CDL, 1998), 491–517; Richard B. Partridge, *Fighting Pharaohs: Weapons and Warfare in Ancient Egypt* (Manchester: Peartree Publishing, 2002); Richard A. Gabriel, *The Military History of Ancient Israel* (Westport, CT: Praeger, 2003); Bridget McDermott, *Warfare in Ancient Egypt* (Stroud: Sutton Publishing, 2004); Anthony J. Spalinger, *War in Ancient Egypt: The New Kingdom* (Malden, MA: Blackwell, 2005); *WANE*; John C. Darnell and Colleen Manassa, *Tutankhamun's Armies: Battle and Conquest during Ancient Egypt's Late Eighteenth Dynasty* (Hoboken, NJ: Wiley, 2007); Robert G. Morkot, *The A to Z of Ancient Egyptian Warfare* (Lanham, MD: Scarecrow Press, 2003); Brad E. Kelle, *Ancient Israel at War, 853–586 BC* (Oxford: Osprey, 2007).

and cultural consideration of warfare and its attendant norms did not occur in a vacuum, after all, but in a dynamic relationship with war-making itself.

The Narmer Palette, dating from c. 3100, is one of the earliest and finest depictions of military victory from the ancient world (figures 1–3). Discovered in the Temple of Horus at Nekhen (Hierakonpolis), it is thought to commemorate the unification of Egypt into a single kingdom.[2] Soldiers march before King Narmer bearing regimental standards (figure 3), leading him to inspect rows of decapitated enemy corpses. The roughly contemporaneous (possibly earlier) Battlefield Palette (figure 28) shows dead bodies being eaten by animals and naked prisoners being led away by Egyptian soldiers. These commemorative palettes were powerful statements of Egyptian military might and the destructive capacity of the king and his army.[3] The Stele of the Vultures, a Sumerian memorial of a quite different type, dates to c. 2500 and memorialises a war between the city-states of Umma and Lagash (figure 4). The surviving fragments of the stele depict ranks of spearmen marching with shields and helmets, as well as the gruesome after-effects of war. The stele takes its name from the carvings of dead bodies being fed upon by vultures following Lagash's victory over Umma.[4]

What these fascinating artefacts reveal is that by the early Bronze Age there were already armies of considerable sophistication operating in the Near East and Mesopotamia. As Albrecht Goetze comments, '[w]ar and warfare were subjects which were continually experienced and practised by the peoples of the Near Eastern world. Victory and defeat spelled out their fate and destiny'.[5] Another scholar paints a particularly bleak picture of first-millennium geopolitics:

> Contemporary evidence gives the impression that neighbours existed to be destroyed or, at least, impoverished; to be reduced to vassalage and/or poverty. Every neighbour was either a potential source of hostility or a potential source of revenue, to be exploited or spoliated, and sometimes as a necessary means to these ends, to be exterminated.[6]

---

2. On the discovery and ambiguities surrounding the Narmer Palette, see Michael A. Hoffman, *Egypt before the Pharaohs: The Prehistoric Foundations of Egyptian Civilization* (London: Routledge & Kegan Paul, 1980), 128–31.

3. The now discredited anthropological 'diffusionist theory' even went so far as to pinpoint the invention of war in ancient Egypt, from where it was supposedly exported to other world cultures. For example, see William J. Perry, *Children of the Sun: A Study in the Early History of Civilization* (London: Methuen, 1923); Grafton Elliot Smith, Bronislaw Malinowski, Herbert J. Spinden, and Alexander Goldenweiser, *Culture: The Diffusionist Controversy* (New York: W. W. Norton, 1927).

4. For the surviving text of the stele, see George A. Barton, *Royal Inscriptions of Sumer and Akkad* (New Haven, CT: Yale University Press, 1929), 23–33.

5. Goetze, 'Warfare in Asia Minor', 130; cf. Trimm, *Fighting for the King*, 1.

6. Thomas Fish, 'War and Religion in Ancient Mesopotamia', *Bulletin of the John Rylands Library* 23 (2) (1939): 387–402 at 390.

FIGURE 1. King Narmer/Menes smiting a prisoner of war under the gaze of the gods: Narmer Palette (recto), c. 3100 BCE. Unknown author, public domain, via Wikimedia Commons.

FIGURE 2. King Narmer/Menes inspecting rows of bound and decapitated prisoners of war, and a pair of entwined lions, symbolising the unification of Upper and Lower Egypt: Narmer Palette (verso), c. 3100 BCE. Unknown author, public domain, via Wikimedia Commons.

FIGURE 3. Egyptian soldiers carrying the regimental standards of the gods: Narmer Palette (verso), c. 3100 BCE. NebMaatRa, CC BY-SA 3.0 licence, via Wikimedia Commons.

FIGURE 4. Vultures carrying away enemy body parts after a battle: Stele of the Vultures, Sumeria, c. 2500 BCE. Sting, CC BY-SA 3.0 licence, via Wikimedia Commons.

Much of the extant evidence does suggest such a world-view, although we should be aware that the ideologies which informed the creation of many of our sources lent themselves to a histrionic recording of events. Histrionics aside, there is no doubt that in the ancient Near East military proficiency was crucial to political survival. Unfortunately for the military historian, there is no survival of a textual tradition discussing military strategy or tactics, and soldiering was almost certainly a craft learned largely through practical experience.[7]

Egyptian military history can be reconstructed through both the material and the textual artefacts that survive from the three major periods of centralised monarchy: the Old Kingdom (c. 2686–c. 2181), Middle Kingdom (c. 2055–c. 1650), and New Kingdom (c. 1552–c. 1069). Some of this evidence can be very full indeed. For example, it was the practice of Egyptian armies during the imperialistic New Kingdom to keep campaign diaries—there was even a designated 'chief military scribe'—which were subsequently deposited in the Theban Temple of Amun-Re. Annals could subsequently be transcribed onto the walls of temples, frequently accompanied by extensive and detailed carved reliefs showing scenes of the army on campaign, engaging in battle and returning victorious, laden with spoils and prisoners of war. In Hatti too, it was part of the king's duties to give account to the gods; this led to an annalistic style being developed by royal scribes for the recording of military deeds.[8] While the iconographic evidence is not as rich in the Hittite archaeological record as it is in the Egyptian, we are fortunate that Egyptian sources depict their Hittite foes on the occasions when those two great powers clashed.

The endurance of Egypt as a recognisable kingdom over the duration of three millennia is testament to the continuing effectiveness of the Egyptian military. Martial prowess was an important facet of Egyptian culture that is often downplayed in favour of its achievements in art and architecture. Ian Shaw argues that 'if the stereotyped image of Egypt is a nation of priests, scribes and embalmers, the real picture must also include the warriors and generals who maintained the stable conditions within which Egyptian civilisation was able to flourish'.[9] The same surely applies to any culture from this region and period. Those societies who could not array substantial military might were unlikely to survive the ongoing struggle for power and resources.

The character of warfare was broadly similar across the cultures of the ancient Near East, especially for those leading states with significant military resources. Armies consisted principally of infantry, including a core force of

---

7. Benjamin R. Foster, 'Transmission of Knowledge', in *A Companion to the Ancient Near East*, ed. Daniel C. Snell (Malden, MA: Blackwell, 2005), 245–52 at 249–50.

8. Raymond O. Faulkner, 'The Battle of Megiddo', *The Journal of Egyptian Archaeology* 28 (1942): 2–15 at 2; Goetze, 'Warfare in Asia Minor', 130.

9. Shaw, *Egyptian Warfare*, 7.

spearmen, archers, and slingers. From the second quarter of the second millennium, chariotry became increasingly prominent in the armies of the most powerful kingdoms. Cavalry also played a role in armies, acting as scouts or messengers, with some cavalrymen possibly fighting from horseback. Unfortunately, there is insufficient evidence for a detailed assessment of how cavalry was tactically deployed, although Egyptian and Assyrian reliefs suggest that it was used as a flanking force in support of the infantry and chariotry.[10]

Armed Forces

Army sizes in pre-modern societies are notoriously difficult to pin down with any degree of certainty, and this is certainly true of the ancient Near East. Hittite texts rarely comment on the size of their armed forces, so that modern estimates of Hittite armies range from anything between two thousand and thirty thousand troops. Howink ten Cate suggests that the lower end of this scale is more likely, with armies in the region of ten thousand troops during the Hittite Old Kingdom (c. 1650–c. 1500).[11] The early Anitta Inscription mentions an army of fourteen hundred infantry and forty teams of horses, which seems entirely credible.[12] King Hattušili I (c. 1650–c. 1620) was able to garrison three thousand troops in two different locations in response to an invasion from Mitanni. Even from early in the Hittite Old Kingdom there existed two military officers who each bore the title 'overseer-of-one-thousand-chariot-fighters', although whether 'one-thousand' refers to the number of chariots or to the number of crew is unclear (Hittite chariots typically carried a crew of three).[13]

Near Eastern army sizes appear to have swelled between c. 1600 and c. 1200. Anthony Spalinger argues that in 1457 the Egyptian pharaoh Thutmose III probably brought somewhere between five thousand and ten thousand troops to fight a Canaanite coalition at Megiddo.[14] From the fourteenth century, Hittite commanders could request three thousand troops for relatively minor expeditions or merely as reinforcements, leading Richard Beal to posit that 'a Hittite field army on a major expedition was well in excess of 10,000'.[15] Others have suggested that major campaign armies could have

---

10. Richard H. Beal, *The Organisation of the Hittite Military* (Heidelberg: Carl Winter, 1992), 190–98; Beal, 'The Organization of the Hittite Military' (PhD dissertation, University of Chicago, 1986), 103–5, 580; Yadin, *Art of Warfare*, 302–3. For references to Hittite commanders scouting the enemy and setting the army on alert, see *LettH*, Letters 7, 12, 13 at 97, 105–7.

11. Beal, 'Organization of the Hittite Military', 341; *AoH*, 72–73.

12. 'The Anitta Inscription', ll. 68–72, in *MHTH*, 27.

13. Beal, *Organisation of the Hittite Military*, 277–79, 282; Beal, 'Organization of the Hittite Military', 341–62.

14. Spalinger, *War in Ancient Egypt*, 36, 83–95.

15. Beal, 'Organization of the Hittite Military', 362.

FIGURE 5. Ramses II fighting at the battle of Kadesh (c. 1274 BCE): Ramesseum, Egypt, mid-thirteenth century BCE. Roland Unger, CC BY-SA 3.0 licence, via Wikimedia Commons.

exceeded thirty thousand,[16] and Hittite sources suggest that their perennial Anatolian enemies, the Kaska, were capable of fielding armies of up to nine thousand troops, including up to eight hundred chariots.[17]

One of the best-documented pitched battles of the Bronze Age Near East was the engagement fought between Egypt and Hatti at Kadesh in c. 1274 (see figure 5). The Egyptian pharaoh Ramses II claims that the combined Hittite forces at Kadesh numbered 37,000 infantry and 3,500 chariots. This included a large number of auxiliary troops recruited from Hittite vassal states. The battle, fought over two days, resulted in a stalemate. It seems reasonable to assume, therefore, that Ramses II's army was of a similar order of magnitude to the Hittite host. If so, Kadesh must have been one of the largest battles of the Bronze Age. Indeed, a military engagement totalling somewhere in the region of eighty thousand to a hundred thousand men can be accounted a massive battle in any era. Yet scholars have defended the possibility of Ramses II's estimate, arguing that at this time both Egypt and Hatti were capable of fielding forces of between forty thousand and fifty thousand men. Spalinger agrees that New Kingdom Egypt could perhaps have fielded thirty thousand to forty thousand troops, especially when one includes the numbers of foreign mercenaries.[18] However, this seems to have been a peak for Bronze Age army sizes.

16. J. G. Macqueen, *The Hittites and Their Contemporaries in Asia Minor* (London: Thames and Hudson, 1986), 56.

17. Glatz and Matthews, 'Anthropology', 56.

18. Beal *Organisation of the Hittite Military*, 291–94; Spalinger, *War in Ancient Egypt*, 36, 202–4, 209–29, esp. Excursus 1.

The later reign of Pharaoh Ramses III (c. 1186–1155) witnessed battles against the Libyans and Sea Peoples in which opposition army sizes could reasonably be estimated at around sixteen thousand.[19]

If we are somewhat hazy about Egyptian and Hittite army sizes, we have even less clarity when considering Israelite armies. The Book of Numbers (1:46 and 2:32) refers to a census of all Israelite males over twenty years of age (and thus able to bear arms), providing a total of 603,550 eligible levies. This is clearly fantastical, and even the army of forty thousand mentioned in Judges (5:8), when compared with the military resources of superpowers such as Egypt and Hatti, must be dismissed as pure fiction. When the Israelite commander Gideon gathered troops for an attack against Midian, Judges (6–8) tells us that thirty-two thousand men were initially recruited. Gideon whittled this number down to ten thousand and then, finally, to three hundred. Gideon's method of selection seems entirely arbitrary, but this final figure of three hundred is at least credible for a minor Levantine power.[20] By the ninth century, the northern Israelite kingdom of Samaria seems to have been able to muster a good-sized fighting force. Assyrian royal inscriptions record that King Ahab of Samaria fielded ten thousand infantry and two thousand chariots against Shalmaneser III at the battle of Qarqar (c. 853). While this figure seems relatively high for what was still only a minor kingdom (especially the number of chariots), it might be explained by the Assyrians counting Samaritan and Judahite forces together. There was also every reason for Assyrian scribes to exaggerate the numbers of Shalmaneser's enemies, in order to emphasise his victory. Whatever the case, Ahab's forces were apparently of similar size to those listed for the kings of Damascus and Hamath, who were also members of the alliance that rose against Assyria.[21]

Such substantial military capabilities obviously required sophisticated machineries of command and organisation. Old Kingdom Egyptian armies were levied regionally on an ad-hoc basis, and there are occasional references to an 'overseer of soldiers'.[22] But from the early second millennium, with the founding of the Middle Kingdom, there was a move towards a royal standing army bolstered by regional conscription and contingents of foreign mercenaries. From the Middle Kingdom onwards, there were commanding officers in charge of recruits and of shock troops, and there appears to have been a clear chain of military command linking the various fortresses and garrisons to the royal centre. By the time of the New Kingdom there was a large standing army, divided into two main corps, in Upper and Lower Egypt, and replete with a

19. Spalinger, *War in Ancient Egypt*, 237.
20. The selection is made by dividing the men on the basis of how they drink from a spring (Judges 7:4–7).
21. See the 'Monolith Inscriptions' of Shalmaneser III, 6th regnal year, in *ANEA*, 1:190; cf. 1 Kings 16:29; 2 Kings 8:3.
22. Shaw, *Egyptian Warfare*, 25; Trimm, *Fighting for the King*, 97–99.

professional officer class. When on campaign, this New Kingdom army could be organised into four divisions, named after the gods Ptah, Re/Pre, Amun, and Seth/Sutekh. It seems likely that a single division on campaign numbered roughly five thousand men.[23]

The use of foreign mercenaries and auxiliaries was common throughout the Near East, and of course vassal states were expected to provide troops to bolster the armies of their overlords. Nubians and, slightly later, Libyans and Sherden were regularly employed as mercenary troops throughout the region. By the first millennium there is also evidence of Hellenes operating as mercenaries in Egypt and elsewhere. Evidence of the composite nature of the Egyptian army is provided in the autobiography of Weni, who served as a military officer during the reigns of the Sixth Dynasty pharaohs Teti, Pepi I, and Merenre I:

> When his majesty [Pepi I] took action against the Asiatic Sand-dwellers, his majesty made an army of many tens of thousands from all of Upper Egypt: from Yebu in the south to Medenyt in the north; from Lower Egypt: from all of the Two-Sides-of-the-House and from Sedjer and Khen-sedjru; and from Irtjet-Nubians, Medja-Nubians, Yam-Nubians, Wawat-Nubians, Kaau-Nubians; and from Tjemeh-land.[24]

Auxiliary units often consisted of former prisoners of war who had been resettled and pressed into military service. Such troops usually retained their particular identity and armaments, as is clearly described in the 'Kadesh Poem' of Ramses II:

> Now his majesty had made ready his infantry and his chariotry, and the Sherden in his majesty's captivity whom he had brought back in the victories of his strong arm. They had been supplied with all their weapons, and battle orders had been given to them.[25]

In the Hittite Kingdom, the Great King was the undisputed commander-in-chief of the military and seems to have regularly led his soldiers on campaign. Below him was a complex web of high-ranking officers and regional

---

23. Yadin, *Art of Warfare*, 112; Shaw, *Egyptian Warfare*, 26–27; Trimm, *Fighting for the King*, 200.

24. 'Autobiography of Weni: Abydos', Cairo Museum 1435, *AEL*, 1:19.

25. 'Kadesh Poem', *AEL*, 2:63. See also Alan R. Schulman, *Military Rank, Title, and Organization in the Egyptian New Kingdom* (Berlin: Hessling, 1964), 37–38; Ziskind, 'Aspects of International Law', 174; Pierre-Marie Chevereau, 'L'Art et la science militaires dans l'Égypte ancienne', *Stratégique* 74–75 (1999) [online publication of the Institut de stratégie comparée (ISC); no pg. nos; article available at http://www.mafhoum.com/press6/160C31.htm (accessed 9 January 2023)]; John Ray, 'Soldiers to Pharaoh: The Carians of Southwest Anatolia', in *CANE*, 2:1185–94; Gary Beckman, 'Foreigners in the Ancient Near East', *Journal of the American Oriental Society* 133 (2) (2013): 203–16 at 209.

commanders, apparently lacking a rigid chain of command. For example, if the king was absent during a campaign, there was no automatic second-in-command. While this duty frequently fell to the crown prince, other leading officers (often princes of the blood) could also be entrusted with command. Yet, with a number of generals of relatively equal status vying for authority, Hittite armies were perhaps occasionally hampered by a lack of command unity.[26] Notwithstanding these competing interests, the system must have been effective enough, because for several centuries the Hittites were the dominant military superpower of the region.

Hittite armies consisted of a standing force of warriors made up of both infantry and elite chariot troops. This standing army performed garrison duties and even seems to have acted as a proto-police force when not on active campaign (a role fulfilled by soldiers also in Egypt). This force seems to have been complemented by soldiers who performed military service as a form of feudal levy connected to landholding.[27] In terms of sheer numbers, infantry constituted the bulk of Hittite forces, as it did in all armies of this region and period. Hittite sources do not specifically discuss the armaments of Hittite infantry on campaign, but the spear and shield were almost certainly the main arms of these troops. Egyptian reliefs depict Hittite infantry armed with spear and shield,[28] and like other infantrymen of the period these troops probably would have carried a variety of other bronze and stone melee weapons such as axes, maces, and daggers. The Mešedi, an elite royal palace guard, carried spears, while another force of elite troops was referred to as 'the men of the golden spear'.[29] Wealthier troops would have carried in addition expensive weapons such as bronze swords, as well as wearing leather and bronze scale armour. Arms and armour could also be acquired through plunder. A

---

26. Beal, *Organisation of the Hittite Military*, 318–19. For an extended analysis of the Hittite military offices, see ibid., 297–520.

27. This standing army was made up of the UKU.UŠ and the *šarikuwa* troops: Beal, *Organisation of the Hittite Military*, 37–55; Trimm, *Fighting for the King*, 99–101. Beal's volume remains the most thorough analysis of the Hittite military, but can be complemented by his original PhD thesis, which offers lengthier discussion of the implements of Hittite warfare: Beal, 'Organization of the Hittite Military', 563–685. For a more concise summary, see also Richard H. Beal, 'Hittite Military Organization', in *CANE*, 1:545–54.

28. Beal, *Organisation of the Hittite Military*, 198–201, 212–31; Beal, 'Organization of the Hittite Military', 605–19; Macqueen, *Hittites*, 59–64; Ian Shaw, 'Socio-economic and Iconographic Contexts for Egyptian Military Technology in the East Mediterranean: The Knowledge Economy and "Technology Transfer" in Late Bronze Age Warfare', in *The Knowledge Economy and Technological Capabilities: Egypt, the Near East and the Mediterranean, 2nd Millennium BC–1st Millennium AD*, ed. M. Wissa (Barcelona: Aula Orientalis, 2010), 77–85 at 79–82.

29. Beal, 'Organization of the Hittite Military', 266–88; *AoH*, 61. See also the Hittite Laws: 'If anyone steals a bronze spear in the gate of the palace, he shall be put to death.' In *LawH*, 116, ¶ 126.

bronze sword of Mycenaean B-type, dating to c. 1370, has been discovered at the Hittite capital of Hattuša; it bears a dedicatory inscription to the Great King Tudhaliya I, celebrating his victorious campaign against Assuwa (a state in western Anatolia).[30]

As in the Egyptian army of the mid-second millennium, the chariot corps was the principal shock force of the Hittites. As Goetze observes, '[c]harioteers were highly trained professionals, and thus useless for any other purpose but war'; they were thus provided with fiefs to maintain themselves and their retainers, rendering military service in return for these land grants.[31] In addition to the standing army, all Hittite subjects were eligible to serve as levies during specific campaigns, or to fulfil garrison duties.[32] This enrolment of the civilian population is indicative of a highly militarised society, in which martial values and customs must have had a significance not necessarily restricted to a small martial elite. Hittite kings also relied heavily on auxiliary troops provided by vassal states. Virtually every Hittite vassal treaty included clauses that stipulated the military obligations of the vassal, and these were treated with the utmost seriousness by the imperial capital. A vassal's failure to fulfil the troop levy was considered a hostile act, potentially leading to military reprisals.[33] Occasionally, manpower could be substituted by monetary payments, which presumably were then used by the Hittite state to hire mercenaries.[34] While we lack specific evidence of how mercenaries operated within Hittite armies, there are several references to 'the mercenary gods' in Hittite treaties—perhaps these deities were understood to represent such troops and bind their oaths of service.[35]

Israelite infantry would have been comparably arrayed to their Egyptian and Hittite predecessors, although by the early first millennium many soldiers,

---

30. 'Bronzeschwert, zufällig entdeckt bei Straßenarbeiten in Eski Örenyeri bei Bogazköy, mit Weihinschrift eines Großkönigs Tuthalija anläßlich eines erfolgreichen Feldzugs gegen Aššuwa.' Horst Klengel, *Geschichte des Hethitischen Reiches* (Leiden: Brill, 1999), 104.

31. Goetze, 'Warfare in Asia Minor', 126.

32. Beal, *Organisation of the Hittite Military*, 56–117; Beal, 'Organization of the Hittite Military', 133–39; Harry A. Hoffner Jr., 'Translations D.—Hittite', in *LCMAM*, 245.

33. Beal, *Organisation of the Hittite Military*, 71–92; Beal, 'Organization of the Hittite Military', 220–39; Trimm, *Fighting for the King*, 118–20, For examples of military obligations within vassal treaties, see *HDT*, 16, 23–24, 29, 37–38, 61, 106, 164–65, 166; *ANEA*, 2:42–45.

34. For example: 'Edict of Tudhaliya IV Releasing Ammistamru II of Ugarit from Participation in War against Assyria', in *HDT*, 183. See also Beal, 'Organization of the Hittite Military', 258.

35. For example: 'Treaty between Muršili II and Manapa-Tarhunta of Land of the Seha River', § 17, 'the mountain-dweller gods, all the mercenary gods of Hatti'; 'Treaty between Muwattalli II and Alaksandu of Wilusa', § 19: 'mountain-dweller gods, the mercenary gods'. *HDT*, 86, 92.

especially elites, would have been carrying iron weapons. The story told by the books of Judges, Samuel, and Kings is of a loose confederacy of tribal armies gradually being restructured into a military force under the command of a king. From the biblical evidence, Saul appears to have been determined to establish a permanent standing army of three thousand men in order to reinforce royal authority, and this was subsequently expanded by David. These troops perhaps originated in the *ne-arim*, a cadre of elite warriors mentioned several times in the Tanakh. From Saul's reign there also appear references to the position of 'army commander', an experienced soldier who acted as second-in-command to the king.[36]

In Egypt, prior to the New Kingdom, it was traditionally the navy rather than the army that possessed the greatest prestige, with aristocrats making up the naval officer class. Armies were transported on the Nile by the royal flotilla, disembarking to lay siege to strategic locations, to engage in land battles, or to launch raids for plunder or punishment. During the New Kingdom the Egyptian seagoing fleet was also expanded to ply the waters of the eastern Mediterranean and Red Sea, for both trade and military purposes.[37] Naval battles occurred, as the intricate reliefs at Medinet Habu testify; these depict a battle raging across a number of ships belonging to the Egyptians and the invading Sea Peoples.[38] It was not until the arrival of the war chariot in Egypt in the mid-second millennium, which heralded the rapid emergence of the chariot corps as a military and social elite, that the navy was ousted from its preeminent social position. During the New Kingdom period, the chariotry corps became the new focus for elite Egyptian warriors. This shift went hand in hand with a policy of territorial expansion which meant that Egyptian wars were increasingly taking place beyond the Nile valley, especially in Syria-Palestine.

The Hittites, by contrast, did not seem at all interested in developing a navy; when pressed, they appear to have relied on their Levantine vassals and allies—cities such as Ugarit—to provide them with the necessary maritime resources. Equally, there is no mention of navies or maritime warfare in the books of the Hebrew Tanakh.

Weapons Technology

It is broadly accurate to say that between c. 3000 and c. 500 BCE military technology changed little as far as the basic forms of weaponry and tactics were concerned. There are two major exceptions to this statement. The first was the

---

36. On references to the *ne-arim*, see 1 Samuel 13:2; 2 Samuel 21:18–21; 22:14–18; 23:18–39; 1 Chronicles 11–23. See also Gerhard von Rad, *Holy War in Ancient Israel*, trans. and ed. Marva J. Dawn (Grand Rapids, MI: Eerdmans, 1991), 75; *KANE*, 2:446–47.

37. See Shaw, *Egyptian Warfare*, 59–64; Spalinger, *War in Ancient Egypt*, 46, 52–59; Morkot, *Ancient Egyptian Warfare*, 150–53; *WANE*, 451–55.

38. Shaw, *Egyptian Warfare*, 61–63.

introduction in the first half of the second millennium of the light war chariot, which quickly came to dominate elite styles of warfare. The second was the transition from stone, copper, and bronze to bronze and iron armaments.

The Bronze Age began in the Near East around 3300, but stone weapons in the form of knives, maces, axe-heads, arrowheads, and sling shot were still in use long after this date. Equally, the transition to iron began around 1200, but this was a gradual process and proceeded at different rates in different places. Iron weapons would have represented the pinnacle of weapons technology at the turn of the first millennium and would have commanded correspondingly high prices. As a result, bronze arms and armour were still abundant throughout the first millennium. As a rule, it seems that the major drivers of military technology were the warring peoples and states of Asia Minor and Mesopotamia, with the kingdom of Egypt often lagging behind in adopting new technology and tactics. By the early first millennium, Assyria had emerged as the leading military power of the region, and could afford to equip its spearmen and archers with coats of iron mail and long straight-bladed iron swords.

The use of archery in war dates back thousands of years in the Near East. Archaeological evidence from the oldest known battlefield, at Gebel Sahaba in modern-day northern Sudan, consists of the remains of fifty-nine skeletons (men, women, and children). These skeletons have been dated to c. 12000– c. 9000, and almost half of the excavated bodies contained flint projectiles.[39] In other words, these people were felled by arrows. A tomb from Old Kingdom Egypt contains scenes of an Egyptian assault upon a city, with enemies pierced by arrows and axe-wielding soldiers dispatching the fallen.[40] Bows are widely attested in the art of the third millennium throughout the region, but it seems likely that the composite recurved bow—considerably more powerful but more technically demanding to manufacture—was not introduced until the late third or early second millennium.[41] Archers primarily fought on foot as part of the main infantry, but the bow remained of fundamental importance to chariot warfare across the region, with warriors shooting from their moving platforms (see figures 5, 6, and 7).[42] Hittite martial culture also held archery in

---

39. *WANE*, 32; compare to the remains found in the Middle Kingdom 'Tomb of the Warriors': ibid., 438–39.

40. Tomb of Inta at Deshashe: McDermott, *Warfare in Ancient Egypt*, 20–21. There is some debate as to whether Egyptians tipped their arrows with poison, although if they did it may well have been restricted to hunting: ibid., 28; Darnell and Manassa, *Tutankhamun's Armies*, 73. See also Adrienne Mayor, *Greek Fire, Poison Arrows, and Scorpion Bombs: Biological and Chemical Warfare in the Ancient World* (Woodstock: Overlook Press, 2004), 63–97.

41. Yadin, *Art of Warfare*, 47, 80; Beal, 'Organization of the Hittite Military', 586.

42. On archery and New Kingdom chariotry, see Yadin, *Art of Warfare*, 80–83, 86–90; Shaw, *Egyptian Warfare*, 31–44; Spalinger, *War in Ancient Egypt*, 117–18, 120–23, 198–99, 237–38; *WANE*, 356–59, 422–25; Darnell and Manassa, *Tutankhamun's Armies*, 70–73, 77–80.

FIGURE 6. Ramses II fighting from chariots, shooting a bow and arrow, and spearing an enemy chief: Temple at Abu Simbel, Egypt, thirteenth century BCE. Dwkriden1, CC BY-SA 4.0 licence, via Wikimedia Commons.

great esteem; indeed, the 'bow was so important a part of the Hittite army that it was used as the symbol of masculinity'.[43] However, we know very little about how archers were actually deployed during campaigns or specific battles.[44]

As mentioned above, spearmen formed the core of ancient Near Eastern armies and thus spears are readily attested in our textual and material sources. Such infantry carried heavy spears tipped with a bronze, and later iron, leaf-shaped head. Spears were used across the social spectrum, including by charioteers. From the Egyptian Middle Kingdom, spears are found deposited in elite graves, and Egyptian pharaohs are represented as killing enemies with spears.[45] Lighter javelins, designed for throwing, are also widely attested, and were again carried in war chariots.[46]

43. Beal, 'Organization of the Hittite Military', 583
44. Beal, *Organisation of the Hittite Military*, 201.
45. McDermott, *Warfare in Ancient Egypt*, 80; Sylvia Schoske, 'Das Erschlagen der Feinde: Ikonographie und Stilistik der Feindvernichtung im alten Ägypten' (Inauguraldissertation zur Erlangung des Doktorgrades [doctoral dissertation], Heidelberg, 1982), 181–95.
46. Beal, 'Organization of the Hittite Military', 605–19; Yadin, *Art of Warfare*, 80.

Infantry spearmen are almost always depicted carrying large shields, which were roughly rectangular and would have been constructed from wood and covered in animal-hide (figures 8 and 9). Early Dynastic and Old Kingdom Egyptian soldiers wore little or no armour but, as time passed, boiled leather, bronze scale, and finally iron scale armour was introduced. Further protection came in the shape of conical leather and later metal helmets of different types, which are depicted in numerous reliefs. As defensive equipment, such as bronze helmets and scale armour, improved during the Late Bronze Age and early Iron Age, shields generally became smaller.[47]

Regarding melee weapons, the most common types were the axe and dagger. Axes were of both tang and socket types, and widely carried.[48] Again, the transition from stone to bronze to iron is apparent. Maces, while common during the third millennium, were effectively replaced by axes at the turn of the second. Nonetheless, maces appear to have held a symbolic and ceremonial importance, and continue to be depicted on reliefs well after this

---

47. Yadin, *Art of Warfare*, 83–85; *WANE*, 324, 422–23.
48. For example, Yadin, *Art of Warfare*, 77–78, 180–85, 222.

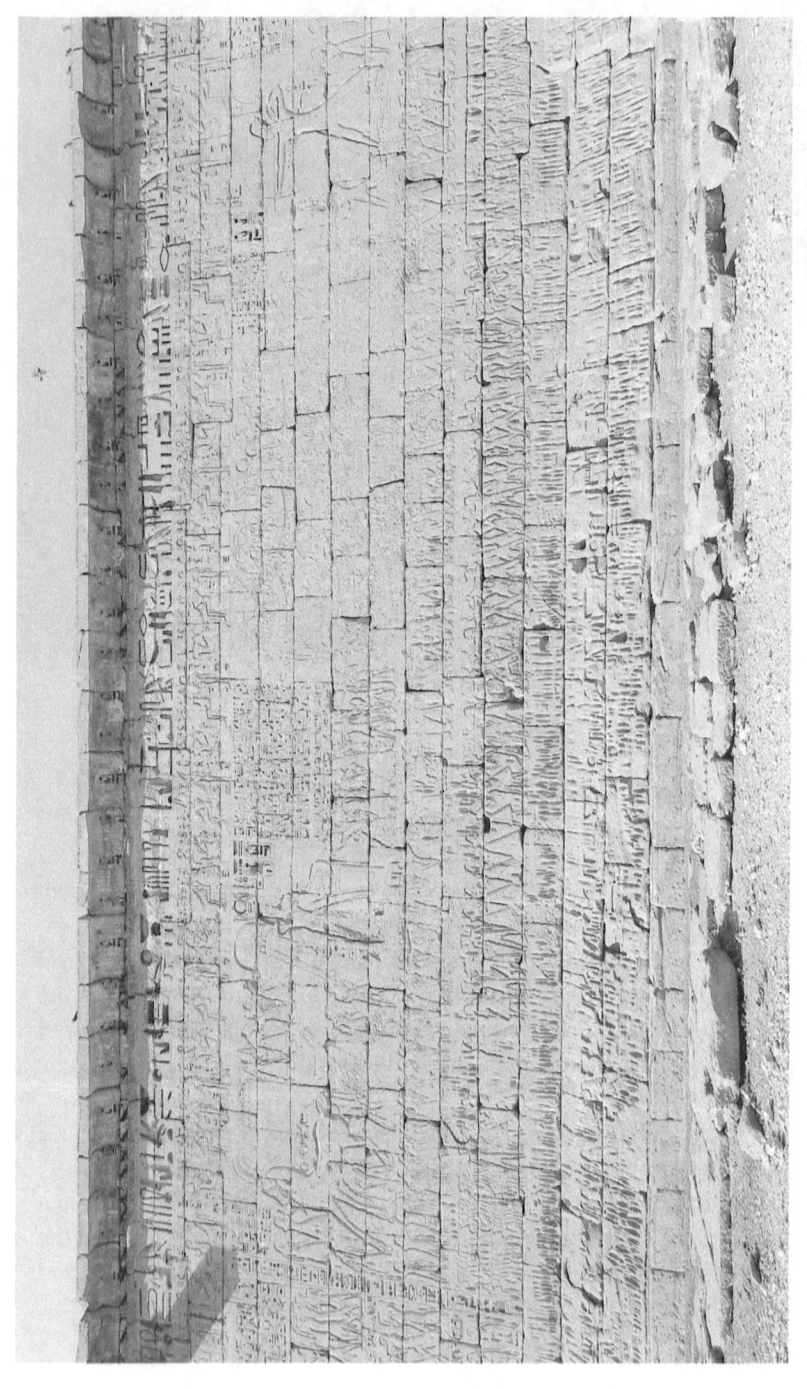

FIGURE 7. Ramses III (right of image) depicted as a great archer fighting the Sea Peoples: Temple of Medinet Habu, Egypt, mid-twelfth century BCE. Olaf Tausch, CC BY 3.0 licence, via Wikimedia Commons.

FIGURE 8. Egyptian model spearmen: grave goods from the tomb of Mesehti at Asyut, Middle Kingdom, c. 2000 BCE. Udimu, CC BY-SA 3.0 licence, via Wikimedia Commons.

FIGURE 9. Egyptian model spearmen: grave goods from the tomb of Mesehti at Asyut, Middle Kingdom, c. 2000 BCE. Cairo Museum, 2022, https://www.ancient-egypt.co.uk/cairo%20museum/cm,%20models/index.htm.

FIGURE 10. Seti I (r. c. 1305–c. 1290/c. 1294–c. 1279 BCE) fighting Libyans (the pharaoh wields a sickle-shaped sword, or *khopesh*): Great Hypostyle Hall, Karnak Temple, Egypt, early thirteenth century BCE. Peter Brand / Karnak Hypostyle Hall Project, University of Memphis.

time.[49] Daggers are depicted in many reliefs from throughout the period, in Egypt, Hatti, and the Levant. Around the mid-second millennium we see the introduction of an elegant curved, sickle-shaped sword called the *khopesh* or *khepesh*: a type of hybrid between a sword and an axe (see figure 10). Straight-bladed swords were also developed from the thirteenth century, possibly an innovation introduced from the Aegean by the migratory and invading Sea Peoples.[50] By the early first millennium such swords were being widely used, and were adopted en masse by the conquering armies of Assyria. It is probably safe to assume, therefore, that similar swords would have been found in Samaritan and Judahite armies of the same period.

The chariot corps were unquestionably the elite shock troops of ancient Near Eastern armies from the second quarter of the second millennium onwards. The war chariot, equipped with eight- or six-spoked wheels, became the most important piece of Late Bronze Age and Iron Age military technology. Being lighter, faster, and more manoeuvrable than the earlier ox- or donkey-drawn 'war carts' of the Sumerian period, the 'true' war chariot was developed in eastern Anatolia at the beginning of the second millennium and was perfected by about 1650.[51] This technology gradually spread across

---

49. *WANE*, 252.
50. Yadin, *Art of Warfare*, 79.
51. Goetze, 'Warfare in Asia Minor', 125–26; M. A. Littauer and J. H. Crouwel, 'The Origin of the True Chariot', *Antiquity* 70 (1996): 934–39; *WANE*, 145–53.

Anatolia, Mesopotamia, Syria, Palestine and, finally, into Egypt during the sixteenth century.[52]

The Hittite and Mesopotamian chariot differed from the Egyptian type in that it was larger and heavier, carrying a crew of three or four warriors rather than two.[53] Since we have no archaeological evidence of Israelite chariotry, it is unclear which type of chariot the Israelite kingdoms preferred. The only known representation of a Judean chariot appears on an Assyrian relief depicting the aftermath of the battle of Lachish (c. 701): an eight-spoked chariot, identical to the Assyrian type, is shown being hauled away as booty, devoid of its crew.[54] The First Book of Kings claims that Solomon 'had 1,400 chariots and 12,000 horses', although even Yigael Yadin's more conservative claim that Solomon may have commanded five hundred chariots is wholly speculative.[55] As mentioned above, in the mid-ninth century Samaria may have been able to field up to two thousand chariots, although by the late seventh century Judah's army had apparently been reduced to just fifty horsemen and ten chariots.[56]

The social status of the chariotry is clear: the chariot constituted the highest level of military technology of the time and so was associated exclusively with military elites. To produce and maintain the equipment, animals, and skilled warriors that made up a chariot crew must have represented a significant cost. The numbers of chariots a state could field would therefore have been commensurate to its wealth and power. In Egypt, images of the pharaoh crushing his enemies under the wheels of his chariot became ubiquitous.[57] Yet we should remember that the bulk of all ancient Near Eastern armies continued to be made up of infantry forces.

---

52. The scholarly consensus is that war chariots were probably introduced to Egypt by the Hyksos, who invaded and ruled most of Lower Egypt between the seventeenth and sixteenth centuries. However, the argument in Ian Shaw, 'Egyptians, Hyksos and Military Technology: Causes, Effects or Catalysts?', in *The Social Context of Technological Change: Egypt and the Near East, 1650–1150 BC*, ed. Andrew J. Shortland (Oxford: Oxbow, 2001), 59–71, problematises this dominant thesis of a relatively straightforward transference of military technology.

53. For a detailed discussion of Hittite chariotry, see Beal, *Organisation of the Hittite Military*, 142–90. Possibly the only Hittite depiction of chariot warfare is a flat stone relief discovered at Hattuša which has been dated to the Hittite Old Kingdom: Andreas Schachner, 'Gedanken zur Datierung, Entwicklung und Funktion der hethitischen Kunst', *Altorientalische Forschungen* 39 (1) (2012): 130–66 at 133–34.

54. See image in Kelle, *Ancient Israel at War*, 35.

55. 1 Kings 10:26; cf. 1 Kings 5:6, which claims that Solomon possessed forty thousand stalls for horses for his chariots and maintained twelve thousand horsemen. See also Yadin, *Art of Warfare*, 285–88.

56. 2 Kings 13:7.

57. For examples, see Schoske, 'Erschlagen der Feinde', 208–11.

Fortifications

One only has to look at the imposing remains of the Egyptian mud-brick fortress of Buhen, or the bases of the massive walls of the Hittite capital of Hattuša, to realise that ancient Near Eastern societies took defensive engineering very seriously. Throughout the Levant, princelings fortified their cities as a necessary means of survival. Egypt, with its natural borders, invested heavily in fortifying the edges of the kingdom, constructing chains of fortresses along the western and eastern delta and along the Cataracts of the Nile to the south.[58] In the late fourth millennium, one of the first acts of King Narmer—having successfully unified the Two Lands of Upper and Lower Egypt—was to construct a massive new fortified capital at Memphis, named Ineb Hedj: 'the White Fortress'. In the early second millennium, a massive mud-brick fortress was constructed at Buhen, guarding the First Cataract and Egypt's southern border (figure 11).[59]

The Hittites were particularly expert in defensive architecture, with one historian describing them as 'the most skilful fortress builders of the Ancient Middle East', and the walls of Hattuša as 'the most grandiose fortification in the ancient world'.[60] By the fourteenth century the multi-level fortified city walls of Hattuša, punctuated with numerous towers and bastions, totalled more than six kilometres (3.7 miles) in length and were eight metres (26 feet) thick in places (figures 12 and 13).[61] Jerusalem, too, must have been an extremely well-fortified city. Although the present walls surrounding the old city were constructed under the Ottomans in the sixteenth century CE, there is ample evidence of walled fortifcations existing much earlier than this. The fact that the city was able to withstand the might of the Babylonian army for two years (589–587) before eventually falling to Nebuchadnezzar is testament to the strength of its defences.

In contrast to the achievements in defensive architecture, siege technology remained quite rudimentary. For example, in the mid-fifteenth century Pharaoh Thutmose III won a quick and crushing victory against the armies of a Canaanite coalition on the plains in front of Megiddo; yet it took the Egyptians a further seven months to capture the city itself. A Hittite Old Kingdom text named the 'Siege of Uršu' mentions the construction of earthen 'siegeworks' and 'a battering ram of Hurrian type', but according to the text such

---

58. A. W. Lawrence, 'Ancient Egyptian Fortifications', *The Journal of Egyptian Archaeology* 51 (1965): 69–94 at 71–93; Shaw, *Egyptian Warfare*, 15–24.

59. *WANE*, 319.

60. Ekrem Akurgal, *The Art of the Hittites*, trans. Constance McNab, photographs by Max Hirmer (New York: Abrams, 1962), 107–8. On fortifications, see also Goetze, 'Warfare in Asia Minor', 127; Macqueen, *Hittites*, 64–73.

61. Yadin, *Art of Warfare*, 91–92.

FIGURE 11. The massive fortified mud-brick walls of the Fortress of Buhen, Upper Egypt, Middle Kingdom, early second millennium BCE. UNESCO, CC BY-SA 3.0 IGO licence, via Wikimedia Commons.

devices had failed to breach the city's walls.[62] A later letter sent to the Hittite king by a provincial military commander named Kaššu reports that, despite sapping and storming the walls of an enemy city, his assaults had been unsuccessful. Kaššu also referred to something called an *epureššar*, which might have been a type of siege tower or elevated archery platform; but evidently this too had failed to breach the city's defences.[63] As was the general rule prior to the introduction of powerful gunpowder artillery in the fifteenth century CE, blockade was probably the most effective (albeit time-consuming) technique for capturing fortified sites. This posed a less immediate danger to one's own forces (not having to risk direct assaults), but we must assume that ancient armies faced the same threats of disease, malnutrition, and counter-attack during sieges as any other army from any other historical period.

As a rule, therefore, a fortified city was a place of refuge where non-combatants and armies could retreat to avoid open battle against superior

62. Gary Beckman, 'The Siege of Uršu Text (CTH 7) and Old Hittite Historiography', *Journal of Cuneiform Studies* 47 (1995): 23–34 at 26.

63. 'No. 111: To the King from Kaššu', *LettH*, 340–44, esp. 341.

FIGURE 12. Defensive rampart, Hattuša, mid-second millennium BCE. China Crisis, CC BY-SA 2.0 licence, via Wikimedia Commons.

FIGURE 13. A modern reconstruction of part of Hattuša's fortified ring wall. Rita1234, CC BY-SA 3.0 licence, via Wikimedia Commons.

forces. Indeed, as is the case for most military history up to the early modern period, sieges and raiding were undoubtedly the dominant forms of warfare in the ancient Near East, with large pitched battles being relatively rare.[64] Such battles would only have taken place when both sides fancied their chances of success and a decisive military result was required for geopolitical reasons, or when one side had run out of other options. The effectiveness of defensive fortifications would certainly have given invading forces an incentive to try to force the enemy into open battle and so avoid the possibility of expensive sieges which could last for months or even years. While there is nothing in our sources to match the legendary decade-long siege of Troy, the tale of the *Iliad* embodies a truth—albeit an exaggerated one—of ancient warfare: that the heavily fortified city was a difficult nut to crack.

When pitched battle did occur, war leaders would have employed tactics that made the best use of the troops under their command. With most armies built around large units of spearmen and archers, commanders must have favoured reasonably large open spaces in which to manoeuvre their phalanxes. On the flanks there likely operated skirmishers armed with slings and javelins, as well as cavalrymen. Battles almost certainly commenced with the deployment of the missile troops. Once the archers and slingers had caused enough damage or panic in the enemy ranks, the phalanxes of spearmen would have advanced into the fray to engage in hand-to-hand combat. Reliefs show axe- and mace-wielding soldiers delivering the killing blow to enemies already struck by arrows.

After the introduction of the chariot, the desire to fight on level open terrain must have only become more urgent, as the shock of the chariot charge would have been nullified by rough terrain covered with obstacles such as waterways and woods. The principal use of the chariot was as a highly mobile platform to transport elite troops quickly around the battlefield, with charioteers carrying bows, javelins, shields, and hand-weapons such as daggers, swords, and axes. It is equally possible that chariots, like cavalry, were deployed on the flanks of the main infantry force.[65] If so, their superior speed could have been used to attempt to outflank and surround enemy forces. Archers would have been able to shoot from moving chariots, but it is likely that warriors also dismounted for hand-to-hand fighting, much like we read in Homeric descriptions of battle on the plains of Troy.[66] Indeed, the story of the *Iliad*, in which virtually all of the fighting takes place on the open plains below Troy's unscalable walls, is surely reflective of a military reality that would have been familiar to ancient Egyptians, Hittites, Israelites, and Hellenes alike.

64. Trimm, *Fighting for the King*, 187–88.
65. Ibid., 191.
66. There is compelling evidence that Hittite and Anatolian culture helped to shape the form of Homeric epic. See Mary R. Bachvarova, *From Hittite to Homer: The Anatolian Background of Ancient Greek Epic* (Cambridge: Cambridge University Press, 2016).

This brief summary has had to paint in broad strokes and cannot provide a detailed assessment of ancient Near Eastern warfare. Nevertheless, it has been sufficient to indicate that military activity could be large-scale and complex, and that military commanders were willing and able to employ a range of different strategies and tactics. The art of war in the ancient Near East was certainly not one-dimensional. For example, the lengthy Egyptian account of the battle of Kadesh makes it clear that the Hittites practised a form of counter-intelligence to misdirect the Egyptian army and subsequently launched an ambush against Ramses II's divided marching columns. Equally, as will be discussed in the chapters that follow, there are numerous examples of commanders launching or falling victim to ambushes and night attacks. In other words, there was tactical flexibility displayed throughout the ancient Near East. But above all else, ancient commanders and soldiers were motivated by a desire to win. Their very survival depended on it.

Egypt, c. 3150–c. 1069 BCE

CHAPTER TWO

Egypt: Historical Introduction

PART I FOCUSES ON two thousand years of Egyptian history, from the turn of the third millennium to the end of the second millennium BCE. During this long period, Egypt experienced a myriad of military and political fortunes. The initial unification of the Two Lands in the closing years of the fourth millennium was a political but also undoubtedly a military achievement. The political stability of the Old Kingdom (c. 2686–c. 2181) and Middle Kingdom (c. 2055–c. 1650) was bifurcated by foreign invasion and dominance, as was the transition from the Middle Kingdom to the New Kingdom (c. 1552–c. 1069). It was during this third and final great kingdom period that the rulers of Egypt fully utilised their military might to pursue imperialist policies, pushing the boundaries of Egypt to their furthest extent into both Africa and Syria-Palestine.

Society and Geopolitics

The popular image of ancient Egypt is of a society excelling in art, architecture, literature, and occult knowledge. From pyramids and sprawling temple complexes to golden death masks and lapis lazuli jewellery, this is a romantic and highly selective picture of ancient Egyptian society and culture. Created as early as the Greco-Roman period, this gilded image rarely leaves space for political or military history and overlooks the essential role that politics and warfare played throughout the history of Egypt.[1] Indeed, it could be argued that the politico-military achievements of the pharaohs were the bedrock upon which Egyptian culture was built, providing a level of territorial security and socio-economic stability that enabled the flourishing of intellectual and artistic pursuits.

---

1. László Kákosy, 'Egypt in Ancient Greek and Roman Thought', in *CANE*, 1:3–14; Helen Whitehouse, 'Egypt in European Thought', in *CANE*, 1:15–31.

CHRONOLOGY: THE PERIODISATION OF EGYPTIAN HISTORY

Among the most influential sources for ancient Egyptian history is the third-century writer Manetho, an Egyptian priest at Heliopolis writing in Greek during the Ptolemaic era. That Manetho should be such an important source is somewhat surprising on account of two factors. First, all of his writings, including his main work the *Aegyptiaca* (*History of Egypt*), survive only in fragmentary form, recovered from later authors such as Flavius Josephus, Sextus Julius Africanus, Eusebius, and Plutarch.[2] Jewish apologists such as Josephus were particularly interested in Manetho's *History*, for within it they sought historical confirmation of the existence of figures such as Abraham, Joseph, and Moses, and moulded the text to achieve this objective.[3] Further liberties were taken by early Christian chronographers such as Eusebius.[4] Second, while Manetho was a native Egyptian author, he was writing in an imported foreign language (Greek) and at least a thousand years after the kingdom of Egypt had fallen from its perch as a geopolitical superpower. By the time Manetho was writing in the early third century, Egypt had been dominated by foreign powers—Kushite, Assyrian, Babylonian, Persian, Macedonian—for more than five hundred years.

The reason why Manetho's *Aegyptiaca* has proven so influential in our understanding of ancient Egypt lies in the method by which he divided Egyptian history chronologically, according to the reigns of successive royal dynasties.[5] This practice of organising the long history of Egypt according to dynasties—from Dynasty 'o' beginning in c. 3150 to Dynasty XXX ending in c. 343—is followed by scholars to this day. Indeed, it has proven so influential that Egyptologists, unlike specialists studying other ancient Near Eastern civilisations, do not follow the archaeologically derived stratigraphic periodisation of the Bronze Age, but prefer the chronological framework derived from Manetho's dynasties.[6]

---

2. Manetho, *History of Egypt and Other Works*, trans. W. G. Waddell (1940; repr. Cambridge, MA: Harvard University Press, 2014), vii–ix, xi–xii, xvi.

3. See Flavius Josephus, *Flavius Josephus: Translation and Commentary*, ed. Steve Mason, 10 vols (Leiden: Brill, 2000–2017), vol. 10: *Against Apion*, trans. John M. G. Barclay (2007), esp. bk 1.

4. Manetho, *History of Egypt*, xvi–xvii.

5. Manetho begins with the reigns of gods, demi-gods and spirits of the dead, who apparently ruled in Egypt for 24,900 lunar years, or 2,206 solar years: ibid., 7.

6. Antonio Loprieno, 'Defining Egyptian Literature: Ancient Texts and Modern Literary Theory', in *The Study of the Ancient Near East in the 21st Century: The William Foxwell Albright Centennial Conference*, ed. Jerrold S. Cooper and Glenn M. Schwartz (Winona Lake, IN: Eisenbrauns, 1996), 209–332 at 210.

While Manetho may have been significantly removed in time from the great pharaohs of the third and second millennia, he had at his disposal a veritable treasure trove of historical resources. As the Loeb translation points out, '[h]e had open access to records of all kinds—papyri in the temple archives (annals, sacred books containing liturgies and poems), hieroglyphic tablets, wall sculptures, and innumerable inscriptions. These records no one but an Egyptian priest could consult and read.'[7] Scholars cannot be sure of the exact sources Manetho consulted, but king lists dating from the New Kingdom can be found on the walls of temples such as Karnak (sixty-one kings, from Menes to Thutmose III) and the Temple of Seti I at Abydos (seventy-six kings, from Menes to Seti I)[8]. Equally crucial to our understanding of Egyptian chronology is the Turin Papyrus, also referred to as the 'Turin Royal Canon', dating from around the reign of Ramses II (c. 1200). Written in hieratic, this papyrus contains a list of over three hundred kings, beginning (as does Manetho) with the mythical age of the gods and providing the reigns of each king in years, months, and days. The Turin Royal Canon divides the kings into dynasties, with the cumulative years of each dynasty recorded: evidence that this chronological practice of dynastic division was already employed in Egypt during the second millennium. Indeed, the practice of creating annalistic king lists actually goes back much earlier, as attested by the Palermo Stone—originally a large black diorite stele but surviving only in fragmentary form—which hails from Dynasty V; that is, some time around 2600. The Palermo list of early kings and events bears a close resemblance to Manetho's later account.[9]

It should be stressed that Manetho's account is far from infallible. Notably, the lengths of certain reigns are impossibly long. Nor did Manetho fully exploit the historical resources available to him.[10] Nevertheless, the value of the *Aegyptiaca* 'lies in the dynastic skeletons which serve as a framework for the evidence of the monuments, and it has provided in its essentials the accepted scheme of Egyptian chronology'.[11] Conceptually, the chronological ordering of Egyptian history has been further organised by modern scholars into the broader periods listed below in Appendix 1. The primary purpose of this periodisation is to distinguish the times when Egypt was effectively unified under a centralised authority (the major 'kingdom' periods) as opposed to

---

7. Manetho, *History of Egypt*, xx.

8. Notably, the Abydos list excludes the Hyksos kings as well as Akhenaten and his immediate successors.

9. Manetho, *History of Egypt*, xxii–xxiv. A close examination of the king lists is provided in Donald B. Redford, *Pharaonic King-Lists, Annals and Day-Books: A Contribution to the Study of the Egyptian Sense of History* (Mississauga, Ontario: Benben, 1986). For translation of the Palermo Stone text, see Nigel C. Strudwick, *Texts from the Pyramid Age*, ed. Ronald J. Leprohon (Atlanta, GA: Society of Biblical Literature, 2005), 65–74.

10. William J. Murnane, 'The History of Ancient Egypt: An Overview', in *CANE*, 2:691.

11. Manetho, *History of Egypt*, xxv.

periods when political authority was fragmented. Such fragmentation could be caused by domestic civil war (First Intermediate), foreign invasion (Second Intermediate), or both (Third Intermediate and Late Period).

Like all schematic models, the neat organisation of Egyptian history into dynasties and kingdom/intermediate periods inevitably hides a much more complex historical reality. Socio-political changes cannot always be satisfactorily mapped onto this schema, and the ideology of royal propaganda did not always keep pace with changing political circumstances. For example, even pharaohs who had palpably lost control of the unified kingdom continued to refer to themselves as 'Lord of the Two Lands'.[12] Such ideological blindness to political reality is comparable to medieval German emperors styling themselves *dominus mundi* (lord of the world). There is also a difficulty in correlating references to specific kings, on the one hand, to specific events or monuments, on the other. This partly arises from Egyptian royal naming conventions: Early Dynastic kings possessed three official names (increasing to five names in later dynasties), and it is not always clear how to assign multiple names to individual kings.[13]

What is offered below, therefore, is a summary of the history of ancient Egypt according to the widely accepted 'periods' discussed above.[14] This is not intended as a comprehensive introduction, but rather as something of a chronological and historical map, aiding readers to situate the ethical developments analysed in chapters 3 and 4.

Pre-dynastic and Old Kingdom Periods, c. 3100–c. 2181

According to ancient Egyptian tradition, the kingdom of Egypt comprised the 'Two Lands' (see Map 1). Lower Egypt encompassed the Nile valley from Memphis (just south of modern Cairo) northwards, where the river splits into the many branches that make up the Nile delta, draining eventually into the Mediterranean Sea. Upper Egypt stretched south from Memphis, all the way upriver to the First Cataract of the Nile and the town of Swenett, near modern-day Aswan. As tradition had it, the Two Lands of Egypt had first been unified by King Menes (c. 3100). Symbolically, this political union was signified by the 'double crown' worn by Egyptians kings, incorporating both the red crown of Lower Egypt and the white crown of Upper Egypt.

12. Murnane, 'History of Ancient Egypt', 693.

13. Alan H. Gardiner, *Egypt of the Pharaohs: An Introduction* (Oxford: Clarendon Press, 1961), 69–71; *KANE*, 1:127.

14. There is a vast literature, too lengthy to list here, on ancient Egypt's long and complex political and cultural history. However, I have found the following concise treatments to be particularly useful in organising the above summary: *KANE*, 1:118–224; Donald B. Redford, *Egypt, Canaan, and Israel in Ancient Times* (Princeton, NJ: Princeton University Press, 1992), 29–213; Murnane, 'History of Ancient Egypt', 691–717; Erik Hornung, *History of Ancient Egypt*, trans. David Lorton (Edinburgh: Edinburgh University Press, 1999).

Previous to unification, during the so-called Archaic Period (c. 3300–c. 3150), a large number of competing autonomous communities had developed along the fertile Nile valley and delta, exploiting the agricultural and trade potential of the river lands and quite suddenly creating large urban centres in the late fourth millennium. This period witnessed rapid societal and economic change—a 'quantum leap'—transforming basic Neolithic villages into far more complex communities; yet the precise catalyst for this transformation remains unclear.[15] Even after the establishment of the unified Egyptian kingdom, these previously independent territories were preserved as administrative districts referred to as *nomes*, administered by nomarchs drawn from local elites. This governmental structure allowed such elites to retain significant local power and influence. Consequently, during periods of weak monarchical authority, some nomarchs sought to assert their influence and autonomy, thus further contributing to the steady disintegration of centralised sovereignty.

The quasi-legendary King Menes is listed as the first ruler of a united Egypt in the Karnak and Abydos king lists, as well as in the Turin Canon and by Manetho.[16] Menes has also been associated with King Narmer, depicted on the famous Narmer Palette of the Naqada III period (figures 1–3). While it remains a contested issue, it is probable that Narmer was the royal Horus name of Menes (Menes being the king's personal name), and that Menes and Narmer were thus one and the same person.[17] Whatever the case, it is now generally believed that the Early Dynastic kingdom did not emerge suddenly as a result of two distinct and well-defined political units—'Lower Egypt' and 'Upper Egypt'—being unified through a single act of conquest by Menes/Narmer. The early kingdom was more likely the result of an Upper Egyptian culture (referred to as 'Late Gerzean' or 'Naqada II' and centred around Hierakonpolis) steadily imposing itself over a politically and culturally diverse northern delta region.[18]

Even if one accepts that Menes/Narmer was a historical king, it is easy to imagine how the consolidation of the Nile valley and delta into a single

---

15. Redford, *Egypt, Canaan, and Israel*, 3. For an extensive analysis of pre-dynastic Egypt, see Hoffman, *Egypt before the Pharaohs*. For a more concise account, see Hornung, *History of Ancient Egypt*, 1–12.

16. A brief historiographical summary of the king lists and the Turin canon can be found in John Van Seters, *In Search of History: Historiography in the Ancient World and the Origins of Biblical History* (New Haven, CT: Yale University Press, 1983), 135–38.

17. One survey of the existing historiographical debate concludes that 'the preponderance of the evidence indicates that Menes was Narmer'. Thomas C. Heagy, 'Who Was Menes?', *Archéo-Nil* 24 (2014): 59–92 at 83.

18. For the most recent discussion, see Lisa K. Sabbahy, *Kingship, Power, and Legitimacy in Ancient Egypt: From the Old Kingdom to the Middle Kingdom* (Cambridge: Cambridge University Press, 2021), 11–27.

kingdom was a long-term project, completed over the course of many years and the reigns of several expansionist rulers. This should not detract from the final achievement. While the exact process of ancient Egyptian unification may remain obscure, the fact remains that, over five thousand years ago, the 'first nation-state in the world, adorned with all the sophisticated trappings of civilization', appeared in the Nile valley.[19]

The early era of political unification and consolidation following Menes/Narmer, referred to as the Early Dynastic Period and including Dynasties I and II, lasted for several centuries, during which time Memphis was developed as a centre of royal power and the Saqqara plateau began to witness the construction of pyramid tombs. The system of hieroglyphics became increasingly sophisticated and, even at this early date, the militaristic elements of Egyptian culture are evident. Objects found in Second Dynasty tombs include the royal epithet 'conqueror of foreign lands'.[20]

By the time Dynasty III took control around 2686, under Pharaoh Senakhte, Egypt had emerged as a stable and powerful centralised political unit. This date is taken by scholars as the beginning of the Old Kingdom, which lasted until the collapse of the Sixth Dynasty around 2181.[21] Over this five-hundred-year period, most of the monumental pyramids were erected. Indeed, the first king of Dynasty III of whom we know anything more than a name is Djoser (Netjerirykhet), the builder of the impressive Saqqaran step pyramid. One could think of these increasingly elaborate royal tombs as the physical expression of Egypt's growing wealth and power, reflected in its extensive trade network through Sinai and the eastern Mediterranean coast, as well as its expansionist policy southwards into Nubia (Kush).[22]

First Intermediate Period, c. 2181–c. 2050

In the early twenty-second century, the authority of the Memphite monarchy under the late kings of Dynasty VI became seriously eroded. Following the death of Pepy II (c. 2216), a series of short reigns gave way to civil war and political fragmentation. It is likely that various nomarchs asserted themselves

---

19. Redford, *Egypt, Canaan, and Israel*, xxi.
20. McDermott, *Warfare in Ancient Egypt*, 9.
21. See Sabbahy, *Kingship, Power, and Legitimacy*, 29–120.
22. Nubia (Kush) refers roughly to the territory south of the First Cataract of the Nile and down as far as the confluence of the Blue and White Niles. Nubia is the term most commonly used in modern scholarship to refer to the region, but was only introduced after the fourth century CE. Prior to this, it was more commonly referred to as Kush (especially from the New Kingdom onwards), although Egyptians also called the region between the First and Third Cataracts 'Wawat', and the region up to the confluence of the Nile 'Yam' or 'Iam'. See Bruce G. Trigger, *Nubia under the Pharaohs* (London: Thames and Hudson, 1976), 35, 40–63; David Connor, *Ancient Nubia: Egypt's Rival in Africa* (Philadelphia: University Museum, 1993), 1–112.

against the financial and military demands of the pharaohs. During the First Intermediate Period (c. 2181–c. 2055), the united monarchy of the Old Kingdom splintered into numerous local principalities, although two principal competing dynasties entrenched themselves at Herakleopolis in the north and Thebes in the south. It took over a century for a dynasty to emerge that was strong enough to realise the ambition of reuniting the Two Lands. Around the beginning of the twenty-first century, Inyotef I, Mentuhotep, and Inyotef II asserted themselves northwards and southwards from their capital at Thebes, creating successful alliances with other nomarchs. Under the Theban kings of Dynasty XI, this expansion eventually culminated in the defeat of the Herakleopolitan kings and the institution of a new unified kingdom—the so-called Middle Kingdom—under Mentuhotep I and his son, Mentuhotep II, between c. 2055 and c. 2010.

Middle Kingdom Period, c. 2050–c. 1650

The Middle Kingdom is often regarded as the high point of ancient Egyptian civilisation. After the initial Theban victories and reunification of the kingdom under Mentuhotep I and Mentuhotep II, there was probably a short period of civil war following the reign of Mentuhotep III. However, Egypt did not disintegrate into competing units as before; rather, the foundation of the Twelfth Dynasty by Amenemhet I (c. 1991–c. 1962) ushered in a remarkably stable political era (c. 1991–c. 1787/83). During this time, literature, theology, ethics, military architecture, and statuary all flourished, sponsored by a royal court which was well funded through a tightly controlled administrative and fiscal system. Documentary evidence for this cultural flourishing includes three separate archives of papyri from the Fayum, as well as plentiful temple and tomb inscriptions. A new fortified administrative base was founded near Memphis, named 'Amenemhet-seizes-the-two-lands', but commonly referred to as Itjtowy.[23] Much of the responsibility for government fell on the shoulders of the royal vizier, a position which had existed since the Old Kingdom. The power of such men is signalled by the fact that changes in royal dynasties often seem to have been brought about by former viziers assuming or usurping the throne.

Egypt also asserted itself abroad, militarily and economically, expanding further into Nubia and Libya, exploiting mining resources in Sinai, and pursuing trade opportunities throughout the region, especially with the wealthy port-cities of the Levantine coast.[24] From the reign of Senusret III (c. 1878–c. 1841), Egypt began to play the role of a true international power, sending regular envoys to cities such as Ugarit and Byblos, and building increasingly

---

23. *KANE*, 1:164.
24. Ibid., 1:144–45; Raphael Giveon, *The Impact of Egypt on Canaan: Iconographical and Related Studies* (Freiburg: Universitätsverlag; Göttingen: Vandenhoeck & Ruprecht, 1978), 51–60.

impressive fortifications along its frontiers, particularly abutting Sinai to the north-east and Nubia to the south, advancing beyond the First Cataract of the Nile. Fortifications south of the First Cataract, such as those at Buhen (figure 11), included double mud-brick walls and watchtowers, and were accompanied by extensive inscriptions. These sites were not only military installations intended for security, but they were monuments of political propaganda, proclaiming the power and authority of the pharaohs and marking the physical boundaries of the Egyptian world.[25] Indeed, the expansion of Egypt's physical borders became an explicit objective for pharaohs of this period. On a boundary stele discovered at the fortress of Heh at the Second Cataract, Senusret III boasted, 'I have made my boundary further south than my fathers, I have added to what was bequeathed to me.'[26]

Memories of the political disunity of the First Intermediate Period influenced the royal propaganda of the Middle Kingdom. In the literature of the period, rebellion and civil war were considered the greatest threats to Egypt and the maintenance of *Ma'at*. Personified as a female deity and symbolised as a single upright feather, Ma'at was the cosmic principle of creation, harmony, justice and order (figure 14). Ma'at was absolutely pivotal to Egyptian religious, social, and political life, and its importance is difficult to overstate.[27] Its antithesis was *Isfet*, a principle which embodied destruction, injustice, and chaos. The Egyptian conception of the cosmos, as well as Egypt's relationship to the wider world, were viewed through the lens of this duality and tension between the opposing principles of Ma'at and Isfet. Three Middle Kingdom 'lament' texts—the 'Prophecy of Neferti', the 'Complaints of Khakheperresonb', and the 'Admonitions of Ipuwer'—all 'decry civil war as the upside-down reversal of the social order'.[28] These royally sponsored texts insisted that only strong kingship and loyal subjects could ensure the proper functioning of society and the cosmos. Unsurprisingly, this was a recurrent theme of Egyptian royal ideology and theologico-political propaganda.

25. Trigger, *Nubia*, 64–85; Shaw, *Egyptian Warfare*, 45–46.

26. 'Boundary Stele of Sesostris III', *AEL*, 1:119.

27. In his authoritative study of Ma'at, Assmann states, 'Die ägyptische Ma'at-Lehre bezieht sich auf den Ort des Individuums in der Gersellschaft, den Ort der Gesellschaft im pharaonischen Staat und den Ort des Staates im Kosmos.' (The Egyptian doctrine of Ma'at was concerned with the place of the individual in society, the place of society in the pharaonic state, and the place of the state in the cosmos.) Jan Assmann, *Ma'at: Gerechtigkeit und Unsterblichkeit im Alten Ägypten* (Munich: Beck, 1990), 18. See also Maulana Karenga, *Maat, the Moral Ideal in Ancient Egypt: A Study in Classical African Ethics* (New York: Routledge, 2004); Siegfried Morenz, *Egyptian Religion*, trans. Anne E. Keep (London: Methuen, 1973), 113–26.

28. Miriam Lichtheim, *Moral Values in Ancient Egypt* (Fribourg: University Press Fribourg; Göttingen: Vandenhoeck & Ruprecht, 1997), 26. For translations of the texts, see *AEL*, 1:139–45, 145–49, 149–63. Also available in *ToS*, 131–43, 144–50, 166–99.

FIGURE 14. Relief of the goddess Ma'at, with feather crown: Temple of Edfu, Egypt. I, Rémih, CC BY-SA 3.0 licence, via Wikimedia Commons.

Second Intermediate Period, c. 1650–c. 1550

During the first quarter of the eighteenth century, the vigour of the Twelfth Dynasty petered out and it was succeeded by the more unstable Thirteenth Dynasty (c. 1786/83–c. 1650). Within a few decades these rulers gradually lost control of the kingdom and Egypt slipped into a second period of political and social fragmentation. It arguably proved more traumatic than the first. While we lack definitive sources for this period, it appears that, for the first one hundred years or so, the fragmentation of power was largely a result of internecine struggles. A rapid succession of rulers from c. 1786 to c. 1648 indicates an unstable and rapidly evolving political landscape.

By c. 1650, however, a powerful new force had arrived in Egypt and established itself in the delta region. 'Infiltration' is probably a more apt description than 'sudden invasion' of its penetration into Egypt.[29] These foreigners, arriving from the north-east, established their capital at Avaris in the Nile delta. They were referred to as 'shepherds' by Manetho and 'chieftains of foreign countries' by the Turin Canon. Later, the Roman-Jewish historian Josephus named these rulers 'Hyksos/Hykoussos', or 'shepherd kings', a garbled version of the original Egyptian terms.[30] Nevertheless, the name Hyksos stuck. From their power base in the delta, the Hyksos kings of Dynasty XV dominated much of Egypt for almost a century. While native dynasties did continue to hold some sort of authority in Upper Egypt, especially around Thebes, the nature of the relationship between the Hyksos kings and their native competitors is obscure.

The identity of the Hyksos themselves remains a subject of debate. Josephus, endeavouring to establish the antiquity of the Hebrew people within the historical record, identified them as early Hebrews.[31] Though a direct connection to the later Hebrews is wishful thinking on Josephus's part, a Levantine origin for the Hyksos is eminently plausible. A stele erected by the Theban king Kamose—who successfully campaigned against the Hyksos in the mid-sixteenth century—refers to the Hyksos king Apophis as 'Asiatic' and 'a man of Retenu', the Egyptian term for Syria-Palestine.[32] Furthermore, the names of Hyksos kings appear to have been of Semitic origin.

The Hyksos were an important political and military presence in Egypt for at least a century. They were alien invaders, hated by the native people, who posed a deep existential threat to Egyptian culture: barbarians who defiled the terrestrial and cosmological harmony of Ma'at. At least, this was the subsequent ideological narrative promoted by the pharaohs of the New Kingdom. If we ignore this shrill propaganda for a moment, the contemporary evidence actually suggests that the Hyksos became acculturated to Egyptian norms quite rapidly, adopting all the traditional trappings and rituals of Egyptian kingship and maintaining numerous native Egyptian elites in order to fulfil court and governmental functions. While foreign invasion must undoubtedly have come as a shock to Egyptians, and especially to the elite, who had most to lose, the fact that the Hyksos were able to rule much of Egypt for almost a century implies that a modus vivendi must have been established. Portraying the Hyksos as debased harbingers of doom was an ideological tool of New

---

29. William C. Hayes, 'Egypt: From the Death of Ammenemes III to Seqenenre II', in *The Cambridge Ancient History*, vol. 2, Part 1: *History of the Middle East and the Aegean Region c. 1800–1380 BC*, ed. I.E.S. Edwards, C. J. Gadd, N.G.L. Hammond, and E. Sollberger, 3rd edn (Cambridge: Cambridge University Press, 1973), 42–76 at 54–64.

30. Flavius Josephus, *Against Apion*, bk 1, § 82 (pp. 55–56).

31. Ibid., bk 1, § 83 (p. 56); bk 1, §§ 88–104 (pp. 59–66).

32. *KANE*, 1:179.

Kingdom rulers, legitimating their own claims to divine authority and discouraging political dissent that might once again render Egypt vulnerable to foreign invasion.

New Kingdom Period, c. 1550–c. 1069

As at the close of the First Intermediate Period, the reunification of Egypt came about as a result of a resurgent military dynasty emerging from Thebes in Upper Egypt and pushing its power steadily downstream along the Nile towards the Mediterranean coast. We know that the Dynasty XVII king Kamose enjoyed a number of successes against the Hyksos (as had his father, Seqenenre Tao), even attacking their capital of Avaris itself. However, it was his brother, Amose, who eventually succeeded in conquering Lower Egypt, defeating the Hyksos and expanding his power north-east into Sinai and Palestine. With Amose, then, the king lists mark the founding of a new dynasty—Dynasty XVIII—and the beginning of the New Kingdom (c. 1552/50–c. 1069).

There is a wealth of information from the New Kingdom available to scholars, comprising royal annals, boundary stelae, documentary texts, temple accounts, correspondence (including the famous El-Amarna letters), tomb biographies, scribal writing manuals, laudatory hymns and poems, and much more besides.[33] The surviving monumental architecture—the great temple of Amun-Re at Karnak, Queen Hatshepsut's funerary temple at Deir el-Bahri, and Ramses II's striking twin temples at Abu Simbel, among many others—give the impression of an assertive and powerful imperial state with considerable resources at its disposal.

It was during the New Kingdom that Egypt reached its military and territorial apogee, extending its control south along the Nile deep into Nubia, and north-east into Syria-Palestine. During this period we can properly speak of an Egyptian empire. Of course, imperialism brought Egypt into frequent military contact with other states and peoples. In Syria-Palestine especially, Egypt clashed with the equally militaristic Mitannian and Hittite empires, fighting numerous battles but also creating one of the best-preserved examples of an ancient international peace treaty (made by Ramses II and Hattušili III in 1259). One of the lasting effects of the Hyksos period was their introduction of a new piece of military technology into Egypt: the light war chariot. During the New Kingdom, the chariotry swiftly emerged as the elite corps within the Egyptian military; concurrently, high military rank became a hallmark of elite status to a far greater extent than in previous periods.[34] From Dynasty XVIII onwards, military officers increasingly dominated the royal court and

---

33. For a revealing collection of international royal correspondence from this period, see *LettGK*.

34. See Schulman, *Military Rank*, for a detailed analysis of the link between military rank and social status during the New Kingdom.

government, and a large standing army was created to meet the needs of garrisoning newly won territory and defending the borders against raids from Libya and Nubia. Indeed, it was during the New Kingdom that the image of the pharaoh as a peerless warrior was most fully realised. Hyperbole is a defining feature of Egyptian royal ideology in general, but New Kingdom propaganda reached a zenith in attributing superhuman abilities to the king and presenting him as a semi-divine being. The kingdom of Egypt, too, was presented as a superpower without equal.

Although royal authority during the New Kingdom appears relatively stable throughout, the period was hardly characterised by political stasis. The New Kingdom witnessed three dynastic changes, a pharaoh (Akhenaten) who embarked on radical religious reforms, a female ruler (Hatshepsut), and the political fallout caused by several royal minorities. Shifts in political circumstances and the idiosyncratic ambitions of individual kings are also evinced by several relocations of the principal royal city. Thutmose I concentrated his administrative and military resources on Memphis, while the importance of Thebes was maintained through the expansion and intensification of the royal cult, centred on the massive Amun-Re temple complex at nearby Karnak. It was at this time that the famous rock-cut tombs of the 'Valley of the Kings' and 'Valley of the Queens' were established near Thebes. The 'heretic king' Akhenaten (c. 1364–c. 1347) introduced a proto-monotheistic royal cult of the Aten (sundisc) and constructed a new royal capital named Akhtetaten/Amarna, near the old city of Hermopolis. This city did not long survive Akhenaten (whose name was excised from official king lists), and his successors swiftly moved the official capital back to Thebes. The Nineteenth Dynasty pharaoh Ramses II built a new administrative and military capital, Pi-Ramses, in the delta region, not far from the earlier Hyksos capital of Avaris. Again, this did not long survive the death of the pharaoh, and Ramses II's successor, Merneptah (c. 1224–c. 1204), reinstituted Memphis as the centre of royal government.

These changes in location were undoubtedly the product of the prevailing domestic and international policies of individual pharaohs of the New Kingdom. It would seem logical that pharaohs most interested in expanding and protecting Egyptian power in the Levant (e.g., Ramses II) would favour a power base in Lower Egypt, allowing for swift mobilisation of military forces for seasonal campaigns into Sinai and beyond. Equally, those pharaohs more concentrated on consolidating their authority within the traditional boundaries of Egypt, or towards Nubia, might prefer a base at Thebes. Unfortunately, this attractive explanation does not always map neatly onto the historical evidence. It is possible, therefore, that Egyptian rulers simply did not think in terms of a single royal capital, and were happy to prioritise different cities at different times for different objectives.

New Kingdom Egypt managed to survive the socio-political cataclysms that so radically impacted the eastern Mediterranean at the end of the thirteenth century. The fading of the Late Bronze Age is associated with the movements of the so-called Sea Peoples, whose identity continues to be contested.[35] In a number of magnificent inscriptions at the Temple of Medinet Habu (figure 7), Ramses III (c. 1184–c. 1152) recorded a series of battles fought in the Nile delta against invading forces that modern scholars have identified with the enigmatic Sea Peoples, as well as other campaigns against Libyans and Nubians. It is notable that, while the great Hittite empire and several other major Levantine states collapsed between c. 1200 and c. 1175, Egypt managed to weather the storm, albeit it a diminished form.

Nevertheless, continuing political instability in Syria-Palestine, a period of regional climatic change and inconsistent Nile flood seasons, and domestic political in-fighting seem to have gradually taken their toll on royal authority. The precise constellation of causes for Egypt's decline remains unclear, but by the death of the last king of Dynasty XX, Ramses XI (c. 1069), Egypt had effectively split into two political units, each controlling a separate geographical region. The rulers of Dynasty XXI controlled Lower Egypt from the new capital of Tanis in the delta, while the Theban high priest of Amun dominated Middle and Upper Egypt as a de facto sovereign.

Thus the beginning of the Third Intermediate Period coincided with the closing years of the second millennium. The next five hundred years witnessed a series of power struggles along the Nile valley, as well as increasing foreign interference. While Egypt remained an important political player during the first millennium, it never again achieved the power and prestige it had enjoyed during the New Kingdom. Periods of relative political unification were imposed under the military strength of foreign kings hailing from Libya (e.g., Sheshonq I, Dynasty XXII: figure 15) and the kingdom of Kush (e.g., Piye, Dynasty XXIV); but these proved short-lived. From the mid-seventh century, Egypt was dominated by foreign powers, including Assyria, Babylon, Persia, Macedonia, and Rome.

Despite periods of foreign domination, Egyptian culture and social structures were able to maintain a remarkable degree of unity and continuity.[36] Foreign rulers were more likely to become acculturated to Egyptian norms and practices rather than impose their own alien customs. Even after Alexander the Great's conquest in c. 332, which ushered in the Hellenisation and, later, Romanisation of Egypt, many traditional Egyptian elements survived. Arguably, it was only the Christianisation and, later, Islamisation of the region that marked a genuine sea change in Egyptian culture and religion.

35. Itamar Singer, '"Old Country" Ethnonyms in "New Countries" of the "Sea Peoples" Diaspora', in *AMILLA: The Quest for Excellence; Studies Presented to Guenter Kopcke in Celebration of His 75th Birthday*, ed. Robert B. Koehl (Philadelphia: Instap Academic Press, 2013), 321–33.

36. Bruce G. Trigger, Barry J. Kemp, David O'Connor, and Alan B. Lloyd, *Ancient Egypt: A Social History* (Cambridge: Cambridge University Press, 1983), 194–95.

FIGURE 15. Sheshonq I (r. c. 943–c. 922 BCE) with triumphal list of conquered cities: Bubastite Portal, Karnak Temple, Egypt. Olaf Tausch, CC BY 3.0 licence, via Wikimedia Commons.

GEOPOLITICS

At the turn of the twentieth century CE, there began construction of a massive dam across the Nile at Aswan (see Map 1). The damming of the river led to the flooding of a long stretch of the Nile valley (as far south as Wadi Haifa in northern Sudan), creating the large body of water that is now called Lake Nasser. Historically, however, the stretch of river near modern-day Aswan marked the first of the Six Cataracts of the Nile. Here was located, during the time of the pharaohs, the frontier town of Swenett. Upstream from this point, as far south as the confluence of the White Nile and Blue Nile (near modern Khartoum), the river was rocky, shallow, and generally unnavigable by larger ships. The First Cataract thus formed a natural southern boundary to the kingdom of Egypt.

Since at least the late fourth millennium, the navigable Nile valley, running north from the First Cataract all the way downstream to the delta region and the Mediterranean coast, had constituted a naturally defined geographical territory in which the ancient Egyptian state and culture developed. Egyptians were thus the people of 'Kmt' (*kemet*), 'the Black Land', referring to the rich alluvial soil of the Nile flood plain. Indeed, in an ancient Near Eastern international matrix where land borders were often hazy and subject to change, Egypt was quite unusual in possessing relatively fixed borders. This, in turn, may have contributed to a heightened sense of ethnic and cultural distinctiveness. This was certainly the opinion of the fifth-century Greek historian Herodotus, who insisted that, because of 'the idiosyncratic climate which prevails there and the fact that their river behaves differently from any other river, almost all Egyptian customs and practices are the opposite of those of everywhere else'.[37] A sense of physical separation from the world beyond the Nile valley was also expressed via Egyptian cosmology, which divided the world between the realm of order (Ma'at), synonymous with the kingdom of Egypt, and the realm of chaos (Isfet), encompassing everything beyond the borders or direct control of Egypt. And yet we should probably be careful not to overstate Egyptian exceptionalism. Our modern perception of ancient Egypt standing apart from the society of Near Eastern nations has undoubtedly been shaped by the Egyptians' own politically motivated and ideologically extreme presentations of Egyptian superiority, as well as the views of later non-Egyptian writers such as Herodotus.[38]

Like any other major state of the ancient Near East, Egypt was deeply involved in the geopolitics of the region. Indeed, during the kingdom periods,

---

37. Herodotus, *The Histories*, trans. Robin Waterfield (Oxford: Oxford University Press, 1998), bk 2, § 35 (p. 108).

38. Loprieno, 'Defining Egyptian Literature', 210; Thomas Schneider, 'Foreigners in Egypt: Archaeological Evidence and Cultural Context', in *Egyptian Archaeology*, ed. Willeke Wendrich (Malden, MA: Wiley-Blackwell, 2010), 143–63 at 147.

when its power was in full flood, Egypt acted as a regional superpower. Its most frequent and most intense relations were with those territories and peoples contiguous with the Nile valley and delta. From the west, 'Libyans' appear as a perennial threat to Lower Egypt, raiding the rich agricultural lands of the delta. To the north-east, through the Sinai Peninsula and into Syria-Palestine (which the Egyptians referred to as 'Retennu', comprising modern Jordan, Israel, Lebanon, and Syria), Egypt sought to assert itself over the thriving city-states and trade routes, competing with other imperialist states such as Babylon, Mitanni, Hatti, and Assyria.

In many ways, the Mediterranean was the highway of the ancient world. So it is unsurprising that Egypt, connected to the Mediterranean as it was, shared trading contacts throughout the eastern Mediterranean and up into the Aegean. The raw material Egypt hungered for most of all was timber, for the Nile valley was almost entirely bereft of large quantities of hardwood suitable for large building projects. The same was also true for much of Mesopotamia, leading to the exploitation (and rapid depletion) of the cedar forests of Lebanon (see figures 31 and 45), famously described in the *Epic of Gilgamesh*.[39] The Levantine ports had always been crucial to this movement of goods. Contact with the Aegean, especially Crete, began as early as the Old Kingdom and intensified over time, especially as Mycenaean culture flourished during the period of the Egyptian New Kingdom. This was also the period when Egyptian imperial power reached its zenith. The remains of statuary from Pharaoh Amenhotep III's fourteenth-century funerary temple is inscribed with a list of Aegean place names, while objects bearing the cartouche of Amenhotep III and other Egyptian pharaohs and queens have been discovered at a number of sites across the Aegean, especially on Crete and at Mycenae in the Peloponnese. Likewise, large amounts of Mycenaean pottery have been found at the site of Amarna, the capital of Amenhotep III's son, Akhenaten, as well as at numerous other sites throughout Egypt.[40]

Another crucial raw material was copper, the essential element of Bronze Age metallurgy. Egypt was able to exploit copper deposits in Sinai from an early period, but the island of Cyprus—or Alashiya, as it was called—was another major source. Indeed, the modern English word 'copper' derives from the ancient Greek name for the island: Kúpros (κύπρος). Contacts between Cyprus and Egypt can be traced back to roughly the eighteenth century, during Egypt's Middle Kingdom. Remarkably, the islanders managed to remain

---

39. Fernand Braudel, *The Mediterranean in the Ancient World*, trans. Siân Reynolds (London: Penguin, 2002), 73–74; *Gilgamesh (Translated from the Sîn-leqi-unninnī Version)*, trans. John Gardiner and John Maier (New York: Vintage Books, 1985), 105–7: Tablet II, col. 5; 133–35, Tablet V, col. 1.

40. Eric H. Cline, 'Amenhotep III and the Aegean: A Reassessment of Egypto–Aegean Relations in the 14th Century BC', *Orientalia* 56 (1) (1987): 1–36; Shelley Wachsmann, *Aegeans in the Theban Tombs* (Leuven: Uitgeverij Press, 1987), 27–28, 103–5, 108, 109–13.

largely neutral during the high point of Egyptian and Hittite conflict in the fourteenth and thirteenth centuries.[41]

By the Egyptian Late Period, kings of the Saite Dynasty (XXVI, c. 664- c. 525), beginning with Psammetichus I, began recruiting Hellenic mercenaries to combat the encroaching power of Persia, even encouraging them to settle near the coast, for example at Naucratis in the western delta.[42] In the fifth century, Herodotus took a strong interest in Egyptian history and religion (see especially Book 2 of *The Histories*), and posited that the Greeks owed the names of most of their gods and religious festivals to the Egyptians.[43] There was even a tradition which claimed that Greek mercenaries, settling in the Nile delta from the seventh century onwards, had adopted their principles of 'liberty' and 'democracy' from Egypt.[44] In the late fourth century, Egypt itself would come under the control of the Macedonian conqueror Alexander the Great. His successors, the Ptolemies, ruled Egypt for three centuries and established a broad and well-trodden bridge between Egyptian and Hellenic culture. The emergence of Neo-Platonism, for example, owed much to both Greek philosophy and Egyptian theology and mysticism. On a more mundane level, scholars still refer to many of the archaeological sites of ancient Egypt by their later Greek names, rather than the original Egyptian (e.g., Hermopolis, Herakleopolis, Heliopolis, Hierakonpolis, Elephantine).

Southwards, Egypt took an active interest in Nubia (modern Sudan and northern Ethiopia), beyond the First Cataract of the Nile, from where a powerful kingdom later developed.[45] This region was endowed with mineral resources as well as being a gateway to the riches (gold, ivory, incense, slaves, etc.) of the African interior and the western coast of the Red Sea (Punt). Egyptian pharaohs struggled with the native Kerma kings for control of northern Nubia (Wawat).[46] The earliest pharaonic rock-cut inscription discovered to date, the Gebel Sheik Suleiman inscription, was found on a hill at the Second Cataract, close to the site of what would later become the massive fortress-town of Buhen, constructed during the Middle Kingdom (figure 11). Dating from the First Dynasty, this early inscription shows that Egyptian rulers were

---

41. Kákosy, 'Egypt in Ancient Greek and Roman Thought', 3–4; A. Bernard Knapp, 'Island Cultures: Crete, Thera, Cyprus, Rhodes, and Sardinia', in *CANE*, 3:1433–49; H. W. Catling, 'Cyprus in the Middle Bronze Age', in *The Cambridge Ancient History*, vol. 2, Part 1: *History of the Middle East and the Aegean Region, c. 1800–1380 BC*, ed. I.E.S. Edwards, C. J. Gadd, N.G.L. Hammond, and E. Sollberger, 165–75 at 174–75.

42. John Baines, 'Kingship, Definition of Culture, and Legitimation', in *Ancient Egyptian Kingship*, ed. David O'Connor and David P. Silverman (Leiden: Brill, 1995), 3–47 at 37.

43. Herodotus, *Histories*, bk 2, §§ 49–59 (pp. 115–18).

44. Aristide Théodoridès, 'The Concept of Law in Ancient Egypt', in *The Legacy of Egypt*, ed. J. R. Harris, 2nd edn (Oxford: Oxford University Press, 1971), 291–322 at 319.

45. William Y. Adams, 'The Kingdom and Civilization of Kush in Northeast Africa', in *CANE*, 2:775–89.

46. Trigger, *Nubia*, 82–102.

already seeking to expand into Nubia at a stage when their own state was still in its political nascency.[47] From the Middle Kingdom onwards, much of Nubia was annexed by Egypt, with the region governed by a 'viceroy of Kush'. After the decline of the New Kingdom, the kingdom of Kush emerged as a powerful state in its own right, and Kushite kings eventually conquered Upper Egypt in the eighth century, installing themselves as the Twenty-Fifth Dynasty.[48]

Communication between the various political communities of the ancient Near East was made possible by the widespread adoption of the cuneiform script and the Babylonian-Akkadian language as the lingua franca of diplomacy. Egypt followed suit in adopting this Mesopotamian practice for its foreign correspondence, and the fourteenth-century El-Amarna letter archive shows the Egyptian state active in a full gamut of international relationships.[49] This included the sending and receiving of ambassadors and envoys, who travelled on safe-conducts and could be provided with armed escorts in their host country. Such missions to Egypt would include diplomatic gift exchanges, the payment of tribute from vassal states, or the sending of foreign princesses destined for diplomatic marriages. New Kingdom pharaohs even appear to have practised a policy of retaining elite foreign hostages at the Egyptian court, especially young heirs, educating and indoctrinating them in Egyptian customs before eventually installing them as vassal rulers.[50] And, as Egypt intensified its exploitation of Nubian gold mines, its bargaining power with the princes and kings of Syria-Palestine and Mesopotamia—all of whom thirsted for gold—increased proportionately.[51]

---

47. Claire Somaglino and Pierre Tallet, 'Gebel Sheikh Suleiman: A First Dynasty Relief After All . . .', *Archéo-Nil* 25 (2015): 122–34.

48. See Trigger, *Nubia*, 138–48.

49. See *The El-Amarna Correspondence: A New Edition of the Cuneiform Letters from the Site of El-Amarna Based on Collations of all Extant Tablets*, trans. Anson F. Rainey, ed. William M. Schniedewind and Zipora Cochavi-Rainey, 2 vols (Leiden: Brill, 2015). For diplomatic practices in the ancient Near East, see J. Margaret Munn-Rankin, 'Diplomacy in Western Asia in the Early Second Millennium BC', *Iraq* 18 (1) (1956): 68–110; Samuel A. Meier, *The Messenger in the Ancient Semitic World* (Atlanta, GA: Scholars Press, 1988); Gary H. Oller, 'Messengers and Ambassadors in Ancient Western Asia', in *CANE*, 3:1465-73; *LIR*, 71–76.

50. C. J. Gadd, 'Assyria and Babylon, c. 1370–1300 BC', in *The Cambridge Ancient History*, vol. 2, Part 2: *History of the Middle East and the Aegean Region, c. 1380–1000 BC*, ed. I.E.S. Edwards, C. J. Gadd, N.G.L. Hammond, and E. Sollberger, 3rd edn (Cambridge: Cambridge University Press, 1975), 21–48 at 23–26; Ziskind, 'Aspects of International Law', 61; David O'Connor, 'Egypt's Views of Others', in *Never Had the Like Occurred*, ed. John Tait (London: UCL Press, 2003), 155–85 at 169; *ILA*, 100; Shaw, *Egyptian Warfare*, 45, 49.

51. William C. Hayes, 'Egypt: Internal Affairs from Tuthmosis I to the Death of Amenophis III', in *The Cambridge Ancient History*, vol 2, Part 1: *History of the Middle East and the Aegean Region, c. 1800–1380 BC*, ed. I.E.S. Edwards, C. J. Gadd, N.G.L. Hammond, and E. Sollberger, 313–416 at 346–53; Margret S. Drower, 'Syria c. 1550–1400 BC', in ibid., 417–525 at 485–87.

So, Egypt's geopolitics and foreign relations were motivated by pragmatic interests concerning security, trade, and wealth. But were its relations with foreign states and peoples solely 'realist', or informed by more intangible ideological concerns? According to David O'Connor, Egyptians made sharp distinctions between themselves and foreigners (*xAstyw*—'people of the hill country/desert region', i.e., not the Nile valley), as well as incorporating their pragmatic experience of international relations 'into their ideological and religious realms'. However, 'neither ideology nor religion were the engines of foreign policy', and like other ancient Near Eastern cultures, Egypt showed little interest in seeking to proselytise.[52]

Nonetheless, there is a degree of disjunction between the highly chauvinistic and ideologically informed portrayal of foreign peoples in sources such as pharaonic temple inscriptions on the one hand, and the actual day-to-day interaction with foreign peoples and states in trade, politics, and war on the other. The 'Nine Bows' was a pejorative term commonly used to describe the Egyptians' traditional enemies to their west, north-east, and south, especially those they referred to as Libyans, Syrians, Nubians, and Asiatics.[53] Yet an examination of Egyptian army lists reveals evidence of Sherdenite, Nehesian, Kebek, Meshwesh, Tjuk, Palestinian, Syrian, Nubian, Hittite, and Ethiopian names.[54] In other words, the 'arch-enemies' of Egypt could equally be recruited to fight in Egyptian armies when it suited Egyptian interests.[55]

It also appears that assimilation into Egyptian society was considered perfectly possible for foreigners; rather than distinctions being made along sharp ethnic lines, it was more a matter of place, language, and habits. Put simply, if one lived in Egypt and practised Egyptian social customs, then one could 'become Egyptian'.[56] An oracle of the god Ammon, recounts Herodotus, declared 'that any land watered by the Nile in flood was Egypt, and that anyone living north of Elephantine who drank the water of the Nile was an Egyptian'.[57] This sense of geographically or, more precisely, fluvially defined identity accorded with the geographical and cosmological dualism of Ma'at and Isfet. If a person entered the land of the Nile, they also entered the land of Ma'at. If they abided by the rule of Ma'at, which was enforced by the pharaoh, they would be acting as an Egyptian: that is, they could be considered properly 'ordered' or civilised. Thus the general Egyptian term for foreigners, which described those peoples beyond the borders of Egypt, was *not* used

---

52. O'Connor, 'Egypt's Views of Others', 155–56, 166; cf. *KANE*, 1:171.
53. See *AEL*, 1:198–99; ibid., 2:36, 40, 53, 77.
54. Ziskind, 'Aspects of International Law', 174; Schulman, *Military Rank*, 37–38.
55. John Baines argues that the ethnic identity of such groups, especially Libyan and Meshwesh, remained crucial, particularly in the Late Period: 'These people were culturally Egyptian but retained a defining ethnic and military identity.' Baines, 'Kingship', 35.
56. Schneider, 'Foreigners in Egypt', 144–45.
57. Herodotus, *Histories*, bk 2, § 18 (pp. 101–2).

to describe people of foreign origin residing within Egypt.[58] This process of acculturation and integration could occur quite rapidly and involve relatively large numbers.[59] During the Middle Kingdom, Second Intermediate, and New Kingdom periods, there is evidence of foreigners integrating into Egyptian society at all levels, from temple slaves to soldiers to government officials.[60]

The concept of proper order and the 'good foreigner' could also be applied to those vassal states that recognised Egyptian suzerainty and were thus considered to be within the ambit of Ma'at. Of course, this recognition of the good foreigner carried with it an implicit understanding that such peoples and states were also subordinate and inferior, for they were only 'good' in so far as they accepted Egyptian overlordship and played by the rules. So, while we can say with relative confidence that Egyptian society was deeply xenophobic, it appears fair to say that its xenophobia was cultural rather than racial in character.[61]

Sources

Considering the quantity, quality, and variety of historical sources that have survived from ancient Egypt, Egyptologists are in the enviable position among scholars of the ancient world in suffering from an embarrassment of riches. As Herodotus exclaimed, Egypt 'has produced more monuments which beggar description than anywhere else in the world'.[62] Indeed, the variety and remarkable preservation of many ancient Egyptian cultural artefacts, from the minute to the monumental, will already be familiar to readers. The remains of Egyptian monumental architecture, for example, are both obvious and impressive, and include royal temples, tombs, palaces, and fortresses. Yet archaeologists have uncovered sprawling urban sites too, filled with the paraphernalia of everyday life.

Egyptologists have also been blessed with innumerable inscriptions and reliefs of varying lengths, subjects, and sophistication, found on temple walls, within tombs (royal and private), on temple and boundary stelae, and on monumental architecture and statuary. While the bulk of analysis in the following chapters concentrates on textual evidence (much of it derived from wall and stele inscriptions), in most cases these texts were accompaniments to striking visual scenes of combat and Egyptian victory over enemies. It was these pictorial representations of warfare that took pride of place, with the text arguably

58. Schneider, 'Foreigners in Egypt', 144, 149; O'Connor, 'Egypt's Views of Others', 170.
59. O'Connor, 'Egypt's Views of Others', 159, 161; Ziskind, 'Aspects of International Law', 191, 201; Dominique Valbelle, *Les Neufs Arcs: L'Égyptien et les étrangers de la préhistoire à la conquête d'Alexandre* (Paris: Colin, 1990), 192–95.
60. Schneider, 'Foreigners in Egypt', 152–54.
61. O'Connor, 'Egypt's Views of Others', 160.
62. Herodotus, *Histories*, bk 2, § 35 (p. 108).

fulfilling only a secondary function. Papyri, felicitously preserved in Egypt's dry desert conditions, have furnished us with annals, sacred books, poetry and other literature. Correspondence, written on both clay tablets and papyri, tells us about the functioning of international diplomacy and trade.[63] Material artefacts are almost endless: palettes, weapons, figurines, jewellery, textiles, ration tokens—the list could go on.

Although it may seem surprising, all these types of sources are of potential relevance to the scholar interested in ethics and war, because all of them tell us something about the values or preoccupations of the society which produced them. A particularly illustrative example is the Narmer Palette. Carved at the end of the fourth millennium (c. 3100, soon after the unification of Upper and Lower Egypt), it is one of the oldest pieces of political propaganda to be discovered anywhere in the world, and one that tells us a great deal about attitudes to war and violence. And yet the intrinsic purpose of the palette itself was to serve as a dish upon which eye make-up could be mixed! Thus I contend that just war scholars—and arguably ethicists more generally—should become much more adroit in examining evidence which sits outside conventional and narrow bodies of literature, and be more willing to consider the quotidian and unexpected.

In terms of accessing the rich written material recovered from ancient Egypt, the real breakthrough came with the discovery of the famous Rosetta Stone in 1799 CE. This stele inscribes a trilingual Ptolemaic decree from c. 196, written in Egyptian hieroglyphics, Demotic, and Greek text; it paved the way for a decipherment of the hieroglyphic script. In 1822 CE, Jean-François Champollion published his transliteration of the stele. Though it took several more years for the hieroglyphic script to be fully deciphered, this breakthrough meant that scholars had increasing access to the expansive written material that had been amassed by archaeologists over the previous fifty years. Archaeological and public interest in ancient Egypt has continued to this day.

In the fifth century, Herodotus remarked that the Egyptians were distinguished 'by a particular practice of recording the history of all peoples'.[64] Modern scholarship has confirmed that the ancient Egyptians were scrupulous in their record keeping, although it has also highlighted the deeply ideological presentation of past events that pervades almost all such records.[65] To give a sense of the number of historical records available, one only has to look at the work of James Henry Breasted, professor of Egyptology at the University of Chicago from 1905 to 1935. Breasted published five volumes of translated historical records from the Early Dynastic Period to the Persian invasion of

---

63. See, for example, *The El-Amarna Correspondence*, trans. Rainey, ed. Schniedewind and Cochavi-Rainey; a selection of the letters is printed in *HST*, 182–214.

64. Herodotus, *Histories*, bk 2, § 77 (p. 124).

65. Van Seters, *In Search of History*, 129–30.

c. 525.[66] Yet even this monumental collection is far from exhaustive, and the mass of evidence discovered since Breasted's time has only increased. More recent contributions that provide a broader array of written material are (to mention just a few) Miriam Lichtheim's three-volume *Ancient Egyptian Literature*, the publication of the vast tablet archive discovered at El-Amarna, and several volumes from the *Writings of the Ancient World* series published by the Society of Biblical Literature.

With so vast a repository of evidence, one might be tempted to think that Egyptologists possess a complete, or near-complete, knowledge of ancient Egyptian society. However, as Amélie Kuhrt observes, attempting to reconstruct Egyptian society based on its written evidence is akin to writing 'the history of Britain using worm-eaten records found in a monastery, a civil service department, a gentleman's private study and perhaps a section of the British Library, all separated by centuries from each other'.[67] Undoubtedly a great deal remains hidden from us, and will likely remain so.

The topic of war can be found throughout this large body of evidence. Andrea Gnirs and Antonio Loprieno have surveyed the presentation of military themes across a broad range of Egyptian literature between the third and the first millennium, and subsequently suggest four main stylistic categories: royal self-portraits and annals (*Selbstdarstellungen*); campaign reports (*Feldzugsberichte*); victory hymns (*Siegeshymnen*); and heroic tales (*Heldenerzählungen*).[68] In terms of sources dealing directly with war, the richest are the annals of individual pharaohs and the campaign records of specific military expeditions and engagements.[69] These are mostly found inscribed on the walls of temples or boundary stelae, but records of campaigns can also be found in a number of tomb biographies of Egyptian elites, such as those of Uni/Weni (Dynasty VI)[70] and Amose son of Ebana (Dynasties XVII–XVIII), and shorter biographical texts, including those commissioned by military officials, can be found on a range of other media, especially statuary.[71] Tombs also

---

66. See *ARE*. See also James Henry Breasted, *A History of Egypt: From the Earliest Times to the Persian Conquest* (1906; repr. Cambridge: Cambridge University Press, 2015).

67. *KANE*, 1:7.

68. Andrea M. Gnirs and Antonio Loprieno, 'Krieg und Literatur', in *Militärgeschichte des pharaonischen Ägypten: Altägypten und seine Nachbarkulturen im Spiegel der aktuellen Forschung*, ed. Rolf Gundlach and Carola Vogel (Paderborn: Schöningh, 2009), 243–308.

69. For a detailed analysis of the most important inscriptions dealing with military matters dating from the New Kingdom, see Anthony J. Spalinger, *Aspects of the Military Documents of the Ancient Egyptians* (New Haven, CT: Yale University Press, 1982).

70. 'Biography of Uni', *ARE*, 1:146–50, §§ 319–24; *ANET*, 227–28; *AEL*, 1:19–20. 'Biography of Amose son of Ebana', *ARE*, 2:3–9, §§ 1–16; *ANET*, 233–34; *AEL*, 2:11–15.

71. For a collection of biographical inscriptions in translation, see Elizabeth Frood, *Biographical Texts from Ramesside Egypt*, ed. John Baines (Atlanta, GA: Society of Biblical Literature, 2007).

preserve paintings depicting soldiers engaged in combat of all forms, such as the Middle Kingdom examples found at Beni Hasan and Thebes;[72] and they provide us moreover with weapons and military paraphernalia—even painted wooden models of soldiers that furnish a vivid image of these ancient warriors (see figures 8 and 9). The excavations of skeletons can also provide insight into traumatic combat injuries (inflicted by weapons such as swords, axes, maces, and arrows), particularly when found in mass graves.[73]

A whole range of other sources informs our attempt to piece together ancient Egyptian norms regarding the ethical, spiritual, and legal ramifications of warfare. There is a rich vein of didactic or 'instructional' literature originating from the Old Kingdom, addressing the proper behaviour of individuals, courtiers, and rulers. Another form of didactic literature, produced during the Middle and New Kingdoms, takes the form prophetic 'laments', warning of disasters that will afflict the kingdom of Egypt as a result of political fragmentation and moral degradation. We also have religious hymns and songs (e.g., the cycle of hymns to Senusret III), or spiritually inclined texts such as 'A Debate between a Man and his Ba [spirit]'. These texts are highly moralistic in tone, displaying the types of personal and political values promoted by the elite. Other literary works, such as the 'Tale of Sinuhe' or the 'Tale of the Eloquent Peasant', provide yet further insights into the legal and ethical norms of Egyptian society.[74]

Surviving diplomatic correspondence and international treaties bear witness to ideological, ethical, and legal paradigms in practice, so to speak. Nevertheless, we must approach such sources with caution, aware that the claims made in a diplomatic letter or vassalage treaty likely represent only one side of an argument and are thus highly partisan. The truth of this is well attested by the serendipitous survival of the Egyptian–Hittite peace treaty brokered in 1259, for which, uniquely, both Egyptian and Hittite versions have been recovered (figures 16 and 17). When these are read side by side, one can see clear differences between the two.[75]

As is almost always the case when dealing with the distant past, we have little hope of knowing what the average soldier—probably pressed into military service—thought about the harsh reality of killing others; or what he thought about the risk of being killed himself. It is possible that such men did not share the confidence of pharaohs like Merneptah or Ramses II, who

---

72. On Beni Hasan, see *ARE*, 1:279–89, §§ 619–39; Yadin, *Art of Warfare*, 58–75; Shaw, *Egyptian Warfare*, 15–18; McDermott, *Warfare in Ancient Egypt*, 59, 77; *WANE*, 94, 422–27. For the tomb of Antef (Thebes, c. 2100), see *WANE*, 447, 454.

73. *WANE*, 15, 27, 32, 438–39.

74. For translations of all these texts, see *AEL* and *ToS*. For further discussion of ethics in Egyptian society, see Lichtheim, *Moral Values*; Morenz, *Egyptian Religion*, 110–36.

75. The Egyptian and Hittite versions of the treaty are translated in *ANET*, 199–203. See discussion below, ch. 3, 'Peace Treaties'.

FIGURE 16. Egyptian–Hittite Peace Treaty (c. 1259 BCE), Egyptian version: Karnak Temple, Egypt. Olaf Tausch, CC BY 3.0 licence, via Wikimedia Commons.

FIGURE 17. Hittite–Egyptian Peace Treaty (c. 1259 BCE), Hittite version: clay tablet. Iocanus, CC BY 3.0 licence, via Wikimedia Commons.

bombastically proclaimed the justice of Egyptian wars and the inevitability of Egyptian victory. Nevertheless, one rare insight comes from a New Kingdom scribal schoolbook. Although probably intended as a tongue-in-cheek parody of other professions, the schoolbook offers us a clue as to how military life might have been regarded by the 'average' (albeit still relatively elite) ancient

Egyptian. The text encourages young scribes to dedicate themselves to their studies in order to avoid the hardships of a soldier's life:

> *The Scribe does not suffer like the soldier:* [He] is called up for Syria. He may not rest. There are no clothes, no sandals. [. . .] His march is uphill through mountains. He drinks water every third day; it is smelly and tastes of salt. His body is ravaged by illness. The enemy comes, surrounds him with missiles, and life recedes from him. He is told: 'Quick, forward, valiant soldier! Win for yourself a good name!' He does not know what he is about. His body is weak, his legs fail him. When victory is won, the captives are handed over to his majesty, to be taken to Egypt. The foreign woman faints on the march; she hangs herself on the soldier's neck. His knapsack drops, another grabs it while he is burdened with the woman. His wife and children are in their village; he dies and does not reach it.[76]

This grim vision of a soldier's experience and fate may be somewhat comical and melodramatic, but no military historian would discount it as far-fetched. Under such difficult circumstances, when survival was not guaranteed, it is easy to understand why high-minded sentiments of justice, righteousness, and honour may have meant little to those Egyptians who found themselves at the sharp end of conflict.

---

76. Papyrus Lansing (P. British Museum 9994), *AEL*, 2:172.

CHAPTER THREE

Egypt: *Ius ad bellum*

CONCEPTUALISING JUSTICE AND WAR

AT THE LEVEL of international relations, the Egyptian state engaged in warfare and diplomacy with a variety of empires, kingdoms, principalities, and nomadic peoples over the course of its long history. While there existed no 'international organizations, law codes or jurists' during the Bronze Age and Iron Age, scholars have long pointed to the existence of what can be described as an international legal community and something of a system of international law operating broadly from the region of the river Nile to the Tigris-Euphrates river system.[1] This did not constitute a specific body of doctrine or legal corpus, but it did constitute a number of, as David Bederman terms them, 'primary obligations'.[2] These obligations included the protection of foreign envoys, the recognition of the status of foreigners living and doing business within a state, standardised rules facilitating the negotiation and conclusion of diplomatic treaties, the undertaking of certain formalities governing the recourse to war, and (more contentiously and limited to specific times and places) the recognition of certain constraints in waging war, designed to enable future reconciliation.[3]

Within this international legal community, Egypt developed its own distinctive ethics of war, as well as partaking in a small number of norms practised across the Near East and Mesopotamia. The distinctiveness of Egyptian just war thought was founded upon three tenets of Egyptian religion and royal ideology that displayed remarkable longevity and consistency from the fourth to the first millennium: first, the cosmological role of Egypt relating

---

1. John Selden, *De iure naturae et gentium iuxta disciplinam ebraeorum* (London: Excudebat Richardus Bishopius, 1640); Munn-Rankin, 'Diplomacy in Western Asia'; *ILA*; *LIR*; *ERCIL*; Ziskind, 'Aspects of International Law', 43–44, 202–3, quotation at 202.

2. *ILA*, 270. See also *ERCIL*.

3. *ILA*, 272; *ERCIL*, 83–87, 163–65, 206–9.

to its importance in maintaining the balance between order (Ma'at) and chaos (Isfet); second, the universal and semi-divine authority of the pharaoh; and third, the superiority of the land of Egypt and its people over all other lands and peoples. As we shall see, these three convictions were at the core of Egyptian thought about the relationship between war and justice.

The history of Egyptian warfare, particularly as it developed during the expansionist and bellicose New Kingdom, has caught the attention of a number of scholars who have explored the logistical, tactical, and technological elements of the Egyptian war machine.[4] In contrast, there has been scant attention paid to ancient Egyptian ethical or legal thought on war.[5] Andrea Gnirs and William Hamblin provide some stimulating if cursory comments pertaining to the justification of Egyptian war, but in Bederman's study of ancient international law Egypt is notably absent from the chapter on war.[6] Bernadette Menu has provided a brief, albeit useful, analysis of the Egyptian

---

4. For example: Faulkner, 'Battle of Megiddo'; Louis-A. Christophe, 'L'Organisation de l'armée égyptienne à l'epoque ramesside', *La Revue de Caire* 207 (1957): 387–405; Yadin, *Art of Warfare*, esp. 77–114; Alan R. Schulman, 'Some Observations on the Military Background of the Amarna Period', *Journal of the American Research Center in Egypt* 3 (1964): 51–69; Schulman, *Military Rank*; Lawrence, 'Ancient Egyptian Fortifications'; J. Kruchten, 'Rétribution de l'armée d'après le décret d'Horemheb', *L'Égyptologie en 1979: Axes prioritaires de recherches* 2 (1982): 143–48; Spalinger, *Aspects of Military Documents*; Spalinger, *War in Ancient Egypt*; Anthony J. Spalinger, 'The Army', in *The Egyptian World*, ed. Toby Wilkinson (Abingdon: Routledge, 2007), 118–30; Shaw, *Egyptian Warfare*; Shaw, 'Egyptians, Hyksos and Military Technology', 59–71; Shaw, 'Socio-economic and Iconographic Contexts', 77–85; Anthony Santosuosso, 'Kadesh Revisited: Reconstructing the Battle between the Egyptians and the Hittites', *The Journal of Military History* 60 (3) (1996): 423–44; Michael G. Hasel, *Domination and Resistance: Egyptian Military Activity in the Southern Levant, ca. 1300–1185 BC* (Leiden: Brill, 1998); Chevereau, 'L'Art et la science militaires'; Andrea M. Gnirs, 'Ancient Egypt', in *War and Society in the Ancient and Medieval Worlds: Asia, the Mediterranean, Europe, and Mesoamerica*, ed. Kurt A. Raaflaub and Nathan S. Rosenstein (Cambridge, MA: Harvard University Press, 1999), 71–104; Donald B. Redford, *The Wars in Syria and Palestine of Thutmose III* (Leiden: Brill, 2003); McDermott, *Warfare in Ancient Egypt*; *WANE*, 308–463; Darnell and Manassa, *Tutankhamun's Armies*; Morkot, *Ancient Egyptian Warfare*.

5. Ziskind's analysis of the rules governing ancient Near Eastern warfare concentrate on Assyrian, Hittite, and Israelite evidence: Ziskind, 'Aspects of International Law', 125–53. David Lorton, Anthony Spalinger, and Barbara Cifola have analysed Egyptian terminology in texts describing military operations, but their studies—though important and useful— are largely restricted to philological and lexicological analysis: David Lorton, *The Juridical Terminology of International Relations in Egyptian Texts through Dynasty XVIII* (Baltimore: Johns Hopkins University Press, 1974); Lorton, 'Terminology Related to the Laws of Warfare in Dynasty XVIII', *Journal of the American Research Center in Egypt* 11 (1974): 53–68; Spalinger, *Aspects of Military Documents*; Barbara Cifola, 'The Terminology of Ramses III's Historical Records with a Formal Analysis of the War Scenes', *Orientalia* 60 (1991): 9–57. I have offered some initial thoughts on why just war scholars should be interested in Egyptian thought: Cox, 'Expanding the History'.

6. Gnirs, 'Ancient Egypt', 72–73, 76–78, 86–89; *WANE*, 353–54, 412–15; *ILA*, 207–66.

legitimation of warfare, in which she notes that 'above all, war was a highly intellectualised act, a fundamental component of ideology'.[7] Menu focuses her discussion of ideology on the three major kingdom periods, observing that as Egyptian territory increased and Egyptian power became more imperial, rulers of the Middle and New Kingdoms were more willing to show themselves as humble servants of the gods in regard to war. In return, the gods were understood to grant the pharaoh martial success and universal dominion over foreign lands. Most fundamental of all, however, was the enduring concept that the pharaoh was the divinely ordained protector of the cosmic principle of order and justice, Ma'at.[8] K. Lawson Younger also considers the key components of Egyptian royal ideology as it relates to conquest accounts from the New Kingdom, stressing the importance of the cosmological dualism between order and chaos in Egyptian figurative representations of pharaonic warfare against foreign enemies.[9] Sa-Moon Kang, similarly, stresses the idea of 'divine war' in Egyptian thought (again, mainly from the New Kingdom), arguing that war was understood as divinely sanctioned and that the gods marched with the pharaoh into battle. Likewise, Anthony Spalinger devotes some attention to the religious implications of New Kingdom militarism and the development of a more aggressive warrior ethos.[10]

Although acknowledging the emergence of an increasingly militaristic aristocratic culture from the late Middle Kingdom onwards, Gnirs and Loprieno argue that war and violence ultimately remained a peripheral theme in Egyptian literary culture, and conclude that 'although there are often descriptions of acts of war, nonetheless there never evolved a real "literature of war"'.[11] Hans Goedicke, meanwhile, offers a fascinating discussion of what is best described as ancient Egyptian military discipline, providing evidence of certain rules of conduct for professional soldiers and mercenaries. Egyptian administrators seemed concerned to restrict the pilfering of goods from civilians, and with prohibiting illicit sexual activity.[12] However, the soldiers' 'code of conduct' seems only to have applied within Egyptian territory, and was primarily directed towards regulating the behaviour of foreign mercenaries serving in Egyptian garrisons. These ideas about proper conduct for soldiers are

---

7. '[S]urtout, la guerre est un acte hautement intellectualisé, un volet fondamental de l'idéologie.' Bernadette Menu, 'La Legitimation de la guerre dans l'idéologie pharaonique', *Droit et cultures* 45 (2003): 49–64 at 49.

8. Ibid., 56–58.

9. Younger, *Ancient Conquest Accounts*, 175–92.

10. Kang, *Divine War*, 86–105; Spalinger, *War in Ancient Egypt*, 70–82.

11. 'Und auch die Feststellung, dass es in Ägypten zwar häufig zu Beschreibungen von Kriegstaten, jedoch nie zu einer echten "Literatur des Krieges" kam.' Gnirs and Loprieno, 'Krieg und Literatur', 299.

12. Hans Goedicke, 'The Rules of Conduct for Egyptian Military', *Wiener Zeitschrift für die Kunde des Morgenlandes* 88 (1998): 109–42.

therefore unlikely to have applied to soldiers whilst they were campaigning beyond the borders of Egypt during a period of active warfare.[13]

While the studies cited above are valuable contributions to our understanding of Egyptian attitudes to war, they represent only a tiny fraction of the total body of scholarly literature dedicated to the history of ancient Egyptian society. The relative scarcity of work on ancient Egyptian war ethics is all the more surprising given that, as will be demonstrated below, the Egyptian state had a very well-developed set of ideas pertaining to the ethics of war. These ideas engaged with issues analogous to later Romano-Christian concepts of proper authority and just cause (so-called *ius ad bellum* criteria), as well as some limited interaction with what are commonly termed *ius in bello* norms of military conduct.

Of course, as noted in the Introduction above, the ancient Egyptians—or any other ancient Near Eastern society—made no such distinction between *ius ad bellum* and *ius in bello* criteria; even the Latin language we now use to describe these categories is anachronistic when applied to the Bronze Age and Iron Age Near East. The two categories should be thought of principally in terms of an analytical schema and comparative tool to highlight how Egyptian concepts and practices articulated values that bear direct comparison to features of later just war thought. These caveats notwithstanding, what is undeniably striking is that, however brutal Egyptian attitudes to war might appear to us, this brutality was rooted in an unshakeable conviction that the possession of justice and the defence of order—on both a terrestrial and cosmological plane—were integral to the wars fought by the Egyptian state.

Concepts of Justice and Law

Before exploring the specific relationship between justice and warfare in ancient Egyptian thought, it will be instructive to consider Egyptian ideas about justice and law more broadly. Ancient Egyptian concepts of good (*nfr*) and evil (*dw*) are evident from tomb inscriptions dating to as early as Dynasty IV (c. 2613–c. 2498), while Ma'at appears as a principle of right action from Dynasty V (c. 2498–c. 2345) onwards. The importance of Ma'at to Egyptian ideas of justice cannot be overstated; as Siegfried Morenz asserts, Ma'at 'forms the core of Egyptian justice'.[14] By the time of the Sixth Dynasty there were increasingly stark contrasts being made between good and evil actions. Miriam Lichtheim points out that the articulation of this intellectual and

---

13. Such selective disciplinary norms, applying only to friendly territory, are not uncommon and can be witnessed in disciplinary ordinances from medieval Europe. See Rory Cox, 'A Law of War?: English Protection and Destruction of Ecclesiastical Property during the Fourteenth Century', *The English Historical Review* 128 (535) (2013): 1381–417.

14. Morenz, *Egyptian Religion*, 12.

theological development is particularly important, showing as it does, firstly, a sense of self; secondly, a recognition of interconnectedness with other persons; and thirdly, a recognition of the existence of a morally right interpersonal and/or social order which should be implemented by an individual's actions.[15]

A brief consideration of Egyptian domestic law is revealing of the way in which Egyptians perceived the complex relationship between justice, injustice, mercy, and punishment. This task is made somewhat more difficult by our lack of a specific 'law code' from ancient Egypt. Given that Sumerian, Akkadian, Hittite, Babylonian, Assyrian, and Israelite law codes have survived from the ancient Near East, it is perhaps surprising that no comparable legal code has survived from ancient Egypt. Nor is there a great deal of evidence from Egypt for the existence of technical legal vocabulary.[16] The lack of extant Egyptian law codes should not, however, be taken to suggest that there was no system of law or legal thought. Egyptian society was deeply legalistic, with law regulating 'the entire day-to-day business of existence in the Nile valley' and 'a structure close to that with which we are familiar'.[17] Middle Kingdom texts point to the existence of systematic collections of laws, although the exact character of Egyptian law codes—customary, positive, or casuistic—remains an area of scholarly debate.[18] The growth of the royal religious cult during the second millennium and the powerful temple system that accompanied it may have actually disrupted the centralised legal system that had developed since early in the Old Kingdom.[19] As the pharaoh's claim to semi-divinity intensified, so also did his claim to be—to borrow a phrase from Roman law—*legibus solutus*: that is, above the law. This is especially pertinent to the issue of justice and war. The king's authority to declare war was coupled with an increasing ability to determine what constituted justice itself, while at the same time his own actions were beyond reproach. In other words, as time went on, royal ideology increasingly posited that the pharaoh was incapable of wrong action.

The range of available legal evidence from ancient Egypt points to quite a severe domestic criminal justice system. This system prescribed a variety of punishments for those who violated Ma'at.[20] As the Old Kingdom 'Instruction of Ptahhotep'

15. Lichtheim, *Moral Values*, 13, 19.
16. Théodoridès, 'Concept of Law', 291.
17. Ibid., 311, 320.
18. See Richard Jasnow, 'Egypt: Middle Kingdom and Second Intermediate Period' (details at n. 20 below), 255.
19. Théodoridès, 'Concept of Law', 292–95, 318.
20. For an overview of ancient Egyptian law from the Old Kingdom to the New Kingdom, see Richard Jasnow, 'Egypt: Old Kingdom and First Intermediate Period'; Jasnow, 'Egypt: Middle Kingdom'; and Jasnow, 'Egypt: New Kingdom', all of which appear in *A History of Ancient Near Eastern Law*, ed. Raymond Westbrook (Leiden: Brill, 2003), 93–140, 255–88, 289–359 respectively. For crime as a 'rebellion' against Ma'at, see also Christopher Eyre, 'Crime and Adultery in Ancient Egypt', *The Journal of Egyptian Archaeology* 70 (1) (1984): 92–105.

advised, 'Punish firmly, chastise soundly, / Then repression of crime becomes an example.'[21] In a similar vein, the so-called 'Memphite Theology' (Old Kingdom, surviving as a New Kingdom copy) asserted that 'justice is done to him who does what is loved, and punishment to him who does what is hated. Thus life is given to the peaceful, death is given to the criminal.'[22]

Crimes against the king (treason/rebellion) or the gods (misappropriation of temple property, tomb robbery) were archetypal capital offences. This was typical across the ancient Near East, and we can see similar sanctions in the Old Babylonian law code of Hammurabi (c. 1755–c. 1750).[23] In Egypt, those found guilty of such crimes faced grisly deaths by impalement or burning.[24] Indeed, as will be discussed below, impalement and the mass burning of enemies were employed by some pharaohs during wartime, and it seems plausible that this practice derived from domestic judicial punishment.

Lesser punishments for wrongdoing included beating (a hundred blows seems to have been standard) and mutilation, which might involve cutting off the nose or ears. Facial mutilation, especially, must have been intended as a very visible projection of the pharaoh's justice and vengeance. It is likely that there was a system of prescribed physical punishments attached to specific crimes; punishment could also be accompanied by compensation to the victim, paid for by the perpetrator or their kin.[25] Imprisonment—for what lengths of time, we do not know—was also possible, as the 'Instructions to King Merikare' (Second Intermediate Period) advised: 'Punish with beatings, with detention, / Thus will the land be well-ordered.'[26] What emerges very

21. 'The Instruction of Ptahhotep', *AEL*, 1:73.
22. 'The Memphite Theology', *AEL*, 1:55.
23. 'The Code of Hammurabi', § 6, in *ANET*, 163–80 at 166.
24. David Lorton, 'The Treatment of Criminals in Ancient Egypt: Through the New Kingdom', *Journal of the Economic and Social History of the Orient* 20 (1) (1977): 2–64 at 14, 26, 28–31, 34–36; Jasnow, 'Egypt: Middle Kingdom', 281–82; Jasnow, 'Egypt: New Kingdom', 344; Kerry Muhlestein, 'Royal Executions: Evidence Bearing on the Subject of Sanctioned Killing in the Middle Kingdom', *Journal of Economic and Social History of the Orient* 51 (2) (2008): 181–208; Muhlestein, *Violence in the Service of Order: The Religious Framework for Sanctioned Killing in Ancient Egypt* (Oxford: Archaeopress, 2011), 34–43, 79–82; Mark D. Janzen, 'The Iconography of Humiliation: The Depiction and Treatment of Bound Foreigners in New Kingdom Egypt' (PhD dissertation, Memphis University, 2013), 250–59.
25. Joyce Tyldesley, *Judgement of the Pharaoh: Crime and Punishment in Ancient Egypt* (London: Weidenfeld & Nicolson, 2000), 60–61.
26. 'Instructions to King Merikare', *AEL*, 1:100. Cf. the Old Kingdom tomb biography of Akhethotep Hemi/Nebkauhor, which records that 'they were locked up in the Great Mansion, or were beaten in the Great Mansion'. Strudwick, *Texts from the Pyramid Age*, 262. The text 'Duties of the Vizier', inscribed within the New Kingdom tomb of Rekhmire, also mentions a 'criminal register which is in the "great prison"': *The Duties of the Vizier: Civil Administration in the Early New Kingdom*, trans. G.P.F. van den Boorn (London: Kegan Paul International, 1988), § 6, R14 (p. 121). The 'great prison', which functioned as a 'place

clearly from the evidence is that a concept of retributive justice prevailed in ancient Egyptian society, and that the broader theological and cosmological principle of Ma'at underpinned it.

Beyond criminal justice, the Middle Kingdom genre of 'instruction' literature gives a particularly lucid insight into the Egyptian sense of justice and right action, at least at an elite level. The 'Instruction of Ptahhotep', an Old Kingdom vizier, counselled that individuals attaining government office should act justly:

> If you are a man who leads,
> Who controls the affairs of the many,
> Seek out every beneficent deed,
> That your conduct may be blameless.
> Great is justice, lasting in effect,
> Unchallenged since the time of Osiris.[27]

The 'Instruction of Ptahhotep' insisted that '[i]n the end it is justice that lasts [...]. / That man endures whose rule is rightness.'[28] This attitude to good government applied all the way up the chain of command, to the very pharaoh himself. King Merikare was instructed, 'Do justice, then you endure on earth [...]. / Beware of punishing wrongfully, / Do not kill, it does not serve you.'[29]

The richly decorated New Kingdom tomb of the vizier Rekhmire (discovered at Thebes), which Breasted described as the 'most important private monument of the Empire', contains inscriptions and reliefs demonstrating a vizier's duties.[30] 'Do not judge unfairly,' commanded Pharaoh Thutmose III when he installed his new vizier, 'God abhors partiality; / This is an instruction, / Plan to act accordingly'.[31] The belief that justice should apply to all,

---

of confinement' and a 'labour camp' was particularly important during Dynasties XXII–XVII: ibid., 126. Compare Breasted's translation of the text in *ARE*, 2:276, § 683. See also Valbelle, *Les Neufs Arcs*, 190, who notes the presence of Asiatics within the great prison during the Middle Kingdom.

27. 'The Instruction of Ptahhotep', *AEL*, 1:64.
28. The text displays a particular distrust of greed in any form (ibid., 1:68–69):
    To be free from every evil,
    Guard against the vice of greed:
    A grievous sickness without cure,
    There is no treatment for it [...]
    It is a compound of all evils,
    A bundle of all hateful things.
29. 'Instructions to King Merikare', *AEL*, 1:100.
30. *ARE*, 2:266. For translations of the text, see ibid., 2:266–95, §§ 663–762. Cf. 'The Installation of the Vizier Rekhmire', *AEL*, 2:21–24.
31. 'The Installation of the Vizier Rekhmire', *AEL*, 2:23. Cf. Breasted's translation: 'It is an abomination of the god to show partiality.' *ARE*, 2:269, § 666. As Breasted goes on to note (ibid., 2:268), the instructions 'are remarkably humane in temper and show a

no matter what their station in society, is embodied in the 'Tale of the Eloquent Peasant', which tells of how a peasant is unjustly robbed of his goods by the avaricious son of a priest. After making a series of elegant petitions to the local magistrate, the peasant eventually obtains redress for his injuries by being awarded all the property of his assailant. Punitive and retributive justice were thus seen to act in concert.[32] Justice and punishment, although severe, were meant to be informed by impartiality and mercy.

At the heart of the Egyptian sense of justice was the principle of reciprocity: that evil deeds bring evil consequences, while good deeds bring good consequences. This might also be compared to the *do ut des* principle—that a thing is given on the tacit understanding that something will be received in return.[33] Or, as the 'Instructions to King Merikare' put it, 'A blow is repaid by its like, / To every action there is a response.'[34] This principle of reciprocity applied to both the living and the dead. The Egyptians believed in judgement after death, whereby an individual's soul would be weighed against Ma'at, symbolised as a feather (figure 18). This was not a universal 'day of judgement' akin to that of Christian apocalyptic thought, but a specific judgement undergone by an individual at the point of death. Each soul was either granted entrance into the blessed afterlife or was immediately destroyed.[35]

In the genre of admonitory texts referred to as 'prophetic' or 'lament' literature, it is exactly these sorts of assumptions that are challenged. In highlighting the perversity of the Egyptian kingdom suffering rebellion or foreign invasion, the authors strove to show how the principle of reciprocity had ceased to function. 'I shall show you the man who did nothing, helping himself, and the man who did something, in want,' prophesied the priest Neferti.[36] In a remarkable text dating from Dynasty XII, in which a man despairs at the hardships of life and enters a kind of moral and metaphysical debate with his *ba* (soul), he bemoans the state of injustice he sees all around him:

> To whom shall I speak today?
> Hearts are greedy,

---

surprisingly high appreciation of justice'. . Cf. Théodoridès, 'Concept of Law', 308; Lichtheim, *Moral Values*, 29.

32. 'The Eloquent Peasant', *AEL*, 1:169–84. See also the 'Inscription of the Statue of Bakenkhons (High Priest of Amun at Thebes, Dynasty XIX)': 'I judged the wretched and the mighty, / the powerful and the weak, / I gave goods to each of them, / For I abhor rapacity.' Cited in Lichtheim, *Moral Values*, 48. Cf. 'Inscription of Beknekhonsu', *ARE*, 3:234–37, §§ 561–68.

33. Lichtheim, *Moral Values*, 36. For more on the principle of reciprocity, see Assmann, *Ma'at*, 58–91, esp. 60–69.

34. 'Instructions to King Merikare', *AEL*, 1:105.

35. Wallis Budge, *Egyptian Religion* (1959; repr. Secaucus, NJ: Citadel Press, 1997), 136; Morenz, *Egyptian Religion*, 183–213.

36. 'The Words of Nerferti', in *ToS*, 137.

FIGURE 18. The weighing of a heart (soul) against Ma'at, as symbolised by a feather: Egyptian Book of the Dead. FinnBjo~commonswiki, public domain, via Wikimedia Commons.

> Everyone robs his comrade's goods. [...]
> One is content with evil,
> Goodness is cast to the ground everywhere. [...]
> None are righteous,
> The land is left to evildoers.[37]

In sum, the Egyptian sense of justice was remarkably egalitarian, holding that everyone, no matter their rank, was deserving of justice (theoretically, at least). At the same time, justice and law were deeply conservative, designed to defend traditional hierarchies, customs, and power structures. Underlying this was a conviction that reciprocity lay at the heart of the cosmic balance: if one wished to receive good things in life and avoid evil things, then one had to act righteously. And to act righteously was to act in accordance with Ma'at. In the *Book of the Dead*, the deceased soul hoping to be admitted into the afterlife had to make a declaration of innocence, confirming,

> I have not done crimes against people [...].
> I have not done any harm [...].
> I have not caused pain [...].
> I have not killed,
> I have not ordered to kill,
> I have not made anyone suffer.[38]

---

37. 'A Dispute between a Man and his Ba', *AEL*, 1:163–69, quotation at 167; cf. 'Dialogue of a Man with his Soul', in *ToS*, 158–59.

38. 'Book of the Dead', *AEL*, 2:125.

The greedy, avaricious, rebellious, or violent person was to be shunned by society. Even if such individuals were not punished immediately, the gods would see to it that they did not escape punishment for long.[39]

Authority

The question of *who* or *what* possesses the proper authority to wage war has been pondered for at least five millennia. The notion that this authority lies ultimately with the gods (or god) is identifiable in many cultures, including those of the ancient Near East. In the Sumerian 'Stele of the Vultures' (c. 2500: figure 4), Eannatum of Lagash claimed that the ruler of Umma had attacked the territory of Lagash 'at the command of his god', and so Lagash, with the help of the god Ningirsu, had defeated Umma in turn.[40] Babylonian kings also cited divine authority, with Hammurabi (c. 1792–c. 1750) and Nebuchadnezzar I (c. 1126–c. 1105) claiming to wage war at the command of the gods Anu, Enlil, and Marduk.[41]

THE EGYPTIAN KING AS AN AGENT OF THE GODS AND A QUASI-DIVINE BEING

Throughout the ancient Near East, divine authority was considered to be mediated through the figure of the king: kings acted as agents of the gods and the executors of their will. Egypt was somewhat anomalous in that, from the Early Dynastic period (c. 3100–c. 2686), the Egyptian king assumed an even greater authority, being regarded not only as an agent of the gods but as a figure who fulfilled a divine office and who eventually attained a quasi-divine status. The precise nature of the pharaoh's (non-)divinity remains a subject of debate. The pendulum of scholarly opinion has swung from a position emphasising the divinity of the pharaoh towards stressing the retention of the monarch's human attributes.[42] Yet the most recent work on Egyptian

---

39. 'The Instructions of Any (Dynasty XVIII)' reads as follows (*AEL*, 2:142; cf. Lichtheim, *Moral Values*, 30):
>Don't rush to attack your attacker,
>Leave him to the god;
>Report him daily to the god,
>Tomorrow being like today,
>And you will see what the god does,
>When he injures him who injured you.

40. Barton, *Royal Inscriptions of Sumer and Akkad*, 25. For other Sumerian examples, see *ERCIL*, 8–19, 26–34.

41. Kang, *Divine War*, 13–14.

42. Proponents of the divine pharaoh thesis included William F. Edgerton, 'The Government and the Governed in the Egyptian Empire', *Journal of Near Eastern Studies* 6 (3) (1947): 152–60 at 153–55; Henri Frankfort, *Kingship and the Gods: A Study of Ancient Near*

kingship has marked a return to the divine pharaoh thesis, and it is common to see references to the 'deified ruler' in the literature, especially in reference to New Kingdom pharaohs such as Amenhotep III and Ramses II.[43]

In one of our earliest artefacts from Egypt, the Narmer Palette (c. 3100: figures 1–3), King Narmer is depicted as uniting the Two Lands of Egypt and smiting his foes under the benign protection of the gods, particularly Horus and Hathor. Similar images of Old Kingdom pharaohs destroying their enemies under the protective gaze of the gods can be found from the reigns of Cheops and Pepy II.[44] The gruesome 'Cannibal Hymn'—from the collection of Old Kingdom inscriptions known as the 'Pyramid Texts'—describes King Unas (c. 2375–c. 2345, Dynasty V) as a god who is nourished by the magical powers of his parent deities:

> A god who lives on his fathers,
> Who feeds on his mothers! [...]
> Who lives on the being of every god, [...]
> Who eats their entrails
> When they come, their bodies full of magic [...]
> It is Kohns, slayer of lords, who cuts their throats for Unas,
> Who tears their entrails out for him,
> He is the envoy who is sent to punish.[45]

This divine aspect of Egyptian kingship was readily linked to the monarch's martial role. Menu interprets the Old Kingdom Pyramid Texts as presenting war as self-legitimising: 'a way for the king to fulfil his obligations with regard to his subjects, and a validation of his functions, regarding his status as

---

Eastern Religion as the Integration of Society and Nature (Chicago: University of Chicago Press, 1948), 24–47, 143–212. Proponents of the human pharaoh thesis include Georges Posener, *De la divinité du Pharaon* (Paris: Imprimerie nationale, 1960), 15–22; Erik Hornung, *Conceptions of God in Ancient Egypt: The One and the Many*, trans. John Baines (London: Routledge, 1983), 139–42; Baines, 'Kingship', 6, 9.

43. David P. Silverman, 'The Nature of Egyptian Kingship', in *Ancient Egyptian Kingship*, ed. David O'Connor and David P. Silverman (Leiden: Brill, 1995), 49–94 at 72, 80, 85, 87; Menu, 'La Legitimation de la guerre', 55. Sabbahy, *Kingship, Power, and Legitimacy*, makes a strong case for 'divine kings' in the Old and Middle Kingdoms. For a summary and partial synthesis of the 'divine' and 'human' arguments, see Paul John Frandsen, 'Aspects of Kingship in Ancient Egypt', in *Religion and Power: Divine Kingship in the Ancient World and Beyond*, ed. Nicole Brisch (Chicago: The Oriental Institute of the University of Chicago, 2012), 47–73.

44. Kang, *Divine War*, 87.

45. 'Pyramid Texts: Unas, Utterances 273–274', *AEL*, 1:36–37. For a detailed analysis of the hymn and its cultural context, see Christopher Eyre, *The Cannibal Hymn: A Cultural and Literary Study* (Liverpool: Liverpool University Press, 2002). See also Robert K. Ritner, *The Mechanics of Ancient Egyptian Magical Practice* (Chicago: The Oriental Institute of the University of Chicago, 1993), 103.

a god-king'.⁴⁶ In an inscription assumed to originate from the temple of the creator-god Atum in Heliopolis, King Senusret I (c. 1971–c. 1926) claimed that 'I was nursed to be a conqueror [. . .] / [. . .] his [Atum's] son and his protector, / he gave me to conquer what he conquered'.⁴⁷ From the Middle Kingdom onwards, Egyptian pharaohs came to associate themselves especially with the high-god Amun-Re.⁴⁸ This was further emphasised during the expansionist New Kingdom. As the son of Amun-Re, the pharaoh possessed an incontestable legitimacy to wage war, not only on behalf of Amun-Re—whose support was tacit—but also on his own authority as a quasi-divine being. This built on earlier royal ideology. During the Old Kingdom, the authority of the terrestrial 'son of Horus' to act with impunity against Egypt's neighbours was so axiomatic that 'no king felt the need to justify such action'.⁴⁹

To reaffirm their relationship with the gods and to emphasise the divine sanction of military ventures, pharaohs visited cult centres—especially the vast Karnak temple complex near modern-day Luxor—prior to embarking on campaigns. Here the pharaoh would 'receive' commands from the god(s).⁵⁰ In an account of the campaign to expel the Hyksos from Lower Egypt (c. 1554–c. 1552/50), the Theban king Kamose declared, 'I went north because I was strong (enough) to attack the Asiatics through the command of Amon, the just of counsels.'⁵¹ During a New Kingdom campaign against the Hittites, Ramses II sought help from his 'father' Amun by asking,

> Do I not walk and stand at your word?
> I have not neglected an order you gave.
> Too great is he, the great lord of Egypt,
> To allow aliens to step on his path!⁵²

A campaign stele discovered in Israel, commissioned by Ramses II's successor, Merneptah (c. 1224-c. 1204), proclaimed that the protection of the gods ensured that all enemies of Egypt were doomed to suffer defeat:

---

46. 'La guerre est à la fois un moyen, pour le roi, de remplir ses obligations à l'égard de ses sujets, et une valorisation de ses fonctions, de son statut de roi-dieu'. Menu, 'La Legitimation de la guerre', 53.

47. 'Berlin 3029', *AEL*, 1:117.

48. For example, Amun-Re is attested on Senusret I's white chapel at Karnak; see Pierre Lacau and Henri Chevrier, *Une chapelle de Sésostris Ier à Karnak*, vol. 2: *Planches* (Cairo: Institut français d'archéologie orientale, 1969), plates 12, 14, 15, 16, 19, 25, 37; plate XXVIII.

49. Donald B. Redford, 'The Concept of Kingship during the Eighteenth Dynasty', in *Ancient Egyptian Kingship*, ed. David O'Connor and David P. Silverman, 157–84 at 165.

50. This was certainly practised during and after the New Kingdom and probably much earlier. See Baines, 'Kingship', 23; Gnirs and Loprieno, 'Krieg und Literatur', 249; Anthony J. Spalinger, 'New Kingdom Triumphs: A First Blush', in *Rituals of Triumph in the Mediterranean World*, ed. Anthony J. Spalinger and Jeremy Armstrong (Leiden: Brill, 2013), 95–122 at 97.

51. 'Carnarvon Tablet I', *ANET*, 232–33. ('Amon' is a variant spelling of Amun.)

52. 'Kadesh Poem', *AEL*, 2:65.

None who attacks her people will succeed.
The eye of every god is after her despoiler,
It will make an end of all its foes.[53]

Effectively, then, the interests and authority of the gods and the pharaoh were considered indivisible and, by the nature of their divine origin, constituted an embodiment of justice and good government. As an extension of this, the divine mandate of the pharaoh to wage war and impose his will on Egypt's enemies was unequivocal. This was articulated particularly forcefully on a stele erected by Thutmose III (c. 1479–c. 1425) in the temple of Amun at Karnak. The inscription imagines the god Amun addressing the king in the following terms:

I gave you valor and victory over all lands.
I set your might, your fear in every country. [. . .]
I made your person's fame traverse the Nine Bows.
The princes of all lands are gathered in your grasp,
I stretched my own hands out and bound them for you.
I fettered Nubia's Bowmen by ten-thousand thousands,
The northerners a hundred thousand captives.
I made your enemies succumb beneath your soles,
So that you crushed the rebels and the traitors.
For I bestowed on you the earth, its length and breadth,
Westerners and easterners are under your command.[54]

According to Thutmose III's political theology, which echoed that of his predecessors, the authority of the pharaoh to wage war was founded upon a divine grant of universal sovereignty over all lands and peoples. The saturation of Egyptian historical texts with themes of the pharaoh's expansive authority led Siegfried Morenz to observe that 'Egyptian history is written as a dogma of sacrosanct monarchy'.[55] Anthony Black, meanwhile, describes Thutmose III's Karnak inscription as 'the earliest record of nationalist imperialism and divinely mandated universal empire'.[56] This ideology of sovereignty was reinforced at the Sed festival, an ancient celebration which marked royal jubilees dating back as early as Dynasty I. The Sed was imbued with symbolic ritual acts emphasising the divine authority of the king. At the culmination of several festivals held for Amenhotep III, for example, the king took a bow and shot arrows towards each of the cardinal compass points, 'which signalled his claim to hold sway over the whole world'.[57]

---

53. 'Poetical Stela of Merneptah (Israel Stela)', *AEL*, 2:75; cf. *ANET*, 376–78.
54. 'Poetical Stela of Thutmose III, Karnak Temple', *AEL*, 2:36; cf. ibid., 2:41. See also *ToS*, 38.
55. Morenz, *Egyptian Religion*, 11.
56. Anthony Black, *A World History of Ancient Political Thought* (Oxford: Oxford University Press, 2009), 24.
57. *KANE*, 1:215.

With this universal claim to sovereignty, any challenge to the Egyptian king's will was interpreted as an act of rebellion. This conceptualisation of universal authority—which rendered all enemies, internal or external, as rebels—served to delegitimise the military actions of enemy peoples at the same time as further justifying the martial actions of the Egyptian state. As will be explored further below, it justified any offensive war as a defensive act to restore the natural political and cosmological order as understood by Egypt. This concept of divine sovereignty and jurisdiction was repeated throughout Egyptian texts and iconography, frequently in relation to war, and highlights the crucial link in Egyptian royal ideology between divine/royal authority, on the one hand, and just warfare on the other.

THE GODS ACCOMPANYING THE PHARAOH IN WAR

There was no surer sign of the pharaoh's divine authority in war than being accompanied on military campaigns by the gods themselves. Amun spoke to Thutmose III, assuring him of his inevitable victories because the god was with the pharaoh and bestowed upon him overwhelming military might:

> The princes of all lands are gathered in your grasp,
> I stretched my own hands out and bound them for you [...]
> My serpent on your brow consumed them,
> She made quick booty of the evildoers.[58]

The presence of the gods could be immediately and viscerally sensed, as in Ramses II's experience of divine intervention at the battle of Kadesh (see figure 5). The 'Kadesh Poem' tells us that, with Ramses fighting in the midst of the battle and on the point of being overwhelmed by the Hittite enemy, the god Amun urged the beleaguered pharaoh to steel himself:

> He called from behind as if near by:
> 'Forward, I am with you [...]
> I prevail over a hundred thousand men,
> I am lord of victory, lover of valor!'[59]

The gods were also believed to be able to affect natural phenomena to provide Egyptian armies an advantage. During Thutmose III's first Syrian campaign, the gods sent a shooting-star against Egypt's enemies, dazzling them and allowing Thutmose to slaughter and scatter his foes at will.[60] A little less spectacularly, the usually violent desert god Seth is said to have transformed

---

58. 'Poetical Stela of Thutmose III', *AEL*, 2:36. The 'serpent on your brow' refers to the Uraeus—a representation of a rearing cobra displayed on the red crown of Lower Egypt.
59. 'Kadesh Poem', *AEL*, 2:66. See also Kang, *Divine War*, 101–2.
60. See Kang, *Divine War*, 104–5.

stormy weather into tranquil summer days in order to aid Ramses II's army on the march. On a more mundane level, the divine protection enjoyed by Egyptian armies was further emphasised (or sought) by the practice of organising battle divisions under the standards of the gods. By the time of the New Kingdom, these four divisions were established under Ptah, Re, Amun, and Seth.[61]

What is beyond doubt is that Egyptian royal ideology was firmly rooted in the concept of the divine authority of the monarch, who ruled as a terrestrial 'son' of the gods and, to some extent, achieved a personal quasi-divine status as time went by. When applied to warfare, this translated into an unambiguous doctrine of legitimate royal authority to declare and to wage just wars on behalf of the Egyptian pantheon. In doing so, the pharaoh was fulfilling his duty to defend the land of Egypt and the cosmological principle of Ma'at, to which we shall now turn our attention.

Just Cause

Asserting that there should *be* a cause for war is an essential first step towards thinking ethically about war, because it implies (at least) three things: first, that war requires a specific cause, and is not simply a pleasure or feckless pastime that needs no explanation or justification; second, that war is not wholly inevitable—if inflicting grievances can be avoided, then there should be no reason to go to war; and third, that there exists some method for the categorisation of licit and illicit actions, whereby some actions or injuries necessitate a military response, while others can be deemed less serious or better resolved via alternative means and/or processes. Therefore, consideration of how (or whether) the concept of *casus belli* existed in Egyptian thought is crucial in order to form a clearer picture of the character of Egyptian ethics of war.

COSMIC HARMONY AND *CHAOSKAMPF*: THE WAR OF ORDER AGAINST CHAOS

The authority of the pharaoh to wage war stemmed not only from his divine office, but also from the unique cosmological status of the kingdom of Egypt. The Two Lands of Upper and Lower Egypt, united as a single kingdom under the pharaoh, were believed to be the terrestrial embodiment of the universal principle of order and justice, Ma'at. In a real sense, Egypt was believed to be a reflection of heaven on earth. This cosmological preeminence made Egypt and

---

61. As they are described in Ramses II's accounts of the battle of Kadesh: *AEL*, 2:64. This custom bears direct comparison to the Israelite practice of carrying the Ark and other 'sacred utensils' into battle, or medieval Christian armies carrying sacred relics (e.g., fragments of 'True Cross').

Egyptians superior to all other lands and peoples.[62] The creative harmony of Ma'at was believed to be perpetually challenged by the chaotic forces of Isfet, which the Egyptians identified terrestrially as foreign peoples beyond their realm and criminal and rebellious elements within it. This belief in the cosmological and terrestrial antagonism between order and chaos is identifiable in a number of ancient Near Eastern and Mesopotamian societies, and is broadly symbolised in the mythological battles of gods or heroes against a destructive beast—often some sort of great serpent.[63] In Egyptian mythology, the struggle of the falcon-headed god Horus against Seth, or the nightly battles of the sun god Ra against the Apep serpent, as well as the ongoing conflict between Ma'at and Isfet, can all be seen within this *Chaoskampf* framework.

This duality of justice and order versus injustice and chaos was easily translated into the dichotomy of peace and war. Ancient Egyptian literature expresses a deep-seated hostility towards 'barbaric' foreigners and the existential threat they posed to civilised society. Such foreign enemies, often referred to generically as the 'Nine Bows', were associated with the chaotic, harsh, and dangerous natural forces of the desert and mountain, as opposed to the tranquil and fertile river lands of the Nile valley. This distinction between barbarism and civilisation was an axiomatic dichotomy in Egyptian ideology.

Egyptian hostility to foreigners is especially vivid in prophetic 'lament' poetry, thought to originate in the Middle Kingdom but surviving only in New Kingdom copies. 'The Words of Neferti', set in the Old Kingdom, recounts the priest Neferti prophesying various catastrophes to be endured by Egypt:

> Destroyed indeed are those things of happiness [...] all happiness has fled, and the land is laid low with pain, by those feeding Syrians who go throughout the land. Enemies have arisen in the East! Asiatics have come down to Egypt; a secure stronghold is lacking [...] I shall show you the land in catastrophe, what should not happen, happening: arms of war will be taken up, and the land will live by uproar.[64]

---

62. Katja Goebs, 'Kingship', in *The Egyptian World*, ed. Toby Wilkinson (Abingdon: Routledge, 2007), 275–95 at 275–81; O'Connor, 'Egypt's Views of Others', 160–61.

63. See, inter alia, Herman Gunkel, *Schöpfung und Chaos in Urzeit und Endzeit* (Göttingen: Vandenhoek & Ruprecht, 1895); John Day, *God's Conflict with the Dragon and the Sea: Echoes of a Canaanite Myth in the Old Testament* (Cambridge: Cambridge University Press, 1985); K. Williams Whitney, *Two Strange Beasts: Leviathan and Behemoth in Second Temple and Early Rabbinic Judaism* (Winona Lake, IN: Eisenbrauns, 2006), esp. the first chapter, 'The *Chaoskampf* in Modern Scholarship', 1–30; Peter Panitschek, 'Zur Gewalttoleranz in der Kriegsführung des frühen Alten Orients', in *'Böser Krieg': Exzessive Gewalt in der antiken Kriegsführung und Strategien zu deren Vermeidung*, ed. Margit Linder and Sabine Tausend (Graz: Grazer Universitätsverlag, 2011), 9–34.

64. 'The Words of Nerferti', in *ToS*, 136–37. The poem is also translated in *AEL*, 1:139–45. For similar themes, see *ToS*, 144–50, 173; *AEL*, 1:145–49, 152.

According to the prophecy, Ma'at would only be restored by the return of a true king:

> Asiatics will fall to his slaughtering, and Libyans will fall to his flame. Rebels belong to his rage, and malcontents to his awesomeness [...]. And the Walls of the Ruler will be built. There will be no letting Asiatics come down to Egypt [...]. Truth will return to its proper place, with Chaos driven outside.[65]

Roughly contemporaneous to this Egyptian lament literature and similar in its concern about the threat posed by uncivilised 'barbarians' was the Sumerian poem 'The Curse of Agade' (c. 2000–c. 1800). The poet describes how a paragon of civilisation—the city of Agade—was laid low by the invasion of the nomadic Gutians, who punished Agade's king, Naram-Sin, for his misdeamenours against the temples of Enlil.[66] The constant defence of Egypt against such catastrophe was one of the principal duties of the pharaoh, and this obligation was articulated from early in the development of royal ideology. An Old Kingdom text cautioned the ruler to be constantly vigilant because '[t]he foe loves destruction and misery [...]. There is no one who has no enemy.'[67]

SELF-DEFENCE

The Defence of Ma'at

The sacred duty of the pharaoh to defend Ma'at formed the foundation of the ancient Egyptian concept of just cause. Almost as influential was the principle of reciprocity that lay at the heart of the Egyptian sense of justice and injustice, as has already been discussed. Essentially, Egyptians subscribed to a basic moral causality which held that good actions brought positive consequences, and evil actions brought negative consequences.[68] 'A blow is repaid by its like, to every action there is a response,' explained the didactic political tract 'Instructions to King Merikare'.[69]

Violence and greed figure as core characteristics of Egyptian contemplations of injustice: 'Mercy has perished, and the fierce man has descended on everyone [...]. They plunder, and every man is taking [from] his fellow [...].

---

65. 'The Words of Nerferti', *ToS*, 139.
66. 'The Curse of Agage', *ANET*, 646–51.
67. 'Instructions to King Merikare', *AEL*, 1:105.
68. Arlette David, 'The Sound of the Magic Flute in Legal and Religious Registers of the Ramesside Period: Some Common Features of Two "Ritualistic Languages"', in *Law and Religion in the Eastern Mediterranean: From Late Antiquity to Early Islam*, ed. Anselm C. Hagedorn and Reinhard G. Kratz (Oxford: Oxford University Press, 2013), 13–39 at 17–19.
69. Lichtheim, *Moral Values*, 36–37, 46.

There are no just men, and the land is left over to the doers of injustice.'[70] When viewed through the lens of the reciprocity principle, it was natural that enemies of Egypt, who were understood as disturbers of peace and enemies of justice, merited the evil consequences of war and defeat. The pharaoh was represented as essentially reactive, responding defensively against the transgressions of others, rather than aggressively and without provocation. As Younger puts it, '[h]is army is dispatched only after others have stirred up trouble, and then only to re-establish the status quo'.[71] Seen in this context, the frequently brutal treatment meted out to foes was justified as part of a cosmological rebalancing process—the reassertion of order against chaos.

Of course, this conception of justice and injustice, and the relative moral status of Egypt and its enemies within this matrix, was entirely stacked in favour of the Egyptians. Since Ma'at was embodied by Egypt, of which the pharaoh was the sole guardian, any assault upon Egypt or Egyptian interests was *ipso facto* unjust. Equally, any Egyptian war in defence of Ma'at was *ipso facto* just. War against the enemy thus became an aspect of the pharaoh's personal battle against the forces of chaos, and the pharaoh was the best—indeed, the only—judge of who or what were to be condemned as the forces of chaos.[72]

It has been suggested that this essentially xenophobic political theology was the product of an exploitative Egyptian elite who, seeking to maintain their legitimacy and wealth, promoted their role as defenders and subjugators of dangerous foreign peoples. No doubt such elites were also the principal benefactors of wealth generated by warfare in the form of campaign spoils, seizure of land, or increased access to foreign trade.[73] This would certainly correlate to the conclusions of anthropologists regarding the increased likelihood of military expansion in highly stratified societies, whereby elites, typically embedded within a martial tradition and competing with one another for resources, seek to increase their wealth and status through warfare.[74] But regardless of the ultimate theological or socio-economic origins of Egyptian xenophobia, the longevity and social pervasiveness of the Ma'at/Isfet

---

70. 'Dialogue of a Man with his Soul (Ba)', *ToS*, 158–59; cf. *AEL*, 1:163–69. The concept of justice was central to Egyptian morality and ethics, particularly to the concept of good government and political authority: for example, see the 'Tale of the Eloquent Peasant in Lichtheim' in *AEL*, 1:169–84 and *ToS*, 54–88.

71. Younger, *Ancient Conquest Accounts*, 184, referring specifically to the *iw.tw* genre of military texts.

72. Spalinger, *War in Ancient Egypt*, 78.

73. O'Connor, 'Egypt's View of Others', 160–61.

74. Fried, 'Warfare', 145–46; R. Brian Ferguson, 'Explaining War', in *The Anthropology of War*, ed. Jonathan Haas (Cambridge: Cambridge University Press, 1990), 26–55 at 30.

world-view, which placed Egypt at the top of the cosmological and terrestrial hierarchy, is evident throughout ancient Egyptian history.[75]

Indeed, the importance of the defence of Ma'at and authority of Amun in Egyptian warfare became so pronounced during the New Kingdom that Bridget McDermott suggests the Egyptians 'came to view their military expansion as a religious crusade'.[76] However, to describe ancient Egyptian warfare in terms of crusade is misleading. Unlike in medieval Europe, no distinction between secular war and holy war existed in ancient Egypt, because the secular and religious objectives of the state were identical. The regime of pharaoh and the regime of Ma'at were indistinguishable, at least in terms of royal ideology. In defending Ma'at, the pharaoh and his subjects were understood to act righteously and piously; in this there is some superficial similarity to the medieval Christian concept of holy war, whereby fighting in defence of the faith earned the warrior spiritual merit. (Crusades were a specific category of holy war, typically declared on papal authority and with indulgences offered to those who took the cross.) Nevertheless, the Egyptian theology of the afterlife was so different from the medieval Christian concept of heaven, sin, penance, and forgiveness that to apply the term 'crusade' to ancient Egyptian warfare tends inevitably to encourage false analogies.

Rather than the Christian concept of crusade, a better analogy may be found in the Islamic concept of *jihad*. In positing a sharp distinction between lands governed by Ma'at and lands ruled by the chaotic forces of Isfet, ancient Egyptian political theology resembles the distinction made in classical Islamic jurisprudence between the *dar al-Islam* (house of Islam; i.e., peace) and the *dar al-Harb* (house of war). Moreover, as in ancient Egypt, Islamic thought made no distinction between the state and religion—thus jihad aimed to defend and expand the Islamic state. As a result, specific undertakings of jihad could be prompted more by political than by religious motives.[77] Yet this should not be taken to imply that religion was irrelevant to such expressions of jihad, because religion—or more precisely, theology—provided the conceptual foundations and justifications for the politico-military enterprise.

---

75. Its longevity can be partly explained by the 'unbroken linguistic and cultural unity [...] accessible through rich and intelligible textual and iconographic records' that bridged the two millennia separating the Early Dynastic period from the New Kingdom and later periods: Trigger et al., *Ancient Egypt*, 189.

76. McDermott, *Warfare in Ancient Egypt*, 85.

77. *Quran: The Final Testament*, trans. Rashad Khalifa (Tucson, AZ: Islamic Productions, 1989), Sura 2.190-95, 216-17, 256; Sura 8.10-16; *Jihad in Medieval and Modern Islam: The Chapter on Jihad from Averroes' Legal Handbook 'Bidāyat al-Mudjtahid' and the Treatise 'Koran and Fighting' by the Late Shaykh-al-Azhar, Mahmūd Shaltūt*, trans. Rudolph Peters (Leiden: Brill, 1977), 3-4; Kelsay, 'Islamic Tradition', 87-89. See also Kenneth A. Goudie, *Reinventing Jihād: Jihād Ideology from the Conquest of Jerusalem to the End of the Ayyūbids (c. 492/1099-647/1249)* (Leiden: Brill, 2019).

Still, there is no evidence of Egyptian warfare being conceived as a spiritual struggle or obligation (as is the case in jihad), and the central role of the pharaoh as a semi-divine ruler and sole source of authority for war similarly problematises any direct comparison with the Islamic political theology of jihad.

Defending Territories against Barbarism

The greatest threat to Ma'at came in the form of attacks from chaotic and barbaric forces beyond the borders of Egypt. Egyptians considered their civilisation so inherently superior that they saw themselves as 'the only true "men" (*rōme*)'.[78] Defending the territorial integrity of the kingdom of Egypt against the encroachment of barbarism was thus the quintessential *casus belli*.[79] In a laudatory hymn to Senusret III (c. 1878–c. 1841), a clear sense of just cause is articulated in describing the king's motivations for defending his southern borders: 'He came and fought [on] his frontier: He rescued him who had been robbed!'[80] The pharaoh is thus depicted as the paradigmatic defender of his people: avenging injuries (in this case, despoliation by Nubian invaders) and preserving the integrity of Egyptian territory. This attitude was widely echoed in Middle Kingdom 'instruction literature', which encouraged prudent rulers thus:

> Strengthen your borders, your frontier patrols,
> It is good to work for the future,
> One respects the life of the foresighted,
> While he who trusts fails.[81]

Considerable resources were expended in fortifying the border zones with Nubia to the south and the Sinai Peninsula to the north.[82] At one of a trio of fortresses designed to repel Nubian incursions along the Second Cataract, the duty of the king to defend his borders was emphasised in a boundary stele erected by the aforementioned Senusret III:

> A coward is he who is driven from his own border [. . .]. The true son is he who champions his father, who guards the border of his begetter. But he who abandons it, who fails to fight for it, he is not my son, he was not born to me.[83]

---

78. Gardiner, *Egypt of the Pharaohs*, 37.

79. Egyptian attitudes to non-Egyptians bear comparison to ancient Greek concepts of the natural animosity that existed between Hellenes and non-Hellenes, or *barbaroi*. See Plato, *The Republic of Plato*, trans. Allan Bloom (New York: Basic Books, 1968), bk 5.470c (p. 150). The third-millennium kings of Sumer and Akkad had come to similar conclusions about their duty to defend Sumerian culture against the threat of foreign invaders associated with eastern mountain peoples: Panitschek, 'Zur Gewalttoleranz', 30–31.

80. 'Hymn IV to Sesostris III', *AEL*, 1:200.

81. 'Instructions to King Merikare', *AEL*, 1:99–101.

82. Lawrence, 'Ancient Egyptian Fortifications', 71ff; Shaw, *Egyptian Warfare*, 15–24.

83. 'Boundary Stele of Sesostris III', *AEL*, 1:119.

Three hundred years later, at the close of the Second Intermediate Period, the highly successful Theban ruler Kamose (c. 1555–c. 1550) justified his wars against the Hyksos and his attempt to reunify the Two Lands on the basis that '[n]o man can settle down, being despoiled by the imposts of the Asiatics. I will grapple with him, that I may cut open his belly! My wish is to save Egypt and *to smite* the Asiatics!'[84] Kamose conceived of his expansion into the Nile delta not as a war of aggression, but as a duty and a right to reclaim Lower Egypt from barbarian invaders. As far as his political rhetoric was concerned, the Theban war against the Hyksos was a defensive war, and Kamose was a saviour of Egypt.

The idea of the pharaoh as a defender of Egypt was translated into literary images of the pharaoh as an impenetrable wall encircling Egypt and protecting its lands, people, and armies. This mural image was promoted throughout the Middle and New Kingdoms: we see Thuthmose III as 'a fortress for his army, a bronze wall'; Amenhotep II as 'a great wall for Egypt, the protection of his army'; and Seti I as 'a great bronze wall, protecting his army'.[85] Ramses II was imagined as 'an excellent wall for Egypt, a buckler of millions, protector of multitudes; he has rescued Egypt when it was plundered, marching against the Asiatics to repel them'.[86] At the battle of Kadesh, this pharaoh was said to be a 'Strong wall around his soldiers, / Their shields on the day of battle'.[87]

From the Eighteenth Dynasty (c. 1550–c. 1295)—a period which witnessed an intensification of Egyptian imperial ambitions—the protective role of the pharaoh came to include the conquered lands in Asia under Egyptian subjugation. We can see this new function in an inscription from a stele placed by Thutmose IV between the paws of the Great Sphinx of Giza, praising his father, Amenhotep II:

> He has taken all of Egypt,
> South and North are in his care.
> The Red Land brings him its dues,
> *All countries have his protection*;
> His borders reach the rim of heaven,
> The lands are in his hand in a single knot.[88]

---

84. 'Carnarvon Tablet I', *ANET*, 232.
85. *LIR*, 83–85.
86. 'Beth-Shan Stela of Ramses II', translation cited from Younger, *Ancient Conquest Accounts*, 177.
87. 'Kadesh Poem', *AEL*, 2:62–63.
88. The Great Sphinx stele at Giza, *Urkunden des ägyptischen Altertums, Abteilung IV: Urkunden der 18. Dynastie*, ed. Kurt Sethe and Wolfgang Helck (Leipzig: Hinrichs; Berlin: Akademie-Verlag, 1906–1958), 1276–83, ll. 5ff, translation cited from Younger, *Ancient Conquest Accounts*, 176 (emphasis added).

Envisaging a proactive protective role, a triumphant hymn to Merneptah designated the pharaoh a liberator of the conquered lands under Egyptian overlordship. Through martial might, the pharaoh became a bringer of order and peace, replacing the chaos that reigned in Egypt's absence:

> Then spoke they, the Lords of Heliopolis [i.e., the Heliopolitan pantheon],
> concerning their son, Merenptah [Merneptah] Satisfied by Truth:
> 'Grant him a lifespan like Re,
> that he may intervene for whoever is oppressed by a foreign country.'[89]

While the propaganda of these expansionist New Kingdom pharaohs asserted the benign aspects of Egypt's military ventures, the importance of maintaining the physical integrity and security of the Two Lands retained its symbolic and political preeminence in royal ideology. Even during Dynasty XX, the last dynasty of the New Kingdom, we see Ramses III proudly recounting his deeds against the Libyans in these familiar terms: 'I turned them back from trampling the border of Egypt.' As a result of his military strength, he boasted, his reign had witnessed a period of peace: 'I was with them as the defence and protection of their limbs [. . .]. I set each man in his security, in their towns.'[90]

FROM SELF-DEFENCE TO DEFENSIVE AGGRESSION

This concept of the pharaoh as the sole protector of his land and people, as well as potentially other lands and peoples, is typical of a centralising and universalising political ideology. Such an ideology is evident in Egypt from at least the early second millennium and, as Liverani notes, according to this ideology 'the only "correct" political solution is universal empire'; the ruler, as the mediator between the gods and humanity, 'is the only one entrusted with the task of keeping the cosmological activity of the gods in good order. All the world must submit to the political authority of the central sovereign, no room being left for rival powers or those sharing the same burden.'[91]

Importantly, however, this centralist and universalist ideology could shift easily into a doctrine of justified aggression and expansion. As Liverani explains, 'non-expansion is considered a failure on the part of the king, a symptom of an inadequacy produced by incapacity, illegitimacy, impiousness

---

89. Kenneth A. Kitchen, *Ramesside Inscriptions: Historical and Biographical*, 8 vols (Oxford: Blackwell, 1969-1990), 4:17, §§ 2-4; 19, § 1, translation cited from Younger, *Ancient Conquest Accounts*, 177.

90. 'Papyrus Harris', *ARE*, 4:201-2, § 405; 205, § 410. Note that Papyrus Harris was actually produced during the reign of Ramses III's son and successor, Ramses IV.

91. *LIR*, 25.

or criminality that has resulted in his abandonment by the gods'.[92] Because those lands beyond the kingdom of Egypt were understood as intrinsically chaotic, military action against them, whether to enrich the centre (i.e., Egypt) or to expand the sphere of civilisation and good order as instituted through the regime of Ma'at (i.e., the rule of the Egyptian king), was always justifiable. Moreover, because of the incessant threat of barbarism, all such military action could be viewed as essentially defensive in nature. The Egyptian concept of self-defence against chaotic and barbaric external forces was therefore extended to what were, to all intents and purposes, aggressive wars to expand Egyptian territory. The tomb autobiography of the high-ranking soldier Ahmose, son of Abana (Dynasties XVII–XVIII), records how Ahmose

> conveyed King Djeserkare [Amenhotep I], the justified, when he sailed south to Kush, to enlarge the borders of Egypt. His majesty smote that Nubian Bowman in the midst of his army. They were carried off in fetters, none missing, the fleeing destroyed as if they had never been'.[93]

This military violence could also be couched in terms of retributive vengeance, as a stele of Merneptah supplicates the gods to 'Grant him a lifetime like that of Re / To avenge those injured by any land'.[94] Violence against morally degenerate enemies such as the Libyans was justified by their crimes, and it was the divinely ordained duty of the pharaoh to avenge these injuries:

> Then said [the god] Ptah concerning the vile Libyan foe:
> 'His crimes are all gathered upon his head.
> Give him into the hand of *Merneptah, Content with Maat,*
> He shall make him spew what he has gorged like a crocodile.'[95]

Enemies of Egypt, then, were viewed as fully culpable and liable to suffer punitive harm.

The Egyptian empire reached its territorial apogee under Thutmose III in the mid-fifteenth century, stretching from beyond the Fourth Cataract of the Nile in the south (modern-day central Sudan) to the river Euphrates in the north-east. Thutmose III left extensive written records of his campaigns in the form of annals inscribed upon temple walls at Karnak (figure 19) as well as a number of surviving stelae. Both the annals and the stelae inscriptions describe the king acting righteously and courageously against foreign threats. Thus, early in his reign, the pharaoh departed from Gaza 'in valor, might, and right, to overthrow that wretched enemy [the prince of Kadesh], to extend the

---

92. Ibid., 46.
93. 'The Autobiography of Ahmose son of Abana', *AEL*, 2:13.
94. 'Poetical Stela of Merneptah', *AEL*, 2:76.
95. Ibid.

FIGURE 19. Annals of Thutmose III (r. c. 1479–c. 1425 BCE): Karnak Temple, Egypt. Jon Bodsworth, https://www.egyptarchive.co.uk, via Wikimedia Commons.

borders of Egypt, his father, mighty and victorious Amun, having commanded that he conquer.'[96]

In the jingoistic 'Poetical Stela of Thutmose III', the pharaoh's authority to subjugate barbarian lands is systematically listed by the god Amun-Re:

> I came to let you tread on those of Asia,
>   to smite the Asians' heads in Retjenu [...]

---

[96]. 'Annals of Thutmose III', *AEL*, 2:30.

I came to let you tread on eastern lands,
>   to crush the dwellers in the realm of god's land [...]
I came to let you tread on western lands [...]
I came to let you tread on lowlanders,
>   Mitanni's regions[97] cringe in fear of you [...]
I came to let you tread on islanders,
>   the sea-borne people hear your battle cry;
I let them see your majesty as the avenger,
>   standing in triumph on his victim's back [...]
I came to let you tread on earth's limits,
>   what Ocean circles is enfolded in your fist [...]
I came to let you tread on border people
>   to bind as captives those upon the sand [...]
I came to let you tread on Nubians;
>   as far as Shat you hold them in your grasp.[98]

It was common for Egyptian inscriptions to revel in the violence that accompanied foreign campaigns and conquest. There is no sense that such violence was considered inappropriate. Indeed, celebrating the martial deeds of the pharaoh was crucial to promoting the valour of the king: 'Now his majesty was in the country of Retenu [...] plundering towns and laying waste encampments of that enemy of the wretched Naharin [...]. Not one of them looked behind him, but was fleeing continually like a *herd* of desert beasts [...] His majesty [...] thus extending the frontiers of Egypt.'[99] The bellicose and coercive subjugation envisioned by Thutmose III bore no resemblance to a benign 'liberation' of foreign peoples, as was suggested in the case of his successors Amenhotep II and Merneptah (see above). One might explain this in terms of a more sophisticated and nuanced imperial ideology emerging as New Kingdom pharaohs matured into their imperial role. But it is just as likely that the two postions were not understood as mutually exclusive, and throughout the New Kingdom pharaohs were happy to promote their capacity for extreme violence against enemies.

The delight that pharaohs took in slaughtering their enemies is indicated by the Karnak inscriptions describing Seti I's (r. c. 1305–c. 1290/c. 1294–c. 1279) wars against the Shasu of Retenu:

> Now as for the good god [Seti], he exults at undertaking combat; he delights at an attack on him; his heart is satisfied at the sight of blood. He cuts off the heads of the perverse of heart. He loves an instant of trampling more than a day of jubilation. His majesty kills them all at

97. Northern Syria and south-west Anatolia.
98. 'Poetical Stela Thutmosis III', *AEL*, 2:37.
99. 'Annals of Thutmosis III', *ANET*, 239–40.

one time, and leaves no heirs among them. He who is spared by his hand is a living prisoner, carried off to Egypt.[100]

As the protector of his kingdom, the pharaoh was thus also the consummate warrior, defending the borders of Egypt through the elimination of the numerous foreign threats that inhabited the lands beyond it.

CONCEPTS OF REBELLION

An abhorrence of rebellion lay at the very heart of Egyptian royal culture and theology.[101] The belief that Ma'at was a divine principle which all peoples should respect and follow was repeatedly emphasised through the identification of enemies, both internal and external, as rebels against Ma'at and royal authority. The non-Egyptian foreigner was the 'prototypical rebel',[102] and much of the justification for aggressive warfare was couched in terms of punitive violence against rebellion. As we have seen, the concept of the pharaoh's universal jurisdiction, bestowed by his role as the guardian of Ma'at, was utilised to justify, on the grounds of self-defence, what were essentially aggressive wars. Because of this universalism, the punishment for rebellion was equally harsh for native Egyptians and foreigners alike. Even domestic criminals were labelled as rebels against Ma'at and consequently subjected to brutal corporal punishments.[103]

Hostility to rebellion was ingrained within Egyptian mythology itself. The Middle Kingdom text 'The Destruction of Mankind' relates how the sungod Re sent the goddess Hathor to destroy mankind because it had rebelled against his authority (there are obvious parallels here with the flood myths of the ancient Near East). Fortunately for mankind, the pleas of the other gods persuaded Re to change his mind, and Hathor only destroyed those humans who dwelled in the desert—that is, non-Egyptians.[104] In the 'Great Hymn to Osiris', the god's punishment of rebels is clearly intended to parallel the actions of the pharaoh:

---

100. 'Seti I, inscription on north exterior wall of great hypostyle hall, Karnak', *ANET*, 254.

101. For texts decrying the evils of civil discord, see *AEL*, 1:139–62; *ToS*, 131–50, 166–99). The Middle Kingdom 'Instructions of King Ammenemes I to King Sesostris I' even imagined the old king Amenemhet/Ammenemes, who had been assassinated, warning his son not to trust anyone: *ANET*, 418–19; *AEL*, 2:135–39; *ToS*, 203–11.

102. Muhlestein, *Violence*, 83.

103. O'Connor, 'Egypt's Views of Others', 156. See also discussion above, 'Concepts of Justice and Law'.

104. 'The Destruction of Mankind' is the first part of a longer text, 'The Book of the Cow of Heaven', which was inscribed inside five New Kingdom royal tombs: Tutankhamun, Seti I, Ramses II, Ramses III, and Ramses VI. See *AEL*, 2:198–99.

Mighty when he fells the rebel,
Strong-armed when he slays his foe.
Who casts fear of him on his enemy,
Who vanquishes the evil-plotters,
Whose heart is firm when he crushes the rebels.[105]

Mirroring the just temperament of the god Osiris, the 'Instructions to King Merikare' urged the pharaoh, 'Do not kill,' and, 'Beware of punishing wrongfully.' But this restraint had its limits: 'Except for the rebel [. . .] / God smites the rebels in blood'.[106]

The Middle Kingdom ruler Senusret I justified horrific acts of violence against those implicated in civil war on the basis that it was a legitimate punishment for rebels who had also destroyed religious property within Egypt:

> as for them that had transgressed against this house (the temple at Tod). My Majesty made a great slaughter among them . . . both men and women, the valleys being filled with rows of cadavers, the mountains bearing sheaves of corpses; the enemy from the 'Terraces' were placed on the brazier—it was death by fire because of what they had done against it . . . the young were sawn up, the children of the enemy were like sacrificial victims.[107]

In this case there was clearly a judgement of corporate guilt, with women and children suffering the same gruesome fate as the men.

The punishment of rebellion was exported beyond Egypt's traditional frontiers as Egyptian imperial power matured. Rebellion features prominently in the records of military campaigns as a cause for war, especially during the New Kingdom. The autobiography of Ahmose, son of Abana claims that the Nubian campaign of Thutmose I (c. 1507–c. 1494) was undertaken, 'to crush rebellion throughout the lands, to repel the intruders from the desert region'.[108] Two generations later, Thutmose III's Megiddo campaign (in Syria-Palestine) was conducted in order 'to kill the treacherous ones who were in it and to give things to those who were loyal to him'.[109] Near the end of his reign, Thutmose III erected a stele at Gebel Barkal recalling how, after the fall of Megiddo, the enemy princes had begged, 'Give us thy breath, our lord!

---

105. 'Great Hymn to Osiris', *AEL*, 2:83.

106. *AEL*, 1:100. See also Lorton, 'Treatment of Criminals', 13–14.

107. From two speeches of Senusret I, cited in Redford, 'Concept of Kingship', 165; see also Muhlestein, 'Royal Executions', 189–93; Muhlestein, *Violence*, 37–39; Janzen, 'Iconography of Humiliation', 304–5.

108. *AEL*, 2:14.

109. 'Armant Stela', *ANET*, 234; cf. 'Annals of Thutmosis III' and 'Poetical Stela of Thutmosis III', *AEL*, 2:29–39.

The countries of Retenu will never repeat rebellion another time!'[110] Six years later, the same pharaoh led a campaign into northern Syria, 'destroying the countries which had been rebellious to him'.[111]

The campaigns of Amenhotep II (c. 1438–c. 1412) were framed in similar terms: 'His majesty proceeded to Retenu on his first victorious campaign to extend his frontiers, made *from* the property *of them who are not* loyal to him.'[112] So we see that the pharaoh's scribes can talk about extending the frontiers of the kingdom in one clause, and yet identify the (presumably foreign) enemy as rebels in the next. Amenhotep was characteristically merciless in his punishment. Upon reaching the town of Ikat, '[h]e surrounded everyone rebellious to him and killed them, like those who have never existed, put on their side, upside down'.[113] Even the Hittite protagonists in Ramses II's great battle at Kadesh were described in the Egyptian sources as 'rebels': a claim that unquestionably had no basis in political reality, but one that was central to the political cosmology of Egyptian royal ideology.[114] These attitudes to enemies and rebellion were preserved until the very end of the New Kingdom. A papyrus produced by Ramses IV, whose reign witnessed a deterioration of centralised royal power, insisted that his grandfather Setnakht 'set in order the entire land, which had been rebellious; he slew the rebels who were in the land of Egypt; he cleansed the great throne of Egypt'.[115]

Motivations for War

While the rhetorical brushstrokes of Egyptian sources paint a picture of wars fought solely with the intention of maintaining the cosmological balance of Ma'at, ruthlessly defending Egypt against barbarians and punishing the crimes of rebels, the reality was somewhat different. Spalinger cautions that 'the Egyptian monarchs were not out to exterminate their enemies, even the major ones'; rather, 'their struggles were over territory and limited advantages'.[116] Annals, campaign reports, battle reliefs, and victory stelae give the impression that the enemy was almost always completely destroyed; but most foreign campaigns lasted just a few months at most, after which the army would return to Egypt and the bulk of the host—its mercenary, auxiliary, and conscripted troops—would disperse. Campaigns of this type were limited in what they could achieve, especially against heavily fortified sites which, given

---

110. 'Gebel Barkal Stela', *ANET*, 238.
111. 'Annals of Thutmosis III', *ANET*, 238.
112. 'Stelae of Amenhotep II', *ANET*, 245.
113. Ibid., 246.
114. 'The serpent on my brow felled my foes, / Cast her fiery breath in my enemies' faces [. . .] / My rays, they burned the rebels' bodies': 'Kadesh Poem', *AEL*, 70.
115. 'Papyrus Harris', *ARE*, 4:199, § 399.
116. Spalinger, *War in Ancient Egypt*, 165.

the rudimentary siege technology of the Late Bronze Age, generally possessed the military advantage. Further challenges were faced when attempting to bring nomadic peoples to heel, as these avoided set-piece confrontations whenever possible. While there is plenty of evidence to suggest that pharaohs did seek pitched battle or besieged fortresses and cities when and where this aligned with their strategic interests, these relatively short-lived campaigns were simply not able to eradicate most enemies. Nor, arguably, was this ever their intent.

Rather than annihilate the enemy, Egyptian pharaohs often sought to utilise military force in order to impose tributary regimes on new territories. Thus Egyptian 'pacification'—that is, the imposition of vassal status—was characterised as a process of imposing order on chaos. Liverani describes this as 'conquest as a cosmic organization', but this cosmic ordering was inherently practical in nature. It consisted of vassal states adhering to the Egyptian economic and political system, defined by agricultural production, government administration and taxation, and the establishment of military garrisons and conscription. It evidently formed the ideological and practical basis of Egyptian foreign policy over the long term.[117]

PROFIT AS A MOTIVATION FOR WAR

As in all ancient Near Eastern warfare, a more basic motive underlay Egyptian military activity: the economy of plunder. The understanding that military victory was rewarded with spoils was 'a doctrine so widely accepted as to be self-evidently true in the Near East'.[118] There were also well-defined systems for collection and distribution of booty instituted for different Near Eastern armies; such systems were obviously widely comprehended by the soldiers who fought and hoped to profit through their efforts.[119] Although a much later text, Xenophon's *Cyropaedia* (written c. 370) succinctly conveys the attitude to enemy property in ancient Near Eastern warfare:

> Friends and allies, thanks be above all to the gods that they have vouchsafed to us to obtain all that we thought we deserved. For now we are in possession of broad and fertile lands and of subjects to support us by tilling them; we have houses also and furniture in them. And let not one of you think that in having these things he has what does not belong to him; for it is a law established for all time among all men that when a city is taken in war, the persons and the property of the

---

117. *LIR*, 92–96.
118. Ziskind, 'Aspects of International Law', 147.
119. See André Aymard, 'Le Partage des profits de la guerre dans les traités d'alliance antiques', *Revue historique* 217 (1957): 233–45. See also below, pp. XXX–XX , XXX–XX, XXX–XX, XXX–XX, XXX–XX, XXX–XX, XXX , XXX–XX.

inhabitants thereof belong to the captors. It will, therefore, be no injustice for you to keep what you have, but if you let them keep anything, it will be only out of generosity that you do not take it away.[120]

Descriptions of the spoils of war are ubiquitous in our extant Egyptian sources. They are used as a literary and pictorial means to indicate the success of a particular campaign or to establish the bravery and praiseworthy deeds of an individual. The epic 'Tale of Sinuhe' begins with the eponymous hero returning from a military expedition to Libya, where he has fought alongside the pharaoh's son and now returns laden with plunder:

> Now his Majesty had sent out an expedition to the Libyan land, with his eldest son at its head, the Perfected God Senwosret, but now he was returning, having carried off Libyan captives and all sorts of cattle without number.[121]

When Kamose attacked Nefrusi, a client town of the Hyksos, the king claimed that 'I attacked him. I broke down his walls, I killed his people, and I made his wife come down to the riverbank. My soldiers were as lions are, with their spoil, having serfs, cattle, *milk*, fat, and honey, dividing up their property, their hearts *gay*.'[122] Later in the New Kingdom, the royal 'Annals' of Thutmose III are replete with boasts of seized plunder from the pharaoh's many campaigns. Such spoils included thousands of slaves, horses, livestock, foodstuffs, and treasures including anything from gold and jewellery to furniture and textiles.[123] Profit appears to have been an influential motivation for a campaign into Retenu in the thirty-third year of Thutmose III's reign, whereby the Egyptian army succeeded in 'plundering towns and laying waste encampments of that enemy'. It was only as an afterthought that the scribes claimed that the campaign also extended the frontiers of Egypt.[124]

More personal accounts also attest to spoils constituting an important motivation for soldiers risking their lives in warfare. The tomb autobiography of a New Kingdom solider named Amenemheb, who served under Thutmose III and was buried at Thebes, recounts the captives and booty he won during several campaigns in Asia. He was also rewarded with the Gold of Valour/Favour after presenting the hands of dead enemies to the king's administrative officers (see figures 20–22).[125] The financial benefits of war

---

120. Xenophon, *Cyropaedia*, vol. 2: *Books 5–8*, trans. Walter Miller (Cambridge, MA: Harvard University Press, 1914), bk 7, ch. 5, §§ 72–73 (p. 293). Also cited in Aymard, 'Le Partage des profits', 248–49.
121. *ToS*, 27.
122. *ANET*, 233.
123. For example, after the Battle of Megiddo: 'Annals of Thutmose III', *AEL*, 2:33–34.
124. 'Annals of Thutmose III', *ANET*, 239–40.
125. 'Biography of Amenemheb', *ANET*, 241.

FIGURE 20. Piling enemy hands after battle: Temple of Medinet Habu, Egypt, twelfth century BCE. Steven C. Price, CC BY-SA 3.0 licence, via Wikimedia Commons.

FIGURE 21. Counting enemy hands after battle: Temple of Medinet Habu, Egypt, twelfth century BCE. Asta, public domain, via Wikimedia Commons.

FIGURE 22. Piling enemy phalli after battle: Temple of Medinet Habu, Egypt, twelfth century BCE. Steven C. Price, CC BY-SA 3.0 licence, via Wikimedia Commons.

could also be enjoyed by veterans in the form of gifts of land, rendered as payment for military service. A stele found at Deir el-Bahri attests how a soldier named Nufer, who served in the armies of Amenhotep I, was rewarded with a 'good plot of land [. . .] as payment for the valor of my arms'.[126] This system of distributing war spoils was carefully administered by the central bureaucracy. The New Kingdom text 'Duties of the Vizier' explains that '[i]t is he who assigns the spoils of war to each town district'. Interestingly, it was also the vizier's duty to oversee the arrest and judgement of anyone involved in illicit plundering *within* Egyptian territory.[127]

The incentive for individual soldiers to enrich themselves through war could also pose problems. For example, when Thutmose III won a significant victory near the city of Megiddo, he was prevented from taking the city itself by the ill-discipline of his troops and their lust for plunder:

> When they [the princes of Retenu] saw his majesty overwhelming them, they fled headlong [to] Megiddo with faces of fear [. . .]. Now if his majesty's troops had not set their hearts to plundering the possessions of the enemies, they would have captured Megiddo at this moment, when the wretched foe of Kadesh and the wretched foe of this town were being pulled up hurriedly so as to admit them into their town.[128]

126. 'Stela of Nufer, Son of Mayor of Thebes (during reign of Amenhotep I)', cited in Lichtheim, *Moral Values*, 53.
127. *Duties of the Vizier*, trans. Boorn, 250, § 17, R26.
128. 'Annals of Thutmose III', *AEL*, 2:32. See also Lorton, 'Terminology', 60, who notes that the king must have recognised such looting as 'legal' plunder.

Having allowed the surviving enemy time enough to retreat behind the fortified walls of Megiddo, it required a long siege before Thutmose was eventually able to take the city.

Today we might baulk at the notion that profit—whether for the state or for the individual—should ever be considered a legitimate cause for war. Nevertheless, we must also be aware that this attitude is not only remarkably recent, but also entirely anomalous when we step back and view the grand sweep of military history. While nineteenth-century American politicking gave birth to the proverb 'to the victor belong the spoils of the enemy',[129] the sense underlying these words—that material reward is legitimate compensation for the risks taken by actors in a conflict—has a very long pedigree indeed. It was a conviction so deeply ingrained in the ancient world that it was never seriously questioned.

On the other hand, it is also worth stressing that material reward is never presented in Egyptian sources as the principal cause or motivation for war. As we have seen, war continued to be viewed in cosmological terms throughout all three major kingdom periods. The defence of Ma'at; the defence of the kingdom's borders against barbarian foreigners; seeking vengeance for injuries; quashing rebellion; the physical realisation of the pharaoh's universal sovereignty through the extension of Egyptian territory and expansion of Egyptian lordship: these were the causes for war that were given pride of place in the sources. Material profit was a natural by-product of war, and in reality was probably an important motivating factor for pharaohs and soldiers alike (most obviously for the numerous mercenary troops who formed a major part of pharaonic armies). However, in terms of the ethics of war, as presented through royal ideology and the funerary monuments of individual soldiers, the primary significance of war spoils was that they served as post-factum proof that the war was justified and that the warrior was brave and loyal. In a context in which victory in war was understood as dependent upon divine favour, war spoils were evidence that the gods had seen fit to reward the just victor with the goods of the unjust enemy. What we take to be uncouth and venal braggadocio about the filthy lucre of war, contemporary Egyptians understood as a material demonstration of divine favour. Even more powerfully, it was a confirmation of the Egyptian kingdom's unique position as a beacon of justice and order in the world.

---

129. The remark is ascribed to US Senator William L. Marcy (1786–1857), made in reference to the 'spoils system' of political appointments within the US government: see Martha Mitchell, 'William L. Marcy', in *Encyclopaedia Brunoniana* (Providence, RI: Brown University Library, 1993), available at https://www.brown.edu/Administration/News_Bureau/Databases/Encyclopedia/search.php?serial=M0120 (accessed 9 January 2023).

CHAPTER FOUR

Egypt: *Ius in bello*

CONCEPTS AND PRACTICES

IN THIS CHAPTER, we shall examine the ideas and mechanisms that governed the conduct of ancient Egyptian warfare preceding, during, and in the aftermath of military operations. In other words, we shall look for norms and actions now traditionally subsumed within the *ius in bello* tradition.

The existence of rules prescribing how violence should be conducted should not be confused with a concern for individual enemies: the one does not necessarily follow from the other. If rules governing military conduct did exist in ancient Egypt, it is possible that they served to enhance as much as to restrain violence. It is a mistake to assume that well-disciplined, rule-based armed forces are by definition merciful.[1] Some of the best trained and most disciplined armies in history, adhering to strong and clearly articulated military customs, have perpetrated some of the most heinous acts of military savagery. One might think of the ancient Romans in Gaul and Germania, the Mongols across Eurasia, the Napoleonic army in eastern Europe and Russia, the British army in India and other colonial territories, the German and Japanese armies during World War II, and the US army in Indo-China, to name but a few. Consequently, we should not take the existence of *in bello* norms as proof of military restraint or of sympathy for the enemy. Indeed, as Donald Redford observes, throughout the ancient Near East the individual person 'was, from the perspective of the state, nought but "a live one" (our "warm body") [...] a "servant (subject)" without even so basic a right as freedom of movement'.[2] If state rulers viewed their own subjects so dispassionately, then we should probably limit our expectations as to whether ancient Near Eastern polities entertained ideas akin to recognising enemy 'rights' in war.

---

1. See Mark J. Osiel, *Obeying Orders: Atrocity, Military Discipline, and the Law of War* (New Brunswick, NJ: Transaction Publishers, 2002), 176, 180.

2. Redford, *Egypt, Canaan, and Israel*, 373.

Declaring War

The opening of hostilities between Egypt and its foes was probably marked by formal declarations of war, albeit there is little direct evidence for this.[3] The start of set-piece battles may also have been heralded by the blowing of trumpets, as indicated by the depiction of trumpeters in various battle reliefs.[4] The recognition within Egyptian martial culture that some formal declaration of war was normative is indicated by criticism of those enemies who *failed* to declare their intentions prior to initiating violence. In representing the stereotypical 'miserable Asiatic', the 'Instructions to King Merikare' claims that such enemies are more like thieves than soldiers, because they do not openly declare hostilities and instead rely upon guerrilla-type ambush tactics:

> He [the Asiatic] fights since the time of Horus,
> Not conquering nor being conquered,
> He does not announce the day of combat,
> Like a thief who darts about a group.[5]

Although falling outside our period, a later example—from the eighth century—is one of the few explicit descriptions we possess of an Egyptian king issuing a declaration of war to his enemy. The victory stele of the Kushite pharaoh Piye (c. 736–c. 712, Third Intermediate Period) records that he commanded his generals to make explicit declarations of battle against his enemy, Tefnakht, prince of Sais. Indeed, Piye went even further in creating the conditions for a set-piece battle, instructing his commanders to permit the enemy additional time to gather more forces:

> Do not attack by night in the manner of draughts-playing; fight when one can see. Challenge him to battle from afar. If he proposes to await the infantry and chariotry of another town, then sit still until his troops come. Fight when he proposes. Also if he has allies in another town, let them be awaited. The counts whom he brings to help him, and any trusted Libyan troops, let them be challenged to battle in advance, saying: 'You whose name we do not know [. . .] form your battle line, and know that Amun is the god who sent us!'[6]

Is this proof of a 'chivalrous' form of warfare? It is possible, but other explanations are more compelling. Pierre-Marie Chevereau argues that Piye's

---

3. Formal declarations of war were common in other ancient Mediterranean societies: Ziskind, 'Aspects of International Law', 125–37; *ILA*, 208ff. There is also some evidence from second-millennium Mesopotamia: *ERCIL*, 51–56.
4. Kang, *Divine War*, 103.
5. 'Instructions to King Merikare', *AEL*, 1:103–4. See also Shaw, 'Socio-economic and Iconographic Contexts', 79.
6. 'Victory Stela of King Piye', *AEL*, 3:69.

command stemmed from his desire to force a single decisive battle on open ground, avoiding the need to embark upon a drawn-out series of skirmishes or sieges.[7] Equally likely is that the king wished to magnify his military achievements by stressing the number of enemy defeated and the courageous manner in which victory was obtained. After all, this victory stele was commissioned by Pharaoh Piye himself, several years after the events took place; it sought to present the pharaoh in the most heroic terms possible. Regardless of Piye's true motivations, the stele does at least indicate that open communication with the enemy prior to large military engagements was considered normal.

Licit and Illicit Weapons and Tactics

Once hostilities had begun, there appear to have been no recogisable restraints imposed upon ancient Egyptian armies. Some efforts to restrict the use of missile weapons were attempted in both ancient Greek and medieval European warfare, although with very limited success.[8] No such restrictions were attempted or considered necessary in Egyptian martial culture; quite the opposite, in fact. As discussed above in the Introduction, archery was prominent throughout the ancient Near East as an elite martial skill, and Egypt was no exception to this. Bows and arrows were frequently deposited as grave goods in elite tombs, indicating their high social status. The falcon-god Horus was associated with elite soldiers and archers, and was addressed as 'Horus the Shooter'.[9] Despite some enemies of the Egyptians being referred to as 'bowmen' (*iwntyw*)[10]—whereby we might expect a pejorative connotation for archery—one of the honorary titles of the pharaoh was 'Mighty of Bows in All Lands'.[11] There are numerous images depicting pharaohs using a bow to fell their enemies, both on foot and from chariots (figures 5–7).[12] In the 'Tale of Sinuhe', the jewel of Middle Kingdom literature, the exiled Egyptian hero fights a duel in which the contestants favour the use of javelins and bows:

---

7. Chevereau, 'L'Art et la science militaires'.

8. Strabo claims that during the War of the Lelantine Plain on the Aegean island of Euboea (c. 700), the belligerents agreed 'that they were not to use long-distance weapons'. *The Geography of Strabo*, trans. Duane W. Roller (Cambridge: Cambridge University Press, 2014), bk 10, pt 1, § 12 (pp. 438–39). In the Middle Ages, the Second Lateran Council (1139 CE) attempted to ban the use of bows and crossbows in wars between Christians: Concilium Lateranense II, canon 29, in *Conciliorum oecumenicorum decreta*, ed. Josephus [Giuseppe] Alberigo et al., 3rd edn (Bologna: Istituto per le scienze religiose, 1973), 203.

9. McDermott, *Warfare in Ancient Egypt*, 24, 151.

10. *AEL*, 1:115.

11. 'Stelae of Seti I', *ANET*, 253; cf. 'Kadesh Poem', *AEL*, 2:62–63. See also Sinuhe's description of the pharaoh's martial prowess: 'None can escape his arrow, none draw his bow.' *ToS*, 30.

12. For example, see Schoske, 'Erschlagen der Feinde', 200–208.

I had escaped his weapons and made them pass by me, with his arrows spent in vain, one after the other, he approached me, and I shot him; my arrow stuck in his neck, he cried out, and fell on his face. I felled him with his own axe, and gave my war cry on his back, while every Asiatic was bellowing.[13]

It was only *after* Sinuhe had felled his opponent with an arrow that he dealt the death blow with the axe belonging to his enemy: the ultimate humiliation. Even with the development of the aristocratic chariot corps during the New Kingdom, the principal weapon of the charioteer remained the bow and arrow.[14]

Any advantage one could gain over the enemy was deemed acceptable, including the use of espionage, ambush, and deceit. Perhaps acting as an early inspiration for the Homeric story of the Trojan Horse, Thutmose III was said to have seized the city of Joppa by hiding two hundred soldiers inside woven baskets that were then smuggled into the city.[15] However, Egypt could also be the victim of deception. Prior to the famous battle of Kadesh, fought between Ramses II and the Hittite emperor Muwatalli II around 1274, the Egyptians captured two Shasu tribesmen who were acting as Hittite spies. After torturing the two spies (see figure 23), the Hittite 'agents' apparently fed their interrogators false information regarding the position of the Hittite forces.[16] This subsequently allowed Muwatalli to ambush the Egyptian divisions 'from the south side of Kadesh [. . .] as they were marching unaware and not prepared to fight'.[17]

This Egyptian narrative of deceit and ambush has been contested by Mario Liverani, who points out that it is inconceivable that such large armies (possibly up to forty thousand men on each side) could have been unaware of one another's position, and that even if no official challenge was issued, then the day of battle was made inevitable after the battle lines were drawn up. Liverani explains the account of the Shasu spies and the so-called 'ambush' by the Hittites as a function of Egyptian royal propaganda: the Hittites being condemned as treacherous precisely because they had defeated the Egyptians (or came very close to doing so). Thus 'it became necessary to demonstrate that this had happened only because the enemy was duplicitous and disregarded the standard modes of combat'.[18] Although the story of the Hittite

---

13. *ToS*, 33.
14. See Yadin, *Art of Warfare*, 80–83, 86–90; Shaw, *Egyptian Warfare*, 31–44; *WANE*, 356–59, 422–25.
15. See 'The Capture of Joppa', *ANET*, 22–23; McDermott, *Warfare in Ancient Egypt*, 44; Spalinger, *War in Ancient Egypt*, 188.
16. 'Kadesh Bulletin', *AEL*, 2:60–61. Note that the beating of the prisoners represented in the carved reliefs is not mentioned in the text.
17. 'Kadesh Poem', *AEL*, 2:64. Cf. 'Kadesh Bulletin', ibid., 61–62: 'the vile Foe from Khatti came with his infantry and his chariotry and the many countries that were with him. Crossing the ford to the south of Kadesh they charged into his majesty's army as it marched unaware.'
18. *LIR*, 120.

FIGURE 23. Captured Shasu spies being tortured (beaten) and interrogated by Egyptians prior to the battle of Kadesh: Temple at Abu Simbel, Egypt, thirteenth century BCE. Public domain, via Wikimedia Commons.

spies and ambush may be nothing more than the invention of Egyptian scribes attempting to conceal the embarrassment of defeat, the fact that this device was employed to condemn Hittite tactics tells us something about Egyptian attitudes to acceptable and unacceptable behaviour in war. As is often the case when reading accounts of military espionage, deceit, and ambush, we encounter blatant ethical double standards. Deceit and ambush, when used by an enemy, could provide an unfair advantage; thus they were considered illegitimate tactics of war *if* utilised by Egypt's enemies. However, as pro-Egyptian stories such as 'The Capture of Joppa' make clear, similar tactics were considered ingenious and praiseworthy when utilised by Egyptians.

Magic

As part of their preparations for war, ancient Egyptians took seriously their communications with the supernatural, attempting to tap into various occult powers. For a kingdom and culture in which politics and everyday life was so deeply entwined with theology and religious ritual, this is hardly surprising. Magic was considered a legitimate instrument of war, with no moral qualms associated with its use. We might guess that such communications occurred all the way down the social scale, with individual soldiers offering votive prayers and carrying magical charms in the hope that such arcane items would lend them protection. Unfortunately, such imaginings of the practices of the average soldier must remain purely speculative.

What we do have evidence for is the routine practice of the state in attempting to harness magical forces to curse enemies through sympathetic magic. This even extended to human sacrifice. Depictions and symbolic images of Egypt's enemies, especially the 'Nine Bows', were rendered upon the floors of

Egyptian palaces, such as the painted pavement at the palace of Amarna.[19] Similar images were even stitched onto the soles of the pharaoh's sandals (such as the pair of ornate sandals found in the tomb of Tutankhamun) in the expectation that the symbolic trampling of the enemy would be magically transmitted into reality.[20]

Even more explicit was the ritual cursing and destruction of objects and figures; such destruction, it was hoped, would weaken the enemy through magic before any physical confrontation took place. So-called 'execration texts', discovered in considerable numbers, consist of figurines and bowls that were inscribed with hieratic curses of Egypt's enemies before being ritually smashed and buried. Over a thousand examples of this type of sympathetic magic have been unearthed at sites across Egypt and Nubia, dating from the late Old Kingdom through to the reign of Amenemhat III in the Middle Kingdom (c. 2200–c. 1808).[21]

Evidence of more grisly magical practices have emerged from archaeological sites. Decapitated human skulls, along with severed limbs and skeletons, have been discovered at Mirgissa and Avaris, indicating the inclusion of ritual execution as part of execration rites.[22] While it is unclear whether the sacrificial victims were foreign prisoners of war or native criminals, these finds establish that ancient Egyptians did not shy away from taking extreme measures when seeking to curry divine favour or harness supernatural power.[23]

Perceptions of the Enemy

The previous chapter discussed how the Egyptian sense of superiority over all foreigners was central to Egypt's conception of just and moral action against its enemies. This provided an almost infinitely broad justification for violence. It is a truism that a vilified and 'othered' enemy is likely to be treated with greater violence than an enemy with whom one shares a sense of shared

---

19. See *KANE*, 1:213.

20. See image in Renate Müller-Wollermann, 'Symbolische Gewalt im Alten Ägypten', in *Extreme Formen von Gewalt in Bild und Text des Altertum*, ed. Martin Zimmermann (Munich: Herbert Utz, 2009), 47–64 at 57. See also McDermott, *Warfare in Ancient Egypt*, 43.

21. Hornung, *History of Ancient Egypt*, 58, 65; Shaw, *Egyptian Warfare*, 9.

22. *ANET*, 328–29; Shaw, *Egyptian Warfare*, 9; Ritner, *Mechanics*, 136–80; *WANE*, 348, 415–18; Muhlestein, 'Royal Executions', 194–96.

23. Ritner, *Mechanics*, 153–54, argues that the Mirgissa sacrifice was performed as a consecration of the adjacent fortress (rather than for any specific military operation); even so, the magical safeguarding of the fortress provides a military context for this ritual. See further Muhlestein, *Violence*, 19–20; Janzen, 'Iconography of Humiliation', 18–21, 314–17; Betsy Bryan, Roxie Walker, Salima Ikram, and Joel Irish, 'Execration and Execution: A Skeleton of a Bound Captive from the Mut Temple Precinct', in *International Congress of Egyptologists XI, Florence (Italy), 23–30 August 2015, Museo Egizio Firenze: Paper and Poster Abstracts* (2015), 22.

humanity and cultural values. Yet in ancient Egypt enemies were routinely denigrated as wicked, evil, wretched, vile: the epitome of Isfet and its chaotic forces.[24] Foreigners, or the 'Nine Bows', were thus regarded with contempt, as evinced by a description of the Nubian enemy on a Twelfth Dynasty boundary stele:

> They are not people one respects,
> They are wretches, craven-hearted.
> My majesty has seen it, it is not an untruth.
> I have captured their women,
> I have carried off their dependents,
> Gone to their wells, killed their cattle,
> Cut down their grain, set fire to it.[25]

During Kamose's expulsion of the Hyksos from their delta capital at Avaris, the Theban king 'speaks' to his opponent in the following terms:

> miserable Asiatic [...] I shall destroy your dwelling-place and cut down your trees, after I have confined your women to the holds of ships.[26]

In being represented as wicked, vile, barbaric, even sub-human—or, as the 'Instructions to King Merikare' puts it, 'the pain of the place where he is'—the foreign enemy was also characterised as essentially weak and cowardly, inevitably succumbing to Egyptian superiority.[27] Enemies are depicted as corn being reaped or as animal prey being savaged by predators who symbolised the pharaoh.[28] Enemies were frequently emasculated or depicted as victims of the pharaohs' sexual conquests; soldiers fleeing in terror were compared to women experiencing the pain of childbirth, while Amenhotep II even imagined conquered states as women whom he had raped: 'violator of the Babylonian [woman], the Byblian maid, the little girl of Alalakh and the old crone of Arrapkha!'[29]

Such wretched and cowardly enemies were considered to be a blight on civilisation. Nonetheless, as far as can be determined from the royal sources at

---

24. Younger, *Ancient Conquest Accounts*, 182–83.
25. 'Boundary Stele of Sesostris III', *AEL*, 1:119.
26. 'War against the Hyksos', fragmentary stele, *ANET*, 554.
27. 'Instructions to King Merikare', *ToS*, 223; *AEL*, 1:103–4, 119.
28. See Arlette David, 'Devouring the Enemy: Ancient Egyptian Metaphors of Domination', *The Bulletin of the Australian Centre for Egyptology* 22 (2011): 83–100.
29. O'Connor, 'Egypt's Views of Others', 156–57; Redford, *Egypt, Canaan, and Israel*, 230. The personification of cities as female, and as victims of sexual violence and destruction, is also evident in the mid-first-millennium prophetic books of the Tanakh. See Brad E. Kelle, 'Wartime Rhetoric: Prophetic Metaphorization of Cities as Female', in *Writing and Reading War: Rhetoric, Gender, and Ethics in Biblical and Modern Contexts*, ed. Brad E. Kelle and Frank Ritchel Ames (Atlanta, GA: Society of Biblical Literature, 2008), 95–111.

least, there was never any doubt that civilisation (embodied in the person of the pharaoh) would emerge victorious. It was only the didactic and politically poignant 'lament literature', discussed in the previous chapter, which entertained the notion of Egypt's defeat by foreign enemies. Yet even this literature foresaw the eventual phoenix-like return and victory of a native Egyptian king.

David Lorton has suggested that the Egyptian term *Xsy* (a common descriptor for Egyptian enemies from the reign of Senusret I onwards), usually translated as 'weak', does not necessarily imply the more pejorative connotations of 'miserable' or 'wretched', or the even more extremely pejorative 'vile', seen in many modern translations. Lorton argues that modern references to the so-called 'vile enemy' may thus be somewhat misleading—intimating a feeling of hatred and disregard not authentic to the original use of the term, which in fact merely belittled the enemy for having been defeated.[30] While Lorton offers a potentially persuasive argument based on linguistic analysis, I think two observations are worth making in response. First, Egyptian royal ideology very much gives the impression that to be weak and defeated was, in itself, a miserable or vile state. Therefore the enemy was miserable or vile *because* he was weak and predestined to be defeated by Egypt. Second, a pejorative translation such as 'vile' seems consistent with the many pictorial reliefs that accompany inscriptions describing enemies as *Xsy*. The scenes of Egyptian chariots trampling scores of enemy soldiers, or of pharaohs mercilessly executing prisoners of war, were not intended to elicit pity from the audience, but rather to instil feelings of majesty, awe, and fear (see figures 1, 2, 5, 6, 7, 10, 15, and 24–27). The reliefs portray a vivid dichotomy between the god-like pharaoh and the broken enemy, who is vile both in his defeat and in the moral-theological sense: the immoral barbarian contrasted with the pharaoh as the embodiment of justice.

While it would be a mistake to interpret Egyptian xenophobia as equivalent to modern expressions of racism, Egypt's politico-military enemies were undoubtedly perceived as alien and inferior in every sense.[31] In this regard, the ancient Egyptian perception of the enemy—in moral, cultural, and religious terms—was simplistic and sharply oppositional: Egypt was good, civilised, and strong; enemies were bad, uncivilised, and weak. Such attitudes were unlikely to give birth to a normative framework of *ius in bello* restraint.

---

30. David Lorton, 'The So-Called "Vile" Enemies of the King of Egypt (in the Middle Kingdom and Dyn. XVIII)', *Journal of the American Research Center in Egypt* 10 (1973): 65–70 at 65–68.

31. As noted above (pp. 77–78), foreigners who lived within Egypt and in accordance with Ma'at could be acculturated into Egyptian society. We need to distinguish between the extreme ideological conception of foreigners contained in the rhetoric and ritual of royal propaganda and the reality of interactions with foreigners in Egyptian society. During the Middle Kingdom and Second Intermediate Period, foreigners are attested in roughly one hundred different professions across the socio-economic spectrum: Schneider, 'Foreigners in Egypt', 152.

FIGURE 24. Thutmose III (c. 1479–c. 1425 BCE) smiting captured enemies: Karnak Temple, Egypt. Markh, public domain, via Wikimedia Commons.

FIGURE 25. Seti I leads Libyan prisoners of war back to Egypt: Great Hypostyle Hall, Karnak Temple, Egypt, early thirteenth century BCE. Peter Brand / Karnak Hypostyle Hall Project, University of Memphis.

FIGURE 26. Bound African prisoners of war: Temple of Abu Simbel, Egypt, thirteenth century BCE. Gary Todd, Xinzheng, China, CC0, via Wikimedia Commons.

And yet, from the Middle Kingdom onwards, Egyptian armies often incorporated foreign mercenaries as well as resettled auxiliary troops from a variety of ethnic backgrounds. The potentially multi-ethnic character of these second-millenium armies problematises any attempt to draw a single line of causation between ideological representations of the enemy, on the one hand, and the brutality of Egyptian military conduct on the other. So, while a process of dehumanisation is plain to see in the stereotypical representations of the enemy adopted by the jingoistic textual and pictorial records of Egyptian warfare, it would probably have been far less easy to draw such sharp distinctions in reality, when men of multiple ethnic backgrounds, fighting on the same or opposite sides, clashed in the heat of battle. What we likely have, then, is a disjunction between state propaganda and military reality—a phenomenon easy to find in the history of almost any political state.

Treatment of the Enemy during War

Brutal treatment of the enemy, both during and after military engagements, was commonplace throughout the history of ancient Egyptian warfare. The killing of enemy soldiers, the execution or enslavement of defeated combatants and non-combatants, and the destruction or looting of enemy property all appear to have been taken for granted. Such actions were not described with

FIGURE 27. Bound Asiatic prisoners of war: Temple of Abu Simbel, Egypt, thirteenth century BCE. Image extracted from four files by Cecioka, Mmelouk, Youssef Alam, and Abumalek Ahmed Mohamed, CC BY-SA 4.0 licence, via Wikimedia Commons.

a sense of regret—as pitiable yet unavoidable evils of war. Rather, extreme violence against the enemy, without distinction between combatants and non-combatants, was presented in essentially positive moral terms: something to be celebrated as evidence of the divine favour enjoyed by individual pharaohs.

The Tombos Stele, from the second year of Thutmose I's reign, gruesomely describes the pharaoh's expedition into Nubia (where the stele was discovered):

> the despoiled Nubian belongs to his grip [...] no escape existed among the evil-of-character [...]. As the Nubian *Iwntyw* have fallen to terror and are laid aside throughout their lands, their stench, it floods their wadis, their blood is like a rainstorm.[32]

In a similar vein, the 'Autobiography of Ahmose, son of Abana' (also recording Thutmose I's Nubian campaign), rejoiced that a 'slaughter was made among them; their dependents were carried off as living captives [...] and that wretched Nubian Bowman [was hung] head downward at the bow of his majesty's ship *Falcon*'.[33] Ahmose, son of Abana, praised similar deeds performed during Thutmose I's later campaign into Syria: 'Then his majesty made a great slaughter of them. Countless were the living captives which his majesty brought back from his victories.'[34]

---

32. Hans Goedicke, 'The Thutmosis I Inscription near Tomâs', *Journal of Near Eastern Studies* 55 (3) (1996): 161–77 at 166. Compare Breasted's translation: *ARE*, 2:30, § 71.

33. 'Autobiography of Ahmose', *AEL*, 2:14.

34. Ibid.

Two generations later, in a campaign against the Naharin, Pharaoh Thutmose III bragged that

> I desolated his towns and his tribes and set fire to them. I captured all their people, carried off as living prisoners [...] and their goods as well. I took away the *very sources of life*, for I cut down their grain and felled all their groves and all their pleasant trees.... I destroyed it; it became a [desert?] upon which there are no trees.[35]

The tomb biography of the soldier Amenemheb, who accompanied Thutmose III on one of his Syrian campaigns, also testifies that in the 'country of Sendjer' (possibly north-west of Hama) the pharaoh 'made [a great] slaughter [among] them. I made captives in the king's presence; I took a hand there, and he gave me the Gold of Favour.'[36]

Clearly these battle descriptions were formulaic, yet they indicate a clear expectation that the mass slaughter and enslavement of the enemy was something to boast about and, in turn, something to be extolled. This attitude also pervaded Egyptian literature. In the 'Tale of Sinuhe' the eponymous protagonist boasts of his actions as a military commander in imitation of royal inscriptions:

> Every country for which I set out, I made my attack on it, and it was driven from its grasslands and wells; I plundered its cattle and carried off its inhabitants, and their food was taken away. I killed the people in it with my strong arm, my bow, my movements, and my excellent plans.[37]

---

35. 'Barkal Stela', *ANET*, 240. See also the description of Kamose's sack of Nefrusi, ibid., 233.
36. 'Biography of Amenemheb', *ANET*, 241.
37. *ToS*, 32.

[130] CHAPTER 4

FIGURE 28. Bound prisoners of war and enemy dead: Battlefield Palette, Egypt, Naqada III period (c. 3300–c. 3100 BCE). Einsamer Schütze, CC BY-SA 3.0 licence, via Wikimedia Commons.

Four motifs dominated Egyptian pictorial and textual representations of battle scenes: the king smiting the enemy, the trampling of the enemy, the king as a lion immobilising the enemy, and the king as a lion devouring the enemy (figure 28).[38] This propagandist iconography dates back to the earliest periods of the Egyptian kingdom. The motif of trampled enemies, for example, was already being used in protohistoric times.[39] Arlette David notes that '[t]extually and iconographically, to be under someone's feet (*xr rdwy*) is to be

38. Cf. Numbers 24:8–9: 'They shall devour enemy nations, crush their bones, and smash their arrows. / They crouch, they lie down like a lion. Like the king of beasts; who dare rouse them?'

39. David, 'Devouring the Enemy', 85–86. See also Aristide Théodoridès, 'Mettres des biens sous les pieds de quelqu'un', *Revue d'égyptologie* 24 (1972): 188–92.

in that person's power; the expression is even used in legal contexts to express possession'.⁴⁰ In other words, the image of trampling was one way to express the fact that enemies had no legal status or 'rights' of their own.

With the introduction of the fast war chariot at the beginning of the New Kingdom, many kings of this period are depicted as trampling and crushing enemies beneath the hooves of their horse-team and the wheels of their chariot (figures 5, 6, and 10).⁴¹ Depictions of the king as a winged lion are evident as early as Dynasty V, while images of the king-lion devouring the head of the enemy (increasingly popular from the reign of Amenhotep III onwards) conveyed 'the absorption of the enemy to make him an integral part of voracious Egypt'.⁴² Beliefs concerning the magical benefits of consuming flesh were of significant antiquity in Egypt. They are a vivid component of the Old Kingdom 'Cannibal Hymn' of the Pyramid Texts, and also appear in the Coffin Texts and elsewhere.⁴³ Whether imagined as bodies to be crushed or 'food' to be consumed, there was no sense of restraint when facing the enemy in war.

WAR AS THE PERSONAL DUEL OF PHARAOH

All of the aforementioned motifs of Egyptian victory were utilised in describing and depicting the personal military deeds of the pharaoh. Indeed, it became increasingly common through the Middle Kingdom period to portray the act of war as an individual struggle of the heroic pharaoh against the enemy. This reached an apogee during the New Kingdom, such that the Egyptian army itself was presented as playing a merely supportive or almost incidental role in the pharaoh's heroic battles. This reductive personalisation of war, transforming it into a struggle between the quasi-divine pharaoh and his wicked enemies, encouraged a deeply moralising and absolutist view of warfare in which few or no restraints were expected or practised.

A laudatory hymn to Senusret III expresses this idealisation of the pharaoh's martial prowess and his ability to defend the kingdom single-handedly:

> Whose slaughter brought death to thousands of Bowmen,
> Who had come to invade his borders [...]
> When he felled thousands who ignored his might [...]
> Unique youth who fights for his frontiers,

---

40. David, 'Devouring the Enemy', 87.

41. Schoske, 'Erschlagen der Feinde', 295–300 provides a number of examples. Cf. 2 Samuel 22:38–43.

42. David, 'Devouring the Enemy', 89, 91, 92. The eating of the head was probably an explicit reference to the destruction of the enemy ruler, as David explains that the hieroglyph *tp* (head) was also used to designate 'headman/chief': ibid., 92.

43. See Ritner, *Mechanics*, 103–4; David, 'Devouring the Enemy', 92. On the 'Cannibal Hymn', see also pp. 95–96 above.

Not letting his subjects weary themselves.
Who lets the people sleep till daylight,
The youths may slumber, his heart protects them.[44]

From the reign of Amenhotep II onwards, the valour of the pharaoh was exaggerated to such an extent that the deeds of the Egyptian soldiery were either ignored or, on occasion, actually denigrated. Both literary techniques served to magnify the heroism of the king, as in this example of Amenhotep II defeating an ambush by Asiatics after crossing the Orontes river:

> His majesty *burst* after them like the flight of a divine falcon [. . .]. Not a single one was with his majesty, except for himself with his valiant arm. His majesty killed them by shooting.[45]

The mass slaughter of enemies by the pharaoh was depicted again and again in pictorial carvings showing him felling enemies with arrows, trampling their bodies under his feet, or riding over enemy corpses with his chariot (figures 1, 2, 5–7, and 10). Egyptian campaign accounts depict victory as inevitable, owing to the supernatural origins and superhuman strength of the pharaoh. There was no sense that a military encounter against Egypt was a 'fair fight': the enemy was doomed from the outset. Royal ideology simply refused to countenance the possibility of defeat, even if such ideology did not always align with the facts.

The sources describing the battle of Kadesh (c. 1274) perfectly encapsulate both of these aforementioned elements: the unique role of the pharaoh in securing victory (contrasted with the cowardice of the Egyptian army), and the disconnect from military reality. This close-fought battle—which in all likelihood witnessed the defeat of Ramses II's army or, at best, a grinding stalemate—was presented in the Egyptian sources as a great victory, albeit a victory that was hard won. Egyptian textual accounts of the battle are provided by the 'Kadesh Bulletin' and the longer 'Kadesh Poem', both of which accompany extensive pictorial reliefs carved on temple walls at Abydos, Luxor, Karnak, Abu Simbel, and the Ramesseum (e.g., figure 5).[46] The 'Bulletin', and more especially the 'Poem', overflow with hyperbole; but while their grip on reality may be tenuous, they undoubtedly convey a powerful sense of the Egyptian concept of martial kingship:

> He [Ramses II] heeded not the foreign multitude; he regarded them as chaff. His majesty charged into the force of the Foe from Khatti and the many countries with him. [. . .] His majesty slew the entire force of

---

44. 'Hymn I to Senusret III', *AEL*, 1:198–99; cf. *ToS*, 30.
45. 'Stelae of Amenhotep II', *ANET*, 245. Cf. 'Barkal Stela' describing Thutmose III's valour: ibid., 240.
46. See 'Kadesh Bulletin' and 'Kadesh Poem', *AEL*, 2:57–62, 62–71.

the Foe from Khatti, together with his great chiefs and all his brothers, as well as all the chiefs of all the countries that had come with him, and their infantry and their chariotry falling on their faces one upon the other. His majesty slaughtered them in their places; they sprawled before his horses; and his majesty was alone, none other with him.[47]

The drama of the battle, which supposedly saw the Hittite chariots ambushing the strung-out Egyptian column, is intensified by the sense of desertion experienced by Ramses II as he single-handedly fights off the might of the Hittite divisions:

> I attacked all the countries, I alone. For my infantry and my chariotry had deserted me; not one of them stood looking back. As I live, as Re loves me, as my father Atum favors me, everything that my majesty has told I did it in truth.[48]

Both the king's isolation and his special ability to seek divine aid is further developed in the more detailed and literary 'Poem', which recounts Ramses II calling directly upon his 'father', the god Amun:

> No officer was with me, no charioteer,
> No soldier of the army, no shield-bearer;
> My infantry, my chariotry yielded before them.
> His majesty spoke: 'What is this, father Amun?
> Is it right for a father to ignore his son? [. . .]
> What are these Asiatics to you, O Amun,
> The wretches ignorant of god? [. . .]
> I am among a host of strangers;
> All countries are arrayed against me,
> I am alone, there's none with me!
> My numerous troops have deserted me,
> Not one of my chariotry looks for me;
> I keep on shouting for them,
> But none of them heeds my call [. . .].'
> I found Amun came when I called to him [. . .]
> I found my heart stout, my breast in joy [. . .]
> I slaughtered among them at my will,
> Not one looked behind him,
> Not one turned around,
> Whoever fell down did not rise.[49]

As the poem progresses, Ramses continues to chastise his troops, contrasting their cowardice with the loyalty of his horses. He brands his soldiers 'cowards',

---

47. 'Kadesh Bulletin', *AEL*, 2:62.
48. Ibid.
49. 'Kadesh Poem', *AEL*, 2:64–66.

wonders why 'Not one among you stood fast / To lend me a hand while I fought!', and ponders how

> I crushed a million countries by myself,
> On Victory-in-Thebes, Mut-is-content, my great horses;
> It was they whom I found supporting me,
> When I alone fought many lands.[50]

It hardly needs to be said that Ramses II did not actually fight the Hittite army at Kadesh single-handedly. Indeed, one might wonder how those Egyptian soldiers who survived the battle responded to these inscriptions. The vast majority would have been illiterate and would never have been permitted access to the temple complexes on which the battle scenes and texts were carved; this was not necessarily the case for the elite chariot corps, however, recruited from the nobility, some of whom would have been literate and would have had access to the royal complexes. How would they have felt about being depicted as craven and disloyal in order to serve the interests of the royal cult? We will never know. What we do know is that a few years after the battle, during peace negotiations with the Hittite king Hattušili III (the younger brother of Muwatalli II), reports of Ramses II's Kadesh reliefs had obviously reached the Hittite court. Hattušili protested about the way in which Ramses was presenting the battle as a great Egyptian victory and, in a pointed example of diplomatic sarcasm, asked his Egyptian counterpart sardonically, '(Really), there was no army and chariotry there?'[51]

Modern historians, emulating Hattušili III's scepticism, should not take accounts of Egyptian battle victories at face value. Nevertheless, what such accounts do convey is a lucid articulation of the Egyptian *ethic* of combat. This ethic was focused solely on legitimating and applauding the destruction of the enemy, whether slaughtered single-handedly by the god-like pharaoh or annihilated by the Egyptian army as a whole. The (idealised) result was the same in either case: the eradication and humiliation of anyone who threatened Egyptian authority and hegemony. In this sense, there is no identifiable ethic of restraint in the Egyptian conduct of war. As we shall see below, this also influenced how enemies were treated in the aftermath of battle and other combat operations.

MUTILATION OF THE DEAD

The deliberate mutilation of enemy dead is an aspect of Egyptian martial behaviour that constituted a purposeful and vindictive violation of the body of the fallen foe, and dates back to the earliest development of the Egyptian state.

---

50. Ibid., 2:67–70.
51. *Die ägyptisch-hethitische Korrespondenz aus Boghazköi*, ed. Elmer Edel, 2 vols (Opladen: Westdeutscher, 1994), 1:24, cited *LIR*, 82 n. 12.

Carved palettes and temple reliefs show the mutilation of enemy corpses, including removal of the eyes, hands, phalli, and head (figure 2). Mutilation of enemy corpses was institutionalised, so that it became standard practice for enemy dead to be counted by the number of hands collected after battle (figures 20 and 21). Such tallies could also be based on the number of ears or phalli harvested from the battlefield (figure 22).

In return for presenting these trophies of war to the army command, Egyptian soldiers were awarded the 'Gold of Valour' (*nbw n qnt*) or 'Gold of Favour' (*nbw n Hswt*),[52] as attested in the 'Biography of Amenemheb': 'I made captives in the king's presence; I took a hand there, and he gave me the Gold of Favour.'[53] Remuneration could also include a share of the living captives. Ahmose, son of Abana boasted that he had 'been rewarded with gold seven times' in return for presenting enemy hands to the pharaoh. During one campaign in Nubia, Ahmose claims that

> His majesty made a great slaughter among them, and I brought spoil from there: two living men and three hands. Then I was rewarded the gold once again, and two female slaves were given to me.[54]

The list of booty taken after Thutmose III's victory at Megiddo included eighty-three hands, while the booty list from Amenhotep III's Ibhet campaign recorded 312. The Great Karnak inscription of Merneptah records the pharaoh returning triumphantly from a war against a Libyan alliance with 'asses [. . .] laden with the uncircumcised phalli of the land of Libya, together with the severed hands of every country which was with them'. The gruesome spoils included 250 hands from the Shekelesh, 790 hands from the Teresh, and over six thousand phalli.[55] During the Ramesside period the pictorial representation of tallying enemy hands or phalli was a recurring motif of monumental art (figures 20–22).[56]

The mutilation of enemy corpses as a means to tally the dead was practised throughout the Bronze Age and Iron Age Near East. Indeed, we can see references to the same practice in the books of the Hebrew Tanakh (see below, pp. 373–78). However, the Egyptian practice of removing body parts from

---

52. Lorton, 'Terminology', 53, 60.
53. 'Biography of Amenemheb', *ANET*, 241.
54. 'Autobiography of Ahmose', *AEL*, 2:12–13.
55. 'Annals of Thutmose III', *AEL*, 2:33–34; 'Semneh Inscription', *ARE*, 2:341, § 854; 'Great Karnark Inscription', *ARE*, 3:247–51, §§ 587–89; Alan R. Schulman, *Ceremonial Execution and Public Rewards: Some Historical Scenes on New Kingdom Private Stelae* (Freiburg: Universitätsverlag; Göttingen: Vandenhoeck & Ruprecht, 1988), 90–91 n. 122. See also Eric H. Cline and David O'Connor, 'The Mystery of the "Sea Peoples"', in *Mysterious Lands*, ed. David O'Connor and Stephen Quirke (London: UCL Press, 2003), 107–38 at 135.
56. Joachim Śliwa, 'Some Remarks concerning Victorious Ruler Representations in Egyptian Art', *Forschungen und Berichte* 16 (1974): 97–117 at 108; Schulman, *Ceremonial Execution*, 90.

enemy corpses must be understood in light of the extreme importance Egyptians attached to the preservation of the deceased body and proper burial, of which the practice of mummification is tangible and obvious proof. This preservation was believed to be vital to the continued existence of the deceased's soul and its passage into the afterlife.[57] This concern is repeatedly emphasised throughout the 'Tale of Sinuhe', and the pharaoh reassures the returning Sinuhe, who has been living in exile for many years, 'Your burial is no small matter; you will not be laid to rest by barbarians.'[58] The deliberate mutilation of corpses—even for apparently mundane purposes such as tallying the dead—must therefore be viewed seriously, as it demonstrated a reversal of the reverence with which Egyptians treated their own dead. The mutilation of enemy corpses in the Egyptian context was thus a deliberate act of violation, intended to convey a message of humiliation, retribution, and warning to existing and potential enemies. One might even interpret wartime mutilation as the ultimate and cruellest punitive act—punishing fallen enemies even after death by denying them proper entry into the afterlife.

The power of this act was most obviously communicated when enemy corpses and body parts were utilised to serve propaganda purposes. Two stelae of Amenhotep II record that the campaigning pharaoh returned from one skirmish proudly displaying '20 hands at the foreheads of his horses'.[59] Nubian prisoners of war were impaled during Akhenaton's reign, leading Alan Schulman to suggest that impalement 'was a regular feature of the punishments meted out to Egypt's defeated enemies'.[60] Impalement was a particularly gruesome and publicly explicit method of violating the body. It was a punishment meted out to domestic criminals and military foes alike, both of whom were branded as 'rebellious'. The Amada stele, commissioned during the fifth year of Merneptah's reign, refers to Libyan prisoners of war being impaled on the outskirts of Memphis; the stele includes what can without doubt be described as an unambiguous determinative hieroglyph, depicting a body being impaled through the midriff by a vertical shaft (figure 29).[61] However, whether impalement was inflicted as a *means* of death (akin to the later Roman practice of crucifixion) or was intended merely as a defilement and public display of the body post-mortem (the prisoner having first been dispatched by some other

---

57. Morenz, *Egyptian Religion*, 198–201.
58. *ToS*, 40.
59. 'Memphis and Karnak stelae', *ANET*, 246.
60. Schulman, *Ceremonial Execution*, 92.
61. Trigger et al, *Ancient Egypt*, 238, fig. 3.16. See also Rainer Hannig, *Die Sprache der Pharaonen: Grosses Handwörterbuch Ägyptisch–Deutsch (2800–950 v. Chr.)*, 5th edn (Mainz: Philipp von Zabern, 2009; Tyldesley, *Judgment of the Pharaoh*, 65. Compare examples of the Israelite king Joshua impaling his enemies (Joshua 8:23–29; 10:19–27) and also in the book of Esther (8:11–9:32). For further discussion of impalement, see below, ch. 10, 'Treatment of Combatants'.

FIGURE 29. Impalement: Egyptian hieroglyphic determinative for impalement, Amada stele of Pharaoh Merneptah, late thirteenth century BCE. After Bruce G. Trigger, Barry J. Kemp, David O'Connor, and Alan B. Lloyd, *Ancient Egypt: A Social History* (Cambridge: Cambridge University Press, 1983), 238, fig. 3.16.

method, perhaps clubbing to the head, as in the smiting scenes discussed below), remains uncertain.[62]

Clearly, the torture and execution of enemies was in no way considered legally or morally problematic by Egyptian society. This is partly explained by the inextricable connection in Egyptian thought between military victory and the restoration of Ma'at. The state had to demonstrate publicly that enemies, as violators of cosmic order and harmony, were not only punished, but completely eradicated. This display formed an essential element of public military triumphs following a successful campaign, which required 'the total abnegation of the opponent, not merely his submission but as well his destruction'.[63] There was no sense here, then, of a desire 'to achieve a victory that avoids rather than assumes the humiliation of the vanquished'.[64] For Egyptians, there could be no tension between victory, peace, and justice, because it was only through absolute victory that peace and justice could be ensured.

Treatment of Prisoners of War

In any examination of the treatment of prisoners of war in the ancient world—regardless of geographical region—it must be stressed that there was no modern equivalent to the legal status of 'prisoner of war'. I use this term simply to refer to those unfortunate people, combatants and non-combatants, who were taken captive as a result of military operations. This applies equally to Egyptian, Hittite, and Israelite warfare.

In Egypt, all prisoners of war were *de iure* the property of the pharaoh. During a campaign or following a successful battle or siege, soldiers were required to submit their captives to the central army administration, which

---

62. Tyldesley, *Judgment of the Pharaoh*, 65–66, assumes that victims were impaled alive.
63. Spalinger, 'New Kingdom Triumphs', 117.
64. A characteristic of classical Greek warfare as posited by Cian O'Driscoll, *Victory: The Triumph and Tragedy of Just War* (Oxford: Oxford University Press, 2019), 51.

was then responsible for redistribution.⁶⁵ After capture, prisoners were afforded no immunities or rights. This applied across the social spectrum, with high-ranking prisoners arguably at greater risk than anyone else.⁶⁶ As Lorton has highlighted, prisoners of war (*sqr-ʿnx*) ceased to possess a juridical status. Previously independent enemies became 'like one who had never existed' (*mì nty n xpr*), while rebels became like 'one who did not exist' (*m tm xpr*). The status of such prisoners appears comparable to the later Roman legal concept of *cives nullius certae civitatis* (citizens of no definite state).⁶⁷

Lacking any kind of status or rights, prisoners of war could expect humiliation and even ritual execution. Evidence for this type of treatment emerges from sources produced throughout the entire period of Egyptian history under investigation, from the late fourth to the late second millennium. The Narmer Palette (c. 3100: figure 2) depicts rows of bound and beheaded enemy prisoners. In the 'Instruction of King Amenemhet' (c. 1950),⁶⁸ the old pharaoh boasts to his son that 'I subjugated Nubians, and I captured Medjai; I made Syrians do the dog-walk'.⁶⁹ The 'dog-walk' presumably referred to prisoners being forced to walk in bonds. Egyptian art shows prisoners of war with their hands bound behind their backs and ropes tied around their necks: literally collared and leashed like a dog (figures 25–28).

Prisoners of war were placed under the control of a 'herald of captures', who supervised the binding, branding, and recording of captives.⁷⁰ Having been stripped of juridical status, such captives were also partly stripped of their human identity. Non-combatants were designated as *skr-nh*, which in earlier periods was used to describe both human captives and non-human plunder such as livestock. By Dynasty XVIII this term was being used to refer specifically to prisoners of war. Equally, just like the earlier usage of the term '*sqr-ʿnx*', the term '*HAq*' or '*HAqt*' (meaning 'spoils'), could refer to either captured persons or inanimate plunder.⁷¹ Thus Egyptian legal terminology aided the transformation

---

65. See references to this system in, inter alia, 'The Biography of Amenemheb', *ANET*, 241; 'Autobiography of Ahmose', *AEL*, 2:13. See also Lorton, 'Terminology', 53, 56–57, and more generally, Lorton, *Juridical Terminology*.

66. The treatment of foreign captives during the New Kingdom is explored in depth in Janzen, 'Iconography of Humiliation'.

67. Lorton, 'Terminology', 54. Lorton observes that in '*sqr-ʿnx*' could be used to apply to persons *and* plunder (e.g., cattle), thus emphasising that human captives were viewed simply as chattels, indistinguishable from other types of booty: ibid., 55–56, 62.

68. The text only survives in New Kingdom copies, but is thought to originate from the reign of Amenemhet I's son Senusret I (c. 1971–c. 1926).

69. *ToS*, 208. Compare the alternative translation in *AEL*, 1:137: 'I repressed those of Wawat, I captured the Medjai, I made the Asiatics do the dog walk.' See also 'Stelae of Amenhotep II', *ANET*, 246, which describe sixteen *maryanu* tied to the pharaoh's chariot. An image of a Nubian tied to the battle chariot of Amenhotep III (limestone stele, Cairo Museum 34032) is printed in Śliwa, 'Victorious Ruler Representations', 115.

70. Ziskind, 'Aspects of International Law', 151.

71. Lorton, 'Terminology', 55–56, 67; David, 'Devouring the Enemy', 84.

of the human war captive into something little more than chattel—a piece of livestock—to be used in whatever way the captor deemed appropriate.

The description of military captives as dehumanised chattels is nowhere more striking than in the twelfth-century Great Harris Papyrus. This remarkable document, composed during the reign of Ramses IV but recounting the deeds of his father Ramses III, is the largest extant papyrus, at over 40.5 metres (133 feet) in length. The record of one campaign declares that '[t]he Sherden and the Weshesh of the sea, they were made as those that exist not, taken captive at one time, brought as captives to Egypt, like the sand of the shore'.[72] The papyrus makes little distinction between plundered humans and plundered livestock:

> I carried away those whom my sword spared, as numerous captives, pinioned like birds before my horses, their wives and their children by the ten-thousand, their cattle in number like hundred-thousands [. . .], chief men of the tribes, branded and made into slaves, impressed with my name; their wives and their children were made likewise. I led their cattle into the house of Amon; they were made for him into herds forever.[73]

Indeed, many of these captured humans and animals were gifted to the temples—especially the Temple of Amun at Karnak—because, as elsewhere in the Near East, plunder was understood to constitute part of the gods' rightful portion in helping to bring about victory.

Elite prisoners do not appear to be have been afforded any special protections, and in fact the humiliation of enemy leaders was essential to the drama of military victory. The custom of the pharaoh placing his foot on the neck of a defeated enemy leader—a potent symbol of humiliating subjugation—had a long pedigree in Egyptian history.[74] The brutality with which even high-status enemy prisoners could be treated is indicated in a gruesome piece of political theatre performed by Amenhotep II:

> His majesty returned in joy of heart to his father Amon, when he had slain with his own mace the seven princes [. . .] who had been put upside down at the prow of his majesty's falcon-boat. [. . .] Then six men of these enemies were hanged on the face of the wall of Thebes, and the hands as well. Then the other foe was taken upstream to the land of Nubia and hanged to the wall of Napata, to show his majesty's victories forever and ever in all lands and all countries.[75]

---

72. 'Papyrus Harris', *ARE*, 201, § 403.

73. Ibid., 202, § 405. Note that McDermott offers a different translation, with the implication that the human slaves *are* the cattle and herds, being literally dehumanised: 'branded and made into slaves, they being stamped by my name, their women and children being dealt with likewise. I brought their herds to the House of Amun, they being made for him as cattle forever.' McDermott, *Warfare in Ancient Egypt*, 118.

74. See images in *ANET*, 248 (§ a), 257, 263 (§ d), 373–74.

75. 'Stelae of Amenhotep II', *ANET*, 248. See also Spalinger, 'New Kingdom Triumphs', 99.

This clearly illustrates the mortal danger faced by captured enemy leaders, yet there is no evidence to suggest that lower status enemies were treated any more mercifully. Two royal stelae record how, during Amenhotep II's second campaign into Asia (c. 1440), the pharaoh ordered a holocaust of enemy prisoners, including women and children:

> He carried off their princes: 34; *merui*:[76] 57; living Asiatics: 231; hands: 372; horses: 54; chariots: 54; *in addition to* all the weapons of warfare, every able-bodied man of Retenu, their children, their wives, and all their property. After his majesty saw the very abundant plunder, they were made into living prisoners, and two ditches were made *around all of them. Behold*, they were filled with fire, and his majesty kept watch over it until daybreak, while his battle-axe was in his right hand, alone, without a single one with him, while the army was far from him, *far from hearing* the cry of Pharaoh.[77]

In ancient Egypt, as in many cultures, fire represented an instrument of ritual cleansing, achieved through the total annihilation of the material substance.[78] Burning was an established punishment in the Egyptian domestic judicial system, as were impalement, mutilation, and permanent enslavement.[79] The fact that enemy prisoners were also subjected to burning (as well as impalement, mutilation, and enslavement) is further evidence that their legal status was equivalent to that of a criminal: that is, they had no legal status. It is also possible that the cleansing properties of fire were deemed appropriate for rebellious enemies requiring purification.

Nevertheless, the burning of prisoners of war appears to have been unconventional (there is little evidence of it in the sources, at least),[80] and precisely

---

76. Probably 'serfs': *ANET*, 247 n. 28.

77. 'Stelae of Amenhotep II', *ANET*, 247. See also Janzen, 'Iconography of Humiliation', 251–55. On the connection between burning and rebellion in Egyptian legal thought, see Anthony Leahy, 'Death by Fire in Ancient Egypt', *Journal of Economic and Social History of the Orient* 27 (2) (1984): 199–206 at 200–203; Muhlestein, 'Royal Executions', 187.

78. The god Thoth killed the serpent demon Apophis by decapitating it and then throwing the corpse into a fire: 'Prayer and Hymn of General Haremhab', *AEL*, 2:102. In the 'Tale of King Cheops' Court', the wife of the courtier Ubainer is burned for adultery: 'The [Majesty of] the Dual King Nebka, the justified, had Ubainer's wife taken away to a plot north of the Residence. Then he had her burnt, [and she became] refuse for the river.' *ToS*, 109.

79. At least one Egyptologist has argued that burning did not become a capital punishment until the Late Period, although this has been convincingly rebutted by more recent scholarship. Lorton, 'Treatment of Criminals', 15, 51, argues for the late introduction of burning. Against this view, see Leahy, 'Death by Fire', 199–206; Muhlestein, 'Royal Executions', 192–94; Tyldesley, *Judgement of the Pharaoh*, 66.

80. Note, however, that 'actual brutality of the kind evinced by Amenophis [Amenhotep] II may have been relatively common. The relatively rare examples may be indicative of general practices normally masked or restricted in literature and art, by the Egyptians' strong sense of decorum in these contexts.' O'Connor, 'Egypt's Views of Others', 157.

what led Amenhotep II to burn these particular prisoners is not clear from the text. He is said to have returned from the campaign with numerous living prisoners as slaves for the temples and for his soldiers, so burning captives cannot have been a blanket policy during the campaign. Of course, the use of fire against enemy property was a long-established terror tactic, and these particular prisoners might simply have been unlucky, suffering the gruesome cost of a lurid political statement.[81] We must also consider the possibility that the whole episode was a fiction of the scribes. The location and modern identity of the two towns from which the prisoners are said to have been seized are unknown to Egyptologists.[82] Yet the specificity of the act, and its repetition on two separate stelae, makes a complete fabrication seem unlikely. Whatever the truth of the episode may have been, it is worth highlighting, yet again, that the texts were designed to express idealised behaviour. As far as the stelae were concerned, the violent actions of the pharaoh were to be understood as awe-inspiring and righteous; there is certainly no hint of criticism or moral condemnation.

While it is not unusual to read in Egyptian accounts about women and children being included among the slaughtered enemy, it is far less common for these non-combatants to appear in art depicting martial scenes. It is striking that in all the numerous carved reliefs of the pharaoh smiting his enemies, the victims are almost exclusively male (see, e.g., figures 1, 6, and 24). Other than the occasional depiction of an Egyptian queen accompanying the pharaoh during the ritual, women and children feature only very rarely in the smiting scenes.[83] This is evidence of the patriarchal nature of ancient warfare and military glory rather than of a recognition of female or infant immunity. Female captives—especially virgins—were a valuable component of military booty and were forced to endure the usual sexual exploitation suffered by so many women caught up in wars over the millennia.[84] For example, after Thut-

---

81. James B. Pritchard certainly interprets it this way: 'This episode was sheer bravura on the part of the pharaoh, of a spectacular nature in order to create a legend of his personal prowess.' *ANET*, 247 n. 40.

82. Ibid., n. 37.

83. One rare example is from the pillared hall (south wall) of the pyramid complex of Sahure (Old Kingdom, Dynasty V, c. 2487–c. 2475), where two children and a woman—possibly the wife and children of the male victim, who is probably an enemy 'prince'—are depicted crouching behind the male victim's foot: D. R. Seton, 'The King of Egypt Annihilating His Enemies: A Study of the Symbolism of Ancient Monarchy' (M.A. dissertation, University of Birmingham, 1971), 7–9.

84. As discussed below, ch. 10, 'Treatment of Women', the Deuteronomic code is unusual in even mentioning appropriate behaviour concerning female captives (Deuteronomy 21:10–14). On the other hand, the disembowelling of pregnant women and the dashing to death of infants is also recorded in the Old Testament (2 Kings 8:12; Amos 1:13; Hosea 14:1), and became a popular trope in medieval chronicle accounts describing the actions of barbarians and heathens. See Rory Cox, 'Asymmetric Warfare and Military Conduct in the Middle Ages', *Journal of Medieval History* 38 (1) (2012): 100–25 at 116–17.

mose III's victory at Megiddo over two thousand prisoners were recorded, including hundreds of women and children.[85]

Amenhotep II's mass holocaust of prisoners of war may have been atypical, but he was not alone in perpetrating humiliating brutalities upon his enemies. During Merneptah's reign, Libyan captives were 'impaled to the south of Memphis, destroyed . . . carried off to Egypt and fire was hurled against their multitude in the presence of their relatives'. As to the remainder, their hands were cut off because of their crimes, and others had eyes and ears removed.[86] Disturbingly, the source appears to say that families were forced to watch the mutilation and burning of their kinsmen.

Significantly, these spectacles were intended primarily for a domestic audience. Captives were usually brought back to Egypt to be executed in a public display of victory and royal power.[87] In other words, such acts were more about projecting an image of punitive and retributive justice to the people of Egypt than they were about terrorising enemy populations, although the latter was undoubtedly a perfectly acceptable by-product. While shocking to modern sensibilities, the status and treatment of prisoners of war in Egypt was fundamentally no different from in other contemporary cultures. Egyptian attitudes and practices mirror other Bronze Age and Iron Age Near Eastern attitudes and practices, as well as later ancient Greek conventions, whereby the victor was entitled to execute, enslave, or ransom enemy soldiers.[88]

ERSCHLAGEN DER FEINDE: SMITING SCENES AND THE EXECUTION OF PRISONERS OF WAR

Of all the motifs of Egyptian art depicting violence, the image of the pharaoh 'smiting his enemies' (commonly referred to in scholarly literature by the German phrase *erschlagen der Feinde*) was both the oldest and most enduring. It first appeared in pre-dynastic times and was repeated all the way through Egyptian history until the late Roman period: a span of over 3,500 years. D. R. Seton provides notes on over 150 examples of the scene, although admits that even this compilation is not exhaustive (see also figures 1, 6, 24, and 30).[89]

---

85. At Megiddo, 340 living prisoners were captured in addition to *maryannu* (elite) captives totalling 38 warriors, 84 children of warriors/princes; also 1,796 male, female, and child slaves, and 103 'pardoned persons': *AEL*, 2:33–34.

86. 'Merneptah Year 4, Amada stela', cited in Schulman, *Ceremonial Execution*, 91–92; Trigger et al, *Ancient Egypt*, 238.

87. Spalinger comments on Amenhotep II's hanging of the Syrian chiefs, 'The reason for this often presumed "barbaric activity" was simple [. . .] it was Amunhotep's wish to demonstrate visually his success.' Spalinger, 'New Kingdom Triumphs', 99.

88. Lanni, 'Laws of War', 480.

89. Seton, 'King of Egypt Annihilating His Enemies', 1–113. See also Śliwa, 'Victorious Ruler Representations', 98–105; Dieter Wildung, 'Erschlagen der Feinde', in *Lexikon*

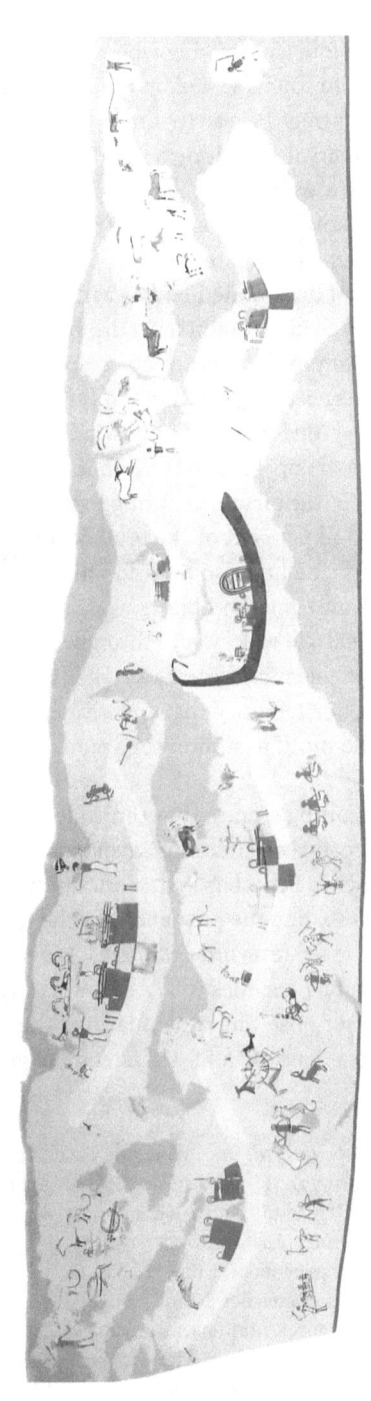

FIGURE 30. Earliest smiting scene, showing a chief smiting three bound prisoners, at bottom left: wall painting (reproduction) from Tomb 100, Nekhen (Hierakonpolis), c. 3500–c. 3300 BCE. Francesco Raffaele, CC BY-SA 3.0 licence, via Wikimedia Commons.

The earliest smiting scene discovered to date is a rock painting from a predynastic tomb at Hierakonpolis (Tomb 100) from around 3400. It shows three bound prisoners kneeling before a chief/king who wields a raised mace in his right hand (figure 30). A more sophisticated image is provided on the slightly later and far more refined Narmer Palette (figure 1), showing King Narmer in what would become the stereotypical smiting pose: right arm raised and wielding a mace ready to deliver the death blow; left hand grasping a kneeling prisoner by the hair. Below the king are the bodies of two further enemies, either already dead or awaiting their violent fate. On the opposite side of the palette, the king inspects two rows of decapitated bodies with heads placed between their legs, leaving the audience in no doubt as to the fate of Egypt's foes.

Smiting scenes were given pride of place on temple pylons, intended to be among the first set of images to meet visitors to the temple (figure 24). At Ramses III's great complex at Medinet Habu, the 'window of appearance'—the balcony on which the pharaoh appeared to the public—was framed on either side by monumental scenes of the pharaoh smiting Egypt's enemies.[90] Temple images account for roughly 40 per cent of the total documented instances of the smiting scene, but the scene has also been found on wadi rock carvings and stelae (public and private), and on objects as diverse as, among others, palettes, ostraca, scarabs, seals, jewellery, and thrones.[91] Notably, in addition to the major temples of Egypt, the smiting scenes are often to be found in territory that was occupied by Egypt or territory that constituted border zones, thus emphasising the role of the motif as a monitory reminder of the pharaoh's power.[92]

In many of the extant smiting scenes, the ethnic identity of the victims is easily identifiable by the stereotyped features of Egypt's main enemies: Nubians, Libyans, and Asiatics. As Sylvia Schoske's systematic study reveals, the Egyptian king could be depicted holding the prisoner(s) by the hair, head, or arms, and wielding a mace, axe, or sickle sword (*khopesh*). Derivatives were possible, including the king impaling enemies with a spear; as a rule, however, the images depict a post-battle or post-war ritual marking the pharaoh's victory over his human enemies as well as the forces of Isfet more generally.[93]

---

der Ägyptologie, vol. 2: *Erntefest–Hordjedef*, ed. Wolfgang Helck and Wolfhart Westendorf (Wiesbaden: Harrassowitz, 1977), 114–17; Schoske, 'Erschlagen der Feinde'; Müller-Wollermann, 'Symbolische Gewalt', 49–56; Martin Zimmerman, *Gewalt: Die dunkle Seite der Antike* (Munich: Deutsche Verlags-Anstalt, 2013), 73–75.

90. Śliwa, 'Victorious Ruler Representations', 116; Schulman, *Ceremonial Execution*, 61–62.

91. See listings in Schoske, 'Erschlagen der Feinde', 21–43.

92. Śliwa, 'Victorious Ruler Representations', 115; Schoske, 'Erschlagen der Feinde', 21–43; Schulman, *Ceremonial Execution*, 8; Müller-Wollermann, 'Symbolische Gewalt', 49–54; Maria Michela Luiselli, 'The Ancient Egyptian Scene of "Pharaoh Smiting His Enemies": An Attempt to Visualize Cultural Memory', in *Cultural Memory and Identity in Ancient Societies*, ed. Martin Bommas (London: Continuum, 2011), 10–25 at 18.

93. Schoske, 'Erschlagen der Feinde', 181–95; David, 'Devouring the Enemy', 84.

While the king and his *ka* (life-force) usually stand alone in the smiting scenes, representing his unqiue responsibility as protector of the realm and destroyer of enemies, virtually all the scenes take place in the presence of a deity or deities, indicating the divine justice enacted through royal violence. Occasionally the king is pictured accompanied by crown princes or, more often, his queen.[94] For example, the smiting scenes found in Ramses II's great temple at Abu Simbel depict his queen as well as his sons and daughters below the main scene.[95] However, taking the smiting scenes as a whole, women and children feature only very rarely.[96] As mentioned above, this was undoubtedly a result of the patriarchal nature of Egyptian warfare and iconographic conventions rather than a recognition of female or infant non-combatant immunity. Depicting the pharaoh triumphing over women and children did little to enhance the king's martial prestige. Equally, in symbolising the victory of good (pharaoh) over evil (enemy soldiers/chieftains), women and children were superfluous to the ideological needs of the scene.[97]

The intimate link between these scenes of ritual slaughter and the concept of justice was reinforced by the prominence of Ma'at as an integral element of the iconography. Of the nineteen private stelae depicting the smiting scene analysed by Schulman, the smiting takes place before the god Ptah in twelve cases.[98] In five of the Ptah stelae, the god is described as 'Ptah, lord of Ma'at',[99] or he is depicted as standing on a Ma'at-shaped pedestal.[100] In a further three stelae, the king himself is described as 'beloved of Ma'at'.[101] Taken together, eighteen of the nineteen stelae include an implicit or explicit reference to Ma'at. There are also reasonable grounds to assume that the final stele, which is badly damaged, also included a reference to Ma'at when pristine.[102]

Thus the smiting scene was intended to represent an act of justice, perhaps the quintessential act of justice: the physical and symbolic defence of Ma'at and the defeat of chaos (Isfet).[103] This scene was so pervasive in public architec-

---

94. A detailed discussion of the persons appearing in the iconography is provided by Schoske, 'Erschlagen der Feinde', 84–171.

95. Ibid., 155–56.

96. See n. 83 above for a reference to one example.

97. On enemies being compared to women as an insult, see above, p. XXX.

98. Schulman, *Ceremonial Execution*, stelae 1, 2, 3, 4, 5, 7, 9, 10, 11, 12, 13, 14.

99. Ibid., stelae 1, 2, 3, 5.

100. Ibid., stelae 1, 2, 3, 4.

101. Ibid., stelae 6, 18, 19.

102. Stele 17 has only the lower legs and feet of the pharaoh preserved, but it is reasonable to assume that this stele would have included some reference to Ma'at, either through the identity of the god, the pedestal on which the god stood, or the king himself. See Schulman, *Ceremonial Execution*, 33.

103. As Jan Assmann says, 'monumental discourse was indeed one of virtue (Egyptian *Ma'at*, which also means justice, truth, and order), of eternity, and of political belonging'. Jan Assmann, *Cultural Memory and Early Civilization: Writing, Remembrance, and Political Imagination* (New York: Cambridge University Press, 2011), 150.

ture that it was even carried over into private monuments. So important was it to royal prestige that it was adopted by the female pharaoh Hatshepsut, as witnessed at her great mortuary temple at Deir el-Bahri. Here, the queen assumed the male gender role of smiting Egypt's enemies:

> Welcome daughter of Amun Re [...]. You shall strike the Libyans and smite the troglodytes—you will cut off the heads of the soldiers you capture. Your tribute will be many men [i.e., enslaved prisoners of war] for the temples of the two lands.[104]

Regardless of her sex, it was necessary that Hatshepsut fulfil the royal role of guardian of Egypt. As a female monarch, she must surely have felt considerable pressure to project an image of herself as a ruler who was the equal of her male predecessors. Nefertiti, the queen of Amenhotep IV (and who possibly ruled the kingdom following her husband's death), was also depicted in the traditional smiting pose, executing enemy prisoners.[105] Both queens could at least draw on the presence in Egyptian theology and mythology of female warriors: for example, the warrior goddesses Sekhmet, Satis, and Anat.

There is significant debate among Egyptologists regarding the historicity of the smiting scenes, and whether they depict real or fictive violence. Some have taken the view that, whilst the earliest scenes probably recorded actual ritual executions, the scenes gradually became merely emblematic rather than reflective of contemporary practice. The smiting scenes are said to have 'assumed the rank of a canonical symbol as early as the Old Kingdom period'.[106] To this extent they fulfilled propagandistic, allegorical, and apotropaic functions pertaining to the defeat of the enemy and the forces of chaos, and should be taken as evidence of the royal myth, not of royal practice.[107] According to Maria Luiselli, the core purpose of the smiting scene was to provide a cultural memory for the quasi-mythical unification of the Two Lands under Narmer/Menes; its continuing use was thus linked to Egyptian identity and 'an attempt to visualize cultural memory'.[108]

However, detailed studies of the smiting scenes have defended the historicity of the executions depicted, arguing that physical actions reinforced the apotropaic function of the ritual act.[109] The scenes, particularly those found

---

104. Cited from McDermott, *Warfare in Ancient Egypt*, 86, commentary to fig. 60.
105. McDermott, *Warfare in Ancient Egypt*, 93.
106. Śliwa, 'Victorious Ruler Representations', 101.
107. G. A. Gaballa, *Narrative in Ancient Egyptian Art* (Mainz am Rhein: Von Zabern, 1976), 128. Cf. Hans Goedicke, 'The Alleged Military Campaign in Southern Palestine in the Reign of Pepi I (VI Dynasty)', *Rivista degli studi orientali*, 38 (3) (1963): 187–97 at 188; Wildung, 'Erschlagen der Feinde', 115–16; David, 'Devouring the Enemy', 84.
108. Luiselli, 'Ancient Egyptian Scene', 20–21.
109. Schoske, 'Erschlagen der Feinde', 450–55, 465; Schulman, *Ceremonial Execution*; Müller-Wollerman, 'Symbolische Gewalt', 64; Muhlestein, *Violence*, 85–91; Janzen,

on private (rather than royal) stelae, may have recorded a specific execution, performed at a specific time and in a specific temple.[110] The sheer frequency and longevity of the smiting motif suggests that the ritual execution of prisoners of war was more than merely artistic fantasy and cannot have been completely abandoned in later periods. The social science theory of 'path dependence' would suggest that the early practice of ritual execution and its rapid integration into the royal myth constituted a 'critical juncture' in Egyptian royal propaganda. The institutional success of this practice as a symbol of political power, testified by its prevalence in the archaeological record, created a 'positive feedback' process, thereby *increasing* the likelihood that future generations within the royal institution were 'locked in' to repeating this ritualised public violence.[111] For Egyptian monarchs to have abandoned the practice of ritual execution entirely, while continuing to utilise it as one of the principal motifs of royal propaganda, would have encouraged unfavourable comparisons with the past, in that the projected image of power (the humiliation and execution of the enemy) was not reinforced by the reality of the present.[112] Schulman even posits that ritual executions may have constituted a type of public festival and holiday.[113] While Jan Assmann's theory of a 'prospective memory' (*prospektive Erinnerung*) in Egyptian art and political culture—whereby inscribed monuments related 'to the present as if to a "future past" [*zukünftige Vergangenheit*]'[114]—has been highly influential, surely no measure of 'prospective memory' would have filled the void of inaction. Unless supported by concrete power, images can quickly lose their potency, as witnessed

---

'Iconography of Humiliation, 308–14. On the broader relationship between Egyptian royal ideology and action, see Muhlestein, 'Royal Executions', 192.

110. Schulman, *Ceremonial Execution*, 48–62, 193–94. While I concur that the smiting motif reflected real-life practice, and 'is not to be dismissed as a mere, stock, scene' (ibid., 57), Schulman's argument in favour of the direct connection between smiting scenes and specific smiting events is not always persuasive.

111. For the application of 'path dependence' to political science, see the seminal article by Paul Pierson, 'Increasing Returns, Path Dependence, and the Study of Politics', *The American Political Science Review* 94 (2) (2000): 251–67. My use of the theory here is intended to be illustrative rather than in earnest.

112. Anthony Black suggests that ancient people 'were probably predisposed to believe (even more than today) that because something was published it was true, and that kings actually possessed the attributes ascribed to them in inscriptions and texts'. Black, *World History*, 30. While there may be some truth in this, it is difficult to see how belief in the reality of a physical act could be maintained for multiple centuries if there was no living memory of the 'real' action itself.

113. Schulman, *Ceremonial Execution*, 46–47, 193–94.

114. Jan Assmann, *Das kulturelle Gedächtnis: Schrift, Erinnerung und politische Identität in frühen Hochkulturen* (Munich: Beck, 1992), 169; Assmann, *Cultural Memory*, 149. Assmann's theory of 'cultural memory' is developed from Maurice Halbwachs's writings on 'social memory'. For an informative overview, see Jan Assmann, *Religion and Cultural Memory: Ten Studies*, trans. Rodney Livingstone (Stanford, CA: Stanford University Press, 2006), 1–30.

in the modern era through the widely publicised vandalism and destruction of political statuary in former Soviet states after 1989, or in Iraq after the toppling of Saddam Hussein's regime in 2003.

This is not to say that *every* ancient Egyptian smiting scene should be thought of as 'historical', in terms of it representing a *specific* execution. Rather, it is to suggest that ritual execution must have existed and survived as a royal practice (at the very least an occasional one) in order for the smiting images—especially the very late images—to have retained any meaningful sense of cultural relevance and political power. In sum, the continued physical practice of ritual smiting was necessary as a point of reference for the symbolic image.

The reluctance of modern scholars to accept the reality of the smiting scenes perhaps stems from an overly romanticised view of ancient Egyptian society and culture.[115] It appears paradoxical that a civilisation capable of such impressive achievements in art, architecture, and literature should also indulge in the cruelty of ritual human slaughter. Yet such paradoxes are commonplace in the histories of highly complex societies. During the Roman republic and empire the public strangulation of prisoners of war was probably a routine feature of ritual military triumphs.[116] In Mesoamerica, very large numbers of prisoners of war (male and female) were sacrificed in both Mayan and Aztec societies, with the decapitation and/or evisceration of the victim playing a central ritualistic and theological role.[117] It would also be worth

---

115. Janzen critiques the 'tendency among Egyptologists to shirk away from brutality in Egyptian sources': Janzen, 'Iconography of Humiliation', 261–317, quotation at 261; cf. Muhlestein, *Violence*, 5–6. Renate Müller-Wollerman takes a conservative approach to the smiting scenes, but does point out that in the otherwise exhaustive *Lexikon der Ägyptologie*, there is no entry for *Gewalt* (violence): Müller-Wollerman, 'Symbolische Gewalt', 47. See Wolfgang Helck, Eberhard Otto, and Wolfhart Westendorf (eds), *Lexikon der Ägyptologie*, 7 vols (Wiesbaden: Harrassowitz, 1972–1992).

116. Donald G. Kyle, *Spectacles of Death in Ancient Rome* (London: Routledge, 1998), 217. The comparison with Rome is particularly striking, and is also made in Schulman, *Ceremonial Execution*, 46. For a lengthier analysis of Roman uses of extreme violence, see Zimmerman, *Gewalt*, 219–339. Note that Mary Beard is more sceptical of the regular execution of elite captives during triumphal processions: Mary Beard, *The Roman Triumph* (Cambridge, MA: Harvard University Press, 2007), 128–32.

117. Christopher L. Moser, 'Human Decapitation in Ancient Mesoamerica', *Studies in Precolumbian Art and Archaeology* 11 (1973): 1–72; Carrie Anne Berryman, 'Captive Sacrifice and Trophy Taking Among the Ancient Maya: An Evaluation of the Bioarchaeological Evidence and Its Sociopolitical Implications', in *The Taking and Displaying of Human Body Parts as Trophies by Amerindians*, ed. Richard J. Chacon and David H. Dye (New York: Springer, 2007), 377–99; Rubén G. Mendoza, 'The Divine Gourd Tree: Tzompantli Skull Racks, Decapitation Rituals, and Human Trophies in Ancient Mesoamerica', in ibid., 400–443. See also the essays in: Elizabeth H. Boone (ed.), *Ritual Human Sacrifice in Mesoamerica: A Conference at Dumbarton Oaks, October 13th and 14th, 1979* (Washington, DC: Dumbarton Oaks, 1984); Vera Tiesler and Andrea Cucina (eds), *New Perspectives on Human Sacrifice and Ritual Body Treatment in Ancient Maya Society* (New York: Springer, 2007).

remembering that the execution of prisoners of war has persisted into the modern era. The Nuremberg executions of high-ranking Nazis in 1946, or the widely publicised use of beheading by Islamist forces fighting in Iraq after 2003, and in Syria between 2014 and 2018, share a set of common characteristics with the killing of military captives in ancient Egypt, Rome, or Mesoamerica. While the specific religious, cultural, and legal dimensions of this act vary considerably (as one would expect), the essential purpose was, and is, remarkably consistent: to communicate a message of power, justice, and retribution to a supportive audience (human and/or divine); and a threat of power, vengeance, and domination to a hostile audience (i.e., the enemy). Seen in this broader chronological and geographical perspective, the execution of comparatively small numbers of prisoners of war should be recognised as a normative rather than an anomalous feature of the history of warfare. Put simply, the ritual execution of military prisoners in ancient Egypt should be regarded as decidedly unremarkable, and there is certainly no evidence to suggest that the punishment vexed Egyptians as ethically problematic.

Ultimately, the historicity of the numerous smiting scenes and the ritualistic slaughter they depict is of secondary importance to our present study. In trying to reconstruct ancient Egyptian attitudes to the ethical aspects of war and violence, it is the 'ideal type' of action displayed in the smiting scenes that is of primary interest. These scenes were intended to convey a very specific message, purposefully created at great cost and effort over a span of thousands of years. What they illustrate is a set of actions which Egyptian rulers *believed* to be demonstrative of justice and punitive retribution. That they obviously wished to communicate this conviction to their gods and their subjects is arguably more important to understanding the Egyptian ethics of war than is speculation on the historical veracity of any individual scene.

Enslavement of Prisoners of War

Bearing in mind that summary execution was a distinct risk for defeated foes in ancient warfare, enslavement could potentially be interpreted as an act of *ius in bello* restraint. Indeed, the Latin term for slave, *serva*, is possibly derived from the verb *servare*, 'to save/to preserve', indicating a historical relationship between enslavement and prisoners of war.[118] Whether enslavement can properly be considered an act of restraint (let alone justice) is perhaps a relative judgement. If the alternative to enslavement is assumed to be something akin to modern expectations of humane detention during war and liberty after war ends, the answer is surely 'No': enslavement cannot be viewed as an act of restraint. However, if the alternative is being summarily executed, mutilated, impaled,

---

118. It should be noted that this etymological/historical link remains contested among Latinists.

flayed, or burnt alive—all real possibilities in the ancient Near East—then the answer is probably 'Yes': enslavement can be viewed as an act of restraint. Nevertheless, such restraint was not necessarily motivated by ethical concerns (i.e., mercy), but rather by a pragmatic concern to profit from enslaved persons, or simply by the impracticality of massacring large numbers of prisoners.

When Ramses II pacified Nubia we are told that '30,000 people were seized as prisoners; but then he (Pharaoh) let them go free, according to his desire that the wretched seed of Kush be not destroyed'.[119] In this case, the 'freed' Nubians were put to work for the state. It may be wise to look for pragmatic rather than ethical motivations for such actions: as we have seen, there was no ethical imperative to grant mercy, and it therefore seems inconsistent to explain the sparing of prisoners of war as an ethically informed act. The freeing of prisoners in this case can be interpreted as part of a process whereby the central authority could 'reconstruct' the subjugated survivors after subduing the hostile 'periphery'.[120]

Some sense of mercy being bestowed by the pharaoh does emerge from the Egyptian texts, however. The grovelling submission of the enemy in return for their lives is a recurring trope, an example of which is provided by the account of the surrender of Megiddo to Thutmose III: 'Now the princes of this foreign land came on their bellies to kiss the ground to the might of his majesty, and to beg breath for their nostrils.'[121] Such displays were intended to convey the pharaoh's majesty and his power over life and death. The phrase 'beg breath for their nostrils' explicitly refers to the sparing of a life: it was often connected to pictorial scenes of the lion-pharaoh using its claws to wrench back the heads of prostrate foes by the nostrils.[122] In the case of Megiddo, the princes sought the pharaoh's mercy through an offering of tribute: 'all the princes captured by his majesty's might [brought] their tribute of silver, gold, lapis lazuli, and turquoise, and carrying grain, wine, and large and small cattle for his majesty's army'.[123] Similarly, during Amenhotep II's first and second campaigns in Asia, several towns submitted to the pharaoh and were consequently spared.[124]

During the New Kingdom there was a concerted policy of reinstalling defeated rulers as puppet kings. Their loyalty was guaranteed by seizing their

---

119. Cited in *LIR*, 93.
120. As posited by Liverani: *LIR*, 93.
121. 'Annals of Thutmose III', *AEL*, 2:33.
122. On the 'Poetical Stela of Thutmose III', Amun-Re says, 'Hearing your battle cry they hid in holes. I robbed their nostrils of the breath of life': *AEL*, 2:36. A number of New Kingdom tomb inscriptions also describe subjugated peoples bringing tribute in return for the 'breath of life', to 'beg breath for their nostrils', or 'begging for peace [. . .] the breath which thou givest!': *ANE*, 248–49. For further discussion, see David, 'Devouring the Enemy', 87–90.
123. 'Annals of Thutmose III', *AEL*, 2:33.
124. 'Stelae of Amenhotep II', *ANE*, 245–47.

dynastic heirs as hostages in Egypt and raising them at court, to be properly schooled in Egyptian customs and civilisation. In time, these adoptive sons of Egypt would inherit their fathers' thrones, thereby increasing the number of loyal and subservient Egyptian vassal states.[125] Regardless of the *Realpolitik* behind this policy, it could be read as an example of mercy. After all, within the politico-military arena, mercy is rarely an act performed within a pristine moral sphere—it is frequently informed by wider strategic objectives.

Of greater relevance to questions regarding the ethics of war is the motivation behind the enslavement or 'sparing' of prisoners. Were prisoners kept alive because of a moral aversion to needless slaughter and a sense of the intrinsic good of preserving human life—what might be termed 'mercy'? Or was enslavement solely the product of an economic incentive to profit from human property and labour? Slaves were an important component of the Egyptian labour force, and crucial to the temple economy especially. In this regard, the 'ethical' aspect of enslaving war captives was determined by the pharaoh's obligation to reward his soldiers and his gods; it was not influenced by any sense of ethical obligation to the captive. Alternatively, enslavement may have been a pragmatic solution to the simple reality that allowing the enemy to go free was considered too great a risk, whereas murdering hundreds or thousands of prisoners of war would have been impracticable, and distasteful even to hardened veterans.[126] None of the aforementioned motivations are mutually exclusive, and it is possible that they all contributed towards creating a norm of enslaving rather than killing the majority of prisoners of war.

Destruction of Property

Just as enemy captives became *de iure* the property of the Egyptian king, to destroy or to preserve as he deemed fit, so too did all enemy property. Much of this seized property was redistributed within the army. Booty constituted an essential element of the soldiers' remuneration, as most domestic troops were unsalaried. Movable enemy property such as foodstuffs would likely be consumed by the campaigning army; valuables, human captives, and any remaining herds of livestock would be transported back to Egypt. Immovable property, on the other hand, was prone to destruction. In the difficult agricultural conditions of much of the Near East, mature fruit trees (including grape vines) were particularly valuable, and therefore vulnerable, not least because it took many years for immature plants to produce a crop (figure 31).[127]

---

125. O'Connor, 'Egypt's View of Others', 169.

126. The military psychologist Dave Grossman has argued that most people, even trained soldiers, display an inherent aversion to using extreme violence against fellow human beings: Dave Grossman, *On Killing: The Psychological Cost of Learning to Kill in War and Society* (Boston, MA: Little, Brown and Company, 1995).

127. For an overview of Egyptian practices regarding the destruction of agricultural

FIGURE 31. Pharaoh Seti I forces enemy chiefs to cut down cedar trees in Lebanon: Great Hypostyle Hall, Karnak Temple, Egypt, early thirteenth century BCE. Peter Brand / Karnak Hypostyle Hall Project, University of Memphis.

The Egyptian records offer a number of examples that indicate the deliberate targeting of agricultural resources, both cereal and arboreal. During Thutmose III's seven-month siege of Megiddo, the Egyptians 'measured the town, surrounded it with a ditch, and walled it up with fresh timber from all their fruit trees'.[128] Thutmose III again targeted agricultural resources in his fifth campaign into northern Syria (29th regnal year): 'Now his majesty destroyed the town of Ardata, with its grain. All its pleasant trees were cut down.' This ravaging tactic was repeated in the following year at Kadesh: 'Arrival at the town of Kadesh. Destroying it. Felling its trees. Cutting down its grain.'[129]

These ravaging tactics were not an innovation of the New Kingdom, but had been employed by Egyptian armies since at least the Sixth Dynasty. The autobiographical account of Weni, a senior soldier during the reign of Pepy I, describes his command of an Egyptian expeditionary force to Asia in the following terms:

This army returned in safety,
    It had ravaged the Sand-dwellers' land.
This army returned in safety,
    It had flattened the sand-dwellers' land.
This army returned in safety,
    It had sacked its strongholds.

---

resources, see Michael G. Hasel, *Military Practice and Polemic: Israel's Laws of Warfare in Near Eastern Perspective* (Berrien Springs, MI: Andrews University Press, 2005), 109–13.

128. 'Annals of Thutmose III', *AEL*, 2:33.
129. 'Annals of Thutmose III', *ANE*, 238–39.

> This army returned in safety,
>> It had cut down its figs, its vines.
> This army returned in safety,
>> It had thrown fire in all its mansions.
> This army returned in safety,
>> It had slain its troops by many ten-thousands.
> This army returned in safety,
>> It had carried off many troops as captives.
>> His majesty praised me for it beyond anything. His majesty sent me to lead this army five times, to attack the land of the Sand-dwellers as often as they rebelled, with these troops. I acted so that his majesty praised me for it beyond anything.[130]

This fascinating passage from a private tomb inscription tells us a number of things about how Egyptian commanders assessed military success. The refrain—repeated seven times—makes clear that the safe return of the army was considered paramount. There is no sense at all of restraint being necessary against the enemy, and Weni boasts of burning enemy property, destroying fruit trees, and visiting widespread devastation upon the enemy's territory. The slaying or enslavement of large numbers of the enemy are presented as key elements of the campaign's success. Weni and his family were clearly proud of these achievements, so much so that they sought to preserve them for eternity in his tomb. Weni's actions were also met with approval by his political masters. The account boasts that Weni was praised by the king and given five further commands.

Even if we assume that Weni exaggerated his achievements, the devastation of territory and non-combatant property that he recounts was a well-established tactic of intimidation, even by the late third millennium. Examples of such violence can be found in most regions from most periods of history. From Pharaoh Pepy I's campaigns, to the medieval English *chevauchées* of the Hundred Years' War (1337–1453 CE), to William T. Sherman's infamous 'March to the Sea' through the US state of Georgia (1864 CE), the objectives of these ravaging operations remained consistent: to terrorise foes into submission, to cripple an enemy's economy in order to reduce military capability, and to provide plunder for the army. Egyptian armies evidently employed this tactic, and there is little reason to doubt its general efficacy (at least in the short term) against political powers of an inferior status to Egypt.

---

130. 'Autobiography of Weni', *AEL*, 1:20. Goedicke convincingly argues that the location of this campaign was not 'Asia', but rather the eastern delta region near Sinai, which was probably not fully incorporated into the kingdom at this time: Goedicke, 'Alleged Military Campaign', 187–97.

Immunities and Diplomacy

SACRED

The concept of religious sanctuary or inviolable sacred spaces during war was almost totally absent from Egyptian martial culture. This may have been the result of the inextricable link between state gods and state wars. The gods were understood to sanction the wars of political communities, and therefore also shared the rewards of success or the humiliation and losses of defeat.[131] It was a simple fact that temples were often repositories of significant wealth, as well as visible symbols of a state's power. Plundering or even destroying such sites was not only profitable, but also projected a powerful message communicating military and political domination. The capture of the enemy's gods—usually in the form of sacred statuary—was thus recognised as a final declaration of victory.[132]

The absence of religious immunities may also be explained by a general lack of concern for non-Egyptian deities and the holy sites associated with them. In contrast, when damage was inflicted on sacred spaces (temples, tombs) during civil conflict *within* Egypt, there is some evidence of remorse on the part of the perpetrators. In the Old Kingdom 'Instructions to King Merikare', the ageing pharaoh expresses regret that his troops had violated tombs near Thebes, as well as monuments in the nome of Thinis, during a civil war earlier in his reign (though he claims this was done without his knowledge):

> Egypt fought in the graveyard,
> Destroying tombs in vengeful destruction.
> As I did it, so it happened,
> As is done to one who strays from god's path [. . .]
> Lo, a shameful deed occurred in my time:
> The nome of This [Thinis] was ravaged;
> Though it happened through my doing,
> I learned it after it was done.
> There was retribution for what I had done,
> For it is evil to destroy,
> Useless to restore what one has damaged,
> To rebuild what one has demolished.
> Beware of it! A blow is repaid by its like,
> To every action there is a response.[133]

---

131. Ziskind, 'Aspects of International Law', 143.
132. Kang, *Divine War*, 46.
133. 'Instructions to King Merikare', *AEL*, 1:102, 105; cf. translation in *ToS*, 221–22, 225.

The literary convention of this genre of texts is to emphasise the evils that result from political disunity within Egypt. The sacrilegious destruction of tombs should therefore be understood as a literary 'proof' of the wickedness of civil war and the benefits of strong centralised monarchy. Ultimately, it is difficult to imagine an Egyptian text displaying similar ideas of remorse regarding the destruction or plundering of sacred spaces beyond the Two Lands of Egypt.

DIPLOMATIC

There is no evidence that universal or specific immunities existed for non-combatant persons or property in Egyptian warfare. However, some limited protection was extended to diplomatic representatives from other political communities. By the early second millennium, regular envoys were being sent between Egypt and the Levantine city-state ports of Ugarit and Byblos.[134] Permanent foreign embassies were not established in Egypt or anywhere else in the ancient Near East, but visiting ambassadors seem to have enjoyed certain guarantees for their property and personal safety during their missions.[135] Despite such diplomatic protocols, foreign envoys could be indefinitely detained by their hosts, even during times of peace.[136] In the fourteenth century, King Kadashman-Enlil of Babylon complained to Pharaoh Amenhotep III that the pharaoh had detained Babylonian envoys for several years and swindled Kadashman-Enlil with a sub-par diplomatic gift:

> In the past, my father used to send an envoy and you would not detain him many days. You used to set him on his way quickly and you used to send a lovely greeting gift to my father. Now, when I sent an envoy to you, six years have you detained him, but in the sixth year you have sent thirty minas of gold that looks like silver for my greeting gift.[137]

Similarly, Aššur-uballit I of Assyria complained to Amenhotep IV about breaches of diplomatic norms concerning the treatment of his ambassadors (although his explanation in the same letter that Egyptian envoys had been delayed in returning from Assyria because their guides had died en route suggests a rather tit-for-tat dispute):

---

134. Shaw, *Egyptian Warfare*, 45–46.
135. Amnon Altman, 'Tracing the Earliest Recorded Concepts of International Law: (5) The Near East 1200–330 BCE', *Journal of the History of International Law* 12 (2010): 101–54 at 150.
136. Munn-Rankin, 'Diplomacy in Western Asia', 99–102, 107–8; Altman, 'Tracing the Earliest Recorded Concepts', 151.
137. EA 3 in *The El-Amarna Correspondence*, trans. Rainey, ed. Schniedewind and Cochavi-Rainey, 1:69. The poor quality or insufficient amounts of gold and gifts sent between kings is a running theme of the royal correspondence between Egypt and its Asiatic competitors.

As for the ambassadors, why are they continually standing outside so that they will die outside? If their standing outside is profitable to the king, then let them stand outside. Outside, let them die! Profit for the king or not, why should they die outside? As for the envoys that we continually send, then doubly, they should keep the envoys alive.[138]

Notably, diplomatic gifts presented to the Egyptian court by independent foreign emissaries were termed *inw*: the same term as was used to describe tribute from vassal states, and a subtle reaffirmation of the ideology according to which all states were subservient to Egypt.[139]

Peace Treaties

Treaties between ancient Near Eastern states originate from at least the early second millennium (but probably earlier), and two types were distinguished by the Akkadian terms *riksu*—a 'parity' treaty between equals—and *ade*—a treaty of subordination confirming an oath of loyalty or vassalage. As with much diplomatic protocol at this time, Akkadian constituted the lingua franca of diplomatic correspondence and contracts, which included defensive and offensive treaties as well as neutrality agreements. Gods were called upon to act as witnesses to treaties, and the swearing of oaths was an essential step in the treaty-making process. To break one's treaty oath was understood not only as a political betrayal but also as a violation of the sacred. Consequently, the offending country was liable to punitive action by both the aggrieved country and its pantheon, which 'included permitting or delegating the human ruler of the aggrieved country to make war'.[140] So we read in the Middle Assyrian 'Epic of Tukulti-Ninurta' how the eponymous Assyrian king (c. 1244–c. 1208) led a punitive war against Kassite Babylon on the grounds that its ruler, Kaštiliaš IV (c. 1232–c. 1225), had violated treaty oaths made to the god Šamaš (Shamash). According to the Assyrian text, even the Babylonian gods abandon Kaštiliaš to his just punishment. Ultimately this resulted in the sack of Babylon, with Tikulti-Ninurta confirming the justice of his war by dedicating the plunder to the Assyrian gods.[141]

The most notable surviving example of an Egyptian peace treaty is the instrument made in 1259 between the pharaoh Ramses II and the Hittite king Hattušili III. It is one of the oldest surviving peace treaties between two

---

138. EA 16 in *El-Amarna Correspondence*, trans. Rainey, ed. Schniedewind and Cochavi-Rainey, 1:133. See also Beckman, 'Foreigners', 208.

139. Younger, *Ancient Conquest Accounts*, 177.

140. Ziskind, 'Aspects of International Law', 126.

141. Peter Machinist, 'Literature as Politics: The Tukulti-Ninurta Epic and the Bible', *The Catholic Biblical Quarterly* 38 (4) (1976): 455–82 at 456–58; Kang, *Divine War*, 19–20.

equal powers that has survived from the ancient world.[142] What is highly unusual—indeed, unique—about the Ramses II–Hattušili III treaty is that both the Egyptian and the Hittite versions have survived, enabling historians to cut through some of the more bombastic royal rhetoric in which both sides indulged, but which was a particular forte of Ramses II's regime.[143] Originally, the treaty was inscribed on silver tablets and presented to both kings, though these are now lost. Fortunately, copies of the more elaborate Egyptian version were carved into the walls of the Temple of Amun at Karnak (figure 16) and also of the Ramaesseum, Ramses II's great mortuary temple.[144] The corresponding Hittite version of the treaty was discovered as a clay tablet copy, unearthed at the Hittite capital of Hattuša in 1906 (figure 17).

In the thirteenth century, Egypt and Hatti were the two imperial superpowers of the Near East, and both had been extending their spheres of influence, northwards and southwards respectively, through Syria-Palestine and along the Levantine coast. The two sides had eventually clashed around 1274, at a major engagement outside the city of Kadesh, with the still youthful Ramses II facing the veteran Hittite king Muwatilli II. This battle, fought over two days, seems to have resulted in a military stalemate—though the exuberant hyperbole of Ramses II's propaganda paints a picture of a hard-won but absolute victory. Sixteen years later, with both kingdoms under increasing pressure from the encroachments of the so-called Sea Peoples, Ramses II agreed upon a *riksu* treaty with Hattušili III (Muwatilli II's successor). This parity treaty was essentially a non-aggression pact as well as a defensive and offensive alliance between the two empires.

---

142. The Egyptian–Hittite treaty itself refers to an earlier (lost) treaty, possibly made during the reign of Horemheb: 'the great ruler of Egypt with the Great Prince of Hatti, the god did not permit hostility to occur between them, through a regulation': *ANET*, 199 n. 6.

143. The Egyptian and Hittite texts are translated in *ANET*, 199–202, 202–3. All quotations below are taken from these translations. See also the translations available in S. Langdon and Alan H. Gardiner, 'The Treaty of Alliance between Ḫattušili, King of the Hittites, and the Pharaoh Ramesses II of Egypt', *The Journal of Egyptian Archaeology* 6 (3) (1920): 179–205.

144. As Pritchard observes, '[s]ince Akkadian was the diplomatic language of the day, the Egyptian text was a translation, edited to give greater prominence to the role of Egypt in granting peace. The Hittite version was probably much closer to the text formally agreed upon, and the two versions should be read together.' *ANET*, 199. Compare the Egyptian 'Poem of Kadesh', commissioned after the battle, which invents a fictitious narrative recording the submission of the Hittites to Ramses II: 'Then the vile Chief of Khatti wrote and worshipped my name [...] "Your servant speaks to let it be known that you are the Son of Re who came from his body. He has given you all the lands together. As for the land of Egypt and the land of Khatti, they are your servants, under your feet [...]. Do not overwhelm us. Lo, your might is great, your strength is heavy upon the land of Khatii. Is it good that you slay your servants, your face savage toward them and without pity? Look, you spent yesterday killing a hundred thousand, and today you came back and left no heirs. Be not hard in your dealings, victorious king! Peace is better than fighting. Give us breath!"': 'Poem of Kadesh', *AEL*, 2:71.

The stated intention of the treaty was 'to cause that good peace and brotherhood occur between us forever'.[145] While acknowledging that conflict had existed between the two states in the past, the treaty bound the rulers to 'the situation which the Re and Seth [Egyptian gods] made for the land of Egypt with the land of Hatti, in order not to permit hostility to occur between them forever', and this was also incumbent upon their subjects, or the 'children of the children', as the treaty puts it.[146] Both kings promised not to invade the territory of the other:

> The Great Prince of Hatti shall not trespass against the land of Egypt forever, to take anything from it [. . .] the great ruler of Egypt, shall not trespass against the land of Hatti, to take from it forever.[147]

They then stated their commitment to a defensive alliance:

> If another enemy come against the lands of User-maat-Re [Ramses II] [. . .] the Great Prince of Hatti shall come to him and the Great Prince of Hatti shall slay his enemy [. . .]. But if another enemy come against the Great Prince of Hatti, [Ramses II] [. . .] shall come to him as reinforcement to slay his enemy.[148]

Remarkably, the agreement to lend mutual military aid even encompassed possible future military support against rebellion in each respective kingdom.[149] The treaty included a number of other military and political details, including a mutual extradition pact concerning refugees from either country, and even a clause in which Egyptian forces could be called to Hatti to support Hattušili's son in the event of a succession crisis.[150] This must surely be the earliest example of formal conditions being agreed upon for international military intervention.

Finally, the treaty was witnessed by 'a thousand gods of the male gods and of the female gods of them of the land of Hatti, together with a thousand gods of the male gods and of the female gods of them of the land of Egypt'. If either side's ruler violated the sacred agreement, these same gods would 'destroy his house, his land, and his servants'.[151]

---

145. *ANET*, 199.

146. Ibid., 199, 200; cf. the Hittite version, ibid., 202. Re and Seth were both Egyptian deities, the former associated with the sun, the latter with the desert and storms. The Hittite version simply has the 'Sun-god and the Storm-god'. Because the treaty binds both sovereigns and subjects, Aristide Théodoridès argues that it 'constitutes an act of public law': Théodoridès, 'Concept of Law', 316.

147. *ANET*, 200.

148. Ibid.

149. *ANET*, 202–3.

150. Ibid., 200, 203.

151. Ibid. David, 'Sound of the Magic Flute', 16, 19, highlights this oath-clause as a further example of the Egyptian concept of retributive justice in practice.

What this treaty shows is that ancient Egyptians conceived of war and peace as existing within a framework of divine and mundane international relations. In terms of the legal conception of war and peace, it demonstrates that there were a sufficient number of shared assumptions regarding the legalism of war to make an international treaty possible in the first place; and all sides agreed that the gods took an interest in the conflicts of states. Moreover, peaceful relations between states were evidently understood as felicitous. The Egyptian scribes imagined the Hittites saying to Ramses II after the battle of Kadesh, 'Very excellent is peace, O Sovereign our Lord! There is no blame in peace when you make it.'[152] Nevertheless, both ethically and legally, war was a perfectly acceptable instrument of retribution and political control. Moreover, it is evident that New Kingdom international relations could at least conceive of future military ventures being subject to the obligations of legal contracts such as those detailed in the Egyptian–Hittite treaty.

At first sight, the Egyptian–Hittite treaty seems to imply that allies of Egypt could achieve a degree of legal symmetry with her; nonetheless, upon closer inspection of the wording of the two versions of the treaty, the Egyptian text repeatedly attempts to subordinate the Hittite ruler to the Egyptian king. In the Egyptian preamble, Hattušili III is introduced as sending his envoy to Ramses II 'in order to beg peace'; and throughout the Egyptian version Hattušili is referred to as the 'Great Prince' or 'Great Chieftain' of Hatti, rather than the 'Great King' of the Hittite version. As Liverani has observed of this linguistic finagling, 'Egypt considers itself so different from any other country that a real parity can be neither culturally conceived nor linguistically expressed: there are as many "chiefs" as you like, but only one "sovereign", namely ours.'[153] Though blatantly a parity *riksu* treaty between two equally powerful imperial states, Egyptian ideology necessitated that this treaty between Ramses II and Hattušili III be interpreted domestically as a vassalic one, whereby an inferior state begged for peace from the all-powerful Egyptian monarch. The resulting relationship—in the eyes of the Egyptians at least—was a one-way submissive obligation, with no necessary corresponding duties on the part of the pharaoh as 'lord'.[154] The rare existence of the other side of the story—the Hittite version of the treaty—serves to remind us always to be wary of the veil of partial fantasy that obscures Egyptian royal texts and images. For although such sources can tell us much about the ideals of Egyptian ethics and power, in so doing they inevitably offer us an incomplete and partisan glimpse of historical reality.

---

152. 'Kadesh Poem', *AEL*, 2:71. Note the rhetorical subjugation of the Hittites, who address Ramses II as 'our Lord'.

153. *LIR*, 39.

154. Ibid., 98, 134; Lorton, *Juridical Terminology*, 76–78, 145–47.

Conclusions to Part I

Taken as a whole, it is manifest that ancient Egyptian attitudes to war existed within a system of ethics that was already quite well developed during the time of the Old Kingdom in the mid-third millennium. Considerations of justice, retribution, and the cosmological balancing of order and chaos were fundamental to the Egyptian concept of war.

Nonetheless, we must conclude that enemy 'rights' were entirely absent from the Egyptian conception, lexicon, and prosecution of war. The variety of sources examined all point towards the conclusion that it was normative within the Egyptian military to treat enemies with extreme brutality. There were no limitations placed on weapons or tactics. Death on the battlefield or summary execution as a prisoner of war was a live possibility, with social rank offering little protection in this regard; indeed, enemy princes may have been at greater risk of ritual execution. The mutilation of enemy corpses was a standard practice, fulfilling both monitory and administrative purposes. All enemy property, movable and immovable, was considered a legitimate target, to be plundered for profit or destroyed as part of a military strategy aimed at the reduction of enemy resources and a political policy of 'shock-and-awe' intimidation. Concerning the treatment of property or persons, no meaningful distinctions were made between combatants and non-combatants, especially when it came to the enslavement of captives. Women and children enjoyed no immunity and were certainly enslaved on a grand scale. In sum, there appears to be almost nothing that could be identified as part of an ancient Egyptian *ius in bello* tradition.

The absence of identifiable *ius in bello* norms in ancient Egypt was the direct consequence of the development of a very potent *ius ad bellum* tradition. The early development of a theologico-political doctrine which insisted upon Egypt's cosmological role as the embodiment of Ma'at and the role of the king as its guardian amidst a sea of chaos was a powerful religious and political teleology upon which to establish an ethics of war. Egyptian royal ideology promoted the unequivocal authority of the divinely mandated pharaoh to wage war in protection of the unique haven of order and truth that was Egypt. Such wars could only be intrinsically just, and it was the king's divine duty to fight them. Egyptian contempt for the 'evil foreigner' endowed the state with an uncontested legitimacy to assert itself—reactively or proactively—against barbarism, while domestic enemies were condemned as wicked rebels who sought to destroy order from within. In this light, the 'Tale of Sinuhe' could easily picture the pharaoh as 'bold, descending on Easterners; his joy is to plunder barbarians', while in the very next stanza describing the same king as 'a lord of kindness, great of sweetness' who '[t]hrough love [...] has conquered'.[155]

---

155. *ToS*, 30.

It is no coincidence that Egyptian just war thought—which stressed unity and authority focused upon the person of the king—was promoted most vigorously during the three periods of centralised monarchy referred to as the Old, Middle, and New Kingdoms. Nevertheless, these periods of strong central authority were punctuated by prolonged periods of civil war, foreign occupation, and fragmented political communities. The Egyptian ethics of war thus developed in conjunction with attempts to reinforce waxing or waning royal power, seeking to buttress centralised authority in the person of the king. What we can reasonably refer to as ancient Egyptian 'just war doctrine' was thus partly the result of an intellectual, political, and military reaction *against* disunity and insecurity. But this is a truism of most political propaganda. Nor does it lessen the importance of this Egyptian just war doctrine, as the conceptual foundations appear to have been remarkably stable during long periods of both stability and instability, from the mid-third to the late second millennium.

It hardly needs to be said that reality is infinitely more complex and fluid than images or texts can communicate. Egyptian sources leaned heavily towards ideological presentations of the glory of Egyptian victories and the utter wickedness and defeat of Egyptian enemies.[156] Pictorial sources tend to distort reality by depicting extremes of practice. The *raison d'être* of Egyptian images and statuary was to show a resolute and strong pharaoh, in order to laud his military deeds, to act as a warning to enemies of the state (external and internal), and to perform an apotropaic function against the material and immaterial forces of chaos. A scene may show the slaughter of captives, but we can only speculate as to how consistent or regular such a practice was in reality. Attempting to depict pragmatic flexibility in the treatment of captives, or even the exercise of 'mercy', would have been antithetical to the objectives of the monument. When depicting and describing the victory of order over chaos, there was little room for nuance. Indeed, when working with Egyptian sources, it is sometimes easy to forget that Egyptians armies did not always win.[157]

Images and texts were also bound by artistic and literary conventions, and pharaohs were not averse to copying texts and reliefs from their predecessors,

---

156. For further discussion, see Barbara Cifola, 'Ramses III and the Sea Peoples: A Structural Analysis of the Medinet Habu Inscriptions', *Orientalia* 57 (3) (1988): 275-306 at 276-77; Cline and O'Connor, 'Mystery of the "Sea Peoples"', 120-32; Younger, *Ancient Conquest Accounts*, 189-91. Though the principal audience for these statements of royal authority were members of the elite and the gods, John Baines notes that regimes such as Ramses II's played a central role in producing and disseminating an extensive range of texts; literary copies of the later New Kingdom show that such texts reached an audience beyond the traditional temple context: John Baines, 'Contextualizing Egyptian Representations of Society and Ethnicity', in *The Study of the Ancient Near East in the Twenty-First Century: The William Foxwell Albright Centennial Conference*, ed. Jerrold S. Cooper and Glenn M. Schwartz (Winona Lake, IN: Eisenbrauns, 1996), 339-84 at 349-52.

157. According to the records of Egyptian scribes, all military undertakings of the pharaoh were considered successful: Spalinger, *Aspects of Military Documents*, 1.

as can be seen at Karnak, where Ramses III appropriated the campaign reliefs of Ramses II.[158] Even at a fundamental technical level, the translation of certain texts remains conjectural, thus producing interpretative controversies.[159] While I would contend that images or texts recording the execution of prisoners or the slaughter of enemies on the battlefield required some basis in reality in order to maintain their symbolic, ideological, and political power, this does not mean that prisoners were *always* executed, or that battles *always* resulted in mass slaughter.

What is significant in the present context, however, is that, for thousands of years, Egyptian kings and elites wished to promote such actions as intrinsically 'good'. Descriptions and images of slaughter, destruction, and enslavement of the enemy expressed ideal types of warlike action. According to the Egyptian ethics of war and the cosmology upon which it was based, only the total annihilation or subjugation of the enemy were 'good' outcomes of war. This represented the victory of Ma'at (order, justice) over Isfet (chaos, injustice). Of course, in reality, not every town could be razed, nor every enemy slaughtered, and it was not always politically astute to execute enemy leaders, or financially astute to burn down vineyards. We know from sources such as the El-Amarna letters that the Egyptians were just as eager as any other imperial power to reap the financial benefits of empire, and this could only be done by preserving the people and resources of subjugated territories.[160] Put simply, the pragmatics and profits of war and politics undoubtedly tended towards at least some degree of restraint. Egyptian diplomacy and foreign policy was more sophisticated than mere brute force, as documents such as the Egyptian–Hittite peace treaty discussed above attest.

This is not to say that Egyptian military leaders were opposed to unleashing extreme violence when it suited their purpose. The defining feature of Egyptian just war doctrine was not that it was prohibitive; quite the opposite, in fact. The defining feature of Egyptian just war doctrine was that it was extraordinarily permissive. And so the unavoidable conclusion is that, fascinatingly, the Egyptian practice of war was probably *less* brutal than the Egyptian ethics of war permitted.

---

158. Śliwa, 'Victorious Ruler Representations', 110, 114–15.
159. *AEL*, 1: vii.
160. O'Connor, 'Egypt's Views of Others', 159.

PART II

Hatti, c. 1650–c. 1200 BCE

CHAPTER FIVE

The Hittites: Historical Introduction

IN A SENSE, the Hittites remain one of the great 'lost' civilisations of history. It is likely that many readers will be unfamiliar with them. In the early twentieth century it could be observed by one scholar that the Hittites were still widely considered 'an insignificant Syrian tribe unknown outside the Bible'.[1] Yet, as we now know, the Hittites were major players in the geopolitics of the ancient Near East. The lifespan of the kingdom of Hatti stretched roughly from 1650 to 1200, bridging in its entirety that period of time which scholars refer to as the Late Bronze Age. Indeed, from c. 1400 to c. 1250 the Hittite kingdom transformed itself into a true empire, dominating Anatolia and much of Syria-Palestine, and emerging as one of the predominant military superpowers of the region.[2]

The Hittites took their name from their capital of Hattuša in central Anatolia (Boğazkale in modern Turkey, about 150 km, or 90 miles, east of Ankara), calling themselves 'men of the Hatti land'.[3] At its height, during the second

---

1. A. E. Cowley, *The Hittites: The Schweich Lectures for 1918* (London: Oxford University Press, 1920), 1.

2. For a sweeping political and cultural history of Anatolia from the Neolithic to late Roman period, see Christian Marek, *In the Land of a Thousand Gods: A History of Asia Minor in the Ancient World*, trans. Steven Rendall (Princeton, NJ: Princeton University Press, 2019).

3. The capital was briefly moved to Tarhuntašša during the reign of Muwattalli II, but Hattuša was reinstated as the capital during the reign of his successor, Muršili III/Urhi-Teshub. Kurt Bittel maintains that the capital was moved south as a response to increased threat from the Kaska: 'It was not because he wanted to be nearer to Syria, at that time the principal scene of foreign entanglements, nor because he considered it easier to cope with an imminent military struggle with Egypt from a southern residence, that Muwattalli gave up the traditional capital [. . . . N]ow we know that he was worried by the exposed situation of the capital on the northern periphery of the empire. Northern barbaric tribes overwhelmed it twice within barely a hundred years.' Kurt Bittel, *Hattusha: The Capital*

half of the fourteenth century, the Hittite empire dominated a territory that stretched from the Aegean Sea in the west, across Anatolia and northern Syria to the banks of the Tigris in the east, and south to the Levantine cities of Byblos and Damascus (see Map 2). The royal capital was encircled by massive fortifcations and was a true ancient metropolis (see figures 12 and 13). Only the kingdom of Egypt could claim to be a serious rival, resulting in both diplomatic interaction and military conflict as the two empires vied to assert their influence throughout the eastern Mediterranean.

At the turn of the twelfth century, now dubbed by scholars as 'the crisis years', there was a series of radical changes in the ancient Near East.[4] Some time around the year 1180 the Hittite kingdom collapsed and its capital of Hattuša was abandoned. Around the same time the Kassite Dynasty in Babylon fell and Mycenean power in the Mediterranean and Aegean also disintegrated. Of the great powers, only Egypt survived the tumultuous changes, albeit much diminished, having lost control of its territories in Syria-Palestine and been forced to fight both land and sea battles in the Nile delta. These battles against the so-called Sea Peoples were immortalised in a series of monumental reliefs at the mortuary temple of Ramses III at Medinet Habu (figure 7). Ramses III notably refers to Hatti among a list of countries that had fallen before the onslaught of the Sea Peoples. However, the exact timescale for Hattuša's abandonment and destruction remains uncertain. When archaeologists discovered extensive evidence of burn-layers, responsibility for the conflagration was initially placed on the Kaska. But disagreement continues as to whether the city had already been abandoned by the time of its final destruction.[5]

Exactly *who* the invasive 'Sea Peoples' were remains a point of scholarly debate, but from c. 1210 to c. 1160 numerous ancient sources from across the region testify to the migrations of sea-borne peoples, attacking coastal centres and penetrating inland, overturning many of the existing power centres.[6]

---

of the Hittites (New York: Oxford University Press, 1970), 21. This is disputed by Itamar Singer, who claims Muwattalli's relocation of the capital was motivated primarily by a southern-focused religious reform: Itamar Singer, 'From Hattuša to Tarhuntašša: Some Thoughts on Muwattalli's Reign', in *Acts of the 3rd International Congress of Hittitology*, ed. Sedat Alp and Aygül Süel (Ankara: Uyum Ajans, 1996), 536–41; *HitP*, 80; cf. Klengel, *Geschichte des Hethitischen Reiches*, 210.

4. William A. Ward and Martha S. Joukowsky (eds), *The Crisis Years: The 12th Century BC: From beyond the Danube to the Tigris* (Dubuque, IA: Kendall Hunt, 1992).

5. Bittel, *Hattuša*, 90; Trevor Bryce, *The Kingdom of the Hittites*, 2nd edn (Oxford: Oxford University Press, 2005), 345; Jürgen Seeher, 'Die Zerstörung der Stadt Hattusa', in *Akten des IV. Internationalen Kongresses für Hethitologie, Würzburg, 4.–8. Oktober 1999*, ed. Gernot Wilhelm (Wiesbaden: Harrossowitz, 2001), 623–34; Andreas Schachner, *Hattuscha: Auf der Suche nach dem sagenhaften Großreich der Hethiter* (Munich: Beck, 2011), 112ff.

6. The Greek mainland offers archaeological evidence of southwards migratory movements from as early as c. 1300. See Redford, *Egypt, Canaan, and Israel*, 242–56, esp. 245. My thanks also to Professor Theo van den Hout for bringing this to my attention.

These were combined with a number of environmental disturbances. A letter from the king of Ugarit to the king of Alašiya gives an impression of the disruption caused by these invasions: 'My father, behold, the enemy's ships came (here); my cities were burned, and they did evil things in my country [...] the seven ships of the enemy that came here inflicted much damage upon us.'[7] Whatever the ethnic background of the Sea Peoples or their precise motivations, these seismic political events helped to bring an end to the highly centralised and geographically extensive kingdoms that characterised the Late Bronze Age Near East. This initiated something of a 'dark age' in ancient Near Eastern history: there is a sharp decline in surviving evidence (especially textual) from c. 1200 to c. 900, seemingly the result of the disintegration of centralised bureaucracies.

Hittite historical records cease during the reign of Šuppiluliuma II (c. 1207–c. 1178). One of our latest records from that king's reign consists of a cuneiform clay tablet, detailing a series of sea and land battles against the island kingdom of Alašiya (Cyprus):

> The ships of Alašiya met me [Šuppiluliuma II] in the sea three times for battle, and I smote them; and I seized the ships and set fire to them in the sea. But when I arrived on dry land, the enemies from Alašiya came in multitude against me for battle.[8]

It is telling that this late document records Hittite military involvement in three naval battles—a form of warfare in which we have virtually no evidence of the Hittites engaging previously. Arguably, this is indicative of a kingdom under increasing strain, forced to commit to military ventures that had not been necessary in earlier years, in which it had little experience and for which it was probably ill prepared.[9]

While the agents of the Late Bronze Age collapse remain contested, it is clear that what followed was a period characterised not by large empires, but by numerous smaller states, focused around a single city and its hinterland. The city-state of Carchemish, for example, survived as a Neo-Hittite power centre ruled by descendants of the Hittite royal family. This period of political fragmentation lasted for around three centuries, until the region witnessed the re-emergence of a newly expansionist Neo-Assyrian kingdom under Adad-Nirari II in the late tenth century. The memory of the once-great kingdom of Hatti began to fade and the Hittites 'disappeared from history'.[10]

---

7. Cited in Bryce, *Kingdom of the Hittites*, 333.

8. Hans G. Güterbock, 'The Hittite Conquest of Cyprus Reconsidered', *Journal of Near Eastern Studies* 26 (2) (1967): 73–81 at 78.

9. On this occasion the Hittites probably relied on the vassal maritime kingdom of Ugarit for its naval resources.

10. Billie Jean Collins, *The Hittites and Their World* (Atlanta, GA: Society of Biblical Literature, 2007), 205.

The Rediscovery of the Hittites

Knowledge of the Hittites has been painstakingly recovered by archaeologists, philologists, and historians over the last two hundred years.[11] Nonetheless, their fame still pales in comparison to other ancient Near Eastern civilisations such as Egypt, Babylon, Assyria, or Persia.

The first step towards rehabilitating the Hittites in the modern historical record began in 1736 CE, when Jean Otter discovered a now famous relief at Ivriz in southern Cappodocia.[12] During the nineteenth century CE there followed the discovery of a series of monumental stone blocks at Hamath (modern Hama), inscribed with a previously unknown hieroglyphic script. The Frenchman Charles Texier discovered the city of Hattuša while looking for the Roman city of Pteria, but was ignorant of who had built it.[13] It was not until 1872 CE that an Irish missionary, William Wright, took a greater interest in these inscriptions and eventually suggested that they were produced by the biblical Hittites. He argued that, far from being a minor tribe, the Hittites had constituted a power centre great enough to challenge the dominance of Egypt.[14]

Crucial to the rediscovery of Hatti's prominence was the decipherment of cuneiform script, followed by the translation of Akkadian cuneiform and Egyptian hieroglyphs a few years later. Newly legible texts revealed numerous references to a land named 'Hatti', although scholars incorrectly assumed that the capital had been at Carchemish.[15] The discovery of a vast horde of diplomatic correspondence at Tell el-Amarna in Egypt revealed letters from the Hittite kingdom written in Akkadian. But the Amarna archive also contained a previously unknown language, identified initially as 'Arzawan'. Further excavations

---

11. For an overview of the challenges facing Hittite historiography and chronology, see Horst Klengel, 'Problems in Hittite History, Solved and Unsolved', in *Recent Developments in Hittite Archaeology and History: Papers in Memory of Hans G. Güterbock*, ed. K. Aslihan Yener and Harry A. Hoffner Jr. (Winona Lake, IN: Eisenbrauns, 2002), 101–9. For a concise overview of Hittite history, see J. G. Macqueen, 'The History of Anatolia and of the Hittite Empire: An Overview', in *CANE*, 2:1085–105. For more in-depth general treatments, see Bryce, *Kingdom of the Hittites*; Collins, *Hittites and Their World*. For a survey of Hittite historical writing, see Hans G. Güterbock, 'Hittite Historiography: A Survey', in *History, Historiography and Interpretation: Studies in Biblical and Cuneiform Literatures*, ed. Hayim Tadmor and Moshe Weinfeld (Jerusalem: The Magnes Press, 1983), 21–35.

12. R. A. Stewart Macalister, 'Exploration and Excavation', in *The Cambridge Ancient History*, vol. 1: *Egypt and Babylonia to 1580 BC*, ed. J. B. Bury, S. A. Cook, and F. E. Adcock, 2nd edn (Cambridge: Cambridge University Press, 1928), 112–44 at 135. Collins, *Hittites and Their World*, ch. 1, provides an excellent summary of the development of modern Hittite historiography.

13. Collins, *Hittites and Their World*, 1.

14. See William Wright, *The Empire of the Hittites* (London: Nisbet, 1884); Macalister, 'Exploration and Excavation', 135.

15. Collins, *Hittites and Their World*, 4.

at Hattuša, as well as later at Ugarit and Alalakh, turned up many more clay tablets inscribed in 'Arzawan'. It fast became clear that this language was in fact the language of the Hittite kingdom, and when Bedrich Hrzony successfully deciphered this language in 1915 CE, Hittite was confirmed as the oldest recorded Indo-European language.[16] A flurry of editions and translations of hundreds of Hittite cuneiform texts followed, although deciphering Hittite hieroglyphs proved more troublesome; notwithstanding some major breakthroughs, hieroglyphic Luwian has still not been completely deciphered.[17]

As a result of these scholarly labours, our knowledge of Hittite civilisation has expanded exponentially over the last century. The ongoing translation of texts and the discovery of new archaeological material means that Hittite history remains dynamic, and much is still provisional.[18] For example, Hittite texts provide hundreds of names of places, but the whereabouts of most remain largely unknown, including the exact location of the Hittite holy city of Arinna—home of the revered Hittite sun-goddess.[19] In attempting to reconstruct and explain Hittite attitudes to war we should thus be aware that future discoveries may yet again shift our understanding of this important and intriguing civilisation.

Chronology

The earliest evidence for the Hittites in Anatolia has been found in Old Assyrian texts dating from the so-called Assyrian Colony period (c. 1920– c. 1740).[20] With regard to the Hittite archives, there is a certain irony in that the earliest historical document is a record of the almost total destruction of the original city of Hattuša. The 'Anitta Chronicle' tells of how a king named Anitta of Kuššara (r. c. 1750) fought and defeated an alliance formed between the kings of Hatti and Zalpa. Anitta first defeated Zalpa and then proceeded to besiege Hattuša, starving its people and eventually capturing the city. Not satisfied with this victory, King Anitta levelled Hattuša, sowed it with weeds, and cursed anyone who tried to resettled the city in the future:

> Hattuša inflicted evil on me [. . .]. But when later it suffered from famine, their deity Halmašuitt (the throne-goddess) delivered it up, and

---

16. *HitM*, 1; Gregory McMahon, 'The History of the Hittites', *The Biblical Archaeologist* 52 (2/3) (1989): 62–77 at 65.

17. Hittite hieroglyphs proved to be a form of Luwian, a closely related Anatolian language in the same sub-family as Hittite: Collins, *Hittites and Their World*, 8.

18. Bryce, *Kingdom of the Hittites*, 3.

19. The location of the holy city of Nerik is now strongly believed to be modern Oymaağaç in Turkey. My thanks to Professor Theo van den Hout for bringing this to my attention.

20. For a useful summary of Hittite chronology and the dating of events and texts, see Bryce, *Kingdom of the Hittites*, Appendix 1, 375–82.

> I took it by storm at night. I sowed cress on its grounds. May the storm-god of Heaven smite whoever should become king after me and should resettle Hattuša.[21]

Anitta's curse obviously proved ineffective. A new dynasty had established itself at Hattuša by c. 1650 and the city remained the royal capital of Hatti (for all but a brief interlude) for the next five hundred years.[22]

The chronology of Hittite kings remains problematic and open to debate, being constructed on both Hittite evidence and comparative dates available from contemporary societies of the region such as Egypt, Babylon, Mitanni, and Assyria.[23] It seems that Hittite scribes never developed a custom of dating administrative documents or recording the lengths of reign of their monarchs. For the chronology of the Hittite kingdom as a whole, philologists and palaeographers use developments in the Hittite language and script to distinguish between the Old (c. 1650–c. 1500), Middle (c. 1500–c. 1350), and New kingdoms (c. 1350–c. 1180).[24] In contrast, there has been a recent trend among historians and archaeologists to divide Hittite political history into just two periods: the Old Kingdom (c. 1700–c. 1400) and the New Kingdom (c. 1400–c. 1180). A date of some time immediately prior to c. 1650 is generally agreed for the reign of King Labarna, the first monarch of the Old Kingdom, while the ascendency of Tudhaliya I, whose reign marks the beginning of the New Kingdom, is accepted as c. 1400.

Roughly speaking, the Old Kingdom represents a period of formation and consolidation in Anatolia; the Middle Kingdom represents a tumultuous period of defence, contraction, and reconquest; the New Kingdom, finally, marks a period of true empire, when Hittite dominion expanded throughout Anatolia and southwards into Syria-Palestine, before collapsing entirely around 1180.[25] Vagaries obstruct the creation of a fixed chronology; what is indisputable, however, is that we have far more evidence from the period c. 1400–c. 1180 than we do for the earlier years of the Hittite kingdom.

---

21. 'Anitta Chronicle, Inscription B', *HST*, 218. Cf. translation provided in Bryce, *Kingdom of the Hittites*, 38; Güterbock, 'Hittite Historiography', 23–24.

22. Rather confusingly, early Hittite kings traced their lineage to the city of Kuššara, although they did not explicitly claim to descend from King Anitta. For a discussion of chronology and the sequence of kings from Anitta of Kuššar to Šuppiluliuma II, see Harry A. Hoffner, Jr., 'Histories and Historians of the Ancient Near East: The Hittites', *Orientalia* n.s. 49 (4) (1980): 283–332.

23. Klengel, 'Problems in Hittite History', 102.

24. On the complex and continued debate regarding the dating of Hittite scripts, see Theo van den Hout, 'A Century of Hittite Text Dating and the Origins of the Hittite Cuneiform Script', *Incontri linguistici* 32 (2009): 11–36.

25. Klengel, 'Problems in Hittite History', 103, 104.

Sources

Scholars now have a wealth of sources through which to explore Hittite culture and society. Early excavations at Hattuša revealed over 10,400 clay tablet fragments, including a Hittite version of the famous Egyptian–Hittite peace treaty of 1259.[26] The Hittite archives have now produced more than thirty thousand tablets and fragments, as well as a single cache of 3,401 seal impressions bearing the names, titles, and genealogy of Hittite kings and their officials.[27] Twenty-six temples have been excavated in the Upper City of Hattuša, revealing the sacred and ceremonial functions of the royal capital. Vast grain silos have been uncovered, showing that the Hittite capital was not only an administrative and religious centre but a major metropolis capable of supporting thousands of inhabitants. Excavations at other Hittite sites have led to the discovery of over three thousand tablets, including ninety-six letters from the reign of Tudhaliya III (c. 1360–c. 1350), a time of considerable vulnerability, when Hatti's enemies launched a series of concentric invasions that threatened to extinguish the Hittite kingdom permanently.[28]

These sources enable a reconstruction of Hittite thought about war.[29] The vast majority of texts were the product of the royal chancery and other scribal offices. It should be remembered that our evidence is as a result dominated by an 'official view of events and history', often serving propagandistic purposes.[30] However, as we are engaged in an assessment of the Hittite ethics of war, the moral norms and political ideals of Hittite society expressed through official propaganda are of greater interest to us than the degree of historicity of reported political or military events.

Of key importance are a number of royal texts in the form of 'annals' or 'manly deeds', commissioned by individual kings. Extant texts exist from only a handful of kings, and even then do not necessarily record entire reigns. It is possible that some kings simply did not feel the need to record their deeds; it

---

26. This led the German archaeologist, Hugo Winckler, to argue correctly that it was Hattuša, not Carchemish, that had been the historic centre of the Hittite kingdom: Collins, *Hittites and Their World*, 6.

27. Theo van den Hout, 'Institutions, Vernaculars, Publics: The Case of Second-Millennium Anatolia', in *Margins of Writing, Origins of Cultures*, ed. Seth Sanders (Chicago: University of Chicago Press, 2006), 221–60 at 223, 225; Bryce, *Kingdom of the Hittites*, xvii, 2; *LettGK*, 170–71; Collins, *Hittites and Their World*, 141–42.

28. *LettGK*, 171. Excavations from provincial sites include Šapinuwa (modern Ortaköy), Sarissa (modern Kusakli), and Tapikka (modern Masat Huyuk).

29. For a useful list of sources pertaining to Hittite warfare, see Victor Korošec, 'The Warfare of the Hittites: From the Legal Point of View', *British Institute for the Study of Iraq* 25 (2) (1963): 159–66 at 159–60.

30. Klengel, 'Problems in Hittite History', 102. See also Van Seters, *In Search of History*, 100–126.

is just as likely that other annals were composed but have been destroyed, or that further archives still await discovery.[31] Hans Güterbock has claimed that these annalistic texts come closest to what we might call "real' historiography, if one has in mind 'the writing of history for its own sake'.[32] Written in the first person and recording the kings' own or their ancestors' military and political exploits, these sources are crucial to our understanding of Hittite attitudes to war. Destruction and plunder are dominant themes, but the sources also reveal evidence of mercy and diplomacy, strategy and tactics. The principal audience for these texts was not the Hittite public, but the Hittite pantheon; in a sense, therefore, they do not represent 'true propaganda'.[33] On the other hand, Hittite kings commissioned the texts in order to stress their achievements and the fulfilment of their duties as pious terrestrial rulers. This, the kings hoped, would gain them access to the divine afterlife. A distinct feature of these texts, compared to equivalent Egyptian or Assyrian annals, is their greater sense of objectivity or, for want of a better word, 'honesty'. That is, they contain references to failures and military defeats, and are not wholly laudatory or bombastic in nature. Some references to the defeats of former kings were undoubtedly intended to enhance the achievements of the present one, but perhaps Hittite kings also believed that there was little point in presenting fictions to the gods, who witnessed the great events on Earth and knew the hearts of men. Nonetheless, we should still view these texts as essentially rhetorical, as they were intended to *persuade* the divine audience of the ruler's righteousness. The scribes were not engaged in writing 'history' in the modern sense of that term. But the texts certainly tell us about paradigms of kingship and martial behaviour within Hittite culture.

The earliest of these texts, the 'Annals of Hattušili I', dates from the Old Kingdom and records Hattušili I's (c. 1650–c. 1620) campaigns from the earlier part of his reign.[34] The second important document purporting to hail from Hattušili I's reign is his so-called 'Testament', which takes the form of a proclamation made by the king in his old age to his high-ranking subjects and warriors. It confirmed Muršili I as his successor and provided instructions on how to govern properly.[35] Both the 'Annals' and the 'Testament' of Hattušili I

---

31. Güterbock, 'Hittite Historiography', 31.

32. Ibid., 30–31. Younger offers a stylistic analysis of the Hittite annals, concluding that '[t]he Hittite imperial ideology was very similar to the Assyrian ideology, although it placed less emphasis on "an ideology of terror" than its Assyrian counterpart'. Younger, *Ancient Conquest Accounts*, 136–63, quotation at 163.

33. Hout, 'Institutions, Vernaculars', 225; Collins, *Hittites and Their World*, 143.

34. Some scholars argue that the 'Annals' refer to highlights from Hattušili I's entire reign: Bryce, *Kingdom of the Hittites*, 63. For an English translation, see 'Annals of Hattušili I', *HST*, 219–22; see also P.H.J. Houwink ten Cate, 'The History of Warfare according to Hittite Sources: The Annals of Hattusilis I (Part I)', *Anatolica* 10 (1983): 91–109; *AoH*, 47–83.

35. 'The Bilingual Testament of Hattušili I', *HST*, 222–28.

are preserved in New Kingdom copies dating from the thirteenth century, meaning that around four hundred years separates the extant texts from the purported events. Nevertheless, there is good reason to believe that these New Kingdom copies preserve what are essentially Old Kingdom texts, and thus record real events, albeit elaborated and modified to cast Hattušili I in a certain light. As copies of much older texts, we can assume they reflect genuine Old Kingdom conventions and attitudes.

Our final significant textual evidence from the Old Kingdom is referred to as either the 'Proclamation' or 'Edict' of King Telipinu (c. 1525–c. 1500).[36] It includes a historical preamble, providing substantial information about the reigns of early Old Kingdom kings, beginning with King Labarna. Significantly, the 'Proclamation' is not wholly laudatory. While it records the achievements of earlier Hittite kings up to the beginning of Telepinu's reign, it also records numerous disasters. The original text dates from the late sixteenth century, but as with the 'Annals' and 'Testament' of Hattušili I, only later New Kingdom copies survive: nine Hittite copies and a fragmentary Akkadian version.[37] This large number of surviving copies indicates that the 'Proclamation of Telepinu' was an important historical and political text and was likely used in scribal training. From this text we can gather that, at the very outset, military success and expansion was a major preoccupation of the Hittite monarchy. From his seat at Kuššara, King Labarna deliberately set out to conquer:

> Once, Labarna was Great King. Then sons, his brothers, and also his in-laws, his kin and his troops were united. The country was small but wherever he went on campaign, he held the enemy lands by force. He destroyed the lands one by one, he made the lands powerless, and he made them the borders of the sea. And each time he returned from campaign, each of his sons went somewhere to a country [. . . that] they each governed.[38]

We see here a stress on political and military unity, a statement of the importance of imposing authority over conquered lands, and an approval of the devastation of enemy lands. Thus the 'Proclamation' presents the Hittite king as a 'restorer of order', with military power being essential to this role.[39]

---

36. Edgar H. Sturtevant and G. Bechtel, *A Hittite Chrestomatby* (Philadelphia: Linguistic Society of America, 1935); extracts available in 'The Proclamation of Telepinu', *HST*, 228–35.

37. Bryce, *Kingdom of the Hittites*, 64.

38. 'Proclamation of Telepinu', §§ 1–4, *HST*, 229–30. Cf. translation given in Bryce, *Kingdom of the Hittites*, 64. There is no contemporary evidence for existence of King Labarna, and it is possible that Telipinu elided Labarna and Hattušili I into a founding 'hero' king. Bryce rejects this, and argues for the existence of two independent personalities: ibid., 65–66.

39. On the 'restorer of order' pattern within the 'Proclamation', see Younger, *Ancient Conquest Accounts*, 127, discussing Mario Liverani, 'Storiografia politica hittita—II: Telepinu, ovvero: Della solidarietà', *Oriens antiquus* 16 (1977): 105–31.

As we enter the Hittite New Kingdom, textual sources that can illuminate Hittite warfare, ethics, and law blossom considerably. Indeed, the century bookended by the battle of Kadesh (c. 1274) at one end and the fall of the Hittite kingdom (c. 1180) at the other is one of the most richly documented periods in ancient Near Eastern history.[40] Significant textual sources include the 'Deeds of Šuppiluliuma I', which were commissioned by his son, Muršili II.[41] The military and political triumphs of Šuppiluliuma I are manifest, for it was during his reign (c. 1350–c. 1322) that the Hittite empire expanded to its greatest extent, especially into Syria-Palestine.[42] Muršili II (c. 1321–c. 1295) also left behind two sets of annals recording his own achievements: the 'Ten Year Annals' and the more detailed 'Comprehensive Annals', the latter of which covers Muršili II's entire reign.[43] These pieces of Hittite political literature are less inclined than their Egyptian or Assyrian counterparts to exaggeration and boasting, and the historical information found within such annals (along with Hittite treaty prologues) is probably fairly accurate.[44]

In addition to these major annalistic sources, the tablet collections of Hattuša have yielded up texts composed in eight different languages, although Hittite diplomatic records were only ever written in Hittite or Akkadian (which the Hittites called 'Babylonian').[45] From among these textual discoveries we can read an 'Apology' of Hattušili III (c. 1267–c. 1237), justifying his usurpation of the throne and laying out his subsequent good deeds (figure 36).[46]

---

40. Itamar Singer, *The Calm Before the Storm: Selected Writings of Itamar Singer on the Late Bronze Age in Anatolia and the Levant* (Atlanta, GA: Society of Biblical Literature, 2011), 3.

41. Hans G. Güterbock, 'The Deeds of Šuppiluliuma as Told by His Son, Muršili II', *Journal of Cuneiform Studies* 10 (1956): 41–68, 75–98, 107–19.

42. For a reassessment of the chronology of Šuppiluliuma's Syrian campaigns, see J. Freu, 'Les Guerres syriennes de Šuppiluliuma et la fin de l'ere amarnienne', *Hethitica XI*, ed. René Lebrun (Louvain-la-Neuve: Peeters, 1992): 39–101.

43. The 'Comprehensive Annals' covered a period of twenty-seven years, but much of the original text is now lost. See Albrecht Götze, *Die Annalen des Müršiliš: Mitteilungen der vorderasiatisch-aegyptischen Gesellschaft 38* (Leipzig: Hinrichs, 1933); Korošec, 'Warfare of the Hittites', 162; Bryce, *Kingdom of the Hittites*, 192–93.

44. Herbert M. Wolf, 'The Historical Reliability of the Hittite Annals', in *Faith, Tradition, and History: Old Testament Historiography in Its Near Eastern Context*, ed. A. R. Millard, J. K. Hoffmeier, and D. W. Baker (Winona Lake, IN: Eisenbrauns, 1994), 159–64.

45. Languages in the archives include Hittite, Akkadian, Hattian, Palaic, Luwian, Hurrian, and Sumerian. Hittite cuneiform was borrowed from Syro-Mesopotamia, and Hittite royal scribes continued to be trained in cuneiform and Akkadian by 'visiting experts' from Assyria and Babylon. It is possible that it was Hittite scribes who introduced cuneiform and Akkadian to the Egyptian royal administration. See O. R. Gurney, *The Hittites*, revised 2nd edn (Baltimore: Penguin, 1962), 117; Collins, *Hittites and Their World*, 104, 141–42; Beckman, 'Foreigners', 208.

46. Albrecht Götze, *Hattušiliš: Der Bericht über seine Thronbesteigung nebst den Paralleltexten; Mitteilungen der vorderasiatisch-aegyptischen Gesellschaft 29* (Leipzig: Hinrichs,

An insight into the emotional turmoil of a ruler afflicted by disaster is provided by the 'Plague Prayers' of Muršili II, in which the desperate king seeks to identify and atone for sins that may have caused a plague that devastated the kingdom over the last two decades of the fourteenth century (see figure 37).[47] We can learn much about Hittite royal administration from preserved royal edicts, decrees, land grants, and oaths. Indeed, one of the largest groups of texts is correspondence between the king and his regional officials, or between these officials and the central administration. In addition to diplomatic and personal correspondence, the central bureaucracy also preserved 'instruction texts', consisting of royal commands to provincial military commanders and political officials.[48] Taken as a whole, such texts 'provide a valuable first-hand record of day-to-day administration in the kingdom's regional centres, and a first-hand view of the conditions, problems and dangers confronting the king's civil and military appointees in these regions'.[49]

A hugely important archive of twenty-four political treaties—the largest single cache of diplomatic instruments from the ancient Near East—has been recovered from Hattuša, giving us a uniquely detailed insight into Late Bronze Age international relations and the political relationships between Hatti, its vassals, and its competitors (see, e.g., figure 32).[50] A Hittite law collection, containing roughly two hundred 'cases', reveals Hittite normative thought about 'right' and 'wrong' action and suitable punishment.[51] Remarkably, these laws display a commitment to applying justice equally across the social spectrum, from slaves to great lords.[52] Importantly, comparative analysis has established that Hittite domestic law and diplomatic contracts had a remarkably deep and lasting influence on the laws and covenants of the Hebrew Tanakh as well as beyond into Greek and Roman traditions.[53] While the influence of ancient

---

1925). English translations are available: 'The Apology of Hattušili III', *HST*, 266–70; William W. Hallo and K. Lawson Younger (eds), *The Context of Scripture*, 4 vols (Leiden: Brill, 1997), 1:199–204. For a biographical discussion of Hattušili III in his historical context, see Theo van den Hout, 'Khattushili III, King of the Hittites', in *CANE*, 2:1107–20.

47. See *HittP*, 47–69.

48. See Jared L. Miller, *Royal Hittite Instructions and Related Administrative Texts*, ed. Mauro Giorgieri (Atlanta, GA: Society of Biblical Literature, 2013).

49. *LettGK*, 170.

50. For a schematic of the formulaic structure of Hittite treaties, see Viktor Korošec, *Hethitische Staatsverträge: Ein Beitrag zu ihrer juristischen Wertung; Leipziger Rechtswissenschaftliche 60* (Leipzig: Weicher, 1931), 12–16; *HDT*, 2–3.

51. See: *LawH*; *LCMAM*, 213–48; *ANET*, 188–97.

52. Korošec, *Hethitische Staatsverträge*, 39, 42; Gurney, *Hittites*, 88–103.

53. The seminal (two-part) comparative study of Hittite and Israelite law is George E. Mendenhall, 'Ancient Oriental and Biblical Law', *The Biblical Archaeologist* 17 (2) (1954): 25–46; Mendenhall, 'Covenant Forms in Israelite Tradition', *The Biblical Archaeologist* 17 (3) (1954): 49–76. These articles are reproduced and published together in George E. Mendenhall, *Law and Covenant in Israel and the Ancient Near East* (Pittsburgh, PA: Biblical Colloquium, 1955). For an extensive collection of comparative texts with historical analysis, see

FIGURE 32. Bronze tablet recording a treaty between the Hittite king Tudhaliya IV and Karunta of Tarhuntašša, c. 1235 BCE. Bjørn Christian Tørrissen, CC BY-SA 3.0 licence, via Wikimedia Commons.

Near Eastern legal traditions on the development of Greek and Roman law has been underestimated, Bruce Wells argues that it 'is becoming increasingly apparent [...] that the Greco-Roman systems have their ancestors to some degree in the Ancient Near East. This points to the Ancient Near East as the source of at least some of the legal ideas and customs that have accompanied human civilizations throughout much of history.'[54] David Bederman has also written at length about the influences and commonalities between successive ancient Mediterranean civilisations in the realm of international law. Rome, especially, was influenced by both Near Eastern and Greek forms, which differed in some of their underlying assumptions, but also shared numerous characteristics regarding sources of obligation, enforcement, sanction, and practices.[55] The ramifications of this argument should give just war scholars, whose subject borrows greatly from Greco-Roman jurisprudence, significant pause for thought, and will be discussed further in the Conclusion to this volume.

Hittite religious records also include a range of material: temple regulations, inventories of cultic sites, ritual instructions, oracular enquiries, and hymns and prayers used in both religious liturgy and for the training of young scribes.[56] Hittite prayers have been described as 'among the most personal and imaginative of Hittite texts', providing 'insights into the intellectual world of Hittite royalty' as well as often pragmatic descriptions of the particular historical circumstances.[57] What is more, these texts reveal 'a sincere "dialogue" between the suppliant and his god, in which he reports all his problems and fears'.[58] In this regard, the prayers are unique in focusing on the king's failures and transgressions as much as, if not more than, his triumphs. They are therefore important sources in helping to unveil the ethical dilemmas and regrets at the heart of the Hittite royal conscience. In doing so, they reveal sustained 'moralistic reflection [...] often characterized by a deeply pessimistic concept of life'.[59]

Religious belief was also expressed in the form of mythology—often a composite of older Near Eastern material blended with Hatti's own religious and literary traditions. Tales of gods and heroes helped the Hittites to place themselves within the cosmos and their cultural environment, and frequently contain didactic elements, indicating right and wrong action and the consequences that follow from each. Indeed, the eclectic mix of influences in Hittite

---

Treaty, Law and Covenant in the Ancient Near East, ed. Kenneth A. Kitchen and Paul J. N. Lawrence, 3 vols (Wiesbaden: Harrossowitz, 2012).

54. Bruce Wells, 'Law and Practice', in *A Companion to the Ancient Near East*, ed. Daniel C. Snell (Malden, MA: Blackwell, 2005), 183–95 at 193.

55. *ILA*, esp. 267ff, 277–78.

56. Gary Beckman, 'The Religion of the Hittites', *Biblical Archaeologist* 52 (2/3) (1989): 98–108, at 98–99.

57. *HitP*, 15.

58. Ibid., 16.

59. Ibid., 17.

FIGURE 33. Hittite rock shrine of Yazilikaya, above the royal capital of Hattuša. Klaus-Peter Simon, CC BY 3.0 licence, via Wikimedia Commons.

mythology is reflective of the religious syncretism of the expanding Hittite state, which sought to incorporate religious and cultural diversity rather than suppress it. Thus Hatti became known as the 'Land of a Thousand Gods'.[60] While the central core of religious and cultural traditions remained relatively stable, arguably it was this cultural flexibility and inclusivity that enabled the kingdom to expand and flourish for six centuries.[61] It is also evidence that religious ideas and ethical norms travelled across the ancient Near East quite freely, from one culture to another, being constantly reshaped. If this was true for theology and cosmology, then it seems reasonable to suppose that it was also true for other areas of life, including warfare and ethics.

Of course, our evidence for Hittite civilisation is not restricted to textual sources. We possess quite rich material evidence in the form of art and architecture, most famously the fortified remains of the city of Hattuša itself, along with the monumental rock reliefs at Yazilikaya, which overlook the royal capital (figure 33).[62] The link here between martial prowess and the divine was strong. Among the deities depicted at Yazilikaya is the so-called Sword God,

---

60. Gary Beckman, 'Religion of the Hittites', 99; Gurney, *Hittites*, 132–33.
61. See *HitM*, 3–4.
62. See, for example, Jürgen Seeher, *Gods Carved in Stone: The Hittite Rock Sanctuary of Yazilikaya*, trans. Giles Shepard (Istanbul: Ege Yayinlari, 2011). On the architecture of the Hittites more generally, see Bittel, *Hattusha*, 24–62; Schachner, *Hattuscha*, 99–109.

THE HITTITES: HISTORICAL INTRODUCTION [179]

FIGURE 34. Procession of twelve deities carrying weapons: Hittite rock shrine of Yazilikaya. Klaus-Peter Simon, CC BY 3.0 licence, via Wikimedia Commons.

and Hittite deities are often represented as carrying weapons (figure 34).[63] However, it must be said that we have very few Hittite reliefs explicitly depicting military activity;[64] for this type of evidence, Hittitologists are largely reliant on contemporaneous Egyptian depictions of Hittites.

In sum, we have a rich variety of sources, speaking to what Liverani terms the 'inner public' (texts possessing 'a celebrative purpose, an underscoring of prestige, a centralized worldview and a disregard for the point of view of the outer partners') as well as 'outer partners' (texts possessing 'an integrative purpose, an underscoring of interest, a symmetrical worldview, and an interest in the point of view of the partner').[65] This collection of evidence paints a rich and varied picture of Hittite society.

Ethnicity and Geography

Hattuša is situated about 150 kilometres (90 miles) east of modern Ankara.[66] Curiously, the Hittites themselves traced their earliest history elsewhere. A certain King Pithana and his son Anitta are said to have expanded their power

---

63. Akurgal, *Art of the Hittites*, 112; Schachner, 'Gedanken zur Datierung', 140, image (*Abbild*) 5.
64. For an example of chariot warfare, see Schachner, 'Gedanken zur Datierung', 133–34, image (*Abbild*) 1.
65. *LIR*, 10.
66. For a good summary of the geography of Hattuša and the Hittite kingdom, and its relationship to Hittite military vulnerabilities, see Macqueen, *Hittites*, 53–56.

from the city of Kuššara (south-east of Hattuša), conquered the city of Neša,[67] and destroyed the city of Hattuša at some time before 1750. King Anitta subsequently moved his royal seat to Neša, and it is notable that even in later years the Hittites referred to their own language as 'Nešite'.[68] Early Hittite kings also traced their lineage to the city of Kuššara, but they did not explicitly claim to be descendants of Anitta. Hattušili I appears to have relocated his seat from Kuššara and established Hattuša as the new royal capital at some point around the middle of the seventeenth century. He also adopted the name of his father, Labarna (or Tabarna), as a title; this subsequently became an adoptive royal title for all future Hittite kings, the equivalent of 'Caesar' in Roman usage.[69] It has been suggested that Labarna and Hattušili I were one and the same person, and that Labarna should simply be read as the Hittite word for 'king'. Alternatively, it may have been Labarna who transferred his base from Kuššara to Hattuša, then adopted the name Hattušili in order to mark a new beginning and tie the royal house to its new territorial seat. Given the paucity of evidence, this remains moot. Whatever the case, it is difficult to exaggerate the importance of Hattušili I to Hittite history. He 'laid the groundwork for the administrative and cultural infrastructure that would define the state until its last days'.[70]

The slightly confusing geography of early Hittite history—split between the city triad of Kuššara, Neša, and Hattuša—is reflective of the fact that the Hittites did not view themselves as a *gens* or *natio* (people/nation) on the basis of a specific ethnic identity. When Hattušili of Kuššara relocated his capital to Hattuša in the land of Hatti (named after the ethnic Hattians, who had inhabited the land since at least the third millennium), his subjects simply began to name themselves 'people of the land of Hatti', whom we call Hittites. These subjects remained ethnically diverse, so it was the land of Hatti—particularly the city of Hattuša itself—that endowed the Hittites with a sense of political 'self'.[71] Ethnic diversity was likely intensified by ongoing Hittite military successes, which resulted in captive populations being transported into the core territory as slaves and soldiers. Language and religion were also extremely pluralistic throughout the Old and New Kingdom periods.[72] So, while the land of Hatti has been described as 'a truly multicultural society united by a central

---

67. Located south of Hattuša and called Kaneš in Old Assyrian sources; it is known today as Kültepe.

68. 'The Anitta Text', *HST*, 216–17; Collins, *Hittites and Their World*, 31.

69. Collins, *Hittites and Their World*, 37. Note that 'Labarna' and 'Tabarna' are used interchangeably.

70. Ibid.

71. Bryce, *Kingdom of the Hittites*, 19; Glatz and Matthews, 'Anthropology', 51.

72. See O. R. Gurney, 'The Hittite Empire', in *Power and Propaganda: A Symposium on Ancient Empires*, ed. Mogens T. Larsen (Copenhagen: Academisk Forlag, 1979), 151–65 at 153; Glatz and Matthews, 'Anthropology', 51.

authority',[73] this should be taken to indicate intense cultural fragmentation across Hittite territories, with distinct communities living near to one another but coexisting relatively harmoniously (perhaps with little direct contact), rather than an integrated multicultural society in the modern sense.

These pluralistic factors influenced how the Hittites saw the world and their place within it. There was a respect for local religious and social customs and a willingness to integrate these local cults into the wider kingdom and empire. There was a recognition that other states had a claim to independent sovereignty. Hittite kings understood that Hatti was but one of several great powers, and they were willing to recognise other great kings as 'brothers'.[74] Be that as it may, the Hittites—like other Near Eastern societies of the period—made a binary distinction between a core 'inner' territory (us/ours) and 'outer' peripheral lands that were presumed to be potentially hostile. The Hittites could find the manners of outer peoples distasteful and even barbaric, although their xenophobia was markedly restrained compared to that of Egyptian ideology.[75] Comparing the political cosmologies of Egypt and Hatti highlights the centralist or universalist elements of pharaonic ideology compared to the multi-centred or pluralistic perspective of Hatti.[76] Unlike the promoters and representatives of pharaonic ideology, Hittite kings never claimed universal authority.

What is clear is that, over the course of the second millennium, Hattuša grew to be a major political, economic, and cultural centre. At the apogee of Hittite power, during the thirteenth century, the walled capital of Hattuša covered an area of at least 168 hectares (414 acres), making it one of the largest cities of the ancient world. The latest archaeological work suggests that the city extended a further two kilometres (1.2 miles) up to the sacred rock

---

73. Collins, *Hittites and Their World*, 219.

74. Ibid.; Richard H. Beal, 'Making, Preserving, and Breaking the Peace with the Hittite State', in *War and Peace in the Ancient World*, ed. Kurt A. Raaflaub (Malden, MA: Blackwell, 2007), 81–97 at 83; *LettGK*, 2; *ILA*, 26–27. The rise of Assyria during the 1200s was initially met with a reluctance from Hittite kings to recognise Assyrian kings as 'brothers' and equals: 'So you've become a "Great King," have you? But why do you continue to speak about "brotherhood" [...] For what reason should I call you "brother"? [...] As my grandfather and father did not call the King of Assyria "brother," you should not keep writing to me about [...] "Great Kingship." It displeases me.': 'No. 104: from King Muwattalli I or Muršili III (Urhi-Teššub) to King Adad-nirāri I of Assyria', *LettH*, 323–24. By the reign of Muwattalli II there had evidently been a shift in attitude, for in a letter to the king of Wilusa (Troy) the Hittite ruler wrote, 'The Kings who are the equals of My Majesty—the King of Egypt, the King of Babylonia, the King of Hanigalbat, or the King of Assyria': 'No. 13: Treaty between Muwattalli II and Alaksandu of Wilusa', *HDT*, 90.

75. Beckman, 'Foreigners', 204.

76. For the comparison of these conceptual frameworks, see *LIR*, especially 18–19, 38–39.

sanctuary of Yazilikiya.[77] The whole site included a royal citadel (Büyükkale), containing royal residences and temples and surrounded by massive fortifications, as well as a lower city, containing markets, grain silos, and the majority of the Hattuša's inhabitants.[78]

Geopolitics

The historical records indicate that the Hittite kingdom, like most kingdoms, was forged in the furnace of war. It has even been said that 'Hittite political history consists of a continuous series of wars'.[79] Over the course of five centuries, the kingdom expanded and contracted quite dramatically, on several occasions. Yet the Hittites were also extremely capable political operators, who developed a sophisticated system of diplomatic relationships based on formal treaties. Conquered territories were legally integrated into the kingdom and empire through vassalage treaties but, in a development seemingly novel to Hatti, treaties were also adapted to serve peaceful diplomacy. The Hittites created peace treaties with co-equal states (such as Egypt), with vassal states over which it effectively ruled directly, and also with a third category of state (*kuirwana*), sitting somewhere between the first two in status: 'a sort of privileged protectorate', in the words of Bederman.[80]

The city-states of Carchemish (conquered by Šuppiluliuma I c. 1324) and Tarhuntašša were ruled by members of the Hittite royal family as 'viceroys', becoming important kings in their own right and enjoying a considerable level of autonomy from the imperial capital. Below this, numerous elite individuals held administrative posts or regional governorships and military commands. Written communications between the king and these officials forms one of the largest components of our surviving textual evidence.[81]

Perhaps most intriguing was the role of the *Tawananna*. This position was always held by a female member of the royal family who primarily fulfilled a religious role as chief priestess, presiding over state cults and royal ceremonies. With religion bound so closely to Hittite concepts of kingship and rulership, this naturally meant that the Tawananna was one of the most influential persons in the kingdom.[82] Nor were these powerful women above political intrigue, with more than one Tawananna being implicated in palace coups. Given their close familial relationship to reigning kings, individual priestesses often sought to further the interests of their immediate male relatives and their claims to the throne.

77. Bittel, *Hattusha*, 25; Schachner, *Hattuscha*, 99–109.
78. Bittel, *Hattusha*, 25, 74.
79. Korošec, 'Warfare of the Hittites', 159.
80. *ILA*, 27.
81. See the sources in *Royal Hittite Instructions*, ed. Miller.
82. Bryce, *Kingdom of the Hittites*, 92–93.

While we are right to think of the Hittite kingdom as a geopolitical superpower during the Late Bronze Age, we must also be aware that the kingdom was potentially quite fragile. The Hittites experienced several very serious reverses, during which the royal capital of Hattuša was sacked and the ruling dynasty almost extinguished. Hittite records inform us that during the reign of Tudhaliya III (mid-fourteenth century),

> the Kaskaean enemy came and sacked the Hatti lands [...]. From the Lower Land came the Arzawan enemy, and he too sacked the Hatti lands [...]. From afar, the Arawannan enemy came and sacked the whole of the Land of Gassiya. From afar, the Azzian enemy came and sacked all the Upper Lands [...]. The Isuwan enemy came and sacked the Land of Tegarama. From afar, the Armatanan enemy came, and he too sacked the Hatti lands [...]. And Hattusa, the city, was burned down.[83]

The damage to the kingdom was so severe that the Egyptian pharaoh Amenhotep III wrote to the king of Arzawa, asking him to 'send me people of the Kaska land. I have heard that everything is *finished*, and that the land of Hattuša is *paralyzed*.'[84]

Achieving military dominance in the ancient Near East was extremely difficult. Hatti was never alone in attempting to establish and maintain military superiority and to exert its influence on Syria-Palestine. The kingdoms of Egypt, Babylon, Mitanni, and Assyria all had similar ambitions at various points in time, seeking to exploit the cities and rich trade routes of Syria and the Levant. The constant threat of incursions from the coastal and island states of the Aegean, and especially from the semi-nomadic Kaskaean (or Gašgaean) peoples of north-eastern Anatolia, brought further challenges and disruption. The Kaska are presented by Hittite sources as the perennial 'barbarians', fundamentally opposed to civilised Hittite society. But all our knowledge of the Kaska is from Hittite sources; the hostility and injustices of the Kaska are therefore viewed entirely from the perspective of an imperial power. As Claudia Glatz and Roger Matthews point out, '[w]ere it possible to write a Kaska history independent of Hittite sources, doubtless the Hittites would seem to be the aggressors, destroyers, and intruders on the Kaska stage'.[85]

Fluctuations in military and political fortune must surely have had an impact upon the Hittite psyche and played an important role in shaping

---

83. Historical preamble to a decree of Hattušili III, in *LettGK*, 181. Bryce suggests that the text may have 'telescoped' a series of events that actually occurred over several years: Bryce, *Kingdom of the Hittites*, 146–47.

84. 'No. 95: From the Pharaoh Nimmuriya (Amenhotep III) to Tarhunta-radu, King of Arzawa', *LettH*, 276; see also *LettGK*, 22. This setback probably occurred during the reign of Arnuwanda I or Hattušili II.

85. Glatz and Matthews, 'Anthropology', 49.

royal ideology, not least the numerous internal conflicts and usurpations that threatened the stability of the crown. Assertions of authority, divine favour, self-defence, just cause, and military achievement must be considered in light as much of the kingdom's instability and weakness as of its durability and strength. Grandiose claims can be the product of a confident political community in rude health, seeking to project its power outwards; however, the loudest claims to authority and righteousness are often made in the face of contradictory claims, or simply because no one is listening. In other words, the propaganda of power can also be a symptom of fundamental political fragility. The experience of defeat may also have triggered some degree of reflection among Hittite elites as to *why* Hatti's enemies were able to overcome it on several occasions. In looking to explain their defeats, Hittite monarchs turned to theological, moral, and legal explanations, whereby wrong action—'sin'—could alienate the good graces of the gods and thus bring about calamity. This critical link between moral action in life and material success in war proved to be a crucial catalyst in the development of genuinely *ethical* reflections about the nature of war within Hittite culture and thought.

CHAPTER SIX

Hatti: *Ius ad bellum*

CONCEPTUALISING JUSTICE AND WAR

Royal Authority and Obligations

Questions regarding the authority to declare and wage war have been central to the development of just war thought. As we saw in chapter 3, from the early third millennium Egyptian pharaohs vigorously asserted their right to wage war, on the basis of a claim to universal authority. How, then, did the Hittite monarchy respond to the issue of authority and warfare over the course of the second millennium, and how did the form of royal authority which evolved in the Hittite state impact upon the ruler's ability to justify wars undertaken in his name?

Theoretically, the Hittite king's authority within his kingdom was absolute. As in other ancient Near Eastern societies, the Hittite monarch's sovereignty was grounded in his divine appointment. This sovereign authority is reflected in the Hittite law collection, which clearly established the king as 'the supreme judge', to whom all Hittite subjects could appeal.[1] This authority was reinforced through sanction. While very few offences merited the death penalty in the Hittite law code (the earliest copies of which date from the Old Kingdom period), challenging or disobeying the judgement of the king was one such capital offence.[2]

Nonetheless, other individuals and institutions held considerable political sway within the Hittite kingdom. The first of these was the *Panku* (meaning

---

1. *LawH*, 4–5.
2. Note that in cases of resisting royal judgement the offender's family was also punished by the destruction or seizure of the offender's property after death: 'If anyone rejects a judgment of the king, his house will become a heap of ruins. If anyone rejects a judgment of a magistrate, they shall cut off his head.' *LawH*, 138, ¶ 173a. See also Hoffner in *LCMAM*, 213–14, 234; Edwin M. Good, 'Capital Punishment and Its Alternatives in Ancient Near Eastern Law', *Stanford Law Review* 19 (5) (1967): 947–77 at 965. Cf. Deuteronomy 17:8–13, which prescribes death for the failure to abide by a court decision.

'all, entire'), an assembly made up of elite warriors and leading officials that effectively served as a royal council and judicial body providing advice to the king.[3] Like most monarchs, the Hittite king relied upon the economic and military support of his elites, and thus the power of the Panku must have fluctuated with the personal power, success, and charisma of individual monarchs. The line between the Panku advising on policy and deciding on policy was probably hazy. Under a strong leader, the Panku would no doubt have fallen into line. In more unstable times, with ineffective or youthful leaders, the power of the Panku must have swelled accordingly.

In terms of individual office-holders, the second-in-command was the king's designated heir, followed closely by the head of the royal bodyguard, the members of which were magnificently named the 'men of the golden spear'. This 'Chief of the Royal Bodyguard' was the highest-ranking official in the kingdom and was frequently entrusted with important military commands during campaigns. This position was usually held by princes of royal blood who were not direct heirs to the throne.[4] The viceroys of Carchemish and Tarhuntašša were also powerful figures within the empire, and the influence of the Tawananna, the chief priestess, should not be underestimated.

In short, when we say that the Hittite king's authority was absolute, we must temper this with the reality that his actions must have been circumscribed by his ability to dominate his elites. The challenges of governing a large and complex kingdom in a world with rudimentary communications technology necessitated a delegation—in reality, a surrendering—of authority, not all of which was easily recovered at the king's will. This state of affairs is perhaps best demonstrated by the many usurpations we find within the dynastic history of the Hittite monarchy.

In the arena of warfare, the king's reliance on his elites would have been particularly striking. The Hittite state operated a socio-economic system that bears some resemblance to medieval European feudalism, with land, slaves, and the spoils of war being bestowed upon elites in return for military service.[5] The king possessed a personal guard and retinue that provided the core of his army, and the hiring of mercenaries was common practice, indicated by several references throughout diplomatic treaties to 'the mercenary gods'.[6] Nevertheless, the king remained reliant on his leading retainers and vassal states to provide the bulk of his infantry and chariotry. This has led one scholar to insist that, although sustaining a principle of hereditary monarchy, the Hittite king was 'merely *primus inter pares*'.[7]

---

3. Bryce, *Kingdom of the Hittites*, 91.
4. Collins, *Hittites and Their World*, 101–2.
5. Bryce, *Kingdom of the Hittites*, 89.
6. For example, see 'No. 12: Treaty between Muršili II and Manapa-Tarhunta of Land of the Seha River', *HDT*, 86, § 17; 'No. 13: Treaty between Muwattalli II and Alaksandu of Wilusa', *HDT*, 92, § 19.
7. Akurgal, *Art of the Hittites*, 86.

Notwithstanding these potential material limits to the exercise of royal power, the ideology of Hittite royal authority was firmly rooted in the divine. Hittite kings did not claim personal divinity—although they did claim to become gods after death[8]—but they were adamant in insisting that they ruled by divine appointment. One ceremonial formula stated that

> Heaven, earth, and the people belong to the storm-god alone. He has made the Labarna, the king, his administrator and given him the entire Land of Khatti. The Labarna shall continue to administer with his hand the entire land. May the storm-god destroy whoever should approach the person of the Labarna, the king, and the borders of Khatti![9]

The divine appointment of the king to rule Hatti was repeatedly stressed in royal documents, from international treaties to private prayers. As Beckman notes, as the king effectively functioned as a steward of the land under the protection of the gods, 'on a human level there could be no legitimate challenge to the rule of the king'.[10]

Preeminent in the Hittite pantheon, and closely associated with the authority and power of the king, was the storm-god Teššub.[11] This great god gave the rule of Hatti to the king, but could also be conceived as bestowing upon the king political authority over certain other subject peoples beyond the lands of Hatti, presumably through the right of conquest. Such a stance is reported in a letter from the king of Ahhiyawa (that is, king of Achaea—probably Mycenae) to Hatti over certain eastern Mediterranean islands contested by the two kingdoms. The king of Ahhiyawa (unsurprisingly) rejected the Hittite king's claim that 'the Storm God gave them to me as subjects'.[12]

---

8. Beckman, 'Religion of the Hittites', 101. A possible exception is Tudhaliya IV, who may have claimed personal divinity during his life: see Stefano De Martino, 'Symbols of Power in the Late Hittite Kingdom', in *Pax Hethitica: Studies on the Hittites and Their Neighbours in Honour of Itamar Singer*, ed. Yoram Cohen, Amir Gilan, and Jared L. Miller (Wiesbaden: Harrassowitz, 2010), 87–98 at 95.

9. Cited by Gary Beckman, 'Royal Ideology and State Administration in Hittite Anatolia', in *CANE*, 1:529–43 at 530.

10. Ibid.

11. Note that Yahweh is also conceptualised as a storm god in the Tanakh (e.g., Psalm 104), and it has been suggested that the Hebrew Yahweh developed from a royal weather god in a similar vein to the Hittite Teššub or the Syrian Baal. See Reinhard Müller, *Jahwe als Wettergott: Studien zur althebräischen Kultlyrik anhand ausgewählter Psalmen* (Berlin: De Gruyter, 2008); Daniel E. Fleming, 'Yahweh among the Baals: Israel and the Storm Gods', in *Mighty Baal: Essays in Honor of Mark S. Smith*, ed. Stephen C. Russell and Esther J. Hamori (Leiden: Brill, 2020), 160–74.

12. Ahhiyawa claimed the islands as an inheritance from the king of Assuwa: see 'No. 99: from the King of Ahhiyawa to the Hittite King', *LettH*, 292. Storm-gods appear in several different manifestations within the Hittite pantheon—likely a result of the integration of various distinct regional cults—but the association with martial strength was consistent. For example, *HitP*, 88, no. 20, §§ 12–15.

The king's authority as political leader was established not only through his selection by the gods to govern the land of Hatti politically, but also through his cultic function as the kingdom's chief priest, essential for mediating human and other worldly interactions with the divine. The interdependent relationship of these two roles is indicated in a prayer of Muwatalli II (c. 1295–c. 1272):

> Divine lords—Sun-goddess of Arinna, my lady, and all the gods of the Land of Hatti, my lords—whose priest I am, who have conferred upon me, from among all others, the rulership over Hatti.[13]

Throughout the Old and New Kingdom periods the storm-god Teššub remained the most powerful deity of the Hittite pantheon and was closely associated with the king, especially in his martial role. However, within the divine pantheon the sun-goddess of Arinna ranked almost on a par with Teššub, and was frequently invoked as representing and protecting the king in his capacity as a governor and a just ruler. This was based on a cosmology in which the sun was an all-seeing and impartial divine entity, embodying justice and overseeing the divine court.[14] The fostering of the royal cult of the sun-goddess shows that Hittite kings did not simply view themselves as warlords ruling through brute force, but rather as representatives of divine justice charged with a duty of good governance. A treaty made between Hatti and Mitanni records that '[a] duplicate of this tablet is deposited before the Sun-goddess of Arinna [...] who governs kingship and queenship in Hatti'. Depositing the treaty in the temple reinforced the fact that the gods bore witness to, and would punish any transgressions of, the oaths sworn by both parties.[15]

We should not be lulled into thinking that the king's association with a female goddess implied any kind of emasculation or feminine gentility. Like other ancient Near Eastern goddesses such as Inanna and Ishtar, the sun-goddess of Arinna was often invoked as 'running in front of the king in battle', smiting his foes and protecting him from harm.[16] One surviving royal prayer

---

13. 'No. 20: Prayer of Muwattalli II', *HitP*, 87.

14. *HitP*, 8. See also prayer of Tudhaliya I: 'O Sun-god, mighty king, son of Ningal! You are establishing the law and custom. Throughout the land you, O Sun-god, are a favoured god.' 'No. 4: Prayers to the Sun-god for appeasing an angry god, 4b', *HitP*, 33.

15. Korošec, *Hethitische Staatsverträge*, 100–102; *ILA*, 143.

16. *AoH*, 48; 'Ten Year Annals of Muršili II', in *HST*, 254–55, §§ 8, 15, 17. In the epilogue to Hammurabi's legal code, the Babylonian king appealed to Inanna to strike down any who rescinded his laws: 'May Inanna, the lady of battle and conflict, who bears my weapons [...] may she shatter his weapons on the field of battle and conflict; / may she create confusion (and) revolt for him! / May she strike down his warriors, / (and) water the earth with their blood! / May she throw up a heap of his warriors' bodies on the plain; / may she show his warriors no mercy!' 'Code of Hammurabi', in *ANET*, 179. Ishtar continued to be venerated as a martial deity throughout the second and first millennium. The Neo-Assyrian king Esarhaddon (r. c. 681–c. 669) rejoiced that 'the goddess Ishtar, goddess of battle and

wonders whether the sun-goddess has 'gone to an enemy land for battle',[17] while an early invocation to the goddess beseeches her protection for the royal couple and her bestowal of military strength:

> She gave them a battle-ready, valiant spear saying: 'May the hostile foreign lands perish by the hand of the *labarna*, and let them take goods, silver and gold to Hattuša and Arinna, the cities of the gods!' [. . .] Whoever are the *labarna*'s first-rank people—his favoured great ones, his infantry, his chariotry and their property—keep them, the aforementioned, alive in the hand of the *labarna* and the *tawannanna*, O most vigorous Sun-goddess!'[18]

In rooting royal authority in the unassailable authority of the gods, Hittite kings simply adopted a widespread Near Eastern practice. The concept of the king as an agent of the gods, and thus also protected by the gods, was explicitly stated in Hittite royal documents, especially vassal treaties and royal edicts: 'The word of Tabarna, Great King, is not to be discarded or broken. Whoever disregards it shall be the legal adversary of the Powerful Storm-god, my lord, of the Sun-goddess of Arinna, my lady, and of all the gods.'[19] Here we see a royal ideology at work that not only sanctioned the king's authority by rooting it in the divine, but by extension presented any challenge or threat to that authority as a challenge to the gods themselves. If individual Hittite kings were really *primi inter pares* in terms of material power, this ideology was intended to raise the royal dignity above the level of other elite competitors.

THE KING'S DUTIES

Endowing kingship with an ideology of divinely mandated rule came with a raft of concomitant duties aimed at maintaining the well-being of the state.[20] The kingdom of Hatti was an agricultural economy and so perhaps the foremost concern was the sustained fertility of the land; as a result, many of the cultic functions of the king were designed to protect or encourage agricultural fecundity. Nevertheless, in terms of the monarch's active participation with his people, the maintenance of justice figured prominently among royal duties. As Martha Roth comments, '[w]hether or not the king was always himself

---

fighting [. . .] remained at my side and broke their line. She broke their battle line'. See Oded, *War, Peace and Empire*, 16.

17. 'No. 8: Muršili's Hymn and Prayer to Sun-Goddess of Arinna', *HitP*, 50.

18. 'No. 3: Invocation of Sun-Goddess of Arinna for Protection of Royal Couple', *HitP*, 26, §§ 6–9.

19. 'No. 29, Edict of Muršili II of Hatti Recognizing the Status of Piyassili of Carchemish', *HDT*, 169.

20. My thanks to Professor Theo van den Hout for his comments regarding the king's duties.

an active participant in the administration of the legal system, he was always its guardian, for the application of justice was the highest trust given by the gods to a legitimate king'.[21] As an active judge and legislator or as a paradigm of moral action, the king symbolised the precepts of justice as demanded by the gods.[22] As a just ruler, the king was also expected to show mercy and be a father to his people. During the Old Kingdom, Hattušili I disinherited his designated heir for the reason that 'he did not cry, he was not kind. Cold he is! He is not kind of heart!'[23]

While prayers rarely feature as a source for the history of the ethics of war, we have such a rich collection of Hittite prayers that it would be foolhardy to ignore them. The Hittite prayer corpus is imbued with moralistic reflections on the importance of justice in the lives of men, and a large number of royal prayers bear witness to the king's obligation to act in accordance with justice. One prayer to the sun-god exclaims, 'You are ruling the land and you are giving victory [...]. The just man is dear to you and you are exalting him.'[24] The prayers provide us with a window, of sorts, into the psyche of Hittite rulers. They reveal individual assumptions about the ordering of the cosmos as well as the deepest anxieties of specific rulers. The solar and storm deities, especially the sun-goddess of Arinna, were by far the most frequently evoked; they functioned as both intercessors on behalf of the king *and* supreme judges in the divine court.[25] Both in form and content, these prayers—usually spoken in the voice of the king—formed a type of legal proceeding between the king and the gods in a divine court. As Itamar Singer explicates, '[t]he defendant is the king, the prosecutor is the offended god, the advocate is the addressed deity (requested to act as an intercessor), and the court of justice is the assembly of gods'; the king would confess or deny his guilt, proffer any mitigating circumstances, and attempt 'the inveigling of the divine judges with flattery (hymns) and presents (vows)'.[26]

What is most remarkable about these prayers, especially when considered from the perspective of the ethics of war and concepts of just cause and injury, is that, from the outset, in pleading his case the king assumed responsibility not only for his own sins but also for those committed by his royal forebears or by his subjects.[27] As evinced by the Hittite law code and from royal prayers, there was a firm belief in Hittite culture that the sin of the father passed down to his heirs, who became responsible for righting any wrongs. (This bears some resemblance to later Hebrew concepts of transferrable familial sin,

21. Roth, *LCMAM*, 4–5.
22. Ibid., 5.
23. 'Bilingual Testament of Hattušili I', *HST*, 224, § 1.
24. 'No. 4c: Prayer of a Mortal', *HitP*, 36, § 1.
25. *HitP*, 8.
26. Ibid., 5–6.
27. Ibid., 10.

passed down from Adam and Eve to their descendants.) A denial of guilt was meaningless in a divine court, as the prayers were usually responding to an affliction or injury already suffered by the ruler, his household, or his kingdom; in other words, the gods were punishing a sin already committed. Nevertheless, as Singer notes, 'the possibilities of exculpation, self-justification, even protestation against unfair punishment, are remarkably manifold in Hittite prayers'.[28]

The moral convictions that define the prayer corpus are also visible in Hittite mythology and fable. A clear division between good and bad action is contained in the didactic tale 'Appu and His Two Sons', probably dating from the Old Kingdom. In this tale the two sons are literally named Wrong (*idaluš*) and Right (*handanza*); Wrong tries to defraud his honest brother Right, but the sun-god adjudicates against him. The end of the tale is lost, but we are led to assume that Wrong will receive his comeuppance, as the tale begins by praising an unnamed deity for punishing evil men and vindicating the righteous: 'He/she it is who always exonerates just men, but chops down evil men like trees, repeatedly striking evil men on their skulls ... until he/she destroys them.'[29]

As to what the Hittites understood to be 'sinful', we can extrapolate from prayers, treaties, mythology, and laws. Robbery, extortion, assault, murder, sexual deviance, oath violation, and impiety are all presented as examples of wrong action. It appears that wrath itself was also perceived as a negative emotion. In one myth the god Telipinu, son of the storm-god, argues with the other gods and goes into self-imposed exile, leaving the land to wither and die. The goddess Kamrusepa is sent after him and helps to reconcile Telipinu by conducting rituals to soothe his anger and the evil associated with it:

> And I have taken from Telipinu, from his body, his evil; I have taken his sin; I have taken his anger; I have taken his wrath; I have taken his pique; I have taken his sullenness [...]. Telipinu, let anger go. Let wrath go. Let sullenness go.'[30]

The myth presents wrath, resentment, evil, and sin as different aspects of a single negative emotion.

The Great King's duty to execute justice also extended to his vassal states. Muršili II intervened in a dispute between Mukish and Ugarit over a matter of

---

28. Ibid.

29. 'Appu and His Two Sons', *HitM*, 63, § 1. For further discussion of this myth, see Harry A. Hoffner Jr., 'Hittite Mythological Texts: A Survey', in *Unity and Diversity: Essays in the History, Literature, and Religion of the Ancient Near East*, ed. Hans Goedicke and J.J.M. Roberts (Baltimore: Johns Hopkins University Press, 1975), 136–45 at 139–40.

30. 'The Disappearance of Telipinu, Version 1', *HitM*, 16, §§ 18, 21. Cf. 'The Disappearance of Telipinu, Version 2', *HitM*, 19, § 20. For an alternative translation, see *ANEA*, 1:87–91, esp. 90. For an examination of this myth, see also Gurney, *Hittites*, 184–90.

lands contested by the two states and, having 'investigated this case, he determined that these cities have belonged to the land of Ugarit since long ago'.[31] Similarly, in a number of political treaties created for the subject principalities of western Anatolia in the wake of Muršili II's defeat of Uhha-ziti of Arzawa (c. 1317),[32] the Hittite monarch positioned himself as a judge and arbiter, keeping the peace between his fractious vassal states. 'If you have some legal dispute,' Muršili stated in a vassal treaty with Targasnalli of Hapalla, 'you shall not act rashly, nor [. . .] be angry. If you yourselves have a resolvable dispute, then set out and come before My Majesty, so that I, My Majesty, can set you on the proper path by means of a judgment.'[33]

Claims to be able to render judgement in international disputes could extend even beyond the traditional spheres of Hittite influence. When Shattiwaza—the usurped ruler of the once mighty Hurrian kingdom of Mitanni—fled to the Hittite court, Šuppiluliuma I seized the opportunity to forge a marriage alliance and utilise Hittite military might to reinstal Shattiwaza as a client king. Notwithstanding the *Realpolitik* behind this decision, in the ensuing treaty, formalising the contract between Hatti and Shattiwaza, the Hittite king portrayed himself as simply enacting the judgement of the gods in this particular legal 'case':

> There was confusion among the Hurrians, and Shutatarra, together with the chariot warriors, sought to kill Prince Shattiwaza. However, he escaped and came into the presence of My Majesty, Šuppiluliuma, King of Hatti, Hero, Beloved of the Storm-god. I, Great King, spoke thus: 'The Storm-god has decided his legal case. As I have taken up Shattiwaza, son of King Tushratta, in my hand, I will seat him upon the throne of his father, so that the land of Mitanni, the great land, does not go to ruin. I, Great King, King of Hatti, have given life to the land of Mitanni for the sake of my daughter.'[34]

The Hittite king claims to have executed the storm-god's legal judgement but also, intriguingly, that his actions were partly motivated by a desire to safeguard Mitanni: so that the land 'does not go to ruin'. Effectively, we have here a justification for military intervention. This should not be interpreted as a selfless or humanitarian intervention: the Hittite king himself states that his actions were ultimately 'for the sake of my daughter' (who through her marriage to Shattiwaza became queen of Mitanni), and this could just as well be read as 'for the sake of myself'. The marriage alliance and the subsequent

---

31. 'No. 31a: Edict of Muršili II concerning Frontiers of Ugarit', *HDT*, 174, § 2.
32. See Treaties 10, 11, and 12, in *HDT*, 69–86.
33. 'No. 10: Treaty between Muršili II of Hatti and Targasnalli of Hapalla', *HDT*, 72, § 10.
34. 'No. 6a: Treaty between Suppiluliuma I of Hatti and Shattiwaza of Mittanni', *HDT*, 44, § 6.

Mitannian dependency was primarily intended to benefit Šuppiluliuma and Hatti. Through securing Shattiwaza's loyalty, Hatti extended its sphere of influence and safeguarded its south-eastern frontier.

The treaty with Shattiwaza is also indicative of the idiosyncratic legalism of Hittite thought, wherein even the gods operated within a legal system. Enemies of the state—those who challenged the authority of the Great King— became *legal* adversaries of the gods. This is why gods feature so centrally in Hittite diplomatic treaties as enforcers of the legal contract sealed between the two parties. War was the terrestrial prosecution of a legal trial in the court of the gods. Given that the Hittites believed divine favour to be dependent upon correct moral action, it stood to reason that the victor would be the state and ruler whom the gods judged to hold the moral 'right'. This divine favour also depended on the proper observation of religious ritual, for which the king, as chief priest, was primarily responsible. 'He was the linchpin of the universe,' as Beckman says, 'the point at which the sphere of the gods met that of human beings.'[35] This cultic role coexisted with the obligation of the king to rule justly, so that Hittite kingship embodied a moral, legal, and religious leadership around which Hittite society was built.

The final crucial aspect of Hittite kingship was the monarch's role as a war leader. Formulaic references to the king as 'hero' underlined the importance of martial prestige as one of the defining features of Hittite kingship. O. R. Gurney posits that during the Old Kingdom the king was first and foremost a war leader, and religious functions accrued to him only later.[36] Royal seal impressions—which possessed signficiant propaganda value, being widely disseminated—often include the formula 'Seal of Tabarna [followed by name of the king], the Great King, the hero'.[37] Seals depict kings accompanied by two hieroglyphs depicting a dagger and a blossom: symbols of the king as a war leader and as a source of fecundity, respectively.[38] Such images are repeated on a monumental scale in the rock reliefs at Yazilikaya (figure 33). Here, Tudhaliya IV (c. 1237–c. 1228/c. 1227–c. 1209) is shown wearing a long sword with an ornate scabbard; facing him, twelve gods are depicted processing in military garb and carrying swords (figures 34 and 35). Elite cultic sites such as Yazilikaya were presumably accessible only to a select few and indicate how kings wished to appear before a divine audience. The representation of gods bearing weapons of war is evidence that martial prowess was vaunted in Hittite society; like the gods, the king was almost always depicted carrying weapons, proof of the central role that war played in Hittite society and culture.

---

35. Beckman, 'Religion of the Hittites', 101.
36. Gurney, *Hittites*, 215.
37. See Akurgal, *Art of the Hittites*, 60–72; Beckman, 'Royal Ideology', 532.
38. Akurgal, *Art of the Hittites*, 74; De Martino, 'Symbols of Power'.

FIGURE 35. King Tudhaliya IV (r. c. 1237–c. 1228/c. 1227–c. 1209 BCE) before the god Šarruma (son of the storm-god Teššub), wearing a long sword: Hittite rock shrine of Yazilikaya. Klaus-Peter Simon, CC BY 3.0 licence, via Wikimedia Commons.

In sum, the Hittite king exercised power through an authority rooted in the divine. As a steward of the land and people, appointed by the gods, the king claimed untrammelled authority within the state. But this was a reciprocal relationship. In return for obedience and service, the king was obliged to rule in a manner appropriate to his divine appointment. He had to act morally, rule according to the law, be merciful to his subjects, fulfil his cultic obligations to the gods, and lead his people to victory in war.

Divine Aid and Victory

There were intimate connections between the king's duties as a war leader, his securing of divine favour, and victory in war. We have already seen that the storm-god Teššub and the sun-goddess of Arinna were frequently invoked to bestow military strength. A good king acted as a kind of divine conduit for his army, channelling the gods' support and strength. Kings beseeched the gods to infuse their warriors with valour: 'Give them a man's valiant, battle-ready, divine weapon! Put beneath their feet the enemy lands, and may they destroy them.'[39]

Through his relationship with the divine, a just king could expect divine protection and military success.[40] Throughout the 'Deeds of Šuppiluliuma', the audience is told that 'the gods helped him' (they 'walked before him' into battle), enabling the king to slay his enemies and reconquer Hittite lands that had suffered encroachment.[41] Such divine support could enable the killing of masses of enemies:

> And the gods helped my father: the Sun Goddess of Arinna, the Storm God of Hatti, the Storm God of the Army, and the Lady of the Battlefield, so that he slew the aforementioned whole tribe, and the enemy troops died in multitude. Furthermore, again he met six tribes [...] and he slew these, too, so that the enemy troops died in multitude. And still another seven tribes he met [...] and slew them, so that the enemy troops died in multitude.[42]

The same convention is followed in other Hittite historiographical texts. In the records of Muršili II, divine help is cited so frequently in connection to military victory that Güterbock comments that it is 'almost a cliché'.[43] The

---

39. 'No. 9: Muršili's Hymn and Prayer to Telipinu', *HitP*, 55, § 11.

40. For example: 'But when my father [Šuppiluliuma I] died, and I [Muršili II], My Majesty, had seated myself upon the throne of my father [...] the gods of my father protected me. I defeated the enemy for him and conquered the entire land of Arzawa.' 'No. 11: Treaty between Muršili II and Kupanta-Kurunta of Mira-Kuwaliya', *HDT*, 74, § 3.

41. Güterbock, 'Deeds of Šuppiluliuma', 78.

42. Ibid., 75–76; cf. ibid., 90–91.

43. Guterbock, 'Hittite Historiography', 34–35.

gods could produce thunder and lightning to terrify enemies, as when the storm-god is said to have 'shot a thunderbolt' (or perhaps a meteor) at the land of Arzawa. They could also raise clouds and storms to veil Hittite armies to make them invisible to their enemies.[44]

In a similar vein to the propaganda of Egyptian pharaohs such as Ramses II (albeit considerably more restrained), Hittite kings claimed to be capable of superhuman martial deeds when endowed with divine support, personally fighting and defeating enemy hordes with minimal help from the army:

> In the morning my father drove down from Tiwanzana [...]. And as my father was driving, he came upon that whole enemy all at once, and my father engaged him in battle. Then the gods helped my father: the Sun Goddess of Arinna, the Storm God of Hatti, the Storm God of the Army, and Ishtar of the Battlefield, so that he smote that enemy.[45]

Nonetheless, moral righteousness on the part of the king and his subjects remained crucial in order to secure divine aid in war. Unlike the ancient Egyptian ethics of war, in which the actions of the monarch were *ipso facto* righteous, the moral righteousness of the Hittite king was not automatically assumed. During the New Kingdom reign of Tudhaliya IV, Hatti faced various threats and military reverses, especially from Assyria. In a prayer to the sun-goddess of Arinna, Tudhaliya's sense of desperation is reflected by his soul-searching: he admits to a lack of proper piety by neglecting certain religious festivals (thus incurring the goddess's displeasure), seeks forgiveness for his sins, and promises to give the goddess her due. By confessing his sins and making the appropriate amendments—that is, by acting righteously—Tudhaliya hoped to be rewarded with divine aid to reverse his military fortunes:

> If you, O Sun-goddess of Arinna, my lady, became angry with me on account of some festivals, take care of me again, O Sun-goddess of Arinna, my lady! May I defeat the enemy! If you, O Sun-goddess of Arinna, my lady, will step down to me, and I shall defeat the enemy, I shall confess my sin before you and never again shall I omit the festivals [...] and if I shall defeat the enemy, when I return from the

---

44. Götze, *Annalen des Muršiliš*, 46, 47–49, 127; Güterbock, 'Hittite Historiography', 35; Moshe Weinfeld, 'Divine Intervention in War in Ancient Israel, and in the Ancient Near East', in *History, Historiography and Interpretation: Studies in Biblical and Cuneiform Literatures*, ed. Hayim Tadmor and Moshe Weinfeld (Jerusalem: The Magnes Press, 1983), 121–47 at 139, 144–45; Kang, *Divine War*, 65–69.

45. Güterbock, 'Deeds of Šuppiluliuma', 76. It is worth noting that, of the four gods specifically cited here as helping the king in battle, the female deities of Ishtar and the sun-goddess of Arinna figure prominently. Compare: 'And the gods helped my father: The Sun Goddess of Arinna, the Storm God of Hatti, the Storm God of the Army [...] Ištar of the Battlefield and Zababa, so that the enemy troops died in multitude.' Ibid., 117–18.

battle-field, I shall go up to Mount Tagurka, and I shall give you thousands [of offerings], and I shall make reparation.⁴⁶

There is even evidence, in a royal edict no less, of Tudhaliya IV contemplating defeat in the ongoing war against Assyria. This edict was sent to the king of Ugarit, releasing him from military obligations against Assyria (itself a sign of political weakness on Hatti's part), and considers the future outcomes of the war:

> While the war with Assyria has not come to an end, the infantry and the chariotry of the king of the land of Ugarit need not come to my aid [...].
> When the war with Assyria has come to an end, *if I, My Majesty, prevail over the king of Assyria, then we will make peace with one another.*⁴⁷

The use of the conditional clause and subjunctive verb—'if I, My Majesty, prevail [...] then we will make peace'—is striking. Whilst Tudhaliya's 'if I prevail' introduces doubt regarding Hittite victory, a contemporaneous Egyptian or Assyrian royal document would never have countenanced the possibility of defeat: victory was always presented as inevitable. When considered alongside royal texts produced by other ancient Near Eastern empires, such sentiments are highly unusual, if not unique. Their expression indicates that Hittite kings were realistic in their assessments of war, were not always confident that their actions had garnered divine approval, and did not take victory for granted.

This is of the highest importance to our analysis of Hittite ethics of war. Arguably, only when a society seriously considers the possibility of defeat can it fully engage with military ethics. Being forced to consider one's own fate in defeat may encourage a greater sense of empathy and restraint. In Hatti, defeat was understood as a result of divine disfavour, which was itself a consequence of immorality on the part of the king, his forebears, or his subjects. A deficiency in justice or piety risked military defeat, and because the Hittites could conceive of their own injustice, they could also entertain the possibility that some of their military actions could be unjust. Here, I contend, we have the beginnings of a genuine engagement with the condition of just cause. Being willing to concede that one's own moral rectitude might be deficient, or one's own cause for war might be morally or legally insufficient, is an important evolutionary step towards an acceptance that others might also have claims to justice in war. One can see how this differs from Egyptian theology and royal ideology, which taught that justice was the absolute preserve of the Egyptian state and pharaoh. Hittite theology and royal ideology did not share this absolutism; as a result, an ethics of war could evolve that was not entirely one-sided. (It also

---

46. 'No. 24: Tudhaliya IV's Prayer to the Sun-Goddess of Arinna for Military Success', *HitP*, 108–9, §§ 1–5.

47. 'No. 37: Edict of Tudhaliya IV Releasing Ammistamru II of Ugarit from Participation in War against Assyria', *HDT*, 183, § 1 (emphasis added).

differs from Israelite thought in this regard, as will be discussed in Part III.) This development was thus a critical step towards the construction of an ethics of war that much more closely resembles a modern understanding of just war thought.

Just Cause

In reconstructing how the Hittite state conceived of and justified war against its enemies, understanding the Hittite concept of *casus belli* is fundamental. During the history of the Hittite kingdom there were certainly causes to which war was deemed a necessary response. As in other ancient Near Eastern polities, war was a 'recognised legal instrument of foreign policy'.[48] In analysing the Hittite evidence, a number of causes for war emerge, each discussed in turn below: first, defence of territory, property, and people; second, restitution of property; third, vengeance (for human and/or divine injuries); fourth, defence of allies; and fifth, suppression of rebellion.

DEFENCE OF TERRITORY, PROPERTY, AND PEOPLE

Self-defence is the most universal and easily recognisable cause for war. It remains the basis for justifiable war to this day, embedded in international law. From the very earliest evidence of Hittite warfare, we can see clear expressions of Hittite kings waging war in response to what they considered direct injuries, threats, and incursions into their territory. Very often, this included references to the perennial enemies of Hatti, the Kaska tribes of north-eastern Anatolia.[49] These tribes recurrently raided lands claimed by the Hittite kingdom, especially when the Hittites were distracted by warfare against other territorially established principalities and kingdoms. King Arnuwanda I (c. 1390–c. 1370) and his queen Asmunikal described Kaskaean ravaging in a prayer to the sun-goddess of Arinna, in which they sought the goddess's support in a defensive war:

> We shall surely continue to tell you gods how the enemies attacked the land of Hatti, plundered the land, and took it away [. . .] and we shall continually bring our case before you [. . .] the temples which you, O gods, had in these lands, the Kaska-men have destroyed and they have smashed your images, O gods. They divided up the priests, the holy priests, the priestesses, the anointed ones, the musicians, the gardeners, and they made them their servants.[50]

---

48. Ziskind, 'Aspects of International Law', 125.

49. The Kaska are mentioned in over two hundred Hittite texts: Glatz and Matthews, 'Anthropology', 53–54.

50. 'No. 5: Prayer of Arnuwanda and Asmunikal to the Sun-Goddess of Arinna', *HitP*, 41–42, §§ 11–18.

From the offences listed in the prayer we can gain a sense of what the royal couple considered the most grievous injuries. In listing them they sought the best chance for 'prosecuting' their case and gaining the support of the divine court. The invasion of Hatti's borders, the plundering of property, the violation of religious sites, and the seizing and enslavement of sacred personnel dedicated to the temples were obviously regarded as heinous crimes, necessitating a military response.[51] The Kaskaean violation of holy temples and their deliberate destruction of sacrosanct images were presumably considered particularly grievous (and persuasive) charges to present before the gods. If this truly occurred—and was not merely a rhetorical flourish on the part of Arnuwanda's scribes—we might wonder at the Kaskaean motivation, as the smashing of sacred images seems to go beyond the simple looting of precious artefacts for profit. Other than wanton destruction in the spirit of revenge, the likeliest reason was that, by destroying Hittite religious symbols, the Kaskaeans were asserting the power of their own deities as well as attempting to weaken the power of the Hittite gods. It also served as a form of psychological warfare, highlighting to the Hittites that their gods had been unable or unwilling to protect them, and that the Hittites, in turn, had disappointed their gods by failing to protect their holy places.

We have many other examples of Hittite kings responding to Kaskaean ravaging as an expression of just defensive warfare. The military activity of Tudhaliya III (c. 1360–c. 1350) exemplified the strategic quandaries typically facing Hittite kings who did not always possess the military resources to defend a large empire against simultaneous attacks:

> And since the troops of the lands of Maša and Kammala kept attacking the land of the Hulana river and the land of Kaššiya, my grandfather [Tudhaliya III] went to attack them. And my father [Šuppiluliuma I] went with my grandfather on the campaign. The gods helped my grandfather, so that he went and destroyed the land of Mašša and Kammala [. . .]. But in the rear the Kaskaean enemy took the weapons up again; and the enemy again destroyed the empty town behind which my father had built fortifications.[52]

In a series of letters between the royal capital and a provincial governor named Kaššu (c. 1300), we see the Hittite royal machinery at work in responding to military threats. We also see the manner in which it viewed its defensive military responses as entirely legitimate:

> [King to Kaššu] Concerning the matters about which you wrote to me: how the enemy is damaging the crops, how in Kappušiya he has

---

51. Note that many of the personnel of the temples would have already been slaves, seized by the Hittites in war and dedicated to the gods as war spoils.
52. Güterbock, 'Deeds of Šuppiluliuma', 65–66.

attacked the property of the Queen, how they have taken one team of oxen belonging to the House of the Queen, and how they have led away 30 oxen and 10 men of the serfs—all this I have heard. Because the enemy thus marches into the land at a moment's notice, you should locate him somewhere, you should attack him.[53]

On this particular occasion the Kaska targeted food resources, apparently provoked by 'a plague of locusts' devouring crops in their own territories.[54] This was not a small-scale problem. The highly mobile Kaska often moved at night, sometimes up to six hundred-strong, and targeted crops and livestock before an adequate Hittite response could be organised.[55]

Conflict between Hatti and territorially defined kingdoms and principalities was also couched in terms of self-defence. In recounting the deeds of his father, Šuppiluliuma, Muršili II describes necessary self-defensive military action:

> because Hatti was attacked by the enemy, and the enemy had taken borderlands of Hatti, my father kept attacking the enemy lands and kept defeating them. He took back the borderlands of Hatii, which the enemy had taken and resettled them.[56]

Hittite kings saw a straightforward relationship between, on the one hand, aggressive actions committed against the Hittite state and, on the other hand, the legitimacy of aggressive military responses to defend Hittite interests. It was the duty of the king to defend both his borders and his subjects. This could come in all shapes and sizes, from contending with the might of the Egyptian or Assyrian empires, to dealing with localised threats from opportunistic warlords: both were discussed drawing upon a similar lexicon of injury, defence, and justice. During the mid-thirteenth century, King Hattušili III had to contend with one such warlord, Piyama-radu, who proved to be an ongoing thorn in his side. Piyama-radu was initially welcomed into the Hittite state, but turned on his patrons as soon as it was profitable for him to do so. He found a ready ally in the king of Ahhiyawa (Achaea), who was always looking to probe Hittite weaknesses in territories bordering the Mediterranean coast. Hattušili III warned Piyama-radu to retreat from the Lukka Lands (dependencies of Hatti in south-western Anatolia) or suffer the consequences, informing him that 'I personally look after my subjects'. Piyama-radu

---

53. 'Letter 14: King to Kaššu', *LettH*, 109. Kaššu held the office of 'Chief of the Army Inspectors' (ibid., 95) and also apparently 'Chief of the Military Heralds', as seen in 'No. 73: From Hulla, the Commander of Chariot Warriors to Kaššu', *LettH*, 227–28.

54. 'No. 24: from the King to Kaššu and Pulli', *LettH*, 130.

55. 'No. 30: from the King to Tatta and Hulla', *LettH*, 140–41; 'No. 42: from the King to [?]', ibid., 163; 'No. 48: to the King from Adad-bēlī', ibid., 174–75.

56. 'No. 12: Muršili II's 'First Plague Prayer to the Assembly of Gods and Goddesses', *HitP*, 62, § 4.

ignored the warning, and Hattušili launched a campaign against him. The king claimed a victory at the city of Iyalanda, but Piyama-radu escaped and Hattušili was forced to return home empty-handed.[57] Nevertheless, his duty to defend his subjects and vassals had presumably been satisfied.

A more complex illustration of Hittite attitudes to defensive force is provided in the historical preamble of a vassal treaty created during Muršili II's reign, informing us that the king of Mira-Kuwaliya 'quarrelled with me, stirred up the land of Pitassa and the Hittites, my own subjects, against me, and would have begun war against me'. This was in spite of the fact that 'I, My Majesty, protected Mashuiluwa, and in no way mistreated him'. Despite this disloyalty and the threat of war, Muršili was willing to pursue a diplomatic resolution. When these overtures were rejected and Mashuiluwa fled into the enemy territory of Masa, Muršili resorted to armed force and 'attacked the land of Masa and destroyed it'. Mashuiluwa was finally captured and, because 'he had offended', was taken as a prisoner of war back to Hattuša.[58]

Muršili presents these events as evidence of an offence committed against Hatti which demanded defensive counter-measures. But the justificatory line between self-defence and what might be termed 'preventive war' was seemingly hazy. Mashuiluwa may have been a threat, but never actually initiated armed conflict. His offence was inciting revolt (we are not given the details) and fleeing into an enemy land: this was taken by Muršili II as sufficient grounds for defensive war. In adopting this stance, Muršili was simply continuing the example set by his father, Šuppiluliuma I, who during his expansionist reign conquered 'other foreign lands' and 'sustained Hatti and secured its borders on each side'.[59] Expanding the Hittite sphere of influence was, in this context, understood as a defensive action, because it secured the borders of the heartland and allowed the kingdom to flourish.[60] In part, this was a symptom of the geopolitical reality of the ancient Near East, where—excluding the relatively well defined and fortified geographical boundaries of Egypt—most state borders were poorly defined and subject to almost constant flux.[61] But such expansion hardly corresponds to our current understanding of self-defence. It is more akin to the later Roman justification of imperial conquest, advocated by the likes of Cicero, that if through conquest the *pax Romana* could be maintained, then even wars for *imperium* were ultimately for the sake of peace.[62]

---

57. 'No. 101: from King Hattušili III to the King of Ahhiyawa ("Tawagalawa Letter")', *LettH*, 300–303. Hattušili admits that part of his forces was ambushed elsewhere.

58. 'No. 11: Treaty between Muršili II and Kupanta-Kurunta of Mira-Kuwaliya', *HDT*, 75.

59. 'No. 12: Muršili I's "First" Plague Prayer to the Assembly of Gods and Goddesses', *HitP*, 62, § 4.

60. 'During his reign the entire land of Hatti did well', as the prayer text says: ibid., 62, § 4.

61. Ziskind, 'Aspects of International Law', 157.

62. Cicero, *On Duties*, bk 1, §§ 35, 38; bk 2, §§ 26–27; cf. ibid., bk 3, § 46. See also Morkevičius, *Realist Ethics*, 70.

RESTITUTION OF PROPERTY

Some of our oldest evidence from Hatti points towards a strongly held belief that armed violence was a legitimate method for restoring stolen property or seeking compensation for property that had been destroyed. This itself was consistent with a legal system that operated on a combination of retributive and compensatory principles. In murder cases, for example, it was the prerogative of the victim's heir to decide whether the murderer should be executed or should survive and pay compensation.[63]

Old Kingdom treaties created between Hatti and independent kingdoms on their border were clear in stipulating a process for resolving cross-border transgressions, compensations, and punishments. A treaty made with Kizzuwatna (c. 1500) stated that if any man from Kizzuwatna entered Hatti and stole property, then he 'must make full twofold restitution to his victim and pay thirty shekels of silver'. If the payment was not forthcoming, then the thief 'must be put to death'. The fines and punishment were identical if the same offence was made by a subject of Hatti entering Kizzuwatna.[64] This echoed older practices enshrined within the Hittite legal code, in which a number of laws deal with the killing or abduction of Hittites and their property.[65] Some of the blood-prices stipulated as compensation for such injuries could be ruinously extravagant.[66] The repercussions of these crimes were not necessarily restricted to a few individuals or households. The 'people' of nations were often implicitly included in international agreements, meaning that crimes against another nation's subjects could potentially violate international accords and thus provide grounds for war.[67]

A deep concern with property was continued into the Middle Kingdom period. An edict issued to vassal military commanders during a border war against the principality of Pahhuwa demanded that they 'will bring the stolen goods' taken by the enemy back to Hatti. There are several clauses on the seizing and returning of property (including slaves), with the king insisting that his servants 'will give back everything which still exists and is visible to the eye. They will not hold back as much as a strand of wool, but will give it back. And they will seize everyone who has escaped.'[68]

---

63. 'Telipinu Edict', in *LCMAM*, 237, ¶ 49.
64. 'Treaty between a King of Hatti and Paddatissu of Kizzuwatna', *HDT*, 13, § 7.
65. *LawH*, 19, ¶ 5.
66. For blood-prices, see *LawH*, 17–29, ¶¶ 1–18; 29–30, ¶ 19a; 143–44, ¶ 180; 147, ¶ 185. It remains unclear what happened if an individual found guilty of murder or kidnap failed to pay compensation. One law suggests that failure to comply would indeed result in harsher penalties: 'If anyone rejects a judgment of the king, his house will become a heap of ruins. If anyone rejects a judgment of a magistrate, they shall cut off his head.' Ibid., 138, ¶ 173a.
67. Ziskind, 'Aspects of International Law', 24–26.
68. 'No. 27a: Indictment of Mita of Pahhuwa and Treaty with the Elders of Several Anatolian Communities', *HDT*, 162–63, §§ 5, 9, 11.

Regarding cross-border relationships, the principles of *lex talionis* and the restitution or compensation of property could, at times, descend into tit-for-tat violence. Tushratta of Mitanni rebuked Šuppiluliuma I for his ingressions into territory bordering Mitanni, warning, 'If you plunder the lands of the west bank of the Euphrates, then I too will plunder the lands of the west bank of the Euphrates.'[69] The principle of restitution could also provoke far more serious reactions. The Assyrian king Tikulti-Ninurta (c. 1243–c. 1207) was aware of the risks of war with Hatti when he wrote to Tudhaliya IV insisting that '[n]o one sinned against your land, no one removed a blade of straw or a splinter of wood from the march of your land'.[70] Similarly, Hattušili III, frustrated at the raiding of Hittite territory by the city of Turira but wishing to avoid all-out war with Assyria, wrote to Adad-nirari I seeking confirmation of Assyria's claim to the city before making a military strike against it:

> When Turira plunders that land [i.e., Hittite territory], they keep taking booty to Turira. My subjects who flee also keep going up to Turira. If Turira is yours, smash it! But you shall not claim the possessions of my subjects who are dwelling in the city. If Turira is not yours, write to me, so that I may smash it. The possessions of your troops who are dwelling in the city shall not be claimed.[71]

Responding to a severe incursion by the Kaska, Šuppiluliuma I marched north from Hattuša and

> arrived in the country and found that the Kaskaean enemy who had come inside the land of Hatti had treated the land very badly [...]. The gods helped my father, so that he slew the aforementioned Kaskaean enemy, the tribal troops, wherever he caught him. And what he held, that my father took away from him and gave it back to the Hittites.[72]

On a separate occasion, Šuppiluliuma I set 'a trap for the enemy' who had invaded Hatti. With the help of the gods the king slaughtered his enemies, seized the 'deportees, cattle, sheep and goods which the enemy held', and 'gave them back to the Hittites'.[73] In both accounts we can detect three essential elements of *ius ad bellum* thought: self-defence of the land and people, revenge for injuries, and restitution of property. Based on these three just causes, unrestrained war against the culpable enemy was considered entirely legitimate.

When the 'Deeds of Šuppiluliuma' claimed that the king gave back stolen property to the Hittites, this was more than just a figure of speech. Remarkably,

---

69. 'No. 6a: Treaty between Suppiluliuma I and Shattiwaza of Mittanni', *HDT*, 42, § 1.
70. *LIR*, 56.
71. 'No. 24b: Letter from Hattušili III to Adad-Nirari I of Assyria', *HDT*, 148, § 1. See also *LIR*, 64–65; Bryce, *Kingdom of the Hittites*, 274.
72. Güterbock, 'Deeds of Šuppiluliuma', 67.
73. Ibid., 78.

when the spoils of war were brought back to Hattuša, any property identified as having been seized from Hittite territory in a previous conflict (including, presumably, slaves), was returned to its former owners.[74] Quite how this process of reclamation functioned we do not know, but its existence is highly unusual and indicative of the seriousness with which the Hittites treated legal property ownership.

The ethical and legal legitimacy of restoring stolen movable property was integrated into a broader understanding of territorial self-defence and reclaiming immovable property. Thus it was perfectly justifiable for Hittite lands that had suffered invasion and annexation by a foreign enemy to be militarily reincorporated into the Hittite kingdom:

> Then my father conquered all of the country of Tumanna and rebuilt it and re-established it and made it again part of the Hittite country [. . .] he went into the country of Ištahara. And since the Kaskaean enemy had taken Ištahara, Hittite territory, my father drove the enemy out of it and rebuilt [. . .] and re-established them and made them again part of the Hittite country.[75]

Even defending people could be seen in light of the king defending his subjects who were, in a sense, the property of the state and the gods. This conception of persons as a form of property was literal in the case of the large indentured population living within Hittite territory. Of course, these attitudes in no way deterred Hittite armies from aggressively seeking vast quantities of enemy plunder during their own offensive campaigns. Nor was such action considered in any way inappropriate. War was a legitimate method to defend or restore property, whether movable or immovable; yet war could also be a means legitimately to acquire territory and goods when such property was seized in a just war of vengeance, to which we shall now turn.

VENGEANCE

If self-defence and the restitution of property were the principal just causes to wage war in ancient Hatti, then vengeance followed closely behind in order of importance. In reality, these three ideal types of just cause were interwoven. Vengeance was often sought in response to enemy actions that had inflicted injuries on Hittite territory, subjects, and property. A war of territorial reconquest following an enemy invasion, for example, was conceived as a self-defensive war that sought to restore property and inflict punitive vengeance on the enemy. The three causes were so tightly entwined that the separate threads are frequently difficult to unravel.

74. Korošec, 'Warfare of the Hittites', 162.
75. Güterbock, 'Deeds of Šuppiluliuma', 91–92.

Nevertheless, vengeance could be a cause of war independent of territorial infringements. Vengeance aimed at punishing the violation of treaty oaths seems to have been particularly common. Such violations were not only a political injury and a slight against the Hittite king, but also implied an insult to the gods, for it was the gods who acted as witnesses to oaths and protectors of justice. Such a conception of treaty violation was already well established in the ancient Near East before the time of the Hittites; it was evident in Mesopotamian states such as Mari in the early second millennium and probably dated back to the third millennium.[76] Seeking vengeance against enemies was thus legitimate and even necessary in order to punish crimes against the Hittite gods and state, and to satisfy mundane and divine demands of justice and honour. In the case of international relations, war was the instrument through which this punishment was executed.[77] This is illustrated in the preambles and clauses of a number of Hittite treaties. One such example is a vassal treaty between Arnuwanda I of Hatti and the 'Men of Ismerika' (southern Anatolia, c. 1380), which stipulated typical demands for loyalty to the Hittite monarchy and listed the various transgressions for which the 'oath gods' would take vengeance:

> No one shall do evil to the King, to the Queen, or to the sons of the King. But if someone does do evil to them, these oath gods shall seize him [. . .] and destroy him, together with his household, his fields, his vineyards, his threshing floors, his oxen, and his sheep, and together with his renown, his progeny [etc].[78]

Violations that required the vengeful intercession of the oath gods opened the door for legitimate military action against the perpetrator; this violence was understood as one aspect of the gods' vengeance.

Beyond clearly spelling out the severity of punishment for oath violation, these clauses (and many others like them) express a clear concept of corporate guilt. The perpetrator would be destroyed along with their household and property. This correlates with Hittite customs that held the son responsible for the offences of the father. When writ large on the international arena, if the offender was a state ruler, this justified the destruction of that prince's 'household': his people, land, and property.

A treaty from the reign of Tudhaliya II (c. 1400) illustrates the seriousness with which Hittite rulers treated oath violation. The historical introduction tells us that Isuwa, a Hittite subject state, threw off Hittite overlordship and began 'hostilities against My Majesty', so that 'I, My Majesty, went in battle

---

76. Kang, *Divine War*, 14–15.

77. Ziskind, 'Aspects of International Law', 87, 126. For examples of curses and punishment of oath-breakers in Hittite treaties, see *HDT*, 22, 24, 29, 35, 52, 53, 113.

78. 'No. 1a: Treaty between Arnuwanda I of Hatti and the Men of Ismerika', *HDT*, 14, §§ 3–4.

against them. I overpowered the land of Isuwa, and the Isuwans fled before My Majesty.'[79] But more was to come. The retreating Isuwans fled to Mitanni, Hatti's oldest rival:

> They went down into the land of Hurri [Mitanni]. I, My Majesty, sent to the ruler of Hurri: 'Return my subjects!' But the ruler of Hurri sent back to My Majesty thus: 'No!' The ruler of Hurri did not return my subjects to My Majesty, but dispatched his infantry and his chariotry. In the absence of My Majesty they plundered the land of Isuwa.[80]

The king of Mitanni's refusal to extradite political refugees and subsequent military intervention on behalf of a rebellious vassal were obviously considered hostile acts by Hatti. Tudhaliya II fumed that, in behaving in such a manner, '[t]he ruler of Hurri transgressed the oath'.[81] This must have referred to a pre-existing treaty made between Hatti and Mitanni. As a result, the Hittites believed they had just cause to wage war against both the rebellious Isuwans and the duplicitous Hurrians.

While this treaty provides evidence of oath violation and the vengeance that this could provoke, it also indicates how political leaders sometimes played fast and loose with treaty obligations and the oaths attached to them. Tudhaliya II had sent messengers to Mitanni, pointedly asking, 'If some land were to free itself from you and turn to Hatti, then how would this matter be?' But the Hurrian king's abrupt response was, 'Exactly the same!' In other words, if the situation had been reversed, the Hurrian king would have expected the Hittites to act in a similar manner, seeking their own political advantage at the expense of a rival.[82] While several scholars have made highly convincing cases for the prominent role of treaty obligations in creating a rules-based international system throughout the ancient Near East, the evidence cited above indicates that the international relations of the region could also be dominated by *Realpolitik*. Treaties and oaths appear as expedient, but far from binding, methods of arbitration and settlement.[83]

A contemporary acceptance of this simple political reality is perhaps indicated by the fact that Hittite kings did not always respond to oath violation with the 'nuclear option' of war. Indeed, Richard Beal observes that 'sometimes the Hittites were very patient, willing to overlook treason, oath-breaking, and even overt military action against Hatti in return for future peace and good behaviour'.[84] Nevertheless, the breaking of oaths still constituted one of the

---

79. 'No. 2: Treaty between Tudhaliya II of Hatti and Sunashshura of Kizzuwatna', *HDT*, 18
80. Ibid., 19.
81. Ibid.
82. Ibid.
83. On the rules-based international system of the ancient Near East, see Ziskind, 'Aspects of International Law'; *LIR*; *ILA*.
84. Beal, 'Making, Preserving, and Breaking', 89.

most important just causes for declaring war. In this sense, international treaties may have had only a limited capacity to restrain war, but they made a substantial contribution to how these wars were justified, providing useful evidence of enemy perfidy and guilt.

Hittite kings could seek vengeance through war for both mundane and divine injuries. In a prayer to the sun-goddess of Arinna, Muršili II bemoaned the devastating impact of a plague in Hatti which had resulted in extensive territories being ceded to enemies in the east and south. He highlighted the terrible effects of this territorial degradation on the cultic devotion enjoyed by the Hittite pantheon:

> The protectorates [. . .] are all in conflict, and they do not respect the gods. They have transgressed the oath of the gods, and they wish to despoil the temples of the gods. May this become an additional reason for the gods' vengeance [. . .] those lands which belong to Hatti [. . .] have declared themselves free from the Sun-goddess of Arinna. They discontinued the payment of their tributes and began to attack Hatti. In the past, Hatti, with the help of the Sun-goddess of Arinna, used to maul the surrounding lands like a lion [. . .]. But now, all the surrounding lands have begun to attack Hatti. Let this become a further reason for vengeance for the Sun-goddess of Arinna. Goddess, do not degrade your own name![85]

Appealing to the gods' sense of personal injury and self-interest, Muršili begged for divine aid to defeat his enemies and punish the crimes committed against the gods and their property:

> Some wish to burn down your temples; others wish to take away your rhyta, cups, and objects of silver and gold; others wish to lay waste your fields, your gardens, and your groves; others wish to capture your plowmen, gardeners, and grinding-women. To those enemy lands give severe fever, plague, and famine [. . .]. To Muršili, the king, and to the land of Hatti turn with favour! [. . .] Give them a man's valiant, battle-ready, divine weapon! Put beneath their feet the enemy lands, and may they destroy them.[86]

The bellicose king Šuppiluliuma I repeatedly exacted revenge on the Kaska, the Arzawans, and other enemies of Hatti for their offences against the kingdom and its gods. Such enemies destroyed towns and stole sacred implements: 'silver, gold, bronze utensils and everything'. In revenge, Šuppiluliuma razed

---

85. 'No. 8: Muršili's Hymn and Prayer to Sun-Goddess of Arinna', *HitP*, 52–53.
86. Ibid., 53.

enemy towns, killed scores of enemy troops, and deported entire communities back to Hatti—all, we are told, with the help of the gods.[87]

As part of the legal and moral process of establishing a just war, Hittite kings would lay 'charges' against their enemies—both human and divine—on the eve of a campaign or at the point of entering enemy territory. An example of this custom was the detailed grievance delivered on the northern-eastern frontier against the Kaska and the Kaskaean gods, citing injuries committed by them against the gods of Hatti and its people:

> O gods of the Kaskean country! We have summoned you before this assembly [...] Hear ye the accusation which we bring against you!
> The gods of the Hatti land have done nothing against you, the gods of the Kaskaean country. They have not put you under constraint.
> But ye, the gods of the Kaskean country, began war. Ye drove the gods of the Hatti land out of their realm and took over their realm for yourselves.
> The Kaskean people also began war. From the Hittite ye took away their cities and ye drove them out of their field and fallow and out of their vineyards.
> The gods of the Hatti land and the Hittite people call for bloody vengeance. The vengeance of the Hatti gods and the vengeance of the Hittite people will be wrought on you, the gods of the Kaskaean country and the Kaskaean people.[88]

Vengeance was not necessarily unlimited and a king *could* choose restraint. When Uhha-ziti, king of Arzawa, broke a treaty and declared war against Hatti in the late fourteenth century, King Manapa-Tarhunta of the Seha River Land was also persuaded to take up arms against his Hittite overlords. Muršili II launched a successful counter-offensive and, 'because Uhha-ziti had transgressed the oath in regard to me, the oath gods seized him, and I destroyed him'. But Muršili was moved to mercy when dealing with Manapa-Tarhunta:

> You backed Uhha-ziti, my enemy, and made war on My Majesty [...]. I would have destroyed you likewise. But you fell down at my feet, and you dispatched old men and old women to me. And your messengers fell down at my feet. You sent to me as follows: 'Spare me, my lord. May my lord not destroy me [...].' Then I, My Majesty, had compassion for you, and because of that I acceded to you and made peace with you.[89]

---

87. Güterbock, 'Deeds of Šuppiluliuma', 66, 67, 68, 78, 83, 91, 92, 93.

88. 'Ritual before Battle', *ANET*, 354–55 (emphasis added). See also Beal, 'Making, Preserving, and Breaking', 91–92; Richard H. Beal, 'Hittite Military Rituals', in *Ancient Magic and Ritual Power*, ed. Marvin Meyer and Paul Mirecki (Leiden: Brill, 1995), 63–76 at 68; *LIR*, 104; Altman, 'Tracing the Earliest Recorded Concepts', 138.

89. 'No. 12: Treaty between Muršili II and Manapa-Tarhunta of Land of the Seha River', *HDT*, 83.

The pitiable act of sending elders (including women) and the unconditional submission offered by Manapa-Tarhunta are clearly represented as having persuaded Muršili to be merciful. Whilst vengeance was entirely legitimate in this case, evidently it did not exclude the possibility of restraint being exercised under certain circumstances.

A Paradigmatic Case: Avenging the Murder of a Hittite Prince
The paradigmatic example from ancient Hatti of a war in the cause of vengeance involved a grievous injury done to Šuppiluliuma I's family. It followed from one of the strangest and most unexpected episodes in the political history of the ancient Near East. During Šuppiluliuma I's siege of the strategically important city of Carchemish (c. 1324), the king was approached by an envoy from the Egyptian queen Ankhesenamun, the widow of the recently deceased Pharaoh Tutankhamun. The young pharaoh's death was itself suspicious, and the queen evidently feared for her own safety and position at court. Her solution was to make the king of Hatti the following offer: '[T]hey say that you have many sons. If you would give me one of your sons, he would become my husband.'[90] Diplomatic marriages between the dynasties of the great states were not unusual; what makes this extraordinary is that in promising to make a Hittite prince her husband, the queen was effectively offering the Egyptian throne to Egypt's greatest rival. Of course, this would provide Ankhesenamum with a mighty ally and ensure her personal safety and position. With a Hittite prince installed as pharaoh of Egypt, Hatti would also have become the unrivalled hegemon of the entire Near East.

Šuppiluliuma was justifiably surprised and suspicious in equal measure, exclaiming, 'Such a thing has never happened to me in my whole life!' He stalled for time, asking for more information and assurances from Ankhesenamum. In the meantime, the Hittites successfully captured Carchemish, installed one of the king's sons as a viceroy to rule the city, and returned to Hattuša to spend the winter. Eventually, the exasperated Egyptian queen wrote back to Šuppiluliuma, urgently insisting, 'Only to you I have written [. . .] so give me one of your sons. To me he will be husband. In Egypt he will be king!'[91] Šuppiluliuma remained wary, fearing a trap and that his son would be used as a political hostage. But he was finally persuaded by the Egyptian envoy that the situation was indeed 'our country's shame' and that the queen's offer was genuine. More likely, the king simply calculated that the potential benefits outweighed the risks. So he sent his son Zannanza to Egypt.

The Hittite prince never met his betrothed. Just as Šuppiluliuma had feared, Zannanza's party was ambushed on route to Egypt and the prince was assassinated. Who bore responsibility for this act remains a mystery, but

90. Güterbock, 'Deeds of Šuppiluliuma', 94. For an analysis of the episode, and Ay's role in Zannanza's murder, see Bryce, *Kingdom of the Hittites*, 178–83.
91. Güterbock, 'Deeds of Šuppiluliuma', 96–97.

Ay—a powerful minister during both Akhenaten's and Tutankhamun's reigns, and who was subsequently crowned pharaoh—remains the prime suspect.[92] Regardless of *who* instigated the assassination, Šuppiluliuma's reaction was predictably wrathful and aimed squarely at the Egyptian state as a whole:

> And when my father heard of the slaying of Zannanza, he began to lament for Zannanza, and to the gods [... and] he spoke thus: 'Oh gods! I did no evil, yet the people of Egypt did this to me, and they also attacked the frontier of my country!'[93]

The murder of Zannanza is presented in the Hittite sources as unequivocally evil: an unjust act committed against Hatti without provocation. Šuppiluliuma sought immediate vengeance by launching an invasion of Egyptian territories in Syria-Palestine, resulting in the defeat of the 'infantry and chariotry of Egypt' and the enslavement of thousands of prisoners of war. This was seen, quite simply, as a justifiable act of vengeance in response to an unjust injury.[94] Moreover, even though the Egyptian court protested its innocence, it is probably safe to assume that the Egyptians themselves expected no lesser retaliation.

Tragically for the Hittites, it was the prisoners of war captured in this short campaign of vengeance that carried a plague into Hatti that would go on to ravage the country for several decades. It was this plague that later lead Šuppiluliuma's son, Muršili II, to question the justice of some of his father's wars.

SUPPRESSION OF REBELLION

From the middle of the seventeenth century, Old Kingdom kings such as Hattušili I pursued a policy of military expansion, bringing numerous small principalities and city-states under Hittite control. By the early fourteenth century, Hatti can be accurately described as a true empire, exercising direct rule over lands beyond the traditional boundaries of the land of Hatti, defeating or conquering formerly powerful kingdoms such as Mitanni, Arzawa, Kizzuwatna, and Carchemish, and imposing indirect rule and a tributary system over many more lands beyond these. At its height, Hattuša dominated a territory that included the majority of what is now Turkey, as well as much of northern Syria and the Levant (including Aleppo, Ugarit, and Byblos); even the island of Cyprus fell under its dominion (see Map 2).

---

92. Even if Ay was not personally responsible, the Egyptian elite would surely have opposed such a transfer of power to a foreign prince: Bryce, *Kingdom of the Hittites*, 183.

93. Güterbock, 'Deeds of Šuppiluliuma', 108. See also Muršili II's reference to this incident: 'No. 11: Muršili II's "Second" Plague Prayer to the Storm-God of Hatti', *HitP*, 58.

94. Güterbock, 'Deeds of Šuppiluliuma', 111; 'No. 11: Muršili II's "Second" Plague Prayer to the Storm-God of Hatti', *HitP*, 58.

But success brought its own challenges.[95] As in any imperial state, political discontent, revolt, and rebellion were a constant source of anxiety for Hittite kings. This anxiety is reflected in the surviving vassal treaties, formulaic components of which were oaths of loyalty to the royal family and promises to report any seditious language or rebellious acts to the royal capital. At a more fundamental social level, Hittite society, like all other societies at this time, was composed of free, semi-free, and unfree persons. Hatti's agrarian economy was dependent on slave and corvée labour, much of which was made up of prisoners of war or their descendants. Revolt was an ever-present concern, so the punishment for insurrection was severe. The Hittite laws decreed, 'If a slave rebels against his owner, he shall go into a clay jar.'[96] Whether this refers to a form of torture or, more probably, is a blunt reference to the slave being executed and cremated (cremated ashes were commonly placed in jars) remains unclear, but in either case the punishment is obviously harsh. Another law, forbidding the stealing of weapons and punishing offenders with death, further reveals concerns about access to weapons among the domestic populace.[97]

Given these socio-political realities, it is unsurprising that the suppression of rebellion features as an important just cause for war. Royal propaganda and official documents display 'a remarkable sensitivity to rumors and accusations directed against the throne', and kings 'were always eager to root out any sign of potential treason against the crown'.[98] In many cases, the threat of rebellion must also have touched upon the basic notions of self-defence and restitution of property, as revolts by vassal states (usually supported by Hatti's peer competitors) often resulted in core Hittite lands being attacked and plundered. The seventeenth-century 'Annals of Hattušili I' details one such example. After two years of successful military conquests, Hattušili was faced by a massive insurrection across his kingdom, coupled with an invasion from Mitanni: 'But in my rear the Hurrian enemy entered the land, and all the countries became hostile to me; only the single city Hattuša remained.'[99] Recovering from this catastrophe, Hattušili did not pause to consider whether

---

95. For an informative overview of the organisation of power and the administrative structure of the kingdom and empire, see Klengel, *Geschichte des Hethitischen Reiches*, 320–87.

96. 'Hittite Laws', in *LCMAM*, 234, ¶ 173b. Compare the slightly different translation in *LawH*, 138–39, ¶ 173b.

97. 'If anyone steals a bronze spear in the gate of the palace, he shall be put to death.' *LawH*, 116, ¶ 126.

98. Harry A. Hoffner Jr., 'Propaganda and Political Justification in Hittite Historiography', in *Unity and Diversity: Essays in the History, Literature, and Religion of the Ancient Near East*, ed. Hans Goedicke and J.J.M. Roberts (Baltimore: Johns Hopkins University Press, 1975), 49–62 at 49.

99. 'Annals of Hattušili I', *HST*, 220, § 5; cf. *AoH*, 48.

the revolting cities had legitimate grievances against Hatti; rather, he asserted his divine authority to crush the rebellious vassal states:

> I am the Great King, the Tabarna, beloved of the sun-goddess of Arinna. She placed me on her lap, held me by the hand, and ran before me in battle. Then I went in battle to the city of Nenašša, and when the people of Nenašša saw me coming, they opened up their city. Thereafter I went in battle to the land of Ulma. The people of Ulma came against me twice in battle, and I defeated them both times. I destroyed Ulma and sowed cress on its territory.[100]

Hattušili I understood and presented his war to reassert control over the kingdom as legitimate, evinced by the support of the sun-goddess, who he claimed fought alongside him and delivered a series of unqualified victories. The different treatment meted out to the cities of Nenašša and Ulma is worth noting, however. As Hattušili continued his reconsolidation of power, cities that submitted voluntarily were spared, whilst those that resisted were destroyed.[101]

The suppression of revolt was also an extension of the concept of just vengeance. Given the Hittite practice of creating legally binding treaties, in most cases rebellious vassals would have violated pre-existing treaty oaths. Even if not, rebellion against the king constituted an injury to the king's honour. Punishing rebellion could thus be justified on at least four grounds: self-defence, restitution of property, vengeance for oath violation, and defence of honour. A document dating from the fifteenth century succinctly conveys these elements of political and personal injury. Referred to as the 'Indictment of Mita of Pahhuwa', it details how the ruler of Pahhuwa committed himself and his country to a standard defensive and offensive alliance with Hatti, necessitating an oath of loyalty to the Hittite king and a promise that Hatti's enemies and friends would be Pahhuwa's enemies and friends.[102] But Mita reneged on his treaty obligations, allied himself with one of Hatti's enemies, and offered sanctuary to prisoners of war absconding from Hittite territory:

> But when Mita arrived back in Pahhuwa he transgressed the oaths [...] he committed an offense even against My Majesty and against Hatti [...]. Then he married the daughter of my enemy Usapa [...]. And concerning my civilian captives he said: 'Let them flee from Hatti and come to me!' Then my civilian captives fled and went to Mita.[103]

---

100. 'Annals of Hattušili I', *HST*, 220, § 6; cf. *AoH*, 48.
101. Salliahšuwa and Parmanna submitted and were spared; Sanahhuitta, Appaya, Alha, Zaruna, and Haššuwa remained hostile, and were destroyed: 'Annals of Hattušili I', *HST*, 220-21, §§ 6-10; *AoH*, 48-50.
102. 'No. 27a: Indictment of Mita of Pahhuwa and Treaty with the Elders of Several Anatolian Communities', *HDT*, 161, § 2.
103. Ibid., 161, §§ 3-4.

The edict urges a number of Anatolian vassals still loyal to Hatti to begin hostilities against Pahhuwa immediately, allowing the king to prepare his main campaign of suppression and vengeance. The injustice of Mita's action is repeatedly stated. We are told that 'Mita continued to cause great offense', that the 'man regularly transgressed the oath', and that he was 'an evil person'.[104] At the same time, in the king's communication to the 'men of Pahhuwa', he offers them the opportunity 'to act loyally' by handing over Mita (along with his family and property) and committing to future annual military levies. Again, we see a strong pragmatic streak to Hittite foreign policy, as this would have certainly been a cost-effective solution in terms of Hittite blood and treasure. 'But', the king warned, 'if the men of Pahhuwa do not carry out these words, but act with contempt for my authority and commence hostilities,' then war was inevitable.[105] Indeed, the king's determination to crush rebellion was so fierce that not only did he command his loyal vassals to wage war against Pahhuwa, but he even threatened to destroy any vassal who ignored his command by delaying or refusing to take the field against the rebels:

> [G]o to Pahhuwa and attack Pahhuwa. Continue to attack it until My Majesty's army arrives. You shall bloody your hands immediately with the men of Pahhuwa. I, My Majesty, will go immediately against whoever does not bloody his hands with the men of Pahhuwa, even before I have gone against Pahhuwa. I will kill him immediately. Furthermore, I will likewise go into battle against Pahhuwa.[106]

This bullish response to rebellion and oath-breaking was not unusual during the history of the Hittite kingdom. A treaty from the early thirteenth century provides a long historical preamble detailing events which had occurred a century earlier, during the reigns of Tudhaliya I and Hattušili II. It records that

> [w]hen Tudhaliya, Great King, ascended to the throne of kingship, the king of Aleppo made peace with him. But the king of Aleppo turned around and settled with the king of Hanigalbat [Akkadian for Mitanni]. Then because of this matter he destroyed them—the king of Hanigalbat and the king of Aleppo, together with their lands. And he dismantled the city of Aleppo.[107]

This act of political betrayal was evidently met with the severest military sanction.

---

104. Ibid., 161, § 1; 162, § 7.
105. Ibid., 163, § 9; 164, § 12.
106. Ibid., 164, § 13.
107. 'No. 14: Treaty between Muwattalli II and Talmi-Sharrumma of Aleppo', *HDT*, 94, § 5; cf. Klengel, *Geschichte des Hethitischen Reiches*, 107.

The preamble also informs us that, a generation later, '[t]he king of Aleppo committed an offence against the king of Hanigalbat, but he also committed an offence against Hattušili, King of Hatti'.[108] According to the historical narrative, Aleppo had acted duplicitously by making alliances with both Hatti *and* its enemy, Hanigalbat (Mitanni). Aleppo, caught between the competing interests of two empires, was surely just seeking to preserve itself. Nevertheless, the city-state had been caught in the act and had clearly committed an offence against both kingdoms. It was absolutely standard practice for alliance treaties to stipulate that one state's enemies and friends became the other state's enemies and friends. Aleppo could simply not be an ally of Hatti and Mitanni simultaneously while these two kingdoms were enemies.

The Hittites were obviously more concerned about the offence to their own state, but it is of particular interest that the Hittites recognised that an injury had also been committed against their enemy, Mitanni. Once again, we are provided with evidence that the Hittites were capable of recognising unjust injuries and just causes for war pertaining to kingdoms other than Hatti alone.

Even when less powerful kingdoms *voluntarily* entered into alliances that effectively made them vassals of Hatti, the breaking of those alliances was interpreted as an act of rebellion that constituted an injury and therefore required vengeance and punishment. A late thirteenth-century treaty narrates such a case concerning the kingdom of Amurru. The former king, Aziru, had chosen to throw off his vassalage to Mitanni and instead pledged allegiance to Šuppiluliuma I.[109] However, during the reign Muwattalli II, Amurru abandoned Hatti and allied itself with Egypt:

> But when Muwattalli [. . .] became King, the men of Amurru committed an offense against him, informing him as follows: 'We were voluntary subjects. Now we are no longer your subjects.' And they went over to the King of Egypt. Then My Majesty's uncle Muwattalli and the King of Egypt fought over the men of Amurru. Muwattalli defeated him, destroyed the land of Amurru by force of arms, and subjugated it. And he made Shapili king in the land of Amurru.[110]

The preamble was at pains to articulate the crime of rebellion committed by Amurru and the punishment that this necessitated. Evidently, there is a degree of exaggeration in describing the war of retribution that followed: Amurru was clearly not 'destroyed' (as the text claims), as Shapili was installed as a client king and his successor, Shaushga-muwa (himself a Hittite prince), agreed the

---

108. 'No. 14: Treaty between Muwattalli II and Talmi-Sharrumma of Aleppo', *HDT*, 94, § 6.

109. 'No. 17: Treaty between Tudhaliya IV and Shaushga-muwa of Amurru', *HDT*, 104, § 3.

110. Ibid., *HDT*, 104–5, § 4. For a discussion of the historical introduction to this treaty, see Bryce, *Kingdom of the Hittites*, 240; *LIR*, 50.

present treaty with Tudhaliya IV.[111] Thus it appears that there was an ideological imperative to stress that rebellion resulted in destruction, but grand strategy had obviously encouraged some restraint.

There is also misdirection contained within the historical account. According to the treaty text, Amurru had been a vassal of Mitanni before voluntarily switching allegiance to Hatti. The truth, however, was that Amurru had been a vassal of Egypt at this time, not of Mitanni. But this presented an inconvenient truth, for it potentially legitimised Amurru's return to Egyptian suzerainty during Muwattalli II's reign. For Tudhaliya IV (the creator of this treaty), such an admission of the long-standing historical relationship between Egypt and Amurru might also have justified any future decision by Amurru to align with Egypt against Hatti.[112] (Mitanni had been destroyed by the time of Tudhaliya IV's reign, so there was nothing to fear there.) Thus, in order to serve Hittite interests, the treaty's preamble literally rewrote history.

In diplomatic correspondence to vassals, Hittite kings were willing to spin the truth to better justify their wars. When Šuppiluliuma I tried to cajole Ugarit into joining a Hittite offensive against the lands of Nuhashshi and Mukish in Syria, he justified the invasion by falsely claiming that 'the kings of the land of Nuhashshi and the king of the land of Mukish [. . .] renounced the peace treaty with Hatti and became hostile to the Great King, their lord'. In reality, these lands were under Mitannian, not Hittite, dominion.[113] What is important to the present study, however, is that Hittite kings did not simply present their wars as being declared without reason. The Great Kings felt compelled to justify their warlike actions, regardless of whether the grounds given for those justifications were strictly truthful. This is testament to a normative just war doctrine in force, shaping politico-military ideas, rhetoric and, to an extent, action.

Such examples serve as an important cautionary tale when attempting to utilise the historical information contained within Hittite diplomatic treaties and international correspondence. These documents are often the best or only evidence we have of political relationships and international relations between certain communities at certain points in time. While undoubtedly providing us with uniquely valuable evidence, the treaties and letters themselves are far from objective sources, and are very much a product of their own political context. They afford us a snapshot of a specific political process that was

---

111. See the loyalty clause of the treaty under discussion, which describes how Shaushga-muwa has been installed as king and given the sister of the Great King as a wife: *HDT*, 105, §§ 6–7.

112. *LIR*, 50.

113. 'No. 19: Letter from Suppiluliuma I to Niqmaddu II of Ugarit', *HDT*, 125–26, § 3. See the later treaty between Šuppiluliuma and Niqmaddu, which refers to this conflict but puts a rather different spin on it: 'No. 4: Treaty between Suppiluliuma I and Niqmaddu II of Ugarit', *HDT*, 34–35, § 2. Compare with Šuppiluliuma's explanation of his wars against Mitannian-sponsored revolts in Isuwa: 'No. 6a: Suppiluliuma I and Shattiwaza of Mittanni', *HDT*, 42–44.

stage-managed and intended to convey a narrative that was certainly manipulated and occasionally mythologised. Yet, in fulfilling this role, they represent the dominant norms, assumptions, and ideals that Hittite monarchs and other political elites were attempting to portray as reality. While as historical narratives they must be treated with a healthy dose of scepticism, as imprints of ethics and ideology they are of indispensable value.

The gravity with which Hittite kings treated rebellion within the kingdom and its dependencies can partly be explained by the history of the Hittite monarchy, which is marked by numerous usurpations and regicides. Hittite kings were paranoid about treason because, in many cases, they had won their own crowns through treachery. Those who had come to the throne through inheritance must have been alive to the possibility of deposition. Usurpation was even embedded within Hittite mythology. In 'The Song of Kumarbi', the god Alalu was deposed as 'king of heaven' by the god Anu after just nine years. After another nine years, Anu was dethroned by the war god Kumarbi, who in turn was usurped by the storm-god Teššub.[114] For immortal beings, a reign of nine years seems remarkably brief! It is tempting to see this myth being forged in the political reality of the Old Kingdom, reflecting the turbulence of Hittite dynastic politics. One could speculate that the myth was created to help justify the actions of usurpers—mirroring and justifying their own ambition in that of the gods. After all, for kings who ascended the throne via rebellion, some attempt had to be made to justify their act to the gods and the people. The best way to do this was to condemn the previous king as impious, unjust, and militarily incompetent.

The most sophisticated example of this form of justificatory propaganda was the so-called 'Apology of Hattušili III', who justified his revolt against his nephew Urhi-Teshub as a response to unjust oppression (figure 36). In acting, he claimed to have executed the will of the goddess Ishtar:

> Yet though I revolted from him, I did not do it sinfully, by raising against him in the chariot or rising against him in the house,[115] but I openly declared war on him saying: 'Thou didst pick a quarrel with me—thou art the Great King, while as for me, of the one fortress thou hast left me, of just that one fortress I am king. Up now! Let Ishtar of Samuha and the Weather-god of Nerrick pass judgement on us.' [...] Then I saw great favour from Ishtar. She deserted Urhi-Teshub, and in none other but her own city of Samuha she shut him up like a pig in a sty [...] and all Hattušas returned to me.[116]

Hattušili presented his revolt, as other types of Hittite warfare were presented, as a form of legal trial against his opponent, testified to by his decision to

---

114. 'The Song of Kumarbi', *HitM*, 40–42. This myth shows parallels with the Greek myth of Zeus and his defeat of his father, Kronos.

115. That is, having Urhi-Teshub assassinated.

116. 'Apology of Hattušili III', cited in Gurney, *Hittites*, 176. This civil war as a major cause for the final weakening of the empire: Singer, *Calm before the Storm*, 14.

FIGURE 36. The 'Apology' of Hattušili III (r. c. 1267–c. 1237 BCE): clay tablet. Edouard d'Erasme, CC BY-SA 3.0 licence, via Wikimedia Commons.

declare war openly rather than 'sinfullly' assassinate his nephew. It was only the righteousness of Hattušili's cause, evinced through the divine support of Ishtar, that enabled his victory. Indeed, his 'Apology' stresses that his triumph against Urhi-Teshub was achieved despite an asymmetry in military power, further proving that the gods supported his legal case. Put simply, Hattušili III's 'Apology' was a propaganda text intended to persuade the gods and his people that he had fought and won a just war.

DEFENCE OF ALLIES

The concept of self-defence was clearly well developed in Hittite ethics from an early date and was consistently deployed as a just cause for war from the Old Kingdom onwards. Equally, the protective duties of the king extended to his political vassals. This is particularly apparent from the surviving diplomatic treaties, most of which date from the New Kingdom (e.g., figure 32). The vast majority of the extant diplomatic instruments are essentially defensive and offensive alliances. Hatti committed itself to defend smaller states in return for their recognition of Hatti's suzerainty, their rejection of Hatti's main competitors, and their commitment to provide Hatti with military service and/or tribute. The treaties thus represent a series of symbiotic political relationships, at the heart of which was the desire for survival through securing military advantages in a highly dynamic, competitive, and dangerous geopolitical system.[117] We know from the history of the Hittite kingdom that the threats to the inner lands and the royal capital were very real: Hatti suffered (and recovered from) several serious invasions before the final collapse of the kingdom about 1180. In creating a sphere of dominance around the traditional homeland in central Anatolia, Hittite kings sought to create buffer zones that would ultimately guarantee the security of Hattuša and the lands of Hatti. The defence of allies was thus a form of self-defence. In return, Hittite kings expected their vassals to defend Hittite interests and continue to take responsibility for defending their own territory. Simply off-loading defence costs onto Hattuša was not acceptable: 'if the enemy marches through your land, and you do no fight him, but even say [. . .] "Go attack, and carry off plunder! I don't want to know anything about it."—then you will thereby have transgressed the oath'.[118]

To provide an exhaustive list of the defensive and offensive clauses contained within all the surviving treaties would be tiresome, especially as many of the clauses are formulaic, such that one treaty largely resembles another in this regard. But a few examples serve to illustrate just how important a consideration this was. A treaty created around the turn of the fourteenth century between Tudhaliya II of Hatti and Sunashshura of Kizzuwatna listed the following obligations:

> § If some other land begins war against His Majesty, Sunashshura must inform His Majesty as soon as he hears of it.
> § If some other land begins war against Sunashshura, His Majesty must inform Sunashshura as soon as he hears of it.
> § If any city in the land of His Majesty begins war—as it is His Majesty's enemy, it will likewise be Sunashshura's—they will fight side by side.

---

117. As Korošec observes, '[d]as Wesen der Hethitischen Vassalitat macht das gegenseitige Schutzverhaltnis aus. Daher ist auch der Großkonig verpflichtet, dem Vasallen nach außen und innen hin Schutz zu gewahren.' (The nature of being a Hittite vassal provided for the mutual duty of protection. Hence the great king also pledged to give protection to his vassal, from external and internal (dangers) alike.) Korošec, *Hethitische Staatsverträge*, 89
118. 'No. 10: Treaty between Muršili II of Hatti and Targasnalli of Hapalla', *HDT*, 73, § 12.

[...]

§ And if some city in the land of Sunashshura begins war—as it is Sunashashura's enemy, it will likewise be His Majesty's—they will fight side by side.

[...]

§ If some land begins war against His Majesty, that land is covered by Sunashshura's oath. His Majesty will request military assistance from Sunashshura, and Sunashshura must provide it to him.[119]

These obligations imposed reciprocal duties on the two rulers, focused on military intelligence and direct military aid, and reflected standard treaty norms. But the language used in this particular treaty to describe the relationship between Hatti as an overlord and Kizzuwatna as a dependent is more unusual. Tudhaliya presents himself as a protector of the people of Kizzuwatna, who are characterised as chattel property: 'Now the people of the land of Kizzuwatna are Hittite cattle and have chosen their stable. They freed themselves from the ruler of Hurri and turned to My Majesty.'[120] In breaking the Hurrian domination of Kizzuwatna, Tudhaliya claims to have a acted as a liberator: 'The land of Kizzuwatna rejoiced exceedingly over its liberation [...]. I, My Majesty, have now given the population of the land of Kizzuwatna its freedom.'[121] While it is true that Hittite influence over Kizzuwatna had gradually increased in the period preceding this agreement, eventually wresting the lands from Mitanni, to style Hatti's effective takeover of the territory as a 'liberation' of the people was a bold justificatory move for what was, to all intents and purposes, an example of Hittite expansionism.

Regardless of how the Kizzuwatnans themselves viewed their so-called freedom, the Hittite king was obviously eager to present his conflict against Mitanni and the annexation of Kizzuwatna that followed from it as licit, motivated partly by a desire to liberate and protect a people oppressed by tyranny. This correlates with a legal strategy contained within Hittite vassal treaties, noted by Viktor Korošec, to compel the inferior signatory to be in 'everlasting gratitude' (*ewigen Dankbarkeit*) for the land bestowed upon him by the Great King.[122] Korošec argues that this represents something of a novel approach in the ancient Near East, with the Hittites attempting to foster loyalty through voluntary subordination and gratitude as opposed to the terrifying intimidation favoured by, for example, the Assyrians.[123] On the other

---

119. 'No. 2: Treaty between Tudhaliya II of Hatti and Sunashshura of Kizzuwatna', *HDT*, 20–21, §§ 20–22, 25, 28.

120. Ibid., 19, § 7.

121. Ibid., § 8. Compare with Hattušili I's claim to have 'freed' the slaves of Hahhi: *AoH*, 52.

122. Korošec, *Hethitische Staatsverträge*, 13.

123. Ibid., 33.

hand, if the vassal failed to show proper gratitude, through failing to supply military assistance or tribute, or allying with Hatti's enemies, it still provided Hatti with grounds to justify punitive action.

The formulaic nature of Hittite defensive/offensive treaties was evident when, around fifty years after the Kizzuwatna treaty, Hatti created an alliance with its old enemy Mitanni (now a shadow of its former self):

> The Hittites shall not do evil to the Mitannians; the Mitannians shall not do evil to the Hittites. When the King of Hatti goes to war, the king of the land of Mittanni shall attack any enemy of Hatti. As someone is the enemy of the land of Mitanni, he shall be the enemy of Hatti. The friend of the King of Hatti shall be the friend of the king of the land of Mitanni.[124]

As one can see, the language and objectives of this treaty are almost identical to those of the earlier treaty made with Kizzuwatna. Another roughly contemporaneous treaty, forging an alliance between Hatti and a conglomerate of small states under the rulership of a certain Tette, laid out similar defensive and offensive principles:

> He shall be at peace with my friend and hostile to my enemy [...]. If some other enemy rises up against the King of Hatti, and attacks Hatti, or if someone carries out a revolt against the King of Hatti, and Tette hears of it, then he must come immediately with his infantry and his chariotry to the aid of the Prince [...]. Or if someone oppresses Tette [...] then the King will come to his aid [...] together with infantry and chariotry, and they will defeat that enemy.[125]

Indeed, the historical preamble to this treaty further underlined the defensive obligations of Hittite kings, claiming that Šuppiluliuma I had previously sent 'infantry and chariotry to his [Sharrupshi's] aid' only *after* king Sharrupshi had begged, 'Save me!'[126]

Of course, vassals were expected to act reciprocally and support the Great King if he faced external invasion or internal revolt. King Alaksandu of Wilusa (Troy) had to promise Muwattalli II that he would send 'infantry and chariotry' if the 'Kings who are the equals of My Majesty—the King of Egypt, the King of Babylonia, the King of Hanigalbat, or the King of Assyria—if someone in this group comes in battle, or if domestically someone carries out a revolt against My Majesty'.[127] It is worth noting that the Hittite king was willing

---

124. 'No. 6a: Suppiluliuma I and Shattiwaza of Mittanni', *HDT*, 45, § 8.

125. 'No. 7: Treaty between Suppiluliuma I and Tette of Nuhashshi', *HDT*, 55–56, §§ 4–6. In spite of this treaty, however, Tette later rebelled against Muršili II and was either killed or removed from the throne: *HDT*, 54.

126. Ibid., 55, § 1.

127. 'No. 13: Treaty between Muwattalli II and Alaksandu of Wilusa', *HDT*, 90, § 11.

to accept the existence of rival monarchs who were 'equals of My Majesty'. Hittite diplomatic forms were evidently more realistic in their assessment of international politics than were those of their Egyptian contemporaries, and were reflected in less absolutist expressions of royal ideology. Around fifty years after the Hatti–Wilusa treaty, during Tudhaliya IV's reign, the list of peer rivals had evolved to reflect new political realities, primarily the destruction of Mitanni (Hanigalbat): 'And the Kings who are my equals in rank are the King of Egypt, the King of Babylonia, the King of Assyria, and the King of Ahhiyawa.'[128]

Up until the end of the New Kingdom, defensive and offensive treaties made between Hatti and its vassals adopted almost identical demands, commitments, and language.[129] Even the famous treaty made between Hattušili III and Ramses II of Egypt adopted the same essential structure and commitments.[130] This treaty between two superpowers of the ancient Near East clearly expresses an assumption that defence—whether self-defence or defence of allies—was a legitimate reason to go to war. An attack on a formal ally was equated with an attack on oneself. In light of the extensive oaths taken as part of treaty processes, to go to war for one's allies was not only justified, but was necessary: a consequence of the obligations that rulers had sworn to uphold.

Pragmatism in Hittite Thought

In spite of the central importance of obligations and oaths to the Hittite diplomatic and politico-military system, there is an undeniable streak of pragmatism evident in Hittite political and religious thought.[131] Hittite diplomatic instruments retained a healthy dose of cynicism regarding the likely behaviour of so-called 'allies'. In clauses outlining joint defensive commitments, the

---

128. 'No. 17: Treaty between Tudhaliya IV and Shaushga-muwa of Amurru', *HDT*, 106, § 11.

129. For example: 'No. 8: Treaty between Muršili II and Tuppi-Teshshup of Amurru', *HDT*, 60–61, §§ 7–8; 'No. 9: Treaty between Muršili II and Niqmepa of Ugarit', *HDT*, 65–66, §§ 2–5; 'No. 10: Treaty between Muršili II of Hatti and Targasnalli of Hapalla', *HDT*, 69–70, §§ 1–3; 'No. 11: Treaty between Muršili II and Kupanta-Kurunta of Mira-Kuwaliya', *HDT*, 77–78, §§ 12–19; 'No. 12: Treaty between Muršili II of Hatti and Manapa-Tarhunta of the Land of the Seha River', *HDT*, 84, § 6; 'No. 13: Treaty between Muwattalli II and Alaksandu of Wilusa', *HDT*, 88–90, §§ 5–12; 'No. 16: Treaty between Hattušili III and Benteshina of Amurru', *HDT*, 102–3, §§ 10–13; 'No. 17: Treaty between Tudhaliya IV and Shaushga-muwa of Amurru', *HDT*, 106–7, §§ 11–13.

130. Most treaties made with vassal states and foreign powers were deposited in the archive of the great temple in Hattuša, reflecting the role of the gods as witnesses to the oaths. However, the Hattušili III–Ramses II treaty was deposited in the royal palace, perhaps evidence of its unusually great political importance. See Bittel, *Hattusha*, 15.

131. Hittite prayers evince not only moralistic reflections but are also, according to Singer, 'characterized by a deeply pessimistic concept of life'. *HitP*, 17.

Hittites remained overtly wary of the dangers of betrayal when committing their army to help defend vassals who may have been less than entirely committed to their alliance, or who were simply attempting to offload the costs of war onto their Hittite patrons:

> But if an enemy arises against you, Targasnalli, and you write to me: 'Send me infantry and chariotry,' and I send you infantry and chariotry, but you do no take them out against the enemy, but somehow betray them to the enemy, you will thereby have transgressed the oath. Or if you request infantry and chariotry from My Majesty [. . .] and you do not make war without hesitation on that enemy with your infantry and chariotry, and your land, but you think as follows: 'Let either the enemy defeat them, or let them defeat the enemy,'—you will have transgressed the oath.[132]

The treaty even foresees the possibility that an ally will fail to protect his own land, preferring instead to simply ignore the problem and allow an invading enemy to carry off plunder.[133]

Hittite cynicism was spelled out even more clearly in a treaty made with Huqqana of Hayasa (probably near modern Armenia), whose allegiance had been secured through marriage to a sister of the Great King. The text explains that recording oaths of loyalty in writing was necessary 'because people are treacherous'.[134] The same phrase—'because people are treacherous'—can be read in treaties from the reigns of Muršili II and Muwattalli II, while the ruler of Wilusa was specifically warned that 'the men of Arzawa are treacherous'.[135] In each case, the treaties sought to forestall the negative implications of mankind's corrupt nature by guaranteeing loyalty through the swearing of oaths and invoking the fearful vengeance of the gods if those oaths should be broken.

A late New Kingdom letter, probably sent by Tudhaliya IV to his mother, is striking in its frankness and echoes this acceptance of the shifting loyalties that characterised international relations:

> But if the men of Lalanda [. . .] have defected, well, the people are treacherous. They have often run off before. When my lord [Hattušili III] fell ill in Ankuwa, at that time they were already on the point of defecting. But when they heard that His Majesty would survive, they did not defect

---

132. 'No. 10: Treaty between Muršili II of Hatti and Targasnalli of Hapalla', *HDT*, 72–73, §§ 10–11.

133. 'Or if the enemy marches through your land, and you do not fight him, but even say as follows to him: "Go attack, and carry off plunder! I don't want to know anything about it."—then you will thereby have transgressed the oath.' Ibid., 73, § 12.

134. 'No.3: Treaty between Suppiluliuma I of Hatti and Huqqana of Hayasa', *HDT*, 30, § 19.

135. 'No. 11: Treaty between Muršili II and Kupanta-Kurunta of Mira-Kuwaliya', *HDT*, 79, § 20; 'No. 13: Treaty between Muwattalli II and Alaksandu of Wilusa', *HDT*, 90, § 12.

after all. But now that they have heard of the death of my lord, they have once again defected … If it is only all of Lalanda which falls, it will be for us a matter of overpowering and conquering it. Were the Lower Land to fall, there would be nothing at all for us to do.[136]

Even mankind's relationship with the divine was viewed partially through a pragmatic lens, with a transactional quality characterising the give-and-take between men and gods. In the Hittite myth 'Song of the god LAMMA', the god Teššub is defeated and replaced as king of the heavens by LAMMA. But the other gods begin to complain to the great god Ea that LAMMA's complacent rule has deleteriously affected the lives of men, so that the gods receive fewer offerings of bread and wine.[137] This reflects a theological understanding within Hittite culture that, although immensely powerful, the gods depended on mankind's devotions in order to flourish. Hittite prayers expended considerable effort in presenting what Itamar Singer terms 'beneficial arguments'; such arguments attempted 'to demonstrate to his gods that it is in their best interest to put an end to the misery of the king and his people', thus indicating a belief that the gods were motivated by self-interest more than by mercy.[138]

This *do ut des* process was clearly invoked in an Old Kingdom prayer to the sun-goddess of Arinna, asking her to support the royal couple and grant military success. The king and queen promise the goddess that, if she grants them victory, 'it will come about that in Arinna your sacrificial bread will be plenty, and the totality of the libation wine will be sweet to you'.[139] An early New Kingdom royal prayer adopts a similar approach, lamenting that the Kaska had ravaged cities in the northern territories, including the holy city of Nerik: 'No one in those lands invokes your names any more, O gods. No one presents to you the daily, the monthly, and the annual seasonal rituals. No one celebrates your festivals and ceremonies.'[140] The royal couple suggest that only by aiding the Hittites would the gods ensure their own well-being.[141] During the

---

136. 'No. 114: to the Queen (Puduhepa?) from Tudhaliya (IV?)', *LettH*, 348–49.

137. 'Song of the God LAMMA', *HitM*, 44.

138. *HitP*, 11.

139. 'No. 3: Invocation of Sun-Goddess of Arinna for Protection of Royal Couple', *HitP*, 27, § 11.

140. 'No. 5: Prayer of Arnuwanda and Asmunikal to the Sun-Goddess of Arinna about Ravages of Kaska Tribes', *HitP*, 42, § 20. This form of 'lamentation' bears close resemblance to Sumerian lamentations for the destruction of Ur and later Biblical lamentations over the loss of Jerusalem: *HitP*, 40.

141. 'Only Hatti is a true, pure land for you gods, and only in the land of Hatti do we repeatedly give you pure, great, fine sacrifices. Only in the land of Hatti do we establish respect for you gods. [...] No one had ever shown more reverence to your rites; no one had ever taken care of your divine goods—silver and gold, rhyta, and garments—as we have.' 'No. 5: Prayer of Arnuwanda and Asmunikal to the Sun-Goddess of Arinna about Ravages of Kaska Tribes', *HitP*, 41, §§ 2, 4. Compare the almost identical appeal and phrasing in 'No. 9: Muršili's Hymn and Prayer to Telepinu', *HitP*, 54–55, §§ 5–8.

great plague that devastated Hatti between the reigns of Šuppiluliuma I and Muršili II, a prayer to the sun-goddess reminded her and her fellow deities of the detrimental effects of the deaths of so many Hittites: 'You have allowed a plague into Hatti, and the whole of Hatti is dying. No one prepares for you the offering of bread and the libation any more.'[142] Evidently, the human–divine relationship was infused with self-interest on both sides.

Underlying this pragmatism, and undoubtedly accentuated by the dangers of war and disease in the ancient world, was a marked sense of man's own mortality.[143] It appears that Hittite monarchs did not desire immortality in the way that Egyptian pharaohs obsessed over it, and were poignantly aware that death ultimately gave meaning to life:

> Life is bound up with death and death is bound up with life. A human does not live forever. The days of his life are counted. Even if a human lived forever, and the evil sickness of man were to be present, would it not be a grievance for him?'[144]

Nevertheless, Hittite kings did believe that they would be judged in the afterlife, and would be required to convince the gods that they had amply fulfilled their duties as king and priest. The importance of acting in accordance to ethical principles must have exercised some influence on their actions in all fields of life—personal, political, and martial. In sum, it would be inaccurate to characterise Hittite culture, politics, or war as essentially pragmatic or 'realist'. Pragmatism featured as but one element, combined with a range of other moral/religious commitments and beliefs.

Guilt and Unjust Cause: Towards an Ethics of War 'Proper'

Some degree of self-reflection is essential in any system of ethics. Concerning ethics of war, recognising one's own capacity to commit injuries is crucial for a system of ethics to be *fully* capable of assessing claims to rectifcatory or reciprocal justice. It is my argument that the Hittites were the first culture to develop such a system of military ethics.

From an early point in Hittite history there was an understanding that kings were capable of unjust action. The Old Kingdom 'Proclamation of Telepinu' refers to the reigns of the kings Hantili and Ammuna, both of whom had

---

142. 'No. 8: Muršili's Hymn and Prayer to Sun-Goddess of Arinna', *HitP*, 52, § 6.
143. 'Wir [...] sind nur Menschen. Wenn nun einer nach seinem Geschick geht, so soll der Überlebende dessen Söhne schutzen.' (We are only humans. If one leaves according to his destiny, so should the survivor take care of his sons.) Korošec, *Hethitische Staatsverträge*, 37.
144. 'No. 4a: Prayers to the Sun-God for Appeasing an Angry God', *HitP*, 32, § 5; cf. 'No. 4c: Prayer of a Mortal', *HitP*, 38, § 11.

ascended to the throne via regicide. We are told that because of their 'crime of blood', both kings suffered defeat at the hands of foreign enemies as an expression of the gods' anger. In the case of Ammuna, who had committed parricide, 'the gods started to seek the blood of Zidanta, his father [...] wherever his troops went on campaign, they did not come back successfully.'[145] Indeed, Telepinu's proclamation was intended to reform the kingdom's system of dynastic succession and put an end to the deeply destabilising series of usurpations that had riven the royal court. In this context, Telepinu's association of usurpation with subsequent military defeat was an attempt to delegitimise and discourage the act of usurpation itself. Nevertheless, for the proclamation to have had any effect, Telepinu must have been appealing to widely held beliefs regarding justice, guilt, and the infliction of divine wrath. War, regarded as the divine trial par excellence, was dependent upon the righteousness of the war leader. It was natural, therefore, that a warlord tainted by blood guilt should suffer defeat in war.

A Hittite king who appears to have genuinely grappled with the problem of injustice and guilt was Muršili II. We have already seen that the context for Muršili's 'Plague Prayers' was a period of social and political crisis for the kingdom. In revenge for the assassination of Prince Zannanza (a younger brother of Muršili), Šuppiluliuma I had ordered a retributive campaign against Egyptian territories in Syria-Palestine. Unknown to the Hittites, some of the prisoners of war captured during this campaign carried a plague which spread over the entire Hittite kingdom, devastating its population.[146] Recurring outbreaks of this pestilence ravaged the kingdom for at least twenty years, probably killing Šuppiluliuma I's immediate successor, Arnuwanda II (c. 1322–c. 1321). Muršili II ascended the throne after his elder brother's death and during his twenty-five-year reign (c. 1321–c. 1295) was at a loss how to respond to the plague or how to stem the erosion of Hittite military and political power which resulted from it. In the so-called 'Plague Prayers', Muršili II appealed to the gods, principally the sun-goddess of Arinna and the storm-god Teššub, to alleviate the sufferings of his kingdom (figure 37).[147] As the upholders of divine justice, the gods were responsible for punishing mankind for evil actions. As the chief priest and protector of his people, it was the king's duty to offer penance and compensation for sins committed. Only then could the guilty party be forgiven and the gods' favour be restored.

The problem for the Hittite king was to identify *what* injustice had been committed. The prayers reveal a process of investigation, carried out by the king's priests, augurs, and scribes, into the exact cause or causes of the gods' anger. The prayers thus constitute perhaps the most exhaustive and explicit

---

145. 'Proclamation of Telepinu', *HST*, 230–31, §§ 11–12, 20–21.
146. 'No. 11: Muršili's "Second" Plague Prayer to Storm-God of Hatti', *HitP*, 58, § 5.
147. For the collection of 'Plague Prayers', see *HitP*, 47–69.

FIGURE 37. One of the 'Plague Prayers' of Muršili II (r. c. 1321–c. 1295 BCE): clay tablet. Osama Shukir Muhammed Amin FRCP(Glasg), CC BY-SA 4.0 licence, via Wikimedia Commons.

self-reflection and self-critique undertaken by any ancient ruler. What emerges is a vivid impression that Muršili II, even as Great King, had a very real sense of his own and his predecessors' fallibility. Accompanying this realisation was the acceptance that Hittite kings could, and had, waged unjust wars.

In Muršili's 'First Plague Prayer' he laments that his people have been dying of plague for twenty years. Having made oracular enquiries, he believes that his father Šuppiluliuma I's usurpation of Tudhaliya the Younger may be the cause of the gods' ongoing displeasure; accordingly, Muršili has performed expiation rituals to expunge his father's sin.[148] Unfortunately, this has failed to have the desired effect, for in the 'Second Plague Prayer' a desperate Muršili laments that his people are still dying and so, through further oracular enquires and searching the royal archive, there have been discovered 'two old tablets' which, he believes, provide answers as to why his kingdom is being punished. The first tablet details certain religious rituals which recent kings have neglected.[149] The second tablet is of greater interest to us, as it reveals how, prior to the murder of Prince Zannanza, Šuppiluliuma I may have broken a treaty oath and waged an unjust war against Egypt in the region of Syria-Palestine. As a fascinating and unique reflection from the ancient world on the possibility of one's own side committing sin and engaging in unjust war, it is worth quoting at length:

> § 4. The second tablet dealt with the town of Kurustamma: how the Storm-god of Hatti carried the men of Kurustamma to Egyptian territory and how the Storm-god of Hatti made a treaty between them and the men of Hatti, so that they were put under oath by the Storm-god of Hatti. Since the men of Hatti and the men of Egypt were bound by the oath of the Storm-god of Hatti, and the men of Hatti proceeded to get the upper hand, the men of Hatti thereby suddenly transgressed the oath of the gods. My father sent infantry and chariotry, and they attacked the borderland of Egypt, the land of Amqa. [...] When the men of Egypt became afraid, they came and asked my father outright for his son for kingship. But when my father gave them his son, as they led him off, they murdered him.[150] My father was appalled and he went to Egyptian territory, attacked the Egyptians, and destroyed the Egyptian infantry and chariotry.
>
> § 5. At that time too the Storm-god of Hatti, my lord, by his verdict caused my father to prevail, and he defeated the infantry and the chariotry of Egypt and beat them. But when the prisoners of war who had been captured were led back to Hatti, a plague broke out among the prisoners of war, and they began to die. When the prisoners of war were carried off to Hatti, the prisoners of war brought the plague into Hatti. From that day on people

---

148. 'No. 12: Muršili's "First" Plague Prayer to the Assembly of Gods and Goddesses', *HitP*, 61–62, §§ 2–6. For the same observation, see also 'No. 11: Muršili's "Second" Plague Prayer to Storm-God of Hatti', *HitP*, 57, § 1.

149. 'No. 11: Muršili's "Second" Plague Prayer to Storm-God of Hatti', *HitP*, 58, § 3.

150. This is a reference to the marriage proposal of Queen Ankhesenamun and the murder of Zannanza, as discussed above in this chapter in the subsection, 'A paradigmatic case: avenging the murder of a Hittite prince'.

have been dying in Hatti. When I found the aforementioned tablet dealing with Egypt, I inquired about it to the god through an oracle saying: 'Has this matter been brought about by the Storm-god of Hatti because the men of Egypt and the men of Hatti had been put under oath by the Storm-god of Hatti?

§ 6 [...] whereupon the men of Hatti themselves suddenly transgressed the word (of the oath), did this become the cause for the anger of the Storm-god of Hatti, my lord?

[...]

§ 8. O Storm-god of Hatti, my lord! O gods, my lords! So it happens that people always sin. My father sinned as well and he transgressed the word of the Storm-god of Hatti, my lord. But I did not sin in any way. Nevertheless, it so happens that the father's sin comes upon his son, and so the sin of my father came upon me too. [...] But because I have confessed the sin of my father, may the soul of the Storm-god of Hatti, my lord, and of the gods, my lords, be appeased again. [...]

§ 9 [...] And since Hatti has made restitution though the plague, it has made restitution for it twenty-fold. Indeed, it has already been that much. And yet the soul of the Storm-god of Hatti, my lord, and of all the gods, my lords, is not at all appeased. Or if you want to require from me some additional restitution, specify it to me in a dream, and I shall give it to you.[151]

It was natural to draw a connection between the prisoners and the cause of divine anger. As physical embodiments of Šuppiluliuma's sin, the prisoners became the instruments of divine vengeance.[152] In the 'Fifth' prayer, Muršili insists that he has not tampered with the tablet recording the historical treaty with Egypt, or invaded the border territories, and generally proclaims his innocence:

To this tablet I did not add any word, nor did I remove any. [...] I do not know whether any of those who were kings before me added any word to it or removed any. I do not know anything, and I have not heard a word of it since. I did not concern myself with those borders which were set for us by the Storm-god [...]. I did not desire from him [pharaoh] anything. Neither did I take anything from his borderland.[153]

---

151. 'No. 11: Muršili's "Second" Plague Prayer to Storm-God of Hatti', *HitP*, 58–60, §§ 4–9.

152. Also recalled in Muršili's 'fourth' prayer: 'When my father went to Egyptian territory, since that day of Egypt, death has persisted in Hatti'. No. 13: Muršili's "Fourth" Plague Prayer to the Assembly of Gods (arranged by localities)', *HitP*, 65, § 5.

153. 'No. 14: Muršili's "Fifth" Plague Prayer to the Assembly of Gods', *HitP*, 67, §§ 8–9.

While Muršili clearly accepted that he was responsible for making good the sins of his father, he was at pains to show that he had not compounded his father's transgressions.[154] Note, however, that compensation was not offered to the Egyptians; rather, restitution was offered to the gods alone.

It seems likely that only the king and a very small circle around him ever read or heard these prayers. We should not assume that royal confessions of fallibility and dynastic wrongdoing were openly publicised. There would have been little theological advantage in disseminating the prayers—as chief priest the king already had the most intimate link with the divine—and it would only have risked tarnishing the royal image in the public domain and diminishing the king's authority.

As has become increasingly obvious from archaeological discoveries, the 'Plague Prayers' confirm that the Hittites kept remarkably thorough records of their diplomatic history, enabling Muršili II's scribes to dig through the royal archives in order to find records of historical treaty obligations. While we are undoubtedly fortunate in possessing a wealth of evidence from Hatti, we are also left wondering just how much has been lost to the ravages of time. If the small portion that survives today tells a story of a thoughtful culture which developed a sophisticated ethics, how deep and more complex still must this culture in fact have been?

The capacity of a Hittite king to err was further intimated in a letter sent by Hattušili III to the king of Ahhiyawa, in which he refers to previous hostility between the two kings over the kingdom of Wilusa:

> But my brother once wrote to me as follows:[155] '[. . .] You have acted aggressively towards me.' But at that time, my brother, I was young; if at that time I wrote anything insulting, it was not done deliberately. We were at enmity [. . .]. Over that matter concerning Wiluša we were hostile, because we have made peace, then what more is there? If one partner confesses his error/sin to the other, then because he confesses his error/sin to the partner, he will not reject him. Because therefore I have confessed my error/sin to my brother, let there be no more hostility me and my brother.[156]

---

154. Singer observes, 'A total denial of guilt is impossible in a divine court. Having said that, the possibilities of exculpation, self-justification, even protestation against unfair punishment, are remarkably manifold in Hittite prayers [. . .]. The discovered sin is regarded as a collective burden on the entire Hittite society.' *HitP*, 10. Cf. 'No. 4a: Prayer of King Kantuzzili', *HitP*, 32, § 6.

155. The term 'brother' in this diplomatic context was an honorific implying equal status between 'Great Kings'; it did not imply a familial relationship. On the ideology of brotherhood between ancient Near Eastern kings, see *LIR*, 135–38.

156. 'No. 101: from King Hattušili III to the King of Ahhiyawa ("Tawagalawa Letter")', *LettH*, 311–12.

In effect, Hattušili admitted culpability for the previous hostility between the two kingdoms. This letter was written at a time of relative political weakness, perhaps explaining Hattušili III's willingness to admit fault in order to secure better relations with Ahhiyawa. But regardless of geopolitics, that a Great King of Hatti was prepared to 'confess his error' in international conflicts with rival states is really quite astonishing.

The identification of Hantili and Ammuna's bloodguilt, Šuppiluliuma's violation of a treaty and the illegal war which followed, and Hattušili III's admission of error in conflict against Ahhiyawa all point to the fact that the Hittites recognised that justice and *injustice* in war existed independently of the kingdom of Hatti. The possession of justice in war was not the monopoly of Hatti, and its kings (albeit only occasionally) countenanced the possibility that rival states could suffer injustice at the hands of the Hittites. In sum, this was the first genuinely *international* conception of just war.

Self-Aggrandisement as a Motive for War

The self-aggrandisement of the Hittite kingdom was considered a legitimate reason to wage war against Hatti's neighbours and competitors. Connected to this was the importance of plunder in Hittite warfare, which prompted Korošec to characterise Hittite warfare as *Raubkrieg* (war for plunder).[157] The 'Proclamation of Telepinu' (late sixteenth century), one of the earliest testaments of Hittite royal history, extolled the aggrandisement of the early Hittite state under King Labarna:

> Once, Labarna was Great King. [. . .] The country was small but wherever he went on campaign, he held the enemy subdued by force. He destroyed the lands one by one, he made the lands powerless, and he made them the borders of the sea.[158]

Thus the 'Proclamation' openly boasts that Labarna's conquests were both expansionist and destructive. Moreover, as the narrative continues to describe the achievements of successive kings after Labarna, the territorial expansion of the kingdom and the destruction inflicted upon enemies is formulaically restated:

> Afterwards, Hattušili was king. [. . .] Wherever he went on campaign, he too held the enemy lands subdued by force. He destroyed the lands one by one, he made the lands powerless, and he made them the borders of the sea. [. . .] When Muršili was king in Hattusa [. . . he] held the enemy lands subdued by force. He destroyed the lands one by one,

---

157. 'Der Krieg gilt als Raubkrieg.' Korošec, *Hethitische Staatsverträge*, 62. This will be discussed further in ch. 7 below.

158. 'The Proclamation of Telepinu', *HST*, 229–30, §§ 1–3.

he made the lands powerless, and he made them the borders of the sea. He went to the city of Halpa. He destroyed Halpa and brought Halpa's deportees and its spoils to Hattusa. Later he went to Babylon, and destroyed Babylon and also fought the Hurrian troops. He kept the deportees and spoils of Babylon in Hatti-land.[159]

There was no attempt here to justify these wars in terms of self-defence or retributive justice; according to the text, the lands were attacked for no reason other than that they were 'enemy lands'. The destruction, despoilment, and subjugation of enemies are presented as victories, intrinsically positive and glorious. Indeed, the violent expansion and enrichment of the kingdom are taken as evidence of a 'golden age' in Hatti's history.[160]

It is possible that territorial aggrandisement was motivated partly by a desire to enhance security: to ensure that Hatti was not swallowed up by a larger rival, perhaps. The 'Ten-Year Annals of Muršili II' explain how, after succeeding to the throne as a young man, the king was forced to appeal to the sun-goddess of Arinna to help him conquer his neighbours in order to prove his strength ('enemy lands have called me a child, they have belittled me') and avoid his own territory being dismantled ('they have begun to try to take your borderlands').[161] Aggrandisement as a means to promote security is also indicated in the policy of appointing Hittite princes to govern newly annexed territory, creating a more permanent political sphere of influence which promoted the security of the kingdom's borderlands, and especially the interior. Notwithstanding the potential security advantages brought about by imperial expansion, enrichment and personal prestige were clearly powerful motivators of Hittite war. Kings made sure that their written records emphasised the wealth they brought back to Hattuša in the forms of war spoils, and through this sought to enhance their own reputation.

A permissive attitude to waging war for the sake of riches and reputation, and without any just cause (in terms of a specific grievance), is suggested in the Old Kingdom 'Political Testament of Hattušili I'. In designating his heir (Muršili I), Hattušili advised the Panku (royal council): 'When it is the third year of his reign, let him go on campaign. [...] Raise him to be your valiant king.'[162] One interpretation of this advice is that Hattušili simply assumed

---

159. Ibid., 230, §§ 5–9.

160. In Hoffner's words, the 'crowning achievement of the Old Kingdom rulers in Telepinu's eyes was the sack of Aleppo and Babylon [...]. These twin military achievements and the rich harvest of booty which they yielded form the climax of that golden age.' Hoffner, 'Propaganda and Political Justification', 52; cf. Klengel, *Geschichte des Hethitischen Reiches*, 53, 58.

161. 'Ten Year Annals of Muršili II', *HST*, 254ff, §§ 6ff. See also Hoffner, 'Propaganda and Political Justification', 50.

162. 'No. 106: The Bilingual Testament of Hattušili I', *HST*, 225, § 8.

that threats and injuries to the kingdom were inevitable, and would of course require the attention of his successor.[163] However, we might also interpret this advice as revealing a concept of war as something prescribed: an activity that is simply necessary to establish a young king's reputation, not as something requiring a specific cause or as a response to a specific injury. Of course, these alternative interpretations are not mutually exclusive. Hittite kings could well have viewed defensive or retributive war as an inevitable annual activity, as well as seeing it as the best way to consolidate royal prestige.

This concept of war obviously had staying power. In the New Kingdom, Hattušili III sent a letter to the new king of Babylon, Kadashman-Enlil II, advising him to go out and wage war without any specific pretext:

> They have said that my brother[164] is a king whose weapons have been stowed and who just sits around [...]. Do not keep sitting around, my brother, but go against an enemy land and defeat the enemy! Against which land should my brother go out? Go against a land over which you enjoy three- or fourfold numerical superiority.[165]

Almost identical advice was given by Tudhaliya IV to the Assyrian court and its young new king Tukulti-Ninurta I: 'Because his father died, and he has just seated himself upon the throne of his father, the campaign on which he goes for the first time should be one on which he enjoys three- or fourfold numerical superiority.'[166] Both letters display the customary understanding of the king as a war leader, whose authority largely rests upon his ability to prove his success in war. Not only did this establish the king's manly qualities, it also provided proof that he enjoyed the favour of the gods. Above all, it was essential that the king should be victorious. The advice to wage war against a weaker foe, over whom 'you enjoy three- or fourfold numerical superiority', emphasises the importance of winning, as well as providing more evidence of the pragmatism of Hittite politico-military thought. The urgent political need to establish a king's domestic authority via victory in war could seemingly override the importance of an identifiable just cause.

Yet we should be cautious before dismissing Hittite ideas of just cause or intention as meaningless in the cut-and-thrust of mundane international relations. The advice cited above could equally be interpreted as evidence of prudential thinking within Hittite military thought: to the effect, that is, that no war should be undertaken without a high probability of success. This

---

163. Korošec, 'Warfare of the Hittites', 159.

164. On the use of the term 'brother' here, see n. 155 above.

165. 'No. 23: Letter from Hattušili III to Kadashman-Enlil II of Babylon', *HDT*, 143, § 14. Similar advice is given by Tudhaliya IV to the Assyrians: see 'No. 24c: Letter of Tudhaliya IV to an Assyrian Nobleman', *HDT*, 150, § 2.

166. 'No. 105: Draft from King Tudhaliya IV to an Assyrian Nobleman Bāba-ah-iddina', *LettH*, 325.

condition is a hallmark of modern just war doctrine.[167] Moreover, since at least the time of Sargon of Akkad (c. 2300), conquest was understood throughout the ancient Near East to bestow a legal right of ownership and was religiously sanctioned by theologies that taught that victory in war was a gift of the gods. Consequently, successful aggrandisement was proof of a ruler's and a people's virtue, which in turn legitimised their military actions. An unrighteous people would simply not enjoy the fruits of conquest.

In the final analysis, as long as it did not violate any pre-existing treaty obligations, conquest (and its concomitant benefits) was understood as a legitimate reason to wage war. If this sounds like a 'code for conquerors', much in the vein of Cicero's later justifications of Roman conquests,[168] it is because that is exactly what it is. This serves to highlight that, from the very origins of just war thought, much of it was primarily designed to permit war for the benefit of the community or, more accurately, of the elite that dominated the community. The Hittite development of what we would now term *ius ad bellum* criteria was self-reflective and highly original, but at its heart it was more permissive than restrictive. It created an ethical framework in which the Hittites could interpret their military actions as legitimate, even righteous, when held against theological demands of right and wrong action. Upholding religious rituals, protecting the property of the gods, and maintaining sworn oaths were central to these theological demands. This framework went hand in hand with jurisprudential norms that demanded retributive and rectificatory justice for injuries against persons and property. As a form of legal process, where the arguments for and against the opposing sides were thrashed out in the court of the gods, the outcome of any particular conflict was decided before it even began: whoever was judged righteous by the gods would be victorious. War was the physical process through which divine judgements were made manifest. To win in war required moral rectitude or a legitimate complaint (and ideally both); victory in war was taken as evidence of the possession of one or the other of these attributes.[169]

For centuries in the West, the doctrine of 'might equals right' has been counterposed to that of 'right equals might'. The two maxims are seen as mutually exclusive. But in the Hittite ethics of war, these maxims were not in conflict; they were complementary. To be righteous bestowed military might, and to be mighty was evidence of righteousness. It was because of this that Hittite kings could not ignore the ethical dimensions of their conflicts.

---

167. For an overview and analysis, see Frances V. Harbour, 'Reasonable Probability of Success as a Moral Criterion in the Western Just War Tradition', *Journal of Military Ethics* 10 (3) (2011): 230–41.

168. Cicero, *On Duties*, bk 1, §§ 35, 38; bk 2, §§ 26–27; bk 3, § 46.

169. On occasion the gods could delay punishment and bestow victory on the unjust, as indicated in Muršili II's 'Plague Prayers' when Šuppiluliuma I's 'unjust' victories against Egypt were later punished by plague.

CHAPTER SEVEN

Hatti: *Ius in bello*

CONCEPTS AND PRACTICES

WE HAVE SEEN in the previous chapter how the Hittites developed *ius ad bellum* thought which conceptualised war in ethical and legal terms. But did concerns for justice affect the actual waging of Hittite warfare? What restraints or customary norms, if any, did they place upon themselves when fighting, and what restraints, if any, did they expect from their enemies? Were certain persons regarded as immune or were certain places considered sacrosanct? Was there an understanding that opposing parties should 'fight fairly', or was the realm of war a realm where normal codes of faith and honour were ignored or simply believed to be irrelevant? In short, was there anything resembling a Hittite *ius in bello* tradition?

Declarations of War

As was demonstrated in the previous chapter, the Hittites developed a highly juridical understanding of war and managed their international relationships through the use of diplomatic instruments. War was frequently the result of one party violating a specific treaty that had been intended to maintain peaceful relations. The transition from peace to war was therefore not only a physical shift in relations, but a conceptual and legal shift that required a specific declaration. Consequently, Hittites usually began their military conflicts with some formal declaration of war.

Letters demanding restitution for specific grievances were dispatched to the opposing party; if these were ignored or refused, a further letter was sent accusing the enemy of unwarranted aggression and referring the dispute to the divine court. This meant it would be settled by war. For example, Muršili II wrote to the king of Azzi several times demanding redress before mobilising his army: 'But you have begun a dispute with My Majesty, and you have come and invaded the land of Dankuwa and depopulated it. So the gods shall stand on my side, and shall decide the case in my favour.'[1]

In its most basic sense, the declaration of war was an open challenge to battle, as an Old Hittite text highlights: 'I came against you: come out! If you do not come, I will subdue you like a bear, and you will die suffocated.'[2] When Šuppiluliuma I went to war against Arzawa, he wrote to its king, 'Come, let us fight!'[3] A similar challenge was issued to the king of Mitanni: 'to thee I wrote thus: "Come! Let us fight!"'

Of course, such invitations were not always accepted. The king of Arzawa 'did not [. . .] come to a battle' against Šuppiluliuma I, nor did the king of Mitanni, who 'stayed in the town of Wašukanni, he did not answer and did not come to a battle. So my father went there after him.'[4] Muršili II issued similar declarations and challenges of war when he succeeded to the throne:

> I sent a messenger to Uhhaziti and I wrote to him: 'My servants who have gone over to you that I requested back from you, you have not given them back to me. You have been calling me a child and you have been belittling me. Now, come! We will battle! May the storm-god, my lord, judge our case.'[5]

A late example, from the reign of Tudhaliya IV, has also been recovered from a text discovered at Ugarit. This describes the Hittite king declaring war in defence of one of his allies; however, in an ongoing diplomatic and military process, it appears that Tudhaliya simultaneously despatched further envoys carrying tablets proposing both war and peace, and that diplomatic manoeuvrings between the two sides continued even amidst the manoeuvrings of war.[6]

Magic, Ritual, and War

Hittite warfare was a highly ritualised activity. Prior to the launching of any Hittite campaign, cultic requirements demanded that commanders and troops undergo purification rituals, while kings made oracular enquiries to determine whether the gods deemed the war just, as well as the wisdom of

---

1. 'Und du hast mit der Sonne Streit begonnen, und bist gekommen und hast das Land Dankuwa überfallen und es entvölkert. Und die Götter sollen auf meine Seite treten und den Prozeß zu meinen Gunsten entscheiden.' 'Ten-Year Annals of Muršili II' (7th regnal year), Götze, *Annalen des Mūršiliš*, 99.

2. Cited *LIR*, 110; cf. *ERCIL*, 52.

3. Güterbock, 'Deeds of Šuppiluliuma', 81.

4. Ibid., 84–85.

5. 'Ten Year Annals of Muršili II', *HST*, 255, § 16. See also *LIR*, 110–12; Korošec, 'Warfare of the Hittites', 163.

6. Sylvie Lackenbacher, 'Nouveaux documents d'Ugarit: I—une lettre royale', *Revue d'assyriologie et d'archéologie orientale* 76 (2) (1982): 141–56, text at 145–49.

specific military operations.⁷ Soldiers underwent a series of rituals designed to instil loyalty, including a curse that 'whoever breaks these oaths and does evil to the king [...] let those oath-gods change him from a man into a woman'. Even chariot horses were purified prior to a campaign in order to remove 'evils' from them, whilst commanders, horses, and weapons could be anointed to impart magical power.⁸

A series of letters, dating from around the reign of Arnuwanda I (c. 1390–c. 1370), reveals that augury played a central role in Hittite military decision-making. In one letter, the king instructs a commander, 'Be very much on your guard toward that enemy, while I am about to make oracular inquiries (whether and how to proceed against him).'⁹ A second letter, about whether the king should attack the city of Takkašta, highlights the lengths to which augurs were willing to go in order to obtain accurate oracles:

> Regarding the fact that we were making oracular observations (of birds) in the towns of Šipišaši, Pišatenitišša, and the land of Malazziya: no bird was actually defeating us, but the birds were *refusing to give us an answer*. Since you, Your Majesty, my lord, were in Kašaša, we situated ourselves in Panāta. But when you, Your Majesty, my lord, marched, since the bird *refused to give* us *an answer*, we drove back to Kašaša, and the birds began *refusing to give* us *an answer* in Kašaša as well. Then we came back to Tapikka and from the base of Tapikka have now carried out the auguries! So let Your Majesty, my lord, be informed! We thoroughly investigated by augury the matter of Your Majesty's planned attack on the town of Takkašta, and we obtained an answer. Regarding the campaign we said as follows: 'His Majesty will successfully attack Takkašta and reap its crops as well.'¹⁰

Prior to any campaign, both the king and the army had to be ritually clean.¹¹ Disease within the army was a major concern and, as in most premodern societies, disease likely killed more soldiers than combat. Accordingly, six different Hittite rituals have survived that seek to expunge disease from the

---

7. Beal, 'Making, Preserving, and Breaking', 91–92; *LIR*, 102; Kang, *Divine War*, 56–63. On the transmission of ritual texts throughout the kingdom's history, see Hannah Marcuson and Theo van den Hout, 'Memorization and Hittite Ritual: New Perspectives on the Transmission of Hittite Ritual Texts', *Journal of Ancient Near Eastern Religions* 15 (2015): 143–68.

8. Beal, 'Hittite Military Rituals', 63–67; Beal, 'Making, Preserving, and Breaking', 91; Goetze, 'Warfare in Asia Minor', 126–29. For the poetic elements of these 'Soldier's Oaths', see Mark Weeden, 'Poetry and War among the Hittites', in *Warfare and Poetry in the Middle East*, ed. Hugh Kennedy (London: I. B. Tauris, 2013), 73–97 at 81–82.

9. 'No. 26: from the King to Pulli', *LettH*, 133.

10. 'No. 50: to the King from Šarla-LAMMA', *LettH*, 180.

11. Demands for ritual purity within Israelite armies, including Uriah the Hittite, are also evident in the Tanakh: Deuteronomy 23:10–15; Joshua 3:5; 2 Samuel 11:10–13.

army or to transfer it to the enemy, mostly via the 'scapegoating' or sacrifice of different animals and people.[12] Ritual cleansing was especially important following a military defeat, which demanded that a 'sin' (the cause of the defeat) be identified, the relevant god appeased, and the army lustrated. These rituals of purification for the army involved animal sacrifices and could even call for the killing of humans. One ritual designed to rid the army of the impurity of defeat involved constructing a gate of hawthorn and cutting in half a human prisoner, a goat, a puppy, and a piglet. The parts of the sacrificial victims were placed on either side of the gate and the troops then marched through this magical doorway. After washing themselves with water from a river, the troops were considered purified.[13]

Despite these gory rituals, the Hittites actually took a very dim view of sorcery when used in the domestic sphere. The Hittite law code shows that image magic and other forms of sorcery were outlawed, with cases being referred directly to the king's court—proof of how seriously it was treated.[14] Nevertheless, image magic was utilised against the state's enemies, with one ritual involving the inscribing of the enemy leader's name on a piece of cedar wood and that of the Hittite leader on a piece of clay. Both objects were then burned in a fire, destroying the wood but hardening the clay. Hittite warfare was understood to be a form of judicial trial or ordeal, and Beal suggests that this ritual symbolised a literal 'trial by fire' ordeal.[15] Asking the gods to curse one's enemies was also considered perfectly acceptable, as attested by several such requests in Muršili II's 'Plague Prayers'. In one prayer, the king asks the gods to '[t]urn the plague, the hostility, the famine, and the severe fever towards Mitanni and Arzawa [. . .]. To those enemy lands give severe fever, plague, and famine.'[16] Hattušili III possibly alludes to something similar in an oracular consultation with the gods, claiming that they have approved 'making the Kaskaen city ill so that they may be defeated'[17]—although whether this is a

---

12. Beal, 'Hittite Military Rituals', 69–76.

13. Goetze, 'Warfare in Asia Minor', 128–29; Gurney, *Hittites*, 151; Beal, 'Hittite Military Rituals', 73–75. For a detailed reconstuction and analysis of Hittite royal rituals from surviving texts, see Hans Martin Kümmel, *Ersatzrituale für den hethitischen König* (Wiesbaden: Harrassowitz, 1967).

14. 'If anyone forms clay for an image (for magical purposes), it is sorcery and a case for the king's court.' *LawH*, 107, ¶ 111. See also Good, 'Capital Punishment', 955–56.

15. Beal, 'Hittite Military Rituals', 67; Beal, 'Making, Preserving, and Breaking', 91.

16. 'No. 8: Mursili's Hymn and Prayer to the Sun-Goddess of Arinna', *HitP*, 52–53, §§ 7, 11. See also 'No. 10: Mursili's "Third" Plague Prayer to the Sun-Goddess of Arinna', *HitP*, 57, § 3; 'No. 12: Mursili's "First" Plague Prayer to the Assembly of Gods and Goddesses', *HitP*, 63–64, § 9. On curse formulae in Hittite treaties, see *ILA*, 144.

17. Cited in Sylvia Hutter-Braunsar, 'Die Terminologie der Zerstörung eroberten Acker- und Siedlungslandes in hethitischen Königsinschriften', in *Der orientalische Mensch und seine Beziehungen zur Umwelt*, ed. Bernhard Scholz (Graz: Grazer Morgenländische Studien, 1989), 201–18 at 214.

reference to a curse imposed by the gods, or literally to some form of biological warfare being utilised by Hattušili III, is unclear.

Tactics of War

BATTLE TACTICS

There is no evidence whatsoever of weapons restrictions in Hittite warfare, nor of any pejorative associations with particular weapon types. In terms of tactics, given that Hittite armies consisted of a core force of chariotry, it is unsurprising that commanders often sought set-piece confrontations in which they could deploy their chariot forces to the best effect. The chariot, though a highly effective mobile platform to deliver shock troops to battle, was limited as to the terrain it could cover. To deploy their chariotry, Hittite commanders probably sought prearranged battles on favourable sites. As in the case of the Trojan war, such a battlefield could often be found outside the walls of a city. Hattušili I says that the 'people of Haššuwa came against me in battle [. . . and] I defeated them'. At the city of Hahha, Hattušili 'gave battle three times in the city gate'.[18] When Šuppiluliuma I 'arrived at the town of Tuwanuwa, he stopped below Tuwanuwa and engaged in fighting Tuwanuwa'. The king engaged in a similar set-piece battle when 'Karanni, king of Hayaša, came to meet him in battle below the town of Kummaha'.[19] Even when fighting the tribal Kaska, Šuppiluliuma I preferred to fight what appear to have been standardised battles.[20]

NIGHT ATTACKS AND AMBUSH

Hittite sources frequently accuse enemies such as the Kaska of resorting to dishonourable tactics such as night attacks, in contrast to seeking set-piece daytime battles.[21] The Kaska could even take advantage of disease within the Hittite army to time the launch of their attacks:

---

18. 'Annals of Hattušili I', *HST*, 220–21 §§ 10, 16.
19. Güterbock, 'Deeds of Šuppiluliuma', 76, 66.
20. '[T]he enemy came with his full force [. . .]. But when it became light and the sun rose, he went to a battle and fought [. . .] And the gods helped my father [. . .] so that the enemy troops died in multitude.' Güterbock, 'Deeds of Šuppiluliuma', 117–18. Note that the god Zubaba—a deity associated with Carchemish—is mentioned in this sequence for the first time as a divine presence helping the Hittite army. During Šuppiluliuma's sack of Carchemish, Zubaba's sanctuaries were specifically spared and respected, and he is now integrated as a god of the Hittite pantheon, lending his support to the Hittites. Compare the almost identical battle sequence of Muršili II against the city of Sapidduwa, cited in Gurney, *Hittites*, 109.
21. For example, Güterbock, 'Deeds of Šuppiluliuma', 92. Note, however, that even when Hittite armies repulsed and defeated night attacks, they were still pragmatic enough to use these victories as a way to force non-violent submissions from other hostile territories and cities: see ibid.

But when the Gašgaeans saw that there was a plague in the army, they seized the population who had again gone into their towns. And some they slew, some they seized. Then the enemy came by night and split up: they went for battle to all the fortified camps which the lords were holding.[22]

Other enemies also utilised night attacks. A letter from a regional Hittite commander based in Syria gives us a first-hand insight into the border struggles and military practices of the Hittite empire and New Kingdom Egypt. The Hittite commander had spent the last five months defending southern Amurru (between Mount Lebanon and the Mediterranean coast) against Egyptian incursions, sustaining heavy losses from enemy night attacks and inclement winter weather:

> My Lord, what is my outlet from here? Now for five months the cold has been gnawing me, my chariots are broken, my horses are dead, and my troops are lost! *My men were attacked over and over again in the middle of the night*, and a battle was waged between them. My men drove them out, and heaped up their equipment and their property. It was within the fortress itself that they were fighting.[23]

Apparently the Egyptian troops—or auxiliary troops operating under the aegis of Egyptian authority—had no qualms about taking advantage of the cover of night to launch their raids. But the Hittite commander is deliberate in his reference to this specific tactic, using it to stress both the pressure on his troops and their enduring fortitude.

In letters sent from the royal capital to regional commanders, the king specifically advised his commanders to be wary of ambushes (*ši-na-ha*) when operating in enemy territory to the north: 'Since Kapapahšuwa is well protected, so that the capture of Kapapahšuwa is not likely to succeed for me, they will keep the territory enclosed on this side of it, and lie in ambush against you [. . .]. So do not do anything rash!'[24] In another letter we learn of a 'cowardly' ambush on a Hittite chariot detachment, resulting in the death of the 'Gold Chariot-Warrior', one of the highest military officers in the kingdom:

> Concerning what you wrote about the enemy, how the enemy set a trap for thirty teams of chariotry from/at Panāta, and that the Gold Chariot-Warrior sought to make a circuit of the *perimeter*, but the enemy killed him from behind—I have heard it all.[25]

---

22. Ibid., 90–91.

23. *LettGK*, 182 (emphasis added). For further examples of night attacks by Hittite enemies, see Beal, 'Organization of the Hittite Military', 30–31.

24. 'No. 22: from the King to Hulla, Kaššu, and Zilapiya', *LettH*, 124–25.

25. 'No. 31: from King to Himmuili', *LettH*, 142. Hoffner believes that we should read this letter as implying that the Gold Chariot-Warrior was killed literally *from behind*, i.e., in an ambush: ibid., 144. On the office of the Gold Chariot-Warrior, see Beal, *Organisation of the Hittite Military*, 173–78; Franca Pechioli Daddi, 'Le cariche d'oro', in *Hittite Studies*

The tenor of the letter—the fact that the king highlights the ambush and the killing of the Gold Chariot-Warrior *from behind*—suggests a caustic assessment of both acts that goes beyond the simple disappointment resulting from a defeat. Indeed, the defeat of the Hittite commander Himuili by ambuscade infuriated Šuppiluliuma I so much that 'he mobilized the troops and chariots of Hatti at once and went into the country of Arzawa', seeking revenge.[26] The association of night attacks with the ever feared and derided Kaska, as well as the presentation of Egyptian night raids as something out of the ordinary, suggests that the Hittites may have held to some norm which taught that night attacks were unacceptable or dishonourable.

In spite of these condemnations from the Hittite sources, we should be cautious before claiming the existence of a strong *in bello* norm which prohibited night attacks and ambushes. Šuppiluliuma I may have been enraged by the Arzawan ambush of Hittite forces, yet this king willingly utilised ambush tactics himself on a number of occasions to defeat forces of invading Kaskaeans:

> And in the country which had been laid waste by its enemy, there stood all of the enemies [. . .]. My father set a trap for them and smote the Gašgaeans. The helpers who had come, those he smote too, so that the Gašgaean troops and the auxiliary troops died in multitude.[27]

Early Hittite historiography clearly records night attacks being utilised successfully as a military tactic. In the eighteenth century, Anitta of Kuššara used the cover of night to capture the city of Neša, although chose to exercise restraint towards the populace: 'The king of Kuššara came down from the city with massed forces and *took Neša by storm at night*. He captured the king of Neša but in no way mistreated the inhabitants of Neša. He treated them as if they were his parents.'[28] King Anitta even conquered the city of Hattuša 'by storm at night'.[29] The seventeenth-century 'Annals of Hattušili I' attests that, during his sixth regnal year, Hattušili 'went to the city of Zippašna. Indeed, *at night I went up to Zippašna*, and I joined battle with them. I piled up dirt on them, and the storm-god appeared in the midst of the land.'[30] These annals were commissioned by the king himself and were originally inscribed upon a golden statue that Hattušili had made in his own likeness. We can assume, therefore, that anything recorded within them had the king's explicit

---

in Honor of Harry A. Hoffner Jr. on the Occasion of His 65th Birthday, ed. Gary Beckman, Richard Beal, and Gregory McMahon (Winona Lake, IN: Eisenbrauns, 2003), 83–92.

26. Güterbock, 'Deeds of Šuppiluliuma', 80.

27. Ibid., 63. For further Hittite ambushes, see ibid., 65, 67, 78.

28. 'The Anitta Text', *HST*, 217, § 2 (emphasis added). Compare the translations in *MHTH*, 24–25; Güterbock, 'Hittite Historiography', 23.

29. 'Anitta Chronicle, Inscription B', *HST*, 218. See also discussion above, ch. 5, 'Chronology'.

30. 'Annals of Hattušili I', *HST*, 221 (emphasis added); cf. *AoH*, 52.

approval.³¹ Hattušili I obviously felt no shame in his use of the night ambush tactic, choosing to record his victory as evidence of his heroic deeds for posterity. The same was true for other Hittite kings too.³²

In the most famous battle fought by the Hittites, at Kadesh in 1274, Muwattalli II launched a surprise attack on Ramses II's army as 'they were marching unaware and not prepared to fight' (according to the Egyptians).³³ The Hittites also apparently executed a strategy of deception prior to the battle itself, deliberately feeding false intelligence to the Egyptians via two Hittite scouts. Unfortunately, we have no Hittite account of the battle and must rely on the Egyptian version of events, which seeks to cast the Hittites in a negative light.³⁴ Muwattalli II would perhaps have presented his strategy and tactics differently.

Yet, as we have already seen in the Egyptian evidence, it is likely that military tactics such as deception and ambush were viewed as morally relative: to be condemned when used by enemies; to be lauded as military genius when employed by one's own side. Indeed, this emerges in one of the oldest and most important Anatolian myths, 'The Illuyanka Tales' (see figure 38). The myth of the struggle between the great serpent Illuyanka and the storm-god is notable for its influence on later Hellenic myths of the victory of Zeus over his father Kronos. It is also notable that, within the Hittite version of the myth, ambush and deceit are utilised by the storm-god (embodying 'good'—Zeus in the Greek version) in order to defeat Illuyanka.³⁵ Two main versions of the

31. 'And I made this golden statute of myself and set it up before the sun-goddess of Arinna, my lady.' Ibid., § 17.

32. See also the description of a night attack by Tudhaliya: 'I, Tudhaliya, drew forth my *tuzzi-* at night. I encircled the *tuzzi-* of the enemy ERÍN.MEŠ [...] I slaughtered the *tuzzi-* of the enemy ERÍN.MEŠ.' Cited in Beal, 'Organization of the Hittite Military', 40–41. For some further references to ambushes in the Hittite royal inscriptions, see Hutter-Braunsar, 'Die Terminologie der Zerstörung', 205–6.

33. 'Kadesh Poem', *AEL*, 2:64–66, quotation at 64. Compare the similar account in the 'Kadesh Bulletin', *AEL*, 2:60–62.

34. For an attempted coverage of the battle of Kadesh from the Hittite perspective (using Egyptian sources), see Bryce, *Kingdom of the Hittites*, 234–41. For a concise overview of the battle and its political repercussions, see Lanny Bell, 'Conflict and Reconciliation in the Ancient Middle East: The Clash of Egyptian and Hittite Chariots in Syria, and the World's First Peace Treaty between "Superpowers"', in *War and Peace in the Ancient World*, ed. Kurt A. Raaflaub (Malden, MA: Blackwell, 2007), 98–120. Liverani, for example, rejects the idea that the massive Hittite army could have surprised the Egyptians: *LIR*, 120–21. See also above, pp. 39–41, 56, 121.

35. For the influence of the Illuyanka myth on later Greek mythology, see Gurney, *Hittites*, 180–81; Alasdair Livingstone and Birgit Haskamp, 'Near Eastern Mythologies', in *A Companion to Greek Mythology*, ed. Ken Dowden and Niall Livingstone (Malden, MA: Wiley-Blackwell, 2011), 357–82 at 372–77. For all principal parallels of this myth (e.g., Yahweh's battle against Leviathan), see Theodor H. Gaster, *Thespis: Ritual, Myth and Drama in the Ancient Near East* (Bristol, CT: Hildreth Press, 1950), 141–42. For Hittite influences on Aegean myth, religion, and epic poetry, see, inter alia, Hoffner, 'Hittite Mythological Texts';

FIGURE 38. The sky-god killing the dragon Illuyanka: Neo-Hittite, from the Lions Gate at Malitiya, c. 850–c. 800 BCE. Georges Jansoone (JoJan), CC BY-SA 3.0 licence, via Wikimedia Commons.

myth survive. In both, the great serpent fights against and defeats the storm-god, ripping out his heart and eyes to rob him of his strength. In one version, the storm-god seeks the help of his daughter, Inara, and a mortal man, Hupisaya, to take back his heart and eyes. They invite Illuyanka to a feast, where they get the serpent so drunk that Hupisaya is able to bind him with a rope. With Illuyanka bound, the storm-god comes and slays the helpless serpent.[36] In a second version, a son of the storm-god marries the daughter of Illuyanka and, at the secret request of his father, asks for the storm-god's eyes and heart as a bride-price. As soon as his organs are restored to him, the storm-god fights the serpent, defeating and killing him.[37]

This myth symbolises the victory of good over evil. But it is intriguing that the Hittite's principal martial deity—the storm-god—resorts to both deception and ambush in order to achieve that victory. Ironically, this allegory of war and victory is, perhaps, the best indicator of how military deceit and ambush were understood in reality. These tactics of war were not intrinsically good or bad, but rather morally neutral.[38] The moral quality of deceit or ambush was endowed by the relevant agent and victim. If it was deemed that the agent was 'good' and the victim deserved defeat, then deceit and ambush in war were wholly legitimate and morally acceptable. But if the agent was deemed

---

Billie Jean Collins, 'Hittite Religion in the West', in *Pax Hethitica: Studies on the Hittites and Their Neighbours in Honour of Itamar Singer*, ed. Yoram Cohen, Amir Gilan, and Jared L. Miller (Wiesbaden: Harrassowitz, 2010), 54–66; Bachvarova, *From Hittite to Homer*.

36. 'The Illuyanka Tales, Version 1', *HitM*, 12; cf. Gurney, *Hittites*, 181, for an alternative translation.

37. *HitM*, 12; Gurney, *Hittites*, 182.

38. This draws a distinction between military deception, on the one hand, and perfidy involving the violation of sacred oaths, on the other. The latter was always considered morally reprehensible.

'bad' and the victim innocent, then deceit and ambush in war were considered dishonourable and cowardly.

This attitude should hardly come as a surprise, nor does it mark a special hypocrisy or inconsistency within Hittite ethics of war. In practice, similar double standards have been a hallmark of virtually every known martial culture, from the ancient world to the present day. We have always been willing to grant greater moral leeway to ourselves than to our enemies.

RAVAGING AND BURNING

If deception, ambuscades, and night attacks occupied an ambiguous and subjective position within Hittite *in bello* norms, there was absolutely no ambiguity regarding the use of ravaging as an integral element of Hittite warfare. The Hittites were well aware of the devastating effects of arson on an agricultural economy, and the Hittite law code proscribed and punished domestic arson of agricultural lands and crops.[39] Realising the value of agricultural lands and produce to their enemies, the Hittites utilised burning, devastation, and plunder as essential military tactics. From the earliest documentary evidence, Hittite royal annals and letters are full of references to the destruction left in the wake of Hittite armies. In the 'Annals of Hattušili I', the king boasts that in the first year of his reign he 'went to the city of Šanahuitta [. . .]. I destroyed its countryside [. . .] and I gave whatever sheepfolds that were in that vicinity to the garrison troops. Thereafter I went to the city of Zalpa and destroyed it.'[40] This trail of destruction was surely designed to cement Hattušili's own authority and popularity within his kingdom, and he followed it up with more campaigns of a similar bent in his second year: 'In the following year I went to the city of Alalah and destroyed it. Thereafter I went to the city of Waršuwa, and from Waršuwa I went to the city of Ikakali. From Ikakali I went to the city of Tašhiniya. I destroyed these lands, but I took their goods and filled my palace with goods.'[41] Expeditions using identical tactics were repeated in Hattušili's third, fourth, and fifth years. But Hattušili was proudest of his achievements in the sixth year of his reign. Emulating the great Sumerian conqueror Sargon of Akkad (c. 2334–c. 2279), he conducted a devastating campaign westwards and became the first Anatolian ruler to cross the Euphrates river. Throughout this campaign the Hittites plundered and burned numerous cities, and

---

39. 'If anyone sets fire to a field, and the fire catches a fruit-bearing vineyard, if a vine, an apple tree, a pear tree or plum tree burns, he shall pay 6 shekels of silver for each tree. He shall re-plant the planting. And he shall look to his house for it. If it is a slave, he shall pay 3 shekels of silver for each tree.' *LawH*, 102, ¶ 105. Compare the Israelite restrictions against destroying fruit trees in Deuteronomy 20:19–20.

40. 'Annals of Hattušili I', *HST*, 219, §§ 1–2.

41. Ibid., 220, § 4. See also *AoH*, 47–48.

Hattušili I cites the razing of Hahha and Haššuwa as proof that his conquests had exceeded the achievements of Sargon:

> No one had crossed the Euphrates River, but I, the Great King, the Tabarna, crossed it on foot, and my army crossed it on foot behind me. Sargon (of Akkad also) crossed it. He fought the troops of Hahha, but he did not do anything to Hahha. He did not burn it down; smoke was not visible to the storm-god of Heaven. But I, the Great King, the Tabarna, destroyed Haššuwa and Hahha, and burned them down with fire. I showed smoke to the sun-god of Heaven and the storm-god.[42]

The records of another of Hatti's most warlike kings, Šuppiluliuma I, are also filled with references to arson and devastation as standard campaign tactics. Over several years of campaigns, Šuppiluliuma's forces burned cities and countryside all over Anatolia and Syria.[43] Some of the territories Šuppiluliuma marched through, like the 'country of Darittara', were 'at peace' with the Hittites, and therefore were not destroyed.[44] This mirrors other cases in which the text records that the king 'slept' at certain towns along his campaign routes, and there is no mention of these settlements being targeted. Hittite commanders were probably making choices of what to destroy and what to preserve on the basis of previous injuries committed by individual towns and cities, and whether or not individual settlements offered immediate submission. This is indicated in one passage recording a punitive raid into Kaskaean territory, during which Šuppiluliuma burned several 'countries' but was moved to clemency at one particular town by the actions of its elders:

> Then he came back into the town of Timuhala. The town of Timuhala was a place of pride of the Gašgaeans. He would have destroyed it, but they were afraid and came to meet him and fell down to his feet; consequently, he did not destroy it, but made it again part of the Hittite country.[45]

Notwithstanding this act of clemency, the rest of the campaign was marked by further destruction of towns and land. This combination of ravaging and

---

42. 'Annals of Hattušili I', *HST*, 221, §§ 19–20; *AoH*, 53–54. The reference to the Sargon stories (Sargon flourished seven centuries before Hattušili), as well as the existence of both Akkadian Babylonian and Hittite versions of the 'Annals', further highlight the fact that the Hittites were partaking in the wider historical tradition and cultural milieu of Mesopotamia at a very early stage in their political development: Güterbock, 'Hittite Historiography', 26–27.

43. Including Sallapa, Zuhhapa, Palhuišša, Kammama, Ištahara, Teššita, Hurna, Dahara, Tapapinuwa, and Šapidduwa—to name just a few. See Güterbock, 'Deeds of Šuppiluliuma', 60, 83, 108–10.

44. Ibid., 109.

45. Ibid., 110.

selective clemency was echoed in a letter written by Hattušili III, in which the king claims to have 'ravaged the land Iyalanda', yet decided to spare 'the city Atriya, a single fortress, for the sake of the city [... and] I did not go after the civilian captives'.[46] Further examples of burning and ravaging from the Hittite texts could be provided ad nauseam.[47] Accounts of the destruction of enemy cities, recorded with the hyperbole typical of royal documents from the ancient Near East, may have been intended to convey a religious message. In cases where cities were said to be completely levelled and sown with weeds, Sa-Moon Kang suggests that the 'whole point of this idea is that the site of the defeated city is to become sacred to the gods and inaccessible to men'.[48] Hittite victory, bestowed by the gods, was therefore seen to produce territorial 'gains' for the gods.

In summary, we can say that the destruction of both movable and immovable property, whether through burning or other methods, was a hallmark of Hittite warfare. In pursuing these tactics of ravaging and burning, in many regards the Hittites were no different to any other Bronze Age or Iron Age society. Success was measured in large part by 'smoke being sent up to the heavens' (to paraphrase Hattušili I), notifying the gods of Hittite conquests. This form of ravaging also had a broader strategic purpose. Agriculture was the basis of all Bronze Age and Iron Age economies. Burning agricultural land, destroying or seizing agricultural produce, and killing or enslaving the land-working populace wrought significant economic damage upon an enemy.[49] A poor enemy was, for a time at least, a crippled enemy. There is nothing within the surviving evidence to suggest that the Hittites considered these tactics as ethically dubious; destruction could even serve a religious function. This was simply how war was waged. On the other hand, Hittite kings were clearly

---

46. 'No. 101: from King Hattušili III to the King of Ahhiyawa ("Tawagalawa Letter")', *LettH*, 302–4. Atriya's survival may have been because Hattušili III simply could not capture it, rather than it being an act of mercy on the part of the king. Other targets included the land of Upu, the city of Qatna, and the land of Amqi, as reported in Egyptian correspondence: *The El-Amarna Correspondence*, trans Rainey, ed. Schniedewind and Cochavi-Rainey, EA 55 (1:401–403), EA 126 (1:657–590), EA 174–76 (1:845–49), EA 363 (1:1239).

47. See also Hutter-Braunsar, 'Die Terminologie der Zerstörung, 206–11.

48. Kang, *Divine War*, 69.

49. As Sylvia Hutter-Braunsar observes, 'die Hethiter durchaus der Tatsache bewußt waren, daß kriegerische Handlungen Zerstörungen der Umwelt bewirken. Dieses Bewußtsein hat bei ihnen aber zu keinen Versuchen geführt, die Zerstörungen möglichst zu vermeiden. Im Gegenteil: Umweltzrstorung wurde bewußt als Kriegstechnik eingesetzt, um dem Feind die notwendigen Lebensgrundlagen zu entziehen.' (the Hittites were certainly aware of the fact that acts of war cause environmental damage. However, this awareness did not lead to any attempts to avoid such destruction as far as was possible. On the contrary: environmental destruction was deliberately used as technique of war in order to deprive the enemy of the necessary means for subsistence.) Hutter-Braunsar, 'Terminologie der Zerstörung', 214.

capable of exercising ad hoc restraint, and in certain cases it was probably economically and sometimes politically more profitable to accept submission and tribute rather than dole out further devastation. And, as will be discussed below, some property was very occasionally treated with a greater sense of reverence.

Raubkrieg: *Plunder and the Spoils of War*

Just as ravaging and burning were considered part and parcel of Bronze Age warfare, the acquisition of plunder was absolutely central to Hittite martial culture and conduct. 'Der Krieg gilt als Raubkrieg'—war was deemed war for plunder—as Korošec described Hittite warfare.[50]

Hittite soldiers were compelled to fight through a form of quasi-feudal service and, unlike mercenaries, received no salaries. Booty was therefore the primary means of remuneration for the majority of the army. In this regard, despoiling enemy lands was neither solely strategic nor necessarily malicious; it was simply understood across the ancient Near East as the inevitable right of the victor. As in Egypt, individual Hittite soldiers had no right to retain booty directly; spoils were surrendered to the central bureaucracy and subsequently redistributed by the king's officers. This centralised process presumably allowed for the identification and restoration of any property that had originally been owned by a Hittite—an idiosyncratic custom discussed in the previous chapter. This serves as a reminder that plundered property must have often passed to and fro between rival communities, with the despoiled becoming the despoiler, and vice versa.

The 'Annals of Hattušili I' describes the king razing a number of cities and territories, but from each of these he also seized plunder. Hattušili paid particular attention to his seizure of religious property and his dedication of these spoils to his own deities:

> Thereafter I went to the city of Zalpa and destroyed it. I took its deities and three palanquins and carried them off for the sun-goddess of Arinna. I carried off one golden ox and one golden rhyton in the shape of a fist to the temple of the storm-god. I carried off the deities that remained to the temple of (the goddess) Mezzulla.[51]

Hattušili boasts of further despoliation of the riches and religious property of Haššuwa and Hahha:

> One golden inlaid table, three silver tables, two golden tables, one golden inlaid throne with arms [...], one palanquin of gold, two

---

50. Korošec, *Hethitische Staatsverträge*, 62; cf. Korošec, 'Warfare of the Hittites, 160.
51. 'Annals of Hattušili I', *HST*, 219–20, §§ 2–3. See also *AoH*, 47–48.

sceptres of stone, plated with gold—these I carried off from Haššuwa to the sun-goddess of Arinna. The Young Woman, Allatum, Hebat, three statues of silver, and two statues of gold—these I carried off to the temple of Mezzulla. One golden lance, five golden maces, five silver maces, two double-axes of lapis-lazuli, one double-axe of gold—these I carried off to the temple of the storm-god [...]. I destroyed Hahha. I took its goods and brought them to my city of Hattuša (two pairs of wagons were loaded with silver): one palanquin, one silver stag, one golden table, one silver table; these deities of Hahha: one silver bull, one boat with prow inlaid in gold, I the Great King, the Tabarna, brought from Hahha and carried off to the sun-goddess of Arinna.[52]

Hattušili was obviously proud of these violent acquisitions. They are cited as physical evidence of his victory: a symbol of his domination over his enemies. But it is also telling that the king made a point of stressing that these material proofs of victory—many of them holding religious value for the communities dispossessed of them—were in turn dedicated to Hatti's own gods. As it was believed that victory was dependent on the gods' support, it was logical that those same gods should share in its spoils. For the king to have acted otherwise would have incurred divine wrath and risked future defeats.

Dedicating war spoils to the gods may have fulfilled a kind of ex post facto justification of the *Raubkrieg* itself. Waging war against one's enemies to acquire plunder for religious dedication was a self-justifying process and a confirmation of Hittite piety. Winning plunder was indicative of divine approval for the war—an illustration that, in practice, might could make right. This imperative to acquire loot for the sake of the gods can be seen in the 'instructions' given to the royal couple by the sun-goddess of Arinna in an Old Kingdom prayer:

> She [the sun-goddess] gave them the royal couple a battle-ready, valiant spear saying: 'May the hostile foreign lands perish by the hand of the *labarna*, and let them take goods, silver and gold to Hattuša and Arinna, the cities of the gods!'[53]

And yet Hittite kings did occasionally appear sensitive to the sanctity of religious spaces. Enemy attacks on Hittite religious property were roundly condemned as acts of barbaric impiety and provided grounds for war.[54] As

---

52. 'Annals of Hattušili I', *HST*, 221, §§ 12–13, 16–17.
53. 'No. 3: Invocation of Sun-goddess of Arinna for Protection of Royal Couple', *HitP*, 26, § 6.
54. For example: 'The enemy lands which are quarrelling and at odds, some are not respectful to you, O Telipinu, or to the gods of Hatti; others wish to burn down your temples; others wish to take away your rhyta, cups, and objects of silver and gold; others wish to lay waste your fallow lands, vineyards, gardens and groves; others wish to capture your plowmen,

far as Hittite acts of war were concerned, there is a suggestion from the Old Kingdom that Muršili I was criticised for his sack of Babylon, the most prestigious cultic centre of Mesopotamia. According to a text from the reign of his successor Hantili I (c. 1590–c. 1560), Muršili's unrestrained ransacking of Babylon 'made the gods sick'.[55] However, it should also be borne in mind that Hantili had usurped the throne and murdered Muršili shortly after the king returned from his Babylonian campaign. Rather than being a genuine condemnation of the destruction of Babylon, the text should probably be read as apologist propaganda produced by the new regime, seeking ways to smear Muršili I in order to justify Hantili's regicide. Nevertheless, the fact that the issue was raised at all is of interest.

As opposed to post facto condemnations of the destruction of sacred sites, there is some evidence of Hittite kings actively protecting religious property and persons. Following Šuppiluliuma I's conquest of Carchemish, Hittite troops took control of the lower town and 'removed the inhabitants, silver, gold, and bronze utensils and carried them to Hattuša'. However, since Šuppiluliuma 'feared the gods', he sectioned off the upper parts of the city where the palaces and temple precincts were located, and 'he let no one into the presence of the deity Kubaba and of the deity KAL, and he did not rush close to any one of the temples. Nay, he even bowed to them.'[56] Šuppiluliuma showed similar restraint elsewhere, being careful to show due respect to the temples of the storm-god:

> I destroyed the Land of Hurna, and the city of Hurna. But because there was a temple of the Storm God of Hurna behind the city of Hurna, I spared it and they did not plunder it. The servants of the god who were behind, I left alone, and they are still there.[57]

Four centuries earlier, the Old Babylonian king Hammurabi may have acted in a similar fashion. In the prologue to his famous law code (c. 1755–1750), Hammurabi boasts that he is 'the warrior, he who spared Larsa'. Larsa, situated in southern Babylonia, was a cult centre of Šamaš.[58]

Some effort to provide a measure of religious immunity is also indicated within a vassal treaty between Muršili II and Kupanta-Kurunta of Mira-Kuwaliya:

---

vinedressers, gardeners and grinding-women. To those enemy lands give severe fever, plague, famine and locusts.' 'No. 9: Muršili's Hymn and Prayer to Telipinu', *HitP*, 55–56, § 13. See also 'No. 5: Prayer of Arnuwanda and Asmunikal to the Sun-Goddess of Arinna about Ravages of Kaska Tribes', *HitP* 41–43, §§ 11–31; *ANET*, 399–400; O. R. Gurney, 'Hittite Prayers of Muršili II', *Annals of Archaeology and Anthropology* 27 (1940): 1–167 at 28–35.

55. Hoffner, 'Propaganda and Political Justification', 56–58.

56. Güterbock, 'Deeds of Šuppiluliuma', 95.

57. Götze, *Annalen des Mūršiliš*, 176–77, translation cited from Beal, 'Making, Preserving, and Breaking', 94.

58. 'The Code of Hammurabi', *ANET*, 164. Hammurabi also claims to have rebuilt cult centres such as Ebabbar and Uruk and 'granted life to Adab', a city of the god Mah: ibid., 164–65.

But if some settlement establishes itself, it shall be your enemy in the same way as it is My Majesty's enemy. Attack it! A single sacred city belonging to Mashuiluwa [the former king of Mira] himself is situated on the Siyanta River, and it shall be exempted from the oath. Protect for yourself this land which I, My Majesty, have given to you.[59]

Clearly the status of the unnamed 'sacred city' resulted in it receiving special treatment in this specific case.

Nevertheless, taken as a whole there is very little evidence of widely recognised *in bello* norms protecting religious property or persons. Most of the evidence suggests that Hittite warfare openly targeted religious property and considered the seizure of religious spoils as perfectly legitimate. As repositories of wealth, temples were natural targets for invading forces. Indeed, in Mesopotamian inscriptions, the capture of an enemy's gods (that is, the seizure of their sacred statuary) was presented as the culminating act of battle and a confirmation of the enemy's defeat.[60]

WAR SPOILS AND ALLIES

The lure of booty was also used by Hittite kings to cajole their vassals into joining military campaigns. King Tuniya of Tikunani was goaded and encouraged by Hattušili I to

> be a man with respect to the man of Hahhum. Devour his food rations like a dog! The oxen which you take shall be your own. The sheep and goats which you take shall be your own. Be a man with respect to him! I from this side, and you from that side.[61]

A letter sent by the Hittite viceroy of Carchemish, Sharri-Kushuh, to King Niqmaddu II of Ugarit promised him spoils in return for putting down a rebellion in the land of Nuhashshi:

> If you begin war with Tette and you, Niqmaddu, take the initiative and attack before I draw near the land of Nuhashshi [. . .] then whatever Niqmaddu takes from the land of Nuhashshi, and whatever troops enter his lands as fugitives he shall retain.[62]

---

59. 'No. 11: Treaty between Muršili II and Kupanta-Kurunta of Mira-Kuwaliya', *HDT*, 76, § 10.
60. Kang, *Divine War*, 46.
61. 'No. 1: Hattušili I to King Tuniya (Tunip-Teššub) of Tikunani', *LettH*, 78. Cf. Güterbock, 'Deeds of Šuppiluliuma', 75–76: 'as an ally Anna was helping, and he attacked Mount Ammuna [. . .] and kept its goods, along with the inhabitants, cattle and sheep'.
62. 'No. 20: Letter from Sharri-Kushuh of Carchemish to Niqmaddu II of Ugarit', *HDT*, 126, § 1. Cf. 'No. 19: Letter from Suppiluliuma I to Niqmaddu II of Ugarit', *HDT*, 125–26, which also tries to persuade Ugarit to join the fight.

Thus we see vassal princes being granted a *selbstandiges Beuterecht* (right of plunder), in the words of Korošec.[63]

The apportioning of spoils of war was taken so seriously by the Hittites that they laid down specific legal agreements in their diplomatic treaties regarding the proper distribution and ownership of war booty. For example, an alliance between Tudhaliya II and Sunashshura of Kizzuwatna explicitly stipulated how movable and immovable property, as well as prisoners of war, would be divided between Hatti and Kizzuwatna in any future joint operations, with a variety of different scenarios envisaged.[64] Equally, a different treaty reassured the ruler of Amurru that any spoils taken illicitly by Hittite soldiers would be restored.[65]

References to plundered silver, gold, and other precious goods can blind us to the reality that, in the majority of cases, the most valuable and abundant forms of plunder were foodstuffs and people. The Hittite kingdom was an agricultural economy, constantly short of manpower and not infrequently afflicted by natural disasters; famine was a harsh reality throughout the history of Hatti. In an age before the utilisation of wind- or water-power, a fundamental shortage of manpower was a consistent feature of the Bronze Age Near East. A fifteenth-century letter from a regional governor appealed to the Great King to supply him with labourers to harvest vineyards: 'They are already ripe for harvesting. If only you would promptly dispatch workers!'[66] Lacking the labourers, the vineyards were being stripped by Kaskaean raiders instead. Given these agro-economic pressures, it is unsurprising that the protection or acquisition of livestock, crops, and slaves were core military objectives for all Hittite rulers. These objectives are openly stated in the context of Šuppiluliuma I's attack on Kašula:

> While he was fortifying Almina, he sent forth Urawanni and Kuwatnaziti, the great 'shepherd', into the country of Kašula in order to attack. And the gods of my father helped them, so that they conquered all of the country of Kašula and brought its population, cattle and sheep before my father. The deportees whom they brought were one thousand.[67]

Of course, Hatti's enemies were driven by almost identical objectives, so that the kingdom was often in the position of having to seek opportunities to rebalance a resource deficit in order to provide security for its own population. News from the frontiers that 'the enemy marched in great numbers in the night, in one place 600 enemy, in another place 400 enemy, and harvested

---

63. Korošec, *Hethitische Staatsverträge*, 55.
64. 'No. 2: Treaty between Tudhaliya II of Hatti and Sunashshura of Kizzuwatna', *HDT*, 21–23, §§ 23–27, 30, 47–49.
65. 'No. 5: Treaty between Suppiluliuma I and Aziru of Amurru', *HDT*, 39, § 7.
66. 'No. 42: from the King to [?]', *LettH*, 163.
67. 'Güterbock, 'Deeds of Šuppiluliuma', 91.

the grain', must have been received in Hattuša with distressing regularity.[68] Moreover, because these food and manpower resources were so essential to the survival of the state and its people, any external assault on them would certainly have been considered a *casus belli*.

Treatment of the Enemy during War

TREATMENT OF COMBATANTS

If one were to read the Hittite sources literally, particularly the royal annals lauding the victories of individual kings, then Hittite warfare must have been extraordinarily bloody. While the texts are often laconic and formulaic regarding the specificities of battle such as troop numbers, movements, timeline, casualties, and so on, the phrase 'the enemy troops died in multitudes' (or variations thereon) appears frequently.[69] Moreover, the texts usually present this butchering of the enemy as being achieved through divine aid, which was itself an implicit assertion of moral righteousness. During battle, no restraints were dictated, observed, or expected between combatants. Combatants sought to kill or disable the enemy by whatever means possible; to kill 'multitudes' of enemy combatants was a sign of military virtue and moral righteousness expressed through divine favour.

Despite this ruthless approach to armed combat, the Hittites did not possess any concept equivalent to the Hebrew *herem* (ban), which required the annihilation of 'everything that breathed'.[70] Nor was there any theoretical or practical distinction made between a more brutal and a more restrained type of warfare, as articulated during the European Middle Ages.[71] For the Hittites, there were simply enemies and there was simply war. After war, former enemies could become slaves, subjects, or even allies.

---

68. *LettGK*, 180.

69. For example, Güterbock, 'Deeds of Šuppiluliuma', 60, 62–63, 68, 75–76, 111–18.

70. For example, Deuteronomy 20:16–17; 13:12–16; Numbers 31:14–18; Joshua 6:20–21; 8:2, 27; 11:14; 1 Samuel 15:3. See discussion below, ch. 10, 'Massacre and the "Doctrine" of *herem*'. See also *ILA*, 209–12; Hans van Wees, 'Genocide in the Ancient World', in *The Oxford Handbook of Genocide Studies*, ed. Donald Bloxham and A. Dirk Moses (Oxford: Oxford University Press, 2010), 239–58 at 242. My thanks to Professor van Wees for bringing this article to my attention.

71. For example, the distinction between *bellum Romanum* (*guerre mortelle*) and *bellum hostile*. For medieval categorisations of 'types' of just and unjust wars, see Maurice H. Keen, *The Laws of War in the Late Middle Ages* (London: Routledge & Kegan Paul; Toronto: University of Toronto Press, 1965), 104; Russell, *Just War*, 129–30; Philippe Contamine, *War in the Middle Ages*, trans. Michael Jones (Oxford: Blackwell, 1984), 282–84; James A. Brundage, 'The Hierarchy of Violence in Twelfth- and Thirteenth-Century Canonists', *The International History Review* 17 (4) (1995): 670–92; Cox, 'Ethics of War', 111–13.

Hittite texts claiming that enemies were slaughtered in vast numbers should be treated with caution, however. Alongside reports that Hittite kings killed the enemy 'in multitudes', we also read that the captives seized in war 'were countless'.[72] While some captives were surely non-combatants, we can assume that significant numbers of defeated combatants were also captured rather than killed. Indeed, the willingness of enemy combatants to surrender to the Hittites and 'seek peace' suggests that they expected a degree of mercy to be shown by the Great King; otherwise there would have been little incentive for them to surrender.[73]

The aforementioned shortage of manpower throughout Hatti may partly explain this practice of sparing enemy combatants and non-combatants. Prisoners of war were exceedingly valuable to the Hittite economy and defeated enemies must have been more attractive as slaves than as corpses.[74] The federated nature of the empire may have further encouraged restraint in combat. Wars were often for the purpose of quelling rebellions or installing sympathetic client princes, so waging wars of annihilation would have made little political or economic sense. Finally, the cosmological assumptions of Hittite culture did nothing to encourage wars of annihilation. While both Egypt and Israel possessed an absolutist interpretation of justice, rooted in cosmologies that encouraged extreme cultural chauvinism, the Hittites never developed either a comparable sense of cultural superiority or a theological imperative which demanded the eradication of certain peoples.

Unfortunately, we have virtually no evidence to inform us of Hittite practice in the immediate aftermath of combat. On the other hand, we have no indication that the Hittites deliberately mutilated their fallen enemies. Unlike the Egyptians—who had strong beliefs about the importance of preserving the body in death, and mutilated enemy corpses as a form of ritual punishment—the Hittites practised cremation.[75] One might speculate, therefore, that the mutilation of enemy corpses would not have had the same religious meaning for them as it did for the Egyptians.

TREATMENT OF NON-COMBATANTS

Non-combatants were viewed as part of the movable property of an enemy territory, and therefore constituted a valuable component of war booty. Combatant and non-combatant captives alike became the chattels of the Hittite king, to be distributed among the army and the temples of the gods. When recalling his conquest of Arzawa, Muršili II plainly stated, 'I have made the

---

72. Güterbock, 'Deeds of Šuppiluliuma', 63.
73. For example, ibid., 65; *LettGK*, 173, 174.
74. Beckman, 'Foreigners', 210.
75. Archaeologists have revealed some of the earliest Anatolian cremation grounds in Hattuša itself: Akurgal, *Art of the Hittites*, 103–5.

civilian captives whom I carried off to Hatti subject to the service obligation.'[76] While the Hittites did enjoy some success in besieging walled cities—for example, the capture of Carchemish by Šuppiluliuma I—simple blockade was probably the most effective (albeit a time-consuming) technique for taking fortified sites. This inevitably dragged non-combatants into warfare.[77] When Muršili II assaulted the city of Puranda and cut off its inhabitants on Mount Arinnanda (c. 1318–c. 1317), he reported,

> I besieged the settlement through hunger and thirst. And when they were oppressed with hunger and thirst, then the prisoners came down and fell at my feet: 'Our lord, do not destroy us! Take us, our lord, into your service and bring us to Hattuša!'[78]

Starving out the defenders and inhabitants of a settlement did not distinguish between combatants and non-combatants, and there is no indication that the Hittites considered such tactics problematic, either in terms of military honour or ethics.

Even elite non-combatants, such as the family members of rival rulers, were liable to become prisoners of war. When the Hittites conquered the land of Nuhashshi its king escaped, but Šuppiluliuma I 'captured his mother, his brothers, and his children, and I brought them to Hatti'.[79] We do not know the fate of these particular prisoners, although their transportation to Hattuša implies, firstly, that even elite non-combatants were not immune from capture or enslavement; secondly, that elite non-combatants were understood to have some political value, whether as trophies of victory or future bargaining tools; and thirdly, that it was not deemed appropriate that elite non-combatants should be summarily executed (proof of restraint, albeit at a low bar). The enemy's abandonment of his women and children actually became a topos of Hittite literature, used as evidence of enemy cowardice and humiliation contrasted with Hittite martial prowess.[80] However, if this literary device had any basis in reality, it suggests that Hatti's enemies may have expected their families to survive in Hittite custody.

---

76. 'No. 10: Treaty between Muršili II and Targasnalli of Hapalla', *HDT*, 73, § 13.

77. Beckman, 'Siege of Uršu Text', 26; Güterbock, 'Deeds of Šuppiluliuma', 95.

78. 'Und den Kolonen setzte ich durch Hunger und Durst zu. Und als es ihnen durch Hunger und Durst drückend wurde, da kamen die Kolonen herab, sie fielen mir zu Füßen: "Unser Herr! Vernichte uns nicht! Nimm uns, unser Herr, zur Untertanenschaft an und führe uns nach Hattuša hinauf!"'. Götze, *Annalen des Müršiliš*, 57.

79. 'No. 6a: Treaty between Suppiluliuma I of Hatti and Shattiwaza of Mittanni (Hittite version)', *HDT*, 43, § 5.

80. Stefano De Martino, 'The Military Exploits of the Hittite King Hattušili I in Lands Situated between the Upper Euphrates and the Upper Tigris', in *Silva Anatolica: Anatolian Studies Presented to Maciej Popko on the Occasion of His 65th Birthday*, ed. Piotr Taracha (Warsaw: Agade, 2002), 77–85 at 83.

TREATMENT OF PRISONERS OF WAR

We have seen that enslavement was a common fate for peoples conquered by the Hittites. As discussed in chapter 4, enslavement *might* be considered a very limited form of restraint; but did the Hittites offer any protections to prisoners of war beyond this very basic gift of life? Or did they routinely brutalise their captives, to serve as a monitory example to others who might oppose them?

The fate of defeated enemies or those who had defected to the Hittites during war was decided by the king himself, seemingly on an ad hoc basis. Conquered civilian populations could be moved en masse across Hittite domains, relocating entire communities away from their ancestral lands.[81] This policy of mass deportation was designed both to enhance the security of frontier regions by removing possibly hostile and rebellious populations and to inject supplies of labour into regions within the kingdom's interior. The importance of these captured civilian populations to the Hittite economy has been discussed above, and is testified to in Hittite diplomatic treaties. Such treaties insisted upon the return of any captives that fled Hittite territory into the lands of client rulers and allies, or fled from the territory of one client ruler to those of another client ruler.[82] Treaties were also concerned with the movement of refugee populations, which could form potentially dangerous semi-autonomous mercenary bands referred to as *hapiru* or *habiru*. In Hatti, *hapiru* were often settled on lands, subjected to royal control, and conscripted into the army as auxiliaries.[83]

Some general distinctions between prisoners of war and domestic slaves appear to have existed. Combatants captured during war were referred to as *appanteš* (from the verb *appant-*, 'to seize'), while non-combatants taken during war were referred to simply as *arnuwala-*, that is, 'booty' or 'plunder'. This distinction probably broke down rapidly during captivity, with all prisoners coming to be referred to as *arnuwala-*.[84] Intriguingly, however, captives who had been taken in war retained a higher social status than ordinary slaves, being described by Goetze as *halbfrei* (semi- or half-free).[85]

---

81. For example, a Middle Kingdom letter reported that '[t]he cities in the territory which were promised to be relocated, they have already relocated those cities. They have already finished that assignment.' 'No. 45: from [?] to [?]', *LettH*, 169.

82. See 'No. 7: Treaty between Suppiluliuma I and Tette of Nuhashshi', *HDT*, 56–57, § 7; 'No. 8: Treaty between Muršili II and Tuppi-Teshshup of Amurru', ibid., 62, § 11; 'No. 9: Treaty between Muršili II and Niqmepa of Ugarit', ibid., 66–67, §§ 7, 11–13; 'No. 10: Treaty between Muršili II and Targasnalli of Hapalla', ibid., 73, § 13; 'No. 11: Treaty between Muršili II and Kupanta-Kurunta of Mira-Kuwaliya', ibid., 81, § 27.

83. 'No. 13: Edict of Hattusili III of Hatti concerning Fugitives from Ugarit', *HDT*, 178; *LIR*, 64–65.

84. Harry A. Hoffner Jr., 'The Treatment and Long-Term Use of Persons Captured in Battle according to the Maşat Texts', in *Recent Developments in Hittite Archaeology and History*, ed. K. Aslihan Yener and Harry A. Hoffner Jr. (Winona Lake, IN: Eisenbrauns, 2002), 61–72 at 61–62.

85. Cited in ibid., 62.

In an attempt to maximise agricultural yields, taxes, and military recruits, many prisoners of war were integrated into the kingdom by establishing them as new communities. Hittite laws indicate that these captives could be assigned fields and agricultural implements, and even exempted from taxes and obligations for the first three years of their resettlement.[86] This distinction in social standing among the unfree population may have been rooted in a perception that being captured in war bestowed upon a prisoner greater honour or respect than was enjoyed by a household slave born into servitude. Or perhaps it reflected a pragmatic realisation that warlike enemy populations had to be treated cautiously—offered a carrot, if you will—if they were to be successfully and peacefully integrated into Hittite society. If prisoners of war truly retained a higher social status than other types of enslaved persons, one might postulate that they also enjoyed better treatment in captivity.

Notwithstanding this differentiation, there is no evidence of a universal policy or strict norms governing the day-to-day treatment of prisoners of war in Hatti. As the majority of such prisoners were destined for use as slave or corvée labour, it would have been in the Hittites' interest to keep them in reasonably good health; yet we can also assume that such captives suffered the usual abuses associated with enslaved individuals. Prisoners of war had no 'rights', and physical violence was undoubtedly threatened and used to enforce obedience. Women especially would have been vulnerable to sexual violence, distributed as they were among the troops as a share of the booty. Some would have become wives or concubines; fulfilling these roles, they would have been integrated into Hittite society and would not necessarily have remained unfree for the duration of their lives.

It goes without saying that the humiliation of those taken into bondage must have been acute, and elite prisoners were sometimes singled out for public humiliation as a form of spectacle and political theatre. After sacking Haššuwa and Hahha, King Hattušili I 'hitched the king of Haššuwa and the king of Hahha to a wagon', leading them in triumph back to the royal capital.[87] However, at least one scholar has noted the relative absence of references in Hittite literature (especially texts describing the ritual conduct of religious festivals) to triumphal processions following victorious military campaigns.[88] Of course, just because we lack ritual prescriptions for how to conduct a military triumph does not mean that these did not take place. Triumphal military processions

---

86. Ibid., 62–64; Beal, 'Making, Preserving, and Breaking', 94. See *LawH*, 47–49, ¶ 40; 107–8, ¶ 112. Compare to similar Egyptian practices: *LIR*, 97–99

87. 'Annals of Hattušili I', *HST*, 221, § 20; cf. *AoH*, 53–54. Compare this to Thutmose I and Amenhotep II hanging elite prisoners from their royal boats: discussed above, ch. 4, 'Treatment of the Enemy' and 'Treatment of Prisoners of War'. For similar practices during Roman triumphs, see Beard, *Roman Triumph*, 107–42.

88. Amir Gilan, 'Hittite Religious Rituals and the Ideology of Kingship', *Religion Compass* 5 (7) (2011): 276–85.

may have been viewed simply as an aspect of military logistics (which were seldom recorded),[89] or perhaps were considered so obvious a celebration that recording them would have been regarded as superfluous.

It appears that the mutilation of free persons was rare in Hatti. Over time, the Hittite law code actually shifted away from corporal punishments, replacing them with monetary fines.[90] The relatively humane character of Hittite laws, and the lack of mutilation scenes in Hittite sculpture and material culture, has led some scholars to claim that the Hittites possessed an unusual respect for human life and individual 'rights'. Others have noted a 'complete absence of that lust for torture and cruelty which characterizes the annals of the Assyrian kings in their victories'.[91] This might lead us to believe that treatment of prisoners of war in Hatti was more enlightened than in other ancient Near Eastern societies.

This praise of Hittite gentility is almost certainly exaggerated. The abuse of prisoners could go beyond humiliation and into the realms of torture and mutilation. Prisoners taken on military campaigns were potential sources of valuable intelligence, and there is no reason to assume that the Hittites shied away from employing torture during their interrogations of captives. A letter from a Hittite commander in Syria-Palestine informs us that, through the interrogation of a captured enemy, the Hittites discovered that the Egyptian pharaoh was preparing an imminent expedition against Hatti.[92] A treaty between Hatti and Kizzuwatna stipulated that any pertinent intelligence gained through interrogations of captured enemies should be communicated to the relevant ruler.[93] It would be naïve to think that such interrogations did not employ physical torture.

Indeed, evidence of prisoners of war suffering deliberate physical harm at the hands of their Hittite captors is provided by several references to the blinding of prisoners. A number of texts discovered at Tapikka (Maşat Höyük) suggest that blinding was used as a method of punishment and intimidation. One text (HKM 102) provides a list of captives available to be ransomed and states their ransom price as well as stating whether they are blind or able to see.[94] As Harry A. Hoffner observes, '[i]t would seem that a rather large proportion of the persons listed on HKM 102 were "blinded" for this to be the accident of battle [. . . and] it appears that the persons were probably blinded after capture, either in order to render them more controllable, as a punishment for the havoc they had wreaked on Hittite personnel, or to humiliate the enemy'.[95] Blinding is mentioned as a punishment for Hittite soldiers who

---

89. As suggested by Gilan: ibid., 283.
90. *LawH*, 4–11; Gurney, *Hittites*, 88.
91. Gurney, *Hittites*, 115; see also Korošec, 'Warfare of the Hittites', 165.
92. *LettGK*, 182–83.
93. 'No. 2: Treaty between Tudhaliya II of Hatti and Sunashshura of Kizzuwatna', HDT, 22, §§ 42–43.
94. *LettGK*, 173–74, 180.
95. Hoffner, 'Treatment and Long-Term Use of Persons', 68.

broke their military oath, so it is possible that these blinded prisoners included those who had taken oaths to serve in the Hittite army but had later rebelled.[96] Kings could threaten even senior commanders with blinding or death as punishments for failure or insubordination.[97] It is thus easy to imagine blinding being used to punish and intimidate the prisoner-of-war population.

Letters exchanged between Hittite officials show that blind prisoners were still put to work; in this case, in a mill-house:

> Concerning the matter of the blind men that you wrote me about: they have conducted all of the blind men up to the city of Šapinuwa. They have left behind here ten blind men (to work) in the mill houses.[98]

Another letter reveals that some blinded mill-house slaves had managed to escape from their captivity in Šapinuwa.[99] Quite *how* a group of blind mill slaves managed to escape from their captors is left unexplained. Captives would not have required their sight to turn grinding-stones, but escaping captivity and evading recapture is a different matter entirely. Perhaps 'blinding' actually referred to the removal of a single eye rather than both?[100] This would certainly have instilled fear into captives, but left the 'blinded' prisoner capable of a wider range of tasks. On the other hand, there is corroborative evidence from later Hebrew sources to suggest that total blinding and forced labour in mills was a common fate for prisoners of war in the ancient Near East. The Book of Judges claims that after Samson's betrayal by Delilah, '[t]he Philistines seized him and gouged out his eyes. They brought him down to Gaza and shackled him in bronze fetters, and he became a mill slave in the prison.'[101] Similarly, after the fall Jerusalem in 586, King Zedekiah of Judah had his eyes put out by King Nebuchadnezzar of Babylon.[102]

---

96. Ibid.; Beal, 'Making, Preserving, and Breaking', 95.

97. 'Say to Kassu and Zilapiya: "As soon as this letter reaches you, come with all haste before His Majesty. If not, (my men) will come to you and blind you on the spot!"' *LettGK*, 180; 'You Pipappa, bring the UKU.UŠ troops across as quickly as possible. Bring them here to the army. If not, you will come (and) you will die!' Ibid., 180.

98. Hoffner, 'Treatment and Long-Term Use of Persons', 68–69; *LettGK*, 173–74.

99. Hoffner, 'Treatment and Long-Term Use of Persons', 69.

100. Also suggested by Hoffner, ibid. This seems more plausible than the captives relying on sighted accomplices, as also suggested by Hoffner.

101. Judges 16:21. Even the report of total blinding in Judges can be problematised, as it could perhaps be interpreted that Samson was only blinded in one eye. When the hero prays for a final gift of strength from Yahweh to pull down the temple upon his Philistine captors, he cries, 'O Lord God! Please remember me, and give me strength just this once, O God, to take revenge of the Philistines, *if only for one of my two eyes*.' Judges 16:28 (emphasis added). Does this imply that Samson deserves vengeance for each of his mutilated eyes, or that only a single eye was mutilated?

102. 2 Kings 25:7.

Hittite commanders were also willing to take the more extreme step of killing enemy captives. The regional governor Kaššu reported to the king that 'behind me the enemy attacked Zikkatta [...]. I expelled him. And sixteen men of the enemy—*including captives* and killed—I felled.'[103] When Šuppiluliuma I defeated a Kaskaean chief named Ariwašu in battle, he 'captured Ariwašu [...] and cut his head off'.[104] We have also seen above that certain military rituals—especially rituals to cleanse the army following a defeat—required human sacrifice. It is highly likely that the sacrificial victims of such rituals were prisoners of war, as also practised in Egypt.[105]

The killing of prisoners of war may have been more likely when captured enemies were regarded as rebels. A treaty between Tudhaliya II and Sunashshura of Kizzuwatna includes five separate clauses detailing the terms of the two kingdoms' defensive alliance against revolt. Each clause demands that captured rebels be executed; furthermore, if either king failed to execute or turn over a rebellious vassal of their fellow monarch, this would result in the dissolution of the alliance and provide grounds for war.[106]

While shocking to modern sensibilities, it remains true that, in the politico-cultural context of the Late Bronze Age, such treatment was relatively mild. We have already seen that Libyan and Nubian prisoners of war suffered impalement in Egypt. The Assyrian king Shalmaneser I (c. 1273–c. 1244) claimed to have blinded 14,400 prisoners,[107] and when the Assyrians received a group of extradited noblemen from Mitanni, the prisoners 'were turned over and impaled in the city of Taite'.[108]

Enslavement, mutilation, or death were not the only outcomes for prisoners of war in Hatti: ransoming or the exchange of hostages could also take place. Such arrangements could be formalised in treaties, such as that with the kingdom of Amurru: '[You] shall not seize a single person of Hatti. If you do not ransom him with alacrity, and do not send him back to the King of Hatti, you will have transgressed the oath.'[109] Or they could be made on an informal or ad hoc basis, necessitated by extraordinary circumstances. In this

---

103. 'No. 16: from King to Kaššu', *LettH*, 114 (emphasis added; the quoted text is from Kaššu's previous report sent to the king, which the king is reciting).

104. Güterbock, 'Deeds of Šuppiluliuma', 118.

105. See above, ch. 4, 'Magic', and ch. 7, 'Magic, Ritual, and War'. See also Gurney's description of the ritual to the god Yarris, which may have involved human sacrifice following a mock battle: Gurney, *Hittites*, 155.

106. 'If the Hittites capture this enemy, they will kill him. If they give him into the custody of Sunashshura, he must kill him.' 'No. 2: Treaty between Tudhaliya II of Hatti and Sunashshura of Kizzuwatna', *HDT*, 20, § 14; see also §§ 13–17.

107. Korošec, 'Warfare of the Hittites', 165.

108. 'No. 6b: Treaty between Shattiwaza of Mittanni and Suppiluliuma I of Hatti', *HDT*, 49, § 2.

109. 'No. 5: Treaty between Suppiluliuma I of Hatti and Aziru of Amurru', *HDT*, 38, § 5. Compare with the Old Babylonian laws of Hammurabi, which also envisaged the

latter case, the Hittites seem to have considered hostage exchange a method of negotiation capable of halting or turning back sizeable invading armies.[110]

Immunities

DIPLOMATIC

While most individuals caught up in ancient Hittite wars were considered fair game and liable to be killed or captured, there did exist a handful of customs that encouraged the protection of certain persons from violence. Foremost among these was the recognition that envoys and ambassadors from foreign sovereigns should enjoy immunity whilst engaged in official diplomatic business with a host nation. Bederman has argued that the 'international law of diplomats and diplomatic protection' was motivated by sheer pragmatism, 'because without it the simplest forms of negotiation between independent polities would have been impossible'.[111] As a major player in the geopolitics of the second millennium, Hatti shared in these diplomatic conventions. Non-hostile interstate relations were characterised by the relatively free coming and going of envoys. As Hattušili III pointedly remarked to the king of Babylon, 'Only if two kings are hostile do their messengers not travel continually between them. Why, my brother, have you cut off your messengers?'[112] Indeed, there is evidence that bilateral diplomacy could be re-established quite soon after even major military confrontations.[113] Yet also implied in Hattušili III's remark is a recognition that *during* war standard diplomatic communications—and presumably any concomitant protections—ceased. This means that it is difficult to classify standard diplomatic immunities as immunities of war per se, as they were more like guarantees of safety during peace.

States did not maintain permanent residences or embassies, so envoys remained quite literally 'guests' within a host kingdom. Ambassadors were obliged to obey the laws and the commands of the sovereign in whose country

---

ransoming of soldiers and the possible return of captured soldiers: 'Code of Hammurabi', § 32, §§ 133–35, in *ANET*, 167, 171.

110. For example, 'Early the following morning Nerikkaili, the man from Taphallu, awoke me and brought me the message: "What do I have in the way of hostages? The enemy who has already invaded Tarittarā numbers 7,000!"' 'No. 49: to the King from Kaššu', *LettH*, 177.

111. *ILA*, 88. See also Ziskind, 'Aspects of International Law', 64–65; *LIR*, 71–76; Beckman, 'Foreigners', 207; Lackenbacher, 'Nouveaux documents d'Ugarit', 149.

112. 'No. 23: Letter from Hattušili III of Hatti to Kadashman-Enlil II of Babylon', *HDT*, 140, § 6.

113. For example, Hittite–Assyrian correspondence following the battle of Nihriya (c. 1237). See Masamichi Yamada, 'The Second Military Conflict between "Assyria" and "Hatti" in the Reign of Tukulti-Ninurta I', *Revue d'assyriologie et d'archéogie orientale* 105 (2011): 199–220 at 203.

they resided, and kings retained the right to detain envoys for as long as they wished. This could amount to considerable periods of time. For example, a number of Assyrian envoys were detained in Hatti for three years.[114] In such cases, we must wonder where the line between honoured guest and imprisoned hostage lay, and it is likely that all ambassadors were viewed both as protected persons and as potential bargaining chips. Occasionally, protection could break down completely. Hattušili III was furious when one of his envoys to Egypt was arrested and apparently condemned to death, with Pharaoh Ramses II ignoring Hatti's calls for the envoy's release.[115] Hattušili's indignation suggests that this violated Hittite expectations of how envoys should be treated.

Protections for diplomats were sometimes enshrined in diplomatic instruments, such as the treaty agreed between Hantili II and Paddatissu of Kizzuwatna (c. 1500–c. 1450): 'If the Great King sends either his son or his subject to Paddatissu, Paddatissu shall not harm him. And if Paddatissu sends either his son or his subject to the Great King, the Great King shall not harm him.'[116] A later treaty with Kizzuwatna, created by Tudhaliya II (c. 1400), formalised similar guarantees of immunity:

> If His Majesty sends his messenger to Sunashshura, Sunashshura must not harm him in any way. He must not ensnare him by means of a magical plant. If Sunashshura sends either his son or his messenger before His Majesty—or if Sunashshura himself comes—His Majesty must not harm them in any way. He must not ensnare them by means of a magical plant.[117]

The inherent suspicion underlying political interactions on the international stage—even between supposed allies—is colourfully illustrated in the final clause, betraying a fear that rulers might seek to bewitch or drug foreign envoys in order to inveigle secret information from them or turn them against their masters. Another clause in the same treaty further underlines that the trustworthiness of envoys was not taken for granted, cautioning that an envoy's oral message should be confirmed by the written document which they carried.[118] In the mid-thirteenth century Hattušili III blamed the incompetence of messengers for the hostile relations between Hatti and the kingdom of Ahhiyawa, and recommended to its king that both sets of envoys should be tried and executed for their mistakes or malice.[119]

---

114. Ziskind, 'Aspects of International Law', 66–67.
115. *LettGK*, 71.
116. 'No. 1: Treaty between a King of Hatti (perhaps Hantili II) and Paddatissu of Kizzuwatna', *HDT*, 12, § 3. Klengel dates this treaty later, to Huzziya II (c. 1450): Klengel, *Geschichte des Hethitischen*, 98.
117. 'No. 2: Treaty between Tudhaliya II of Hatti and Sunashshura of Kizzuwatna', *HDT*, 22, §§ 44–45.
118. Ibid., 24, § 59.
119. *LettGK*, 64–65.

On the one hand, these treaties provide evidence that certain protections for diplomats were widely recognised. On the other, the fact that such protections had to be stated repeatedly in diplomatic instruments implies that universal immunities for envoys and ambassadors were weaker than has been claimed. After all, if there were standardised and broadly enforced norms regulating the treatment of diplomats, why was there a requirement to specify such protections in individual treaties? This implies that sovereigns were pessimistic as to whether their representatives would genuinely be immune from violence unless a foreign ruler had been bound to a specific code of conduct by a treaty oath. In other words, diplomatic immunity may have been widely practised between international actors in the ancient Near East, but it was not taken for granted.[120] This conclusion is supported by other treaty stipulations that demanded the arrest and imprisonment of enemy envoys who sought to communicate covertly with Hittite vassal states (the suspicion being that they would seek to seed rebellion). Such envoys were regarded as enemy messengers to be intercepted, and thus they were not protected by any blanket form of immunity.[121]

Ambiguity regarding the personal safety of individuals granted safe-conducts is revealed by the interactions between Hattušili III of Hatti, the king of Ahhiyawa, and a duplicitous warlord named Piyama-radu, who had formerly been a Hittite vassal but later began raiding Hittite territories and allied himself with Ahhiyawa.[122] Hattušili offered Piyama-radu a safe-conduct to negotiate, which Piyama-radu rejected, forcing Hattušili to seek the intervention of the king of Ahhiyawa:

> Why did he [Piyama-radu] not come to meet me? If Piyama-radu says: 'I feared a plot to murder me,' did I not send to him my own son, the crown prince? Did I not give my son these instructions: 'Go, assure him with an oath, take his hand, and conduct him to me'? And concerning the plot to kill him because of which he is afraid, is murder a thing permitted in the land of Hatti? It most certainly is not.[123]

Hattušili III was so affronted by Piyama-radu's suspicion that he launched into an explanation of exactly how such guarantees operated in Hatti:

> Now safe conduct works this way in Hatti: If they send [...] to someone, they may not harm him. [...] 'Come, make your case before me

---

120. See also Meier, *Messenger*, 128, 137–41; *ILA*, 107.

121. For example, 'No. 27a: Indictment of Mita of Pahhuwa and Treaty with the Elders of several Anatolian communities', *HDT*, 163, 164, §§ 12, 16.

122. For more on the incorrigible Piyama-radu, see *LettGK*, 203–7; Bryce, *Kingdom of the Hittites*, 224–27, 290–93.

123. 'No. 101: from King Hattušili III to the King of Ahhiyawa ("Tawagalawa Letter")', *LettH*, 305.

[. . .]. But if you are not satisfied, then my man will escort you back into the land of Ahhiyawa in the same manner as he came here with you.[124]

Not only did Hattušili emphasise that the guarantee of safety was absolute, but he also offered an 'exchange': one of his closest courtiers would remain in Ahhiyawan territory as a hostage.[125] Yet Piyama-radu, who had an impressive track-record of flagrantly violating oaths of service and loyalty, remained doubtful that any safe-conduct offered in war was a true guarantee of immunity.

In sum, it appears that in Hatti diplomatic immunities were conventional and taken for granted during periods of peaceful relations, whereas during open conflict assumptions of immunity ceased and diplomatic communication came to rely upon the issuing of safe-conducts. However, these safe-conducts were themselves not above suspicion.

NON-COMBATANT

As regards immunities or protections pertaining to anyone other than individuals engaged on official state-level diplomacy, there is very little evidence. We have already mentioned the very occasional protection of priests, but a further example merits attention. An extremely rare reference to the behaviour of an army *returning* from a military campaign contains fascinating instructions for protecting non-combatants and their property:

> After the campaign no one shall steal a man, woman, son, daughter, slave, slave girl, ox, sheep, horse, mule, ass, silver, gold [. . .] bronze, or copper implements.[126]

This proclamation, issued to a number of Anatolian communities under Hittite control, is particularly concerned with the rape of women: 'And when you march [. . .] after the campaign you shall not violate the wife or daughter of a man, nor shall you injure them.'[127]

These are extremely significant regulations, pointing to a concern for non-combatants very rarely seen in this period. But it is important to note that the ordinances pertain specifically to conduct *after* a campaign. The protections thus appear to be designed to protect Hittite territories and subjects in the path of a returning army, especially an army containing allied contingents.

---

124. Ibid., 307–8.

125. 'Otherwise, let this charioteer remain in his [Piyama-radu's] place, while he [Piyama-radu] is coming and while he comes back there.' The charioteer is named as Dabala-Tarhunta, a close friend of the king and married to a member of the queen's family. Ibid., 308.

126. 'No 27a: Indictment of Mita of Pahhuwa and Treaty with the Elders of Several Anatolian Communities', *HDT*, 165, § 18.

127. Ibid., 165, § 18.

Rape, for example, was illegal in the Hittite kingdom; the pre-existing law of the land was simply being asserted.[128] There is no evidence of rape or plunder being prohibited *during* a campaign: that is, in enemy territory. As a result, this text, while constituting an important piece of evidence for structures of military discipline, cannot be taken as evidence of prohibitions against rape or assault of non-combatants during war itself.

Making Peace

Peaceful settlement was almost always a possibility during Hittite wars. Like the treatment of prisoners, '[p]eace making was the king's business'.[129] Local commanders were empowered to take the surrender of the enemy but were required, in the words of one king, to 'keep sending to My Majesty the Kaskaean men who are coming to make peace'.[130] Indeed, it appears that some regional governors were reluctant to commit themselves in peace negotiations, preferring to delegate responsibility to others. Kaššu, a 'Commander of the Military Heralds', was reprimanded by Hulla, 'Commander of the Chariot-Warriors', for his unwillingness to take action on his own authority and for allowing the enemy to play for time:

> Regarding what you wrote to me, as follows: 'Lord, if only you would drive down here! The Kaska men keep saying: "If only the Commander of the Chariot-warriors would drive here, we would make peace!"' You keep writing to me like that! But are *you* not a lord too? Furthermore, they call you Commander of the Military Heralds, and I am Commander of the Chariot-warriors. Why have you actually deferred to me? Why have you not met with their envoys?[131]

Even rebellious vassals could be forgiven and reinstalled as rulers, as long as they made peace and submitted to Hittite overlordship. We have already seen the overtures made to the repeatedly disloyal Piyama-radu. Later in the New Kingdom, Tudhaliya IV was willing to bestow the principality of Mira to the son of its rebellious former ruler:

---

128. 'If a man seizes a woman in the mountains and rapes her, it is the man's offence, but if he seizes her in her house, it is the woman's offence: the woman shall be put to death. If the woman's husband discovers them in the act and kills them, he has committed no offence.' *LawH*, 156, ¶ 197. Cf. *LCMAM*, 237. The assumption here is that in a city the woman could cry for help and be heard; failing to do this implies consent, and thus adultery. Compare the almost verbatim repetition of this law in Deuteronomy 22: 25-29 (see discussion below in ch. 10, 'Treatment of of Women').

129. Beal, 'Making, Preserving, and Breaking', 81, 83-84.

130. 'No. 16: from King to Kaššu', *LettH*, 113.

131. 'No. 73: from Hulla, the Commander of Chariot Warriors to Kaššu', *LettH*, 227-28. Cf. 'No. 54: to the King from Kašturrahšeli', ibid., 189-90.

Your father [...] was coveting my border territories [...]. Then I, My Majesty, too opened hostilities and defeated your father. But I, My Majesty, took you up [...] and treated you in a brotherly fashion [...]. You recognized My Majesty as overlord.[132]

Hittite law and culture demanded that the son share in the guilt of the father, but Tudhaliya's decision in this case shows the flexibility and pragmatism of Hittite foreign policy.

Conclusions to Part II

By this stage I hope it is evident that a case for the existence of a Hittite ethics of war should be taken very seriously. In terms of *ius ad bellum* thought, the Hittites developed a complex and sophisticated range of considerations concerning whether or not a war was just. The authority of the king as a representative of the gods was crucial, but wearing the crown was not necessarily enough in itself to make a king righteous, or a war just. This element of scepticism may have stemmed from the long history of usurpation that plagued the Hittite monarchy, or the slightly less centralised character of Hittite political power when compared to some of their peers; whatever the cause, there was a definite recognition in Hittite culture that their own kings could err. In such cases, divine punishment for waging unjust wars could be terrible, and responsibility for correcting moral and legal transgressions could be passed down from one king to another. This is most notable in the case of Šuppiluliuma I and his son, Muršili II.

The Hittites also recognised that just wars had just causes. Self-defence was the principal cause for war, but the restitution of property, vengeance for divine and mundane injuries (especially the violation of oaths), and the defence of allies all ranked as important and legitimate reasons to go to war. War was regarded as a form of legal process, prosecuted in the court of Hatti's gods, and as such it was also a type of ordeal or *judicium deorum*. To win in war, one had to be righteous, in terms both of the personal moral qualities of the king (indicated primarily through his upholding of the state cults) and of the legitimacy of the cause for which he was fighting. Crucially, the recognition that even the Hittites themselves could occasionally lack these attributes, and could thus engage in unjust wars, witnessed the first serious engagement with justice in international relations as something objective rather than wholly subjective and chauvinistic. The importance of this development cannot be overstated.

And yet the Hittites also countenanced and justified wars which were overtly aggressive and self-aggrandising. This was particularly the case during the Old Kingdom, such that both Gurney and Korošec have suggested

---

132. 'No. 102: from King Tudhaliya IV to Tarkašnawa of Mira ("Milawata Letter")', ibid., 317.

an evolution in Hittite attitudes to warfare between the Old and New Kingdoms, from understanding war in terms of plunder, to understanding it in legal terms. Korošec draws parallels between the increasing legalisation of Hittite warfare and the evolution of the Hittite law code, which gradually mitigated severe corporal punishments and introduced monetary fines and other more 'humane' forms of punishment.[133] These observations are largely valid, but underestimate the degree to which the legal and moral dimensions of war, expressed primarily through the bestowal of divine favour and victory, were already evident in the Old Kingdom. Concepts of just war undoubtedly became more complex during the course of the second millennium, but the building blocks were already apparent in Hatti by the late seventeenth century. Even wars of self-aggrandisement were understood in moral terms. The gods' approval was necessary to win wars, *ergo* victory in war was indicative of the gods' approval. For the Hittites, 'might equals right' and 'right equals might' were complementary rather than oppositional concepts. This was indeed a 'code for conquerors', developed to serve Hittite interests. Even so, this does not detract from the fact that, fundamentally, the Hittites viewed war as an activity contained within moral and legal parameters. For the Hittites, war always had moral and legal dimensions.

The moral and legal dimensions of war carried over into its practice, but in a far more limited way. There are only the basic outlines of what one could call Hittite *ius in bello* customs. Declarations of war were commonly issued, and clearly regarded as the appropriate way to open hostilities: they were a formal declaration of intent, a chance to air grievances before the gods, and a mark of the shift in legal and diplomatic relations between the opposing parties. Certain tactics, such as night attacks and ambushes, were frowned upon when used by enemies but were lauded when successfully employed by the Hittites themselves. In combat, there were no norms dictating how Hittite troops should treat their enemies. In defeat, enemies enjoyed no 'rights', although enemy combatants who surrendered could hope to be spared from death. Indeed, prisoners of war clearly *were* spared regularly, perhaps even normally. Slaves were a source of profit and labour, and Hatti was chronically short of manpower. Combatants and non-combatants were enslaved on a grand scale, although some prisoners of war could enjoy preferential treatment and even full integration into Hittite society, with many eventually fighting in Hittite armies.

It seems clear that no meaningful immunities existed for groups of people classed as non-combatants. All types of people were taken as prisoners of war, and kings even boasted of the numbers of 'civilian captives' taken as booty. The only evidence we have of non-combatant immunity is the occasional ad hoc protection of temple priests, or the immunities offered to diplomats

---

133. Gurney, *Hittites*, 113–14; Korošec, 'Warfare of the Hittites', 164, 166.

engaged in negotiations. A similar condition applied to movable and immovable property: religious sites and goods could occasionally be spared on the whim of individual kings, but this was very far from a concrete norm.

Therefore, while the ancient kingdom of Egypt may lay claim to the earliest development of just war thought, it is in Hatti that we find the origins of a truly sophisticated and nuanced ethics of war. What I mean by this is that, while Egypt may have conceived of war as a moral and legal activity, there was no space in Egyptian ethics for the consideration of Egyptian injustice. Egypt's wars were always just and always legitimate; Egypt's enemies were always wicked and always wrong. The Hittites, in contrast, believed that they had to make a convincing case for their wars: quite literally, that they had to *justify* them. Hittite kings were able to entertain the notion that they might not be in the right, and that their wars might not be successful. Whether to the gods or to men (or both), Hittite kings felt compelled to prove that they were morally upright and that they waged war in response to injuries committed by their enemies. Ultimately, it was through victory that the Hittites found proof of their righteousness.

PART III

The Israelites, c. 1000–c. 450 BCE

CHAPTER EIGHT

The Israelites: Historical Introduction

ANCIENT ISRAEL SITS somewhat uncomfortably in the company of Egypt and Hatti. Compared to these imperial superpowers of the ancient Near East, the Israelites were, in terms of the geopolitical history of the region, not much more than a footnote. They were relatively minor political players operating in a highly dynamic and dangerous political landscape. Between c. 1000 and c. 450, Israelite communities were battered by storms blowing from Egypt, Assyria, Babylon, and Persia. Suffice to say, they did not escape from such storms unscathed. The northern Israelite kingdom of Samaria and the southern Israelite kingdom of Judah (see Map 3) both fell to military conquest—by Assyria in the late eighth century and by Babylon in the early sixth century, respectively.[1] Even beyond this period, the Hellenistic and Roman ages brought about significant changes for Israelite communities in the Near East. Following a tenacious but failed rebellion against Rome, the Jerusalem Temple was destroyed in 70 CE and a large portion of the community from Judea was sent into exile.

In spite of the minor geopolitical status of the Israelite kingdoms, there are several compelling reasons to include ancient Israelite culture in this study. First, the Israelites produced wonderfully detailed accounts of their own religion, history, and culture; collectively, these texts are now referred to

---

1. Most scholars date the creation of the kingdom of Samaria to the late tenth century (c. 930)—that is, following the death of Solomon. The royal capital of Samaria was created by Omri in the ninth century, although the original capital was possibly at Shechem. Scholars also use the terms 'kingdom of Israel', 'kingdom of Northern Israel', or simply 'Northern Kingdom'. I will use the term 'kingdom of Samaria' to differentiate it clearly from the (potentially fictional) 'united kingdom of Israel' which preceded it (ruled by the kings Saul, David, and Solomon), and its historical southern Israelite competitor, the kingdom of Judah.

as the Tanakh.[2] In the West, this is better known as the Hebrew Bible or, to Christians, the Old Testament. As a source of ancient theology, political ideology, and attitudes to war, the Tanakh is a goldmine. War is a dominant topos within the text as a whole, leading to Julius Wellhausen's influential articulation of the inextricable link between war, Israel, and Yahweh:

> The name 'Israel' means 'El does battle,' and Jehovah was the warrior El, after whom the nation styled itself. The [army] camp was, so to speak, at once the cradle in which the nation was nursed and the smithy in which it was welded into unity [. . .]. There was Israel and there was Yahweh.'[3]

As another scholar describes the Tanakh, 'it is essentially a violent book with an obvious bias toward strife'.[4]

Compared to textual evidence from other ancient Near Eastern cultures, the Tanakh provides a uniquely detailed narrative of the history of the Israelite people, their relationship with their god, and their various travails, successes, and failures. As a composite document—written, collected, and redacted over several centuries—it also provides an aperture through which a historian can view a changing landscape of just war thought. Additionally, as a composite text, the Tanakh includes texts hailing from a much broader social context than the vast majority of our evidence from Egypt or Hatti, which tends to be royal and bureaucratic. While anything written in an age before mass literacy must be described as 'elite' to a certain degree, the Tanakh at least provides remnants of Israelite thought from sources other than royal propaganda.[5]

Nevertheless, if the Tanakh is a goldmine for the intellectual historian, it is also a minefield.[6] It is an immensely complicated artefact in terms of the history of its textual composition and redaction, as well as the vast amount of hermeneutical exegesis that has accrued around it in the Judaic, Christian, and Islamic traditions. Debates continue to rage in various branches of scholarship regarding its historicity and meaning, and the majority of these

---

2. All quoted passages from the Tanakh are taken from the standard English translation of the Hebrew Masoretic Text: *The Jewish Study Bible*, ed. Adele Berlin and Marc Zvi Brettler; consulting editor Michael Fishbane, 2nd edn (New York: Oxford University Press/ Jewish Publication Society, 2004).

3. Julius Wellhausen, *Prolegomena to the History of Israel, with a Reprint of the Article 'Israel' from the 'Encyclopaedia Britannica'*, trans. J. Sutherland Black and Allan Menzies (1885; repr. Charleston, SC: BiblioBazaar, 2006), 531.

4. Gerardo Zampaglione, *The Idea of Peace in Antiquity*, trans. Richard Dunn (Notre Dame, IN: University of Notre Dame Press, 1973), 192.

5. The elite and non-elite components of Israelite and Judahite ethics are explored in Crouch, *War and Ethics*, 65–116.

6. The overview in Niels Peter Lemche, *Ancient Israel: A New History of Israelite Society* (Sheffield: JSOT Press, 1988), 29–73, provides a succinct introduction to many of the problems posed by the Tanakh.

debates are coloured to some degree by theological, and occasionally political, commitments. Whilst the greater part of such debate need not concern us in our focus on the ethics of war, it will be necessary to discuss some of the key points concerning textual composition and dating. Ultimately, this is because it bears on what we can say about Israelite attitudes to war relating to different periods. A text composed in the sixth century but claiming to date from the tenth century (or earlier) poses obvious problems concerning a reconstruction of contemporary attitudes to war. First and foremost, what does 'contemporary' mean when reading such a text? Should we read it simply as a reflection of sixth-century attitudes, or do we read it as the summation of a long and relatively stable tradition dating back to the tenth century or earlier? How do we account for the problem of anachronism? Similarly, if we take the text as a faithful representation of tenth-century norms, can we assume that such norms were still relevant in the sixth century, or is it rather an example of outdated and sentimentalising history, composed as a piece of didacticism or contemporary critique?

It is important to state that I approach the Tanakh as a complex historical artefact, not as a piece of revealed theological truth. Readers will also notice that I favour the term 'Yahweh'. This is not the only name given to the Israelite god in the books of the Tanakh. The names El and Jehovah (the enunciated form of Yahweh) also appear. Of the two, El is the more ancient; indeed, the literal translation of *Israel* (*Yisra'el* in Hebraic) is 'El fights'.[7] Thus the very name Israel is rooted in theological conceptions of divine violence. To avoid confusion, I have preferred the name Yahweh throughout. Readers will also notice that I eschew the standard capitalisation of 'God' in reference to Yahweh, or 'He/Him' in the third person (except in quoted text). Again, this is because I approach Israelite theology in the same way as other theologies. There is no convention to capitalise 'god(s)' or 's/he' when referring to deities such as Amun, Isis, Ishtar, Teššub, Aššur, and so on; thus, I see no reason to capitalise references to Yahweh.

The second reason for including the Israelites in this study is that, as relatively minor kingdoms, Samaria and Judah provide a useful point of comparison to the great imperial powers of Egypt and Hatti. The Israelites developed their attitudes to war under the shadow, and sometimes under the direct domination, of more powerful empires. What impact did this have on Israelite ethics of war? Susan Niditch, for example, identifies a potent strain of 'tricksterism' in Israelite attitudes to war and violence, observing that '[d]eception is one of the ways marginal people imagine themselves improving their situation at the expense of those with greater power'.[8] As a result of the domination

---

7. Rudolf Smend, *Yahweh War and Tribal Confederation: Reflections upon Israel's Earliest History*, trans. Max G. Rogers (Nashville, KN: Abingdon Press, 1970), 27.
8. *WHB*, 110.

of the Levantine region by imperial states such as Egypt, Hatti, Assyria, and Babylon, it is perhaps reasonable to suppose that the Israelites—with limited politico-military resources—may have developed attitudes to the ethics of war significantly different from those of the major powers. On the other hand, it is just as likely that the domineering influences of Egypt, Hatti, Assyria, and Babylon to some extent rubbed off on the practices and attitudes of the Israelites.

Connected to this point concerning the Israelites as a minor military power, it is noteworthy how military defeat and enforced exile were integral elements of Israelite history. Much of the Tanakh was written or revised in the period immediately following the fall of Judah and the fifty years of Babylonian exile which a large component (although far from the whole) of its populace endured. What impact did this traumatic event have on Israelite identity and concepts of war as expressed in their sacred literature? In the shadow of defeat, Hebrew scribes may have exaggerated the military achievements of Israel's past as a means to cope with the disappointment of the present. Or perhaps the seeds of defeat were found in the past, the result of a long-term accumulation of sinful practices—Yahweh's punishment for violations of the Covenant. In either case, the political reality of the period c. 600–c. 450—when the Tanakh approached a form close to what we have today—must have fundamentally shaped the way that Israelite scribes projected their sense of ethics and war onto the past.

The third reason to include ancient Israelite thought in a study of the origins of the concept of just war is the remarkable influence it has had on later global culture, not least the Western just war tradition. It hardly needs stating that the Tanakh has played a foundational role in Jewish theology and ethics, especially in dialogue with the oral traditions enshrined first and foremost within the Mishnah, then later within the Talmud. Within the Islamic tradition, one could also look to the influence of the Torah (the first five books of the Tanakh) on the Quran, the Hadith, and the subsequent juridical development of the doctrine of jihad in Shari'a reasoning.[9] Moreover, the Patriarchs of the Hebrew Bible—especially Abraham (Ibrahim)—are venerated as prophets and ancestors in the Quran.

However, it was the incorporation of the Tanakh almost wholesale into the Christian Bible which guaranteed its subsequent 'internationalisation'. It also engendered an exceptionally high level of engagement with Israelite thought by Christian theologians, canon lawyers, and commentators. This trend continues today and shows no sign of abating. The availability of Greek translations of the Tanakh was crucial in this process, with the Torah ('Pentateuch' in Greek—literally 'five books') being translated in the mid-third century, followed by the

---

9. For a useful sketch of the Tanakh's influence concerning war within Judaism, Christianity, and Islam, see Craigie, *Problem of War*, 21–32.

longer Septuagint around the turn of the second and first centuries. These were joined by the Latin 'Vulgate' translation of Saint Jerome in the late fourth century CE.

Viewed through this Christian lens, the stories, attitudes, and norms of the Tanakh, known to Christians as the Old Testament, influenced untold numbers of believers, including political leaders, military commanders, and soldiers. Moreover, in the Christian (as well as in the Jewish and Islamic) tradition, the books of the Old Testament were, of course, read as sacred texts containing universal truths. This quite clearly endowed such texts with a unique authority, and so elevated the war ethics expressed within them to a status of both theological and moral 'truth'.

Saint Augustine of Hippo is frequently identified (incorrectly, as it happens) as the 'father' of the just war tradition. In truth, his writings on war were rather disparate, and what has come to be understood as Augustine's 'doctrine' of just war was more the product of medieval canon lawyers, especially the twelfth-century CE canonist Master Gratian.[10] Yet Augustine's treatment of war, along with that of his Christian predecessors and successors, is inconceivable without the Tanakh.[11] The general acceptance that violence can be both necessary and justifiable within a Christian framework, as well as the image of Yahweh as a potentially warlike and wrathful deity, was inherited almost wholesale from the Old Testament, not the New. With its message of love, meekness, suffering, and self-sacrifice, the New Testament, if taken in isolation, could not provide a compelling theological, philosophical, or legal justification for war. As a result, Christian commentators from the third century CE onwards repeatedly turned to the Old Testament as they attempted to explain and justify Christian warfare. Thus the influence of the Old Testament can be seen in discussions of the just war as it developed in the Christianised West from the second to the twenty-first century CE; in turn, these discussions helped to shape modern international law. One can state with absolute confidence, therefore, that the Western just war tradition would look quite different were

---

10. See *Augustine: Political Writings*, ed. E. M. Atkins and R. J. Dodaro (Cambridge: Cambridge University Press, 2001), xxiv; Johnson, 'St. Augustine', 25–28; Cox, 'Gratian', 34–35.

11. For example, Augustine points to Yahweh's justified destruction of Sodom (Genesis 19:24–25), and the need to physically chastise erring sons (Proverbs 3:12), and also cites David as a model warrior approved by Yahweh: *Augustine: Political Writings*, ed. Atkins and Dodaro, 207, 209, 216. In his *Questions on Numbers* (part of his *Questions on the Heptateuch*), q. 44 (Numbers 21:24–25), Augustine states that the Israelites waged just wars because 'safe passage was denied, which should have been available under the most equable law of human society'. Saint Augustine, *Questions on the Heptateuch*, introduced and annotated by Joseph T. Lienhard, trans. Joseph T. Lienhard and Sean Doyle, in *The Works of Saint Augustine: Writings on the Old Testament*, ed. Boniface Ramsey with a gen. intro. by Joseph T. Lienhard (New York: New City Press, 2016), 3–476 at 300. For discussion of this passage, see below, pp. 327–28.

it not for the Israelite Tanakh. So, while the Israelites may have been no more than bit-players on the geopolitical stage of the ancient Near East, the influence of their religious and cultural heritage on the world has been several orders of magnitude greater than they or their contemporaries could have envisaged.

In sum, the remarkable detail offered by the Tanakh as an ancient text, the character of the Israelite kingdoms as minor political communities fighting for survival in a region dominated by great powers, and the enduring impact of Israelite beliefs and attitudes on later global cultures of war all warrant the inclusion of Israelite thought in this study.

Sources

EVIDENCE OUTSIDE THE TANAKH

Given the surfeit of scholarship on the history and thought of the Israelites, there is remarkably little explicit evidence of ancient Israelite society outside of the Tanakh. Israel—as a place or a people—is not mentioned at all in Egyptian or West Asian sources until the very end of the thirteenth century. Even after that, the documentary evidence is scanty at best. From the turn of the twelfth to the middle of the eighth century—that is, the entire period supposedly covering the exodus, the conquest of Canaan, the creation of the unified kingdom of Israel, and the rupture of the united monarchy into the kingdoms of Samaria and Judah—only five or six allusions to Israel or Israelite rulers can be gleaned from the historical record, and even some of these have been called into question.[12]

The earliest reference to Israel is found on a victory stele from the reign of Pharaoh Merneptah (r. c. 1213–c. 1203), commemorating a successful Egyptian campaign against the Libyans. While focusing on the victories against the Libyans, the laudatory poem ends by praising the pharaoh's subjection of all enemy peoples, including those of Canaan:

> Canaan is captive with all woe.
> Ashkelon is conquered, Gezer seized,
> Yanoam made non-existent;
> Israel is wasted, bare of seed.[13]

Thus the reference to Israel on the so-called Israel Stele is not much more than a single entry in an appendix. A number of ambiguities also remain. It is unclear whether the term 'Israel' refers to a people, a state, or a region. Indeed, there is debate as to whether the Egyptian hieroglyphs can be translated as

---

12. Redford, *Egypt, Canaan, and Israel*, 257.
13. *AEL*, 2:77. See also *ANET*, 378; *ANEA*, 1:231.

'Israel' at all, or if another translation would be more accurate.[14] Finally, as James B. Pritchard notes, 'the text is not historical [...] but is rather a poetic eulogy of a universally victorious pharaoh'.[15] Ultimately, therefore, it tells us very little. This distinct lack of historical evidence for an early united Israelite kingdom—the kingdom of Saul, David, and Solomon—has led a number of scholars to maintain that a unified Israelite kingdom simply did not exist, and that the concept of a unified historical 'Israel' did not come into existence until the post-exilic period of the late sixth century and later.[16]

Further references to 'Israel' do not appear again until the second half of the ninth century. Two fragmentary inscriptions discovered at Tel Dan (close to the modern border between Israel and Lebanon), probably dating from the second half of the ninth century, may have been commissioned by King Hazael of Aram. The inscriptions refer to the killing of a 'king of Israel'—*possibly* a reference to Jehoram (son of Ahab), king of Samaria.[17] A more substantial reference comes in the form of a victory stele also dated to the mid- to late ninth century, created by Mesha, king of Moab (c. 855–c. 830).[18] The 'Moabite Stone' or 'Mesha Stele' is a fascinating artefact in its own right, but it has mainly been discussed for its narration of Mesha's victory over King Omri of Samaria (Israel):

> Now Omri, king of Israel oppressed Moab many days, for Kemosh was angry with his land [...] but I prevailed over him and over his house. Now Israel utterly perished forever.[19]

Mesha claims to have attacked and sacked the Israelite cities of Ataroth and Nebo, proscribing several thousand men and women for the Moabite god, Ashtar-Kemosh. At Nebo, Mesha 'took from there the vessels of Yahweh, and [...] hauled

---

14. See Gösta W. Ahlström, *Who Were the Israelites?* (Winona Lake, IN: Eisenbrauns, 1986), 37–43; Othniel Margalith, 'On the Origin and Antiquity of the Name Israel', *Zeitschrift für die Alttestamentliche Wissenschaft* 102 (2) (1990): 225–37; Alessandra Nibbi, 'Some Remarks on the Merenptah Stela and the So-Called Name of Israel', *Discussions in Egyptology* 36 (1996): 79–102; Niels Peter Lemche, *The Israelites in History and Tradition* (Louisville, KY: Westminster John Knox Press; London: SPCK, 1998), 35–38. For a defence of the 'maximalist' translation and the location of Israel within Canaan, see Michael Hasel, 'Merenptah's Reference to Israel: Critical Issues for the Origin of Israel', in *Critical Issues in Early Israelite History*, ed. Richard S. Hess, Gerald A. Klingbeil, and Paul J. Ray Jr. (Winona Lake, IN: Eisenbrauns, 2008), 47–60.

15. *ANEA*, 1:231.

16. See especially Philip R. Davies, *In Search of Ancient Israel* (Sheffield: JSOT Press 1992), who argues that the 'biblical Israel' is a literary construct, while 'ancient Israel' is a scholarly construct. Cf. Gottwald, *Politics of Ancient Israel*, 16–22.

17. 'Tel Dan Stele Inscription', *HST*, 305–7. For a critique of the claims made by biblical scholars regarding these inscriptions, see Lemche, *Israelites in History*, 38–43, 62.

18. 'Moabite Stone', *HST*, 311–30.

19. Ibid., 312–13. Kemosh was the principal deity of Moab.

FIGURE 39. King Jehu of Samaria (kneeling) (r. c. 842–c. 815 BCE) pays tribute to the Assyrian king Shalmaneser III: the 'Black Obelisk' of Shalmaneser III, mid-ninth century BCE. GFDL, CC BY-SA 3.0 licence, via Wikimedia Commons.

them before Kemosh'.[20] Thus, the Moabite Stone also provides the oldest unequivocal reference to the god Yahweh outside the books of the Tanakh.

The usually rich Assyrian sources are equally sparse when it comes to references either to Israel as a united kingdom or to the Israelites as a distinct people. A single possible reference has been identified, from one of the Kurkh Monoliths of Shalmaneser III, constructed at some time between c. 879 and c. 852. One of the inscriptions record Shalmaneser III's battle at Qarqar (c. 853) against a large coalition of forces, including those of Ahab of Israel, who provided two thousand chariots and ten thousand infantry.[21] This is the only specific reference to 'Israel' in Assyrian or Babylonian sources. Such sources refer instead to the northern kingdom of Samaria as the 'House of Omri', 'Land of Omri', or simply 'Samaria'.[22] A later inscription from Shalmaneser III's 'Black Obelisk' refers to a tribute payment from 'Jehu, son of Omri' (figure 39).[23] The records of the campaigns of Tiglath-Pileser III (c. 744–c. 727) in Syria and Palestine mention both Jehoahaz of Judah and the defeat of, and extraction of tribute from, Menahem of Samaria.[24] Tiglath-Pileser III's successor, Sargon II (c. 722–c. 705), boasted of conquering Samaria (c. 722) after a three-year siege and the taking of 27,290 prisoners, in addition to fifty chariots.[25]

20. Ibid., 313.
21. *ANEA*, 1:190. Cf. 1 Kings 16:29; 2 Kings 8:3. See also above, ch. 1, 'Armed Forces'.
22. Kelle suggests that 'Israel' could have designated a group of vassal states, including Samaria, Moab, Edom, and Judah: Brad Kelle: 'What's in a Name?: Neo-Assyrian Designations for the Northern Kingdom and Their Implications for Israelite History and Biblical Interpretation', *Journal of Biblical Literature* 121 (4) (2002): 639–66.
23. *ANEA*, 1:191; cf. ibid., 192.
24. Ibid., 1:193–94; cf. 2 Kings 15:17.
25. *ANEA*, 1:195; cf. 2 Kings 17:4.

THE TANAKH

The ancient Near Eastern documentary record yields very few clues about Israelite history prior to the eighth century. The period from the supposed patriarchal age all the way down to the destruction of the kingdom of Samaria is essentially bereft of documentary evidence. Unfortunately, this sparsity is also true for the archaeological evidence more broadly. While there is rich evidence of human settlement throughout the Levant during the second and early first millennia, not a single artefact or site testifies to the existence of the Israelites *specifically*: that is, as a people distinct from the other Semitic peoples of the region. There is no explicit archaeological evidence of a united Solomonic kingdom of Israel existing in the tenth century, nor any evidence of a sophisticated or powerful polity in either Judah or Samaria prior to the ninth century.

The core problem for the field of biblical archaeology is, as Amelie Kuhrt succinctly puts it, that 'the archaeological evidence rarely fits comfortably with the Old Testament text'.[26] For example, the rapid and devastating Israelite conquest of Canaan, recounted in the books of Joshua and Judges, is flatly contradicted by the material record. Cities such as Jericho, Ai, and Gibeon had either been in ruins for centuries or had yet to be founded when Joshua's 'conquest' is said to have occurred in the Late Bronze Age.[27] With a dearth of archaeological evidence or corroborative documentary evidence, biblical scholars have been forced to fall back almost exclusively on the text of the Tanakh itself in order to reconstruct the history of Israel, Samaria, and Judah. The stark truth is that without the Tanakh we would know barely anything at all about these societies, and any attempt to reconstruct a political, military, or religious history of the ancient Israelites would be all but impossible.[28]

This over-reliance on the Tanakh has encouraged an uncritical approach, exaggerated by the special authority bestowed on the text in the Judaic, Christian, and Islamic traditions. As one biblical scholar recognises, '[s]o much of what we do as biblical historians involves "taking things on faith" in more than one sense of the phrase'.[29] Donald Redford, an eminent historian of the Near East, excoriates many biblical historians for routinely taking the sources at face value and failing to assess critically the reliability or originality of the evidence. Redford offers an analogy, explaining the hazards of biblical 'history' by comparing the reconstruction of Israelite history on the basis of the Tanakh to a reconstruction of early British history on the basis of Arthurian legend.[30]

---

26. *KANE*, 2:431.
27. See, inter alia, Lemche, *Ancient Israel*, 110–14; *KANE*, 2:431.
28. For a scholarly yet unusually accessible analysis of Israelite historiography, see Van Seters, *In Search of History*, esp. 209–353.
29. *WHB*, 11; cf. Gottwald, *Politics of Ancient Israel*, 13–14.
30. Redford, *Egypt, Canaan, and Israel*, 260–62.

Despite the notable inadequacies of some biblical scholarship, it remains the case that the Tanakh is a fascinating and important source. The bulk of it is written in Hebrew, although some late books (Ezra, Daniel) contain Aramaic. In its current form, the Tanakh is divided into three parts: the five books of the Torah, or Law (Genesis through Deuteronomy), referred to in Greek as the Pentateuch; the books of the *Nevi'im*, or Prophets, which includes the 'Former Prophets' (Joshua through Kings[31]) and 'Later Prophets' (Isaiah through Malachi); and finally the books of *Ketuvim*, or Scriptures (Psalms through Chronicles).[32] As the introduction to the English translation of the standard Masoretic text proudly and justifiably asserts, '[t]he ancient Near Eastern world produced no other work of comparable length in the span of time its narrative covers or in the inclusiveness of the literary genres and sources incorporated into it'.[33] To give some comparison, the Tanakh is around twice the length of Herodotus's *Histories* (composed c. 440).[34] It is remarkable that this combination of myth, religious practice, folklore, and cultural memory was ever collected into a single whole, or that it should have survived to the present day, albeit with modification. More remarkable still has been its influence on world religion and history.

The Internal Chronology of the Tanakh

Based solely on the Masoretic text, the major events described within the Tanakh roughly follow the internal chronology listed here in Appendix 2.[35] The problem with this chronology is that it is contradicted by far more compelling archaeological and documentary evidence from the region. For example, the conquest of Canaan under Joshua is dated to the same time as the well-documented Canaanite campaigns of Pharaoh Thutmose III, which were followed by Amenhotep II's campaigns and deportations of the local population. It goes without saying that the Egyptian and Israelite conquests could not have occurred simultaneously. Similarly, the period of Judges as recounted in

---

31. Samuel and Kings were each originally considered single books in the Hebrew tradition. The third-century Greek Septuagint (translated c. 225) divided both of these lengthy books.

32. It should be noted that variant versions of the texts exist in the form of the third-century Greek Septuagint, the Samaritan Pentateuch, the Dead Sea Scrolls, and the Old Testament as contained in the Syriac Peshitta.

33. *JSB*, 6–7.

34. The *Histories* runs to almost 250,000 words, while the Tanakh runs to around 450,000.

35. For examples of the vigorous debate regarding composition and dating, see Rolf Rendtorff, *The Problem of the Process of Transmission in the Pentateuch* (Sheffield: JSOT Press, 1990); Rendtorff, 'Between Historical Criticism and Holistic Interpretation: New Trends in Old Testament Exegesis', in *Congress Volume: Jerusalem, 1986*, ed. J. A. Emerton (Leiden: Brill, 1988), 298–303; Niels Peter Lemche, 'The Old Testament—A Hellenistic Book?', *Scandinavian Journal of the Old Testament* 7 (2) (1993): 163–93.

THE ISRAELITES: HISTORICAL INTRODUCTION [279]

the Tanakh was concurrent with the Egyptian and Hittite empires in Asia and Egyptian dominance in Canaan. Until c. 1200, Egypt controlled coastal cities such as Gaza, Jaffa, Beth Shean, and Aphek. Other than the single instance on the 'Israel Stele' of Merneptah (c. 1208), no Egyptian or Near Eastern source makes any reference to the Patriarchs, a nation or people of Israel, a military leader called Joshua, or any of his tribal successors.[36] If such a people or persons existed, then they were evidently not considered important enough for other states to discuss; they certainly were not embarking on mass conquests in the region of Canaan.

The Tanakh also proves itself consistently ignorant of historical realities, especially concerning the second millennium. If one were to read the Tanakh alone, one would have no sense that the territories in which the stories play out were actually dominated by Egypt and Hatti during the mid-second millennium, and largely ruled by Egypt in the late second millennium. The military campaigns and tributary systems of Egypt and Hatti, or the major Egyptian dynasties of the Amenophids, Thutmosids, or Ramessides, make no appearance. The Tanakh continues to confuse Egyptian history well into the first millennium.[37]

Anachronisms contained in the supposedly early historical books include common references to iron—chariots, weapons, implements—when this technology was either unavailable or extremely rare.[38] Camels make a number of appearances in episodes set in the second millennium, yet were not domesticated in the Near East until the ninth century.[39] The Phoenician city of Sidon is often cited as a major centre—reflecting its status from the sixth century onwards—but Tyre, the dominant Phoenician port of the Late Bronze Age and Early Iron Age, is overlooked.[40] Even the two latest texts in terms of composition, the books of Daniel and Esther (second century), are set three to four hundred years earlier, during the Persian period of the late sixth and fifth centuries.[41]

This historical time-flattening has led to the misconception of the Tanakh as a pre-exilic compendium of texts, dating all the way back to Moses's authorship of the Torah some time in the second millennium.[42] In truth, the many contradictions and anachronisms of the Tanakh were the product of a text composed and redacted largely between the seventh and third centuries, yet

36. *KANE*, 2:425; Redford, *Egypt, Canaan, and Israel*, 258–58.
37. As Redford concludes, '[b]iblical writers of the seventh to sixth centuries BC[E] lacked precise knowledge of Egypt as recent as a few generations before their own time'. Only toponyms give some 'echo' of this Egyptian heritage: 'Land of Ramesses' (Genesis 47:11); city of Ra'amses (Exodus 1:11). Redford, *Egypt, Canaan, and Israel*, 257–58.
38. Judges 1:19; 4:3, 13; 1 Samuel 13:19–21.
39. Judges 6:5; 7:12; 8:21, 26.
40. Joshua 11:8, 13:4; Judges 1:31, 10:6, 19:28; Redford, *Egypt, Canaan, and Israel*, 277.
41. *KANE*, 2:418–19.
42. Doubts about Moses's authorship of the Torah have existed since at least the eighteenth century: ibid., 2:420.

claiming to be much older. Of course, this does leave open the possibility that the later redactors were drawing from much older oral traditions and historical artefacts. Parts of the Tanakh are surely very ancient: the Song of Deborah and the Decalogue, for example, are stylistically and substantively archaic, and probably have their origin in the second millennium. But taken as a whole, the text likely coalesced into its current form in the period between the Babylonian conquest of Judah in 586 and the era of Persian dominance during the fifth and fourth centuries: essentially, the first half of the Second Temple Period (c. 516–70 CE). Variations between the Hebrew Tanakh and the Greek Septuagint (translated from the Hebrew in Alexandria c. 225) indicate that the text had still not completely crystallised by the third century. Some very late additions, such as Balaam's prophecy with its reference to Rome (*Kittim*),[43] may have been added as late as the first century CE, thus extending the compilation period to include the entire Second Temple Period. Other variants of the Israelite narrative exist in the form of the Samaritan Torah (or Samaritan Pentateuch), the Dead Sea Scrolls, and the Syriac Peshitta.

Even if one accounts for the late composition of the Tanakh, the historian faces other challenges regarding the reliability of the narrative. As Norman Gottwald observes,

> the late compositors of the Hebrew Bible were so preoccupied with and limited by the horizons of their commitment to fashion a new 'Israelite-Jewish' community following the destruction of the states of Israel [Samaria] and Judah, that their ideological perspective altogether cancels out any interest on their part in reporting the actual history of Israel before the collapse of those states.[44]

Furthermore, the Tanakh is steeped in a southern Judahite perspective which adopted an increasingly ardent Yahwism. The version of Israelite history presented is one that critiques the Samaritan kingdom, its dynasties, its people, and its religious practices. Samaria's own voice is almost silent. Consequently, our image of Israel and Israelite thought has been fashioned by only 'one branch of self-identified Israelites'.[45] This raises serious doubts regarding the extent to which *any* of the narrative recounting a united Israel, constructed as it is from a Judahite perspective and with a specific ideological agenda, can really be taken as reflective of Israelite history as a whole.

The 'Documentary Hypothesis'/'Critical Thesis'

Building on the pioneering nineteenth-century work of Karl Graf and Julius Wellhausen, biblical scholars have long debated the literary processes that led to the creation of the Tanakh as we know it now. Perhaps the most important

---

43. See Numbers 24:3–9, 17–24.
44. Gottwald, *Politics of Ancient Israel*, 1–2.
45. Ibid., 17.

development within this scholarship was the emergence of the so-called documentary hypothesis. This approach meticulously analyses linguistic conventions within the Tanakh and cross-references citations of specific events, practices, and laws in order to construct a chronology of textual composition. It posits the existence of four distinctive 'authors' or 'schools' responsible for the various books of the Tanakh, and has come to be regarded as the 'critical orthodoxy'.[46]

Beginning with the 'second' creation story (Genesis 2:4), a lively narrative style uses the name Yahweh (Jehovah) exclusively for the Israelite god; this 'author' is thus identified as the 'Yahwist', or 'J' author. Within the J narrative, Yahweh is anthropomorphised and accessible, interacting with humanity. J betrays a definite bias towards the history of southern Israel and the Davidic dynasty, indicating that it was probably written in the southern kingdom of Judah. Dates for J have ranged from the tenth century (Solomon's royal court) to the post-exilic fifth century.

A contrasting narrative, beginning with Abraham, refers to the Israelite god as Elohim or El. This narrative is thus identified as the 'Elohist' or 'E' author. Elohim is presented as a transcendental and distant deity, up until his revelation to Moses. The Elohist provides the majority of the Covenant Code (Exodus 20:22–23:19), and its 'history' concentrates more on the northern territories of Ephraim, possibly indicating a Samaritan authorship. Dates for E range from the late ninth to the fourth century. However, some portions of text are so difficult to differentiate between the Yahwist and the Elohist that they are identified as 'JE'.[47] These two textual traditions may have converged as a result of Samaritan refugees entering Judah after the fall of the northern kingdom in the late eighth century.[48]

A distinctive ideological tone, at pains to emphasise Yahwist monotheism, is adopted by the so-called Deuteronomist, also referred to as 'D'. The Deuteronomist is believed to be responsible for the relatively coherent historical narrative spanning the books of Deuteronomy, Joshua, Judges, Samuel, and the two books of Kings.[49] The Deuteronomist focuses on the crucial importance of Israelite fidelity to the Covenant, and warns of the terrible consequences that violations of Yahweh's law will bring about. The Deuteronomist bestows the responsibilities for all cultic ritual upon the tribe of Levi,

---

46. *JSB*, 5–6. Over the last two centuries, composition dates have generally been revised to reflect later dates of authorship.

47. For example, on the Covenant, Exodus 20:22–22:33.

48. *KANE*, 2:422.

49. The 'Deuteronomistic historiography' thesis, which proposes that the books of Deuteronomy through Kings are the product of a single redactional effort, completed during the Babylonian exile of the mid-sixth century, is principally associated with Martin Noth's *Überlieferungsgeschichtliche Studien* (1943). This is available in English in two 'parts': Martin Noth, *The Deuteronomistic History* (Sheffield: JSOT Press, 1981); Noth, *The Chronicler's History* (Sheffield: JSOT Press, 1987). Noth was convinced that the Deuteronomist was editing (rather than inventing) older historical material.

demarcating a closing off of religious authority that is absent from J and E. Some scholars have identified the initial creation of Deuteronomy as being part of King Josiah of Judah's religious and political reforms of the mid-seventh century,[50] but much of the Deuteronomistic material is more likely to be exilic or post-exilic, compiled from around the mid-sixth century.

Deuteronomy itself is of the utmost importance to concepts of war. Gerhard von Rad attached special significance to Deuteronomy as the basis for his influential holy war thesis, stating that 'Deuteronomy is in the whole Old Testament by far the richest source concerning concepts and customs of holy war [...] it is thoroughly saturated from the first to the last chapter by an outspoken war ideology'.[51] Moreover, through the Deuteronomistic composition and redaction of many other books of the Tanakh, it 'contributed that additional element of militant spirit and programmatic irreconcilability which has so frequently alienated people'.[52] Others have described the programmatic Deuteronomistic 'ban' (the complete annihilation of enemy persons and property in war) as 'created at the writing desk' and thus not a reflection of 'any real circumstances'.[53] Suffice to say, the dating of Deuteronomistic material continues to be hotly debated.[54]

Finally, a late and highly formalised style displays a particular concern with proper religious practice, especially the organisation of the priesthood and the regulation of the cult after the time of Moses and Aaron. This author, almost certainly post-exilic, has subsequently been identified as the 'Priestly Code', or simply 'P'. Like the Deuteronomist, P is concerned with the demarcation of religious authority, decreeing that only descendants of Aaron could perform cultic sacrifices.[55]

As even this very brief summary should indicate, the Tanakh is an intricate and intertwined literary web. Extricating single strands is extremely difficult.

---

50. For example, Moshe Weinfeld, *Deuteronomy and the Deuteronomic School* (Oxford: Clarendon Press, 1972; repr. Winona Lake, IN: Eisenbrauns, 1992). For an accessible overview of Josiah's reforms, see Israel Finkelstein and Neil Asher Silberman, *The Bible Unearthed: Archaeology's New Vision of Ancient Israel and the Origin of Its Sacred Texts* (New York: Simon & Schuster, 2002), 275–95.

51. Rad, *Holy War*, 115.

52. Ibid., 116.

53. Weinfeld, *Deuteronomy*, 167. Cf. Michael Walzer, 'The Idea of Holy War in Ancient Israel', *The Journal of Religious Ethics* 20 (2) (1992): 215–28 at 224; Norman Solomon, 'Judaism and the Ethics of War', *International Review of the Red Cross* 87 (858) (2005): 295–309 at 297 n. 8.

54. Erik Eynikel, *The Reforms of King Josiah and the Composition of the Deuteronomistic History* (Leiden: Brill, 1996), 7–31, provides a detailed albeit rather difficult summary of much of the key historiography. See also Albert de Pury, Thomas C. Römer, and Jean-Daniel Macchi (eds), *Israel Constructs Its History: Deuteronomistic History in Recent Research* (Sheffield: JSOT Press, 2000); Van Seters, *In Search of History*, 322–53.

55. For a useful overview, see *JSB*, 'Introduction'; KANE, 2:421–22.

For example, most scholars agree that P is the latest of the four 'authors', yet P is responsible for the creation story of Genesis 1 (one of two creation stories: cf. Genesis 2:4), which now forms the beginning of the Tanakh and Christian Bible. P also contributes to Exodus, Leviticus, Numbers, and several other books. Paradoxically, then, the 'oldest' parts of the Tanakh—in terms of its internal narrative chronology—are actually the work of the latest author and were probably not compiled until the fifth to the third century. This single example gives some sense of the complexity of composition, and the pitfalls of reading the Tanakh as a simple, chronologically arranged narrative.

This summary, painted in broad strokes, does little justice to the extraordinary scholarly effort invested in developing and refining the documentary hypothesis. Nevertheless, the sketch broadly represents the current consensus among biblical scholars regarding the composition of the Tanakh. What, then, are the ramifications for reading the Tanakh as a historical source? First, all sophisticated scholars agree that the Tanakh does not provide a neat record of historical events. Second, we must recognise that references to events said to have taken place in the second millennium probably contain limited or possibly no historical truth. Certain episodes might preserve cultural memories of real events, but as traditions evolve over time they inevitably warp, taking on the imprint of the practices, norms, and experiences of the communities they serve at any particular time. Martial and ethical traditions are not immune from this process; arguably, they are particularly susceptible to it, as they are constitutive of the self-identity, norms (ideational and applied), and pragmatic considerations of individual societies. Thus martial and ethical traditions will always, to a significant degree, be aligned to contemporary or near-contemporary reality. It stands to reason, therefore, that the texts of the Tanakh tell us more about the conceptual world of Israelites of the mid-first millennium (when the texts were composed or compiled) than they do about Israelites of earlier periods.

Major Historical Events according to the Tanakh's Narrative

According to the Tanakh, the principal events of Israelite history follow a timeline that essentially begins—leaving aside the patently mythical Creation, Fall, and flood stories—with the patriarch Abraham leading a nomadic life, perhaps as a mercenary, throughout the Levant (see Appendix 2). Compelled by famine, Abraham's successors spent several generations sojourning in Egypt, until the Israelites eventually fled that country in a mass exodus, led by the prophet Moses. Forty years of wanderings in the Sinai Peninsula and other territories followed, during which time Moses received the Decalogue and forged the Covenant between the Israelites and Yahweh. Upon Moses's death, the Israelites crossed the river Jordan under the military leadership of

Joshua, and thereupon began a rapid 'conquest' of Canaan, lasting just seven years.[56] A period of 'Judges' (tribal warlords) followed, during which the Israelite tribes' settlement of Canaan and the surrounding lands was consolidated, although conflict with their new neighbours continued. Eventually, as a result of military expediency, to combat the growing threat of the Philistines, leadership of the tribes was unified under a monarchy, with Saul elevated to the kingship. The new monarchy was militarily effective, but descended into civil war between Saul and the mercenary warlord David. The usurper David was finally victorious. However, the Davidic dynasty of the united monarchy lasted only as long as the reign of David's son and successor, Solomon. Upon Solomon's death, the united kingdom of Israel splintered into two states: the northern kingdom of Israel, which eventually settled on the city of Samaria as its capital; and the southern kingdom of Judah, with Jerusalem as its capital. In the following generations, Samaria and Judah alternated as allies and enemies, while at the same time fighting for survival amidst the greater powers of the region. Samaria's demise came in about 722, when it was conquered by the Assyrian kings Shalmaneser V and Sargon II. Judah survived as a much-depleted entity until about 587, when it too was conquered, by Nebuchadnezzar, king of Babylon. The destruction of the Jerusalem Temple and the forced relocation of a significant portion of the population marked the beginning of the so-called 'Babylonian Exile', which lasted until the Persian king Cyrus conquered Babylon around 539 and permitted the Israelites to return to their lands. Darius I allowed the rebuilding of the Jerusalem Temple (c. 520–c. 516). This Second Temple Period (not specifically recounted in the Tanakh) lasted through Persian, Hellenic, and Roman domination, until the final destruction of the Jerusalem Temple by the Roman general Titus in 70 CE.

The historicity of much of this narrative, particularly those parts covering the period prior to the ninth century and the emergence of the two kingdoms of Samaria and Judah, has thus far proved impossible to confirm. It is likely that Yahweh (*Yhw*) emerged around the middle of the second millennium as one of a number of hero-creator gods in Canaan, perhaps among the 'Shasu' peoples in the region around Moab and Edom.[57] But the evolution and assertion of Yahwist monotheism came much later in Israelite history, certainly not before the first millennium, and possibly as late as the post-exilic period. No Egyptian sources mention the sojourn or the exodus, despite the fact that Numbers 1:1–46 calculates the number of Hebrew adult males leaving Egypt as 603,550 (implying a total Hebrew population of around two million!). Moreover, the Exodus account itself is clearly of late authorship, and

---

56. Joshua 14:7–10ff. For an excellent summary of the geographical course of the conquest and the major regions and cities involved (according solely to the Tanakh), see Redford, *Egypt, Canaan, and Israel*, 263–64.

57. Redford, *Egypt, Canaan, and Israel*, 382.

its geographical information regarding Egypt is from the Saite period (c. 664–c. 525) or later.[58]

Some have argued that 'if the Israelites had invented their history, it seems more likely that they would have portrayed themselves as the original inhabitants of their land rather than as interlopers with a humiliating background as slaves'.[59] But this fails to stand up against comparative evidence from other cultures. Imagine for a moment that Virgil's *Aeneid* was the only extant source from ancient Rome. We would read a foundation account of how Rome was built by Trojan exiles who had suffered humiliating defeat at the hands of their bitterest enemies, and had arrived as interlopers in Italy. The popular cycle of Brut chronicles in medieval England, 'recording' the settlement of England by Aeneas's son Brutus, continued and expanded this Virgilian tradition. Exactly the same could be said of the American story of 'manifest destiny', created in the nineteenth century CE to heroise a story of persecution and exile from Europe resulting in the conquest and colonisation of the 'promised land' of North America (a story much inspired by the biblical narratives of Exodus and Joshua). The truth is that themes of heroic peoples rising phoenix-like from the ashes and possessing land by right of conquest is a powerful trope across many cultures, regardless of historicity.

Conquest

For many modern adherents of the Abrahamic faiths, the terrifyingly violent conquest of Canaan, as recounted in the Tanakh, poses a number of moral problems. Such readers can be comforted in the knowledge that the conquest narrative, as recounted in the books of Joshua and Judges, is almost entirely fictional.[60] While there remains disagreement regarding the extent to which the narrative is ahistorical, and exactly when it was composed (from late eighth century to post-sixth century), the majority of scholars now reject the idea of a massive Israelite military conquest of Canaan, either as a swift or a more drawn-out process. Primarily this is because the archaeological and comparative documentary evidence belies it.[61] There is also the fundamental conundrum of explaining how a group of nomads, with no siege equipment,

---

58. Ibid., 408–10.
59. *JSB*, 104, 106.
60. Smend, *Yahweh War*, 23–24. There is still some disagreement regarding the extent to which the narrative is ahistorical: *KANE*, 2:427; *JSB*, 455.
61. Ahlström, *Who Were the Israelites?*, 2–3, 5ff; Israel Finkelstein, 'Patriarchs, Exodus, Conquest: Fact or Fiction?', in Israel Finkelstein and Amihai Mazar, *The Quest for the Historical Israel: Debating Archaeology and the History of Early Israel; Invited Lectures Delivered at the Sixth Biennial Colloquium of the International Institute for Secular Humanistic Judaism, Detroit, October 2015*, ed. Brian B. Schmidt (Atlanta, GA: Society for Biblical Literature, 2007), 41–55; Finkelstein and Silberman, *Bible Unearthed*, 72–96.

managed to overcome fortified cities that had successfully resisted attacks from great military powers such as Egypt, Hatti, and Assyria.[62]

Theories of the emergence of a distinctive Israelite polity in Canaan have varied over the past century. Moving away from a picture of swift military conquest, the German scholars Albrecht Alt and Martin Noth described nomadic or semi-nomadic pastoralists infiltrating Canaan both forcefully and peacefully, establishing pioneer settlements and gradually integrating with the native population.[63] Alongside this new interpretation was the theory of a 'confederation' or 'amphictyony' of twelve Israelite tribes united around a cultic shrine to Yahweh. The name of this amphictyony, it was claimed, was 'Israel'.[64] Building on the idea of a religious amphictyony, George Mendenhall posited a socio-economic model of a peasant revolution by *habiru* (becoming 'Hebrew') pastoralists and mercenaries. During the period of Judges, this loose federation of semi-nomadic tribes was bound together by a religious covenant, and the 'text of that covenant is the Decalogue'.[65] Adapting Mendenhall's peasants' revolt theory, Gottwald proposed that the Israelite polity was not ethnically distinct from Canaan, but rather originated from within a Canaanite group of agriculturalists who rejected the oppressive burden of city-state government. The glue binding this group of radicals together was their worship of Yahweh.[66] However, as for the other theories already mentioned,

---

62. Redford, *Egypt, Canaan, and Israel*, 264. Despite the glaring deficiencies in evidence, the conquest thesis (in various forms) was defended in a number of influential works during the twentieth century and continues to be defended in more conservative biblical literature. For example: William Foxwell Albright, *The Archaeology of Palestine*, revised edn (Harmondsworth: Penguin, 1960), 112–13, 118–19; Albright, *From the Stone Age to Christianity*, 274–89; John Bright, *A History of Israel*, 3rd edn (1959; Philadelphia: Westminster Press, 1981), 129–33, 137–43; Yigael Yadin, *Hazor: The Rediscovery of a Great Citadel of the Bible* (London: Weidenfeld & Nicolson, 1975); Shmuel Yeivin, *The Israelite Conquest of Canaan* (Istanbul: Nederlands Historisch-Archaeologisch Instituut in het Nabije Oosten, 1971); Abraham Malamat, 'Conquest of Canaan: Israelite Conduct of War according to Biblical Tradition', *Revue internationale d'histoire militaire* 42/Édition de la Commission israelienne d'histoire militaire (1979): 25–52.

63. Albrecht Alt, *Essays on Old Testament History and Religion*, trans. R. A. Wilson (Oxford: Basil Blackwell, 1966), esp. 165–69, 175–83; Martin Noth, *The History of Israel*, revised 2nd edn, trans. Peter R. Ackroyd (London: A. and C. Black, 1960), 68–84. Volkmar Fritz, 'Conquest or Settlement? The Early Iron Age in Palestine', *The Biblical Archaeologist* 50 (2) (1987): 84–100, posits an adapted version of the 'infiltration hypothesis', which he terms the 'symbiosis hypothesis' (98). This is developed further in Fritz, *The Emergence of Israel in the 12th and 11th Centuries BCE*, trans. James W. Barker (Atlanta, GA: Society of Biblical Literature, 2012), esp. 82–139.

64. Noth, *History of Israel*, 53–138; Rad, *Holy War*, 41–42, 65–66, 117–18, 126. Both Noth and von Rad based their models on the Greek amphictyonies of the Archaic period.

65. Mendenhall, 'Ancient Oriental and Biblical Law', 28; cf. Mendenhall, 'Covenant Forms', 62–63; George E. Mendenhall, 'The Hebrew Conquest of Palestine', *The Biblical Archaeologist* 25 (1962): 66–87.

66. Norman K. Gottwald, *The Tribes of Yahweh: A Sociology of the Religion of Liberated Israel, 1250–1050 BCE.* (London: SCM Press, 1980); Gottwald, *Politics of Ancient Israel*.

there is little or no archaeological evidence to support a theory of social revolution in Canaan, and the evidence points to a relatively impoverished Palestinian 'elite' who bore little resemblance to the wealthy and over-mighty aristocrats of the peasant revolution thesis. Consequently, both the 'amphictyonic theory' and the 'revolt theory' have attracted strong criticism and have largely been rejected.[67]

While we will probably never know precisely how the Israelite polity (or polities) emerged, what is abundantly clear from reading the Tanakh is how central the idea of conquest was to the sense of Hebrew identity it sought to create and foster. This highly militaristic vision of Israelite history and identity was likely a product of the seventh or sixth centuries, a period of intense stress for Israelite communities, following the collapse of Samaria and the intensifying political peril faced by Judah. In religious, cultural, social, and political terms, the creation of the conquest narrative—of a people arriving from far away and seizing the land of Canaan by strength of arms under the direction of an omnipotent deity—was intended to establish an unquestionable claim to the land through the rights of possession bestowed by military conquest.[68] Following the exile, this story of military might would have been all the more potent to a people humiliated by military defeat and dispossessed of their land; the conquest narrative would have provided a sense of pride in past military glory, and a hope that such glories might return in the future.

Geopolitics

Were the Israelite states more or less the same as other ancient Near Eastern states, or were they different in fundamental respects?[69] This question, posed by Gottwald, is an important one. In the West, with our Judeo-Christian cultural heritage, we are accustomed to thinking of the ancient Israelites as atypical and special; yet there is no reason why this should have been the case. If we accept that large swathes of the political history of Israel, Samaria, and Judah has been invented or exaggerated by the Tanakh and by later faith traditions, it is equally possible that their distinctiveness has been exaggerated, too.

If the Book of Judges tells us anything, it is of how a number of small tribal communities, led by individual warlords, struggled to assert themselves

---

67. See, inter alia, Roland de Vaux, *The Early History of Israel*, trans. David Smith, 2 vols (London: Darton, Longman and Todd, 1978), 2:695–715ff; Van Seters, *In Search of History*, 274; Ahlström, *Who Were the Israelites?*, 6–9, 15–21; Lemche, *Ancient Israel*, 106–9; Redford, *Egypt, Canaan, and Israel*, 265–68; J. Maxwell Miller and John H. Hayes, *A History of Ancient Israel and Judah*, 2nd edn (Louisville, KY: Westminster John Knox Press, 2006), 54–83. Lemche, *Israelites in History*, 104–8, stresses that the 'amphictyony' had no historical basis but serves as a literary construct.

68. Lemche, *Ancient Israel*, 112–14.

69. Gottwald, *Politics of Ancient Israel*, 3. A question also pursued in Crouch, *War and Ethics*.

throughout Canaan around the turn of the first millennium. No doubt these Israelite warlords fought each other as much as they fought Ammonites, Philistines, Edomites, Moabites, and other neighbours. Indeed, it is possible that Israelite warlords emerged from these very same communities, just as it is possible that they had their origins among the 'Sea Peoples'. These petty Israelite warlords would have made only relatively minor impressions on the geopolitics of the region, and the lack of any contemporary sources testifying to their existence suggests that they were ignored, tolerated, or dominated by superior powers. Such powers would have regarded them either as annoyances or as pawns in the regional power game.

Whether by some act of collective political will (as described in the Book of Samuel) or by the emergence of a charismatic and successful warlord (possibly named Saul), these Israelite tribes may have coalesced into a single political unit at the very turn of the first millennium. The period of 'United Monarchy' under Saul, David, and Solomon perhaps saw an enlarged Israelite state emerge as a regional player within Canaan, possibly even the wider Levant. But if so, there is no evidence to suggest it was of any consequence beyond this. Stories of royal visits from far-off kingdoms such as Sheba (1 Kings 10; 2 Chronicles 9) are pure inventions.[70] The texts of the Tanakh devote disproportionate attention to the 'United Monarchy', most of which is found in the books of Deuteronomistic history (Deuteronomy, Joshua, Judges, Samuel, Kings). Much of the material is patently unhistorical, and the narrative of events is structured in such a way as to express a theological message of initial military and political success born through piety, contrasted with later politico-military decline brought about by impiety.

Given its central importance to the Israelite foundation myth, and how elements of this myth have impacted upon claims associated with the modern state of Israel, the 'United Monarchy' is one of the most contested aspects of Israelite history in modern archaeological and historical scholarship. Scholars still lack any corroborative contemporary references to Saul, Solomon, or David from the era in which they are supposed to have flourished, and only a single (disputed) later reference to the 'House of David' exists from the inscription discovered at Tel Dan mentioned above. There is evidence of new fortifications being constructed in Canaan around the tenth and ninth centuries, which

---

70. Amihai Mazar, 'The Search for David and Solomon: An Archaeological Perspective', in Israel Finkelstein and Amihai Mazar, *The Quest for the Historical Israel: Debating Archaeology and the History of Early Israel; Invited Lectures Delivered at the Sixth Biennial Colloquium of the International Institute for Secular Humanistic Judaism, Detroit, October 2015*, ed. Brian B. Schmidt (Atlanta, GA: Society for Biblical Literature, 2007), 117–39 at 138. The kingdom of Sheba is usually identified as the kingdom of Saba, in Yemen, which came to prominence as a trading hub for incense and spices between the eighth and seventh centuries—that is, far too late for Solomon's kingdom, but precisely the date when the Deuteronomistic authors probably began compiling the 'history' of Israel.

could be owed to the emergence of a wealthier centralised kingdom with access to greater resources. However, we possess no royal inscriptions or other epigraphic evidence attesting to the existence of this hypothesised kingdom, and not a single archaeological structure can be indisputably attributed to a united kingdom of Israel—despite the fact that the territory of modern Israel is one of the most intensively excavated areas in the world.[71]

It is perfectly plausible that a united kingdom of Israel never actually existed and was the invention of later Judahite writers. This could have been a royal project under a centralising king such as Josiah, or an even later, post-exilic attempt to forge a united Israelite identity whilst living under colonial domination.[72] Given our current state of knowledge, we are unable to say anything of substance about the politics, statecraft, or military institutions of the 'United Monarchy'.[73] On the other hand, if a united Israelite kingdom did exist, then there is every reason to concur with Gottwald's assessment that 'Israel's political experience is likely to have been roughly parallel to the fortunes of other ancient Near Eastern polities'.[74] The Tanakh indicates that Solomon entered into a variety of international treaties, from agreeing parity treaties and trade alliances with regional powers such as the Pheonician city-states to imposing vassal treaties on less powerful neighbours.[75]

According to the Tanakh, the period of Israelite political unity was brief. The united kingdom of Israel apparently splintered during the contested reign of Solomon's son, Rehoboam, perhaps in the final quarter of the tenth century. Even before this, the unity of the young kingdom had been fragile. Saul's throne was usurped by David, who in turn faced regional revolts, including one led by his own son Absalom.[76] The Tanakh records how Solomon's grip on his northern territories had weakened, so that he eventually lost control of Edom, Aram Zobah, and Damascus. It was perhaps to be expected, then, that

---

71. *KANE*, 2:437–38, 447–48.

72. For essays considering both sides of the debate regarding the historicity of a united Israel, see Lowell K. Handy (ed.), *The Age of Solomon: Scholarship at the Turn of the Millennium* (Leiden: Brill, 1997). See also Finkelstein, who defends the thesis that David and Solomon were historical figures but argues that the 'united kingdom' was a Deuteronomistic product of Josiah's religious and political reforms in the late seventh century: Israel Finkelstein, 'King Solomon's Golden Age: History or Myth?', in Israel Finkelstein and Amihai Mazar, *The Quest for the Historical Israel: Debating Archaeology and the History of Early Israel; Invited Lectures Delivered at the Sixth Biennial Colloquium of the International Institute for Secular Humanistic Judaism, Detroit, October 2015*, ed. Brian B. Schmidt (Atlanta, GA: Society for Biblical Literature, 2007), 107–16.

73. Redford, *Egypt, Canaan, and Israel*, 311. For a useful summary of how biblical scholars have traditionally mapped Israelite political development according to the Tanakh, see Gottwald, *Politics of Ancient Israel*, 15–27.

74. Gottwald, *Politics of Ancient Israel*, 26.

75. 2 Samuel 8:6; 10:10; 1 Kings 4:21; 5:12. See also *ILA*, 29.

76. See, for example, 2 Samuel 15 and 20.

the northern Israelite population, afforded inferior status by the southern Judahite elites centred on Jerusalem, sought to break away during the instability created by Solomon's death.

It is from this point that the geopolitical history of the 'two Israels'—Samaria and Judah—becomes much more credible. Excavations at Samaria show evidence of a working royal capital, replete with fortifications, a palace and citadel, extensive buildings, and official seals indicating the workings of a government bureaucracy.[77] This capital was established by Omri, who ascended the throne c. 876 and created a marriage alliance with Judah.[78] There is contemporary evidence, particularly from Assyria and Moab, of this kingdom being referred to as the 'Land of Omri' (Bīt Humri). According to 2 Kings 9–10 (cf. 2 Chronicles 22), the Omrides ruled Samaria until usurped by a military commander named Jehu, who ruthlessly purged the former ruling dynasty. As the larger and more assertive of the two Israelite kingdoms, Samaria was frequently embroiled in conflict (including with Judah) and also caught the attention of Egypt and Assyria, leading ultimately to its doom. Around the year 737 Samaria formed an alliance with Edom and Damascus in order to oppose Judah and Assyria. When Damascus was conquered by Tiglath-Pileser III after a two-year siege (c. 732), this alliance was dismantled and a significant portion of Samaria's territory was annexed by Assyria. A decade later (c. 724–722), when Samaria yet again tested the limits of Assyrian political patience, Shalmaneser V and Sargon II smashed what was left of the kingdom, prompting many of its people to flee south to Judah.

While Assyrian military power may have landed the killing blow against Samaria, arguably it was internal instability as much as external pressure that had finally sealed the northern kingdom's fate. The institution of kingship in Samaria was never challenged, but possession of the throne became the subject of bitter and bloody internal feuding, leading to rapid changes of ruler and little predictability in the line of succession. This also generated myopic and inconsistent politico-military policies, with competing dynasts flip-flopping between Egyptian and Assyrian alliances.

In Judah, the Davidic dynasty continued to rule from Jerusalem until its fall around 587. However, the political autonomy of Judah was effectively extinguished at the same time as Samaria's fall, for it was clearly in no position to resist the might of the Neo-Assyrian empire. Judah's vassal status in relation to Assyria was confirmed by treaty around 700, mirroring (with the exception of Tyre) the fate of the Phoenician city-states. Judah was able to survive in this form as a subjugated state for over a century, passing from Assyrian to Babylonian vassalage. However, the Tanakh suggests that various Judahite kings bridled under foreign domination. Indeed, the sack of Jerusalem and the exile

---

77. *KANE*, 2:464.
78. 1 Kings 16:23–28.

of its elites, around 587, came about after a failed revolt against Babylonian overlordship.

It was during the years of Babylonian exile that monotheistic Yahwism fully emerged. When the Persian king Cyrus conquered Babylon (c. 539) and permitted the Judahite exiles to return to Jerusalem (c. 538), this more radical strain of the Yahweh cult was imported back into Judah.[79] It was also during the Persian period that 'literate returnees' began to form the Tanakh as a collection of texts bearing a close resemblance to the one we have today, and they did so under considerable Persian influence.[80] As Niditch observes, these priestly elites 'played an important role in preserving images of war in ancient Israel although the activity of actual, independent armies was over for the time being'.[81] Thus the ethics of war expressed in the Tanakh were preserved and/or formulated by a group of men who were starkly aware of the consequences of war (defeat, humiliation, and exile), but who had probably never fought in a war themselves. It had been fifty years since the fall of Jerusalem; not only were priestly scholars excluded from military service by virtue of their religious function, but with average life expectancy in the ancient world being much lower than today, it is unlikely that any of the surviving returnees had been older than children in 587. Indeed, most of the returnees must have been born in exile. If any Judahite returnees had fought in wars during the half-century of exile, it would have been as auxiliary or mercenary troops in the armies of Babylon. What affect did this have on Israelite attitudes to the ethics of war in the post-exilic period? It is possible that war texts were influenced by Assyrian and Babylonian norms, adopted during periods of relocation within the territories of these empires. If the authors and compilers of the Tanakh had no direct knowledge or experience of *Israelite* warfare (i.e., fighting for an Israelite state according to Israelite conventions, rather than fighting for Babylon or other non-Israelite states), did it make their approach to war more idealistic, more circumspect, more pacificist, or more belligerent?

Transmission from Egypt, Hatti and Assyria

Oral transmission has always been an important means of spreading culture, but from the late second to the mid-first millennium knowledge of writing was spreading beyond royal administrators to private persons, expanding the

---

79. Karen Armstrong, *A History of God: The 4000-Year Quest of Judaism, Christianity and Islam* (New York: Ballantine Books, 1993), 62.

80. Reinhard G. Kratz, *The Composition of the Narrative Books of the Old Testament*, trans. John Bowden (London: T&T Clark, 2005), 319–22.

81. Susan Niditch, 'War and Reconciliation in the Traditions of Ancient Israel: Historical, Literary, and Ideological Considerations', in *War and Peace in the Ancient World*, ed. Kurt A. Raaflaub (Malden, MA: Blackwell, 2007), 141–60 at 144.

literate population considerably.⁸² Israelites partook in this process of cultural transmission that had been occurring throughout the Near East and eastern Mediterranean from at least the Early Bronze Age. Since the late nineteenth century CE, scholars have recognised the Mesopotamian and western Asian influence on Israelite mythology and theology. The Israelite creation stories in Genesis have much in common with the wider Near Eastern and Mesopotamian cosmological concept of *Chaoskampf*—the war of a deity against primordial chaos. This concept is embedded in the stories of the Babylonian *Enūma Eliš* creation cycle.⁸³ Equally, the characters of Adam, Eve, and Noah have roots in earlier myths such as those of Gilgamesh and Atra-Ḫasīs.⁸⁴ It is notable that Yahweh only fully emerged as a resplendent divine warrior *and* sovereign creator in the post-exilic period, apparently borrowing from aspects of the Canaanite god Baal and the Babylonian god Marduk.⁸⁵ Later Hebrew apocalyptics, such as the Book of Daniel, show elements of Persian Zoroastrian dualism.⁸⁶ The religious rites described in Exodus 29 and Leviticus 12 bear close similarities to earlier Hittite and Hurrian blood rites, possibly transmitted via cities such as Ugarit.⁸⁷

Egypt, too, exerted an influence on Israelite culture, although its influence on Israelite historical literature has generally been underestimated or overlooked in favour of Canaanite or Mesopotamian evidence.⁸⁸ The story of Moses recounted in Exodus bears marked similarities to the Egyptian 'Tale

---

82. Foster, 'Transmission of Knowledge', 245, 248.

83. See the translation of *Enūma Eliš* printed in W. G. Lambert, *Babylonian Creation Myths* (Winona Lake, IN: Eisenbrauns, 2013), 51–133, especially Tablet IV, containing Marduk's struggle against Tiamat. See also 'The Slaying of Labbu', ibid., 361–65.

84. *Gilgamesh*, 57–58, Tablet I, col. i; W. G. Lambert, A. R. Millard, and M. Civil, *Atra-Ḫasīs: The Babylonian Story of the Flood, with the Sumerian Flood Story* (Winona Lake, IN: Eisenbrauns, 1999).

85. Gunkel, *Schöpfung und Chaos*; Frank Moore Cross, *Canaanite Myth and Hebrew Epic: Essays in the History of the Religion of Israel* (Cambridge, MA: Harvard University Press, 2021), esp. 112–44 on the 'Song of the Sea'; Day, *God's Conflict*; John J. Collins, 'The Mythology of Holy War in Daniel and the Qumran War Scroll: A Point of Transition in Jewish Apocalyptic', *Vetus Testamentum* 25 (3) (1975): 596–612 at 596–99; Whitney, *Two Strange Beasts*, 1–30; Crouch, *War and Ethics*, 22–24; Shawn W. Flynn, *YHWH is King: The Development of Divine Kingship in Ancient Israel* (Leiden: Brill, 2014), 91–118.

86. Collins, 'Mythology of Holy War', 601–8.

87. Yitzhaq Feder, 'A Levantine Tradition: The Kizzuwatnean Blood Rite and the Biblical Sin Offering', in *Pax Hethitica: Studies on the Hittites and Their Neighbours in Honour of Itamar Singer*, ed. Yoram Cohen, Amir Gilan, and Jared L. Miller (Wiesbaden: Harrassowitz, 2010), 101–14 at 110. See also Yitzhaq Feder, *Blood Expiation in Hittite and Biblical Ritual: Origins, Context, and Meaning* (Atlanta, GA: Society of Biblical Literature, 2011).

88. Younger, *Ancient Conquest Accounts*, 166; R. J. Williams, '"A People Come Out of Egypt": An Egyptologist Looks at the Old Testament', *Vetus Testamentum Supplements* 28 (1974): 231–52.

of Sinuhe', which dates from Dynasty XII (early nineteenth century) but is found in a number of later copies.[89] Archaeological evidence reveals Egyptian votive objects circulating throughout Canaan and the later Israelite kingdoms, although Raphael Giveon argues that the 'absence of any preaching by the prophets against Egyptian religion' is evidence that the penetration of Egyptian religion into Canaan 'can not have been deep'.[90] Nonetheless, further links to Egypt can be seen in the iconographic and economic sphere. While Egyptian political power waned in the early first millennium, the continuing importance of Egypt as an economic centre is indicated by the Iron Age Israelite states adopting Egyptian systems of weights, measures, and numerals.[91] And Bederman argues persuasively for the existence of a Near Eastern legal and diplomatic tradition which was transmitted westwards to Greece and Rome, via Egyptian, Phoenician, and Israelite interactions.[92]

The importance of Near Eastern cultural transmission to Israelite culture is perhaps most marked in Israel's covenant tradition—that of the formal legal relationship between Yahweh and the people of Israel (expressed most clearly in the Decalogue and Joshua 24). As Mendenhall established in two seminal articles, the Israelite Covenant was closely modelled on Hittite and Assyrian legal and diplomatic instruments, especially vassalage treaties.[93] In the Israelite version, Yahweh became the great king and the Israelite people were his vassals, bound to Yahweh under oath and to each other by a sacred truce.[94] Just as copies of ancient Near Eastern treaties were traditionally deposited in temples, so Deuteronomy tells us that the Israelites deposited the two stones of the Decalogue in the Ark: the portable shrine of Israel.[95] Therefore Israel shared in 'what might be called [a] cross-fertilization of legal traditions',

89. *ToS*, 3–7.

90. Giveon, *Impact of Egypt on Canaan*, 13–14. Younger contrasts the Egyptian policy in the Levant—where 'there were no deliberate attempts to impose Egyptian cults upon the people of the Levant'—with the policy of 'Egyptianization' carried out in Nubia: *Ancient Conquest Accounts*, 185–89, quotation at 188.

91. Although these systems seem to have been transmitted indirectly, via the Phoenician cities. See Giveon, *Impact of Egypt on Canaan*, 13, 14, 99; Redford, *Egypt, Canaan, and Israel*, 337, 366.

92. *ILA*, 3, 47, 150. Cf. *LIR*, which was published in the same year and shares many of the same conclusions.

93. Mendenhall, 'Ancient Oriental and Biblical Law', 25–46; Mendenhall, 'Covenant Forms'. Mendenhall relied upon Korošec's masterful analysis of Hittite legal instruments in *Hethitische Staatsverträge*.

94. Mendenhall, 'Covenant Forms', 57, 64. For further analysis of the Near Eastern origins of the Israelite covenant, see Meredith G. Kline, *Treaty of the Great King: The Covenant Structure of Deuteronomy: Studies and Commentary* (1963; repub. Eugene, OR: Wipf and Stock, 2012). On the influence of Near Eastern treaty formulae and law, see also Weinfeld, *Deuteronomy*, 59–157.

95. Mendenhall, 'Covenant Forms', 64–65.

dating back to the Code of Hammurabi and the Hittite Law Code.[96] Mendenhall further proposed that Deuteronomy, rather than being merely a 'pious forgery' of seventh-century Judah, actually represented a 'continuity of the old traditions' of covenant law and the amphictyonic model dating back to the second millennium.

This covenant tradition formed the basis of Israel's relationship with Yahweh, created the authority by which Israelite monarchs ruled, and even provided the foundation for the reconstruction of 'just law' in the post-exilic period, as well as a continuing sense of a unified Israelite identity and religion.[97] It is to these issues, which directly correspond to concerns of *ius ad bellum* thought, that we shall now turn.

---

96. Mendenhall, 'Ancient Oriental and Biblical Law', 33, 37. See also Albrecht Alt's essay, 'The Origins of Israelite Law', in Alt, *Essays on Old Testament History*, 79–132.

97. Mendenhall, 'Ancient Oriental and Biblical Law', 44; Mendenhall, 'Covenant Forms', 71–74. However, Gottwald argues that there is no evidence for the existence of a special 'covenant politics' determining the political behaviour of the Israelite states: Gottwald, *Politics of Ancient Israel*, 247.

CHAPTER NINE

The Israelites: *Ius ad bellum*

CONCEPTUALISING JUSTICE AND WAR

MOST DISCUSSIONS of ancient Israelite ethics of war adopt a framework of analysis created by rabbinic commentary on the Mishnah. This approach distinguishes two categories of war in ancient Israelite thought: *milhemet mitzva* (obligatory war) and *milhemet reshut* (optional war).[1] The former is characterised by an unrestrained and excessively brutal form of warfare; the latter by a more restrained and rules-based approach to prosecuting war. However, the redaction of the Mishnah and the composition of the Jerusalem Talmud and Babylonian Talmud (second to eighth centuries CE) reflect attitudes significantly divorced from the thought-world and events described within the Tanakh.[2] As Norman Solomon observes, '[r]abbinic discussion of war lacks firm contact with political reality; the rabbis' legislation on warfare is historical reconstruction or messianic speculation, not the operational law of an actual Jewish State'.[3] It stands to reason, therefore, that the rabbinically derived categories of 'obligatory' and 'optional' war are not the only, or even the most revealing, way to think about ancient Israelite ethics of war. Furthermore, one of the major concerns of those modern biblical scholars (whether

---

1. Occasionally *milhemet mitzva* is replaced in scholarly literature by the term *milhemet hova*: both terms imply an absolutely necessary and obligatory war, in contrast to *milhemet reshut*. To avoid confusion, I have preferred *mitzva* throughout. Norman Solomon also includes a third category of 'preemptive/preventive war' when discussing later Jewish ethics of war: Solomon, 'Judaism', 298.

2. Rabbinic commentaries on the Mishnah and Talmud continued long after this period too. One of the most influential medieval commentaries, for example, was the *Kitabl al-Siraj* of Maimonides (Moses ben Maimon), composed around 1168 CE. For the development of later Jewish thought on the ethics of war, see: Solomon, 'Judaism'; Norman Solomon, 'The Ethics of War in Judaism', in *The Ethics of War in Asian Civilizations: A Comparative Perspective*, ed. Torkel Brekke (Abingdon: Routledge, 2006), 39–80.

3. Solomon, 'Judaism', 297–98.

[295]

Jewish or Christian) who approach the Tanakh as divinely revealed wisdom or even universal 'truth' is that the texts should be shown to be coherent and free from contradictions.[4] I have no such objectives or constraints.

As in the preceding chapters on Egypt and Hatti, my examination of the ethics of war in ancient Israel will utilise the conceptual framework of the later just war tradition, divided broadly between issues that fall respectively within the *ius ad bellum* and the *ius in bello* range of norms. As analytical categories, these are no more or less historically valid or authentic than the rabbinical categories of *milhemet mitzva* and *milhemet reshut*. However, utilising the ideal types of the just war tradition will enable a better comparative perspective of Israelite ethics of war, placing it alongside our analysis of Egypt and Hatti, as well as modern cultures. I build on some initial (although largely overlooked) work by Robert Good, who highlighted the benefits of approaching the Israelite evidence from a jural notion of just war. Good posited that a legalistic war ideology—the concept of war as a divine legal judgement—could be traced through the whole of the Tanakh, back to the archaic texts of the Song of Deborah and Poem of Miriam. As a result, Good argues, 'we can speak of the *just* war in ancient Israel without doing violence to the historical evidence'.[5]

Israelite Holy War?

The tendency for modern biblical scholars to examine ancient Israelite warfare and ethics according to Late Antique and early medieval rabbinic categories has been reinforced by the enduring influence of Gerhard von Rad's thesis of 'holy war'. The 'institution' of holy war in ancient Israel, as conceived by von Rad, fits neatly with the type of war described as *mitzva* ('obligatory') in the Mishnah and Talmud. While von Rad was not the first to recognise the importance of Yahwist theology to depictions of war in the Tanakh, nor the first to apply the term *der heilige Krieg* to ancient Israelite warfare, it is his holy war thesis that has become the starting point for most modern discussions of Israelite warfare.[6]

---

4. This is particularly evident in Christian 'divine warrior studies' scholarship; for example, Gelston, 'Wars of Israel', 326–27; Craigie, 'Yahweh is a Man of Wars', 183–88; Craigie, *Problem of War in the Old Testament*; Millard C. Lind, *Yahweh is a Warrior: The Theology of Warfare in Ancient Israel* (Scottdale, PA; Kitchener, Ontario: Herald, 1980); Longman and Reid, *God is a Warrior*; Cross, *Canaanite Myth*, 91–110.

5. Robert M. Good, 'The Just War in Ancient Israel', *Journal of Biblical Literature* 104 (3) (1985): 385–400 at 399.

6. See Friedrich Schwally, *Semitische Kriegsaltertümer, Heft 1: Der heilige Krieg im alten Israel* (Leipzig: Deiterich/Weicher, 1901). For an extensive although still not exhaustive list of works pursuing the 'holy war' and 'Yahweh war' thesis, see Jacob L. Wright, 'Military Valor and Kingship: A Book-Oriented Approach to the Study of a Major War-Theme', in *Writing and Reading War: Rhetoric, Gender, and Ethics in Biblical and Modern*

Von Rad understood holy war to be a central cultic institution of the pre-monarchical period of Israelite history.[7] This institution was intimately linked to the Covenant with Yahweh and the 'amphictyony' uniting the tribes. Following accounts in the books of Joshua, Judges, and Samuel, von Rad identified a distinct type of war fought at the command of, and by the grace of, Yahweh. When waging such wars, Israelites apparently possessed an 'utterly unshakeable certainty of victory, which was the characteristic defining all holy war'.[8] In prosecution, these Yahwist holy wars were uncompromising in their employment of violence. The reason why such brutality was necessary, argued von Rad, was because holy wars were fought for the very survival of Israel as a people and a nascent nation. In essence, therefore, holy wars were defensive wars.[9] The notion that holy war was waged in order to purify a territory (the risk of religious pollution could not brook less extreme measures) was, von Rad claimed, a later 'modernizing' insertion by the Deuteronomistic author, intended to justify the massacre of peoples described in the conquest narrative.[10] While von Rad admits that the historical evidence points against a swift conquest of Canaan (as described in Joshua), he posits that the holy war, waged by the 'amphictyony' of Israelite tribes, was the ideal type of Israelite warfare prior to the monarchic period. After the foundation of the monarchy, this holy war institution—with its uncompromising and impolitic stance on international relations—clashed with royal interests and policies, and was thus rarely utilised.[11] Its memory was preserved by the prophets, who chastised individual kings for deviating from the ideal.[12] Indeed, von Rad admitted that the uncompromising character of the holy war suggests that it was always more of an ideal than a reality, even in the pre-monarchic period.[13] Nevertheless, the accounts of the war of Deborah and the uprising of Israel against the Philistines, led by Saul, are archetypal examples of the type of war von Rad had in mind.[14]

Yet there was a problem of explaining why the clearest stipulations on the format of holy war are contained in Deuteronomy, which was not composed until at least the seventh century—well after the period when the holy war supposedly had its heyday. Von Rad's explanation was that during the period

---

Contexts, ed. Brad E. Kelle and Frank Ritchel Ames (Atlanta, GA: Society of Biblical Literature, 2008), 33–56 at 33 n. 4.

7. Rad, *Holy War*, 51.
8. Ibid., 42–44.
9. Ibid., 65.
10. Ibid., 117–18.
11. Von Rad, ibid., 59, claims that Saul's war against the Ammonites (1 Samuel 11) is one example of the holy war surviving into the monarchical period.
12. Ibid., 97.
13. Ibid., 52; cf. ibid., 69.
14. Ibid., 59–60.

of Assyrian dominance, Judah had been forced to rely more heavily on the older system of citizen militia to meet its military needs. It was the revival of this 'ancient' tribal militia that revivified the older religious military traditions, including the holy war institution, and inspired the text of Deuteronomy.[15] So Deuteronomy did not create the institution of holy war; it simply rediscovered an older tradition that had suddenly become relevant again, albeit for a limited time. In practical terms, the institution of holy war was finally brought to an end by the defeat and death of the Judahite reformer King Josiah.[16]

Von Rad's thesis is persuasively argued. Unfortunately, it is also highly speculative and lacks any substantive evidence. The term 'holy war' (*milhamah qedoshah*) does not appear at all in the Tanakh (indeed, it appears in no ancient Near Eastern text),[17] and since the critique of von Rad's thesis by Rudolf Smend (among many others), the term 'Yahweh (YHWH) war' has become more common among scholars. For Smend, the war of Yahweh—an archaic development associated principally with the figure of Moses—predated any possible development of an Israelite amphictyony.[18] The change in terminology indicates a move away from conceiving early Israelite warfare as a religious institution with a specific set of rules governing cause and conduct, instead seeing this institutionalised aspect as a later, Deuteronomic invention.[19] 'Yahweh war' implies a broader concept, of war waged on the command, authority, approval, or behalf of Yahweh, and recognising him as ultimately determining victory. However, this broader concept of war could be waged by any Israelite group, for any number of causes and by any number of means.[20] Some have argued that it is simply anachronistic to speak of 'holy war' during this period at all, because neither the Israelite nor the Assyrian texts ever make a distinction between 'religious' and 'secular', or between 'defensive' and 'offensive', wars. Moreover, the concept of 'divine war' (that is, war involving the gods in some way) was absolutely normal across the entire

---

15. Ibid., 124–25.

16. Ibid., 128.

17. Ziskind, 'Aspects of International Law', 153; Norman K. Gottwald, 'Holy War in Deuteronomy: Analysis and Critique', *Review and Expositor* 61 (4) (1964): 297–310 at 297; Craigie, *Problem of War*, 49–50.

18. 'The war of Yahweh [. . .] would have actually been the original element of what in time was destined to become the religion of Israel. To this original element the amphictyonic element was later added.' Smend, *Yahweh War*, 134. The phrase 'Yahweh war' appears in: Exodus 17:17; Numbers 21:14; 1 Samuel 17:47; 18:17; 25:28. See also Gwilym H. Jones, '"Holy War" or "Yahweh War"?', *Vetus Testamentum* 25 (3) (1975): 642–58.

19. Kang argues that the hallmarks of YHWH war began to accrue from the Davidic kingdom onwards, although his assertions regarding the 'historical realities' of battles described in Exodus, Judges, and Kings should be treated with extreme caution: Kang, *Divine War*, 114–222.

20. Jones, '"Holy War" or "Yahweh War"?', 648.

region throughout the third to first millennia.[21] Essentially, almost all wars were 'divine wars' in one way or another, and so to look for a separate category of 'holy war' is futile.

A common theme in the reassessment of von Rad's holy war thesis is that, if such a concrete concept of religious war ever existed, it existed only in the minds of the Deuteronomistic authors.[22] According to A.D.H. Mayes, 'the holy war is more a matter of an interpretation of past events and a schematization of accounts of them than an actual method of waging war'; thus, as a cogent ideology, the holy war is 'a result of the systematizing of Deuteronomy'.[23] Gottwald posits that Deuteronomy may 'have preserved old pieces of legislation from previous centuries', but argues that 'there is little evidence that these notions of holy war were taken literally by any of the kings from Saul onward'; rather, they were a type of rallying cry and motivator, firing the martial spirit of the soldiery.[24] Whatever the (contested) dating or authorship of Deuteronomy, Gottwald points out that the holy war ideology expressed therein was removed from a real-world experience of warfare: it was a 'theoretical dogma', and 'the writer had little or no first-hand experience of what he was talking about'.[25]

Justice, Authority, and Divine Aid in War

Blessed is the Lord, my rock,
who trains my hands for battle, my fingers for warfare;
my faithful one, my fortress,
my haven and my deliverer,
my shield, in whom I take shelter,
who makes peoples subject to me.[26]

As in other ancient Near Eastern cultures we have encountered thus far, authority was central to the ancient Israelite conception of war. The Tanakh tells us, however, that—in contrast to the other cultures we have discussed— the Israelites only adopted a monarchical system relatively late in their political development, perhaps between the late eleventh and early tenth centuries. Prior to the crowning of Saul as the first king of Israel (1 Samuel 8:19–22), the

---

21. Manfred Weippert, '"Heiliger Kreig" in Israel und Assyrien: Kritische Anmerkungen zu Gerhard von Rads Konzept des "Heiligen Krieges im alten Israel"', *Zeitschrift für die Alttestamentliche Wissenschaft* 84 (4): 460-93 at 490-92; Altman, 'Earliest Recorded Concepts', 110; Collins, 'Mythology of Holy War', 598.

22. Fritz Stoltz, *Jahwes und Israels Kriege: Kriegstheorien und Kriegserfahrungen im Glauben des alten Israel* (Zurich: Theologischer Verlag, 1972).

23. A.D.H. Mayes, *Deuteronomy* (London: Oliphants, 1979), 292.

24. Gottwald, '"Holy War" in Deuteronomy', 306-7.

25. Ibid., 307.

26. Psalm 144:1-2.

Israelites had apparently been ruled by a variety of tribal chieftains and charismatic religious prophets. According to the biblical narrative, Abraham was a paterfamilias who led his tribe into Egypt. Generations later, Moses emerged as a divinely inspired prophetic leader who led the Israelites out of Egypt and sealed their covenant with Yahweh, all the while struggling to contain their complaints, unruliness, and religious transgressions. The Tanakh presents the Israelites during the story of the Wanderings and the conquest of Canaan as a 'nation'—in the sense that they were a single people, a *natio/gens*, of common stock united under Yahweh—but they are not portrayed as a political state with a fixed political hierarchy. This Israelite *natio* consisted of twelve semi-autonomous tribes, each with its own internal hierarchy.[27]

Moses eventually handed over the reins of authority to Joshua, a war leader par excellence, who in many ways appears in a monarchical guise. Moses and Joshua were certainly portrayed as exercising sovereign-like power and authority, but neither of them is ever described as a 'king' of the Israelites. As the Book of Judges (21:25) says, '[i]n those days there was no king in Israel; every man did what was right in his eyes'.

Although political authority was not centralised, the compilers of the Tanakh were explicit in articulating the singularity of Yahweh's divine authority. This was crucial in Israelite thought on war, and was also connected to the prominence of law and justice as a defining feature of good rulership. This began with Moses's presentation of the Decalogue, which had, explicitly, a divine origin.[28] David, always the model of just kingship for the compilers of the Tanakh, was approvingly described as a king who 'executed true justice among all his people'.[29] His dying words are a paean to justice and piety:

> He who rules men justly,
> He who rules in awe of God
> Is like the light of morning at sunrise.[30]

Nevertheless, there was not an intrinsic connection between the righteousness of a ruler, on the one hand, and political success, on the other. Even a king like Josiah, responsible for the seventh-century religious reforms of Judah and presented as an ideal king in the image of David, failed to increase

---

27. Even on the eve of the conquest of Canaan, two and a half tribes decided to separate themselves from the main body of Israel, settling permanently on the eastern side of the river Jordan on the recently conquered pastoral lands of Jazar and Gilead. Moses and Joshua agreed to this settlement, on the condition that these tribes sent their fighting men over the river Jordan to aid in the conquest of Canaan: Numbers 32; Deuteronomy 3:12–20; Joshua 1:12–15.

28. Hector Avalos, 'Legal and Social Institutions in Canaan and Ancient Israel', in *CANE*, 2:615–31 at 617.

29. 2 Samuel 8:15.

30. Ibid. 23:3–4.

Judah's security and was himself killed in battle against an Egyptian army at Megiddo.[31] Josiah had been caught between the waning political fortunes of Assyria and the waxing political power of Neo-Babylonia, which had found an ally in Egypt. As the head of a small state caught up in the competitive power games of larger neighbours, King Josiah was representative of all Israelite rulers of the first millennium. Josiah gambled on Assyria, and lost. Other Israelite kings fared better; yet those who flourished politically were not necessarily remembered fondly in the books of the Tanakh. For the authors, compilers, and redactors of this complex text, an individual's relationship with Yahweh and their fidelity to the Covenant (as judged by the compilers) were always the crucial considerations.

THE AUTHORITY OF THE KING AS WAR LEADER

In Egypt and Hatti, the king was the preeminent authority within the state, and it was tacitly acknowledged that this authority translated directly into the realm of war. The absence of a comparable political figure in the early political structure of Israel is an idiosyncratic feature of early Israelite history as provided by the Tanakh. If political authority was fragmented and contested, we might expect the authority to go to war to be similarly diffuse. However, the bulk of the Tanakh was probably composed or compiled in the period between c. 750 and c. 450. During this period, monarchy was the dominant political system of the Near East. Those Hebrew scholars who played a part in creating the texts of the Tanakh as we have them today were thus embedded in political systems in which monarchy was the norm. Whether under the kings of Samaria, Judah, Assyria, Babylon, or Persia, Hebrew scholars were shaping their texts within the context of monarchical systems of government. Therefore, while many books of the Tanakh purport to represent the words, attitudes, and ethics of a pre-monarchical Israelite culture, the reality is that all of these accounts were composed in a world of kings. As we shall see, this influenced the ways in which authority in general, and the authority to wage war specifically, was represented in the Tanakh. Effectively, what we see is a system of *ius ad bellum* thought that prioritised a singular source of authority. This authority was not human but divine: that of the god Yahweh. In the human realm, authority to wage war was vested in individual war leaders by Yahweh. Prior to Saul, these war leaders were not technically monarchs, but fulfilled the functions of kings in all but name.

The best extant sources for Near Eastern just war thought from between the twelfth and sixth centuries are the Hebrew Tanakh and a series of royal Assyrian inscriptions.[32] Both Israelite and Assyrian sources stress the impor-

---

31. 2 Kings 22:8–23, 25; 23:29.
32. Altman, 'Earliest Recorded Concepts', 105–6.

tance of divine support in war, mediated through the king or, in the Israelite case, Yahweh's chosen representative—whether prophet, tribal chief, or king. In determining whether to embark on military campaigns, both Israelite and Assyrian procedures required supplication to the god(s) through divination, either through extispicy (the study of the entrails of sacrificed animals) or prophecy. In both cases, the intimate link between mundane and divine military authority was reinforced.

With the establishment of the Israelite monarchy under Saul, a human institution was created which at least *assumed* an authority to wage war without relying constantly on explicit divine sanction. Indeed, it was the pressing need for self-defence and the people's desire for military leadership that pushed Israel to appoint a king in the first place, in spite of Samuel's warnings against this course of action:

> But the people would not listen to Samuel's warning. 'No,' they said. 'We must have a king over us, that we may be like all the other nations: Let our king rule over us and go out at our head and fight our battles.'[33]

In 1 Samuel we are explicitly presented with a view of monarchical authority as originally rooted in war. Yahweh's choice to anoint Saul as the first king seems to be based purely on his physical prowess: he is said to be the most handsome of the Israelites and 'a head taller than any of the people'.[34] In ancient literature such gifts are typically the attributes of the warrior; neither intellect nor piety were identified as reasons for Saul's elevation to kingship. This emphasis on physical prowess further underlines the essential role of the king as a warrior and the creation of Saul's kingship as a 'definitive army kingship'.[35] This being the case, the authority of the Israelite king to wage war must have been taken for granted, for he was first and foremost a war leader.

The role of the king as a war leader was confirmed through Saul's initial military actions. Though vastly outnumbered by his Philistine enemies, he immediately declared all-out war on Israel's neighbouring states:

> After Saul had secured his kingship over Israel, he waged war on every side against all his enemies: against the Moabites, Ammonites, Edomites, the Philistines, and the kings of Zobah; and wherever he turned he worsted [them]. He was triumphant, defeating the Amalekites and saving Israel from those who plundered it. [...] There was a bitter war against the Philistines all the days of Saul.[36]

---

33. 1 Samuel 8:19–20. Samuel had warned against appointing a king: ibid. 8:10–18.
34. 1 Samuel 8:2.
35. Rad, *Holy War*, 75; cf. Wright, 'Military Valor and Kingship', 36–46.
36. 1 Samuel 14:47–48, 52. Saul gathered three thousand troops; the Philistines mustered thirty thousand chariots and six thousand horsemen, in addition to numerous infantry: ibid. 13:1–5.

As God's anointed, Saul's authority to engage in warfare was not questioned, and his victories evinced his divine approval.[37] This model of kingship was much closer to those of Hatti and Assyria than to Egypt.[38]

YAHWEH AS A GOD OF WAR

As previously noted, the literal translation of 'Israel' is 'El battles', and from the early stories of the Tanakh the Israelite god is presented as a martial deity.[39] In 'The Song of the Sea' (Exodus 15:1–18), an archaic poem contained within Exodus and possibly one of the oldest compositions in the Torah, Moses exalts his god as a god of war:

> The Lord, the Warrior;
> Lord is His name!
> Your right hand, O Lord, glorious in power,
> Your right hand, O Lord, shatters the foe!
> Who is like You, O Lord, among the celestials.[40]

As the Israelites fled Egypt, Yahweh chose to compel the Egyptians to pursue the Israelites into the Red (or Reed) Sea as a means to display his divine power through a miraculous martial victory:

> And I will stiffen the hearts of the Egyptians so that they go in after them; and I will gain glory through Pharaoh and all his warriors, his chariots and his horsemen. Let the Egyptians know that I am Lord, when I gain glory through Pharaoh, his chariots, and his horsemen.[41]

---

37. As Yahweh's anointed, Saul apparently enjoyed a measure of immunity. When David discovered Saul (his enemy) sleeping in a cave, he refused to harm 'God's anointed': 1 Samuel 24:5–17; 26:6–25. There is also an implication that slaying Saul while he was asleep would have been dishonourable.

38. Redford, *Egypt, Canaan, and Israel*, 367–69.

39. See Patrick D. Miller Jr., *The Divine Warrior in Early Israel* (Cambridge, MA: Harvard University Press, 1973).

40. Exodus 15:3, 6, 11. The 'Song of the Sea' is dated as early as the thirteenth century or as late as the fifth century. Its archaic literary form is indicative of either a genuinely antique poem or the product of a deliberately archaizing style. See Gregory T. K. Wong, 'Song of Deborah as Polemic', *Biblica* 88 (1) (2007): 1–22 at 1 n. 1; E. Zenger, 'Tradition und Interpretation in Exodus XV 1–21', in *Congress Volume Vienne 1980*, ed. J. A. Emerton (Leiden: Brill, 1981), 452–82 at 456–58; Alan J. Hauser, 'Two Songs of Victory: A Comparison of Exodus 15 and Judges 5', in *Directions in Biblical Hebrew Poetry*, ed. Elaine R. Follis (Sheffield: JSOT Press, 1987), 265–84. In the 'Song of the Sea', supposedly sung by Moses, Yahweh is still conceived as one of *many* gods, although later monotheistic interpretations claimed that 'celestials' referred to the angels of Yahweh's divine court rather than other gods. See commentary to Exodus 15:11, *JSB*, 137. On the jural notion of war in the 'Song of Miriam', see Good, 'Just War in Ancient Israel', 398.

41. Exodus 14:17–18.

Yahweh's motivation in provoking the Egyptians, which resulted in the annihilation of the pharaoh's army, was presented primarily in terms of glorifying the Israelite god and spreading his martial fame. It was not explained or justified in ethical terms pertaining to just punishment. This is not to say that the story is devoid of punitive elements. Most notably, Exodus describes at length how Egypt is afflicted by ten plagues, causing significant death and destruction, including the targeted killing of children. This is presented as retributive justice in the face of the pharaoh's refusal to allow the Israelites to leave his country.

But the story of the parting of the Red Sea and the extermination of the pharaoh's army indicates the importance of stressing Yahweh's role in achieving a *military* victory against Egypt.[42] Exodus makes clear that it was Yahweh who 'stiffened the heart of Pharaoh king of Egypt, and he gave chase to the Israelites'.[43] According to the text, then, the pharaoh was not acting wholly of his own volition, and Yahweh deliberately engineered the conditions which brought about the military victory, albeit a miraculous one, for the Israelites.

The image of Yahweh as a warlike deity, upon whose authority Israelite warfare hinged, crops up repeatedly in the Tanakh. In the 'Song of Hannah', the image of Yahweh as breaker of foreign nations is highly reminiscent of earlier language used in Egypt to describe the pharaonic domination of the 'Nine Bows' through the power of Amun:

> The bows of the mighty are broken,
> And the faltering are girded with strength. [. . .]
> The foes of the Lord shall be shattered;
> He will thunder against them in the heavens.[44]

The claims of martial strength endowed by the patron god can also be found in the 'Song of David'—a prayer made by King David of Israel on his deathbed. It emphasised martial glory and the subjugation of foreign powers:

> I pursued my enemies and wiped them out; [. . .]
> I destroyed them, I struck them down;
> They rose no more, they lay at my feet.
> You have girt me with strength for battle,
> Brought low my foes before me,
> Made my enemies turn tail before me [. . .].
> Peoples I knew now must serve me.[45]

Nevertheless, the power of Yahweh as a martial deity could also be turned against Israel. On the banks of the river Jordan, at the cusp of the conquest

---

42. See also Lind, *Yahweh is a Warrior*, 49–50.
43. Exodus 14:8.
44. 1 Samuel 2:4, 10.
45. 2 Samuel 22:38–44.

of Canaan, Moses told his people of the terrible consequences promised by Yahweh if the Israelites betrayed their Covenant:

> I will sweep misfortunes on them,
> Use up My arrows on them [. . .].
> The sword shall deal death without,
> As shall the terror within.[46]

Here, Yahweh was presented as both divine judge and warrior, as well as a jealous and wrathful god.

This image of a fearsome warlike deity, ready to pass judgement, is repeated throughout Deuteronomy 32. While the Deuteronomist obviously wished to produce a sense of awe and appropriate fear of Yahweh's power, the author(s) also sought to confirm the unique status enjoyed by the Israelites as Yahweh's chosen people. Ultimately, the god would take violent vengeance against peoples who harmed the Israelites and refused to acknowledge his exclusive claim to divine authority:

> There is no god beside Me.
> I deal death and give life;
> I wounded and I will heal [. . .].
> When I whet My flashing blade
> And My hand lays hold on judgment,
> Vengeance will I wreak on My foes [. . .].
> I will make my arrows drunk with blood—
> As My sword devours flesh—
> Blood of the slain and the captive
> From the long-haired enemy chiefs.[47]

Yahweh's position as divine judge and god of war placed him at the source for all legitimate warlike actions conducted by Israel. He is capable of bestowing universal sovereignty over nations to the Israelite king, who 'can smash them with an iron mace'.[48] This sovereign and warlike image of Yahweh manifested in post-exilic prophetic writing which envisaged the god's terrible vengeance upon the nations (especially Edom), foretelling that 'the hills shall be drenched with their blood'.[49]

---

46. Deuteronomy 32:23, 25.
47. Ibid. 32:39, 41–42.
48. 'But I have installed My king on Zion, My holy mountain [. . .]. Ask it of Me, and I will make the nations your domain; your estate, the limits of the earth. You can smash them with an iron mace, shatter them like potter's ware.' Psalm 2:6, 8–9. For further statements of Yahweh as a universal sovereign and judge, see Genesis 18:25; Isaiah 34; Psalms 82; 96:10, 13; 98:9. See also Thomas Krüger, '"They Shall Beat Their Swords into Plowshares": A Vision of Peace through Justice and Its Background in the Hebrew Bible', in *War and Peace in the Ancient World*, ed. Kurt A. Raaflaub (Malden, MA: Blackwell, 2007), 161–71 at 169–70.
49. Isaiah 34:2–3.

With very few exceptions, wars waged by the Israelites without Yahweh's explicit approval ended in defeat. We see, therefore, that the wars of the Israelites were founded upon two fundamental assumptions. The first was that Yahweh's authority was required to fight a legitimate war. The second—dependent upon the first—was that Yahweh's divine support was essential to success in warfare. Israel's military defeats were explained in terms of Yahweh withholding his support in order to punish the Israelites for their transgressions against the Covenant; indeed, Yahweh could even actively strengthen Israel's enemies.[50]

YAHWEH AND CONQUEST

Bestowing legitimate rights of conquest was arguably Yahweh's most important function in the narrative of the Tanakh. The Israelites only emerge as a defined political entity as a result of Moses and Joshua leading them to the Promised Land of Canaan in order to complete a military conquest, decreed by their god. When Moses ascended Mount Sinai for the first time (Exodus 19:16ff), Yahweh's promise of territorial conquest was a crucial feature of the Covenant between the deity and his people. The Israelites had no claim to Canaan except the promise of Yahweh. The books of Joshua and Judges also stress the numerical and technological inferiority of the Israelites, making it clear that Israel had no hope of conquering Canaan without divine aid.[51] Yahweh strengthened the Israelites in battle, but also engaged in a type of preternatural biological warfare, removing the population while leaving the infrastructure unharmed:

> I will send forth My terror before you [. . .]. I will send a plague ahead of you, and it shall drive out before you the Hivites, the Canaanites, and the Hittites. I will not drive them out before you in a single year, lest the land become desolate and the wild beasts multiply to your hurt. I will drive them out before you little by little, until you have increased and possessed the land.[52]

When Joshua renewed the Covenant between Israel and Yahweh, the god reminded his people of the debt they owed to him, having been gifted a conquered land already replete with agricultural and urban infrastructure:

> I have given you a land for which you did not labor and towns which you did not build, and you have settled in them; you are enjoying vineyards and olive groves which you did not plant.[53]

---

50. Numbers 14:41–45; Deuteronomy 28:7, 49–57; Joshua 7:4ff; Judges 2:11ff. See also Susan Niditch, 'War and Reconciliation', 143.
51. See Joshua 7:4–5; 11:1–9; 17:16–18; Judges 1:19; 1 Samuel 13ff.
52. Exodus 23:27–30.
53. Joshua 24:13.

The Tanakh's authors thus gave Yahweh sole credit for the conquest, as well as reminding the Israelites that they enjoyed the fruits of other peoples' labours only through the grace of their god. In terms of both legitimacy and capability, the Tanakh presents the conquest of Canaan as entirely reliant upon Yahweh.

The author(s) of Deuteronomy were determined to negate any claim to mundane authority alone in the arena of politics or war. Political and military authority—and by extension, political and military success—had to be rooted in the divine. Moreover, it was stressed that it was not the Israelites' own virtues or military skill that enabled their military conquest, but rather the sins of the Canaanites as judged by Yahweh:

> Know then this day that none other than the Lord your God is crossing at your head, a devouring fire; it is He who will wipe them out [. . .]. And when the Lord your God has thrust them from your path, say not to yourselves, 'The Lord has enabled us to possess this land because of our virtues'; it is rather because of the wickedness of those nations that the Lord is dispossessing them before you.[54]

Prior to the crossing of the Jordan, Yahweh is described as physically 'giving' victory to the wandering Israelites. After Moses smashed the tablets of the Decalogue and was called to ascend Sinai for a second time (Exodus 34:10ff), the role of Yahweh as a god of conquest remained at the heart of his relationship with Israel.[55] Later, Yahweh tells Moses not to fear King Og of Bashan, who has marshalled troops against Israel, 'for I give him and all his people and his land into your hand'. This resulted in the Israelites defeating King Og and massacring all his people, 'until no remnant was left him; and they took possession of his country'.[56] When the aged Moses assigned Joshua as his successor to lead the Israelites across the Jordan and begin the conquest proper, the old prophet emphasised the role of Yahweh as conqueror:

> The Lord your God Himself will cross over before you; and He Himself will wipe out those nations from your path and you shall dispossess them [. . .]. The Lord will deliver them to you, and you shall deal with them in full accordance with the Instruction that I have enjoined upon

---

54. Deuteronomy 9:3-4.

55. 'I hereby make a covenant [. . .]. Mark well what I command you this day. I will drive out before you the Amorites, the Canaanites, the Hittites, the Perizzites, the Hivites, and the Jebusites.' Exodus 43:10-11. Cf. almost identical language in Exodus 23:23, 28.

56. Numbers 21:33-35; cf. Deuteronomy 3:1-11. The Amorite king, Sihon of Heshbon, who had denied free passage to the Israelites, had already been dealt with in a similar manner: Numbers 21:21-25.

you.[57] Be strong and resolute, be not in fear or in dread of them; for the Lord your God Himself marches with you: He will not fail you or forsake you.[58]

Conquest, as conceived here, is not victory over foreign peoples leading to their subjugation and exploitation by a new overlord, but an annihilation—a purification, essentially—enabling the settlement of a land wiped clean of corrupting foreign influences.

YAHWEH WITH THE ARMY

The authority of Yahweh in war, especially in identifying legitimate targets for attack, was reinforced through the god's presence within the Israelite army itself. Yahweh was understood to accompany the army on campaign and fight in front of it in battle.[59] With the creation of the Ark as a locus for the manifestation of Yahweh's presence, there was even a visual and tangible quality to this divine support.[60] During the Israelites' march through the wilderness, the Ark's progress in the vanguard marked Yahweh's role as a protective war leader: 'When the Ark was to set out, Moses would say: Advance, O Lord! May Your enemies be scattered, And may Your foes flee before You!'[61] When Moses dispatched the army on a specific campaign, it was accompanied by a Levite priest carrying the sacred utensils and ready to sound the trumpet blasts to call the attention of Yahweh.[62] For von Rad, it was the 'blast of the trumpet' that signalled the mustering of the Israelite 'amphictyony' for a holy war.[63]

Deuteronomy 20 prescribed a set of pre-battle rituals, stipulating that the religious exhortations of priests should prefigure the specific tactical instructions of the commander.[64] The priests confirmed the presence of Yahweh in the army, thus also confirming divine support and the guarantee of victory: 'For it is the Lord your God who marches with you to do battle for you against your enemy, to bring you victory.'[65] Such rituals and speeches would have

---

57. That is, the instructions for conducting war given in Deuteronomy 20, which commands the total destruction of the Seven Nations.

58. Deuteronomy 31: 3–6.

59. Rad, *Holy War*, 44–45.

60. Exodus 25:8ff; Numbers 10:35; Joshua 10:14, 42; Judges 4:15; 7:22; 1 Samuel 4:3; 7:10; 14:15, 20; 2 Samuel 11:11. Smend is sceptical that the Ark was ever truly the central sanctuary of the so-called amphictyonic period: Smend, *Yahweh War*, 76–97.

61. Numbers 10:35.

62. Ibid. 31:6. The *JSB* commentary notes that the sacred utensils included the Ark as well as the Urim and Thummim. Cf. 2 Samuel 4:3–11. For discussion of the Ark in battle, see Kang, *Divine War*, 208–12.

63. Rad, *Holy War*, 41–42.

64. 'When the officials [priests] have finished addressing the troops, army commanders shall assume command of the troops.' Deuteronomy 20:9.

65. Ibid. 20:4.

served to boost the morale of troops about to enter battle, and the Levitical confirmation of Yahweh's presence in the army may have acted as a form of official declaration of war—a point of no return.[66]

Because the texts claimed that Yahweh inhabited the Israelite camp, they also mandated certain observances regarding the physical and spiritual purity of the troops and the army's environment. Abstinence from masturbation or sexual intercourse was required, and any individual partaking in such activity had to undergo ritual purification. Latrines had to be located outside the camp, so as not to offend Yahweh with unpleasant odours as he walked among the tents.[67] It was explained that '[s]ince the Lord your God moves about in your camp to protect you and to deliver your enemies to you, let your camp be holy; let Him not find anything unseemly among you and turn away from you.'[68] In short, Yahweh's presence was conceived as a physical manifestation of the deity in support of the army.

Yahweh's martial authority, power, and presence were nowhere better established than through direct intervention in battle. Yahweh's intervention was comprised either of *promises* of direct intervention in future battles, or immediate intervention in a conflict as it unfolded. Promises of victory were often accompanied by a quid pro quo: the Israelites would receive divine aid but must act in a manner pleasing to Yahweh in return (effectively the *do et des* principle). For example,

> When My angel goes before you and brings you to the Amorites, the Hittites, the Perizzites, the Canaanites, the Hivites, and the Jebusites, and I annihilate them, you shall not bow down to their gods in worship or follow their practices, but shall tear them down and smash their pillars to bits.[69]

The god's intervention in war could manifest itself in a variety of forms, and there are references to blazing stars, earthquakes, flood, fire, cloud, and plagues striking terror into the enemy. This mirrored patterns of divine warfare and divine intervention found throughout the ancient eastern Mediterranean (including Greece) and Mesopotamia.[70]

Given the mortal risks of war, as well as the game-changing nature of divine intervention when it came to battle, it is not surprising that Israelite war leaders strove to gain any insight as to whether they could rely on divine support. Such oracles could be positive, such as those received by David before defending the

---

66. Jones notes the importance of ritual before, during, and after battle in so-called 'Yahweh War': Jones, '"Holy War" or "Yahweh War"?', 648–49.

67. Deuteronomy 23:10–14; see also Joshua 3:5; 1 Samuel 21:4–5; 2 Samuel 11:10–13.

68. Deuteronomy 23:15.

69. Exodus 23:23–24.

70. As explored by Weinfeld, 'Divine Intervention'. For a comparative analysis highlighting some of the analogues between the Israelite and Assyrian models, see Weippert, '"Heiliger Kreig" in Israel'.

people of Keilah.⁷¹ However, when Saul failed to receive an oracle from Yahweh prior to waging war against the Philistines, in desperation the king turned to a female diviner and necromancer—the infamous witch of En-dor—to get answers.⁷² Unfortunately for Saul, the ghost of Samuel foretold his defeat and death, along with the death of his sons. This, according to Samuel's ghost, was Yahweh's punishment for Saul's previous failure to kill all the Amalekites.⁷³ In a similar vein, the Samaritan and Judahite kings Ahab and Jehoshaphat consulted numerous oracles from a number of prophets to determine whether they should declare war against Aram. Only the pious Micaiah cast doubt on the motivations of King Ahab and warned the kings against war, predicting disaster. Refusing to heed Micaiah's warning and preferring the more favourable oracles, the Israelite kings marched to war and were swiftly defeated.⁷⁴

In the majority of cases, however, Israelite war leaders appear to have tacitly assumed that they enjoyed Yahweh's support in war. It is possible that some early references to war oracles were excised by post-exilic redactors, perhaps uncomfortable in depicting war leaders repeatedly resorting to oracles. Such practices smacked of non-Yahwist ritual magic and prophecy (such as in the case of Saul and the witch of En-dor), and would thus have conflicted with the ideological agenda of the redactors. In Deuteronomy the promise of Yahweh's military intervention was included within the terms of the Covenant. If Israel remained faithful, then the 'Lord will put to rout before you the enemies who attack you; they will march out against you by a single road, but flee from you by many roads'.⁷⁵ On the eve of their entry into Canaan, foreseeing the many dangers facing them, promises of divine military aid were intended to quell the fear of the Israelites: 'When you take the field against your enemies, and see horses and chariots—forces larger than yours—have no fear of them, for the Lord your God, who brought you from the land of Egypt, is with you.'⁷⁶

In the narrative of the Tanakh, the first full-scale battle fought by the Israelites, towards the end of their wanderings in the wilderness, was against an Amalekite army. We are given no explanation for the Amalekite attack, but simply told that 'Amalek came and fought with Israel at Rephidim'.⁷⁷ Deuteronomy claimed that the Amalekites surprised the Israelites while on the march, cutting down the weak stragglers at the rear of the column.⁷⁸ The older Exodus text, in contrast, portrayed the contest as a conventional pitched

---

71. 1 Samuel 23:1–5.
72. Ibid. 28:1–25.
73. Ibid. 28:17–19.
74. 1 Kings 22:1–40.
75. Deuteronomy 28:7.
76. Ibid. 20:1.
77. Exodus 17:8.
78. Deuteronomy 25:17–18. This single act of aggression by Amalek was given as a justification for the Israelites to destroy the Amalekites and to 'blot out the memory of Amalek from under heaven': ibid. 25:19.

battle. Moses instructed Joshua to muster the fighting men and do battle with the Amalekites the following day (hardly indicative of a rapid 'hit-and-run' attack), explaining that he would watch over the battle from a nearby hill, 'with the rod of God in my hand'. As the fighting got under way, 'whenever Moses held up his hand, Israel prevailed; but whenever he let down his hand, Amalek prevailed'. With Yahweh's power channelled through the rod, 'Joshua overwhelmed the people of Amalek with the sword'.[79]

This episode highlights a number of important tropes. First, Yahweh was willing and able to intervene to ensure military victory for Israel. In the engagement against the Amalekites, Yahweh's martial vigour was manifested through his chosen people, endowing the Israelite troops with the power to overcome their foes. It is made explicit that Yahweh's power was essential for the Israelite victory, as the text stressed that every time Moses lowered his rod—the conduit of divine power—the Israelites were beaten back.

It is also notable that Moses himself did not fight in the battle, nor in any other battle described in Exodus or Numbers.[80] This may simply be that the storyteller considered it inappropriate and unrealistic for a man who is said to be over a hundred years old to be fighting in a battle. But it was more likely driven by a concern for ritual purity. Moses was Yahweh's prophet and priest par excellence, and just as the Levites were later excused from military service because of their role as priests and attendants to the tabernacle (Numbers 1:47–53), Moses too had to remain ritually pure and abstain from bloodshed as a prerequisite for his intimate relationship with Yahweh. But there was clearly a distinction made between shedding blood, on the one hand, and enabling bloodshed, on the other. In the destruction of the Egyptians at the Red Sea and the Amalekites at Rephidim, Moses did not contaminate his hands with blood, but nevertheless played a pivotal role as the conduit of divine power, leading to the annihilation of both enemy armies.[81]

The battle against the Amalekites is far from being a unique example of Yahweh's willingness to directly intervene in war. Yahweh even provided cultic instructions for the Israelites' pre-battle ritual: 'When you are at war in your land against an aggressor who attacks you, you shall sound short

---

79. Exodus 17:8–16. Compare the role of the rod during the battle against Amalek to Yahweh's instructions to Moses to 'lift up your rod and hold out your arm over the sea' to divide the waters of the Red Sea. This command and gesture was repeated to bring the waters back over the Egyptian army: Exodus 14:16, 21, 26–28.

80. After Moses's killing of an Egyptian (Exodus 2:11–15)—which precipitates his flight from Egypt—there is no other record of him personally shedding blood. Arguably, it was this act of violence that symbolised the metamorphosis of Moses into the defender of Israel and Yahweh's anointed prophet.

81. In the Christian tradition, similar distinctions, between exhorting warriors to fight a just war and personally commanding the shedding of blood or shedding blood by one's own hand, have been made. For the development of these debates, see Lawrence G. Duggan, *Armsbearing and the Clergy in the History and Canon Law of Western Christianity* (Woodbridge: Boydell, 2013).

blasts on the trumpets, that you may be remembered before the Lord your God and be delivered from your enemies.'[82] Yet the most famous example of trumpets being used by the Israelites to call Yahweh to arms, at the city of Jericho, clearly *preceded* any military aggression from the inhabitants of Jericho: the Israelites launched an unprovoked attack on the Jerichoans, not vice versa.[83] According to the Book of Joshua (6:1–27), an angel commanded Joshua to perform the ritualised marching and trumpet blowing around the city for seven days. As promised, on the seventh day the great walls of Jericho collapsed and the Israelites sacked the city. With the exception of the prostitute Rahab and her family (who had earlier hidden and saved some Israelite spies), everything within the city—inhabitants and spoils—was proscribed (*herem*) and destroyed as a sacrifice to Yahweh.[84]

Yahweh also delivered the city of Ai and its people into Joshua's hand,[85] and later provided a spectacular victory over five Amorite kings (of Jerusalem, Hebron, Jarmuth, Lachish, and Eglon) by bombarding them with massive hailstones. Indeed, the text is at pains to point out that 'more perished from the hailstones than were killed by the Israelite weapons'.[86] According to the Book of Judges (7), Yahweh aided Gideon in leading the Israelites in rebellion against the subjugation of Midian and Amalek; in doing so, the god purposefully reduced the size of the Israelite army from thirty-two thousand arrayed troops to just three hundred picked men. This was so that none could doubt that Yahweh's divine might, *not* Israelite strength in arms, would achieve victory.

Late in the history of the kingdom of Judah, Yahweh responded to the pleas of King Hezekiah by intervening to relieve Sennacherib of Assyria's siege of Jerusalem:

---

82. Numbers 10:9.

83. Joshua 6:1–27. The story of Jericho perhaps provided the inspiration behind the later ritual prescription in Numbers 10:9 that the Israelites should sound trumpets to call the attention of Yahweh. The Book of Numbers belongs largely to the 'Priestly' tradition and, alongside the Book of Leviticus, is the latest of the books of the Torah/Pentateuch. The bulk of the text is almost certainly post-exilic in date, with elements dating to as late as the Roman period (e.g., the prophecy of Balaam: Numbers 24). See also discussion above, ch. 8, 'The Tanakh': 'The "documentary hypothesis"/"critical thesis"'.

84. The story has no basis in reality. Archaeological investigation has established that Jericho was destroyed in the early to mid-Bronze Age and was all but deserted by the late second millennium. The city did not possess any significant walls until well after the ninth century—that is, several centuries later than the purported events described in the book of Joshua. See Redford, *Egypt, Canaan, and Israel*, 264.

85. Joshua 8:1–35. The conquest of Ai is yet another anachronism, as this city was not settled until the early first millennium.

86. Joshua 10:1–43, quotation at v. 11. For further references to stones from heaven in the Tanakh, as well as in the Assyrian and Greek traditions, see also Weinfeld, 'Divine Intervention', 140–41. For a comparison to the miraculous thunderbolt (which Younger translates as 'meteor') described in the Hittite 'Ten Year Annals of Muršili', see Younger, *Ancient Conquest Accounts*, 208–10.

> He shall not enter this city:
> He shall not shoot an arrow at it,
> Or advance upon it with a shield,
> Or pile up a siege mound against it.
> He shall go back
> By the way he came; He shall not enter this city—declares the Lord [...].
> That night an angel of the Lord went out and struck down one hundred and eighty-five thousand in the Assyrian camp, and the following morning they were all dead corpses. So King Sennacherib of Assyria broke camp and retreated, and stayed in Nineveh.[87]

Of course, such intervention was only a temporary relief, as the post-exilic authors of 2 Kings were perfectly aware.

THE ABSENCE OF MEDIATED DIVINE AUTHORITY AND MILITARY DEFEAT

The pivotal role played by divine authority and aid in the Tanakh's accounts of Israelite warfare is perhaps best illustrated by those occasions when Israelites go to war *without* Yahweh's approval and aid. Deuteronomy recalls an instance when Moses warned the Israelites not to attempt any military actions because Yahweh had removed himself from the army: 'But the Lord said to me, "Warn them: Do not go up and do not fight, since I am not in your midst; else you will be routed by your enemies."'[88] The Israelites ignored this warning and, predictably, were promptly crushed by the Amorites at Hormah (Deuteronomy 1:44). The message is unambiguous: the removal of divine authority and support to wage war doomed this military venture to failure. Later in Deuteronomy, Yahweh warned the Israelites that if they violated their Covenant with him, they would suffer defeat in war: 'The Lord will put you to rout before your enemies; you shall march out against them by a single road, but flee from them by many roads; and you shall become a horror to all the kingdoms of the earth.'[89]

This theme of divine alienation and military defeat is recurrent throughout the books of the Tanakh. The assault against the city of Ai was initially unsuccessful because, unbeknownst to the Israelite leadership, a soldier named Achan had seized and withheld spoils from Jericho. This act violated the ban Yahweh had placed on the city, which demanded that *everything* should have

---

87. 2 Kings 19:32–36.
88. Deuteronomy 1:42.
89. Ibid. 28:25. See also ibid. 28:49–57, where the reference to Israel's defeat by a nation from afar is likely a reference to either Assyria or Babylon.

been dedicated as a herem offering. As punishment for this impiety, Yahweh removed his divine support during the first assault on Ai:

> So about three thousand of the troops marched up there; but they were routed by the men of Ai. The men of Ai killed about thirty-six of them, pursuing them outside the gate as far as Shebarim, and cutting them down along the descent. And the hearts of the troops sank in utter dismay.[90]

The wholesale removal of divine aid on this occasion was caused by the specific sin of just a single individual (Achan), an ordinary soldier otherwise of no special note. Once Achan's sin was discovered, and he and his entire household were condemned to death by holocaust, Yahweh's support was restored and Ai conquered and razed.[91]

In other episodes, the sins of the Israelites tend to be more general, or are committed by leaders or kings, and often included the proscribed worship of other gods. In the Book of Judges, Yahweh is described as being 'incensed at Israel' because of their devotional treachery, declaring that 'I for My part will no longer drive out before them any of the nations that Joshua left when he died'. So it came to pass that the Israelites 'could no longer hold their own against their enemies', and their lands were ravaged and overrun.[92] When Jehoahaz became king of Samaria, his actions angered Yahweh to such an extent that 'He repeatedly delivered them [the Samaritans] into the hands of King Hazael of Aram and into the hands of Ben-hadad son of Hazael'.[93] These defeats left King Jehoahaz with a much-reduced army: punishment for his impiety.[94] The gradual Assyrian conquest of the kingdom between c. 732 and c. 720 was interpreted in a similar manner. The Second Book of Kings explains that

> [t]his happened because the Israelites sinned against the Lord their God [...]. They worshipped other gods and followed the customs of the nations which the Lord had dispossessed before the Israelites [...]. The Lord was incensed at Israel and He banished them from His presence [...]. So the Israelites were deported from their land to Assyria, as is still the case.[95]

---

90. Joshua 7:4–5. The fact that just thirty-six casualties were described as a 'rout' perhaps indicates the true, much smaller, size of Israelite armies.
91. Ibid. 7:1–8:35.
92. Judges 2:14, 21.
93. 2 Kings 13:3–7.
94. Jehoahaz was 'left with a force of only fifty horsemen, ten chariots, and ten thousand foot soldiers; for the king of Aram had decimated them and trampled them like the dust under his feet': ibid. 13:7.
95. Ibid. 17:7–22. Regarding the Assyrian invasion, see also ibid. 17:3–12; 18:9–12.

In the face of Israelite breaches of the Covenant, even the presence of the Ark was no guarantee of Yahweh's military intervention. The First Book of Samuel recounts how, having acted with impiety, the Israelites were routed by the Philistines, 'who slew about four thousand men on the field of battle'.[96] Determined to reverse their losses, and confident in the power of the Ark, the Israelite Elders commanded that the Ark should be brought from Shiloh and that once again they should take the field against their foes. Even the Philistines appear to have feared the Ark.[97] And yet, once again, the Israelites were routed, suffering thirty thousand casualties. Worse still, the Ark itself was captured and taken off as spoil.[98] Here, the awful military consequences of Yahweh refusing to intervene in battle were writ large for the Israelites: massacre, humiliation, and the loss of the Ark, Israel's most sacred symbol of their relationship with the divine.

In political and historical terms, the most catastrophic defeats in Israelite history were the destruction of the two kingdoms of Samaria and Judah. The collected books of Kings, Chronicles, and the Prophets are very clear about *why* these kingdoms were destroyed in turn. The leaders and people of both kingdoms had angered Yahweh: they had worshipped other gods, ignored the Decalogue, and broken the Covenant. The fall of Samaria and Judah, the destruction of the Jerusalem Temple, and the final exile of the Israelites from their promised land was the most potent demonstration of what horrors befell them when divine support was absent from their military ventures.

The message of the books of the Tanakh, repeated loudly and clearly, is that Yahweh was absolutely pivotal to the Israelites' military success. It was his authority that bestowed legitimacy on a military enterprise, just as his intervention guaranteed victory. In contrast, it was Yahweh's displeasure and absence that guaranteed defeat. Yahweh's ability to determine either victory or defeat underscored the god's fundamental role in all Israelite warfare. Human individuals—whether prophet or king—could aspire to lead the Israelites in war, but ultimately the authority for waging just wars and the power to win them was rooted first and last in Yahweh alone.

Just Cause

As we have seen, the concept that wars are waged as a result of a certain provocation or a recognised injury is very ancient indeed. It goes back to at least the early third millennium, and was probably understood long before this. From the books of the Tanakh there emerges substantial evidence of Israelite wars being justified on account of specific grievances. Yet there are also instances

---

96. 1 Samuel 4:2.
97. Ibid. 4:6–9. Note the assumption in v. 9 that those defeated in war will be enslaved.
98. Ibid. 4:10–11.

of Israelite violence being prosecuted without any obvious pre-existing injury or 'just cause'. The most glaring and significant example is the conquest of Canaan itself. As recounted in the Tanakh, this conquest was not prosecuted on account of any specific injury done by the Canaanites against the Israelites. Rather, the invasion was launched because Yahweh had deemed these nations unfit to inhabit the land and thus gifted it to the Israelites. The 'injustice' committed by the Canaanites was an injustice not against any particular person or state but, apparently, against Yahweh. Equally, the decision that the land of Moab would not form part of the territory bestowed to Israel was made by Yahweh alone.[99]

This approach to war bears more in common with Egyptian concepts of foreigners as inherently barbarous and wicked than with any physical or legal concept of human injury. As was demonstrated in Part I above, the dualistic conflict between Ma'at and Isfet bestowed on the pharaoh a permanent right to wage war against non-Egyptians because they threatened the cosmological order and its terrestrial reflection in Egypt. Yahweh's universalist claims to authority and punitive justice, directed at the Canaanites, echo this absolutist tradition.

The existence of certain legitimate just causes for war was certainly recognised in the Levant of the late second millennium, the period in which the Israelite conquest of Canaan is supposed to have occurred. While the modern scholarly consensus is that no such conquest took place (see discussion in chapter 8), it remains possible that the narrative of Joshua and Judges preserves or reflects vestiges of historical norms in force at the end of the second millennium. As a point of comparison, Middle and Neo-Assyrian evidence (c. 1200–c. 1050 and c. 900–c. 650) points towards the existence of well-established just causes for war, articulated through royal ideology.[100] Bustenay Oded has argued that the 'Assyrians sanctioned war as a legitimate means of pursuing their goals and spreading their hegemony', but nevertheless 'possessed the notion of *causa iusta*' and 'were sensitive to the religious and moral aspect of warfare'.[101] Oded identifies twelve categories of grievances that could each constitute a *causa belli* emerging from the Assyrian royal inscriptions: by divine command; to punish evildoers; as a response to hostilities; to protect a political protégé and aid allies; to combat and punish usurpers; to punish violations of an oath of loyalty; to quell rebellion; to enforce order

---

99. 'And the Lord said to me [Moses]: Do not harass the Moabites or provoke them to war. For I will not give you any of their land as possession; I have assigned Ar as a possession to the descendants of Lot.' Deuteronomy 2:9.

100. See Oded, *War, Peace and Empire*; Mario Liverani, 'The Ideology of the Assyrian Empire', in *Power and Propaganda: A Symposium on Ancient Empires*, ed. M. T. Larsen (Copenhagen: Akademisk Forlag, 1979), 297–317. For comparative treatments of Assyria and Israel, see Weippert, '"Heiliger Kreig" in Israel'; Younger, *Ancient Conquest Accounts*; 61–124; Crouch, *War and Ethics*.

101. Oded, *War, Peace and Empire*, 177–79.

and peace; to punish sinners against the gods; to enforce the right of reprisal; to demonstrate force and glory; and to assert the Assyrian king's rightful dominion over the world. Among these varied just causes for war, self-defence against the unprovoked aggression of enemies was the most commonly cited. In sum, the Assyrians believed that '[e]very war must have a *iusta causa*'.[102]

These articulations of the intimate connection between justice and war reflected the belief that the Assyrian king's wars were enacted on both terrestrial and cosmological planes. It certainly appears that Assyrian kings were confident enough in their own justifications of violence to wage a type of warfare that was essentially limitless in terms of *in bello* conduct. Assyrian texts and bas-reliefs are far from squeamish about describing bloody massacres, brutal tortures, and campaigns of devastation committed against enemies.[103] Whether such descriptions were faithful representations of reality is another matter entirely, of course, but they do demonstrate an ideological confidence in the legitimacy of Assyrian violence. As we have seen in our treatment of Egyptian thought concerning the pharaoh's duty to defend Ma'at (order) against Isfet (chaos), Assyrian kings also envisioned themselves engaged in a *Chaoskampf*. Much later, this ideology of a king defending the cosmic order by warring against chaotic enemies was displayed in Israelite thought.[104]

SELF-DEFENCE

Defending Territory

The ethical norms of the ancient Near East widely accepted that conquest endowed a conqueror with a lawful claim to territorial ownership. This meant that once a new territory was annexed the conquerors could claim any subsequent defence of it as lawful and just. This concept of conquest and ownership is likely to be extremely ancient, and its religious sanction was already operational in Old Kingdom Egypt and in Sumer under Sargon of Akkad.[105] The Israelite concept of war, being so closely bound to the story of Israel's territorial manifestation in Canaan, perhaps unsurprisingly also incorporates ideas of territorial self-defence.

The story of the Israelite conquest of Canaan is an exemplar of this ancient notion of divinely sanctioned conquest. It is notable that Yahweh's promise of land ownership appears very early in the narrative arc of Israel's history as presented in the Tanakh; indeed, it occurs even before the name 'Israel' was bestowed upon Jacob. The promise of territory was a personal promise made

---

102. Ibid., 45, quotation at 178; see ibid., 45–59 for discussion of evidence concerning self-defence.
103. See also discussion of Assyrian atrocities below, pp. XXX–XX.
104. Crouch, *War and Ethics*, 29.
105. Ziskind, 'Aspects of International Law', 35, 41.

by the god to Abraham/Abram: 'To your offspring I assign this land, from the river of Egypt to the great river, the river of Euphrates.'[106] Although the Genesis text long postdates the supposed period of the united kingdom of Israel, the purpose of the passage was to confirm the Israelites' territorial claims in Canaan by vesting these claims in divine authority and ancient heritage. Consequently, any later defence of these conquered territories would have to be viewed as legitimate and just.

One can find a few brief but uncomplicated references in the Tanakh to defending or reclaiming 'stolen' land. For example, during Samuel's 'reign' as judge, the Israelites sought to reconquer land from the Philistines: 'The towns which the Philistines had taken from Israel, from Ekron to Gath, were restored to Israel; Israel recovered all her territory from the Philistines.'[107] This military action was presented as essentially defensive, aimed at recovering stolen territory. Even after the united kingdom of Israel splintered into the separate kingdoms of Samaria and Judah, King Ahab of Samaria proposed a joint operation with King Jehoshaphat of Judah to reconquer Ramoth-gilead, a territory apparently once part of the Solomonic kingdom but now held by Aram.[108] The reclamation of this former Israelite territory was presented by Ahab as a just cause for war, despite the fact that Israel and Judah had been at peace with the Arameans for the previous three years.[109] Given these peaceful relations, King Jehoshaphat appears to have harboured some doubts about the legitimacy of such an attack, insisting that oracles should be consulted prior to the launching of a military operation. The seemingly avaricious motivations of Ahab—who is presented in the pro-Judaean 1 Kings as a degenerate leader who has strayed from the path of Yahweh—can be inferred from the prophecies of Micaiah: the prophet foretells that a war with Aram will end in Ahab's death. Nevertheless, Ahab ignores Micaiah's warning and marches on Ramoth-gilead, where he is promptly hit by a fluke shot from an Aramean archer, dying shortly afterwards and so fulfilling the prophecy.[110] Unfortunately, the text does not provide any further information on the outcome of the battle or the relative justice of the competing claims to Ramoth-gilead. Instead, the battle and the death of Ahab acts as a literary device to illustrate Yahweh's vengeance against an iniquitous (Samaritan) Israelite king. Nevertheless, this text is indicative of two sets of norms relating to war. The first norm, legalistic in character, is indicated by Ahab's attempt to justify the war against Aram in terms of reclaiming lost territory, thus demonstrating the concept of territorial defence as a just cause for war. The second norm,

---

106. Genesis 15:18.

107. 1 Samuel 7:14.

108. For Ramoth-gilead as part of the Solomonic kingdom, see 1 Kings 4:13. It is also mentioned as an Israelite settlement in Joshua 20:8; 21:36; Deuteronomy 4:43.

109. 1 Kings 22:1–5.

110. Ibid. 22:6–38.

moralistic in character, is indicated by Jehoshaphat's doubts regarding Ahab's claims and intentions, as well as by Micaiah's warning not to declare war against Aram. This demonstrates an attempt by the author to highlight the iniquity of Ahab's motives (waging war solely for profit and self-aggrandisement rather than for the glory of Yahweh), and thus the injustice of this particular war against Aram.

The most detailed account of a territorial dispute involving the Israelites, in which the principle of justified territorial self-defence appears front and centre, is furnished in the Book of Judges (11:4–32). The episode, supposedly taking place prior to the establishment of the monarchy, also provides a glimpse of diplomatic processes operating between rulers of relatively minor states, with envoys carrying attempts at negotiation or declarations of war.

The text recounts how both the Israelites and Ammonites asserted competing claims to a number of territories, including those formerly held by the Arameans. Time clearly plays an important role for both parties: the appeal to historical possession is portrayed as intrinsic to determining legal ownership. At the outset we are told that the 'Ammonites went to war against Israel', prompting the elders of Gilead to appoint Jephthah as their commander and chief.[111] As chief, Jephthah's first act was to send messengers to the king of Amon, asking, 'What have you against me that you have come to make war on my country?' The king of Amon replied with a historical claim to significant tracts of land currently dominated by the Israelites: 'When Israel came from Egypt, they seized the land which is mine, from the [river] Arnon to the [river] Jabbok as far as the [river] Jordan. Now, then, restore it peaceably.'[112] In response to this historically founded legal challenge, Jephthah offered his own series of sophisticated historical and legal arguments, utilising the Exodus account in order to historicise Israel's claims and rebuff those of Amon. This series of arguments and counter-arguments was all delivered through envoys.

To begin, Jephthah rebuffed the initial claim made by the Ammonite king—that the Israelites had invaded Ammonite territory during the exodus—, explaining that his people had never actually entered Amon or Moab:

> Israel did not seize the land of Moab or the land of the Ammonites [...]. Israel sent messengers to the king of Edom, saying 'Allow us to cross your country.' But the king of Edom would not consent. They also sent a mission to the king of Moab, and he refused. So Israel, after staying at Kadesh, travelled on through the wilderness, skirting the land of Edom and the land of Moab. They kept to the east of the land of Moab

---

111. Judges 11:4. Again, this emphasises the strong link between military and political authority. The elders had previously exiled Jephthah.

112. Ibid. 11:12ff.

until they encamped on the other side of the [river] Arnon; and, since Moab ends at the Arnon, they never entered Moabite territory.[113]

Having established that the wandering Israelites had not violated Ammonite territory during the exodus, Jephthah then recounted how and why they came to dominate Amorite land:

> Then Israel sent messengers to Sihon king of the Amorites, the king of Heshbon. Israel said to him, 'Allow us to cross through your country to our homeland.' But Sihon would not trust Israel to pass through his territory. Sihon mustered all his troops, and they encamped at Jahaz; he engaged Israel in battle. But the Lord, the God of Israel, delivered Sihon and all his troops into Israel's hands, and they defeated them; and Israel took possession of all the land of the Amorites, the inhabitants of that land.[114]

Thus Jephthah rejected the initial Ammonite claim to this disputed land on the basis that, prior to the Israelite conquest, the territory formerly belonged to the Amorites, *not* the Ammonites.[115] Further, Jephthah identified the denial of passage and unprovoked aggression against the Israelites as causes for war against the Amorite king of Heshbon. Victory against the Amorites was made possible by divine favour and intervention, and thus the subsequent Israelite possession of Amorite land was legitimate—not only as a justified response against legal grievances and armed aggression, but, more importantly, according to the divine authority of Yahweh.

Having explained that the god of Israel had bestowed the formerly Amorite land on Israel, Jephthah mocked the Ammonite claim to it by asking, rhetorically, whether the Ammonites would willingly give up land which *their* national god, Kemosh (or Chemosh), had gifted *them*?[116] But this was not the end of the correspondence. Jephthah continued his legal rebuttal of Amon's claims by challenging his rival to explain why, if Amon truly had a claim to these lands, the Ammonites had taken no action for three hundred years:

---

113. Ibid. 11:15–18. Cf. Numbers 20:18–20.
114. Judges 11:19–21; cf. Numbers 21:23–25.
115. This claim is somewhat contradicted by Numbers 21:26. Following the Israelite defeat of the Amorites, 'Now Heshbon was the city of Sihon king of the Amorites, who had fought against a former king of Moab and taken all his land from him as far as the Arnon.' This suggests that at least some of the territory in question had indeed at one time been Ammonite (i.e., Moabite), and was subsequently invaded by the Amorites.
116. 'Now, then, the Lord, the God of Israel, dispossessed the Amorites before His people Israel; and should you possess their land? Do you not hold what Kemosh your god gives you to possess? So we will hold on to everything that the Lord our God has given us to possess.' Judges 11:23–24. Note that Jephthah does not challenge the existence of Kemosh, but assumes that each people had its own national deity. See also *WHB*, 125–26; Good, 'Just War in Ancient Israel', 395.

While Israel has been inhabiting Heshbon and its dependencies, and Aroer and its dependencies, and all the towns along the Arnon for three hundred years, why have you not tried to recover them all this time? I have done you no wrong; yet you are doing me harm and making war on me. May the Lord, who judges, decide today between the Israelites and the Ammonites![117]

This fascinating exchange highlights a number of important issues: the original grievances that led to the Israelite conquest of Amorite territory; the divine sanction of Israelite military action; the divine bestowal of land by national gods; the importance of time in establishing ownership, and the importance of time in determining the legitimacy of a military response.

According to medieval or modern Western just war doctrine, self-defence (including territorial defence) must be prosecuted *incontinenti*—that is, immediately—in order to be ethically legitimate. While there has always been debate concerning what exactly constitutes an 'immediate' response, and exactly how much elapsed time between injury and armed response is ethically acceptable (it was difficult to muster a medieval army in less than a week, for example), it is fascinating to see parallel arguments being made by the author of Judges 11. For Jephthah, even *if* the Ammonites had a claim to the disputed lands, three hundred years was simply too great a hiatus to make a valid claim on the territory.[118] Put simply, Jephthah argued that time and the length of possession contributed to legal ownership.

Ultimately, Jephthah leaves the case to be judged by Yahweh in the divine court.[119] In all, the correspondence is highly reminiscent of the type of legal-ethical approach to war pioneered by the Hittites, with Jephthah essentially 'presenting' his legal case to Yahweh via the medium of his correspondence with Amon. This also corresponds to Liverani's observations of ancient war as a form of legal ordeal, with guilt established according to which party inflicted

---

117. Judges 11:26–27.

118. Compare the (pseudo-)Aristotelian concept of just vengeance of injuries, in which elapsed time seems unimportant: 'Let us take up the same method with regard to the most important aspects of war and peace. These are the reasons to wage war on others: "Since we were wronged before, now that the opportunities have come, we must defend ourselves against those who did the wrong," or "Since we are being wronged now we must make war either on behalf of ourselves or our kinsmen or our benefactors, or to help allies who are being wronged, or for the sake of the city's advantage, or its good reputation, resources, or power, or something else of that sort."' Aristotle, *Problems*, vol. 2: *Books 20–38: Rhetoric to Alexander*, ed. and trans. Robert Mayhew and David C. Mirhady (Cambridge, MA: Harvard University Press, 2011), ch. 2, § 26 (pp. 492/3). See also O'Driscoll, 'Rewriting the Just War Tradition', 3.

119. Good attaches great importance to Judges 11, concluding that '[w]e are, in short, justified in speaking here of a preexilic concept of war as an expression of divine *legal* judgment': Good, 'Just War in Ancient Israel', 395.

the first injury: 'Hence the necessity of going back in time and interpreting the events of the past in their causal relations, until a fixed point is reached when the enemy committed the original wrong.'[120] If this story of the Israelite–Ammonite dispute possesses any degree of historicity, then we might assume that the 'case' was presented in very similar terms by Jephthah in his private supplications to Yahweh, just as Hittite Great Kings went in supplication to the storm-god and the sun-goddess of Arinna before going to war against their enemies.

According to the Book of Judges, the king of Amon's response to these carefully crafted historical and legal arguments was to ignore Jephthah's overtures and continue his aggression against Israel.[121] Jephthah, in turn, was obviously not willing to gamble his success in war on the strength of his historical and legal case alone. In order to guarantee Israelite victory against the king of Amon, Jephthah made the following vow to Yahweh:

> If You deliver the Ammonites into my hands, then whatever comes out of the door of my house to meet me on my safe return from the Ammonites shall be the Lord's and shall be offered by me as a burnt offering.[122]

Yahweh accepted the oath, intervened in favour of Israel, and the Ammonites were decisively beaten.[123] Tragically, when Jephthah returned victorious from battle, the first thing that came out of his house was his young daughter. Knowing that the vow to Yahweh must be honoured, the girl was sacrificed.[124] The tale calls to mind the Greek myth of Agamemnon's sacrifice of his daughter Iphigenia in order to assuage the goddess Artemis and permit the passage of the Achaean fleet to Troy.[125] More importantly, the tragic element of Jephthah's victory reiterates that the ethical framework of Israelite thought is inherently unstable if viewed from the perspective of interstate relations, as

120. *LIR*, 104.
121. Judges 11:28.
122. Ibid. 11:30–31.
123. Ibid. 11:32.
124. Ibid. 11:34–40.
125. This story of Iphigenia does not appear in the *Iliad*, but is developed in a number of other classical Greek sources, including the fifth-century tragedy by Euripides, *Iphigenia at Aulis*. For an extended and provocative analysis of the importance of sacrifice in Greek culture and religion, see Burkert, *Homo necans*. While it may be tempting to see some connection between the story of Jephthah and the Homeric Agamemnon, the trope of sacrificing family members is actually quite common in ancient mythology, and occurs elsewhere in the Tanakh, such as the near-sacrifice of Isaac (Genesis 22). King Mesha of Moab is also said to have sacrificed his son to the god Kemosh in order to turn back an Israelite attack (2 Kings 3:24–25). In the Hittite *Tale of Illyunka*, the storm-god sacrifices his mortal son in order to defeat the serpent. Indeed, the sacrifice of a child by a parent is the central story of the collection of religious texts that came to lean most heavily on the Tanakh: the New Testament and the sacrificial crucifixion of Jesus of Nazareth.

opposed to Israelite–Yahweh relations. The death of Jephthah's daughter was only necessitated by the personal oath made to Yahweh in return for his intervention against the Ammonites. This support was apparently entirely separate from the relative ethical or legal strength of Israel's case against Amon, for which Jephthah had provided compelling proof in his diplomatic missives. If the key consideration in determining whether the Israelites had just cause to go to war had been the relative justice or injustice of the two states' territorial claims, then Jephthah's votive oath to Yahweh should have been unnecessary or irrelevant. If that was the case, why did the Israelite leader feel compelled to make such a vow, and to bind himself to what would prove to be such a tragic commitment? Why was it not sufficient for Yahweh to judge the case on 'legal facts' alone?

The answer is that the ethics of war in the Tanakh are rooted in the personal relationship between the Israelites and Yahweh. Ultimately, it was Jephthah's personal relationship with Yahweh, bolstered by his votive oath, that ensured Israel's victory. The exhaustive legal arguments presented to the king of Amon, and the relative ethical and legal status of Israel's claims as regards to the disputed territory, appear to have been of secondary importance, at best.

This episode reveals two distinctive and potentially conflicting currents of thought. The first—recourse to detailed legal arguments and appeals to historical ownership—provides a valuable insight into how territorial self-defence was justified in the international relations of the first millennium. For Robert Good, this exchange embodies the jural ideology of war in ancient Israel, furnishing proof that the Israelites envisaged Yahweh as a judge who accepted the existence of reciprocal rights and duties between different peoples. War functioned to maintain those rights and duties, and thus Israelite ethical thought transcended the concept of Yahweh as a deity fighting for or judging in favour of Israel because of his 'special care' for his chosen people; rather, it attained a level of ethical sophistication that could accept that Yahweh would judge cases on the basis of ethical or legal merit, with judgements possibly going against Israel.[126] However, in placing so much weight on the Jephthah/Amon case, Good is arguably using an exception to prove a norm. It must be remembered that the Tanakh contains *many* more examples of Yahweh aiding Israelites in war purely on a partisan 'special care' basis, rather than because of any evidence of Israelite claims to just cause. We should also remember that Jephthah won the war against Amon after beseeching and receiving Yahweh's help on the basis of a contract of exchange (a promised votive offering), so the incident in no way proves Yahweh's impartiality.

The second, conflicting, current of thought evinces the theological imperative of the author(s) of the Book of Judges. These priestly authors, obsessed

---

126. Good, 'Just War in Ancient Israel', 399–400.

with the covenantal relationship, required that the story serve a specific didactic purpose, showing how and why Yahweh intervened in earthly affairs and how individual Israelites should behave in relation to their god. Whether or not Amon had a plausible legal claim to the disputed territory was a nonstarter for such authors, who considered all the lands of Canaan to be a gift from Yahweh to the people of Israel. For these priestly authors, the core moral lesson of the Israel–Amon dispute was the crucial importance of keeping faith with Yahweh, which manifestly generated real-world benefits (albeit at the cost of Jephthah's innocent daughter).

Defending People

Recourse to arguments of justified defence of people (rather than territory) are quite rare in the Tanakh.[127] In part, this is because the books of the Tanakh more often present the Israelites as military aggressors and conquerors than as victims. On other occasions, the justice of self-defence is implicit rather than articulated, such as the when the Amalekites attack the Israelites in the wilderness.[128] While neither Exodus nor Deuteronomy display a need to justify the Israelites' armed response to this attack, the outrage provoked by the attack is evident in the subsequent promise made by Yahweh and Moses to 'blot out the memory of Amalek from under heaven'.[129]

Nonetheless, explicit articulations of defence of people as just cause for war can be found. When the Canaanite king of Arad attacked the Israelites in the wilderness (taking some of them captive), they responded by beseeching Yahweh to grant them vengeance for this crime: 'Then Israel made a vow to the Lord and said, "If you deliver this people into our hand, we will proscribe their towns."' Yahweh granted Israel's request and 'delivered up the Canaanites; and they and their cities were proscribed'.[130] The annihilation of the people and cities of Arad was in no way proportionate to the raid on the Israelite column, yet this episode does broadly conform to notions of self-defensive violence, albeit of a kind that veers more towards vindictive justice than immediate self-defence.[131]

---

127. For later rabbinic commentaries on self-defence in Talmudic writings, see Solomon, 'Judaism', 298–99.

128. Exodus 17:8–16; Deuteronomy 25:17–19.

129. Exodus 17:14–16; Deuteronomy 25:19.

130. Numbers 21:1–3. The *JSB* commentary notes that archaeological excavations show no evidence of a settlement at Arad in the second millennium.

131. It could be judged that there is a vindictive element to the response against Arad, as the initial attack had ceased by the time the Israelites supplicate Yaweh for vengeance. Nevertheless, the reaction by the Israelites is immediate (in the sense that they did not embark on any other ventures between the injury and the response) and thus within the norms of self-defence.

At the opposite end of the biblical narrative we see one of the most interesting examples of self-defensive violence appearing in the Book of Esther, where we encounter a case of preemptive—even preventive—self-defence.[132] In this tale set in the court of the Persian king Ahasuerus, the royal councillor Haman urges the king to kill all the Hebrews in his kingdom, having accused them of sedition. However, the virtuous and beautiful Esther, favourite wife of the king, persuades him that the Hebrews are loyal subjects. She then obtains his permission for her people to defend themselves preemptively by striking first against Haman and those plotting to kill them. This results in several thousand deaths, including those of the ten sons of Haman, who are impaled at Esther's request.[133] Throughout, Esther's actions are presented as entirely noble, and the deaths of the Hebrews' would-be attackers as wholly justified.

The potential complexities and inconsistencies of the concept of justified self-defence within the Tanakh is hinted at in an episode concerning King David. Having received reports that the people of Keilah were suffering violent Philistine raids, David consults with Yahweh as to whether or not he should attack the Philistines. Receiving Yahweh's affirmation, David subsequently defeats the raiders, saves the inhabitants of Keilah, and seizes spoils from the defeated enemy (1 Samuel 23:1–5). At first glance, the defence of Keilah appears to conform to the image of David as an ideal king, fulfilling his role by defending his subjects. The text certainly presents the people of Keilah as innocent victims of unjust aggressors. But if so, why did David feel compelled to seek Yahweh's approval prior to going to Keilah's defence? Surely it was the king's duty to defend his subjects, and in this case—a border raid—such defensive violence must have been permissible, even obligatory?

David's oracular consultation can be subjected to several layers of interpretation. The first is that the author of the Book of Samuel simply assumed that it was always necessary to consult oracles prior to any military venture, regardless of how just or unjust the proposed expedition might appear. Given the widespread use of oracular consultation concerning military matters throughout the ancient Near East, this is eminently plausible. An additional layer of reading could interpret David's actions as proof of prudential concerns about the possibility of success: because Israelite tradition taught that military victory was dependent upon Yahweh's approval and intervention, to have waged war without Yahweh's approval would have invited disaster. Yet another layer of reading suggests that the ethics of war in ancient Israelite thought were based on shifting sands, held hostage by the seemingly ad hoc whims of Yahweh. The god's grand strategy—focused on achieving his divine eschatological plan for Israel—resulted in a series of events that could appear ethically inconsistent.

---

132. Esp. Esther 3:13–4:17; 8:11–9:32.

133. Ibid. 9:13–30. The text implies that it is the corpses which are impaled, rather than impalement being the means of death.

Israel's penitential journey towards salvation required both victory and defeat, defensive and offensive violence, restraint and massacre. Indeed, from the post-exilic perspective of the author(s) of the Book of Samuel—writing *after* the collapse of Samaria and Judah—the terrible demands of Yahweh's salvific plan would have appeared all too real and immediate. Within this eschatological framework, Israelite commanders such as King David could never blithely assume Yahweh's support for a particular military venture, regardless of how 'obvious' the case for permissibility might appear to human observers. Consequently, even self-defensive violence to protect people required oracular approval.

This facet of Israelite thought undermines any attempt to argue for a casuistic understanding of *iusta causa* in Israelite war ethics. According to the authors, compilers and redactors of the Tanakh, Israel was always the centre of Yahweh's concerns, whether for good or ill. These ancient scholars interpreted the defeat of Israel in war as a punishment for Israelite sins against Yahweh, not as an affirmation of the justice of the victor. As a rule, injustices committed by the Israelites against other peoples or states were entirely irrelevant to the outcome of their wars. Likewise, Israelite victory in war does not provide any specific commentary on the relative injustice of their enemies. There are many examples of the Israelites defeating enemies who have committed no identifiable injury against them.

THE DEFENCE OF 'RIGHTS': FREE PASSAGE

Throughout the ancient Near East, passage across the territory of a foreign state was not a right, but a privilege, and required formal consent. If free passage was granted, then the person or group received the full protection of the laws of that state. If passage was refused, then any subsequent trespass would be interpreted as an act of war.[134] These diplomatic norms, dominant throughout the second and first millennium, shaped the narrative of Israel's movement from Egypt to Canaan.

Near the city of Kadesh, Moses twice requested free passage across Edomite territory, promising not to take anything from the land. Despite these reassurances, 'Edom answered him, "You shall not pass through us, else we will go out against you with the sword" [. . .]. And Edom went out against them in heavy force, strongly armed.'[135] Given the descriptions of the Israelite force—a vast column of nomadic troops and people—it is perhaps understandable that Edom would have been hesitant to grant the Israelites free passage across its lands. On this occasion no fighting ensued, as Moses prudently decided to alter course in order to circumvent Edomite territory.

---

134. Ziskind, 'Aspects of International Law', 154–57.
135. Numbers 20:18, 20. Cf. Deuteronomy 2:18–23.

A short time later, a similar request for free passage was made to Sihon, king of the Amorite city of Heshbon, and Moses was again rebuffed: 'But Sihon would not let Israel pass through his territory.' Not only did the Amorites marshal troops on their borders, but King Sihon proceeded to attack the Israelites: 'Sihon gathered all his people and went out against Israel in the wilderness. He came to Jahaz and engaged Israel in battle.' However, the Amorites were defeated and Israel subsequently 'took possession of their land' and city.[136]

Both the Edomite and Amorite cases support the claim that in the ancient Levant free passage was a privilege rather than a right, and thus denial of free passage could not in itself be considered just cause for war. At Kadesh the Israelites were denied free passage but were not otherwise molested, so peacefully diverted their course. Nor does the text imply that Moses was surprised by Edom's denial of passage, or that the Israelites considered Edom's denial a cause for war. The Amorites also denied Israel free passage, but the cause for war came about because the Amorites attacked the Israelites at Jahaz, thus provoking a violent response. While the subsequent brutal annihilation of the Amorites could hardly be described as proportional, it did, nonetheless, stem from a simple act of self-defence.

It is worth reiterating that the cause for war against the Amorites on this occasion was *not* their denial of free passage to the Israelites, but rather their attack on them at Jahaz. Even by the time that Marcus Tullius Cicero was writing in the first century, one can find no mention in his comments on war that free passage was considered a right. It seems that Cicero shared the ancient Near Eastern assumption that free passage remained a privilege that could be either granted or denied.[137] In light of this, we can see that when Saint Augustine came to write his *Questions on Numbers* in the late fourth century CE, the bishop of Hippo anachronistically misinterpreted the meaning of these verses. Augustine asserted that free passage was a 'just right of human society' and argued, therefore, that its denial by the Amorites provided the Israelites with a just cause for war.[138] He did not call attention to the fact that the Edomites had also denied passage to the Israelites, nor that the Israelites only

---

136. Numbers 21:21–25.

137. The *Glossa ordinaria* to *Decretum magistri Gratiani* (see n. 140 below), C. 23, q. 2, c. 3, provides some evidence in Roman civil law that passage should be free: 'For although to cross another's field is not law, as above, D. 1 c. 1., yet, because this transit was necessary and harmless, they ought not to have forbidden it, as at *Digest* 39.3.2.5. Also, because it was a public road, and no one is forbidden to make use of a public road, as at *Codex* 3.34.11. Ioan.' My thanks to Professor Giulio Silano for providing this passage.

138. Augustine, *Questions on Numbers*, q. 44, c. 20 (Numbers 21:24–25), cited in *Decretum magistri Gratiani*, in *Corpus iuris canonici: Editio lipsiensis secunda post Aemilii Ludouici Richteri*, ed. A. Friedberg, 2 vols (Leipzig: Tauchnitz, 1879–81), vol. 1, Pars secunda, C. 23, q. 2, c. 3. See also Augustine, *Questions on the Heptateuch, in, Writings on the Old Testament*, ed. Ramsey, 300.

fought King Sihon because he attacked them. Nevertheless, Augustine's commentary on Numbers 21:24–25 was later incorporated into Gratian's *Decretum* (c. 1140 CE), an immensely influential Latin canon law compendium, which subsequently led to the principle being widely accepted in the Western just war tradition.[139]

THE DEFENCE OF ALLIES

The defence of allies features only rarely as a cause for Israelite war. King Solomon is reported as allying himself with Egypt and other states through diplomatic marriages, although we are given no information regarding any military aid resulting from these alliances.[140] After coming to terms with the Gibeonites, Joshua marched out in defence of Gibeon against a combined Amorite host, which he crushed with the aid of Yahweh.[141] There are two occasions when the kingdoms of Samaria and Judah are reported as embarking as allies on campaigns against Aram, Elam, and Moab;[142] however, these campaigns were offensive rather than defensive in nature, and the two Israelite kingdoms were seemingly more often enemies than allies.[143]

Late in the history of Samaria and Judah, both kingdoms sought the military aid and protection of larger states such as Assyria, Egypt, or Babylon (see, e.g., 2 Kings 16:5–9), but not always to their advantage. Around 609, King Josiah of Judah, acting as an ally of Assyria, died in battle against an Egyptian expeditionary force at the Megiddo Pass, while his son, Jehoahaz, was later taken to Egypt as a prisoner of war.[144] Such examples furnish some evidence

---

139. '"*Innoxius transitus filiis Israel negabatur, atque ideo iusta bella gerebantur.*" Notandum sane est, quemadmodum iusta bella gerebantur a filiis Israel contra Amorreos. Innoxius enim transitus negabatur, qui iure humanae societatis equissimo patere debebat.' ('Harmless transit was denied to the children of Israel, and so they waged just wars.' It is to be noted how just wars were waged by the children of Israel against the Amorites. For harmless transit was being denied, which by the most just law of human society should have been permitted to them.) *Decretum magistri Gratiani*, C. 23, q. 2, c. 3, citing Augustine, *Questions on Numbers*, q. 44. My thanks to Professor Caroline Humfress and Professor Bruce Frier for their comments on this subject.

140. 1 Kings 3:1; 11:1–8.

141. Joshua 10:5–10. The text says that after Joshua's destruction of Jericho and Ai, 'the people of Gibeon had come to terms with Israel and remained among them' (ibid. 10:1). They had only done so, however, by tricking the Israelites into thinking that their envoys had come from *outside* the territory of Canaan (ibid. 9:3–27), and were thus not proscribed by Yahweh's ban on the nations.

142. 1 Kings 22:1–40; 2 Kings 3:5–27. On the motivation of the war against Aram in 1 Kings 22:1–40, see also *WHB*, 129.

143. For Samaria and Judah as enemies, see 1 Kings 15:6, 16; 2 Kings 14:7–14; 16:5–9; 2 Chronicles 28:9–11, 14–15.

144. 2 Kings 23:29–30; 2 Chronicles 35:20–24. See also Redford, *Egypt, Canaan, and Israel*, 448; Miller and Hayes, *Ancient Israel and Judah*, 460–62.

of Israelite rulers engaging in military-political alliances, yet the episodes are not presented by the compilers of Kings and Chronicles as articulations of Israelite rulers fighting in defence of justice. Rather, the general tone is that the kings of Samaria and Judah had long fallen into iniquity, and their military actions and failures merely foreshadowed the inevitable disasters that would come to afflict both kingdoms.

One explicit example of justified defence of allies—albeit an alliance based on bonds of kinship rather than politics—presents itself in Genesis (14:11–16). The kings of Elam, Goiim, Shinar, and Ellasar had invaded the plains around Sodom and Gomorrah and captured Lot and his household. Lot's uncle, the patriarch Abraham/Abram, immediately raised a war-band to rescue his nephew and retrieve his stolen property:

> When Abram heard that his kinsman had been taken captive, he mustered his retainers, born into his household, numbering three hundred and eighteen, and went in pursuit as far as Dan. At night, he and his servants deployed against them and defeated them; and he pursued them as far as Hobah, which is north of Damascus. He brought back all the possessions; he also brought back his kinsman Lot and his possessions, and the women and the rest of the people.[145]

The narrow parameters of Abraham/Abram's defensive actions—defending his family's honour—do not seem to have been motivated by a broader ethical concern or sense of obligation to defend political (rather than personal) allies.

The paucity of references to defensive alliances within the Tanakh is best explained by the way in which the Israelites are depicted as a unique religio-political community, constantly beset by ungodly foreigners. As the chosen people of Yahweh, Israel's exalted status and its Covenant with its god did not encourage alliances with other, non-Yahweh worshipping, peoples. In fact, quite the opposite: such peoples were viewed as an existential threat to Israel's religious purity. The Tanakh broadly depicts the Israelites as either invulnerable because of their divine support from Yahweh, or doomed because of their breaches of the Covenant. Neither position really requires political allies, as it is understood that rival states will either be subjugated in the good times or will be an instrument of Yahweh's wrath in the bad times. Politico-military alliances would therefore detract from the focus on Yahweh as the ultimate arbiter of Israelite military destiny, and serve as something of a narrative obstacle to the didactic moralism of the texts.

---

145. Genesis 14:14–16. Abraham even pointedly refused to keep any spoils for himself, giving them back to the king of Sodom. Note that King Melchizedek of Salem, while congratulating Abraham, assumed that Yahweh was to be credited for the victory: Genesis 14:18–20.

VENGEANCE AND PUNISHMENT

Vengeance and retributive justice were powerful drivers of war in ancient Israelite thought. War was an extreme but apparently common means to redress injuries suffered by Yahweh or the Israelites, allowing Yahweh's universal sovereignty and judgement to be enacted in the mundane world. The destruction of people and property, wrought through warfare, was consistently utilised as an effective means of retribution. Even the conquest account of Joshua 9–12 can be described as embodying an ideology of revenge and terror.[146]

This attitude to war as a tool of retributive justice is encapsulated in one of the final acts of Moses prior to the prophet's death. Yahweh communicated his wish, via Moses, that the Midianites should be destroyed in revenge for their historical sins against Israel. (Notably, these sins did not include any overt military aggression committed by Midian.) The sins of Midian included hiring a diviner, Balaam, to curse Israel before it could assault Midian (Numbers 22:7) and the insidious influence of Midianite women on Israelite men, enticing them into idolatry at Baal Peor.[147]

> The Lord spoke to Moses, saying, '*Avenge the Israelite people* on the Midianites; then you shall be gathered to your kin.'[148] Moses spoke to the people, saying, 'Let men be picked out from among you for a campaign, and let them fall upon Midian *to wreak the Lord's vengeance on Midian*.'[149]

The Israelites proceeded in fact to muster twelve thousand men, accompanied by priests sounding trumpets and carrying the sacred utensils, and attacked Midian, exterminating every male, including all five kings of the Midianites and the diviner Balaam.[150]

A similar example is furnished in Deuteronomy, with Moses instructing his people to remember the historical injury inflicted by the Amalekites (Exodus 17:8–17) and to do all in their power to wreak a terrible vengeance:

> Remember what Amalek did to you on your journey, after you left Egypt—how, undeterred by fear of God, he surprised you on the march, when you were famished and weary, and cut down all the stragglers in your rear. Therefore, when the Lord your God grants you safety from all

---

146. Younger, *Ancient Conquest Accounts*, 233–34.
147. Numbers 25:6, 14–18. On the demonisation of 'alien women' in the Book of Numbers, see Susan Niditch, 'War, Women, and Defilement in Numbers 31', in *Women, War, and Metaphor: Language and Society in the Study of the Hebrew Bible*, ed. Claudia V. Camp and Carole R. Fontaine (Atlanta, GA: Scholars Press, 1993), 39–57 at 45. See also *WHB*, 78–89.
148. 'be gathered to your kin': i.e., to die.
149. Numbers 31:1–3 (emphasis added).
150. Ibid. 31:4–8.

your enemies around you, in the land that the Lord your God is giving you as a hereditary portion, you shall blot out the memory of Amalek from under heaven. Do not forget!¹⁵¹

This passage in Deuteronomy could be read as a preparatory justification for the much later destruction of Amalek achieved during the reign of King Saul:

> Thus said the Lord of Hosts: 'I am exacting the penalty for what Amalek did to Israel, for the assault he made upon them on the road, on their way up from Egypt. Now go, attack Amalek, and proscribe all that belongs to him. Spare no one, but kill alike men and women, infants and sucklings, oxen and sheep, camels and asses!'¹⁵²

Several generations separated the period of the Wanderings from the period of Saul's kingship. So, in this case, the passage of time does not appear to have been a limiting factor on the exaction of justified vengeance: an interesting observation, given Jephthah's mocking of the Ammonites for delaying so long in seeking to reclaim the disputed Amorite territory (see above, pp. 319–24).

Though clearly presented as an act of retributive justice, the genocidal vengeance inflicted upon Midian and Amalek was in no way proportional to their original crimes. This was not an example of the *lex talionis* in practice, which Mendenhall claims was a law originally intended to ensure 'a measure of protection'.¹⁵³ Indeed, even Saul's minor act of *in bello* restraint—taking King Agag of Amalek prisoner rather than killing him outright, and permitting some of his troops to seize booty rather than burning everything as herem—was chastised by the prophet Samuel as an act of impious disobedience.¹⁵⁴ For this single infraction, Yahweh forsook Saul and anointed David as his political rival (1 Samuel 17). Wars of vengeance demanded by Yahweh allowed for no mitigation of hostilities; they were absolute statements of justice, in which the execution of violence was similarly absolute.

The ruthless proscription of Midian and Amalek in vengeance for their historical offences against Israel, as well as the mercy shown to the Kenites in repayment for their historical good will, underlines the principle of reciprocity (although certainly not proportionality) at work in Israelite conceptions of

---

151. Deuteronomy 25:17–19. Cf. Jeremiah 50:15, 28; 51:3–11, where the Babylonians are condemned as plunderers and thus deserving of vengeance.

152. 1 Samuel 15:2–3.

153. Mendenhall, 'Ancient Oriental and Biblical Law', 39–40.

154. '"Why did you disobey the Lord and swoop down on the spoil in defiance of the Lord's will?" Saul said to Samuel, "But I did obey the Lord! I performed the mission on which the Lord sent me: I captured King Agag of Amalek, and I proscribed Amalek, and the troops took from the spoil some sheep and oxen—the best of what had been proscribed—to sacrifice to the Lord your God at Gilgal.' 1 Samuel 15:19–21.

the relationship between justice and war.[155] The moral of the story is that, regardless of time, evil actions beget evil consequences while good actions beget good consequences.[156] In both cases, 'justice' was ultimately served.

Vengeance could also be a legitimate cause for war in disputes *within* the Israelite nation, best illustrated by the war against the tribe of Benjamin, during which vengeance was understood as necessary on both an individual and a communal level.[157] The roots of this specific conflict lay in the brutal gang rape and murder of a Levite concubine within the Benjaminite town of Gibeah.[158] The other Israelite tribes were obliged to take action, resulting in a punitive war against the tribe of Benjamin. Having received oracular approval from Yahweh, the tribal alliance 'routed the Benjaminites before Israel'. Twenty-five thousand Benjaminite troops were killed in battle, while many more were massacred in the aftermath and their property razed.[159]

Israel itself was subject to retributive wars, as Yahweh avenged himself on his chosen people for breaches of the Covenant. The moral and eschatological purpose of such wars were often articulated through prophecy, such as Ahijah's prediction of the Assyrian conquest of the kingdom of Samaria in revenge for King Jeroboam's blasphemous devotions to the goddess Asherah.[160] In a similar vein, the prophet Jeremiah—himself a witness to the Babylonian conquest of Judah—intoned against the corrupted Davidic dynasty. He prophesied that retribution would come in the form of plagues and famine sent by Yahweh, followed by the military might of Babylon.[161] As presented in the Book of Jeremiah, Nebuchadnezzar and his armies were conceptualised as a *flagellum dei*, a divine instrument to realise Yahweh's judgement against Israel; Babylonian victory was not a product of Babylon's own righteousness.[162] Thus

---

155. 'Saul said to the Kenites, "Come, withdraw at once from among the Amalekites, that I may not destroy you along with them; for you showed kindness to all the Israelites when they left Egypt." So the Kenites withdrew from among the Amalekites.' Ibid. 15:6.

156. Samson was lauded for killing numerous Philistines in order to avenge his personal honour, though his pretexts for violence were spurious, to say the least: Judges 14:19–15:20.

157. Ibid. 19:1–20:48.

158. The callousness of the Levite towards his concubine is shocking in itself, and the 'crime' consists of the affront to the Levite's property and honour rather than the violent sexual assault and killing of the woman: ibid. 19:25–30.

159. There is some repetition of information and different numbers of dead given at Judges 20:29–37 compared to ibid. 20:38–48. Despite having Yahweh's support, the tribal alliance suffers two successive defeats by the Benjaminites, losing thirty thousand men.

160. 1 Kings 14:14–15.

161. Jeremiah 21:4–7.

162. Jeremiah predicted that Yahweh would eventually avenge himself against Babylon for its cruelties, excesses and insolence: See Jeremiah 50:1–51:64, which foretells the conquest of Babylon by Persia.

we return once again to the conclusion that the Tanakh's ethics of war were focused entirely on Israel's relationship with Yahweh, rather than Israel's legal or political relationship with other states.

CRUSHING REBELLION

Political overlordship was often a fragile state of affairs in the ancient Near East, mainly because it necessitated projecting power over significant distances but with only rudimentary communications technology. Small states were constantly jockeying for increased autonomy, while great states were always seeking ways to tempt or coerce their competitors' vassals into new alliances. Even within the domestic political sphere, ruling dynasties experienced challenges to their authority, proving vulnerable to internal dissent and dynastic usurpation. Like their political predecessors and contemporaries, Israelite rulers were also forced to contend with rebellion in various forms, and developed various ethical approaches to justify its punishment through armed force. Jacob Wright gives a list of no less than twelve 'putsches' listed in the books of Samuel and Kings, and stresses the crucial link between martial prowess and political power within Israelite society.[163]

The Tanakh conceived Israel first and foremost as a religious community given political form. It is unsurprising, therefore, to see rebellion conceived in theological terms. In Deuteronomic law, any Israelite settlements found guilty of breaking the Covenant and worshipping other gods—that is, rebelling against Yahweh and separating themselves from the Israelite religio-political community—were to be subjected to extreme punitive violence. In such cases, the greater community of Israel was obliged to wage herem war against the 'rebels' in the following manner:

> [P]ut the inhabitants of that town to the sword and put its cattle to the sword. Doom it and all that is in it to destruction: gather all its spoil, into the open square, and burn the town and all its spoil as a holocaust to the Lord your God. And it shall remain an everlasting ruin, never to be rebuilt.[164]

Insisting on the 'nuclear option' of herem proscription against those Israelites guilty of rebellion against Yahweh demonstrated the gravity of this crime in the eyes of the zealous author(s) of Deuteronomy.

With regard to rebellion considered as a political rather than a strictly theological crime, we see a variety of responses (with the caveat that, when discussing cultures in which religious sanction and political authority were

---

163. Wright, 'Military Valor and Kingship', 39–40.
164. Deuteronomy 13:16–17. Compare the punishment (being stoned to death) for individuals guilty of the crime of idolatry: ibid. 17:2–7.

so intimately entwined, political acts always retained a degree of religious significance). Israelite kings inevitably viewed rebellion as a legitimate cause for punitive war and acted energetically to suppress it, but the texts frame the higher justice of their actions as dependent upon the moral status of the individual ruler.

The kingdom of Samaria seems to have experienced a number of destabilising usurpations over the course of its history. Indeed, according to the tradition of the Tanakh, the kingdom was itself born out of rebellion, when Jeroboam of Samaria led a revolt against Solomon's son Rehoboam (1 Kings 12). While the separation of Samaria from Judah was presented as a sign of Israel's long-term degeneration, even the pro-Judahite author(s) of the Book of Kings painted Rehoboam as a harsh and unjust king.

Rebellion in Samaria was a bloody affair. The usurper Abimelech is said to have murdered all seventy sons of Jerubbaal (Abimelech's half-brothers) in order to seize the throne, aided by the inhabitants of Shechem.[165] This crime was obviously a form of political rebellion in itself, as Abimelech and the Shechemites removed the legitimate royal heirs. As an act of fratricide on a massive scale, the crime also possessed a religious element, imitating and magnifying the crime of Cain. When the people of Shechem themselves later rebelled against Abimelech's tyrannical rule, his response was swift and merciless. The king ambushed the city, massacred the inhabitants, and sowed the ground with salt. When some of the unfortunate Shechemites sought refuge in a tower (or tunnel, in alternative translations), Abimelech torched the entrance and burned everyone inside: 'about a thousand men and women' in all.[166]

Such harsh treatment of rebels aped the Deuteronomic proscriptions for rebellion against Yahweh. While the Shechemites had not overtly rebelled against Yahweh worship, their fate had been prophesied as punishment for their betrayal of the seventy sons of Jerubbaal.[167] Thus the principle of reciprocity was enforced by the ultimate fate of the Shechemites. Reciprocity can also be seen at work in the fate of Abimelech himself. After dealing with the Shechemites, he faced further rebellions, including one by the people of the town of Thebez. In his eagerness to smite the rebels and attack the town's stronghold, the king was mortally wounded by a woman dropping a millstone on his head. So ignominious was this that Abimelech begged his attendant to finish him off with a dagger, so that no one could say that he was killed by a woman.[168] Through this humiliating death, 'God repaid Abimelech for the evil he had done to his father by slaying his seventy brothers'.[169]

---

165. Judges 9:1–5. See also *WHB*, 124.
166. Ibid. 9:42–52.
167. Ibid. 9:7–20. 'God likewise repaid the men of Shechem for all their wickedness. And so the curse of Jotham son of Jerubbaal was fulfilled upon them.' Ibid. 9:57.
168. Ibid. 9:53–54.
169. Ibid. 9:56.

Beyond internal politicking and power struggles, rebellion by weaker states against Samaritan or Judahite domination could spur Israelite rulers to war. But the justice of suppressing rebellion against Israelite overlordship does not appear to have been assessed according to any consistent ethical, legal, or political framework, other than the individual ruler's relationship with Yahweh. More often than not, Samaritan and Judahite kings were found wanting in this regard. King Joram of Samaria enlisted the aid of Judah and Edom in attempting to quell the rebellion of Moab, but failed to defeat it after King Mesha sacrificed his own son to the god Kemosh in order to drive away the Israelites.[170] A later Joram (son of Jehoshaphat), king of Judah, launched a night-time ambush against Edom in order to quell an Edomite rebellion. Again, the Israelites were defeated, and 'Edom fell away from Judah, as is still the case'.[171] In both cases, the failure of the two kings to quell rebellions is explained by their failure to rule in a manner that was pleasing to Yahweh.

And yet political rebellion could actually be directly sanctioned by Yahweh's prophets. Most notable was David's rebellion against Saul, stemming initially from Saul's paranoia that David's victory against Goliath had overshadowed his own prestige. David, meanwhile, was presented as a loyal captain who insisted upon his innocence.[172] Nevertheless, the prophet Samuel makes it clear that Yahweh had anointed David as king of Israel, removing his favour from Saul because of the old king's failure to eradicate the Amalekites.[173]

The potentially fickle nature of Yahweh's favour and its political ramifications can also be read of in the story of Jehu of Samaria. When Jehu—military commander of King Joram of Samaria—was anointed king by the disciples of the prophet Elisha, he betrayed and assassinated Joram to seize the throne. Jehu then also murdered King Ahaziah of Judah (who had been visiting Joram), without any provocation.[174] The texts justify these acts of political rebellion and assassination by lauding Jehu's religiously inspired zealotry: he immediately effected bloody purges against Jezebel (wife of the former king of Samaria, Ahab, and mother of Joram), the seventy princes of the House of Ahab, and all the priests and worshippers of Baal in both Samaria and

---

170. 2 Kings 3:5–7, 26–27.

171. Ibid. 8:16–22, quotation at v. 22. The underhand tactics pursued by Joram—an ambush and a night attack—are perhaps utilised by the author(s) to further highlight Joram's lack of heroism and righteousness.

172. 1 Samuel 18–24, 26:1–27:4.

173. Ibid. 15:35–16:14. Ultimately, it is not David but the Philistines who bring about the death of Saul (ibid. 31).

174. 'Thereupon Joram turned his horses around and fled, crying out to Ahaziah, "Treason, Ahaziah!" But Jehu drew his bow and hit Joram between the shoulders, so that the arrow pierced his heart; and he collapsed in his chariot [. . .]. On seeing this, King Ahaziah of Judah fled along the road to Beth-haggen. Jehu pursued him and said, "Shoot him down too!" [And they shot him] in his chariot at the ascent of Gur, which is near Ibleam. He fled to Megiddo and died there.' 2 Kings 23–24, 27.

Judah.[175] In this case, Jehu's rebellion was unambiguously legitimised by the author(s) of the Book of Kings.

War for Aggrandisement and Profit

The Danite tribe of Israelites provide a particularly egregious example of unprovoked warfare aimed at aggrandisement and profit. Having failed to oust the inhabitants of certain Canaanite territories 'allotted' to them by Joshua, the Danites turned their attention to the otherwise peaceable territory of Leshem, which had not figured in the allotted portions assigned to the tribes by Joshua.[176] Undeterred, the Danites 'captured it and put it to the sword; they took possession of it and settled in it.'[177]

A more detailed version of this story of ruthless Danite military expansionism was provided in the Book of Judges, with Leshem instead referred to as Laish.[178] Judges records how the tribe of Dan 'was seeking a territory in which to settle', so the elders dispatched spies into the surrounding lands. The spies discover the town of Laish, where 'they observed the people in it dwelling carefree, after the manner of the Sidonians, a tranquil and unsuspecting people, with no one in the land to molest them and with no hereditary ruler'.[179] Quickly reporting back to their elders, the spies urged immediate military action against this idyllic community:

> Let us go at once and attack them! For we found that the land was very good, and you are sitting idle! Don't delay; go and invade the land and take possession of it, for God has delivered it into your hand. When you come, you will come to an unsuspecting people.[180]

The tribal elders heeded this advice, and the Danites

> proceeded to Laish, a people tranquil and unsuspecting, and they put them to the sword and burned down the town [. . .]. They rebuilt the town and settled there, and they named the town Dan, after their ancestor Dan who was Israel's son.[181]

The campaign was evidently nothing more than a brutal land grab. The claim made by the spies that Laish had been delivered to the Danites by Yahweh was not supported by a specific oracle or by a prophetic announcement, while the

---

175. Ibid. 9:30–10:28. Jehu's 'just' slaughter of the seventy princes fulfilled Elijah's prophecy concerning the sinful House of Ahab; it is a mirror-image of Abimelech's unjust killing of his seventy brothers: Judges 9:1–52; 2 Kings 10:1–11, 16–17; 2 Chronicles 22.
176. Joshua 19:40–46.
177. Ibid. 19:47.
178. Judges 18:1–13, 27–31.
179. Ibid. 18:7.
180. Ibid. 18:9–10.
181. Ibid. 18:27–28.

Laishians themselves are repeatedly described as peaceful and innocent. Taken as whole, the text provides no evidence that the Danites had any just cause to wage war against Laish.[182] On the other hand, there is no overt condemnation or criticism of the Danites' actions at Leshem/Laish in either Joshua or Judges. While it is true that the Danites are not portrayed in a flattering light, the passages basically adopt a neutral stance, neither praising nor condemning the Danites' unprovoked extermination of a peaceable community.[183]

The Danites were not the only Israelite tribe guilty of unprovoked aggression. Following their internecine war against the combined Israelite tribes, the Benjaminites launched an unprovoked attack on Shiloh in order to acquire female concubines, in a story much like that of the Roman rape of the Sabine women.[184] Even the paradigmatic Israelite ruler, David, indulged in such behaviour. During the period that David served the Philistine king Achish of Gath, he launched a series of brutal raids for plunder against communities of Geshurites, Gizrites, and Amalekites. To keep his raiding secret from King Achish, David pursued a ruthless policy:

> When David attacked a region, he would leave no man or woman alive; he would take flocks, herds, asses, camels, and clothing [. . .]. David would leave no man or woman alive to be brought to Gath.[185]

Regardless of this profit-driven savagery, the text presents David as a hero, justifying his violence against the victim communities merely on the basis that David had *not* been attacking his fellow Israelites. When David's base at Ziklag was attacked by the Amalekites in revenge, David pursued and killed the raiders. This was presented as a legitimate response, and the cause of the attack (David's own brutal raiding of Amalekite territory) or the possible injustice of David's military activities in the region was never questioned.[186] We are left with the distinct impression that, as Yahweh's anointed, David's actions were *ipso facto* just. David's personal relationship with Yahweh, combined with his guiding principle of not harming Israelite interests, was taken as proof of his moral virtue. Again, this is indicative of the prevailing trend in Israelite thought on war: that it was the relationship with Yahweh, not the moral character of the deeds themselves, which determined the ethical quality of warlike actions.

---

182. For von Rad, this was a clear example of a war for *Lebensraum* rather than a holy war undertaken by the 'amphictyony' of Israel under the authority of Yahweh: Rad, *Holy War*, 64.

183. The Danite abduction of a Levite priest and religious utensils from the house of the Israelite Micah on the road to Laish is clearly depicted as an act of bullish coercion (Judges 18:13–26). The description of this thuggish behaviour was perhaps intended to reflect the aggressive and unruly character of the tribe.

184. Judges 21:15–24. Compare to Livy, *Ab urbe condita*, bk 1, ch. 9, §§ 8–16, in *Livy in Thirteen Volumes*, vol. 1: *Books 1 and 2*, trans. B. O. Foster (London: William Heinemann; New York: G. P. Putnam's, 1919), 34–39.

185. 1 Samuel 27:6–27, quotation at vv. 9, 11.

186. Ibid. 27:30.

Subsequent Davidic kings, however, were far more liable to criticism by the authors and compilers of Hebrew scripture. For these authors and redactors, the reigns of later Israelite kings marked a deterioration in the relationship with Yahweh, signalled by the fracturing of Israel and the decline of its two splintered kingdoms. The dangers of hubris and of pursuing aggrandising wars without Yahweh's support were illustrated by the fate of the bellicose young king of Judah, Amaziah. Having defeated the Edomites (2 Kings 14:7), Amaziah challenged the Israelite kingdom of Samaria to war. The rival kings engaged in full diplomatic military ritual, including a challenge, response, and declaration of hostilities:

> Then Amaziah sent envoys to King Jehoash son of Jehoahaz son of Jehu of Israel, with this message: 'Come, let us confront each other.' King Jehoash of Israel sent back this message to King Amaziah of Judah [. . .]: 'Because you have defeated Edom, you have become arrogant. Stay home and enjoy your glory, rather than provoke disaster and fall, dragging Judah down with you.' But Amaziah paid no heed; so King Jehoash of Israel advanced, and he and King Amaziah of Judah confronted each other at Beth-shemesh in Judah.[187]

Unfortunately for the impetuous and hubristic Amaziah, nemesis caught up with him: the Judahites were routed, Amaziah was captured, and Jehoash of Israel breached the walls of Jerusalem and carried off 'all the gold and silver and all the vessels that there were in the House of the Lord and in the treasuries of the royal palace, as well as hostages'.[188] Thus the king of Judah, being estranged from Yahweh, was punished for an unjust war against his fellow Israelites.

Israelite Ius ad bellum *Thought and the Relationship with Yahweh*

Israel's success or failure in war was determined by the nature of its relationship with Yahweh (a relationship which was highly dynamic), not by its ethical or legal relationship with its enemies. Israel's success in war was not a commentary on its claim to justice or injustice *in a specific war* or in relation to a specific enemy, but rather a witness to its ongoing positive or negative relationship with its god, Yahweh.

In adopting this stance in relation to just cause, Israelite thought was perhaps representative of broader cultural and political trends. Amnon Altman argues that ancient Near Eastern political propaganda was frequently more interested in the relationship between a ruler and a deity than in the particular

---

187. 2 Kings 14:8–11; cf. 2 Chronicles 25:17–21.
188. 2 Kings 14:12–14. King Amaziah was captured but apparently not executed, as he lived *beyond* the end of Jehoash's reign (ibid. 14:17–18).

causes of specific wars.[189] While Altman's assertion does not do justice to Hittite thought on war, which was far more legalistic and possessed at least some objective qualities, it does ring true for Egyptian ethics of war, which assumed that justice was generated through the pharaoh's unique relationship to Ma'at. The Israelite tradition focused on Yahweh as a singular deity, although the principle remained much the same: the justice of war was ultimately determined by one's relationship with the divine—the embodiment and font of justice—and was not dependent on the relations between different peoples and their subjective claims to goods, territory, and 'rights'.

On the one hand, this renders an ethico-legal category such as 'just cause' highly mutable, perhaps even irrelevant, because seemingly identical injuries might elicit Yahweh's support on one occasion but not on another (e.g., attacks by the Amalekites in the wilderness as compared to attacks by the Babylonians on Jerusalem). Without Yahweh's support, any military response to an injury lacked both legitimacy and likelihood of success. To reiterate, this is because it was Israel's relationship with Yahweh that determined the justice of Israelite warfare, not the mundane grievances and actions of the conflicting parties themselves. In this sense, there was in fact no concept of reciprocity or impartiality in Israelite conceptions of *iusta causa*, as has been claimed by some scholars.[190] In cases of Israelite defeat, Yahweh did not provide a judicial decision in favour of Israel's enemies (who, by not recognising Yahweh's divine sovereignty, were *ipso facto* unjust), but rather rendered a decision *against* Israel as a means of punishment. Only in certain prophetic imaginings of the future was it conceived that other nations would recognise Yahweh's universal sovereignty and, consequently, his mandate to act as arbiter and judge in international disputes.[191] So we see the oft-cited prophecy of Isaiah, so beloved of modern peacemakers that it is inscribed opposite the United Nations Headquarters in New York city (figure 40):

> Thus He will judge among the nations
> And arbitrate for the many peoples,
> And they shall beat their swords into plowshares
> And their spears into pruning hooks:
> Nation shall not take up
> Sword against nation;
> They shall never again know war.[192]

---

189. Altman, 'Earliest Recorded Concepts', 111.

190. Gelston, 'Wars of Israel', 329–31; Good, 'Just War in Ancient Israel', 388–90.

191. For example, Isaiah 4:2; Micah 4:3; Joel 4:1–19. These prophets flourished in the second half of the seventh century, but the oracles are probably post-exilic, dating from between 539 and 332. See Krüger, '"They Shall Beat Their Swords"', 162–63.

192. Isaiah 2:4. Compare the version of this prophecy in Micah 4:1–5. As Krüger comments, '[t]here is a relatively broad consensus in present research that the nearly identical

FIGURE 40. The 'Isaiah Wall', New York City. Jim Henderson, CC0 licence, via Wikimedia Commons.

But even within this prophecy there is little doubt that Yahweh will judge against the Nations and in favour of the Israelites. (Thus such a judgement cannot be interpreted in terms of an 'ordeal', as the outcome is effectively predetermined and partisan.)[193] Moreover, not all the prophets were as optimistic as Isaiah. Although far less prominent in Western culture, it is important to note that a mirror-image of Isaiah's prophecy was provided by the prophet Joel, who foresaw the ploughshares once again beaten into swords:

> Proclaim this among the nations:
> Prepare for battle!

---

oracles of Isaiah 2:2–5 and Micah 4:1–5 did not originate in the times of the prophets Isaiah and Micah, that is, roughly, the second half of the seventh century, but in the period of Persian dominion over Jerusalem and Judah, between 539 and 332—more probably in the first of this period than in the second': Krüger, '"They Shall Beat Their Swords"', 163.

193. As posited by Richard Preß, 'Das Ordal im Alten Testament', *Zeitschrift für die Alttestamentliche Wissenschaft* 51 (1933): 121–40, and also refuted by Good, 'Just War in Ancient Israel', 391.

> Arouse the warriors,
> Let all the fighters come and draw near!
> Beat your plowshares into swords,
> And your pruning hooks into spears.
> Let even the weakling say, 'I am strong.'[194]

In addition, there are other prophetic visions in which peace is only attained through the complete annihilation of non-Yahwist nations.[195]

Ultimately, then, Good's attempt to portray Israelite war ideology as intrinsically jural, with Yahweh acting as an impartial judge bound by reason and standards of reciprocity (as opposed to a partial sovereign recognising no limits), is unconvincing.[196] This is not to say that Israelite war ideology was unaffected by legal tradition; quite the opposite—ancient Near Eastern legal traditions deeply influenced Israelite concepts of war. Rather, it is to say that ancient Near Eastern legal thought, when touching upon the relationship between political communities, national gods, and divine judgement, did not have the same concept of reciprocal justice and obligations as we possess in the modern era. Put simply, ancient national gods—and Yahweh is arguably the archetype of a vindictive national god—were never thought of as impartial. Their worshippers *expected* them to be partisan and judge in their favour: that is why they worshipped them.

And yet the books of Isaiah and Micah expressed an idea that justice (albeit a partisan Yahwist/Israelite interpretation of justice) could eventually spell the end of war among nations:

> Then justice shall abide in the wilderness,
> And righteousness shall dwell on the farm land.
> For the work of righteousness shall be peace,
> And the effect of righteousness, calm and confidence forever.[197]

This universalising conception of justice and its potential to end conflict between nations shows that Israelite authors did indeed grapple with the nature of the relationship between war and justice. Crucially, it clearly indicates their belief that in a 'perfect world' of justice there would be no need for war.[198] Such a belief was, most likely, based on the presumption that war was the result of injustice; eradicate injustice, and one would thereby eradicate the need for war.

---

194. Joel 4:9–10.
195. 'Come and see what the Lord has done, how He has wrought desolation on earth. He puts a stop to wars throughout the earth, breaking the bow, snapping the spear, consigning wagons to the flames.' Psalm 46:9–10.
196. Good, 'Just War in Ancient Israel', 387–88.
197. Isaiah 32:16–17; cf. Krüger, '"They Shall Beat Their Swords"', 169.
198. Krüger, '"They Shall Beat Their Swords"', 163.

All this should not be taken to imply that specific physical injuries were unimportant in Israelite thought on war. Israelites were as likely to respond to invasion or raiding as any other group. But the 'justice' of that military response was not determined by the fact of an invasion or raid in itself, because, as in all things, such injuries had to be considered as possible expressions of Yahweh's divine will and salvific plan. Israelite authors, therefore, could not classify the justice or injustice of physical or legal injuries purely on the basis of their mundane characteristics, but instead had to consider all injuries as possible expressions of the divine will. Some injuries would be just punishment for Israelite violations of the Covenant (making Israelite success in war unlikely). Others would be an opportunity for the Israelites to confirm their favoured status with Yahweh and benefit both spiritually and materially.

This conceptual construction of just cause as determined by the relationship between the Israelites and their god is remarkably stable throughout the Tanakh. It is an attitude also evinced in the Israelite legal codes, which show that 'purity of religion was incomparably more important to the Hebrews than to any other ancient Near Eastern culture'.[199] It was also translated into ethico-legal considerations of war. Essentially, when the Israelites stood in favour with Yahweh, their military actions were almost always legitimate and justified. Conversely, if the Israelites forsook the strictures of the Covenant, then injuries by enemies and defeat in war were deserved punishments inflicted according to the will of Yahweh.

---

199. Good, 'Capital Punishment', 977.

CHAPTER TEN

The Israelites: *Ius in bello*

CONCEPTS AND PRACTICES

THE TASK OF identifying the existence of *in bello* norms in Israelite warfare is made difficult by the fact that the Tanakh contains surprisingly little detailed information concerning set-piece battles or military campaigns. Battles certainly appear, but the authors provide limited information concerning the ebb and flow of military confrontations, or how specific units were marshalled in preparation for battle or directed during it. As a result, modern scholars of ancient Israelite warfare have had to rely almost entirely on comparative Egyptian, Hittite, and Assyrian evidence for reconstructing Israelite battle tactics.[1]

This is compounded by the fact that many battles, especially those supposed to have taken place prior to the period of the monarchy, were almost certainly fictional or largely obscured by legend. Even battles occurring later, which may possess a greater degree of historicity, were probably 'recorded' by scholars writing long after the event. Moreover, such scholars lacked intimate knowledge of, or interest in, the minutiae of military manoeuvres. The Tanakh's accounts of battle were often intended to celebrate (or occasionally criticise) a specific king or commander. The primary motivation of the authors, however, was to glorify Yahweh and emphasise the god's role in determining victory. As a result, miraculous battlefield events and miraculous outcomes were of more interest than the mundane military realities of battle.

An idiosyncratic feature of the Tanakh when compared to other ancient Near Eastern battle accounts is the unusual provenance of the accounts themselves. The vast majority of our Egyptian, Hittite, or Assyrian accounts of battle were

---

1. For example, Yadin, *Art of Warfare*, 49–50, 71–73, 100–108, 302–12; Hasel, *Military Practice and Polemic*; Michael G. Hasel, 'Assyrian Military Practices and Deuteronomy's Laws of Warfare', in *Writing and Reading War: Rhetoric, Gender, and Ethics in Biblical and Modern Contexts*, ed. Brad E. Kelle and Frank Ritchel Ames (Atlanta, GA: Society of Biblical Literature, 2008), 67–81; Crouch, *War and Ethics*; Trimm, *Fighting for the King*.

commissioned by kings, royalty, and other high elites drawn from the civil, military, or religious bureaucracy. In many senses they are 'official' documents. The books of the Tanakh, by contrast, appear to have been largely created by authors and redactors operating at a less exalted level of society.[2] Although undoubtedly representing an elite—male, literate, priestly—the social context of the texts of the Tanakh cannot be considered equivalent to a victory stele erected by an Egyptian pharaoh, or the historical introduction to a vassal treaty ratified by a Hittite king.

Deuteronomy and Ius in bello

The Tanakh is unique among ancient Near Eastern texts in providing a set of specific instructions about how wars against Israel's enemies should be conducted. The principal source of these *in bello* regulations is Deuteronomy 20:10–20, and further stipulations relevant to *in bello* conduct can be found elsewhere in Deuteronomy and the Second Book of Kings.[3] While the instructions provided in Deuteronomy 20 outline eight principles for military conduct, these represent different literary traditions and war ideologies within the corpus.[4] The stipulations provided in Deuteronomy 20 are certainly not comprehensive prescriptions for military conduct; yet the fact that such stipulations were articulated at all is highly significant, demonstrating mid-first millennium Israelite authors engaging with ethical categories of military action and distinguishing between different types of politico-military opponents. Deuteronomy would also deeply influence later Christian thought about just conduct in war.

The first half of Deuteronomy 20 (vv. 1–9) outlined the role of priests in boosting the morale of the army, defined eligibility criteria for military service, and established a command structure for Israelite hosts. The second half of the chapter (vv. 10–20) provided rules for parleying with the enemy prior to battle, the conduct of sieges, and what type of people and goods were subject to destruction or capture.

Because the consideration of *in bello* norms found in Deuteronomy 20 is so unusual, it has been the subject of considerable scholarly excursus. Deuteronomy 20 will be discussed in various contexts below, but especially in the sections dealing with sieges and arboreal resources. However, it must be stressed that Deuteronomy cannot be taken as straightforward evidence for military prescriptions regulating early Israelite warfare. Deuteronomy is, at

---

2. The importance of showing a sensitivity to the social origins of the Israelite texts underlies Crouch's comparative approach: Crouch, *War and Ethics*, 4–9.

3. See Deuteronomy 20:1–9, 10–18, 19–20; 21:10–14; 23:10–11, 12–15; 24:5; 25:17–19; 2 Kings 3.

4. Rad, *Holy War*, 117–23; Gottwald, '"Holy War" in Deuteronomy', 298; *WHB*, 66–68.

the earliest, a mid-seventh century text; it is likely that much of it is post-exilic (mid-sixth century or later). So, while it is possible that Deuteronomy 20 preserved older martial traditions, it is also possible that it reflected purely post-exilic theological attitudes to war, removed from the actual experience of Israelite warfare.

Declaration of War

It is probably safe to assume that Israelite battles followed the pattern of their contemporaries, albeit on a smaller scale. For set-piece confrontations, commanders would probably have sought open, flat terrain, to best utilise the mobility of their chariotry. Israel's politico-military competitors would have possessed similar armaments and capabilities, and it may have benefited both sides to use envoys to negotiate some arrangement regarding the place and time of battle.[5] As we have seen in the Egyptian and Hittite cases, evidence for specific declarations of war remains pretty sparse.[6] It might also be wise to differentiate between a declaration of war, on the one hand, and a challenge to battle, on the other. While the two types of communication may often be conflated, the question of timing is important.

A declaration of war announces the beginning of hostilities, marking a transition from peace to war. Today, we think of this as a formal shift in the international legal framework governing relations between nation-states. Something comparable may have been recognised in the ancient Near East, because the declaration of war between major states often marked the failure of a pre-existing treaty. The breakdown of the legal relationship established by the treaty was, therefore, a formal shift in a legal/contractual relationship between two or more states. Notification of this shift was performed by the declaration of war. A challenge to battle *could* perform the same function—and indeed challenges to battle sometimes accompanied declarations of war. However, a challenge to battle frequently indicated that hostilities had already begun.

Assyrian records from the eighth and seventh centuries—a period which witnessed Assyrian conflict with both Samaria and Judah—provide examples of both types of martial communication. Ursa, the enemy of Sargon II (c. 722–c. 705), sent the king 'a messenger with a challenge to attack and mingle in

---

5. It is claimed in the Book of Judges that during the slow conquest of Canaan the Judahites failed to dominate the plains because the inhabitants possessed iron chariots: Judges 1:19 (cf. ibid. 4:13). This anachronistic reference to iron chariotry existing in the mid- to late second millennium serves to illustrate first-millennium military technology available to Samaria, Judah, and their competitors.

6. For some Assyrian examples of 'challenges' to battle, see *LIR*, 110–12. Altman discusses a few examples from Assyria, Babylonia, and Israel: Altman, 'Earliest Recorded Concepts', 111–14.

battle'.⁷ Conforming to the 'battle challenge' type, this suggests that Ursa and Sargon II were already open enemies. In contrast, the later annals of Aššurbanipal (c. 686–c. 628) recorded the Assyrian king issuing a declaration of war to Indabibi/Indabigash, a king of Elam, who had given sanctuary to Assyrian rebels:

> I sent the following (message) to Indabigash through his messenger: 'Because you have not sent (back) these people, I am coming to destroy your cities. I will carry off the people of Susa, Madaktu (and) Hildalu. I will hurl you from your royal throne, and I will place another on your throne.'⁸

This declaration shows the relationship between Assyria and Elam passing from peaceful to hostile, and the legal relationship between the two rulers shifting. It thus marked a formal initiation of Assyrian hostilities against Elam.

There is some evidence of similar declarations of war and challenges to battle being made in the Tanakh. In the long diplomatic exchange between Israel and Moab recorded in Judges (11:12–40), Jephthah's unsuccessful manoeuvrings end with a declaration of war, framed as a forced response to Moab's unjust aggression: 'I have done you no wrong; yet you are doing me harm and making war on me. May the Lord, who judges, decide today between the Israelites and the Ammonites!'⁹ In contrast to Jephthah's sophisticated legal arguments, perhaps the bluntest challenge to battle in the Tanakh is that made by King Amaziah of Judah to King Jehoash of Samaria: 'Then Amaziah sent envoys to King Jehoash son of Jehoahaz son of Jehu of Israel, with this message: "Come, let us confront each other."'¹⁰

The series of military stipulations that appear in Deuteronomy 20 include what appears to be a rule instituting the proper declaration of hostilities prior to combat: 'When you approach a town to attack it, you shall offer it terms of peace.'¹¹ At the very least, this implies a minimum level of communication between Israel and enemy cities prior to the commencement of hostilities. But, as Altman notes, this precept is more a 'call to submit' than an offer of peace, 'motivated by the drive to save time, resources and lives of the attackers rather than from humane feelings'.¹² Deuteronomy 20:10 did not envisage

---

7. Oded, *War, Peace and Empire*, 51–52.
8. Daniel David Luckenbill, *Ancient Records of Assyria and Babylonia*, 2 vols (Chicago: University of Chicago Press, 1926–27), 2:341, § 878. The Assyrian cylinder text goes on to claim (§ 879) that the threat of war by Assyria caused such panic in Elam that Indabibi/Indabigash was killed by his own people and another king put in his place.
9. Judges 11:27.
10. 2 Kings 14:8; 2 Chronicles 25:17.
11. Deuteronomy 20:10.
12. Altman, 'Earliest Recorded Concepts', 114.

the Israelites offering terms of mutually beneficial peace, but a choice between enslavement or death, as the following verses make clear:

> If it responds peaceably and lets you in, all the people present there shall serve you at forced labour. If it does not surrender to you, but would join battle with you, you shall lay siege to it; and when the Lord your God delivers it into your hand, you shall put all its males to the sword.[13]

Deuteronomy 20:10 thus has more of the character of a challenge to battle than a declaration of war. It envisions an Israelite army approaching a town in full battle array, having already entered the enemy's territory. Under such circumstances, a declaration of war would have been rather superfluous. If a declaration of war were to serve any real procedural purpose, it would be required *prior to* entering the enemy's territory, as the crossing of the border without permission was, in itself, an act of war. We have already seen examples of this norm being enforced when the Edomites and the Amorites refused to allow Israel to traverse their territories during the Wanderings.[14] Deuteronomy 20:10 is thus better understood as a direct challenge to battle and a call for submission—issued with the assumption that war had already been declared—rather than as the initiation of a legal procedure marking the imminence or opening of war.

Deuteronomy 20:10 is representative of pragmatic attempts to mitigate military costs for the Israelites, while promising an enemy some limited guarantees as to how they would be treated if they surrendered. But the fact that this 'peace guarantee' only really offered the enemy a life of servitude is indicative of how dire their situation would be if defeated in combat; the Deuteronomist clearly assumed that those who refused to surrender and were subsequently defeated by arms could expect no *ius in bello* restraints whatsoever.

This ritual call for submission was not universally observed by the Israelites. Deuteronomy stipulated that it was only to be offered to 'towns that lie very far from you, towns that do not belong to nations hereabout'.[15] According to later rabbinical exegesis, wars against such foes were *reshut* (optional) because they concerned territory beyond Canaan, and so not gifted by Yahweh. For those towns and peoples within Canaan that Yahweh had proscribed (the 'Seven Nations': Hittites, Girgashites, Amorites, Canaanites, Perizzites, Hivites, and Jebusites), war was *mitzva* ('obligatory'), and no offer of submission was to be extended: 'In the towns of the latter peoples, however, which the Lord your God is giving you as a heritage, you shall not let a soul remain

---

13. Deuteronomy 20:11-13. See ibid. 20:10-15, which applies to towns that 'do not belong to nations hereabout'—i.e., do not belong to the seven proscribed nations—and thus booty can be kept rather than offered as herem to Yahweh.
14. Numbers 20:18-20; 21:21-23; Deuteronomy 2:18-36; Judges 11:15-18.
15. Deuteronomy 20:15.

alive."[16] In the towns of the Seven Nations, men, women, and children were to be destroyed as herem to Yahweh, ensuring that there would be no corruption of the people of Israel.[17] Yet it is clear from elsewhere in the Tanakh that the type of herem practices envisioned in Deuteronomy were never consistently applied by Israelite armies.[18]

What emerges from the Tanakh is the clear sense that Israelite thought on war differentiated between states of peace and states of war. As a result, it was normative, although not universal, to communicate with enemies regarding the transition between these two states, informing them of their status as enemies or challenging them to a trial of arms.

Ritual, Magic and War

In ancient Near Eastern religions there was typically a fine line between supplication to, and manipulation of, the supernatural. Humble prayer is often difficult to differentiate from magic proper. Many ritual interactions with the divine betrayed a mechanical quality, whereby an operation was completed in the expectation of a specific result, such as the offer of sacrifice resulting in the supernatural debilitation of an enemy. The hazy distinction between prayer and magic can be seen in one example from the royal inscriptions of Aššurnasirpal II of Assyria (r. c. 883–c. 859), who recorded that 'because of my voluntary offerings and my prayers, the goddess Ishtar, who loves my priesthood, approved of me and made up her mind to make war and battle'.[19] On the one hand, these offerings were a supplication; on the other hand, Aššurnasirpal certainly expected (and apparently received!) a specific result: Ishtar's supernatural intervention in battle.

Biblical scholars have noted the importance of 'customs of a ritual and cultic nature' in Israelite warfare but have been markedly reluctant to describe these practices as instances of magical operations.[20] This has more to do with the theological commitments of many biblical scholars—who are unwilling to describe Old Testament practices as magical—than the character of the operations themselves. Yet it is telling that one of the few works dedicated to analysing this aspect of ancient Israelite culture concludes that 'ancient Israel was a "magic society"'.[21]

16. Ibid. 20:16.
17. Ibid. 20:17–18.
18. Gottwald, '"Holy War" in Deuteronomy', 299.
19. Oded, *War, Peace and Empire*, 23.
20. For example, Jones, '"Holy War" or "Yahweh War"?', 649, observes that Moses's use of the rod in the battle against Amalek bears a 'close resemblance to sympathetic magic', but is reluctant to name it specifically as magic. Rad, *Holy War*, 71, admits to 'magical residues' in accounts of Israelite wars.
21. Frederick H. Cryer, *Divination in Ancient Israel and Its Near Eastern Environment: A Socio-Historical Investigation* (Sheffield: JSOT Press, 1994), 324.

Israel's emergence as a coherent *military* nation in Exodus began with acts of magic and demonstrations of occult power. Before the Israelites left Egypt, Aaron won a magical contest against Egyptian priests; not only was Aaron's rod/wand magically transformed into a snake, but the greater power of Yahweh magic was demonstrated when the magical snake devoured the snakes of the Egyptian priests.[22] Supernatural plagues were then unleashed on Egypt, and in each case Aaron's magical rod/wand played a key role in conducting Yahweh's occult power.[23] These lethal supernatural interventions can and should be understood as opening volleys in the narrative of Israel's wars to acquire the Promised Land. Exodus specifically described the Israelites leaving Egypt *as an army*—'Now the Israelites went up armed out of the land of Egypt'—led by Yahweh in the form of a supernatural pillar of fiery cloud.[24]

The harnessing of supernatural aid in war via ritualised prayer or sacrificial exchange can be found in a number of other places in the Tanakh. The magical role of the rod/wand in war was demonstrated by Moses during the battle against the Amalekites.[25] We have already seen how Jephthah's victory over the Ammonites ultimately cost him the life of his daughter: a particularly powerful sacrificial exchange.[26] The Israelite hero Samson also exchanged his own life for a gift of supernatural strength, enabling him to kill thousands of Philistines by single-handedly bringing down a temple upon them.[27] The prophet Samuel conducted magical operations prior to a battle against the Philistines, ordering the Israelites to fast, confess their sins, and pour libations. Samuel then ritually sacrificed a lamb to Yahweh in exchange for supernatural aid:

> For as Samuel was presenting the burnt offering and the Philistines advanced to attack Israel, the Lord thundered mightily against the Philistines that day. He threw them into confusion, and they were routed by Israel.[28]

The significance of magical operations in accounts of Israelite warfare is nowhere better illustrated than at the famous siege of Jericho. After the Israelites crossed the river Jordan under their new commander, Joshua, they were instructed by Yahweh to perform a mass purification ritual which necessitated

---

22. Exodus 7:11–12.
23. Ibid. 7:14–12:30.
24. Ibid. 13:18, 21–22; 14:24. On the motif of fire and cloud as symbols of divine intervention in Israelite and ancient Near Eastern warfare more generally, see Weinfeld, 'Divine Intervention', 131–40, 143–45.
25. Exodus 17:8–16.
26. Judges 11:30–40. Niditch notes that '[v]ows to the deity, promises in exchange for divine favors, are common in Israelite war descriptions'. *WHB*, 32.
27. Judges 16:23–30.
28. 1 Samuel 7:7–11, quotation at v. 10. See also Judges 20:26–28 for similar operations and war oracles.

the circumcision of all the fighting men.[29] After a period of recovery, an angel appeared to Joshua and promised to deliver the great walled city of Jericho, instructing Joshua to perform a specific seven-day ritualised perambulation of its walls, accompanied by the Ark and the sounding of trumpets.[30] On the seventh day the walls crumbled and the Israelites carried out the instructions of Yahweh: 'They exterminated everything in the city with the sword: man and woman, young and old, ox and sheep and ass [. . .]. They burned down the city and everything in it.'[31] Clearly, this was only made possible by the magical rituals preceding it.

War-magic could also be used *against* Israel by its enemies. Balak, king of Moab and Midian, hired the magician Balaam to 'put a curse upon this people for me [. . .]. I can thus defeat them and drive them out of the land.'[32] King Mesha of Moab (perhaps the same king who commissioned the 'Moabite Stone') performed a particularly extreme act of war-magic.[33] Faced with a concerted Israelite assault on his city of Kir-haresheth, Mesha resorted to sacrificing his own son to the god Kemosh:

> Seeing that the battle was going against him, the king of Moab led an attempt of seven hundred swordsmen to break a way through to the king of Edom; but they failed. So he took his first-born son, who was to succeed him as king, and offered him up on the wall as a burnt offering. A great wrath came upon Israel, so they withdrew from him and went back to their own land.[34]

Even the Hebrew text accepts that this astonishing sacrifice was potent enough to ensure the enemy's victory.

As a rule, attempts by Israel's enemies to harness supernatural powers through magical rituals are condemned in the Tanakh and presented as proof of the iniquity of other nations.[35] In contrast, magical operations performed by Israelite prophets or priests were presented as miraculous and unambiguously positive: proof of Yahweh's love for his chosen people. Israelite thought

---

29. Joshua 5:2–12.
30. Jericho possessed no walls in this period: see above, ch. 9 n. 84.
31. Joshua 6:21, 24.
32. Numbers 22:3–6, at v. 6. The curse was never performed because Yahweh appeared to Balaam and ordered him not to curse the Israelites (ibid. 24:1–11). Nonetheless, Yahweh and Moses condemned this attempted use of magic and in vengeance ordered the subsequent destruction of the Midianites (ibid. 31:8).
33. The stele describes ongoing conflict between King Mesha of Moab and Israel, although Mesha's stele claims that at that point 'Israel utterly perished forever'. See translation and commentary in *HST*, 311–30, quotation at 313.
34. 2 Kings 3:26–27.
35. Compare with the near sacrifice of Isaac in Genesis 22. For condemnations of human sacrifice in the Tanakh, see Leviticus 18:21; 20:2–5; Deuteronomy 12:31; 18:10; Jeremiah 7:30–31; 19:5. See also *WHB*, 42–46.

concerning the ethical permissibility of war-magic was thus highly partisan and did not exclude the possibility (even desirability) of Israelites employing it. And although the Tanakh was at pains to dismiss the deities of other nations as false and impotent, real anxieties persisted that supernatural resources could and would be weaponised against the Israelites by their enemies.

Weapons and Duels

There is no evidence for any restrictions on weapons in Israelite warfare. The books of the Tanakh refer to the full range of ancient armaments, including swords, daggers, spears, bows, slings, and chariots. Israelite thought betrays no sense of moral judgement pertaining to any of these weapons, nor any moral judgement regarding those who wielded them. However, some weapons were more prestigious than others, and indicative of social rank. This is evident in the famous duel between David and the Philistine Goliath. The story is generally regarded as a very late reworking of one or more earlier legends which described Israelites defeating enemy heroes descended from the giant race of the Raphah; there is even another Goliath (a Gittite), killed by the hero Elhanan.[36]

The asymmetry of the David–Goliath duel is marked by the young shepherd boy being armed with only a wooden staff and a sling—low-cost and low-status weapons—while the warrior-hero Goliath carries expensive arms and armour. These include a coat of mail weighing five thousand shekels of copper and a spear with a haft as thick as a weaver's beam, topped with a spearhead weighing six hundred shekels of iron.[37] Goliath is said to be insulted not only by David's youth but also by his lack of conventional high-status war gear:

> And the Philistine called out to David, 'Am I a dog that you come against me with sticks?' The Philistine cursed David by his gods.'[38]

As far as Goliath was concerned, the disparity between the lightly armed boy and the heavily armed elite veteran showed a distinct lack of respect. David's lack of conventional battle-gear was emphasised again when, after felling Goliath with his slingshot, David had to use Goliath's own sword to decapitate his fallen foe.[39]

Though David killed his opponent from a distance and with a low-status weapon rather than in hand-to-hand combat with a high-status forged weapon,

---

36. This 'early' Goliath is also described as bearing a spear with a shaft 'like a weaver's bar' (2 Samuel 21:19; cf. 1 Samuel 17:19). See also the defeat of Saph by Sibbecai, and an unnamed 'giant of a man' with six fingers and toes, killed by Jonathan (2 Samuel 21:18–22; cf. 1 Chronicles 20:6).
37. 1 Samuel 17:1–7.
38. Ibid. 17:43. David refused Saul's offer to be armed with the king's own battle-gear: ibid. 17:38–39.
39. Ibid. 17:49–51.

this act was presented not as cowardly or ethically dubious but as one of divinely inspired bravery and skill. Our modern Western image of warrior duels consisting of hand-to-hand combat (with no role for missile weapons) is almost entirely the product of popular images of the European Middle Ages. Such an image is not an accurate representation of ancient Near Eastern and Mediterranean duels, for which warriors used ranged weapons such as throwing javelins and bows.[40] The 'Tale of Sinuhe', an early-second-millennium Egyptian text which enjoyed widespread dissemination throughout the Near East, includes a story in which the eponymous hero fights a duel against an 'Asiatic' champion. This duel begins with the throwing of spears and shooting of arrows:

> Then his shield, his axe, his armful of javelins fell to me: after I had escaped his weapons and made them pass by me, with his arrows spent in vain, one after the other, he approached me, and I shot him; my arrow stuck in his neck, he cried out, and fell on his face. I felled him with his own axe, and gave my war cry on his back, while every Asiatic was bellowing.[41]

The use of ranged weapons by both Sinuhe and his opponent, as well as Sinuhe's use of his enemy's axe to deliver the coup de grâce, are so similar to the David–Goliath text that it seems likely that the popular Sinuhe tale acted as a literary model for the later David–Goliath duel. The point is that, considered in the light of ancient duelling practice, David's use of a ranged weapon to defeat his opponent was not unusual or dishonourable.[42] What made David's victory against Goliath atypical was that the Israelite was not equal to the Philistine in social or military status, and that his missile weapon was a sling—the weapon of a peasant—rather than a bow or a javelin, the traditional weapons of a warrior.

The David–Goliath duel gives a rather confusing picture of customary martial norms—apparently adhering to some whilst transgressing others.

---

40. 1 Samuel 17:6 states that Goliath carried a bronze javelin. Further examples can be found in Homer's *Iliad*. The duel between the Trojan, Paris Alexander, and Menelaus, king of Sparta, opens with both warriors casting javelins before advancing to fight with swords. The same occurs in the duel between Achilles and Hector. See *The Iliad*, trans. Richard Lattimore (Chicago: University of Chicago Press, 1961), bk 3, ll. 340–82; bk 22, ll. 270–94. Compare also to the deadly spear, named the *Gáe Bulg*, belonging to the Celtic hero Cú Chulainn, as recounted in the mythology of the Ulster Cycle. My thanks to Francis Eaves for pointing out the similarities.

41. *ToS*, 33. For a discussion of the composition and potential problems of this passage, see Hans Goedicke, 'Sinuhe's Duel', *Journal of the American Research Center in Egypt* 21 (1984): 197–201. Goedicke posits that the passage indicates that Sinuhe followed an Egyptian rather than Asiatic custom of fighting a duel with bow and dagger, rather than a full panoply of arms: ibid., 199.

42. From the late eighteenth century CE, the pistol—a ranged weapon—became the favoured weapon of European and North American duellists, thus arguably reverting to a more ancient style of duelling. See Lorenzo Sabine, *Notes on Duels and Duelling, Alphabetically Arranged, with a Preliminary Historical Essay*, 3rd edn (Boston, MA: Crosby, Nichols, and Company, 1859), 30.

For example, the Philistines and Israelites line up in battle array on opposite hills, indicating a standardised set-piece battle on agreed terrain. Challenges of battle were issued, along with the specific challenge to single combat. Customary rules of engagement were to be observed in the duel: the winning side would take all, the defeated would become slaves to the victor.[43] Yet Goliath was forced to repeat his challenge once a day for forty days, and the lack of response from the Isrealites was presented as shaming and indicative of a lack of faith (that Yahweh would protect them). When David eventually stepped forward—a youthful shepherd, not a soldier—Goliath was insulted because he expected to confront a social equal. In victory, Goliath would gain no honour in killing a boy; in defeat, he risked a disgraceful death. In this sense, Saul violated a customary norm dictating equality of combatants by permitting David to fight; Saul himself seemed aware of this problem.[44]

The importance of this 'honour norm' of equality of combatants can be witnessed in the ritualised, brief, and exceedingly deadly combat between twenty-four young warriors (*ne'arim*) drawn from the armies of Abner (Ishbaal/Ish-bosheth's general)[45] and Joab (David's general). This duel may have failed to avoid further hostilities, but the equal status of the *ne'arim* of both armies created the proper conditions for a contest in which honour could accrue, even in death (see figure 41).[46] This was starkly contrasted with a situation that developed in the *aftermath* of the battle, when Abner was repeatedly challenged by the youth Asahel, Joab's younger brother: 'Abner again begged Asahel, "Stop pursuing me, or I'll have to strike you down. How will I look your brother Joab in the face?"' Abner, the veteran general, understood that he would gain no prestige from the youth's death (quite the opposite), and that killing Asahel would infuriate the young man's more senior bloodrelatives. When Asahel 'refused to desist, Abner struck him in the belly with a backward thrust of his spear and the spear protruded from his back. He fell there and died on the spot.'[47] Forced into killing Asahel against his own wishes, Abner would later be assassinated by Joab in revenge.[48]

---

43. 1 Samuel 17:9.

44. Ibid. 17:33–39.

45. Ishbaal ('man of Baal': see 1 Chronicles 8:33; 9:39), Saul's son, is referred to more commonly in the Judahite texts of 1 and 2 Samuel as Ish-bosheth. The earlier name suggests an ongoing veneration for Baal among the early Israelites, which the later monotheising redactors attempted to disguise by changing the name to Ish-bosheth, meaning 'man of shame'.

46. 'Abner said to Joab, "Let the young men [*ne'arim*] come forward and sport before us." "Yes, let them," Joab answered. [. . .] Each one grasped his opponent's head [and thrust] his dagger into his opponent's side; thus they fell together.' 2 Samuel 2:14, 16. Yadin stresses that the *ne'arim* were elite troops and that this was a (quite literally) deadly serious encounter which was intended to forego the necessity of a full battle: Yadin, *Art of Warfare*, 266–67.

47. 2 Samuel 22–23.

48. 'When Abner returned to Hebron, Joab took him aside within the gate to talk to him privately; there he struck him in the belly. Thus [Abner] died for shedding the blood of Asahel, Joab's brother.' Ibid. 3:27.

FIGURE 41. Aramean warriors duelling: Palace of Kapara, Tell Halaf, c. tenth–ninth century BCE. Pergamon Museum, CC BY-SA 3.0 licence, via Wikimedia Commons.

After the death of Goliath and the flight of the Philistines,[49] David mutilates Goliath's body and carries his head to Jerusalem as a war trophy, even taking it to his audience with Saul.[50] David's mutilation of Goliath's body reflected a

49. The reaction of the Philistines to Goliath's defeat also appears to have violated a norm governing the highly formalised martial ritual of the duel. Though Goliath had vowed that, if an Israelite 'bests me in combat and kills me, we will become your slaves', upon seeing their champion struck down the Philistines immediately fled, leaving their camp to be looted by the Israelites rather than submitting themselves to Saul: 1 Samuel 17:9, 51–53.

50. 'David took the head of the Philistine and brought it to Jerusalem; and he put his weapons in his own tent. [. . .] Abner took him and brought him to Saul, with the head of the Philistine still in his hand.' Ibid. 17:54, 57.

THE ISRAELITES: *IUS IN BELLO* [355]

FIGURE 42. Assyrian soldiers carrying decapitated heads: Palace of Nimrud, Assyria, c. 865–c. 860 BCE. © Trustees of the British Museum.

grisly but not uncommon practice of the ancient Near East.[51] We have already seen the fourth-millennium Narmer Palette depicting rows of beheaded enemy corpses (figure 2). In the mid-first millennium, when the Tanakh was compiled, decapitation of defeated foes was commonly practised by the Neo-Assyrians (see figures 42 and 43). The Assyrian King Esarhaddon (r. c. 681–c. 669), for example, made a point of decapitating two enemy princes and hanging their severed heads around the necks of their nobles.[52] The symbolic power of the

51. See also 2 Samuel 4:1–12; 2 Kings 10:7–8; 2 Chronicles 22.
52. Oded, *War, Peace and Empire*, 19.

FIGURE 43. Assyrian attack on the Egyptian city of Memphis (c. 667 BCE), with soldiers carrying decapitated heads: Palace of Nineveh, Assyria, c. 645–c. 635 BCE. Osama Shukir Muhammed Amin FRCP(Glasg), CC BY-SA 4.0 licence, via Wikimedia Commons.

FIGURE 44. Perseus decapitating Medusa: terracotta pithos, Greek, c. 670 BCE. Musée du Louvre, Paris, public domain, via Wikimedia Commons.

head as a war trophy can be found across time and in many different cultures, whether encapsulated in mythology as in the Greek story of Perseus and Medusa (figure 44), in war-magic such as the *tzantza* shrunken heads of the Jivaroan tribes of the Amazon, or in the gruesome propaganda videos of the so-called Islamic State and other radical jihadist groups of the twenty-first century CE.

Ambushes and Night Attacks

As we have seen in both Egyptian and Hittite sources, the moral quality of victories won through ambush were usually subject to partisan interpretations.[53] The Israelites adopted similar attitudes to ambush. When the Amalekites ambushed the Israelites in the Wilderness, this act was condemned by Moses in Deuteronomy:

> Remember what Amalek did to you on your journey, after you left Egypt—how, undeterred by fear of God, he surprised you on the march, when you were famished and weary, and cut down all the stragglers in your rear. Therefore [...] you shall blot out the memory of Amalek from under heaven. Do not forget![54]

The Deuteronomist presented this ambush as an underhand and unethical act of war. Indeed, even many years after the event, it justified the complete annihilation of Amalek.[55]

Notwithstanding Moses's ire against Amalek, however, there are numerous examples in the Tanakh of ambushes and night attacks being successfully utilised by Israelites, and there is no evidence of such tactics being criticised. In some cases these tactics were directly commanded by Yahweh.[56] When Lot's uncle, Abraham, was abducted during an attack on the city of Sodom, Lot stealthily took advantage of both the cover of darkness and the element of surprise: 'At night, he and his servants deployed against them and defeated them;

---

53. See above, pp. 121–22, 238–43. The famous sixth/fifth-century Chinese general Sun Tzu insisted that '[w]arfare is the Tao of deception': Sun Tzu and Sun Pin, *The Complete Art of War*, trans. Ralph D. Sawyer, with Mei-chün Lee Sawyer (Boulder, CO: Westview Press, 1996), bk 1, 41. On martial attitudes to ambush in medieval Europe, see David Whetham, *Just Wars and Moral Victories: Surprise, Deception and the Normative Framework of European War in the Later Middle Ages* (Leiden: Brill, 2009).

54. Deuteronomy 25:17–19. Note that some of these details are not given at Exodus 17:8–17.

55. '"Thus said the Lord of Hosts: I am exacting the penalty for what Amalek did to Israel, for the assault he made upon them on the road, on their way up from Egypt." [...] Saul destroyed Amalek from Havilah all the way to Shur, which is close to Egypt, and he captured King Agag of Amalek alive. He proscribed all the people, putting them to the sword.' 1 Samuel 15:2, 7–8.

56. See also Malamut, 'Conquest of Canaan', 47–50.

and he pursued them as far as Hobah.'[57] The most famous Israelite war leader, Joshua, repeatedly used ambush tactics to gain victory. Marching to the aid of his allies the Gibeonites, Joshua conducted a forced march through the night in order to launch a lightning attack against the Amorites: 'Joshua took them by surprise, marching all night from Gilgal. The Lord threw them into a panic before Israel: [Joshua] inflicted a crushing defeat on them.'[58] Prior to assaulting the town of Bethel, the Judahites captured one of its inhabitants and forced him to show them into the town. Stealthily taking the inhabitants unawares, the Judahites 'put the town to the sword'.[59]

There were several occasions when Yahweh himself directed the Israelites to take advantage of ambushes and night attacks. Following the conquest of Jericho and the punishment of Achan, Yahweh commanded Joshua to progress to the city of Ai and 'set an ambush against the city behind it'.[60] Yahweh specifically ordered Joshua to hold out a javelin, reminiscent of the magical rods used by Aaron and Moses, as a signal to launch the ambush.[61] When Joshua was faced by a combined Canaanite host 'as numerous as the sands on the seashore',[62] Yahweh bolstered him by saying, 'Do not be afraid of them; tomorrow at this time I will have them all lying slain before Israel. You shall hamstring their horses and burn their chariots.' Joshua immediately ambushed the Canaanites at the Waters of Merom, 'and pounced upon them [...] crushed them, letting none escape.'[63]

During the internecine punitive war against the Benjaminites, the combined Israelite host received a command from Yahweh to 'put men in ambush against Gibeah on all sides'.[64] The result was a crushing victory:

> [T]he Israelite ambush was rushing out from its position at Maareh-geba [...] and the battle was furious. Before they realized that disaster was approaching, the Lord routed the Benjaminites before Israel. That day the Israelites slew 25,100 men of Benjamin, all of them fighting men [...] for they relied on the ambush which they had laid against

---

57. Genesis 14:15.

58. Joshua 10:9–10. The text states that the combined Amorite army included the kings of Jerusalem, Hebron, Jarmuth, Lachish, and Eglon: ibid. 10:5–43.

59. Judges 1:25. Compare the surprise attack against the Canaanites at ibid. 4:4–16. King Joram of Judah attempted to launch a surprise night attack on Edom, but failed: 2 Kings 8:16–22.

60. Joshua 6–7; 8:2.

61. 'As soon as he held out his hand, the ambush came rushing out of their station. They entered the city and captured it; and swiftly they set fire to the city.' Joshua 8:18–19. Archaeology proves this story to be purely fictional: the settlement of Ai had been abandoned for a thousand years by c. 1200, with only a tiny village established on the ruins. See *KANE*, 2:429.

62. Joshua 11:4.

63. Ibid. 11:6–8.

64. Judges 20:28–29.

Gibeah. One ambush quickly deployed against Gibeah, and the other ambush advanced and put the whole town to the sword.⁶⁵

In sum, ambush and night attacks were considered a legitimate and ethically acceptable tactic of war in the world-view of the Tanakh's authors. In light of Israel's politico-military history, such a stance makes sense. Early Israelite forces were probably rather piecemeal, operating in small bands bound by parochial kinship ties. Such bands of roving warriors and raiders were named *habiru* (or *abiru*, *apiru*) in Egypt, Hatti, and Mesopotamia, and the ethnic designation 'Hebrew' possibly originates from this general term.⁶⁶ If the early Israelites can be identified among these *habiru* communities, then ambushes and surprise night attacks would have been essential tactics in the repertoire of these opportunistic raiders and auxiliary troops. Even after the emergence of the Samaritan and Judahite kingdoms, Israelite rulers found themselves in the shadow of great empires such as Egypt, Assyria, and Babylon, against whom they had no prospect of matching arms on equal terms. There is a good chance that the survival of martial legends glorifying the use ambushes and surprise attacks aligns with the pre-monarchic and post-monarchic military realities of Israelite communities and their dominant military modus operandi. This is what Niditch describes as the Israelite military ethos of 'tricksterism'.⁶⁷ Such tactics have always found favour with nomadic or highly mobile groups, or with commanders who find themselves outmanned and 'outgunned' by opponents possessing superior resources. These Israelite martial traditions, borne out of military pragmatism, were then translated into ethical norms that legitimated the use of ambush as a morally permissible—occasionally even divinely ordained—tactic of war.

Deceit and Assassination

Ancient societies depended heavily upon oral communication and oral contracts, which demanded high levels of trust. Perfidy, as a specific form of deceit involving the breaking of an oath, was a serious breach of social conventions, as it undermined the contractual and communicative principles on which ancient societies were built. Deceit more generally implied the breaking of

---

65. Ibid. 20:33–37. For details of how the ambush was organised, see ibid. 20:38–48.
66. See Genesis 12–14 on Abraham as an itinerant mercenary. *Habiru/apiru* was used as a general term referring to a variety of linguistic and political groups, not to a single group of 'Hebrews', although 'Hebrew' may have developed later as an ethnic reference. See Mendenhall, 'Hebrew Conquest', esp. 71–73; Vaux, *Early History of Israel*, 1:105–12, 209–16; Stuart A. West, 'The Habiru and the Hebrews: From a Social Class to an Ethnic Group', *Jewish Bible Quarterly* 7 (3) (1979): 102–7 at 107; Ahlström, *Who Were the Israelites*, 11–21; Anson Rainey, 'Shasu or Habiru: Who Were the Early Israelites?', *Biblical Archaeological Review* 34 (6) (2008): 51–55.
67. *WHB*, 110.

trust, and touched upon notions of both personal and national honour. Such treachery could also provoke the fury of the gods in whose name oaths were sworn. (It is significant that the very basis of Israelite identity and community, as conceived by the Tanakh, was constituted by an oral covenant with Yahweh.) Deceit, therefore, was typically cast in a negative light, regardless of which side was guilty of committing it. While assassination need not involve deceit, several examples of assassination in the Tanakh did in fact require a level of treachery. Thus discussion of these murders within a broader context of deceitful behaviour does not seem inappropriate.

One could cite Cain's fratricide as the first example in the Tanakh of treacherous violence, although of course this was not imagined as taking place within a warlike setting.[68] Later in Genesis, the story of the rape of Jacob's daughter Dinah provides a more protracted account of premeditated deceit and violence which targeted a rival polity. Following the sexual assault of Dinah by Schechem, a Hivite prince, Schechem's father Hamor, recognising that his son had offended Jacob and his kin (there is little concern for Dinah herself from either party), offered Jacob anything he wished as a brideprice for his daughter.[69] In answer, Jacob's sons, 'speaking with guile because [Schechem] had defiled their sister Dinah', insisted that all the Hivite men must undergo circumcision before their sister or any other Hebrew woman could intermarry with them.[70] However, this was intended as a ruse to provide Dinah's brothers with an opportunity to take revenge. After the male Hivites had undergone the surgery,

> [o]n the third day, when they were in pain, Simeon and Levi, two of Jacob's sons, brothers of Dinah, took each his sword, came upon the city unmolested, and slew all the males. They put Hamor and his son Schechem to the sword, took Dinah out of Schechem's house, and went away. The other sons of Jacob came upon the slain and plundered the town, because their sister had been defiled. They seized their flocks and herds and asses, all that was inside the town and outside; all their wealth, all their children, and their wives, all that was in the houses, they took as captives and booty.[71]

Simeon and Levi, along with their brothers, believed their act of deceitful violence to be justified because of the insult to their family's honour. But when Jacob discovered what his truculent sons had done without his knowledge, he realised the dire repercussions of their actions:

> Jacob said to Simeon and Levi, 'You have brought trouble on me, making me odious among the inhabitants of the land, the Canaanites and

---

68. Genesis 4:1–16.
69. Ibid. 34:1–31.
70. Ibid. 34:13–16, quotation at v. 13.
71. Ibid. 34:25–29.

the Perizzites; my men are few in number, so that if they unite against me and attack me, I and my house will be destroyed.'[72]

Simeon and Levi's treachery and disproportionate brutality apparently shamed Jacob and risked triggering a cycle of vengeance against him and his kin. So great was Jacob's concern that he and his household fled the territory.[73] Even years later, on his deathbed, Jacob cursed his sons and their progeny for their compulsive love of violence:

> Simeon and Levi are a pair;
> Their weapons are tools of lawlessness.
> Let not my person be included in their council,
> Let not my being be counted in their assembly.
> For when angry they slay men,
> And when pleased they maim oxen.
> Cursed be their anger so fierce,
> And their wrath so relentless.[74]

Other Israelites utilised deceit in order to murder their opponents. Abimelech, son of Jerubbaal/Gideon, assassinated all but one of his seventy brothers in order to raise himself to be king. But Abimelech's death at the hands of a woman was proof of divine punishment for his fratricidal treachery.[75] Joab, King David's commander-in-chief, deceived the unsuspecting Abner and murdered him within the walls of David's palace: 'When Abner returned to Hebron, Joab took him aside within the gate to talk to him privately; there he struck him in the belly. Thus [Abner] died for shedding the blood of Asahel, Joab's brother.'[76] David was furious when he learned of Abner's assassination, claiming that Abner was undeserving of such a death and condemning Joab's actions as 'savage'. David even forced Joab and his personal guard to perform an act of public contrition, rending their clothes and wearing sackcloth during Abner's funeral.[77]

Another high-profile assassination took place during David's reign, although apparently not under his aegis. A pair of assassins arrived at David's court to deliver the head of Ish-bosheth—Saul's son and David's dynastic rival—to the king. Unfortunately for the assassins, they failed to receive the greeting they were hoping for from David:

> 'The man who told me in Ziklag that Saul was dead thought he was bringing me good news. But instead of rewarding him for the news, I seized him and killed him. How much more, then, when wicked men have killed a blameless man in bed in his own house! I will certainly

72. Ibid. 34:30.
73. Ibid. 35:1–5, 9–10.
74. Ibid. 49:5–7.
75. Judges 9:1–5, 42–57.
76. 2 Samuel 3:27.
77. Ibid. 3:33–34.

avenge his blood on you, and I will rid the earth of you.' David gave orders to the young men, who killed them; they cut off their hands and feet and hung them up by the pool in Hebron.[78]

David's contempt for the assassins was a product of his high opinion for the sacrality of monarchy and his own personal code of honour. When David had chanced upon Saul sleeping in a cave, he had refused to harm the man who was hunting him, because Saul was Yahweh's 'anointed', and because to kill a man in his sleep was cowardly.[79] It seems to have been the violation of honour norms that infuriated David: these dictated that, as in the armed duel, violence should be conducted according to certain rules of etiquette. Putting it simply, all of the aforementioned assassinations (including the potential assassination of Saul) appear to have violated norms concerning personal honour and sacred kingship.

A late example of assassination appears in the Book of Jeremiah, when the Babylonians had put a certain Gedaliah in charge of the rump state of Judah.[80] However, Gedaliah was assassinated by a small group of Judahite malcontents led by Ishmael son of Nethaniah. Ishmael's treachery was made all the worse by his acceptance of Gedaliah's hospitality, and by the fact that although Gedaliah had been forewarned of Ishmael's murderous intent, he had refused to sanction a preemptive strike against him.[81] These examples evince deep concerns regarding the ramifications of violating oral covenants and bonds of trust.

Despite the widespread antipathy shown towards deceit and assassination, there are nevertheless a number of stories within the Tanakh that recount Israelites committing precisely such deeds and being praised for doing so. After all, deception may be a means for the marginalised or impuissant to strike back at those with greater power, as suggested by Niditch's heuristic of Israelite 'tricksterism'.[82] Ehud the Benjaminite carried out a daring assassination during a period in which, we are told, Moab had dominated Israel for eighteen years.[83] Seeking to relieve Israel of this burden and 'raised up' by Yahweh, Ehud took advantage of his role as an official envoy responsible for delivering Israel's tribute to Moab. He gained a private audience with the obese King Eglon by feigning that he had a secret message for the king:

> Ehud said, 'I have a message for you from God'; whereupon he rose from his seat. Reaching with his left hand, Ehud drew the dagger from

---

78. Ibid. 4:1–12, at v. 12.
79. 1 Samuel 24:5–17; cf. ibid. 26:6–25.
80. According to Jeremiah (40:7), those Judahites who had not been exiled were 'the poorest in the land', although in reality they likely constituted a sizeable portion of the Judahite population. This serves to remind us that the view provided by the Tanakh's authors and redactors is an elite view, and its interests were firmly focused on elite Israelite experiences.
81. Jeremiah 40:7–41:15.
82. *WHB*, 106–122; Niditch, 'War and Reconciliation', 147–48, 153–54.
83. Judges 3:15–30.

his right side and drove it into [Eglon's] belly. The fat closed over the blade and the hilt went in after the blade—for he did not pull the dagger out of his belly—and the filth came out.[84]

Ehud made good his escape through a window, and the success of this divinely sanctioned assassination was cemented shortly afterwards by a battle in which Israel slaughtered ten thousand Moabites.[85]

The Book of Judges provides an even more remarkable case of assassination. Having launched a surprise attack against the Canaanites, the Israelites managed to rout their enemies, forcing the Canaanite general Sisera to flee and seek refuge in the tent of Jael, the wife of Heber the Kenite. Feigning hospitality and offering to hide Sisera from his pursuers, 'Jael came out to greet Sisera and said to him, "Come in, my lord, come in here, do not be afraid." So he entered her tent, and she covered him with a blanket.'[86] Unfortunately for Sisera, Jael's intentions were far from hospitable:

> Then Jael wife of Heber took a tent pin and grasped the mallet. When he was fast asleep from exhaustion, she approached him and stealthily drove the pin through his temple till it went down to the ground. Thus he died.[87]

This assassination was unequivocally norm-violating. It shattered the accepted sanctity of hospitality, in which guests were protected persons. Moreover, as we saw above in the case of David refusing to kill Saul, to murder a sleeping foe was considered cowardly. Finally, for a soldier to die by the hand of a woman would have been widely understood as a deeply shameful death—all the more so for a military commander who had fled the field.[88] Yet despite the socially provocative nature of the act, the assassination of Sisera is openly lauded in the 'Song of Deborah', in which Jael is described as 'most blessed of women'.[89]

Assassination is also presented positively in the story of Jehu's bloody coups in Samaria and Judah. Jehu is said to have usurped the throne of

---

84. Ibid. 3:19–22.
85. Ibid. 3:23–30.
86. Ibid. 4:18.
87. Ibid. 4:21; cf. ibid. 5:24–27.
88. For the problems posed by both Jael and Deborah as female 'warriors', see Gale A. Yee, 'By the Hand of a Woman: The Metaphor of the Woman Warrior in Judges 4', in *Women, War, and Metaphor*, ed. Claudia V. Camp and Carole R. Fontaine (Atlanta, GA: Scholars Press, 1993), 99–132.
89. The 'Song of Deborah' reads (Judges 5:24–27):
   Most blessed of women be Jael [...]
   Her [left] hand reached for the tent pin,
   Her right for the workmen's hammer.
   She struck Sisera, crushed his head,
   Smashed and pierced his temple.
   At her feet he sank, lay outstretched,
   At her feet he sank, lay still;
   Where he sank, there he lay—destroyed.

Samaria by assassinating King Joram and purging seventy princes of the House of Ahab.[90] Not content with this bloodshed, Jehu also assassinated King Azahiah of Judah along with forty-two of his kinsmen, thus securing the throne of Judah in addition to that of Samaria. The text made no attempt to hide the brutality of Jehu's power-grab, yet he is presented as a pious reformer of Israelite and Judahite corruption, acting as Yahweh's 'anointed'.[91]

All these examples of deceit or assassination possess different characteristics. Some were condemned while others were condoned, even lauded. It appears that it was the moral character of the victim(s) that determined the perceived permissibility or impermissibility of the act of assassination. Eglon and Sisera were foreign enemies and were thus *ipso facto* liable to harm. The Israelite victims of Jehu's bloody purge were presented as corrupt and impious, and their assassinations were excused by a text which sought to emphasise the importance of reformatory zeal. In contrast, Abner, Ish-bosheth, and the brothers of Abimelech were portrayed as honourable and undeserving of their manner of death; thus the assassins were condemned. Finally, the Hivite victims of Simeon and Levi were viewed as liable to harm because of the injury incurred by Dinah's rape, but Jacob judged his sons' vengeance to be disproportionate to the original insult, as well as politically reckless. Taken as a whole, assassination appears to have been viewed as a morally problematic act of violence, because it often required deceit; nevertheless, it was an act which *could* be employed to achieve morally positive outcomes, and was subsequently justified under certain circumstances.

Siege Warfare

Deuteronomy 20:10–11 instructs as follows: 'When you approach a town to attack it, you shall offer it terms of peace. If it responds peaceably and lets you in, all the people present there shall serve you at forced labor.' Submission and enslavement is perhaps marginally preferable to death for some and enslavement for the survivors, but the exact meaning of the offer to serve the Israelites 'at forced labour' (*lā-mas waʻăbādūkā*)[92] is the subject of scholarly disagreement and variant translations.[93] The offer to submit and become a

---

90. 2 Kings 9:22–28.

91. Ibid. 10:1–11, 12–14, 16–17; 2 Chronicles 22. On the contested historicity of Jehu's coup and reforms, see *WHB*, 73.

92. From 'Deuteronomy 20:11', Bible Hub, https://biblehub.com/text/deuteronomy/20-11.htm (accessed 9 January 2023).

93. Alternative translations render this as 'all the people found therein shall become tributary to you, and they shall serve you.' 'Devarim—Deuteronomy—Chapter 20', Chabad.org, *The Complete Jewish Bible, with Rashi Commentary*, https://www.chabad.org/library/bible_cdo/aid/9984/jewish/Chapter-20.htm (accessed 9 January 2023); cf. 'Deuteronomy 20:11', Bible Hub, https://biblehub.com/text/deuteronomy/20-11.htm (accessed

tributary vassal obviously involved a prospect very different from the enslavement of the entire population. Which translation offers a more faithful rendering of the original meaning is difficult to determine from the historical context of either the second or first millennium, as both policies were practised across the region during this period. In this particular case it seems pertinent that mass deportation and forced labour was the ultimate fate of many Israelites after the successive Assyrian and Babylonian conquests of Samaria and Judah. A threat of enslavement would surely have resonated loudly with the redactors of Deuteronomy, perhaps making the more severe translation more likely.

Leaving aside the contested meaning of Deuteronomy 20:11, from the perspective of the Israelites, the enemy's acceptance of the invitation to submit would have avoided a costly siege and escalade, as well as potentially preserving the population as an economic resource. Whether the offer was motivated by pragmatic reasoning or by humanitarian concerns, or both, is difficult to gauge. But the mass of evidence from throughout the region points towards the former. Deuteronomy certainly displayed little humanitarian concern for the enemy city if it refused to submit:

> If it does not surrender to you, but would join battle with you, you shall lay siege to it; and when the Lord your God delivers it into your hand, you shall put all its males to the sword. You may, however, take as your booty the women, the children, the livestock, and everything in the town—all its spoil—and enjoy the use of the spoil of your enemy, which the Lord your God gives you.[94]

This is reflective of standard ancient Near Eastern practice, which assumed that defeated cities were entirely at the mercy of the conqueror. Men of military age were killed because they posed a threat, women and children were profitably enslaved, and all other goods were divided as spoils among the victors.

Deuteronomy is unusual, however, in that it went on to make a distinction between *types* of enemies. Verses 10–14 applied strictly to enemies encountered *beyond* the territories promised by Yahweh: 'Thus you shall deal with all towns that lie very far from you, towns that do not belong to nations

---

9 January 2023). The Latin Vulgate (derived from the Greek Pentateuch), renders it 'si receperit et aperuerit tibi portas *cunctus populus qui in ea est salvabitur et serviet tibi sub tributo*' (if it accepts and opens its gates to you, all the people therein shall be spared and serve you under tribute): *The Latin Vulgate Bible* http://www.latinvulgate.com/, Deuteronomy 20:11 (emphasis added) (accessed 9 January 2023). Mayes observes that 'the Hebrew word *mas* is not an abstract concept, but a collective noun denoting those people conscripted for forced labour': Mayes, *Deuteronomy*, 294. This sense of *mas* as a collective noun referring specifically to people would seem to indicate that it was indeed enslavement of a group of individuals that was being envisaged, not the more abstract concept of a city becoming tributary.

94. Deuteronomy 20:12–15.

hereabout.'[95] Cities belonging to those 'nations hereabout'—that is, the Seven Nations inhabiting the Promised Land—were denied any opportunity for clemency.[96] This was a demand for complete herem destruction of people and goods, as already outlined in Deuteronomy 7.[97] This annihilation was justified on the grounds that these peoples would corrupt the Israelites and 'lead you into doing all the abhorrent things that they have done for their gods'.[98]

According to the Book of Joshua, the conquest of Canaan did indeed follow these lines. With the exception of the Hivites of Gibeon, who tricked the Israelites into forming a non-aggression pact,[99] all the other cities of the Nations were proscribed:

> Apart from the Hivites who dwelt in Gibeon, not a single city made terms with the Israelites; all were taken in battle. For it was the Lord's doing to stiffen their hearts to give battle to Israel, in order that they might be proscribed without quarter and wiped out, as the Lord had commanded Moses.[100]

It is likely that the books of Joshua and Deuteronomy were both completed and edited into a single 'history' (also containing Judges, 1 and 2 Samuel, and 1 and 2 Kings) at about the same time, either during the reign of Josiah of Judah (c. 640–c. 609) or during the Bayblonian exile (c. 586–c. 538).[101] Deuteronomy was later included as one of the five books of the Torah in the post-exilic period. Ironically, then, the stipulations of Deuteronomy 20 were probably written down at a time when Israel's military institutions and capabilities had effectively ceased to exist. But the Book of Joshua may contain much older elements:

---

95. Ibid. 20:15.

96. Ibid. 20:16–17. Michael Fishbane suggests that this herem proscription was a late addition by the Deuteronomist to more ancient siege laws contained in Deuteronomy 20:10–14: Fishbane, *Biblical Interpretation in Ancient Israel* (Oxford: Clarendon Press, 1985), 200–202.

97. 'When the Lord your God brings you to the land that you are about to enter and possess, and He dislodges many nations before you—the Hittites, Girgashites, Amorites, Canaanites, Perizzites, Hivites, and Jebusites, seven nations much larger than you—and the Lord your God delivers them to you and you defeat them, you must doom them to destruction: grant them no terms and give them no quarter.' Deuteronomy 7:1–2. Cf. ibid. 7:5, 16, 24–25.

98. Ibid. 20:18; cf. ibid. 12:1–3.

99. Joshua 9:1–27. While the Gibeonites were spared, it is also implied that they were enslaved, becoming 'hewers of wood and drawers of water'. The pact with the Gibeonites was later broken by Saul, who killed a number of them. As a punishment, Yahweh afflicted Israel with famine: 2 Samuel 21:1–2. See also Joseph Blenkinsopp, 'Are There Traces of the Gibeonite Covenant in Deuteronomy?', *Catholic Biblical Quarterly* 28 (2) (1966): 207–19.

100. Joshua 11:19–20.

101. For the earlier date, see Eynikel, *Reforms of King Josiah*. For the exilic date: Noth, *The Deuteronomistic History*. See also above, ch. 8 n. 49.

predating, that is, the composition of Deuteronomy 20.[102] This compositional history is important with regard to how we interpret the siege prescriptions contained in the aforementioned texts. In the passage quoted above, the text states that 'not a single city made terms with the Israelites; all were taken in battle. For it was the Lord's doing to stiffen their hearts to give battle to Israel'. This implies that the cities had a *choice* to come to terms, but refused to do so. This conflicts with the stipulations of Deuteronomy 20:16–17, which demanded that cities of the Nations should *not* be offered any terms for surrender. In the Joshua passage, the refusal of the cities to seek terms with Israel is presented as a justification for their destruction (notwithstanding that Yahweh himself is, in a direct sense, made responsible for their belligerence because he 'stiffened their hearts'). What we may be seeing in Joshua 11:19–20, therefore, is a relic of Israelite practice from before the composition of Deuteronomy 20. This earlier military practice assumed that terms of surrender could indeed be offered to all enemies, including those in Canaan.[103] Arguably this reflected good military and political strategy: the exercise of military pragmatism. In contrast, the more extreme stipulations introduced by Deuteronomy 20 were probably a later theologically inspired radicalisation of customary military norms, intended to emphasise the physical and spiritual separation of the Israelites from their Canaanite neighbours. As such, the Deuteronomic stipulations are unlikely to provide an accurate image of pre-exilic Israelite military practices.[104]

The Second Book of Kings provides points of comparison on how Jerusalem itself was treated during two successful sieges by the Babylonians. During the first siege of Jerusalem in c. 597, King Jehoiachin of Judah surrendered in the face of a massive Babylonian army:

> King Nebuchadnezzar of Babylon advanced against the city while his troops were besieging it. Thereupon King Jehoiachin of Judah, along with his mother, and his courtiers, commanders, and officers, surrendered to the king of Babylon. The king of Babylon took him captive in the eighth year of his reign.[105]

Nebuchadnezzar emptied the treasure stores of the royal palace and the Temple of Solomon (although did not destroy either of these), and exiled King Jehoiachin to Babylon, along with the royal household and all the elites and artisans of the city. He then installed Jehoiachin's uncle, Mattaniah/Zedekiah,

---

102. *JSB*, 462.
103. Cf. 2 Samuel 10:19.
104. In contrast, Philip Stern maintains that Deuteronomy 20 was produced during the heyday of the kingdom of Samaria, implying that Israelite kings may have actually implemented herem proscriptions during wartime: Philip D. Stern, *The Biblical Herem: A Window on Israel's Religious Experience* (Atlanta, GA: Scholars Press, 1991).
105. 2 Kings 24:11–12.

as a puppet ruler in his place.[106] The prompt capitulation of Jerusalem probably encouraged the Babylonians to show considerable restraint. Furthermore, Jehoiachin was seemingly treated well in exile, as he was later given a pension by the fabulously named King Evil-merodach.[107]

In contrast, when King Zedekiah rebelled nine years later and provoked a second siege (c. 589–c. 587), the Babylonians took far more extreme measures against their recalcitrant vassal. Not only did Nebuchadnezzar sack the city and burn the temple (2 Kings 25:8-17), but his treatment of Zedekiah was markedly more violent:

> [T]he Chaldean troops pursued the king, and they overtook him in the steppes of Jericho as his entire force left him and scattered. They captured the king and brought him before the king of Babylon at Riblah; and they put him on trial. They slaughtered Zedekiah's sons before his eyes; then Zedekiah's eyes were put out. He was chained in bronze fetters and he was brought to Babylon.[108]

The change in treatment of the royal household is stark: the royal heirs were massacred while the rebellious king was mutilated and ritually humiliated.

Two key factors probably influenced the Babylonian response. First and foremost, Zedekiah had refused to surrender, foregoing the opportunity for clemency and forcing the Babylonians to besiege Jerusalem for seventeen months before finally taking the city by escalade. The massive commitment of time and resources that this necessitated—as well as the political embarrassment for the dominant empire of the region—would have motivated the Babylonians to wreak severe retribution upon Judah. Second, having been installed as a Babylonian vassal, Zedekiah's revolt clearly marked him as a rebel; thus his punishment was that of an oath-breaker rather than a standard political opponent. Both factors required Babylon to make a political statement, as much as a military or legal statement, in their treatment of Jerusalem and its royal family, communicating to other would-be rebels the terrible consequences of resisting or betraying Babylonian suzerainty.

Destroying or Preserving Trees

Trees were a precious and dwindling resource in the ancient Near East, and even the cedars of Lebanon had been seriously depleted by the turn of the first millennium (see figures 31 and 45). As a valuable piece of immovable property, trees, orchards, and gardens were routinely targeted by ancient Near Eastern armies as an effective means of devastating an enemy's agricultural

---

106. Ibid. 24:13-16, 17.
107. Ibid. 25:27-30.
108. Ibid. 25:5-7.

THE ISRAELITES: *IUS IN BELLO* [369]

FIGURE 45. Transportation of Lebanese cedar: Palace of the Assyrian king Sargon II, at Dur Sharrukin, Assyria, late eighth century BCE. Musée du Louvre, Paris, public domain, via Wikimedia Commons.

resources or drawing him out of a city for battle.[109] Assyrian royal inscriptions from the reigns of Shalmaneser III to Tiglath-pileser III (c. 859–c. 727) frequently recorded the destruction of arboreal resources. Such destruction was emphasised particularly in campaigns that had failed to achieve their primary

---

109. For an amusing but informative discussion on the practicalities of destroying fruit trees, see Victor Davis Hanson, *A War Like No Other: How the Athenians and Spartans Fought the Peloponnesian War* (New York: Random House, 2005), 35–37.

military objective, such as the capture of an enemy city, probably as a scribal device to focus attention on something more 'positive'.[110] The destruction of trees was also highly symbolic, showing the defeat of the enemy and the resources necessary for life; it was presented as just punishment for enemies (especially rebels) and therefore carried moral significance.[111]

Given the widespread occurrence of arboreal devastation in ancient Near Eastern warfare, the stipulations of Deuteronomy 20:19-20 prohibiting the destruction of certain trees during siege operations are of particular interest:

> When in your war against a city you have to besiege it a long time in order to capture it, you must not destroy its trees, wielding the ax against them. You may eat of them, but you must not cut them down. Are trees of the field human to withdraw before you into the besieged city? Only trees that you know do not yield food may be destroyed; you may cut them down for constructing siege-works against the city that is waging war on you, until it has been reduced.[112]

Notably, this passage has had an enduring impact on the Western just war tradition and has found its way, through the influence of jurists such as Hugo Grotius, into modern international law.[113]

The protection of trees (a commodity that, once felled, took a generation to re-grow) could be understood as a sensible precaution; but was it an *ethical* injunction? Or was the prohibition of felling trees a critique of Neo-Assyrian practices of arboreal devastation, as proposed by biblical scholars as early as the eighteenth century CE?[114]

Deuteronomy 20:19 portrayed trees as helpless bystanders—'Are trees of the field human to withdraw before you?'—and thus not deserving of destruction. However, Deuteronomy also made a distinction between trees which yielded food (perhaps including vines), which were to be protected, and those that did not yield food, which could be felled to construct siege-works. The stipulation that even non-food yielding trees should be felled *only* for siege works is

---

110. Bustenay Oded, 'Cutting Down Orchards in Assyrian Royal Inscriptions: The Historiographic Aspect', *Journal of Ancient Civilizations* 12 (1997): 93–98 at 93, 98. See also Jeremy D. Smoak, 'Assyrian Siege Warfare Imagery and the Background of a Biblical Curse', in *Writing and Reading War: Rhetoric, Gender, and Ethics in Biblical and Modern Contexts*, ed. Brad E. Kelle and Frank Ritchel Ames (Atlanta, GA: Society of Biblical Literature, 2008), 83–91, esp. 85–86.

111. Oded, 'Cutting Down Orchards', 96–97.

112. Deuteronomy 20:19-20.

113. Jacob L. Wright, 'Warfare and Wanton Destruction: A Reexamination of Deuteronomy 20:19-20 in Relation to Ancient Siegecraft', *Journal of Biblical Literature* 127 (3) (2008): 423–58 at 424–26.

114. Wright convincingly rejects the 'Assyrian critique' thesis: ibid., 426–27, 445–48.

indicative of a general sense that trees should not be destroyed merely for the sake of harming an enemy.

A prudential motive for Deuteronomy 20:19-20 is perhaps more convincing than an ethical or 'humanitarian' one. During a siege, the preservation of food-yielding trees had the obvious advantage of acting as a source of sustenance (depending on the season) for the besieging army itself.[115] Cutting down such trees would only have exacerbated the logistical demands of feeding a static army. Moreover, if the Israelites were investing a city with the aim of conquering it and controlling it, then destroying the valuable natural resources of that city would have been counter-productive. In preserving trees, the Israelites may have had an eye on their own future agricultural interests.[116]

It has been suggested that prohibitions against destroying trees were intended exclusively for intra-Israelite warfare, so as 'to ameliorate, in a spirit of self-interest, the barbarities of intertribal conflicts'.[117] This reasoning relates to quite widespread scholarly interpretations of *ius in bello* restraints as evolving in part as insurance policies for elite combatants—a method of protecting their interests and security even in defeat. There is no reason to dismiss such an interpretation entirely. However, the preservation of trees made sound strategic sense in *any* ancient Near Eastern conflict aimed at acquiring or recapturing territory, not just in internecine conflicts between Israelite communities. Michael Hasel has attempted to defend a late second-millennium (rather than a mid-first-millennium) origin for Deuteronomy 20:19-20 by setting the verses against a context of Egyptian and Assyrian siege practices. Hasel argues that the prohibitions on felling food-yielding trees were prudential instructions created for Israelite armies during the conquest of Canaan.[118] While thought-provoking, Hasel's hypothesis remains speculative and is rooted in a desire to create a Mosaic provenance for Deuteronomy

---

115. Assnat Bartor, '"When you go forth to war against your enemies . . .": Narrative Reading of Deuteronomic Warfare Legislation', in *The Reception of Biblical War Legislation in Narrative Contexts: Proceedings of the EABS Research Group 'Law and Narrative'*, ed. Christoph Berner and Harald Samuel (Berlin: De Gruyter, 2015), 1-21 at 18-19.

116. Deuteronomy 20:19 has continued to be a source of contested interpretation up to the present day. As Solomon observes, '[i]n its biblical context this is a counsel of prudence rather than a principle of conservation; however, rabbinic tradition has applied it generally as a prohibition of waste, and modern Jewish environmentalists have quarried this tradition in support of their pleas for conservation'. Solomon, 'Judaism', 300. For example, Mayes states that vv. 19-20 are 'concerned specifically with prohibiting undue devastation of the country': Mayes, *Deuteronomy*, 293-94.

117. Ziskind, 'Aspects of International Law', 142. A view defended at length by Wright, 'Warfare and Wanton Destruction', 423-58.

118. Michael G. Hasel, 'The Destruction of Trees in the Moabite Campaign of 2 Kings 3:4-27: A Study in the Laws of Warfare', *Andrews University Seminary Studies* 40 (2) (2002): 197-206; Hasel, *Military Practice and Polemic*; Hasel, 'Assyrian Military Practices'.

and to defend the historicity of the conquest. As a result, it has failed to persuade most scholars.[119]

Whether the authors of Deuteronomy 20:19–20 were motivated by prudential or by ethical concerns, there is no evidence that this stipulation to protect trees was ever in fact observed by pre- or post-Deuteronomic Israelite armies. Indeed, the protections for trees outlined in Deuteronomy 20 are contradicted elsewhere in the Tanakh. During the Israelite campaign against Moab narrated in 2 Kings 3, Yahweh commanded the kings of Samaria and Judah to 'conquer every fortified city and every splendid city; you shall fell every good tree and stop up all wells of water; and every fertile field you shall ruin with stones'.[120] This directive for agricultural and arboreal devastation was carried out to the letter.[121] There seems little reason to doubt that Israelite armies prior to the sixth century followed the common practice of targeting arboreal resources during raids of enemy territory, as in the episode just cited, but perhaps preserved such resources in territories that they intended to subjugate.

Defending a prudential reading of Deuteronomy 20:19–20 leads to the conclusion that either the verses contain the kernel of an older tradition, or that the Deuteronomistic author(s) were engaging with contemporary military reality. If we assume that Deuteronomy largely dates from the exilic or post-exilic period, then we must wonder *why* the authors felt compelled to create prudential rules for Israelite armies that no longer existed. If the inclusion of the stipulations was genuinely an ethical protest against an unnecessarily destructive practice (as Mayes asserts: see above, n. 116), then it was a weak protest, because it was not consistent enough for the Deuteronomist to excise the destruction of trees ordained and described in 2 Kings 3:19–25. Moreover, an ethical protest with

---

119. Mayes, representing the consensus, comments that '[t]he deuteronomic law takes up again in vv. 19–20, where, however, there is probably no pre-deuteronomic basis [. . . it is a] deuteronomic protest against a practice considered unnecessarily destructive': Mayes, *Deuteronomy*, 294, 296. See also reviews of Hasel's *Military Practice and Polemic* by Jacob L. Wright, *Journal of Biblical Literature*, 125 (3) (2006): 577–79, and by Scott Morschauser, *The Catholic Biblical Quarterly* 68 (4) (2006): 731–32.

120. 2 Kings 3:19. Compare to the Deuteronomic command to fell trees associated with non-Yahweh cultic sites: 'You must destroy all the sites at which the nations you are to dispossess worshipped their gods, whether on lofty mountains and on hills or under any luxuriant tree. [. . . Put] their sacred posts to the fire, and cut down the images of their gods, obliterating their name from that site.' Deuteronomy 12:2–3.

121. 2 Kings 3:24–25. Note that many English translations of the Bible, following the King James translation, dispense with the direct reference to fruiting trees and instead render the phrase in 2 Kings 3:25 as 'felled all the good trees', repeating the wording of ibid. 3:19: *The Holy Bible: King James Version* (n.p.: World Bible Publishers, 2005). The Latin Vulgate, however, maintains the original reference to fruiting trees in 2 Kings 3:25—'omnia ligna fructifera succiderunt' (they cut down all the fruit-bearing trees)—as well as referring to fruiting trees in ibid. 3:19: 'et universum lignum fructiferum succidetis cunctosque' (and [you] shall cut down every fruit-bearing tree). *Latin Vulgate Bible*: http://www.latinvulgate.com/ (accessed 9 January 2023).

no Israelite army to hear it seems futile, and it is implausible that such a protest was aimed at an Assyrian, Babylonian, or Persian audience.[122] It is more likely, I think, that Deuteronomy 20:19–20 tapped into widely held prudential military concerns about preserving arboreal resources that were still very much alive in the mid-first millennium, when the Deuteronomy text was taking shape. These concerns were inserted by the Deuteronomist to make the 'Mosaic' rules of war appear more realistic and convincingly 'historical'. They were not an ethical or ideological protest, but they did reflect a Near Eastern military reality that had been recognised for centuries.

Treatment of the Enemy during War

TREATMENT OF COMBATANTS

Just as in the case of Egyptian and Hittite representations of war, a literal reading of the Tanakh will lead to one simple conclusion: that Israelite warfare was horrifically brutal. There is ample evidence throughout the text that enemy combatants rarely enjoyed mercy, and the slaying of scores of opponents was routinely presented not only as a positive act, but as a divine command of Yahweh. In the narrative of Israel's early history, concerns such as discrimination or proportionality in war are entirely absent. During Israel's flight from Egypt, Yahweh wiped out Pharaoh's entire army using the waters of the Red Sea, so that 'not one of them remained'.[123] Yahweh was also willing to engage in biological warfare against the peoples of Canaan, promising the Israelites, 'I will send a plague ahead of you.'[124] A zero-sum policy towards enemy combatants is visible in Judges (4:12–16) when an entire Canaanite army under the command of Sisera—nine hundred chariots plus infantry—was put to the sword, so that not a single man survived. Even Sisera, who managed to flee the battlefield, was shortly afterwards murdered by having a tent peg hammered through his head whilst asleep.[125]

Severe treatment of enemy combatants resulted from Joshua's victory against a coalition of five Amorite kings, with Joshua refusing to allow the defeated enemy to escape. Instead, the Israelite war leader ordered that they should be ruthlessly hunted down and killed:

> 'But as for the rest of you, don't stop, but press on the heels of your enemies and harass them from the rear. Don't let them reach their towns, for the Lord your God has delivered them into your hands.'

---

122. Wright also rejects the 'Assyrian critique' thesis, although on different grounds: Wright, 'Warfare and Wanton Destruction', 426–27, 445–48.
123. Exodus 14:28.
124. Ibid. 23:28.
125. Judges 4:17–21; above, p. 363.

When Joshua and the Israelites had finished dealing them a deadly blow, they were wiped out, except for some fugitives who escaped into the fortified town.[126]

Following this massacre, Joshua proceeded to ritually humiliate the five captured kings, ordering his commanders, 'Come forward and place your feet on the necks of these kings.'[127] The slaughter and subsequent humiliation was intended to publicise Israel's ruthless mode of war—'For this is what the Lord is going to do to all the enemies with whom you are at war'—and finally the royal prisoners were 'put to death and impaled on five stakes'.[128] On this occasion it seems that the kings were already dead before their bodies were impaled; here, impalement was a monitory display of bodily desecration.[129] A much later episode, set during the Persian period, recorded Esther demanding that the ten sons of Haman should similarly be impaled. This was done, although like the Joshua episode the victims were apparently already dead.[130]

There are other references to impalement in the Tanakh, although not necessarily performed by Israelites. The bodies of Saul and his sons were impaled by the Philistines after their death in battle, while all of Saul's remaining male heirs (except for the lame Meribaal) were handed over to the Gibeonites by David, who 'impaled them on the mountain before the Lord'.[131] The exquisitely detailed Assyrian victory panels from Sennacherib's palace of Nineveh depict the siege and sack of the Judahite city of Lachish in retaliation for Hezekiah of Judah's rebellion against Assyrian overlordship. The carved reliefs include a scene showing captured Judahite soldiers being impaled outside the city's walls (figure 46).[132] The interior-decorating choices of Assyrian kings certainly did not shy away from depicting scenes of appalling violence: the images of impaled Judahites at Lachish were accompanied at Nineveh by a raft of equally grisly scenes, including one relief of captured Elamites being flayed alive (figure 47).

---

126. Joshua 10:19–20.

127. Ibid. 10:24.

128. Ibid. 10:25–26. For the relationship of Joshua 10:16–27 to the Assyrian tradition, see Younger, *Ancient Conquest Accounts*, 220–25. Compare to the stipulations on the execution of criminals at Deuteronomy 21:22–23. For further discussion of the treatment of enemy kings, see below, 'Killing Kings'.

129. An opposing view is offered in the later Book of Amos (2:1), which actually condemns the desecration of enemy bodies, citing the burning of the bones of the king of Edom as one of Moab's transgressions which would be punished by Yahweh.

130. Esther 9:6–14.

131. 1 Samuel 31:1–12; 2 Samuel 21: 5–9. Kuhrt notes that this appears to have been a convenient excuse for David effectively to extinguish Saul's line of succession: *KANE*, 2:452–53.

132. Compare to the Assyrian impalement of Mitannian noblemen recorded in a Hittite treaty: above, p. 258.

THE ISRAELITES: *IUS IN BELLO* [375]

FIGURE 46. Assyrian soldiers impaling Judahites outside the city of Lachish: Palace of Nineveh, Assyria, c. 700–c. 692 BCE). Osama S. M. Amin, https://etc.worldhistory.org/photos/siege-lachish-reliefs-british-museum.

Joshua's brutal treatment of the Amorite kings and troops is reminiscent of the inscriptions of the Assyrian king Aššurnasirpal II (c. 883–c. 859), who boasted of killing, burning, mutilating, and flaying his enemies:

> I approached the city Tēla [...]. They did not submit to me. In strife and conflict I besieged and conquered the city. I felled 3000 of their fighting men with the sword [...]. I burnt many captives from them. I captured many troops alive: from some I cut off their arms and hands; from others I cut off their noses, ears, and extremities. I gouged out the

FIGURE 47. Assyrian soldiers flaying Elamites: Palace of Nineveh, Assyria, c. 700–c. 692 BCE). © Trustees of the British Museum.

eyes of many troops. I made one pile of the living and one of heads. I hung their heads on trees around the city. I burnt their adolescent boys and girls. I razed, destroyed, burnt, and consumed the city.[133]

While such acts will strike modern readers as evidence of sadistic cruelty, Aššurnasirpal II claimed to be a ruler 'who has always acted justly with the support of Ashur and Shamash', and—on grounds identical to Joshua's claim of divine guidance by Yahweh—to have acted because the god Aššur 'has commanded me to take possession of, subdue and govern countries and dangerous mountain regions'.[134] Similarly, when Sargon II crushed a rebellion led by the

---

133. *The Royal Inscriptions of Mesopotamia, Assyrian Periods*, vol. 2: *Assyrian Rulers of the Early First Millennium BC, I (1114–859 BC)*, ed. A. Kirk Grayson (Toronto: University of Toronto Press, 2002), 201, cols i.113–ii.1. Prior to reaching Tēla, Aššurnasirpal claimed to have committed comparable atrocities at the city of Kinabu: 'I [...] approached the city of Kinabu, the fortified city of Hulāiia [...]. I felled with the sword 800 of their combat troops, I burnt 3000 captives from them. I did not leave one of them alive as a hostage [...]. I made a pile of their corpses. I burnt their adolescent boys and girls. I flayed Hulāiia their city ruler and draped his skin over the wall of the city Damdammusa. I razed, destroyed and burnt their city.' Ibid., col. i.106–10. Aššurnasirpal II's texts are particularly gruesome, but the violence of the Neo-Assyrian royal style can be seen throughout the inscriptions collected in the volume, from Tiglath-pileser I onwards.

134. Cited in Oded, *War, Peace and Empire*, 11, 39.

city of Hamath and flayed its king, he claimed he did so in order to establish 'peace and harmony'.[135] However, the claim that the Assyrians were unique in their acts or boasts of cruelty simply does not hold up against the evidence.[136] The victory stele commissioned by Mesha of Moab, recording his wars against Israel, boasted that he 'slew all the people of the city [Ataroth] as a spectacle(?) for Kemosh and Moab'. When Mesha assaulted the city of Nebo, the king 'took it and slew all, seven thousand male citizens and foreign men[,] seven thousand men, female citizens, foreign women and female slaves. For Ashtar-Kemosh I had it put to the ban.'[137] Clearly, these acts were not presented in a bashful or regretful tone.[138] The Israelites of the Tanakh also indulged in numerous boasts of massacres and mutilation of defeated peoples, including women and children.

The history of the Israelite monarchy was steeped in stories of ruthlessness shown to Israel's military enemies. Saul's coronation as king was sealed by his victory over an Ammonite army encamped before Jabesh-Gilead; the Israelites obliterated their camp so that 'no two were left together'.[139] During the siege of Jabesh-Gilead, the Ammonite commander had shown himself equally willing to mutilate combatants and non-combatants alike, responding to the city's proposal of surrender in these terms: 'Nahash the Ammonite answered them, "I will make a pact with you on this condition, that everyone's right eye be gouged out; I will make this a humiliation for all Israel."'[140]

When Saul felt his royal authority was under threat from David, who sought the hand of the king's daughter in marriage, he demanded 'no other bride-price than the foreskins of a hundred Philistines, as vengeance on the king's enemies'.[141] Believing that such a demand was impossible for David to fulfil without getting himself killed in the process, Saul was unhappily surprised when 'David went out with his men and killed two hundred Philistines; David brought their foreskins and they were counted out for the king, that he

---

135. *ANEA*, 1:196.

136. For the claim that the Assyrians were uniquely cruel amongst Near Eastern societies, see Altman, 'Earliest Recorded Concepts', 115–16; Yadin, *Art of Warfare*, 384–87; Mordechai Cogan, '"Ripping Open Pregnant Women" in Light of an Assyrian Analogue', *Journal of the American Oriental Society* 103 (4) (1983): 755–57 at 755. Others argue that the Assyrians were probably no more or less cruel in practice than most of their predecessors and contemporaries: see Ziskind, 'Aspects of International Law', 151; Crouch, *War and Ethics*, 40–43.

137. 'Moabite Stone', *HST*, 313. Referring to the sacrificial ban, the Moabite stele uses the same root *hrm* as found in biblical texts. See *WHB*, 31.

138. Such histrionic boasts do not necessarily reflect reality. Mesha's claim that he slaughtered his Israelite foes must be contrasted with this detail appearing later in the stele: 'I dug the trenches for Qarho with the prisoners of Israel' (i.e., some Israelite prisoners of war evidently survived Mesha's massacre). 'Moabite Stone', *HST*, 313.

139. 1 Samuel 11:1–15, quotation at v. 11.

140. Ibid. 11:2.

141. Ibid. 18:25.

might become the king's son-in-law.'¹⁴² Laying aside the total absence of any justification for killing two hundred Philistines (it is merely a ruse for Saul and an act of bravado for David), the mutilation of enemies to supply war trophies was obviously considered both normal and praiseworthy. (See figure 22 for an Egyptian example of phalli as war trophies.) Moreover, the text does not actually specify whether David's victims were combatants or simply the closest available Philistine villagers.

MASSACRE AND THE 'DOCTRINE' OF *HEREM*

War is ever-present in the Tanakh. When we compare it with other religio-historical texts from the second or first millennium, we see that there is nothing unusual about this. What is striking, however, is the ubiquity of accounts of massacre within the Israelite corpus. Entire populations—women, children, the old, the lame—were purposefully put to the sword. On some occasions the slaughter even included domesticated livestock, as well as the ritual destruction of crops and inanimate objects seized from the enemy. In many cases, this was said to have been done at the direct command of Yahweh.¹⁴³

These episodes of stark and brutal military violence can be grouped together as examples of the biblical 'ban' (*herem*), which biblical scholars have explained either as a special type of holy war or as an invention of the Deuteronomist. Von Rad notably envisioned the ban as the cultic 'highpoint and the conclusion of the holy war'.¹⁴⁴ It must be considered, however, that modern biblical scholars—discomfited by accounts of divinely mandated genocidal violence—have been too willing to discount such extreme practices as fiction. In one of the most sophisticated examinations of Israelite ethics of war to date, Susan Niditch is surely correct when she observes that this dismissal of the massacre accounts says more about the normative theological expectations of biblical scholars than it does about ancient Israelite thought.¹⁴⁵

The term *herem* (root: *hrm*) originated in a sacrificial meaning of 'devote to destruction', and derivations of *herem* appear in a number of Near Eastern cultures.¹⁴⁶ In Israelite thought, it implied an act of sacrifice to Yahweh.¹⁴⁷ For

---

142. Ibid. 18:27.

143. Women and children could still be massacred without any reference to the herem imperative, as in David's killing of non-combatants in Negev during his service as a mercenary (*habiru*) for the king of Gath (1 Samuel 27:6–27). See also Gottwald, '"Holy War" in Deuteronomy', 299.

144. Rad, *Holy War*, 49.

145. *WHB*, 9, 41–42. Cf. Crouch, *War and Ethics*, 174–89.

146. For other Near Eastern parallels of the 'ban', see Stern, *Biblical Herem*, 19–88.

147. Good, 'Capital Punishment', 971. Niditch differentiates between two 'banning ideologies': one treating the killing of the enemy as a sacrifice to Yahweh, the other treating the killing of the enemy as an execution of divine justice. See *WHB*, 28–55, 77; Niditch, 'War and Reconciliation', 144–45.

the sake of maintaining a linear narrative and a degree of coherence, we will examine the major examples of massacre in the order in which they appear in the current form of the Tanakh. Most of the examples appear in the books of Numbers, Deuteronomy, Joshua, and Judges—that is, those books which narrate the establishment of the Israelite nation through conquest. However, it should be remembered that the Book of Numbers was predominantly the product of the late 'Priestly' author (c. sixth century), although may contain older Jahwist/Elohist components (c. tenth to eighth century).[148] Deuteronomy, Joshua, and Judges are now considered part of a single revised Deuteronomistic history, although the Book of Judges perhaps contains older tribal traditions.[149] The books of Samuel and Kings, which might be said to better represent an authentic monarchical outlook, contain less evidence for herem practices. Put simply, the majority of our evidence for military massacre derives from texts that were either composed or heavily redacted around the time of the exile. As such, they reflect a predominantly theological rather than a political or strictly historical interest.[150]

In terms of narrative chronology, the earliest reference to 'annihilating' an enemy—in the sense of complete destruction—appears in Exodus, as Yahweh explains to Moses how the conquest of Canaan will unfold. The god emphasises the importance of purging non-Yahwist religious practices from the land.[151] The first indications of massacres actually taking place occur from the beginning of the conquest narrative, from Numbers 21 onwards: that is, prior to the stipulations of Deuteronomy 20. The books of Numbers and Deuteronomy recount victories over two Transjordanian kings, although they differ in their presentation of the violence. Referring to the Amorites under King Sihon, Numbers says that 'Israel put them to the sword, and took possession of their land'.[152] But when Moses 'remembered' this event in Deuteronomy, he provided greater detail:

> Sihon with all his men took the field against us at Jahaz, and the Lord our God delivered him to us and we defeated him and his sons and all his men. At that time we captured all his towns and we doomed every town—men, women, and children—leaving no survivor.[153]

---

148. *JSB*, 281.
149. Ibid., 462–64, 509.
150. A point also made by Crouch, *War and Ethics*, 178–81.
151. Exodus 23:23–24; cf. ibid. 23:27–33; 24:10–14.
152. 'But Sihon would not let Israel pass through his territory. Sihon gathered all his people and went out against Israel in the wilderness. He came to Jahaz and engaged Israel in battle. But Israel put them to the sword, and took possession of their land, from the Arnon to the Jabbok, as far as [Az] of the Ammorites, for Az marked the boundary of the Ammorites.' Numbers 21:21–24.
153. Deuteronomy 2:32–34.

This language is that of the ban (*herem*): proscribing enemies as a process of religious cleansing. Deuteronomy was far more explicit than Numbers in stating that even women and children were included in the sacrificial massacre, although on this occasion the Israelites were permitted to retain non-human booty rather than surrendering everything to holocaust.[154]

The same morphing of language and ideology from Numbers to Deuteronomy is visible in the account of the conflict against King Og of Bashan. While Numbers makes it clear that some kind of massacre took place—'They defeated him and his sons and all his people, *until no remnant was left him*; and they took possession of his country'[155]—Deuteronomy recounts the same event with greater emphasis on the eradication of people:

> So the Lord our God delivered into our power King Og of Bashan, with all his men, and we dealt them such a blow that no survivor was left. At that time we captured all his towns; [...] sixty towns, the whole district of Argob [...]. We doomed them as we had done in the case of King Sihon of Heshbon; we doomed every town—men, women, and children—and retained as booty all the cattle and the spoil of the towns.[156]

Yahweh's gift of victory was thus repaid by offering human lives to the god; at the same time, this served the purpose of cleansing the land of religious practices that risked corrupting the Israelites. The slaughter of the Midianites (Numbers 31) was presented in a similar light, of cleansing Israel of corruption. The initial slaughter of the adult males and the burning of Midianite villages and towns was not comprehensive enough for Moses, who insisted that even the women and children should be butchered, allowing an exception only for virgin girls.[157] The Midianite women, especially, were to be blamed for enticing Israelite men to worship Baal.

The importance of cleansing Canaan through massive acts of bloodshed was dealt with specifically in Deuteronomy, as Moses communicated Yahweh's instructions to his people:

> When the Lord your God brings you to the land that you are about to enter and possess, and He dislodges many nations before you—the Hittites, Girgashites, Amorites, Canaanites, Perizzites, Hivites, and Jebusites, seven nations much larger than you—and the Lord your God

---

154. Cf. ibid. 20:14–18.

155. Numbers 21:33–35 (emphasis added). Compare Israel's subsequent conflict against the Midianites, during which they followed the command of Yahweh 'and slew every male', including the five kings of Midian (ibid. 31:7–8).

156. Deuteronomy 3:3–6.

157. Numbers 31:1–12, 15–20. Niditch proposes that this minor exception—of sparing the virgin girls—means that Numbers 31 cannot be classified alongside the other 'ban texts' in which all human life was extinguished. Niditch, 'War, Women, and Defilement', 47.

delivers them to you and you defeat them, you must doom them to destruction: grant them no terms and give them no quarter.[158]

The massacre of the Nations was presented as necessary because otherwise they would turn Israel from Yahweh worship (Deuteronomy 7:4–5). Thus Yahweh commanded, 'You shall destroy all the peoples that the Lord your God delivers to you, showing them no pity.'[159] This demand for religious purity, achieved through ruthless killing, also applied to any Israelite community who were found guilty of transgressing the Covenant and worshipping other deities.[160] Likewise, the 'Song of Moses' offered a more poetic, though no less terrifying, warning of the warlike violence Yahweh that would inflict upon his enemies.[161]

It is notable that throughout Deuteronomy there is no attempt to dilute accounts of massacre—quite the opposite, in fact, as the Deuteronomist revelled in Israel's crushing victories over its enemies. It is a distinct feature of the Israelite texts that massacres were presented as divine commands. While the Egyptian, Hittite, and Assyrian traditions certainly portrayed their gods as providing their followers with the authority and power to destroy their terrestrial enemies, they rarely, if ever, framed their most excessive acts of violence as direct *commands* from a deity. The Israelite conception of divinely mandated massacre, in the sense of a direct command rather than tacit approval, was something unique to the Israelite tradition of war.

Examples of military massacres were certainly not limited to the books of Numbers and Deuteronomy; the bulk of the examples are, perhaps unsurprisingly, found in the books dealing with the conquest of Canaan. Books describing episodes of massacre, such as those of Joshua and Judges, are likely to contain older material than the book of Deuteronomy, despite Deuteronomy's appearance of laying down the 'original' stipulations for such action. In terms of composition, therefore, the 'command' to enact herem probably postdates the tradition of action, complicating any simple causal explanation of herem violence based on a reading of Deuteronomy as the starting point for the practice.[162]

---

158. Deuteronomy 7:1–2. Mayes opts for a less violent interpretation of the verse: 'the command represents [. . .] an ideal: all forms of intermingling with non-Israelites are rejected'. Mayes, *Deuteronomy*, 183. Note that 'Hittites' in the list of Nations does not refer to the Late Bronze Age Hittite empire, but to the diffusion of Iron Age Neo-Hittite city-states in the Levant.

159. Deuteronomy 7:16.

160. Ibid. 13:16–17. Cf. ibid. 17:2, which prescribes stoning to death for individuals guilty of idolatry.

161. 'Song of Moses' at Deuteronomy 31:30–32:44, esp. 32:41–42. On Hellenic/Roman Jewish interpretations of the command to annihilate the Nations, see Louis H. Feldman, 'The Command, according to Philo, Psuedo-Philo, and Josephus, to Annihilate the Seven Nations of Canaan', *Andrews University Seminary Series* 41 (1) (2003): 13–29.

162. Moreover, the Israelites 'doom' the two Amorites kings in Deuteronomy 2 and 3—that is, narratively prior to the command received from Yahweh in ibid. 7 and 20.

After the death of Moses, the first large-scale herem massacre took place at Jericho. After the walls of Jericho miraculously collapsed (with no offer of peace having been made), the Israelite army 'exterminated everything in the city with the sword: man and woman, young and old, ox and sheep and ass [. . .]. They burned down the city and everything in it.'[163] Finally, Joshua cursed anyone who might attempt to re-establish Jericho in the future.[164] He followed up this massacre at Jericho with the devastation of Ai. Having successfully feigned a retreat, the Israelites counter-attacked and 'slaughtered' the army of Ai, 'so that no one escaped or got away'.[165] Nor did this mark the end of the bloodbath:

> When Israel had killed all the inhabitants of Ai who had pursued them into the open wilderness, and all of them, to the last man, had fallen by the sword, all the Israelites turned back to Ai and put it to the sword. The total of those who fell that day, men and women, the entire population of Ai, came to twelve thousand. Joshua did not draw back the hand with which he held out his javelin until all the inhabitants of Ai had been exterminated.[166]

The Israelites seized and retained spoils from the city, 'in accordance with the instructions that the Lord had given to Joshua', and then burnt Ai to the ground, turning it 'into a mound of ruins for all time, a desolation to this day'.[167] The king of Ai, who had been captured alive, 'was impaled on a stake until the evening'; eventually, the corpse was flung in front of the city's entrance and stones placed on top of it, where the narrator claims it remains 'to this day'.[168] The tone of the narrator's account of the massacre at Ai is clearly laudatory, while the gruesome killing of the king and the desecration of his body was obviously monitory. The narrator was not shy about highlighting the killing of non-combatants, with women and children specifically numbered among the twelve thousand dead.

Joshua continued his unremitting slaughter of combatant and non-combatant populations during his campaigns against the Amorites. At Makkedah, the Israelites 'put it and its king to the sword, proscribing it and every person in it and leaving none that escaped'.[169] Victories at Libnah, Lachish,

---

163. Joshua 6:21, 24. Only the prostitute Rahab and her family were spared the massacre, having earlier helped the Israelite spies to escape from the city. From the booty, only the silver, gold, copper, and iron objects were preserved and 'deposited in the treasury of the House of the Lord.' See Joshua 6:1–27.
164. Ibid. 6:26.
165. Ibid. 8:22.
166. Ibid. 8:24–26. The function of Joshua's javelin as a conduit of Yahweh's power and authority is very similar to that of Moses's rod against the Amalekites: see Exodus 17:8–16.
167. Joshua 8:27, 28.
168. Ibid. 8:23, 29.
169. Ibid. 10:28.

Gezer, Eglon, Hebron, and Debir followed the same pattern: 'Thus Joshua conquered the whole country [...] with all their kings; he let none escape, but proscribed everything that breathed—as the Lord, the God of Israel, had commanded.'[170] In the region of Negeb and the coastal plain, the Israelites captured Hazor and 'proscribed and put to the sword every person in it. Not a soul survived, and Hazor itself was burned down.'[171] The peoples of the hill country of Judah and 'from the entire hill country of Israel' were proscribed too.[172] From these cities the Israelites 'kept all the spoil and cattle [...] as booty. But they cut down their populations with the sword until they exterminated them; they did not spare a soul.'[173]

The conquest under Joshua was thus presented as a relentless series of massacres. Under Joshua's leadership, the Israelites unseated thirty-one kings, and the text approvingly describes the death and destruction inflicted upon Israel's foes.[174] What is particularly striking, in terms of ethics, is that in the majority of cases Israel's violence was unprovoked, with no injury having been sustained.

The death of Joshua did not spell an end to these massacres. When the Judahites captured Jerusalem 'they put it to the sword and set the city on fire.'[175] During King David's reign, the army commander Joab is said to have persevered for 'six months until he had killed off every male in Edom'.[176] In a later campaign against the Edomite city of Seir, King Amaziah of Judah massacred ten thousand men from the city during battle and subsequently killed another ten thousand prisoners of war.[177]

The normative force of the ban in Israelite literature and the 'ideology of legitimate genocide'[178] is nowhere better illustrated than in the punishments inflicted upon those Israelites who failed to fulfil herem proscriptions with the appropriate rigour. On the few occasions when Israelite commanders opted to exercise mercy or political prudence (taking enemy leaders prisoner rather than summarily executing them) or preserving some of the spoils of war as booty for their troops, they were chastised and condemned by representatives of Yahweh. Ultimately, they themselves were punished for transgressing

---

170. Ibid. 10:40.
171. Ibid. 11:10–11.
172. Ibid. 11:21.
173. Ibid. 11:14.
174. Ibid. 12:1–24.
175. Judges 1:8. Note that this conflicts with Judges 1:21, which claims that the 'Benjaminites did not dispossess the Jebusites inhabitants of Jerusalem; so the Jebusites have dwelt with the Benjaminites in Jerusalem to this day'. (The Jebusites were among the proscribed Seven Nations.)
176. 1 Kings 11:15–16.
177. 2 Chronicles 25:11–12.
178. Wees, 'Genocide', 242.

divine commands.[179] The authors of the Tanakh envisioned the use of extreme violence against non-conformist Israelite communities. When the town of Jabesh-Gilead failed to provide troops in the internecine war against the tribe of Benjamin,

> the assemblage dispatched 12,000 of the warriors, instructing them as follows: 'Go and put the inhabitants of Jabesh-Gilead to the sword, women and children included. This is what you are to do: Proscribe every man, and every woman who has known a man carnally.'[180]

Although these descriptions of herem violence are detailed and highly emotive, they cannot be read as simple records of Israelite military deeds. The assertion of Israel's religious purity and physical separation from pernicious religious influences was crucial to the writing programme of the scholars who created the Tanakh, especially from the seventh century onwards. Practices of herem in the Tanakh thus probably reflect 'varying interpretations at different periods in Israel's history or in different narrative circles', as Norman Gottwald puts it.[181] Similarly, Hans van Wees observes that the 'genocidal campaigns claimed for the early Israelites [. . .] were largely fictional'.[182] One only has to look at the archaeological record, as well as the internal inconsistencies between Deuteronomy, Joshua, Judges, Chronicles, and Kings to appreciate this. Yet this ideology of massacre did not spring up *ex nihilo* in the seventh or sixth century. As we have seen, earlier states such as Egypt frequently presented themselves as carrying out large-scale enemy massacres during war. States contemporary to the Israelite kingdoms, such as Assyria, also performed atrocities during the first millennium. Nor was Israel unique in endowing massacre with a theological sheen. The ninth-century Moabite king Mesha boasted of slaughtering seven thousand Israelite men and women as herem to glorify his god, Kemosh.[183] In her comparison of the Israelite and Assyrian literary traditions, Carly Crouch concludes that 'by boiling *ḥērem* down to a particular expression of the cosmic struggle against chaos it becomes eminently clear that the ideology underlying *ḥērem* is fundamentally identical to that which undergirds Assyrian military action, even though it uses different language'.[184]

---

179. See Deuteronomy 13:17; Joshua 7; 1 Samuel 15, 30; Leviticus 27:29.

180. Judges 21:10–11. Four hundred virgins from Jabesh-Gilead were brought back, leading Niditch to observe that this was a cynical use of the ban in order to obtain wives for the quasi-ostracised Benjaminites: *WHB*, 70–71.

181. Gottwald, '"Holy War" in Deuteronomy', 300.

182. Wees, 'Genocide', 242.

183. 'Moabite Stone', *HST*, 313; cf. 2 Kings 3:26–27. See also above, pp. 275–76, 377. On the close parallel between the Moabite and Israelite formulae of herem, see also Gottwald, '"Holy War" in Deuteronomy', 301; Stern, *Biblical Herem*, 41–49, 219–20.

184. Crouch, *War and Ethics*, 182.

Episodes of herem massacre said to have occurred during the conquest of Canaan but not written down until at least the late eighth century (and probably considerably later), probably had little relevance to early first-millennium Samaritan or Judahite military practice. When the accounts of putting enemy populations to the sword were composed or redacted to reflect their current form, the Israelites were in no position to execute such policies. To explain this, Crouch has argued that as the external threat of 'chaos' became ever greater in the mid-first millennium (in the form of Assyrian and Babylonian incursions), Samaritan and Judahite military ideology responded by espousing more extreme programmes of herem violence in order to restore a sense of cosmological 'order'.[185] Daniel Smith-Christopher, meanwhile, argues that the stories of genocide were added to older war stories by post-exilic authors and were the product of 'postexilic feelings of revenge'; as such, 'the biblical battle narratives are angry fantasies [. . .] directed within the community'.[186] Absolute power over an enemy—which the ideology of the ban epitomises—was the antithesis of the contemporary military reality for these later writers, for whom Israelite victory through sheer force of arms was nothing more than a cultural memory at best. Equally, the authors and audience of the books of Numbers, Joshua, Judges, Deuteronomy, and Kings would have understood these massacre accounts as 'historical' stories that did not—and need not—reflect contemporary practice. And yet the books of the Tanakh are, inescapably, didactic religious texts. As such, descriptions of acts performed at the explicit command of Yahweh were intended to inspire, if not emulation, then admiration. In terms of ancient Israelite attitudes to ethical conduct in war, we cannot dismiss such stories as meaningless or irrelevant.

TREATMENT OF NON-COMBATANTS

Non-combatants are often depicted in the Tanakh as victims of war. We have seen above how, on certain occasions, they could be slaughtered en masse as votive devotions to Yahweh. There is almost no evidence that the Israelites afforded non-combatants any special accords or immunities in war. Indeed, a precedent for targeting children specifically was established early in the narrative of the Tanakh, by Yahweh himself, who murdered all the first-born sons

---

185. Ibid., 182–89.
186. Daniel L. Smith-Christopher, 'Gideon at Thermopylae?: On the Militarization of Miracle in Biblical Narrative and "Battle Maps"', in *Writing and Reading War: Rhetoric, Gender, and Ethics in Biblical and Modern Contexts*, ed. Brad E. Kelle and Frank Ritchel Ames (Atlanta, GA: Society of Biblical Literature, 2008), 197–212 at 209–11. Niditch has suggested that herem doctrine might indicate Israelite ethical discomfort caused by the horrors of war, especially offensive wars without any real ethical justification. By removing the responsibility for killing from human hands to Yahweh's command, the Israelites could 'offload', so to speak, the ethical ramifications of their violence. Niditch, 'War and Reconciliation', 146; *WHB*, 50–51.

of Egypt.[187] Elsewhere, the fate of non-combatants was often determined by the whims or ire of individual military commanders. The bellicose Abimelech responded to local rebellions by burning down a tower at Shechem containing a thousand men and women, and attempted to do the same at Thebez.[188] When David conquered Jerusalem from the Jebusites, he ordered the killing of the lame and the blind in revenge for a taunt the Jebusites had made during the siege.[189]

Non-combatants were spared only when a specific agreement had been made in return for services rendered, as in the case of Rahab and her family surviving the proscription of Jericho (Joshua 6), or there existed a specific incentive to keep them alive, as with the four hundred virgin girls from Jabesh-Gilead (Judges 21). The women and children of defeated enemies could be valuable commodities and were widely accepted in the ancient Near East as part of the spoils of war. When the Israelites defeated the Midianites, for example, they took 'the women and children of the Midianites captive [...] and they brought the captives, the booty, and the spoil to Moses, Eleazar the priest, and the whole Israelite community'.[190] Moses, however, was outraged that these captives had been preserved, and demanded instead that all the male children and the non-virgin females should be butchered as herem devotions. The women, whom Moses accused of having seduced some Israelites to commit idolatry, were especially to blame:

> Moses said to them, 'You have spared every female! [...] Now, therefore, slay every male among the children, and slay every woman who has known a man carnally; but spare every young woman who has not had carnal relations with a man.'[191]

One could speculate that Moses's reaction and demand that the women and children should be slaughtered was presented by the author(s) as an exceptional demand, intended to show the prophet's unwavering dedication to the Covenant. After all, the Israelites had clearly believed these people to be

---

187. Exodus 11:1–12:36. Exodus seems to attempt to justify Yahweh's slaughter of the Egyptian children by presenting it as retaliatory, stating that initially the pharaoh had given orders for all Hebrew male children to be killed (ibid. 1:16–22). Compare King Herod of Judea's 'massacre of the innocents' in the New Testament (Matthew 2:16–18).

188. Judges 9:49, 51–2.

189. 2 Samuel 5:6–8. That the lame and the blind were said to be 'hateful to David' may have been an attempt to explain the later prohibition on the blind and the lame from entering the Jerusalem Temple (ibid. 5:8). In contrast, Yadin posits that David's killing of the blind and lame was rooted in an ancient military oath ritual, evident from a Hittite text, whereby troops swore loyalty on punishment of being struck blind and deaf. The Jebusites thus paraded their blind and lame as a threat—showing that their troops had taken oaths to defend their walls to the death. Yadin, *Art of Warfare*, 269–70.

190. Numbers 31:9–12.

191. Ibid. 31:15–18.

valuable, as their assumption had been that they should preserve them as booty. During their sweeping conquest of Canaan, as recounted in the Book of Judges, many enemy populations were indeed made to do 'forced labour': that is, they were enslaved.[192]

The dashing to death of infants or the disembowelling of pregnant women was a highly emotive *topos* that occurs in several places,[193] although only in the case of Menahem were these acts performed by an Israelite.[194] The polemic of such stories was aimed at condemning the non-Israelite perpetrator (e.g., Amos 1:13) or highlighting the sufferings inflicted upon those who turn their back on Yahweh (e.g., Hosea 14:1). Michael Walzer, following Max Weber, suggests that the list of 'historical war-crimes' cited in the prophecy of Amos (Amos 1–2) consisted of 'a kind of international law that was recognised, if not consistently observed, by both Israel and its neighbours.' Walzer sees the prophet's indictments as representing a baseline of *in bello* prohibitions, 'a code for co-existence [...] to guarantee the survival of the parties, if only so that they can fight again', including prohibitions against 'the killing of women and children'.[195] However, such an interpretation appears overly optimistic and selective, especially given that Amos's predictions of Yahweh's vengeance include wiping out entire populations; this surely undermines any interpretation of Amos which claims an implicit critique of such actions.[196]

As far as can be gathered from the evidence of the Tanakh, the status of non-combatants during war was extremely perilous, and their safety could certainly not be taken for granted. Whether they became casualties of direct military violence or theologically inspired massacre, or victims of commercially driven enslavement or mass plundering of their property, Israelite ethical thought on war provided no privileged space for non-combatants, and nothing approaching a principle of *in bello* immunity.

Treatment of Prisoners of War

As has already been stated above, we cannot necessarily take these accounts of mass killing at face value. In ethical terms, most of the texts of the Tanakh were more than happy to condone the massacre of combatants and non-combatants

---

192. E.g., Judges 1:27–33.
193. 2 Kings 8:12; 15:16; Amos 1:13; Hosea 14:1.
194. 'At that time, [marching] from Tirzah, Menahem subdued Tiphsah and all who were in it, and its territory; and because it did not surrender, he massacred [its people] and ripped open all its pregnant women.' 2 Kings 15:16. For further discussion of the topos, see Cogan, '"Ripping Open Pregnant Women"; Crouch, *War and Ethics*, 93–94, 106–7; Wees, 'Genocide', 241.
195. Walzer, 'Idea of Holy War', 221. Cf. Max Weber, *Ancient Judaism*, trans. and ed. Hans H. Gerth and Don Martindale (Glencoe, IL: The Free Press, 1952), 302.
196. Amos 1:5, 8, 11, 12; 2:2.

FIGURE 48. Assyrian soldiers amputating prisoners of war, with severed heads hanging from city walls: embossed bronze band from the Balawat gates, reign of Shalmaneser III (r. c. 858–c. 824 BCE), Assyria. © Trustees of the British Museum.

alike. However, while large-scale massacres undoubtedly took place from time to time, motivated by a variety of reasons, there was scant economic or pragmatic rationale to encourage such acts. In short, defeated populations were more valuable alive than dead. But this did not guarantee that prisoners of war would be treated benignly. The Israelites were apparently capable of brutalising their war captives, and there are references to prisoners across the social spectrum being subjected to extremely cruel treatment. When the king of Bezek was defeated and captured, his Israelite captors 'cut off his thumbs and his big toes. And Adoni-bezek said, "Seventy kings, with thumbs and toes cut off, used to pick up scraps under my table; as I have done, so God has requited me."'[197] The text presented this form of mutilation as conventional, with Adoni-bezek reflecting that he himself had treated seventy other defeated kings in the same manner. The convention of subjecting prisoners of war to such punishment is further suggested by an Assyrian relief depicting soldiers amputating the hands and feet of prisoners (figure 48).

After an Israelite victory over Moab, King David summarily executed many of the prisoners according to their height:

> He made them lie down on the ground and he measured them off with a cord; he measured out two lengths of cord for those who were to be

197. Judges 1:6–7.

put to death, and one length for those to be spared. And the Moabites became tributary vassals of David.[198]

David presumably used this measurement of height, akin to the much later Mongolian practice of 'measuring against the linchpin' (executing any enemy prisoner taller than the height of a wagon wheel's axle), as a means to determine which prisoners were of military age. By executing all the adult males, David sought to subjugate the Moabites as vassals by denying them any substantial military power. Perhaps the most explicit reference to the mass killing of prisoners of war pertained to the ever-belligerent Amaziah of Judah, who ordered that ten thousand Edomite prisoners should be thrown to their deaths: 'They threw them down from the top of Sela and every one of them was burst open.'[199]

That Israelite political elites, in turn, feared becoming prisoners of war is indicated by Saul's actions in his final battle against the Philistines. Having been grievously wounded, the king asked his arms-bearer: 'Draw your sword and run me through, so that the uncircumcised may not run me through and make sport of me.' When his attendant refused, 'Saul grasped the sword and fell upon it'.[200] A desire to avoid humiliation and secure an honourable death were at play here, grounded in a fear of more prolonged agonies if taken alive. Saul feared that he would become 'sport' for his enemies. The king's fears were apparently justified as, according to the text, the Philistines took Saul's body and impaled it on the walls of Beth-shan, next to the bodies of his sons.[201] Indeed, perhaps Saul's fear that his enemies will 'run me through' actually referred to impalement whilst still alive.

Israelite kings were the not the only abusers of prisoners of war described in the Tanakh. When Samson was taken prisoner by the Philistines, his captors 'gouged out his eyes [...] and shackled him in bronze fetters, and he became a mill slave in the prison'.[202] Intriguingly, this double punishment of blinding and forced mill-labour was exactly the same fate as experienced by prisoners of war recorded in earlier second-millennium Hittite administrative texts (discussed above, ch. 7, 'Treatment of Prisoners of War'), which begs the question as to whether this was routine treatment for male prisoners of war across the ancient Levant. Finally, after the Babylonians crushed the rebellion of Zedekiah of Judah, many Judahite elites were executed as part of the

---

198. 2 Samuel 8:2.
199. 2 Chronicles 25:11–12.
200. See 1 Samuel 31:1–12, quotation at vv. 4–5.
201. Saul's armour was also taken and deposited in the temple of Ashtaroth; later, the Israelites of Jabesh-Gilead removed the bodies under the cover of night and cremated them: ibid. 31:10–12. For an alternative version of Saul's death, see 2 Samuel 1:6–16.
202. Judges 16:21.

reprisals, including leading priests and military officials.[203] No doubt this was aimed at crippling the human infrastructure of the Judahite state in order to make it more compliant.

In contrast to the hyperbolic descriptions of sanguinary Israelite rulers routinely abusing or massacring their prisoners of war (most of which incidents are said to have occurred during the conquest period), there is a handful of examples which suggest that kings of Samaria and Judah enjoyed a reputation as *malkhei hesed*—'merciful kings'.[204] During the reign of Ahab of Samaria (mid-ninth century), Ben-hadad of Aram repeatedly attacked the kingdom but was eventually defeated by the Israelites in battle:

> His ministers said to him [Ben-hadad], 'We have heard that the kings of the House of Israel are magnanimous kings. Let us put sackcloth on our loins and ropes on our heads, and surrender to the king of Israel; perhaps he will spare your life.'[205]

Ben-hadad's ministers were proved correct. Ahab and Ben-hadad subsequently negotiated a peace treaty which established shared trading rights between the two kingdoms, and Ben-hadad was released unharmed.[206] Nevertheless, King Ahab was subsequently condemned for his restraint by an unnamed prophet of Yahweh, who said to him, 'This said the Lord: Because you have set free the man whom I doomed, your life shall be forfeit for his life and your people for his people.'[207] Clearly, mercy and political pragmatism could be at odds with theological absolutism.

A variant example of Israelite mercy appears in 2 Kings 6:12–23. In response to an Aramean attack, the prophet Elisha prayed for protection to Yahweh, who responded by sending a host of angels to strike the Arameans with a blinding light. The incapacitated Arameans were then led by Elisha into the city of Samaria itself:

> When the king of Israel saw them, he said to Elisha, 'Father, shall I strike them down?' 'No, do not,' he replied. 'Did you take them captive with your sword and bow that you would strike them down? Rather, set food and drink before them, and let them eat and drink and return to their master.'[208]

---

203. 2 Kings 25:18–21. The Babylonians also sacked the city of Jerusalem and burned the Temple: ibid. 25:8–17.

204. Solomon, 'Judaism', 299.

205. 1 Kings 20:31.

206. Ibid. 20:34. Cf. 2 Kings 6:24–32, which gives an alternative history, recounting the siege of Samaria by Ben-hadad of Aram.

207. 1 Kings 20:43. On the conflict between pragmatic royal interests and prophetic interests, see also Niditch, 'War and Reconciliation', 145.

208. 2 Kings 6:21–22.

Why, on this occasion, Yahweh preferred mercy was not explained by Elisha. But the fact that Aram was not one of the Seven Nations proscribed in the books of Deuteronomy and Joshua may be one explanation.[209]

The intervention of the prophet Oded was also decisive in deciding the fate of Judahite prisoners of war captured in one of the many internecine conflicts between Samaria and Judah. Returning to Samaria with two hundred thousand prisoners ('women, boys, and girls'), King Pekah of Samaria was commanded by Oded to release his captives:

> Do you now intend to subjugate the men and women of Judah and Jerusalem to be your slaves? [... L]isten to me, and send back the captives you have taken from your kinsmen, for the wrath of the Lord is upon you![210]

Accordingly, the captives were fed, clothed, and escorted back to Jericho unharmed.[211]

While these examples are important evidence of restraint being shown by Israelites towards their prisoners of war, it must be noted that these acts of restraint were far outnumbered by acts of violence. Moreover, in the Elisha episode the king's initial assumption was that he should *execute* the prisoners—he was only prevented from this action when Elisha informed him that Yahweh willed otherwise. Similarly, in the Oded episode, the prisoners were only freed because they were fellow Israelites and thus under the protection of Yahweh. Notwithstanding the bond of kinship, it had evidently been King Pekah's intention to enslave these Judahite prisoners of war.

KILLING KINGS

As potentially high-value political prisoners, we might expect enemy kings or leaders to have been routinely offered some degree of immunity within Israelite warfare. However, the Tanakh furnishes numerous instances of kings being mutilated and/or killed but records very few instances of them being spared or bartered for political advantage.

The Book of Numbers boasted that the Israelites slew all five kings of Midian (Evi, Rekem, Zur, Hur, and Reba),[212] and after the destruction of Ai and its people, Joshua impaled the king of Ai on a stake and desecrated his corpse.[213] Some time later, having annihilated an allied Amorite host composed of armies from Jerusalem, Hebron, Jarmuth, Lachish, and Eglon, Joshua had the five

---

209. See also *WHB*, 98–99, 136.
210. 2 Chronicles 28:10–11.
211. Ibid. 28:14–15.
212. Numbers 31:7–8.
213. Joshua 8:20–29.

cowering Amorite kings dragged out of a cave. He proceded to ritually humiliate them in front of the entire Israelite army and finally 'had them put to death and impaled on five stakes'. Afterwards, their bodies were flung back into the cave in which they had sought refuge.[214] The formulaic descriptions of Joshua's victories during his Canaanite conquest invariably include the slaughter of the defeated population and the slaying of the enemy king. This occurred at Makkedah, Hazor, and Negeb, as well as throughout the hill region and the coastal plain more generally: 'from Mount Halak, which ascends Seir, all the way to Baal-gad in the Valley of the Lebanon at the foot of Mount Hermon', where 'he captured all the kings there and executed them'.[215]

When the list of defeated kings is tallied up, we see that Moses was said to have killed two kings while Joshua killed thirty-one.[216] The Book of Joshua presented this list as unambiguous proof of victory and divine favour. Indeed, some scholars have suggested that a post-exilic redactor of the Book of Joshua sought to demonise Canaanite kings specifically, depicting them in the conquest narrative as almost solely culpable for Canaanite sins against Israel. In other words, the redactor sought to show that the real 'enemy' was the kings, not their people.[217] While this is an interesting argument, it does rather overlook the indiscriminate slaughter of the populace which inevitably accompanied the demise of these kings. If the enemy's guilt was genuinely believed to stem from the king, it is still difficult to identify any sympathy for the common people; rather, the texts appear to display an assumption of corporate guilt rendering all enemy persons culpable and thus liable to harm.

The precedent established by Moses and Joshua was seemingly emulated by their successors. When the tribes of Judah and Simeon successfully advanced against the Canaanites and Perizzites and captured King Adonibezek, they mutilated and enslaved the deposed monarch, so that he died shortly afterwards in Jerusalem.[218] After the military hero Gideon captured two Midianite kings, Zebah and Zalmunna, in battle, he claimed that he would have spared them if they had not been responsible for the deaths of his own brothers:

> 'As the Lord lives, if you had spared them, I would not kill you.' And he commanded his oldest son Jether, 'Go kill them!' But the boy did not

---

214. Ibid. 10:22–27.
215. Ibid. 10:28–43; 11:10–17; 12:1–24, quotation at 11:17.
216. Ibid. 12:1–24.
217. Lawson G. Stone, 'Ethical and Apologetic Tendencies in the Redaction of the Book of Joshua', *Catholic Biblical Quarterly* 53 (1) (1991): 25–36; L. Daniel Hawk, 'Conquest Reconfigured: Recasting Warfare in the Redaction of Joshua', in *Writing and Reading War: Rhetoric, Gender, and Ethics in Biblical and Modern Contexts*, ed. Brad E. Kelle and Frank Ritchel Ames (Atlanta, GA: Society of Biblical Literature, 2008), 145–60.
218. Judges 1:5–7.

draw his sword, for he was timid, being still a boy. Then Zebah and
Zalmunna said, 'Come, you slay us; for strength comes with manhood.'
So Gideon went over and killed Zebah and Zalmunna.[219]

This passage has been interpreted as representative of the importance of reciprocity, fair play and respect; that is, an ancient form of the chivalric ethos.[220] This seems an overly generous interpretation of Gideon's actions. If we are to draw medieval parallels, the custom of the feud seems more pertinent, with Gideon exacting blood vengeance on the Midianite kings for spilling the blood of his own kin. The essentially familial context of the feud was reinforced by Gideon's desire to 'blood' his young son by having him perform the executions, physically confirming his kin's prosecution of vengeance and thus achieving an equilibrium of violence within the logic of the feud.[221] Zebah and Zalmunna understood this logic: they accepted their fate without pleas for mercy.

Even when the Israelite royal instinct was to preserve the life of enemy kings, this could be overridden by the more uncompromising demands of Yahweh's prophets. In a war against the Amalekites, Saul had captured King Agag of Amalek alive and had apparently granted him immunity.[222] This could either be taken as evidence of elites sparing elites (the 'insurance policy' thesis) or be seen as a prudential exercise in mercy for political advantage; indeed, both of these motivations could act in concert. It was relatively common in the ancient Near East for defeated rulers to be reinstalled by their conquerors as puppet kings, usually with hostages being kept at the victor's court to ensure good behaviour. However, upon learning of Saul's act of restraint, the prophet Samuel reprimanded the king for his clemency and insisted that Agag should die. Fearing divine punishment, Saul assented to Samuel's demands in order to 'please Yahweh':

> Samuel said, 'Bring forward to me King Agag of Amalek.' Agag approached him with faltering steps, and Agag said, 'Ah, bitter death is at hand!' Samuel said: 'As your sword has bereaved women, So shall your mother be bereaved among women.' And Samuel cut Agag down before the Lord at Gilgal.[223]

Samuel's moralising remark to Agag sought to place the death sentence within a framework of retributive justice: Agag had killed sons and husbands, so now

---

219. Ibid. 8:19–21.
220. *WHB*, 90, 99–100; Niditch, 'War and Reconciliation', 147.
221. On the medieval feud see, inter alia, Paul R. Hyams, *Rancor and Reconciliation in Medieval England* (Ithaca, NY: Cornell University Press, 2003); Susanna A. Throop and Paul R. Hyams (eds), *Vengeance in the Middle Ages: Emotion, Religion and Feud* (Farnham: Ashgate, 2010); Belle S. Tuten and Tracy L. Billado (eds), *Feud, Violence and Practice: Essays in Medieval Studies in Honor of Stephen D. White* (Farnham: Ashgate, 2010).
222. 1 Samuel 15:13–20.
223. Ibid. 15:32–33.

he too must die. This was a justification of sorts, but what the episode really emphasises is that kings captured in war had no 'right' to immunity in the Israelite tradition. Moreover, Agag's execution has the character of a human herem sacrifice, with the enemy king slaughtered by a priest 'before the Lord at Gilgal'.[224]

Nor were kings safe in internecine Israelite struggles. When David split away from the house of Saul, the head of his competitor Ish-bosheth was delivered to him by a pair of assassins (albeit apparently not at David's command, and against his wishes).[225] Even queens were not immune from violence. After Jehu's bloody coup d'état in Samaria, which soon spilled over into Judah, the usurper not only killed both kings, but then also sought out Jezebel, the reviled wife of Ahab and mother of the slain King Joram, and ordered that she should be defenestrated: '"Throw her down," he said. They threw her down; and her blood spattered on the wall and on the horses, and they trampled her.'[226]

Clearly, in ancient Israelite thought, royalty and elite status was no guarantee of safety in either international war or domestic power-politics. This attitude appears to mirror Assyrian practices, in which 'violence enacted against enemy persons is at its most extreme and its most explicit in the descriptions of the treatment(s) of opposition leaders and their followers'.[227] We have also seen similar brutal treatment of elites in the context of ancient Egyptian military violence. Evidently, the risks of war applied to everyone in the ancient Near East, regardless of social status.

TREATMENT OF WOMEN

One of the unusual features of Deuteronomy is its stipulations regarding the treatment of certain women captured as prisoners of war. Deuteronomy 21 describes a process whereby such women could be properly incorporated into Israelite households:

> When you take the field against your enemies, and the Lord your God delivers them into your power and you take some of them captive, and you see among the captives a beautiful woman and you desire her and would take her to wife, you shall bring her into your house, and

---

224. Compare with the agreement between King Ahab of Samaria and Ben-hadad of Aram in 1 Kings 20.

225. 2 Samuel 4:1–12.

226. 2 Kings 9:33. Somewhat incongruously, Jehu then ordered that Jezebel (or what was left of her) should be given a burial, as befitted her royal rank: '"Attend to that cursed woman and bury her, for she was a king's daughter." So they went to bury her; but all they found of her were the skull, the feet, and the hands.' Ibid. 9:34–35.

227. Crouch, *War and Ethics*, 39.

she shall trim her hair, pare her nails, and discard her captive's garb. She shall spend a month's time in your house lamenting her father and mother; after that you may come to her and possess her, and she shall be your wife. Then, should you no longer want her, you must release her outright. You must not sell her for money: since you had your will of her, you must not enslave her.[228]

We should be clear about what the stipulations did *not* do: they did not provide any substantial protection for the female captive. While the text established an initial period in which the captive was able to mourn the death of, or separation from, her parents, Deuteronomy also licensed the eventual rape of the captive—'you may come to her and possess her'—and certainly did not afford her any 'rights' in the modern sense of that term. There has been an exegetical tendency to interpret the month-long period of mourning as being on humanitarian grounds, or the 'legal respect for the female captive as a person', as the *Jewish Study Bible* puts it.[229] But the female captive was given no choice regarding sexual congress, and while she could not be sold as a slave afterwards, the captor retained the right to dismiss her from his household after the rape; thus the victim did not enjoy the full protections of marriage.

Rather than expressing humanitarian concerns, the restrictions detailed in Deuteronomy 21 may have originated as a form of taboo, during which time the foreign captive was 'purified'. The woman had to 'discard her captive's garb' and alter her physical appearance in order to be safely integrated into the Israelite religious community. In other words, the taboo period was not designed with the mental or physical well-being of the captive in mind; rather, the taboo period fulfilled a socio-religious function rooted in a concern for the purity and homogeneity of the Israelite community. It also ensured the familial honour of the male captor. The waiting period prior to the commencement of sexual relations was used to confirm that the woman was not already pregnant, thus guaranteeing that any future children were indeed sired by the captive's new master.[230]

To lend more force to this 'taboo' interpretation, we can compare attitudes to rape, and legislation concerning it, in Israelite law. In all cases, rape was viewed through a patriarchal lens, in which the requirements of protecting male honour took precedence over the well-being of women. In the early example of the rape of Dinah (see discussion above, 'Deceit and Assassination'), the vengeance enacted by the sons of Jacob against the Hivites was

---

228. Deuteronomy 21:10–14.
229. *JSB*, 414. For further discussion, see Niditch, 'War and Reconciliation', 156–57; Susan Brooks Thistlewaite, '"You may enjoy the spoil of your enemies": Rape as a Biblical Metaphor for War', in *Women, War, and Metaphor: Language and Society in the Study of the Hebrew Bible*, ed. Claudia V. Camp and Carole R. Fontaine (Atlanta, GA: Scholars Press, 1993), 15–75 at 65–66.
230. Niditch, 'War, Women, and Defilement', 50–53.

motivated primarily by wounded family honour, rather than by concern for Dinah.[231] The brutal rape and murder of the Levite's concubine by a gang of men in Gibeah resulted in a punitive war against the tribe of Benjamin, but at no point was the principal concern the horrific fate of the enslaved woman (Judges 19–20). This accords with Susan Brooks Thistlewaite's observation that '[r]ape in the Hebrew Bible is theft of sexual property'.[232] Indeed, the Levite's host in Gibeah even offered his own daughter (i.e., his own property) to the gang of rapists in an attempt to save face and protect the property of his house guest.[233] Without a hint of irony, the Book of Judges follows up the account of the Benjaminite war by describing how, in punishment for not sending men to help prosecute the aforesaid war, the collected tribes decreed that Jabesh-Gilead should be proscribed, sparing only four hundred virgin maidens as wives for the tribe of Benjamin.[234] Not content with this haul of fresh concubines, the Benjaminites soon launched an unprovoked attack against Shiloh, securing yet more sex-slaves.[235]

How do these attitudes to rape compare with the treatment of rape under Israelite law? Again, we must turn to Deuteronomy, which sought to tie female complicity in sex acts to female culpability:

> In the case of a virgin who is engaged to a man—if a man comes upon her in town and lies with her, you shall take the two of them out to the gate of that town and stone them to death: the girl because she did not cry for help in the town, and the man because he violated another man's wife. [. . .] But if the man comes upon the engaged girl in the open country, and the man lies with her by force, only the man who lay with her shall die, but you shall do nothing to the girl. [. . .] He came upon her in the open; though the engaged girl cried for help, there was no one to save her.[236]

The text quoted above clearly assumes that, in the cramped living conditions of ancient urban communities, any cry for help would be audible to a neighbour. Therefore, if no one heard a cry, the woman was assumed to have consented to the sex act. In contrast, if the rape took place outside a town, the

---

231. Genesis 34:1–31. See also the discussion of the Dinah story in Thistlewaite, '"You may enjoy the spoil"', 69–71. On the broader relationship between sexual violence and martial violence in Genesis 34, Judges 19, and 2 Samuel 13, see Alice A. Keefe, 'Rapes of Women/Wars of Men', in *Women, War, and Metaphor: Language and Society in the Study of the Hebrew Bible*, ed. Claudia V. Camp and Carole R. Fontaine (Atlanta, GA: Scholars Press, 1993),, 79–97.

232. Thistlewaite, '"You may enjoy the spoil"', 62.

233. Judges 19:22–26.

234. Ibid. 21:1–11.

235. Ibid. 21:15–24. In the 'Song of Deborah', the Canaanite women of Sisera's household presume that their master must be delayed because he is dividing the spoil of a 'damsel or two for each man', with the clear implication of sexual conquest: Ibid. 5:30.

236. Deuteronomy 22:23–27.

woman was considered blameless, because no one would hear her and be able to intervene.²³⁷ Remarkably, this Deuteronomic law on rape appears to have been taken almost verbatim from the second-millennium Hittite law code.²³⁸ The influence of Hittite diplomatic instruments on the form of the Israelite Covenant has already been noted in chapter 8, but it is fascinating to see this influence of the Hittite law code surviving into the first millennium, probably via the Neo-Hittite city-states of the Levant.²³⁹

None of the examples given above provide evidence of women being valued as anything more than slaves, concubines, or potential wives. Women were not autonomous or fully legal persons, and any sexual gratification to be gained from them during or after conflict was considered part of the spoils of war. As Thistlewaite observes, 'biblical writers did not recognize rape in war under their own designations of rape as theft of sexual property [. . .] since no sexual property holder was left alive to be offended'.²⁴⁰ While it is true that even the very minimal protection for female captives outlined in Deuteronomy 21 is more than exists from anywhere else in the ancient Near East, the driving force for this treatment of female captives was a desire to maintain the religious purity of the community and the honour of the male captor. So, while the Hellenistic Jewish philosopher Philo of Alexandria (d. c. 50 CE) urged that women 'have the privilege of exemption from war service' because of 'their natural weakness', the Tanakh contains nothing so explicit regarding female immunity.²⁴¹

War Spoils

The capture of spoils was an integral component of ancient warfare. The seizure and permanent occupation of an enemy's territory and towns could obviously be considered part of the spoils of war, but discussions of war booty more usually referred to the movable property of the enemy. Such movable

---

237. Ibid. 22:28–29 stipulates that if a man rapes a virgin who is not engaged, he must pay a fine of fifty shekels of silver to the girl's father and take her as a wife, with no right to divorce her in the future. For further discussion, see Thistlewaite, '"You may enjoy the spoil"', 63–64.

238. 'If a man seizes a woman in the mountain(s) (and rapes her), it is the man's offence, and he shall be put to death, but if he seizes her in (her) house, it is the woman's offence: the woman shall be put to death. If the (woman's) husband finds them (in the act) and kills them, he has committed no offence.' *LawH*, 156, ¶ 197; cf. *LCMAM*, 237. On the dates of the surviving legal corpus, see Hoffner in *LCMAM*, 213–14. See also Victor H. Matthews and Don C. Benjamin, *Old Testament Parallels: Laws and Stories from the Ancient Near East*, revised 3rd edn (New York: Paulist Press, 2006), 119.

239. For further discussion of the Hittite influence on Israelite Covenant forms and law, see Mendenhall, 'Ancient Oriental and Biblical Law'; Mendenhall, 'Covenant Forms'; Mendenall, *Law and Covenant*. See also the useful collection of comparative sources in *Treaty, Law and Covenant*, ed. Kitchen and Lawrence.

240. Thistlewaite, '"You may enjoy the spoil"', 69.

241. Philo of Alexandria, *On the Special Laws*, cited in Solomon, 'Judaism', 299.

property included foodstuffs, textiles, furniture, metalwork (including tools, weapons, and ornaments), and religious objects of various types. Movable property also included living booty such as livestock and human captives. As we have seen above, it was expected that non-combatant women would be seized in war. With human prisoners constituting a major component of military spoils, ancient warriors must have had a good sense of what individual captives were worth. The Book of Leviticus even specified the equivalent value of a human life vowed to Yahweh.[242]

Nevertheless, the Tanakh presents a complicated relationship between Israelites and war spoils. The source of this complication was the demand made by Yahweh to destroy, under certain circumstances, all manner of goods seized in war. In the ancient Near East it was normative for spoils to be dedicated to national deities—Egyptian, Hittite, Babylonian, Assyrian, and a multitude of lesser kings and princelings bestowed vast amounts of treasure upon the shrines of their various gods. In Egypt, for example, the temples and associated priesthoods of the principal gods were greatly enriched through the monarchy's military success; they became among the wealthiest and most powerful institutions in the land, owning vast tracts of land and huge numbers of slaves, even to the point of challenging royal authority at times. Israelite practice, as presented in the Tanakh, does not fit neatly into this mould. Those who were too covetous of war riches could be subjected to critique, such as when the dying Jacob rejected his son Benjamin and his future tribe:

> Benjamin is a ravenous wolf;
> In the morning he consumes the foe,
> And in the evening he divides the spoil.[243]

The primary cause of complications, however, was the level of destruction demanded by Yahweh of valuable war spoils in the form of herem offerings. This was juxtaposed against the standard practice of bestowing spoils upon a deity's cult site. For example, when the Philistines captured the Ark from the Israelites in battle, rather than destroy it, they 'took the Ark of God and

---

242. This may be a reference either to herem sacrifices or pledging chattels to the service of the Jerusalem Temple and the Levite priesthood. Adult males (twenty–sixty years) were valued at fifty shekels of silver; adult females (twenty–sixty years) at thirty shekels; male and female youths (five–twenty years) at twenty and ten shekels respectively; male and female elders (above sixty years) at fifteen and ten shekels; and male and female infants (up to age five) at five and three shekels respectively. See Leviticus 27:1–8, 29. Compare the values of humans and animals specified in the Hittite Law Code: *LawH*, 18–21, ¶¶ 3–7; 23–4, ¶ 10; 29–30, ¶ 19; 143–44, ¶ 180; 147, ¶ 185. Hoffner has also compiled useful tables of prices, wages, and fees for a wide range of objects, services, and penalties as taken from the laws: ibid., 7–11, Tables 2–4.

243. Genesis 49:27.

brought it into the temple of Dagon and they hung it up beside Dagon'.[244] Displaying defeated cult symbols in the precincts of national gods was conventional, as it established the power of one's own god(s) over those of one's enemies. On the Moabite Stone, meanwhile, Mesha declared that when he sacked the Israelite city of Nebo, he 'took from there the vessels of Yahweh, and [. . .] hauled them before Kemosh'.[245] It may be significant that in both of these cases, the cult items were transported rather destroyed. This was probably on account of their intrinsic value—such items were frequently constructed from valuable materials—but might also indicate an abiding fear of items imbued with religious power. It was perhaps considered safer to devote such items to one's god(s), whose occult power could nullify that of the enemy's gods, rather than risk supernatural retaliation by destroying the cultic symbols and property of enemy gods.

Yahweh, by contrast, was understood to demand the annihilation of valuable enemy people, property, and religious symbols. No exceptions were to be made. When Achan admitted to concealing a handful of spoils from Jericho (a mantle and some silver and gold), he and his entire household—his sons, daughters, ox, ass, and sheep—were stoned to death and burned along with the stolen booty.[246] However, the temptation and popular pressure to preserve valuable war spoils was intense. After Saul's defeat of Amalek, he allowed his troops to keep some of the best livestock.[247] When he was upbraided by the prophet Samuel for failing to fulfil Yahweh's commands, Saul claimed that he 'was afraid of the troops and [. . .] yielded to them'.[248] Like Achan's crime, this had severe consequences. Saul's failure to destroy King Agag and all the Amalekite property was said to be the reason for the king's rejection by Yahweh, the anointing of David as Yahweh's chosen king, and the civil war that followed.[249]

Yahweh was not always so ungenerous in responding to the material desires of his followers, and on many occasions permitted Israelites to retain booty as their own. After Achan's crime of concealment had been punished, Yahweh promised all the spoils of Ai to the Israelites—all, that is, except for the lives of the inhabitants, who were to be put to the sword for Yahweh.[250] The same norm applied for many of the conquests made by Joshua, whereby the 'Israelites kept all the spoil and cattle' but exterminated the human

---

244. See 1 Samuel 5:1–5, quotation at v. 2. Unfortunately for the Philistines, during the seven months that the Ark was in their possession, Yahweh threw down the statue of Dagon and sowed illness and haemorrhoids throughout their lands: ibid. 5:6–6:1.
245. 'Moabite Stone', *HST*, 313.
246. Joshua 7:1–26.
247. 1 Samuel 15:13–21.
248. Ibid. 15:24.
249. Ibid. 17ff.
250. Joshua 8:1–31.

populations.²⁵¹ After David's victory over Goliath, the Israelites pursued and killed the fleeing Philistines, then 'the Israelites returned from chasing the Philistines and looted their camp'.²⁵²

The fair distribution of war spoils was intrinsic to good relations within ancient military communities, and partly explains Saul's reluctance to deny his troops their share of the Amalekite plunder. The Book of Numbers provided a detailed list of booty taken from the Midianites, with clear guidelines on how it should be apportioned between Yahweh, the priestly Levites (who were not permitted to fight), the army commanders and soldiers, and the community at large.²⁵³ When David defeated a band of Amalekite raiders, he insisted that the spoil should be fairly distributed among his six hundred troops, including those two hundred men who had remained behind to guard the baggage and did not directly participate in the battle. This became 'a fixed rule for Israel, continuing to the present day'.²⁵⁴

Aside from its financial value, war booty could also fulfil a potent symbolic function as a physical embodiment of victory. David claimed both the war gear and head of Goliath, carrying and displaying the head as a trophy of victory.²⁵⁵ Later, chronicling his successes as king, the Book of Samuel recorded David's numerous military victories, the expansion of his kingdom, and the seizure of huge quantities of copper, silver, and gold 'from all the nations he had conquered'; these treasures he 'dedicated to the Lord'.²⁵⁶ As a result of the pious largesse of Israelite rulers, the Jerusalem Temple—like the shrines of other national deities—became a treasure storehouse, as the frequent emptying of it by invading armies testifies.²⁵⁷ Of course, this also testifies to the fact that not all treasure was destroyed; indeed, it is likely that the zealously ideological conquest accounts, in which the herem destruction of spoils was described, did not reflect historical Israelite practice.

Religious Property

Facing an Assyrian invasion led by King Sennacherib (r. c. 705–c. 681), Hezekiah of Judah prayed to Yahweh for aid, despairing that 'the kings of Assyria have annihilated all the nations and their lands and have committed their gods

---

251. E.g., ibid. 11:14.
252. 1 Samuel 17:53.
253. Numbers 31:25–54. The amount of booty listed is clearly fantastical. For example, thirty-two thousand slaves are said to have been captured from Midian.
254. See 1 Samuel 30:1–31, quotation at v. 25. Yadin described this act as 'one of the first of the military regulations of his [David's] army': Yadin, *Art of Warfare*, 276.
255. 1 Samuel 17:54–57.
256. 2 Samuel 8:10–11.
257. For example, 1 Kings 14:25–26; 2 Kings 18:13–16; 24:10–14; 25:8–17.

to the flames and have destroyed them'.²⁵⁸ The wanton destruction of religious property during war was recorded by the Assyrians themselves, such as in the bellicose bragging of King Aššurbanipal (c. 669–c. 631):

> The *zikkurat* (temple tower) of Susa [...] I destroyed [...]. The sanctuaries of Elam I desecrated. Its gods (and) goddesses I counted as powerless ghosts. Their secret groves, into which no stranger (ever) penetrates, whose borders he never (over)steps—into these my soldiers entered, saw their mysteries, and set them on fire.²⁵⁹

In light of the religiously infused logic of the period, there was good reason for depriving the enemy of their cultic sites. When conquerors removed a defeated state's sacred images they were not only symbolically celebrating their victory and humiliating the enemy, but also removing the defeated state's medium for divine communication and aid. In Hatti, the 'land of the thousand gods', such cultic images were generally deposited in Hittite temples and could be assimilated into the Hittite pantheon as lesser gods. In Assyria, defeated gods could be treated with respect but were also liable to be bestowed as 'slaves' upon the Assyrian great gods, or simply destroyed altogether.²⁶⁰

According to the First Book of Kings, the Jerusalem Temple, so meticulously constructed by Solomon, survived intact for just one generation before it was stripped by the invading army of Pharaoh Shishak (possibly Sheshonq I; see figure 15) of Egypt, during the reign of Solomon's son Rehoboam:

> In the fifth year of King Rehoboam, King Shishak of Egypt marched against Jerusalem and carried off the treasures of the House of the Lord and the treasures of the royal palace. He carried off everything; he even carried off all the golden shields that Solomon had made.²⁶¹

In the sixth century the Jerusalem Temple was stripped bare by the Babylonians after King Jehoiachin of Judah ('who did what was evil in the eyes of the Lord') rebelled against Babylon but was forced to surrender to Nebuchadnezzar.²⁶² Zedekiah, Jehoiachin's successor, failed to learn the lesson and eventually he too rebelled and was defeated. This led to more severe reprisals:

---

258. Isaiah 37:18–19.
259. Cited in Altman, 'Earliest Recorded Concepts', 128.
260. Ibid., 127–28.
261. 1 Kings 14:25–26; cf. 2 Chronicles 12:2–9. The biblical Shishak and his sack of Jerusalem may be identifiable with the pharaoh Sheshonq I (c. 945–c. 924), founder of the Twenty-Second Dynasty, who led an Asiatic campaign around the year 930. However, a fragmentary stele from Karnak and a triumphal scene on the south wall of the hypostyle lists 154 towns destroyed during Sheshonq I's campaign, but does not mention Israel or Judah by name. See *ANEA*, 1:187; Redford, *Egypt, Canaan, and Israel*, 312.
262. 2 Kings 24:13. The royal household and over eight thousand Judahites were sent into exile in Babylon: ibid. 24:10–16.

rather than loot the Temple (there can have been precious little left to steal), the Babylonians destroyed it along with the great buildings of the city:

> Nebuzaradan, the chief of the guards, an officer of the king of Babylon, came to Jerusalem. He burned the House of the Lord, the king's palace, and all the houses of Jerusalem; he burned down the house of every notable person [...] tore down the walls of Jerusalem on every side [...] broke up the bronze columns of the House of the Lord, the stands, and the bronze tank that was in the House of the Lord; and they carried the bronze away to Babylon [and] took whatever was of gold and whatever was of silver.[263]

When we turn our attention to the conduct of Israelite armies, the sense of the vulnerability of religious property is only enhanced. The theological drive of the Tanakh's post-exilic redactors, who were determined to assert Yahwist monotheism, presented Israel as distinctly uncompromising towards any aberrant religious practices. As tangible expressions of non-Yahweh worship, cult shrines and sacred groves (as well as their priests) were to be deliberately targeted for destruction. The importance of destroying religious property was introduced very early in the story of Israel. Foretelling the conquest of Canaan in the book of Exodus, Yahweh outlined the two-pronged thrust of the Israelite attack: he would lay low the enemy while his followers would destroy their sacred places:

> When My angel goes before you and brings you to the Amorites, the Hittites, the Perizzites, the Canaanites, the Hivites, and the Jebusites, and I annihilate them, you shall not bow down to their gods in worship or follow their practices, but shall tear them down and smash their pillars to bits.[264]

This message, and the imperative of destroying religious sites, was again emphasised by Yahweh during Moses's second ascent of Sinai. Indeed, it was a central tenet of the Covenant:

> Beware of making a covenant with the inhabitants of the land [...]. No, you must tear down their altars, smash their pillars, and cut down their sacred posts; for you must not worship any other god, because the Lord, whose name is Impassioned, is an impassioned God.[265]

In spite of this warning, some Israelites violated the Covenant by taking Moabite women as sexual partners and partaking in ceremonies dedicated to

---

263. Ibid. 25:8–9, 13, 15.
264. Exodus 23:23–24.
265. Ibid. 34:12–14.

Baal-peor. In revenge, Yahweh ordered Moses to impale the ringleaders and wage war against the Midianites.[266]

On the eve of invading Canaan, Moses reminded the Israelites of Yahweh's edict to destroy the enemy's sacred sites—their religious symbols were not even to be taken as spoils: 'you shall tear down their altars, smash their pillars, cut down their sacred posts, and consign their images to the fire'.[267] Moses warned, 'You shall consign the images of their gods to the fire; you shall not covet the silver and gold on them and keep it for yourselves.'[268] In case this message had failed to register with his audience, it was repeated a third time:

> You must destroy all the sites at which the nations you are to dispossess worshipped their gods, whether on lofty mountains and on hills or under any luxuriant tree. Tear down their altars, smash their pillars, put their sacred posts to the fire, and cut down the images of their gods, obliterating their name from that site.[269]

Given the prominence of these violent exhortations within the narrative, there are surprisingly few explicit references to this type of systematic destruction of religious sanctuaries and symbols actually being carried out by the Israelites. Perhaps, when the books of Joshua and Judges described the herem proscription of towns and communities during the conquest, the authors naturally assumed that this included the destruction of religious sites as described in Exodus and Deuteronomy. Samson's final suicidal act was to destroy the temple of the Philistines, pulling the building down upon himself and thousands of his captors. While Samson himself had no role in choosing this 'target' (it was simply the place where the Philistines had chained him), the miraculous destruction of the enemy's temple was clearly intended to convey a powerful religious symbolism.[270]

In contrast, when David defeated the Philistines at Baal-peratzim, the Israelites seized the idols as booty rather than destroying them then and there: 'The Philistines abandoned their idols there, and David and his men carried them off.'[271] This discrepancy was noticed by the authors of the later Book of Chronicles, which reported the same incident in different terms, stressing that David had in fact destroyed the images of Baal rather than keeping them as spoils: 'And they abandoned their deities there, and David commanded, and they were burnt with fire.'[272]

---

266. Numbers 25:1–9, 16–18.
267. Deuteronomy 7:5.
268. Ibid. 7:25.
269. Ibid. 12:2–3.
270. Judges 16:23–30.
271. 2 Samuel 5:17–21.
272. 1 Chronicles 14:12. Cf. Isaiah 46:1–2; 37:19.

When Israelite rulers were specifically credited with destroying religious property, this more commonly referred to shrines *within* Israelite territory and constructed, in breach of the Covenant, by Israelites themselves. Numerous Israelite kings from Solomon onwards were apparently guilty of this crime. In response, King Hezekiah of Judah fervently instituted a number of religious reforms, including the destruction of shrines and the smashing of idols within and beyond Judahite territory, so that 'the Lord was always with him; he was successful wherever he turned'.[273] Ironically, Hezekiah's bellicosity caught the attention of Sennacherib of Assyria, who forced Judah's political submission and Hezekiah was consequently compelled to strip the Jerusalem Temple (including the gold plates off the doors) to pay the required Assyrian tribute.[274] Thus Hezekiah's desecration of non-Yahweh shrines was lauded as pious, yet his political actions resulted in his desecration of Yahweh's holiest cult site. The hubris implied by this series of events goes unremarked by the author(s) of the Book of Kings.

Perhaps most surprising of all, when Jehoash of Samaria attacked Jerusalem in response to the unwarranted aggression of King Amaziah of Judah, the Second Book of Kings tells us that the northern Israelite king looted the Jerusalem temple, seizing 'all the gold and silver and all the vessels that were in the House of the Lord'.[275] Here, then, we have an example of an Israelite king violating the sanctity of supposedly the most sacred Yahweh shrine, treating it simply as a source of booty. Nor did religious shrines offer any guarantee of refuge for those seeking protection, even within Israelite territory. According to the Book of Exodus, individuals accused of murder could be seized from the sanctuary of an altar by an 'avenger of blood'—that is, a kinsman of the slain.[276]

In sum, Israelite warlords probably followed a pattern similar to that of other ancient Near Eastern warlords: seizing wealth and statues from sacred sites so as to enrich themselves and demonstrate their power. Abducted images of gods were probably used to fulfil a religio-political function, being placed in Israelite temples to exhibit their subjugation or ritually destroyed as part of victory ceremonies. It is also possible that religious statuary was simply stripped of any precious materials and then discarded, although fears of the persisting latent power of occult images would probably have necessitated their destruction. Occasionally, however, a more violent approach may have been adopted (akin to Aššurbanipal's treatment of Elam)—demolishing, smashing, or burning sacred sites and images in situ as an act of overt political domination and/or punishment of the defeated community.

Whatever the exact mechanics may have been, we can conclude that there was no norm of immunity for religious property in ancient Israelite culture,

---

273. 2 Kings 18:1–8.
274. Ibid. 18:13–16.
275. Ibid. 14:12–14.
276. Exodus 21:14; cf. Deuteronomy 19:12.

and probably not in Israelite warfare either. If it escaped destruction, religious property was treated as part of the spoils of war, like spoil from other sources. Thus first-millennium Israelite military culture and practice appears to be in line with ancient Near Eastern military culture and practice more generally, which manifestly lacked any normative protections for religious property or persons. Any tradition of restraint that may have existed in the early first millennium was thoroughly expunged by the Tanakh's exilic and post-exilic redactors, who sought to reconstitute Israelite history to emphasise the violent purging of non-Yahwist cults in Israel's past. Asserting a thoroughly uncompromising version of Yahwist monotheism and Israelite exceptionalism, such authors and redactors left behind only faint hints of the pragmatism of their warrior forbears—such as Saul's gift of Amalekite property to his army, or the discrepancy between David's actions as described in the Second Book of Samuel (5:17–21) and in the later First Book of Chronicles (14:12). Such political and military leaders would surely in fact have preferred to seize valuable religious property as spoil than consign it all to the flames.

Personal Immunities

PRIESTS

Most non-combatants were afforded no meaningful protections in Israelite military culture. But were there any customary immunities for special categories of non-combatant persons: namely, priests and ambassadors?

The Tanakh sought to confirm the preeminence of Yahweh over all other gods or, in its more radical monotheistic statements, the non-existence of other gods. It should come as little surprise, therefore, that priests dedicated to competing religious traditions were not accorded any immunity from violence; indeed, they were ruthlessly targeted. For example, after Jehu's military takeover of Samaria and Judah, all the priests and worshippers of Baal were gathered together and promptly massacred.[277] This echoed the actions of the prophet Elijah during the reign of Ahab of Samaria, who challenged and then slaughtered 850 priests of Baal and Ashera on Mount Carmel.[278] The slaughter necessitated both an act of deception (violating a promise of safe-conduct) and shocking brutality.[279] Similarly, when the so-called 'ancient' scroll was

---

277. 2 Kings 10:18–28.

278. 1 Kings 18:19–40. The massacre orchestrated by Elijah was, in part, revenge for Jezebel's killing of Yahweh's prophets (ibid. 18:4).

279. Bucking the scholarly trend, Frances Flannery posits that a post-exilic reworking of 1 Kings 18–19 'has crafted a tightly woven critique of Eliahu's [Elijah's] warlike behaviour'. Frances Flannery, '"Go back by the way you came": An Internal Textual Critique of Elijah's Violence in 1 Kings 18–19', in *Writing and Reading War: Rhetoric, Gender, and Ethics in Biblical and Modern Contexts*, ed. Brad E. Kelle and Frank Ritchel Ames (Atlanta, GA: Society of Biblical Literature, 2008), 161–73 at 172.

discovered in the Jerusalem Temple during the reign of Josiah, it prompted a spate of reforms which included the killing of priests of non-Yahweh cults.[280]

If the Tanakh presented the killing of non-Yahweh priests as desirable in the domestic sphere, then we would hardly expect it to express a commitment to priestly immunity in the military sphere. However, other than the murder of the priest Balaam and the general descriptions of slaughter in the conquest accounts discussed above, there are very few explicit references to the killing of enemy priests specifically.[281]

Concerning protections for Yahwist priests, which may have been of relevance to internecine Israelite conflict, some sense of immunity is indicated by the separation of the role of the priest from the rest of the Israelite community. The tribe of Levi was dedicated to guarding the Tabernacle and performing religious duties, and were to physically separate themselves from the army encampment.[282] This was a matter of ritual purity, for in handling the sacred utensils and the Ark and in performing religious rites, priests could not pollute themselves by shedding human blood. The descendants of Aaron became the priestly *Kohanim* caste and were exempted from military duties. It was taboo for Levite priests even to touch a corpse.[283] Moses, the archetypal prophet of Yahweh, did not physically take part in combat, but rather directed Yahweh's power from a distance.[284]

The immunity of Yahwist priests *within* Israelite military culture is suggested by the outrage associated with the single blatant act of violence against them. During the civil war between Saul and David, the priest Ahimelech sheltered David in the Levite city of Nob, and, interpreting this as an act of treachery and rebellion, Saul ordered the execution of the city's priests:

> And the king commanded the guards standing by, 'Turn about and kill the priests of the Lord, for they are in league with David; they knew he was running away and they did not inform me.' But the king's servants would not raise a hand to strike down the priests of the Lord. Thereupon the king said to Doeg, 'You, Doeg, go and strike down the priests.' And Doeg the Edomite went and struck down the priests himself; that day, he killed eighty-five men who wore the linen ephod. He put Nob, the town of the priests, to the sword: men and women, children and infants, oxen, asses, and sheep—[all] to the sword.[285]

The refusal of Saul's Israelite troops to perform the command was clearly intended as a literary device to underline Saul's madness as well as the reprehensibility of his actions. Only an Edomite, who as a Gentile had no concern for Yahweh's law

---

280. 2 Kings 22:8–23:25.
281. For the killing of Balaam, see Numbers 31:8.
282. Ibid. 1:47–53.
283. Leviticus 21:1–2, 11.
284. Exodus 17:8–16.
285. 1 Samuel 22:6–19.

or the priest's inviolability, was willing to carry out the order. To stress the blasphemy and moral fall of the king further, the narrator adds that Saul proscribed the entire city in a perverse imitation of Yahweh's ban on the Nations.

ENVOYS AND AMBASSADORS

The Tanakh offers sparse evidence of either hospitality or hostility being shown to foreign envoys or ambassadors.[286] The account of the assassination of Eglon was based on what can only be described as a serious breach of diplomatic norms by the Israelite Ehud, who exploited his role as an envoy to approach Eglon privately and murder him.[287] When a young Amalekite messenger arrived at the court of David and reported that he had delivered the coup de grâce to Saul (at Saul's own request), David had the Amalekite executed.[288] Though the young soldier was not an official diplomatic envoy of Amalek, this is hardly indicative of concrete immunities for foreign messengers to the court.

In turn, David's own envoys suffered mistreatment in Ammon. Having been sent to offer David's condolences on the death of their king, the Ammonites suspected the Israelites of espionage. The envoys were seized and suffered the humiliation of having half their beards shaved off and their clothes rent in two, after which they were sent packing. David was predictably infuriated by this insult, citing a breach of diplomatic norms as a cause for his subsequent war.[289] That David saw the mistreatment of his envoys as a cause for war suggests that there did exist a normative expectation that envoys were to be treated respectfully at foreign courts, and were not to be harmed. Seeing it in this light, we may indeed be witnessing the force of this peremptory diplomatic norm, in that this breach was exceptional enough to justify war and be considered worthy of mention within the narrative.

Finally, in characteristically bloody fashion, the Samaritan usurper Jehu butchered Judahite nobles unfortunate enough to time their diplomatic visit to the Judahite royal court during his ruthless purge of the kingdom. The kinsmen of Ahaziah (the Judahite king assassinated by Jehu), who had come to pay their respects to the royal family, were seized and then slaughtered 'at the pit of Beth-eked, forty-two of them; he did not spare a single one.'[290]

---

286. For further analysis, see Meier, *Messenger*, 36–42, 116–19, 186–190ff.

287. Judges 3:15–30, and discussed above, 'Deceit and Assassination'.

288. 2 Samuel 1:14–16.

289. Ibid. 10:1–19. Envoys were considered a personification of the state and its gods, therefore to 'offend an ambassador was an insult to the sending nation, and was an invitation for war': *ILA*, 75.

290. 2 Kings 10:13–14. While Second Kings records that Jehu murdered Jehoram and Ahaziah, the author of the Tel Dan stele—possibly Hazael of Aram—claims, 'I killed Jehoram, son of Ahab, king of Israel and I killed Ahaziahu, son of Jehoram, king of the house of David. And I set their towns into ruins and turned their land into desolation.' 'Tel Dan stele', *HST*, 307.

Overall, then, immunity for diplomatic personnel was presented inconsistently throughout the Tanakh. One finds examples of diplomatic protections being ignored by both Israelites and non-Israelites, as well as examples of anger when such protections were ignored. As in the case of ambushes, deceit, and assassination, the morality of such breaches appears to have been dependent on how the texts viewed the particular personage responsible.

Conclusions to Part III

The evidence examined over the last three chapters has provided copious examples of just war thought in ancient Israelite culture. However, just as in the cases of Egyptian and Hittite just war thought, this positive assertion must be accompanied by several important caveats.

First and foremost, while there is compelling evidence for strains of *ius ad bellum* thought about war, evidence for equally well-developed *ius in bello* thought or customs is largely absent. Another important caveat is that, analogous to the Egyptian case, Israelite ideas of just war were highly partisan and absolutist. And yet, as in Hatti, the Israelites recognised their own capacity for sin. There are frequent references to Yahweh's chosen people acting against the wishes of their deity and thus violating their covenant with him. Both commoner and king was capable of sin; indeed, the kings of Samaria and Judah were targets for vitriolic criticism, and even a great king like Solomon was understood to be capable of impious corruption. As the story of Israel, Samaria, and Judah unfolds in the Tanakh, these sins become increasingly stark, and finally lead to the destruction of the Israelite kingdoms and the humiliation of their rulers and peoples.

Even here, however, Israelite ethics remained highly partisan. Israel's enemies might have triumphed over it, but not because they were intrinsically righteous or held a legitimate political grievance. Rather, Yahweh utilised Israel's enemies as a convenient stick to beat the Israelites with, in punishment for their violation of the Covenant. Even in defeat, Israelite war ethics gave no space to accord justice to their non-Israelite enemies, and the legal or ethical relationship between Israel and its enemies was often not considered at all. Central to this conception of war was the relationship between Yahweh and Israel itself, which throughout the varied books of the Tanakh consistently remained the point of focus for assessments of the justice of particular military activities.

In spite of these caveats, a number of assertions can still be made concerning the character of Israelite war ethics. There was a well-developed understanding of the necessity of proper authority to wage war, and this authority was rooted in an individual's relationship with Yahweh. While Yahweh was the ultimate authority and arbiter of justice, his anointed ruler—whether a 'judge' such as Joshua or a monarch such as David or Hezekiah—could wage war under his authority and according to his commands. As long as an individual honoured Yahweh and the Covenant, and did what was pleasing to the diety, then it was assumed that he had the necessary authority to wage just war. However, if a war leader (such as Saul), or even an individual within that war leader's army (such as Achan), violated the Covenant and thus altered the terms of the relationship with Yahweh, authority to wage war in Yahweh's name and, importantly, with Yahweh's aid, could and would be swiftly removed. To this extent, authority to wage war began and finished with Yahweh.[291] As an extension of this divine authority, Israelite texts—especially those recounting the story of the conquest of Canaan—were at pains to show Yahweh's physical presence and supernatural support of Israelite armies. Such support was crucial for military victory.

Israelite war ethics also displayed a concern for just cause, although not always in the sense in which we understand just cause in modern just war doctrine. The permissible defence of territory appears to have been a relatively straightforward assumption within Israelite thought, and the retributive purpose of war also played a major role. Indeed, the punishment of a wide range of injuries was a common justification for war. It must be stressed that, in many cases, the 'injury' was not suffered by the Israelites themselves, but by Yahweh. The justification for the invasion of Canaan was entirely on this basis. There were even occasions when the absence of physical injury was so blatant that the Israelites appear solely as an unreasonable aggressor (such as at Jericho, or Ai, or Leshem/Laish). Yet these aggressive wars were presented as permissible, on the basis of Yahweh's 'gift' to the Israelites or his condemnation of the foreign nations involved.

This is where the Israelite concept of just cause differs substantially from modern conceptions: the actions of the enemy were only of secondary importance in establishing just cause. This may sound somewhat paradoxical, but actually further emphasises that Israelite war ethics, as formulated in the Tanakh, were entirely focused on the Israelites' perceived relationship with Yahweh, and *not* on the Israelites' mundane relationship with their neighbours and enemies. Just like the ancient Egyptian perception of foreigners as representative of Isfet (injustice, destruction, disorder), Israelite thought (as it appears in the Tanakh) perceived all non-Yahwist, non-Israelite peoples as inferior and unjust. Such peoples could never possess 'just cause' against Israel, but might nevertheless be utilised by Yahweh to chastise Israelites for violations of the Covenant.

Other familiar just causes were deemed less important, or at least were given far less attention. The defence of people (rather than territory) or of allies was given short shrift by the authors and redactors of the Tanakh. The

---

291. See also Lind, *Yahweh is a Warrior*, who makes a similar argument but on *very* different assumptions about the historicity of the scriptural texts.

relative justice of rebellion and its suppression was dependent on the relative moral/religious standing of the individual who was rebelling, although there does seem to have been a certain respect for the sacrality of the monarch as the representative of Yahweh's authority.

When we consider norms usually associated with the *ius in bello* tradition, the picture is very different. There were certainly no prohibitions on types of weapons, with Israel's most famous warrior and king, David, using a peasant's sling. Nor were there restrictions on tactics, with ambushes and night attacks even being ordered by Yahweh himself. Supernatural powers and magical rods were frequently taken advantage of during battles, although the authors of the Tanakh—as well as modern biblical scholars—presented these as categorically different from directly comparable uses of magic by the Israelites' enemies. In truth, the distinction is interpretive rather than substantive, betraying a desire to present Yahweh-magic as a type of 'true' and 'proper' supernatural power in contradistinction to the 'false' and 'improper' magical operations of non-Yahwist peoples.

Deceit and assassination occupied an ambiguous moral position within Israelite thought, being both condemned and praised. Assassination, in particular, appears as a morally neutral action per se—its moral status being determined by the motivations of the assassin and the character of his or her victim. Whereas some assassinations and deceptions were considered unacceptable, to assassinate or deceive wicked persons for the greater good of the Israelite community and in the service of Yahweh was ethically permissible and even laudable.

Even the oft-cited prescriptions of Deuteronomy 20 and 21, regardless of when they were actually composed or what historical period they best represent, offer little in the way of substantive *in bello* ethical norms. A close analysis reveals a set of ordinances inspired by pragmatic military requirements or taboo-based concerns regarding the integration of aliens into Israelite communities. I see no evidence that the Deuteronomic ordinances were inspired by ethical or humanitarian concerns for individuals, places, or objects during wartime. Devastation of property and the targeting of non-combatants was considered an essential element of Israelite warfare. Prisoners of war were given no normative protections, and this included enemy elites, who could be mutilated and impaled. Enemy priests and religious sites were particularly vulnerable to exceptionally harsh treatment.

This is not to say that *in bello* norms were completely absent from the Israelite martial tradition. Like other ancient Near Eastern societies, declarations of war and challenges to battle appear to have been part of the war-making process, and duels appear to have followed certain customary and ritualistic rules of engagement. However, the apparent frequency with which Israelites exploited ambush tactics indicates that an open challenge to battle was not strictly necessary.

Similarly, standard Near Eastern diplomatic norms regarding the immunity of envoys appear to have been acknowledged, if not always observed. Likewise, when a treaty was agreed with the Gibeonites (despite their deception), Joshua felt compelled to honour its terms. Later Samaritan and Judahite kings were said to have concluded treaties with various states across the region, although they also appear to have broken these treaties with some regularity, albeit frequently to their own detriment. Israelite rulers were not atypical in acting in this manner; the dynamic international relations of the second- and first-millennium Levant shows warlords, princelings, and kings constantly jockeying for position and seeking their own advantage, often regardless of existing political commitments.

Taken as a whole, there is scant evidence to suggest anything more than the bare bones of a *ius in bello* framework within Israelite war ethics. The vague protections implied by the prudential stipulations of Deuteronomy 20 are counterbalanced by numerous references to the gratuitous mass killing of non-combatants and the destruction of property. Thus the case for the existence of Israelite *in bello* norms is comparable to that for Egypt and for Hatti: at best, they were ad hoc and extremely limited and provided no guarantees of restraint or protection in any area of warfare. When viewed in a Near Eastern context encompassing the period c. 3000–c. 450, the Israelites were broadly unremarkable in their attitudes to the conduct of war and conformed to widespread regional attitudes and practices.[292]

A brief overview of the difficulties and debates involved in dating the texts of the Tanakh was provided in chapter 8. In light of these complexities, it should be evident to readers that, in reflecting upon Israelite just war thought as presented in the Tanakh, it is impossible to say with certainty to what extent it reflected historical attitudes to war at any specific point in time. Throughout Part III, I have maintained a cautious dating of the Tanakh, placing most of the texts in their current form in the period immediately prior to, during, and following the Judahite exile of the sixth century. Though it is likely that various elements of Israelite thought on war were shaped by cultural and military traditions dating back to the early first millennium (possibly earlier), we lack sufficient corroborative evidence to graft these intellectual positions onto historical practices of Israelite warfare during the first millennium, and certainly not onto those of the second millennium.

The most we can say with any degree of confidence, I believe, is that the war ethics outlined in this and the preceding chapters can be taken as representative of the views of elite Israelites in the period from roughly 750 to 450 BCE, when the majority of the Tanakh assumed its final form. The texts containing these views were compiled, written, and rewritten by scholars, rather

---

292. Crouch reaches the same conclusion when comparing the first-millennium kingdoms of Samaria and Judah to Neo-Assyrian military practices: Crouch, *War and Ethics*, 96.

than actual warriors, but they were surely intended for a wider audience that would have included Israelites drawn from various, including military, backgrounds. Moreover, although independent Israelite armies effectively ceased to exist during the sixth century, this did not entail the termination of Israelite experiences of war. Whether as victims of regional military violence, or serving as auxiliaries and mercenaries in the armies of Assyria, Babylon, Persia, and other smaller polities, Israelites continued to accrue experiences of war. Such roles were entirely compatible with the martial ideas contained within the Tanakh, for it was as mercenaries and raiders (*habiru*) that the Israelites were imagined as first appearing on the geopolitical stage of the Near East. Whilst undoubtedly providing an idealised and ideological world-view and history, the texts of the Tanakh must have retained at least a degree of relevance and credibility in the eyes and ears of their audience. After all, texts which presented a world-view totally at odds with the expectations and values of their contemporaries would not have enjoyed the prestige and authority enjoyed by those of the Tanakh.

CONCLUSION

The Characteristics of Ancient Just War Thought

ONE OF THE fundamental questions posed by this study has been whether ancient Near Eastern states conceived of wars as either 'good wars' or 'bad wars', and, building on this conceptual and moral distinction, whether they developed what could accurately be described as 'just war thought'. In answer to this question, there has emerged substantial evidence of just war thought in each of the societies examined. Evidence of just war thought has emerged from a variety of sources, including royal annals and campaign diaries, public and personal art and architecture, mythology, literature and poetry of various types, personal prayers, administrative correspondence, diplomatic legal instruments, and law codes. This evidence points to the fact that Egyptians, Hittites, and Israelites did indeed conceive of war as good or bad, just or unjust.

What is perhaps most striking is that for each society there is substantial evidence of patterns of thought addressing *ius ad bellum* concerns. The highly sophisticated and militaristic kingdoms of the Middle and Late Bronze Age sought to enhance and maintain their imperial power with the help of the gods, so they were particularly attuned to claims of authority and justice, and how those played out in the arena of warfare and international relations. In Egypt and Hatti, the development of just war thought was closely tied to royal ideology. While we do have numerous sources that were not *direct* products of the monarchical regimes, it is fair to say that the majority of such sources reflect an elite culture which closely mirrored, and probably attempted to emulate, the dominant ideology of the royal centre.

Even after the decline of the Egyptian and Hittite empires, interest in the relationship between authority, justice, war, and divine favour continued in expansionist states such as Neo-Assyria and, to a lesser extent, Neo-Babylon. It was in this cultural and political milieu that the Israelites emerged as political players. We will probably never know for certain whether a united Israelite kingdom was a historical reality or not, and we can be even less confident about the processes that led to the emergence of the Israelites as an identifiable people in the ancient Levant. What we can say is that both Samaria and Judah were embroiled in Levantine politics and warfare by the early first millennium, and that by the mid-first millennium the authors and redactors of the Tanakh showed an active interest in questions of authority, justice, and war. Throughout their telling of Israelite history, these interests were focused on establishing the Israelites' sovereignty over the land of Canaan, as well as conveying a sense of eschatological purpose governed by Yahweh's providential plan. More often than not, stories about war were refracted through this eschatological lens, so that narratives of terrestrial warfare frequently became vehicles for reflection on cosmological questions about Yahweh's power in the world and the destiny of the Israelites as a chosen people.

Despite the political, social, and cultural differences between each of the three principal societies examined, their patterns of *ius ad bellum* thought display numerous similarities. In all three, the ultimate source of authority for waging war was divine: a national deity or deities of some description. In the cases of Egypt and Hatti, this divine authority was mediated exclusively through the king, and in Egypt the monarch came to be personally endowed with a quasi-divine authority. In Israel, divine authority could be mediated through a number of different persons—prophets, war leaders, kings—but all were considered to be empowered by Yahweh. In all three societies, the war leader acted as a protector of his (or in Egypt, occasionally her) people, and this was closely tied to broader notions of just rulership, whereby the king was obligated to uphold the domestic laws, peace, security, and cultic rituals of the realm.

In Egyptian, Hittite, and Israelite thought there were also clear concepts of the legitimacy of self-defence. The most important aspect of this form of violence was the defence of territory and the defence of property, which could extend to war being used as a means to restore stolen property. The defence of people was secondary to this, although it remained a legitimate cause for war. It should also be remembered that people were frequently viewed as a form of property, or synonymous with territory, so ideas of self-defence rooted in rightful ownership could be understood as the root of defensive war for the state's territory *and* subjects.

Punitive violence also featured prominently in all three societies, and was essentially considered an extension of self-defensive violence. Seeking vengeance against enemies for various injuries was commonly accepted as a form of just punishment and a legitimate cause for war. Importantly, wars of vengeance could be prosecuted on the grounds of both mundane and divine injuries. Wrongs done to the gods (such as the sacking of their sanctuaries) were certainly understood as deserving of punishment, and such wars were prosecuted with the full expectation of divine support. In Israelite thought especially, punitive violence could be presented solely in terms of avenging injuries to Yahweh, regardless of whether the Israelites themselves had suffered physical injuries at the hands of their opponents. Indeed, the account of the conquest of Canaan was presented almost entirely in these terms.

The justified defence of allies appears as a recurring theme, although it is far more prominent in Hittite and Egyptian than in Israelite evidence. Two factors go a long way towards explaining this, one geopolitical, the other theological. First, Hatti and Egypt were major political powers that controlled numerous vassal states, and it was a political reality that vassal states would appeal for military aid from their overlords. Indeed, it was standard for diplomatic treaties to state explicit conditions for military aid from vassal and suzerain alike. As a result, Hittite and Egyptian royal ideology presented such aid as part of the obligations and actions of the just monarch. The Israelites never achieved a comparable level of geopolitical power, and so were not forced to think about the moral and legal ramifications of alliances to quite the same extent. Nevertheless, if we had access to a historical corpus of Samaritan or Judahite diplomatic treaties (which these kingdoms surely produced), such instruments would likely provide evidence for concepts of just defence of allies within Israelite political thought. Secondly, the theologically driven narrative of the Tanakh presents the Israelites as a people uniquely close to Yahweh and entirely dependent upon the god's favour for their political success. Such a narrative was less inclined to highlight the Israelites or Israelite kingdoms as working with, or dependent upon, non-Israelite and non-Yahwist political communities, whether as overlords or as allies.

Finally, all three of these ancient societies show a distinct concern for the repression of rebellion within the state and amongst vassals. They interpreted such acts as a just cause for war, and all three justified the use of extreme violence to quell sedition or revolts. The royal institutions in all three societies suffered perennial problems of internal instability, with many Egyptian, Hittite, Samaritan, and Judahite monarchs facing challenges to their authority from within their respective kingdoms or empires. Usurpation and/or assassination were a real threat for ancient Near Eastern kings and princes. It was natural, therefore, that royal ideology—which strove to bolster royal authority—should readily justify wars to quash internal challenges to the monarch. In Egypt especially, rebellion was presented as a crime more heinous than external aggression (which was to be expected from the barbaric forces of Isfet), because it represented a perversion of the harmony of Ma'at within Egypt itself. It is notable that, as Egyptian power and ideology became more imperialistic and grandiose during the course of the second millennium, external enemies were increasingly conceptualised not as autonomous external competitors, but as rebels.

The Absence of Ius in bello Norms in Ancient Near Eastern Just War

This study has looked in depth at ancient attitudes regarding *how* wars should be fought. It has discussed attitudes to weapons, acceptable and unacceptable tactics, the treatment of enemy combatants, non-combatants, and prisoners of war, and the treatment of property, of religious sites, of women, and of envoys.

The inescapable conclusion is that there was very little which could be described as *ius in bello* thought in any of the ancient societies examined, let alone an identifiable *ius in bello* tradition. There is no evidence that certain types of weapons were considered illicit, and in fact missile weapons such as bows and javelins were considered elite arms and were closely associated with ideals of warrior masculinity. Even the humble sling features prominently in the story of Israel's most famous warrior king, David. Similarly, tactics were not subject to any normative moralising, although we do see some variation in how certain tactics were presented, dependent upon *who* was using them. Ambushes, night attacks, and deception were all vaunted when used to achieve victory for one's own side; in contrast, when the same tactics were utilised by an enemy, they were generally described as cowardly or dishonourable. The oft-cited 'laws' of Deuteronomy 20 concerning the conduct of siege warfare were prudential rather than humanitarian in essence. They were pragmatic, not ethical, restraints, and they were certainly not 'laws' in any meaningful sense. They allowed for cities to be taken without the risk and expense of assault or siege. Enemies were offered nothing more than their lives, and even those were forfeited in bondage to their conquerors. Likewise, while a city's valuable arboreal resources could be spared, the benefits of this boon were intended not for the city's current inhabitants, but for its Israelite conquerors. Deuteronomy 20 thus represented rational military and economic policy; it more resembles a military handbook for conquerors than a codification of *ius in bello* norms.

The use of assassination seems to have inhabited a moral grey area. Across our sources we have seen assassination both justified and condemned, while assassins were both praised and punished. The factors determining *how* assassins and assassination were judged morally appears to have been dependent upon the identity of the victim(s), the identity and motivations of the assassin(s), and the identity of the political leader who either benefited from or was injured by the death of the victim. Thus the 'Tale of Sinuhe' begins by describing the shock and dread caused by the assassination of the old pharaoh, Amenemhat I; the Hittite 'Deeds of Šuppiluliuma' fiercely condemns the Egyptian assassination of the Hittite prince Zannanza; the Book of Samuel describes David's brutal punishment of the assassins responsible for murdering Saul's son Ishbosheth, and David's fury at Joab for murdering Abner. In contrast, the 'Apology of Hattušili III' justifies the usurpation and killing of King Urhi-Teshub; the Book of Judges praises the Benjaminite Ehud for his assassination of the

Moabite king Eglon and lauds Jael for the killing of the Canaanite commander Sisera; and the account of Jehu's killing spree in Samaria and Judah in the Book of Kings is presented as a pious purge of corrupted elites.

In general, assassination was treated cautiously in the sources and more often than not interpreted as a deviant moral act. If we bear in mind that many of our most detailed sources were commissioned by royal regimes, this should hardly come as a surprise. While it is true that numerous ancient kings came to power through usurpation and possibly assassination, new rulers looking to consolidate their own power must have been inclined to cover up such behaviour rather than publicise it. It would hardly be to the advantage of a new king to praise the use of assassination when he was now the main target for internal or external competitors.

Broadly accepted customs for waging war between states were limited to issuing formal declarations of war and/or challenges to battle. We have seen evidence of war leaders issuing such declarations and challenges, and we have also seen criticism of certain enemies for launching attacks without first issuing a declaration or challenge. Yet the irregularity of such declarations and challenges means that we are hard pressed to describe their use as a 'rule' or 'law' of war. Again, this goes back to the subjective criticism of surprise attacks such as ambush and night raids, which the Egyptian and Hittite sources usually associate with politically loose-knit or nomadic enemies such as the Sherden or Kaska. However, this did not stop Egyptian or Hittite commanders from utilising such tactics when it served their own purposes. The Israelite material notably contains numerous references to ambush being an effective tactic, at times even specifically commanded by Yahweh.

Envoys appear to have been granted some degree of immunity and freedom of movement. However, it should be stressed that these protections designed to enable communication between states and the performance of ambassadorial duties were largely restricted to times of peace, not war. Once hostilities commenced, it appears that most protections ceased to be recognised, and even safe-conducts were mistrusted. Even during periods of peaceful relations, foreign envoys never enjoyed a true guarantee of safety, and remained vulnerable to being detained or abused by their hosts.

Other individuals could not expect even these basic protections. During combat itself there were no binding customs of ritualised capture and ransom, and the iconographic evidence shows us soldiers systematically dispatching injured enemies on the ground. The fate of prisoners of war can only be described as insecure. Vast numbers of combatants and non-combatants alike were enslaved, although summary execution was also possible. High-status prisoners were occasionally released for political and pragmatic reasons, but enemy leaders were also liable to become the focus of retributive acts of political theatre, forced to endure public humiliation, torture, and death. There is evidence to suggest that their deaths could be particularly gruesome, with punishments such as impalement mentioned with relative frequency. The broad cultural acceptance of such behaviour throughout the ancient Near East is indicated in one of the foundational ancient texts, the *Epic of Gilgamesh*, which was circulating in various forms from at least the early second millennium (including a Hittite version).[1] A crucial episode in the story comes when the heroes, Gilgamesh and Enkidu, enter the sacred cedar forest and mercilessly slay its guardian, Humbaba; they do so despite the fact that their foe has already been defeated in battle and is begging for his life.[2] Thus mythic literature, in this moment, merely reflected wider socio-military realities.

While victors were entirely at liberty to kill their captives, it is likely that most prisoners of war escaped such a fate and endured a range of experiences. The luckiest might avoid enslavement altogether and instead become part of a vassal state owing annual tribute to their conquerors. Others might experience deportation and resettlement, providing corvée labour and possibly even military service for their new masters. Less fortunate prisoners might be gifted as slaves to temples (part of the gods' spoils) or as rewards to soldiers for their military service. Such prisoners were often branded and became legal non-entities. The most unfortunate—likely adult males who posed a potential security threat—could find themselves blinded or mutilated in some way, and put to work as mill slaves or in other forms of hard labour.

Women enjoyed no immunities in war and were often targeted as war spoils. The only advantage women and children appear to have enjoyed was that, rather than being butchered, they were more likely to be taken as living captives. For those women taken into captivity, many would have been used as sex-slaves and/or for domestic and manual labour. Others—especially younger unmarried women and girls—would be taken as wives by their captors. The regulations for the treatment of female captives provided in Deuteronomy 21 envisaged exactly this kind of fate, and describe a process whereby non-Israelite women could be integrated into the Israelite community without fear of religious pollution. Even so, Egyptian and Israelite sources do speak with relative frequency of the massacring of women and children along with adult males, occasionally in very large numbers. While the historicity of such massacres must remain open to question, the sources reveal no moral condemnations of such violent acts. Rather, they are more often presented as entirely justified and laudable.

Just as men, women, and children enjoyed no customary protections in war, so we have seen that all property was vulnerable to violence. No distinctions or discriminations were made between combatant and non-combatant property, nor between secular and religious property. Movable property was taken as plunder or destroyed. Immovable property was routinely razed,

---

1. *ANET*, 73.
2. *Gilgamesh*, 144–47, Tablet V, col. vi; cf. *The Epic of Gilgamesh*, trans. Maureen Gallery Kovaks (Stanford, CA: Stanford University Press, 1989), 44–47, Tablet V.

especially during punitive raids that were not intended to establish permanent control over a territory. Some immovable commodities such as orchards and vineyards could be preserved, but this seems to have been motivated entirely by pragmatic (primarily economic) concerns: conquerors wanted to preserve the economic base of the territories they were hoping to colonise or subjugate, and impoverished populations without resources could not pay taxes or tribute. Again, while the descriptions of slaughter and destruction were undoubtedly hyperbolic, they reveal the absence of any ideational restraints or immunities.

As centres of wealth, temples were routinely targeted by invading armies. Examination of a very large number of sources reveals no more than six examples of some sort of protection being offered to religious sites, or expressions of regret that sacred sites were sacked. Such protective action or subsequent regret (which implies a belief that the destruction was somehow illicit) thus appears to have been exceptional. Normally, indeed, the capture or destruction of the images of enemy gods possessed a potent symbolic meaning and was part of the propaganda of war. As well as providing wealth, the stripping of enemy temples and sacred statuary confirmed the judgement of the divine court: it emphasised the righteousness of the victors and the humiliating punishment of the guilty.

Of our surviving Near Eastern sources, the Tanakh is by far the most extreme in its attitude to the necessity of destroying enemy religious sites. Unlike in the Egyptian or Hittite traditions, targeted destruction of religious property was presented as a duty demanded by Yahweh, with religious spoils often condemned to destruction as *herem* offerings. Yet we must wonder if this mid-first-millennium theological retelling of Israelite history was truly reflective of early first-millennium Samaritan and Judahite practice. Israelite warrior chieftains and kings must have valued the precious metals and treasures found in enemy temples as much as did any of their contemporaries. They would surely have been loath to obliterate such wealth. (Indeed, a king of Samaria is even recorded as looting the temple of Jerusalem itself!) Hints of this historical reality can be found within the pages of the Tanakh, with Israelite war leaders and soldiers taking spoils for themselves rather than dedicating them to destruction, as demanded by Yahweh's prophets.

In sum, Egyptian, Hittite, and Israelite customs pertaining to *in bello* conduct appear to have been extremely limited in scope and (at best) ad hoc and very occasional in application. From the early fourth millennium to the mid-first millennium, there was no widely acknowledged or observed *ius in bello* tradition operating cross-culturally, nor any individual *ius in bello* traditions operating within specific martial cultures. This was true across the entire region and period, from pre-dynastic Egypt to the fall of the kingdom of Judah. The methods by which wars were fought were dictated largely by pragmatic and prudential concerns. Victory—or at least avoiding defeat—was the primary motivation. This applied to kings as well as to soldiers, because the grave consequences of defeat bore on every individual, regardless of one's place in society. Equally, many could hope to profit by the material spoils of victory, from the soldier on campaign to the priest or priestess in their temple back at home. The only privilege in ancient Near Eastern warfare was the privilege of the victor to act in whatever way they wished.

The Pernicious Effects of Prepotent Ius ad bellum *Traditions*

The absence of *ius in bello* thought or practices in ancient Egyptian, Hittite, or Israelite warfare can be substantially explained by two causal factors. The first was that there was no equivalent to the modern liberal concept of the individual, and as an extension of this, no normative recognition of individual 'rights' within war.[3] This is clearest to see in the mass enslavement of prisoners of war, which was standard across the region and period, and rendered the war captive literally a legal non-entity. Arguably there is a cautionary tale here for modern military practices and the ways in which captured non-state/sub-state actors, stripped of legal status, have been treated in conflicts since 2001. The second—and more influential—causal factor was the nature of each society's development of vigorous *ius ad bellum* traditions of thought. These *ius ad bellum* traditions were so confident and so inflexible in their claims to authority and justice that they simply nullified *in bello* considerations. This too should give modern just war theorists pause for thought.

EGYPTIAN

Egyptian just war thought was absolutist in the sense that it depicted war in black-and-white moral terms. The very early development of theological understandings of the Two Lands as the terrestrial embodiment of Ma'at was crucial to the concomitant development of a royal ideology of just war. On the one hand, Egyptian concepts of justice were universalising, in that Egyptian theology posited the cosmological principle of Ma'at as a universal embodiment of justice and order. Not only was Ma'at understood as a universal principle of justice to which all peoples should be subject, but from at least the Middle Kingdom onwards, the pharaoh also projected universalising claims to sovereignty. In projecting such claims, all enemies—internal and external—were understood as rebellious and unjust, and thus any military action against them was justified on the basis of retributive justice or simple self-defence.

---

3. For a lively comparative account of the history of individual 'rights', see Micheline Ishay, *The History of Human Rights: From Ancient Times to the Globalization Era* (Berkeley: University of California Press, 2004). On the impact of liberal doctrines of international law on 'rights', see the classic study by Marti Koskenniemi, *The Gentle Civilizer of Nations: The Rise and Fall of International Law, 1870–1960* (Cambridge: Cambridge University Press, 2001).

On the other hand, Egyptian concepts of justice were highly chauvinistic. Because justice and Ma'at were synonymous, and because Egypt was the terrestrial embodiment of Ma'at, justice and the kingdom of Egypt were effectively one and the same thing. There could be no justice except Egyptian justice; there could be no just ruler except the Egyptian king, who was a semi-divine guardian of Ma'at. Embodying both justice and righteous sovereignty, the actions of the Egyptian state and pharaoh were automatically just. Ideologically, Egyptian monarchs were incapable of morally wrong action. It was natural, therefore, for Egyptian rulers and people to believe in the justness of Egypt's military defence. According to theology and royal ideology, all lands beyond Egypt represented the antithesis of justice: Isfet. They were lands dominated by chaos and barbarism, and the struggles that took place on the terrestrial plane were understood as mirroring those that took place on the celestial. War against Egypt's political enemies was thus transformed into a cosmological war of order and justice against chaos, in which the gods could not allow the wicked to triumph over the good. Extending the boundaries of Egypt and the dominion of Ma'at was thus intrinsically good and justified. This was a truly imperialistic just war doctrine. Egyptian kings assumed the approval of the gods in all their ventures, especially when it came to war. Royal ideology found it very hard to conceive of the Egyptian pantheon punishing the king, because the king was himself a demi-god. This is why Egyptian royal and elite sources work so hard to present all Egyptian military actions as successful, to the extent that defeats were either ignored entirely or were reworked by Egyptian scribes as hard-won but ultimately glorious victories.

In light of such a highly chauvinistic and absolutist *ius ad bellum* tradition, there was scant moral space left for the evolution of norms aimed at limiting warfare or protecting the enemy. Egyptian just war thought was rooted in the idea of the *Chaoskampf*—the fight against chaos—and in such a war it was irrational to think in terms of restraint. Chaotic threats to Egypt had to be not only eliminated, but annihilated. The Egyptian just war tradition thus gave permission for any form of military action.

ISRAELITE

A parallel form of universalism combined with chauvinism is also a defining feature of Israelite just war thought. As in Egypt, the absence of an Israelite *ius in bello* tradition can be explained by the conception of war as a cosmological struggle of order against chaos. In place of the semi-divine pharaoh standing at the epicentre of this battle, the Tanakh inserts the divine figure of El/Yahweh/Jehovah. The elevation of Yahweh to a preeminent divine position was accompanied by the claim that the god enjoyed universal sovereignty, and so the god was the sole authority empowered to make judgements regarding the justice of war. War could certainly be conceived as a means to prove Yahweh's superiority—an end justifiable in and of itself—as it was throughout the books describing the exodus from Egypt and the conquest of Canaan. However, while the compilers of the Tanakh presented Yahweh as a supreme deity, the god's focus remained firmly fixed on the Israelites. Through the creation of the Covenant—the vassal treaty which bound the people to their divine 'Great King'—the Israelites were uniquely placed to wage just wars. Yahweh's terrestrial representatives—whether prophets such as Moses, war leaders such as Joshua, or kings such as David—were endowed with the authority to wage all types of warfare (defensive, aggressive, retributive, and so on) only in so far as they were conduits of Yahweh's divine authority and power; but as such, these war leaders and the soldiers they commanded were understood to fulfil Yahweh's providential plan for his chosen people.

The relationship between the Israelites and other human communities were almost entirely irrelevant when seen through the lens of Yahweh's salvific plan. Consequently, the mundane details of the political and military interactions of Israelites with other political communities were also of secondary importance. In all matters, it was primarily the Israelites' relationship with Yahweh that was determinative. Victory in war was something that Yahweh could give or take away from the Israelites—it had very little to do with the nature of the relationship between the Israelites and their enemies. If the Israelites had a legitimate mundane grievance against a foe, this did not guarantee their success in war if they themselves had also sinned against Yahweh in some way (usually by a violation of the Covenant). Military defeat by an enemy could be used by Yahweh as a means of punishing his people for some transgression against him, or could be interpreted as a necessary step along the path of providence. Such defeats did *not* imply that enemies of Israel were 'good' or 'just' in any way, or that they possessed a just cause to wage war.

The moral quality of Israelite war was therefore refracted through two lenses. The first lens was that of Yahweh's divine providence, which meant that the Israelites could never be certain if a specific war would turn in their favour or not. The story of the Tanakh is, after all, one of both victory and defeat: the glories of the conquest followed by the slow decline and final destruction of the Israelite kingdoms. This was because both victory and defeat had purpose in Yahweh's salvific plan. This theological reasoning was perhaps a natural response for post-exilic authors and redactors struggling to make sense of the fall of the Israelite kingdoms and the humiliation and exile of their people.

The second lens, equally important, was the nature of the relationship between Yahweh and his people (or the rulers that represented them) at any specific moment in time. Yahweh was represented as granting numerous military boons to the Israelites when they or their leaders obeyed the Covenant, for the relationship was based on reciprocal duties: territorial conquest and victory in arms were intrinsic to Yahweh's duties as a warrior god. However, when rulers or people disregarded their obligations to Yahweh, the god was more than willing to punish them severely, utilising military defeat by their enemies as a weapon of divine retribution. Crucially—and this cannot be stressed enough—such military defeats were understood as judgements *not* on the relative justice of the Israelites vis-à-vis their enemies, but on the justice of the Israelites vis-à-vis their god. Israelites might have absolutely no mundane grievance against a foe, but might still expect Yahweh's aid in war. This line of thinking defines justifications for the conquest of Canaan itself. The crucial point being made by the authors of the Tanakh was that, when waging war, the most important consideration (by far) was whether the Israelites remained faithful to their covenantal relationship with Yahweh. Yahweh would judge whether or not they were deserving of victory first and foremost on this basis rather than on that of mundane questions about property ownership or legal transgressions. If Yahweh turned against the Israelites and inflicted military defeat upon them, it was not because of particular crimes the Israelites had committed against external non-Israelite peoples, but because of crimes against their god. For the authors of the Tanakh, the gradual political and military decline of the Israelites went hand in hand with the growing alienation of the people and their kings from Yahweh and the Covenant. The Babylonian exile and the complete destruction of Solomon's temple was the final tragic proof of this truth.

Although the theological reasoning underpinning Egyptian and Israelite just war thought was different, the result was broadly similar. In both Egyptian and Israelite thought, justice was a remarkably one-sided affair. The enemy's claim to justice was effectively irrelevant. Indeed, conceptually it was almost a contradiction in terms that a non-Israelite could possess a claim to justice, just as it was absurd that a barbarian embodying Isfet could have a just claim against Egypt. This highly chauvinistic and absolutist *ius ad bellum* tradition of thought had little room for moralising about the humane treatment of the enemy. At best, enemy persons and property represented economic resources and could be subjugated as vassals; at worst, they represented chaos, religious profanity, and a future threat to the Israelite community, and needed to be expunged.

The most extreme (and probably the latest, in terms of the Tanakh's composition) expressions of Israelite violence are contained in the conquest narrative, and depict Israel's enemies as requiring complete destruction. This presents the violence of war as a form of purification, the herem annihilation of the enemy and all of their property mirroring a ritualistic sacrificial offering to the god. These herem offerings were perhaps also a form of payment to the deity for new territory, conforming to the principle of *do ut des* common throughout ancient Near Eastern religions. Yet if we accept that the conquest account is largely fictional (as most scholars do), then we must also accept that its theologically inspired violence is also fictional. The violence depicted was a result of Yahwist redactors around the time of the exile attempting to promote an increasingly ardent monotheism. Their aim was to contrast the 'successes' of the religiously pious early Israelites with the disasters of the Samaritan and Judahite kingdoms, and to explain these disasters as a consequence of an alienation from Yahweh. It is significant, however, that a doctrinally charged account of pious action was expressed through the depiction of extreme violence. The moral message was not that pious peoples act mercifully towards their enemies, but that a proof of piety was the willingness to commit the most atrocious violence against persons external to the religiopolitical community. As in Egyptian just war thought, hyperbolic accounts of the destruction of the enemy on a vast scale served a theological and ideological purpose, confirming the victory of the just against the unjust, and the cosmological victory of order over chaos.

HITTITE

Hittite just war thought shares many similarities with both the Egyptian and Israelite traditions. The same principles of just cause can be seen, with self-defensive and retributive violence featuring prominently. Hittites were also concerned with ideas of proper authority, and recognised that authority ultimately stemmed from the gods. The storm-god Teššub and the sun-goddess of Arinna were especially prominent in this regard, and the Great King was their chosen representative. As in Egyptian and Israelite thought, the Hittites were convinced that victory in war was only possible with divine support, and that such support was dependent upon the proper execution of justice. Unlike the Egyptians and Israelites, the Hittites took a more open-minded (or less self-assured) approach to the question of *which side* had a superior claim to possessing justice or being the victim of injustice. Taken as a whole, there is a palpable concern in Hittite thought about the nature and quality of mundane actions, both their own and those of their enemies. It was a recurring feature of the Hittites' appeals to the 'court of the gods' to carefully describe, before embarking on a campaign, how and why they were waging war, detailing the injuries they had suffered as a result of the terrestrial crimes of their enemies. Clearly, this was an important process in convincing the gods that the Hittites were embarking on a just war and were thus deserving of divine support.

This is where we begin to see a genuine divergence from Egyptian and Israelite just war thought. Although the Hittites were undoubtedly given to partisan interpretations of the righteousness of their own cause (something of which all political communities are guilty, across all periods and regions), the Hittite understanding of war was the most legalistic, interpreting war as a form of legal trial or ordeal in which the judgement of the divine court was played out on Earth. As a result, the Hittite just war tradition evinces a more balanced interpretation of justice in the realm of war. Hittite kings were less confident about maintaining the favour of the gods and seem to have been alive to the possibility that they, or more often their forebears, were capable of committing errors. Defeat in war was tied to the (dis)ordered relationship between gods and men, and more specifically between the gods and their chief priest, the Great King. Some of these human–divine acts of injustice were solely internal to the Hittite realm (such as failing to offer proper worship to a god or goddess) but, crucially, acts of injustice could also be rooted in transgressions against external peoples and states. Thus we see concern about the legal violation of an international treaty; and we see an apology to a foreign king concerning unjust claims to a contested territory.

This willingness to contemplate the possibility of error on the side of the Hittite monarch generated a degree of objectivity in Hittite ethical thought on war that was simply absent from other ancient just war thought. This distinguishes the Hittite from both the Egyptian and the Israelite just war traditions, as well as from those of the Assyrians and Babylonians. It is this degree of objectivity, arguably rooted in the deeply legalistic and pluralistic bent of Hittite society, that marks Hittite just war thought as genuinely innovative.

Notwithstanding this innovation, however, it would probably be a mistake to conclude that the Hittite practice of war was any less brutal than that of its contemporaries. Having presented their case to the gods, the Hittites waged war with the same conviction of righteousness as their peers. The fact that the Great King was going to war in the first place, based undoubtedly on the outcome of numerous oracles, was evidence that he believed he was in the right. Royal soul-searching about past crimes only occurred in the wake of defeat or natural disaster. While Hittites may have been slightly more cautious about *declaring* war, once the decision for military action had been taken they were no more likely than any of their peers to grant their enemies privileges based on moral reasoning or cultural obligations. We still read plenty of throwaway lines in Hittite royal sources about enemies being slaughtered in droves, while plundering enemy property was considered an obvious privilege and even an attraction of war.

What differentiated the Hittites from their Egyptian or Israelite counterparts was that they were far less likely to believe that there was a *moral imperative* to eradicate their enemies. Hittite sources show very little inclination towards such convictions, except perhaps when they discuss the crimes of the hated Kaska. As a rule, they do not indulge in gory details about putting enemies to the sword, and describe battles and campaigns in a laconic, matter-of-fact style. Moreover, the Hittites evidently preferred to use prisoners of war as corvée or bondage labour, and throughout the history of their kingdom showed considerable political flexibility in forgiving or reinstalling client kings who had proven themselves less than reliable.

In the final analysis, then, it must be concluded that ancient just war thought did almost nothing to lessen the violence of ancient warfare. In fact, the *ius ad bellum* traditions which evolved from theological and ideological convictions arguably encouraged a more brutal, 'zero-sum' attitude to war.

The Egyptian, Hittite, and Israelite *ius ad bellum* traditions were highly permissive with regard to *in bello* conduct. In all three societies, extreme violence was morally permissible, on the basis of deeply held theologico-political beliefs. These just war traditions were aligned to broader cultural beliefs and practices, and as such were comfortably integrated within each society. Thus Bederman's claim that 'all ancient States saw the need for limitations and immunities to be impressed on the conduct of warfare', and that there was a 'common core of ideas leading to the exercise of restraint by ancient States in armed conflict', simply does not stack up against the weight of evidence for the period prior to c. 450 BCE.[4]

The Restraining Hands of Prudence and Pragmatism

Despite the almost total absence of any meaningful *ius in bello* norms in the ancient Near East, there is good reason to think that the unlimited violence permitted within Egyptian, Hittite, and Israelite just war traditions was frequently–perhaps even typically—mitigated in practice. Pragmatism must have been a driving force in restraining some of the more extreme ideological and cosmological claims. First and foremost were issues of practicality and strategy. In the pre-industrial age, massacring hundreds or thousands of prisoners of war was no easy task. It must have taken time and cannot have been pleasant work for even the most grizzled veteran. Massacre also had quite narrowly defined strategic benefits. While such an extreme action might be used selectively to terrorise an enemy into submission, it was only effective if at other times army commanders showed restraint. If an enemy could only expect annihilation, regardless of circumstances or surrender, then every enemy would have been sure to fight tooth and nail to the last man. So, if the point of massacre was to encourage submission without the need for costly extended campaigns and sieges, then the very nature of the tactic required that it be used selectively rather than indiscriminately. The point is not that massacring people was morally or legally prohibited; rather that it was not always practically feasible or strategically useful.

Massacre must also be viewed within the context of the ancient Near Eastern labour-intensive agricultural economy. Due to low demographic density in many territories, labour shortages were a genuine problem, meaning that people were often more valuable alive than dead. Whether as agricultural or

---

4. *ILA*, 265. Indeed, despite the generalisation of Bederman's claim, his evidence for such a conclusion is drawn almost exclusively from Greco-Roman material and cannot be taken as representative of the more ancient Near East. Nevertheless, his assertions regarding the development of a 'law of nations' providing customary norms for the treatment of envoys, treaty processes, and certain formalities leading to the declaration of war (ibid., 272) remain convincing, and have been discussed in the preceding chapters.

household slaves, concubines, or indentured auxiliary troops, there were many ways in which prisoners of war could be put to use. Indeed, with the expansion of empires in the mid-second millennium, there was an incentive for imperial powers such as Egypt and Hatti to preserve conquered populations in order to reap the benefits of tribute and other forms of vassal service. Again, the killing or mutilation of prisoners of war—especially high-ranking ones—might be used as a show of force to deter future revolts, but there was little benefit in killing or disabling too many.

In reality, it is likely that very little differentiated the ways in which Egyptians, Hittites, and Israelites waged war. The same is probably true of Assyrians, Babylonians, and Mitannians too, along with the rest of the ancient Near Eastern and Mesopotamian states. The only real difference would have been one of scale, or determined by the objectives of a specific campaign: territorial conquest, punitive raid, or plunder. Violence was obviously a deliberate feature of warfare; for combatants and non-combatants alike there were no normative protections to alleviate it. In defeat, extreme violence as an act of retribution or political admonition was possible. The loss of one's property and wealth must have been taken for granted. Enslavement was likely. The only real hope that defeated peoples could cling to was that the enemy would be motivated more by greed than by bloodlust, or simply have other more pressing military objectives to pursue, and so move on before inflicting too much damage.

Ancient Just War Traditions

At last, we are in a position to be able to describe ancient Egyptian, Hittite, and Israelite cultures as having developed genuine just war *traditions*. In each case, there is a clear chronological development of patterns of ethical thought, with expressions of just war thought becoming more explicit over time. In Egypt, royal claims to justice and authority in war were strengthened through each kingdom period, reaching their apogee in the imperialistic New Kingdom. There were frequent references to the past, antique literature and myths were recirculated, and some pharaohs simply lifted texts and images wholesale from their forebears. In Hatti, too, we see the careful preservation of texts by a sophisticated royal bureaucracy, so that kings could demand that their scribes search the royal archives for historical references and proofs. The practice of composing royal annals and appending lengthy historical preambles to diplomatic treaties ensured that the claims and deeds of royal forebears could be used as inspiration for current and future leaders. Kings were sure to repeat and expand prior claims to authority and justice, as well as learning from—and possibly atoning for—the mistakes of their predecessors. In the case of the Tanakh, we have a clear example of a source that was the product of a lengthy (re)interpretation of textual and oral histories. The just war claims contained within it represent a definite tradition of thought, whereby ideas from a range of periods were reformulated according to contemporary needs and objectives.

This does not mean that the just war thought of each society emerged as a monolithic just war *theory*, systematically articulated and defended. Rather, it developed in the form of increasingly sophisticated theologico-political doctrines, based on both theological beliefs and royal ideology (which were themselves intertwined). Ideas were promoted through a variety of channels. Royal ideology propagated just war doctrine via monumental architecture and iconography, cult and ritual, dedicatory stelae, campaign records and annals, diplomatic correspondence, and legal instruments. Public and private literary texts, poetry, mythology, and prayers also reflected on good and bad deeds, as well as on military service to the state and to the gods. Taken together, these ideas and practices produced individual traditions consisting of broadly coherent doctrines about war and justice that circulated in each culture and were elaborated over time. Though broadly coherent and consistent, such doctrines could also contain contradictory elements, as do all cultural systems.[5] The creation of this 'loose' type of doctrine, as opposed to rigorous analytical theory, is entirely typical of ethical thought about war across all epochs, and of the history of just war thought more specifically. But these ancient Near Eastern just war traditions represent the earliest evidence for just war thought in the history of human civilisation.

A widely respected political theorist once asked me, very sensibly, whether a just war doctrine which is so partisan that it can only ever envisage its own side as just can actually be described as a proper just war doctrine.[6] The answer is, surely, that it can: because, like concepts of justice, just war thought is subjective. If a system of just war does not map precisely onto our *own* system of just war, or our expectations of what such a system should look like, this does not invalidate it. The difference is one of degree, not of type. The highly partisan just war traditions developed within the Egyptian and Israelite (and to a lesser extent, Hittite) cultures served their purposes very well, providing a coherent ethical framework in which these peoples could wage war without compromising their religious beliefs, moral convictions, or legal systems.

Taken as a whole, Hittite ethical thought on war was the most sophisticated just war thought of the ancient Near East. One might draw some compelling comparisons between Hittite thought and the so-called 'regular war' tradition that emerged tentatively with Raphaël Fulgosius in the early fifteenth century CE, and more substantively in the Enlightenment work of Christian Wolff and Emer de Vattel.[7] Hatti could be said to have believed in the 'perfect

---

5. Geertz, *Interpretation of Cultures*, 17–18.

6. I have taken the liberty of paraphrasing the excellent question posed by Professor Chris Brown during a panel at the 2019 Toronto ISA Convention. My thanks to Chris for the question, and to Cian O'Driscoll for reminding me of it.

7. Reichberg, 'Ius ad bellum', 16–17; Pablo Kalmanovitz, *The Laws of War in International Thought* (Oxford: Oxford University Press, 2020), 77–80.

rights' of a plurality of peer states, and recognised the importance of 'reason of state' in determining when, where, and why going to war was legitimate. On the other hand, this would tend to overlook the continued importance of the supernatural in Hittite thought. Reason of state could not be divorced from divine approval, because victory in war depended upon divine support. Consequently, the state (or rather, the king) was never entirely free to determine what was a just war on its authority alone, and a religious sanction had to be superadded. The comparison with regular war also breaks down when considering *in bello* restraints. Early modern regular war theorists—recognising that claims to just cause were too contentious in a system of equally sovereign states—advocated for a doctrine of 'belligerent equals', pinning their hope on *in bello* norms to restrain the viciousness of war.[8] However, as we have seen, no comparable *in bello* norms were developed in Hatti or anywhere else in the ancient Near East.

Nevertheless, the Hittite just war tradition can be described as a genuinely ethical form of just war thought, in the sense that sophisticated ethical engagement requires a degree of self-reflection and even self-criticism. The emergence—albeit tentative—of this type of self-reflection and objectivity is evident in the Hittite just war tradition, and the significance of this development occurring 3,500 years ago should not be underestimated.

Does this qualify Hittite thought to be recognised as 'proper' just war doctrine? This is probably the wrong question to ask. It is more constructive, I think, to consider historical just war traditions in terms of relative complexity, sophistication, or nuance. Was Egyptian or Israelite just war thought as sophisticated or nuanced as Hittite just war thought? No. Was Hittite just war thought as sophisticated or nuanced as treatments by Thomas Aquinas or Hugo Grotius? Clearly not. But though modern just war thought rejects much of what Aquinas and Grotius took for granted, no one would think to dismiss Aquinas or Grotius as major contributors to the body of just war thought *in toto*.[9] The same holds true for many other pre-modern contributions to just war scholarship, and should also hold true for ancient just war doctrines. Though by today's standards we may find aspects of ancient doctrine

---

8. Kalmanovitz, *Laws of War*, 79–80, 97–126.

9. Aquinas's principal analysis of war can be found in St Thomas Aquinas, '*Summa theologiae*': *Latin Text and English Translation, Introduction, Notes, Appendices and Glossaries*, ed. Thomas Gilby O.P. et al., 61 vols (London: Blackfriars; New York: McGraw-Hill, 1964–81), vol. 35: *Consequences of Charity (2a2ae. 34–46)*, ed. and trans. T. R. Heath O.P. (1972), Questions 40–42. The most authoritative treatment of Aquinas's thought on war is Gregory Reichberg, *Thomas Aquinas on War and Peace* (Cambridge: Cambridge University Press, 2017). For Grotius, see Hugo Grotius, *The Rights of War and Peace*, ed. Richard Tuck, from the edition of Jean Barbeyrac, *Major Legal and Political Works of Hugo Grotius*, 3 vols (Indianapolis: Liberty Fund, 2005). An excellent new introduction to Grotius's thought is provided by Randall Lesaffer and Janne E. Nijman (eds), *The Cambridge Companion to Hugo Grotius* (Cambridge: Cambridge University Press, 2021).

unfamiliar, even objectionable, that does not invalidate it as constituting a genuine manifestation of just war thought. Modern criticisms that ancient just war frameworks were not objectively 'fair' to enemies would undoubtedly have struck ancient thinkers and warriors as absurd, just as modern cosmopolitan just war arguments, for example, would surely have flummoxed a thinker such as Aquinas or Grotius.

From Ancient to Modern Just War Traditions?

Having established that there were indeed just war traditions developing in the Near East from as early as c. 3000 BCE, one of the two ancillary claims this study set out to test was whether ancient Near Eastern just war thought is analogous to, perhaps even homologous with, that body of later thought associated with the Greco-Roman and Christian just war tradition.

Claims regarding the existence of customary 'laws of war' restraining Greek warfare have circulated for some time and been broadly accepted.[10] Essentially, this argument proposes that, with the emergence of agonal hoplite warfare in the early first millennium, archaic Greece witnessed the gradual emergence of culturally mandated rules of war. Certain of these rules were either abandoned or reinforced during the internecine violence of the Peloponnesian War (c. 431–c. 404), so that by the fifth century there appears to have been a set of established norms which applied to intra-Hellenic warfare and included conditions such as formal declarations of war, periods of truce for sacred holidays, ransoming of prisoners, and, to some degree, the immunity of non-combatants.[11]

However, several scholars have vociferously challenged the existence of such military norms in archaic and classical Greece, highlighting the lack of evidence to prove that they were ever universally recognised or regularly enforced.[12] As Hans van Wees argues, 'what stands out [. . .] is not a moral

---

10. For example, see: Hanson, *A War Like No Other*, 180–82, 299–302; Ober, 'Classical Greek Times'; Ober, 'Rules of War'; Lanni, 'Laws of War'. On Roman norms, see Alan Watson, *International Law in Archaic Rome: War and Religion* (Baltimore: Johns Hopkins University Press, 1993); Raymond, 'Greco-Roman Roots'; Barrandon, 'La Transgression', 97–123.

11. Michael M. Sage (ed.), *Warfare in Ancient Greece: A Sourcebook* (London: Routledge, 1996), 127–34; M. D. Goodman and A. J. Holladay, 'Religious Scruples in Ancient Warfare', *The Classical Quarterly* 36 (1) (1986): 151–71; Ober, 'Classical Greek Times', 12–13.

12. Pierre Ducrey's classic studies of prisoners and warriors in Greek warfare highlighted the disparity between theoretical protections and military practice: Pierre Ducrey, *Le Traitement des prisonniers de guerre dans la Grèce antique: Des origines à la conquête romaine* (Paris: E. de Boccard, 1968), esp. 271ff; Ducrey, *Guerre et guerriers dans la Grèce antique* (Paris: Payot, 1985), 64–66, 239–55. Recent revisionist interventions include: Peter Krentz, 'Deception in Archaic and Classical Greek Warfare', in *War and Violence in Ancient Greece*, ed. Hans van Wees (London: Duckworth, 2000), 167–200; Krentz, 'Fighting by

code of restraint but, in Nietzsche's words, "a tigerlike urge to annihilate".[13] The image of ancient Greek warfare as a highly ritualised and norm-governed practice may be significantly detached from the historical reality of conflict. In other words, it may have borne a much closer resemblance to Thucydides's famous account of the Melian Dialogue, frequently taken as a paradigmatic example of political realism. For those unfamiliar with this text, Thucydides recounts how, during the Peloponnesian War, the militarily superior Athenians informed the unfortunate Melians—who wished to remain neutral—that 'the standard of justice depends on the equality of power to compel and that in fact the strong do what they have the power to do and the weak accept what they have to accept'.[14] The Melians, who bravely (or foolhardily) opted to fight for what they reasonably claimed to be a just cause, were promptly slaughtered or enslaved.[15]

The works of Plato in the mid-fourth century offer a clear engagement with war as an ethical problem. War was not to be left to private individuals, but was rather the monopoly of the public authority. Any violation of this law, insisted Plato, should be punishable by death.[16] In the *Republic*, the character of Socrates identifies resource competition as the origin of war: the desire for luxurious living necessitating the acquisition of resources from neighbouring communities. More importantly, Socrates/Plato goes on to make an important ontological distinction between wars fought between Greeks, and wars fought between Greeks and barbarians (βάρβαροι/*barbaroi*—literally 'babblers', i.e., non-Greek speakers):

---

the Rules: The Invention of the Hoplite Agon', *Hesperia* 71 (1) (2002): 23–39; Hans van Wees, *Greek Warfare: Myths and Realities* (London: Duckworth, 2004); Wees, 'Defeat and Destruction'; Wees, 'Genocide'. More equivocal views are taken by Jérôme Wilgaux, 'Trangressions et sanctions divines en temps de guerre en Grèce ancienne', in *La Transgression en temps de guerre: De l'Antiquité à nos jours*, ed. Nathalie Barrandon and Isabelle Pimouguet-Pedarros (Rennes: Presses Universitaires de Rennes, 2021), 49–64; Isabelle Pimouguet-Pedarros, 'Guerre, norms et transgressions dans le monde grec', in ibid., 65–81.

13. Wees, 'Defeat and Destruction', 106. On the brutality of Roman war as a comparison, see also Zimmerman, *Gewalt*, 219–36.

14. Thucydides, *The Peloponnesian War*, trans. Rex Warner, with an introduction and notes by M. I. Finley (Harmondsworth: Penguin, 1954), bk 5, § 89 (p. 402).

15. While Thucydides has often been viewed as a proponent of realism, this overlooks the nuances of his historical work. His account may well be dispassionate, but nowhere does he laud acts of barbarity, and he consistently portrays those who take a humane attitude toward their enemy in a positive light, regardless of whether these humane actions were motivated by ethics or self-interest. For example, see the Athenian debate regarding the fate of Mytilene: Ibid., bk. 3, §§ 36–50 (pp. 212–23). See also Paul A. Rahe, 'Justice and Necessity: The Conduct of the Spartans and the Athenians in the Peloponnesian War', in *Civilians in the Path of War*, ed. Mark Grimsley and Clifford J. Rogers (Lincoln: University of Nebraska Press, 2002), 1–32.

16. Plato, *The Laws*, trans. Trevor J. Saunders (Harmondsworth: Penguin, 1970), bk 12 (pp. 489, 507).

[W]hen Greeks fight with barbarians and barbarians with Greeks, we'll assert they are at war and are enemies by nature, and this hatred must be called war; while when Greeks do any such thing to Greeks, we'll say that they are by nature friends, but in this case Greece is sick and factious, and this kind of hatred must be called faction.[17]

Seen in this way, armed conflict is an expression of hatred (as Freud would also later explain it); as such, it would seem to have a negative moral nature. And yet Socrates/Plato identifies conflict between Greeks and barbarians as natural, for it is the expression of the fact that they are 'enemies by nature'. According to Platonic cosmology, what is natural cannot be immoral; at worst, it can only be regarded as morally neutral. This natural conflict is what Socrates/Plato terms 'war' in the proper sense, and he distinguishes between this and the 'unnatural' type of internecine conflict fought between Greeks, which, he argues, is not really war at all but rather a species of disease that he terms 'faction'. This, being unnatural, is 'a wicked thing'.[18]

So we have two distinct categories of conflict: 'war', which is natural; and 'faction', which is unnatural. Crucially, however, it is only for the second category of conflict that Socrates/Plato introduces ideas of normative restraint. These include what we would now term proportionality and non-combatant immunity, and are intended to aid future reconciliation between fellow Greeks:

'Therefore, as Greeks, they won't ravage Greece or burn houses, nor will they agree that in any city all are their enemies—men, women, and children—but that there are always a few enemies who are to blame for the differences. And, on all these grounds, they won't be willing to ravage lands or tear down houses, since the many are friendly [. . .].'

'I for one,' he [Glaucon] said, 'agree that our citizens must behave this way toward their opponents; and toward the barbarians they must behave as the Greeks do now toward one another [i.e., without restraint].'[19]

Therefore, while advocating for *in bello* limitations during intra-Hellenic conflict, Plato argued in favour of limitless violence directed against non-Greeks in 'proper' wars. Aristotle followed this line of thought, stating that intra-Hellenic warfare was a 'disease', while the wars fought by Greeks against barbarians were natural and therefore legitimate and virtuous. Aristotle quoted the poet Euripides, claiming that '[i]t is meet that Hellenes should rule over barbarians'. With the teleology of the political state being the attainment of the life of virtue (the 'good' life), Aristotle maintained that governments must be organised with a view to military strength as a means to defend the

17. Plato, *Republic*, bk 5.470c (p. 150).
18. Ibid., bk 5.470d (p. 150).
19. Ibid., bk 5.471a–b (p. 151).

common good of the community (which included law, justice, etc.) against barbarism and other external threats.[20] Plato and Aristotle were therefore no less chauvinistic or xenophobic in their understanding of war than the exponents of earlier, Near Eastern traditions upon which, possibly, they drew indirectly. Their ethical analyses of war relied on a fundamental dichotomy between Hellenes and non-Hellenes that was akin to the Egyptian/non-Egyptian or Israelite/non-Israelite dichotomies, so that even wars of conquest which resulted in 'mastery over those who deserve to be slaves' could be understood as morally permissible.[21] The Greek philosophers may have claimed that war was not an end in itself and should only be waged 'for the sake of peace';[22] but the peace they envisaged was something wholly beneficial to Hellenic society and involved no concern for the welfare of barbarian enemies.

Plato's long-lived maxim that war should be for the sake of peace passed into the Roman tradition, appearing in important works such as Cicero's *De officiis* (*On Duties*), whence it was repeated by Augustine, Gratian, and many others.[23] Cicero stressed that justice and warfare should be closely related, and that warring parties must possess just cause and proper authority.[24] According to Arthur Nussbaum, this constituted the 'invention' of Western just war doctrine and was 'the foremost Roman contribution to the history of international law'.[25]

While Cicero was concerned that every just war should produce peace (that is, a peace suitable to Roman interests), he was more concerned than Plato or Aristotle that war should be used as a legal instrument to restore justice to its *status quo ante bellum*.[26] In this regard, Cicero interpreted the justice and legality of war within a framework of both natural law and customary law, embodied as the 'law of nations' (*ius gentium*). The natural right to self-defence (*vim vi repellere*, 'to repel force with force') was the most immediate and clear-cut justification for war, but the right to recover goods

---

20. Aristotle, *Politics*, bk 1.1252b.5-9 (p. 2) (quote); bk 2.1267a.18-28 (p. 35); bk 3.1280b.39 (p. 65); bk 5.1308a.25-30 (p. 125); bk 7.1328b.7-10 (p. 167); Aristotle, *Rhetoric to Alexander*, ch. 2, §§ 26-32 (pp. 492/3-496/7).

21. Aristotle, *Politics*, bk 7.1333b.37-1334a.10 (p. 178).

22. Plato, *Laws*, bk 7 (p. 292). Cf. ibid., bk 1 (p. 51). Aristotle, *Nicomachean Ethics*, trans. Martin Ostwald (Upper Saddle River, NJ: Prentice Hall, 1999), bk 10.1177b.5-6 (p. 289); Aristotle, *Politics*, bk 7.1333a.34-35 (p. 177).

23. Augustine, Letter 189 to Boniface, § 5, in *Augustine: Political Writings*, ed. Atkins and Dodaro, 217; *Decretum magistri Gratiani*, C. 23, q. 1 c. 3. See also Barnes, 'The Just War', 780.

24. Cicero, *On Duties*, bk 1, § 34 (p. 14); Marcus Tullius Cicero, *On the Republic; On the Laws*, trans. Clinton W. Keyes (Cambridge, MA: Harvard University Press, 1928), *On the Republic*, bk 3, ch. 23, § 35 (pp. 211/12). See also Cox, 'Ethics of War', 102-4.

25. Arthur Nussbaum, *A Concise History of the Law of Nations* (New York: Macmillan, 1947), 17; Nussbaum, 'Just War', 454.

26. Russell, *Just War*, 18-19.

(*repetitio rerum*) and a punitive right to avenge injuries (*iniuriae ulciscuntur*) followed close behind.[27] If one accepts (as Cicero did) the Aristotelian assertion that man is naturally a political animal who seeks a life of virtue, then defence of the political state could be justified on grounds of natural self-defence. War was conceived as an enterprise which could correct injustice when diplomatic overtures had failed.[28] Cicero's legal approach to war was built on long-established Roman religious tradition, the so-called fetial law (*ius fetiale*), which stipulated that after a formal request for restitution was issued by the Roman state, the guilty party was given thirty-three days to redress the wrong or surrender those responsible. If no conciliatory action was forthcoming, then war was formally declared with the full approval of the gods.[29] This process was designed to make it crystal clear that Rome was the victim rather than the aggressor (regardless of the reality), and that its war was thereby entirely necessary and justified.

For a man who served as a Roman governor and consul, it is hardly surprising that Cicero reserved the right to declare war to the public authority. Ancillary to this, individuals who fought in war had to be official representatives of the state. Cicero stated very clearly that 'it is not lawful for one who is not a soldier to fight with the enemy'.[30] The private individual could only use violence in self-defence or, if necessary, in the immediate (*incontinenti*) defence of a neighbour.

However, while Cicero parroted the 'war for peace' platitude—'wars, then, ought to be undertaken for this purpose, that we may live in peace, without injustice'—he was just as eager as any Egyptian pharaoh to defend war for the glory of empire, now rooted in ideas of universal Roman authority. He argued that Roman *imperium* produced greater security; its expansion, therefore, was justified for the sake of peace and the protection it offered to Rome's allies. Moreover, offensive wars were intended to defend the empire against violent rivals and so could, once more, be justified as essentially defensive.[31] For present readers, now well-versed in Egyptian justifications for wars in defence of Ma'at, this Ciceronian reasoning appears strikingly familiar. Essentially, it created the conceptual space to justify *all* Roman wars on the basis of universal Roman *imperium* and the *pax Romana*.

Although Cicero undoubtedly viewed war through a legalistic lens—incorporating natural, religious, and customary law—he seems to have relied

27. Cicero, *On Duties*, bk 1, § 11 (p. 6) and § 13 (pp. 6–7).
28. Ibid., bk 1, § 34 (p. 14). For Cicero's definition of injustice: ibid., bk 1, § 23 (p. 10).
29. Ibid., bk 1, § 36 (pp. 15–16). See also Watson, *International Law in Archaic Rome*, 27–28, 62–63.
30. Cicero, *On Duties*, bk 1, § 37 (p. 16).
31. Ibid., bk 1, § 35 (pp. 14–15) (quote). Cf. ibid., bk 1, §§ 20, 23, 34–38, 80; bk 2, §§ 26–29; bk 3, §§ 22–23, 46–49, 86–88; Cicero, *On the Republic*, bk 3, ch. 23, §§ 34–35 (pp. 209/10–211/12).

upon an ethic of military honour to regulate military excesses, hoping that soldiers would be moved by principles of *humanitas* and *honestum*.[32] In terms of how war should be conducted, Cicero recommended that states should conduct themselves honourably, that oaths should be observed (even with the enemy), that poison or treachery should be shunned, and that justice should be maintained 'even towards the lowliest'.[33] Enemies who surrendered should be spared, as should those who had fought honourably, and punishment should not be excessive.[34] Significantly, however, Cicero drew a distinction between fighting for empire and glory, on the one hand, and fighting defensive wars against mortal enemies on the other. He remarked that 'wars in which the goal is the glory of empire are waged less bitterly', whereas in defensive wars notions of restraint were discarded because 'the question was not who would rule, but who would exist'.[35] This is reminiscent of the Tanakh's justification of wars of genocidal annihilation against the Seven Nations (because these peoples contested the promised land of Canaan itself), whereas more restrained forms of warfare were recommended against peoples who inhabited the lands beyond Canaan. For both Israelites and Romans, existential conflicts were defined by their savagery and lack of restraint.

Rome also distinguished between peer enemies (*hostes*) and those it considered too uncivilised or politically inferior to attain this status (*latrones, inimici*). Importantly, it was only in wars against *hostes* that certain norms were considered applicable, especially regarding the conclusion of truces or treaties. Wars against *inimici/latrones* were effectively viewed as armed conflict against savages and/or criminals, in which case the Roman state was under no *in bello* obligations whatsoever.

Taken as a whole, Greco-Roman thought on war showed a distinct tendency towards creating a broad platform for unlimited violence against enemies who were considered either culturally inferior and/or existentially threatening. In doing so, it mirrored similar patterns of justification apparent in Near Eastern cultures at least a thousand years or more earlier. Whether Greeks and Romans created such frameworks wholly independently or were adopting and adapting Near Eastern forms is impossible to say with any degree of certainty. All we can do is point out that the similarities exist.

That such similarities in ethical thought about war can develop independently is suggested by the evidence found in China from the first millennium BCE onwards, where a highly influential school of 'Legalist' scholars

---

32. John von Heyking, 'Taming Warriors in Classical and Early Medieval Political Theory', in *Ethics, Nationalism, and Just War: Medieval and Contemporary Perspectives*, ed. Henrik Syse and Gregory M. Reichberg (Washington, DC: Catholic University of America Press, 2007), 11–35 at 18–19.

33. Cicero, *On Duties*, bk 1, §§ 35, 39–41; bk 3, § 99.

34. Ibid., bk 1, §§ 35, 39; bk 2, § 18.

35. Ibid., bk 1, §§ 34–8. See also ibid., bk 2, § 26; bk 3, §§ 46–49, 86–88.

developed tenets of *Machtpolitik* that helped to establish the ideological basis of the Qin empire.[36] The paradigmatic text, *The Book of Lord Shang* (late fourth to early third century), championed the enhancement of state power against rivals and the development and control of agricultural and military resources. This was backed up by a legal code based on punishment and reward: the 'Two Handles', as the mid-third-century *Han Feizi* described them.[37] Aggressive war for territorial aggrandisement, with no limitations on conduct, was treated by the Legalists as a positive enterprise. Meanwhile, texts such as the *Strategems of the Warring States* were almost wholly pragmatic in their approach to the utility of war.[38] It is true that Confucian, Mohist, and Daoist texts treated aggressive wars far more negatively, but they also justified war for defensive and punitive causes.[39] Chinese thinkers such as Mengzi/Mencius (c. 372–c. 289) left the door open for wars of conquest, permitting such military action if a state acted out of benevolent concern for an oppressed people.[40] As the fourth-century military treatise *Sima Fa* put it, '[i]f one must attack a state out of love for their people, then attacking is permissible'.[41] Yet it is easy to see how this doctrine of virtuous conquest could be read simply as a justification for imperialism.

All of the aforementioned traditions, including those of the ancient Near East, had analogous concepts of what constituted the various just causes to go to war, and all of them recognised the importance of proper authority. We have seen that the fundamental building blocks of *ius ad bellum* criteria were

---

36. I am not an advocate of the 'Axial Age' hypothesis posited by Karl Jaspers and successive scholars, mainly because it fails to account for significant intellectual and cultural developments prior to the first millennium BCE. To incorporate such developments, we are left with the overly broad concept of 'axiality', as proposed by Jan Assmann. See Karl Jaspers, *Vom Ursprung und Ziel der Geschichte* (Frankfurt am Main: Fischer Bücherei, 1959); S. N. Eisenstadt (ed.), *The Origins and Diversity of Axial Age Civilizations* (Albany: State University of New York Press, 1986); Jan Assmann, 'Axial "Breakthroughs" and Semantic "Relocations" in Ancient Egypt and Israel', in *Axial Civilizations and World History*, ed. Johann P. Arnason, S. N. Eisenstadt, and Björn Wittrock (Leiden: Brill, 2005), 133–56; Robert N. Bellah, 'What is Axial about the Axial Age?', *European Journal of Sociology* 46 (1) (2005): 69–89; John D. Boy and John Torpey, 'Inventing the Axial Age: The Origins and Uses of a Historical Concept', *Theory and Society* 42 (3) (2013): 241–59.

37. Ping-cheung Lo, 'Varieties of Statecraft and Warfare Ethics in Early China: An Overview', in *Chinese Just War Ethics: Origin, Development, and Dissent*, ed. Ping-cheung Lo and Sumner B. Twiss (Abingdon: Routledge, 2015), 3–25 at 5–7; David A. Graff, 'The Chinese Concept of Righteous War', in *The Prism of Just War: Asian and Western Perspectives on the Legitimate Use of Military Force*, ed. Howard M. Hensel (Farnham: Ashgate, 2010), 195–216 at 197–98.

38. Graff, 'Chinese Concept', 197.

39. Lo, 'Varieties of Statecraft', 8–12; Lewis, 'Just War in Early China', 189–90.

40. Lo, 'Varieties of Statecraft', 8.

41. Cited in Graff, 'Chinese Concept', 202; cf. Lewis, 'Just War in Early China', 188; Lo, '*Art of War* Corpus', 404.

apparent across Egyptian, Hittite, and Israelite just war thought, and the basic concerns regarding causes for war and authority to wage war are directly comparable to later just war traditions. When it came to the practical business of fighting wars, each of these three traditions was marked by a refusal to grant any privileges to the enemy. This was coupled with a striking pragmatism which recognised that while victory in war was determined by divine judgement, victory was also a necessity for survival and personal liberty.

But whether such similarities were ultimately derived from the same conceptual rootstock as later Greco-Roman and Christian just war traditions, and thus constitute a genealogical lineage, is impossible to say with any degree of certainty. That just war ideas were transmitted transculturally seems likely, but cannot be proven conclusively. Given its geographical location, Egypt has always occupied a liminal space between Europe, the Middle East, and Africa. Egypt figured prominently in Israelite history as narrated by the Tanakh: as a place of refuge and prosperity (Genesis 12:10–20; 37:28–50:25); as a place of oppression and exodus (Exodus 1:1–15:6); as a politico-military ally (1 Kings 3:1; 9:16); and as a military threat (1 Kings 14:25–26; 2 Chronicles 36:3–4). Hans Goedicke has argued that Egyptian religion was far more monistic than traditionally envisioned, and Jan Assmann has been the most prominent champion of the thesis that Mosaic monotheism can be traced back to Egyptian royal theology.[42] As one of the dominant cultural forces in the Levant at the turn of the first millennium BCE, it does not strain credibility to think that any number of norms might have been transmitted from Egyptian into Israelite culture. There seems little reason why ideals concerning justice and war should not have been included in this process. We can certainly point to striking similarities between the narrative of the duel in the 'Tale of Sinuhe' and the story of David and Goliath, for example.

From at least the New Kingdom onwards, Egyptians also had contact with Aegean Greeks.[43] Herodotus was surely not alone in believing that the Hellenic world owed a great deal to Egypt in terms of theology and mythology. The Hellenistic conquest of Egypt in the fourth century provided a further

42. Hans Goedicke, 'Unity and Diversity in the Oldest Religion of Ancient Egypt', in *Unity and Diversity: Essays in the History, Literature, and Religion of the Ancient Near East*, ed. Hans Goedicke and J.J.M. Roberts (Baltimore: Johns Hopkins University Press, 1975), 201–21; Jan Assmann, *Politische Theologie zwischen Ägypten und Israel* (Munich: Carl Friedrich von Siemens Stiftung, 1995); Assmann, *Moses the Egyptian: The Memory of Egypt in Western Monotheism* (Cambridge, MA: Harvard University Press, 1997); Assmann, *Of God and Gods: Egypt, Israel, and the Rise of Monotheism* (Madison: University of Wisconsin Press, 2008). The link between Egypt, monotheism, and Moses dates back to Freud's 1939 work *Der Mann Moses und die monotheistische Religion*, available in English as Sigmund Freud, *Moses and Monotheism*, trans. Katherine Jones (London: Hogarth Press and Institute of Psycho-Analysis, 1939).

43. See Wachsmann, *Aegeans*; Cline, 'Amenhotep III and the Aegean'; O'Connor, 'Egypt's Views of Others', 166–67.

conduit for cultural transmission, and even the definitive version of Homer's *Iliad* was edited in Alexandria, at the mouth of the Nile delta. Egypt was partially assimilated into Hellenic, Roman, and early Christian culture for over nine hundred years (c. 331 BCE–c. 616 CE), before being integrated into the Islamic world. In a very real sense, therefore, the history of Egypt is entwined with the histories of these later cultures and religions.

Equally, the Hittites engaged in political contact and military aggression with the Mycenaeans, and I have already noted traces of Hittite myths in Greek mythological cycles.[44] Between Hatti and Egypt, meawhile, there was obviously enough conceptual and legal common ground for them to negotiate a sophisticated defensive and offensive alliance in the thirteenth century. It is also likely that pharaonic claims to divine kingship encouraged Hittite Great Kings to assert comparable claims towards the end of their empire.[45] One can also point to the remarkable debt that the Israelite Covenant owes to the genre of Hittite vassal treaties, or the apparent lasting influence of the Hittite law code on Israelite conceptions of rape.

Given the practice of enslavement and deportation in the wake of Near Eastern wars, there must also have been significant movements of people across political and cultural boundaries. Importantly, this could include peoples who were subsequently integrated into the conqueror's military machine as auxiliaries or mercenaries; such warriors would surely have preserved elements of their idiosyncratic martial cultures, integrating them with those of their new masters. Finally, Rome became acquainted with the norms of Near Eastern international relations via its interactions with Egyptians, Phoenicians, Carthaginians, Israelites, and others. As the Roman empire matured into a pan-Mediterranean superpower, its diplomatic practices in the region became ever more closely aligned to long-established Near Eastern forms of international relations.[46]

In other words, cultural interaction and transmission undoubtedly took place over time, so that lines of influence between Egyptian, Hittite, Israelite, Greek, Roman, Christian, and Islamic just war thought are eminently plausible. One might speculate that the similarities appear close enough, and the opportunities for transmission numerous enough, for fine threads of continuity to exist. But we simply cannot say for certain, and so must be content with speculation.

The one avenue which encourages a less cautious approach is the influence of the Tanakh on later Jewish, Christian, and Islamic thought, which was (and is) both substantial and incontestable. As has been discussed, much of the most extreme war material in the Tanakh was likely a product of the exilic and post-exilic period up to about 450. Later, faced with continuing political and

---

44. See above, ch. 7 n. 35. See also Dowden, *Uses of Greek Mythology*, 169.
45. De Martino, 'Symbols of Power', 95.
46. *ILA*, 47, 278.

social challenges in the wake of Hellenic and Roman invasions, an even more radical form of Yahwism evolved and was linked to a sense of nationalism, producing the militarism of the Maccabees and the violence of the Zealots.[47] With the emergence of rabbinical commentary, which took shape in the form of the Mishnah and Talmud, Judaism created a reformulated tradition of just war based on the foundations of the Tanakh.[48]

The Tanakh, in the form of the Old Testament, provided a crucial theological foundation for justifications of Christian warfare. Early Christian apologists such as Ambrose of Milan (d. 397 CE) and Augustine of Hippo (d. 430 CE) found in the Old Testament a pre-existing just war tradition that could be adopted and adapted to their needs. It was incorporated into a Stoic and legalistic Romanised concept of political authority and justice, but retained the essential components and chauvinism of its Israelite foundations. Israelite ideas of just cause and divine authority were not significantly altered. However, rather than the relationship between the Israelites and Yahweh being front and centre to questions of justice and authority, in the hands of Christian theologians it became the tripartite relationship between Christ, his followers, and the Roman emperor as Christ's agent of terrestrial authority. War, victory, and defeat were still ultimately seen as part of divine providence, centred on the narrative of salvation. But, just like the redactors of the Tanakh, Christians continued to believe that there could be no hope of victory in war if they did not faithfully maintain their duties to Yahweh/Christ.

The influence of the Israelite just war tradition has continued even up to the modern era. In 1948 the Israeli Military Rabbinate was established concurrently with the Israel Defense Forces (IDF), evincing a continuing relationship between Yahwism, military activity, and the hope for military success. To this day it is a legal requirement that every IDF unit be accompanied by a representative from the Military Rabbinate.[49] The Rabbinate's official 'Prayer for the Well-Being of the Israel Defense Forces' implores, 'May He lead our enemies under our soldiers' sway and may He grant them salvation and crown them with victory. And may there be fulfilled for them the verse: "For it is the Lord your God, Who goes with you to battle your enemies for you to save you."'[50] In a similar vein, General Bernard Montgomery's address to

---

47. Redford, *Egypt, Canaan, and Israel*, 470.

48. For introductory surveys of this later Jewish tradition, see Solomon, 'Judaism'; Michael Walzer, 'The Ethics of Warfare in the Jewish Tradition', *Philosophia* 40 (2012): 633–41; Daniel F. Polish, 'Just War in Jewish Thought', in *The Concept of Just War in Judaism, Christianity, and Islam*, ed. Georges Tamer and Katja Thörner (Berlin: De Gruyter, 2021), 1–41.

49. 'Military Rabbinate', Israel Defense Forces website, https://www.idf.il/en/minisites/military-rabinate/ (accessed 9 January 2023).

50. 'Jewish Prayers: Prayer for the Well-Being of the Israel Defense Forces', Jewish Virtual Library, https://www.jewishvirtuallibrary.org/prayer-for-the-well-being-of-the-israel-defense-forces (accessed 9 January 2023).

the 21st Army Group (5 June 1944), as they prepared for the D-Day Landings, declared, 'We have a great and a righteous cause. Let us pray that the Lord Mighty in Battle will go forth with our armies, and that his special providence will aid us in the struggle.'[51] In the now famous battle speech given to the Royal Irish Regiment by Lieutenant Colonel Tim Collins on the eve of the 2003 invasion of Iraq, Collins made several references to the Old Testament, reminding his troops that Iraq was 'the birthplace of Abraham'. Collins also cautioned his soldiers to show restraint in taking human life, warning that, 'I know of men who have taken life needlessly in other conflicts. I can assure you they live with the mark of Cain upon them.'[52]

Notwithstanding such influences, that traditions of just war thought developed in various cultures around the world—cultures with demonstrably few or no contacts with one another—suggests that just war thought does not require any sort of singular Ur-culture. Rather, it is a way of thinking about large-scale violence that frequently goes hand in hand with complex social life, cultural systems, and states.

Ius pro bello *and the Origins of Just War Thought*

Ancient Near Eastern just war traditions represent the earliest evidence for just war thought. The importance of this discovery cannot be overstated, for it shows that the human urge to intellectualise and justify large-scale organised violence is very ancient indeed. It tells us something poignant about the fundamental intellectual and emotional needs of human communities when engaged in the killing of other humans, as well as the requirements and ambitions of socio-political structures of authority.

Following from this, is it accurate to say, therefore, that societies engage in ethical reflection on war as a self-legitimating and self-justifying process resulting directly from the necessity or desire to wage war? As I posited at the beginning of this book, a concept of justice is required for any complex society to flourish, and is designed to mitigate violence and unpredictability within the community. War does not just challenge such violence-limiting norms; it

---

51. 'General Montgomery's message, Operation Overlord—Normandy Landings', D-Day and Battle of Normandy Encyclopedia, https://www.dday-overlord.com/en/d-day/files/montgomery-message (accessed 9 January 2023). See also Craigie, *Problem of War*, 33.

52. 'Iraq is steeped in history. It is the site of the Garden of Eden, of the Great Flood and the birthplace of Abraham. Tread lightly there. [. . .] It is a big step to take another human life. It is not to be done lightly. I know of men who have taken life needlessly in other conflicts. I can assure you they live with the mark of Cain upon them.' Lieutenant Colonel Tim Collins' Eve-of-Battle Speech' (19 March 2003), 'Royal Irish: The Irish Soldier in the British Army' website, https://www.royal-irish.com/stories/lieutenant-colonel-tim-collins-eve-of-battle-speech (accessed 9 January 2023).

inverts them.[53] And yet, even in war, most people want 'to act or to seem to act morally'.[54] This was no less true for the ancient world than for the modern. In the ancient world, belief in some form of afterlife was almost universal, and the quality of a soul's experience after death was dependent upon an individual's actions during life. The principle of moral reciprocity was key to this understanding: good actions invited good consequences; evil actions invited evil consequences. This meant that individuals were concerned about the moral qualities of their actions and could not afford to be flippant about killing other humans. Warriors concerned with the afterlife could not simply kill and be done with it; rather, they wished to ensure that their act of killing was not anathema to their cultural or religious values, thus not preventing their reintegration into the community after war or hindering their final passage into the afterlife. In the ancient Near East, in which religion infused all aspects of life, the norm-defying violence of war thus required sacralisation. The emergence of ethics of war therefore seems to be rooted in a need to sacralise the act of killing, especially mass killing, in order to remove guilt from the individual and the community. So began the process of sacralising killing by framing it in terms of ethical or moral justifications. Most obviously, this focused on the wickedness of the enemy and thus the necessity of their death. (Arguably, when all else is stripped away from modern just war doctrine, this remains, at heart, the principal justification for war.) This desire to sacralise the act of killing may also have been grounded in a psychological repugnance (conscious or subconscious) towards killing other members of the same species; there is certainly compelling psychological research to suggest that most soldiers have a powerful aversion (initially, at least) to harming or killing other human beings.[55] One could imagine just war doctrine as a psychological coping mechanism, seeking to assuage the trauma of killing by disguising it as an essentially positive moral act (or at the very least not a negative one).

Directly linked to this, the emergence of ethics of war was also surely grounded in the fear of death. We too often forget that just war doctrines are

---

53. This aligns with Burkert's observation about the friction between early human social life and the increasing lethality of weapons-based hunting: 'what was allowed and necessary in one realm was absolutely forbidden in the other. [...] Peace must reign within the group, for what is called for outside, offends within.' Burkert, *Homo necans*, 19, 21. On the so-called 'hunting hypothesis', which contentiously posits that military virtues were grounded in aggressive genetic traits, see Robert Ardrey, *The Hunting Hypothesis: A Personal Conclusion concerning the Evolutionary Nature of Man* (New York: Atheneum, 1976).

54. Walzer, *Just and Unjust Wars*, 20.

55. See Grossman, *On Killing*. See also Burkert, *Homo necans*, 16, 20–21; *LIR*, 86–87; *WHB*, 20–25. Freud thought otherwise, and asserted that 'primaeval man [...] had no objection to someone else's death; it meant the annihilation of someone he hated, and primitive man had no scruples against bringing it about'. Freud, 'Thoughts for the Times', 292.

designed not only to justify the act of killing, but to rationalise and/or sacralise the very real risk of death. Warriors of all periods and places want to know that if they have to sacrifice their lives, it is a sacrifice worth making. Believing one's own side to be righteous and enjoying divine favour must have endowed soldiers with a sense of confidence in their own victory, psychologically distancing the prospect of their own deaths.[56] At the same time, it must also have made the thought of their own deaths more tolerable, as they could be confident that they were dying for a worthwhile cause. War is humanity's most lethal activity and has to be understood conceptually and symbolically precisely because of the concrete danger it poses. Assessed in purely material terms, the risk of war to individuals might often seem to outweigh the potential rewards. And though the attitudes and experiences of the average soldier from the ancient world remain all but hidden from us, we can assume that the ethical and martial values expressed through the elite sources—the subject of the foregoing analysis—were disseminated throughout society through channels such as religious practice, military training, royal appearances, public art and architecture, and the myriad other ways in which members of any society are indoctrinated into dominant modes of thought. The development of ethics of war is, therefore, perhaps an inevitable feature of complex societies: a kind of socio-evolutionary imperative, rendering a physically perilous and psychologically traumatic activity, which many individuals might sensibly wish to avoid, a symbolically meaningful one.

Violence and war are not the same things: war is infinitely more complex; war has to be 'constructed' from simple violence. The development of just war thought was an intrinsic, perhaps even an integral, part of that process of construction, persuading individuals to accept or ignore the physical and metaphysical costs of waging war, as well as reinforcing the potential benefits. Modern commentators on just war, especially those approaching the subject from the perspective of analytical moral philosophy, have tended to ignore the simple fact that violence between human communities predates the ethics of war. Communities were fighting before they began articulating *why* they were fighting, or indeed *if* they should be fighting at all. Both law and ethics tend to be reactive, so it is self-evident, I would argue, that concepts of justified violence were not created *ex nihilo* as exercises in abstract ethical reasoning; rather, they were created in response to the reality of large-scale violence. Consequently, we cannot divorce ethics of war from collective experiences and acts of war. As Bernard Williams phrased it in his essay on the relationship between political theory and political action, '[i]n the beginning was the deed'.[57] Equally, as Rosemary Kellison cautions, it is important to remember that ethics of war

---

56. Cf. *LIR*, 113.

57. Bernard Williams, *In the Beginning Was the Deed: Realism and Moralism in Political Argument*, ed. Geoffrey Hawthorne (Princeton, NJ: Princeton University Press, 2005), 18–28.

are the products of *people*.⁵⁸ It belies historical reality to propose that systems of ethics, especially ethics of war, are morally autonomous in the Kantian sense (i.e., sprung from universal duties). Ethics of war evolve to service the needs of the war society and the warrior, not the duties of some fanciful universal morality. Just war traditions were (and are) shaped by the dominant cultural values of specific societies as well as by the exigencies and realities of war itself. As a result, we should not be surprised to find just war thought expressed in diverse sources—mythology, prayers, royal annals, campaign reports, art, and so on—because all of these express broader cultural beliefs and ideas about social life.

This does not mean that just war traditions in the ancient Near East were purely a veil for pragmatic power games. Ideas shaped action just as action shaped ideas. As we have seen from the very earliest articulations of just war thought, societies and warriors have displayed a consistent desire to imagine themselves as 'good' and 'righteous' and 'just'. As a result, they have been perfectly capable of imposing obligations on themselves in order to satisfy these idealistic demands, whether paying tribute to a god, performing rituals to avoid taboo and pollution, or suffering corporal punishment as a form of penance. In most cases, just war thought is a synthesis of ideational convictions and material requirements.

It also does not mean that just war thought has to remain fixed to specific war experiences. Some of the most radical claims to universal authority made by ancient monarchies came about during periods of political instability, as rulers attempted to bolster their political power in the face of endogenous and/or exogenous challenges. We have seen that the increasingly radical just war thought espoused by the Tanakh's redactors was only loosely connected to the historical military experiences they were attempting to describe and to explain. As Israelites suffered devastating military defeat, some reacted by crafting just war thought that was not only more permissive, but more demanding of extreme violence.

The fact remains that archaeological evidence from a range of ancient cultures indicates that ancient societies were more inclined to praise warlike actions than to condemn them. For almost every known ancient culture around the world, archaeologists have discovered evidence of martial traditions: elite warriors buried with war gear, votive and propitiatory offerings of warrior sculptures and weapons, images of warlike deities. To this we can add a plethora of textual evidence which suggests that ancient societies did more than accept warfare: they glorified it. This assessment appears true for the majority of cultures, regardless of time or place. The proliferation of martial symbolism and themes pervading all aspects of modern culture(s) confirms

58. Rosemary Kellison, *Expanding Responsibility for the Just War: A Feminist Critique* (Cambridge: Cambridge University Press, 2019), 1–2, 9, 15.

that this trend remains alive today. The uncomfortable truth is that societies often *want* to wage war (or fantasise about their ability to do so), especially those members of society who profit most from war spoils or from territorial expansion. To do so, they require ethical systems that maintain their self-image as 'righteous' and 'good', convincing their populations that killing is permissible (even laudable) and that dying is an acceptable risk.

The ancient evidence suggests that societies began engaging in ethical reflection on war as a self-legitimating and self-justifying process, resulting directly from the necessity or desire to wage war. Such a conclusion forces us to address two modern claims that seek to describe the essence of the historical Western just war tradition. In a 1983 encyclical, the US Catholic bishops claimed that Christian just war thought 'begins in every case with a presumption against war' (*ius contra bellum*).[59] James Turner Johnson, in contrast, has vociferously critiqued the bishops' interpretation and offered in response a characterisation of Western just war thought as being defined by a 'presumption against injustice'.[60]

Neither of these characterisations fits the ancient just war thought examined throughout this study. The bishops' assertion of a 'presumption against war' underlying the Christian tradition clearly fails to stand up to historical examination and derives from a misreading of the scriptural and canonistic evidence, as well as a fundamental misunderstanding of the historical roots of the Christian and Hebrew tradition. As for Johnson's 'presumption against injustice', we have seen that justice was indeed a primary concern for the Egyptian, Hittite, and Israelite traditions, but lying at the heart of their just war doctrine was not a presumption against war or injustice, but rather a *presumption in favour of war*.

Our modern English word 'presumption' derives directly from the Latin verb *praesumere*, meaning 'to anticipate'. All ancient just war thought *anticipated* war, accepting it as a reality. As has been shown, the primary aim of all such doctrine was not to restrain or condemn war, but to legitimate it. Ancient just war thought cannot be described in terms of a 'presumption against injustice' and certainly not a 'presumption against war'. Rather, the defining quality of ancient just war thought was that it anticipated war and sought to portray its violence as compatible with the dominant religious and cultural norms of the

---

59. 'The Challenge of Peace: God's Promise and Our Response; ('A Pastoral Letter on War and Peace by the National Conference of Catholic Bishops, 3 May 1983'), PDF available at https://www.usccb.org/upload/challenge-peace-gods-promise-our-response-1983.pdf (accessed 9 January 2023).

60. James Turner Johnson, 'The Broken Tradition', *The National Interest* 45 (1996): 27–36; Johnson, 'The Just War Idea: The State of the Question', *Social Philosophy and Policy* 23 (1) (2006): 167–95. See also a useful analysis of the debate in Serena K. Sharma, 'The Legacy of *Jus Contra Bellum*: Echoes of Pacifism in Contemporary Just War Thought', *Journal of Military Ethics* 8 (3) (2009): 217–30.

individual society. In this sense, just war thought was a presumption *for* war, because by aligning war with systems of morality, it effectively enabled more war. And at no point did ancient just war thought seriously question the necessity or legitimacy of war itself. If we need a pithy Latin phrase to sum up this anticipation and justification of war, then it might best be described as *ius pro bello*. Ancient peoples assumed the reality, even the desirability, of war. In so doing, they sought to provide ethical and legal grounds to sacralise and justify warfare, thus giving birth to what I have identified as nascent just war traditions. In many senses, these traditions were self-legitimising. Just causes could include self-defence and retribution, but could also include self-aggrandisement, glory, and profit. I would argue that this is, in fact, a surprisingly common feature of just war thought throughout the ancient world, and arguably through the Middle Ages and up to the beginning of the modern era too.

Ius pro bello, *or Just Realism?*

The earliest doctrines of just war were not characterised by a presumption against injustice and certainly not by a presumption against war. Instead, they were geared towards legitimising war and warriors. This finding challenges a number of modern preconceptions about the history of the just war. But does it reduce ancient just war thought merely to a strain of pragmatism or political realism?

Strictly speaking, just war thought is opposed to doctrines of realism.[61] Realist scholars have long cast doubt on the ability of normative obligations to constrain the violence of war, an attitude embodied in Clausewitz's oft-cited claim that '[w]ar is thus an act of force to compel our enemy to do our will. [. . .] Attached to force are certain self-imposed, imperceptible limitations hardly worth mentioning, known as international law and custom, but they scarcely weaken it.'[62] Classical realism claims that the natural state between polities is one of competition and mistrust; interactions between political communities are essentially amoral, and the relationship between war and justice is irrelevant, notwithstanding any claims to the contrary.[63] 'Wars

---

61. The opposition between just war thought and realism is clearly described by Walzer, *Just and Unjust Wars*, 3–20.

62. Carl von Clausewitz, *On War*, ed. and trans. Michael Howard and Peter Paret (1976; repr. New York: Everyman's Library, 1993), bk 1, ch. 1, § 2 (p. 83). Ironically, Clausewitz almost immediately contradicts this claim when he contrasts the wars of 'civilised' and 'savage' peoples: 'If wars between civilized nations are far less cruel and destructive than wars between savages, the reason lies in the social conditions of the states themselves and in their relationship to one another. These are the forces that give rise to war; the same forces circumscribe and moderate it.' Ibid, bk 1, ch. 1, § 3 (p. 84).

63. For a summary of classical realist thought and its proponents, see Steven Forde, 'Classical Realism', in *Traditions of International Ethics*, ed. Terry Nardin and

among states cannot settle questions of authority and right,' claims the neo-realist scholar Kenneth N. Waltz, 'they can only determine the allocation of gains and losses among contenders and settle for a time the question of who is the stronger.'[64] As one post-positive critic of the just war tradition sums it up, 'Just War conditions provide a cover which allows power to do what power can do'.[65] Or, expressed more pithily, 'just wars are just war'.[66]

As we have seen, in the ancient Near East there was an intimate connection between theologico-political ideology, on the one hand, and military necessity or ambition on the other. The development of this relationship was informed, in many instances, by what would now be described as pragmatism. It should not be forgotten that societies are the creative force behind systems of ethics and justice, and societies are ready to alter such systems in response to real-world demands. Whether in defence of the state or for the aggrandisement of the state, presenting war as a morally positive endeavour clearly had material advantages. There was a tangible sense in which 'might makes right' and 'right makes might' were equally true—two sides of the same coin.

In sum, characterising ancient just war thought as *ius pro bello* underlines the claim that societies engage in ethical reflection on war as a self-legitimising and self-justifying process resulting directly from the necessity or desire to wage war. Building on this conclusion, perhaps a re-examination of medieval and modern just war thought—whether from the Western, Islamic, Hindu, or Chinese traditions—might highlight that such traditions are also best described as *ius pro bello*.

Ultimately, I think this would undermine some modern attempts to present just war doctrines (historical and contemporary) as primarily geared towards providing a set of *questions* about war. As has been demonstrated, the earliest just war thought emerged as a deliberate attempt to provide answers about war that were intentionally predetermined to permit war and enable

---

David R. Mapel (Cambridge: Cambridge University Press, 1992), 62–84. More nuanced realist approaches to war and political morality can be found in, for example, David R. Mapel, 'Realism, War and Peace', in *The Ethics of War and Peace: Religious and Secular Perspectives*, ed. Terry Nardin (Princeton, NJ: Princeton University Press, 1997), 54–77.

64. Kenneth N. Waltz, *Theory of International Politics* (1979; repr. Long Grove, IL: Waveland Press, 2010), 102, 112. Some realist scholars have sought to highlight the connections between realism and just war thought. Valerie Morkevičius argues that 'the theoretical parallels between realism and just war thinking are so significant that we should see the two traditions as sharing the middle passageway': Morkevičius, *Realist Ethics*, 10–11. See also Valerie Morkevičius, 'Power and Order: The Shared Logics of Realism and Just War Theory', *International Studies Quarterly* 59 (1) (2015): 11–22; Barry Paskins, 'Realism and the Just War', *Journal of Military Ethics* 6 (2) (2007): 117–30.

65. Ken Booth, 'Ten Flaws of Just Wars', *The International Journal of Human Rights* 4 (3–4) (2000): 314–24 at 317.

66. Ibid., 316. See also Andrew Fiala, *The Just War Myth: The Moral Illusions of War* (Lanham, MD: Rowman and Littlefield, 2008).

warriors, glorifying both war and warriors in the process.[67] And I think we should be very sceptical of any attempt to portray just war theorising as a morally neutral or objective endeavour.

Yet this book is not a realist account of just war thought. Neither ancient nor contemporary just war thought can be reduced to mere political pragmatism. One of the key assumptions underlying this study is that communities (historical and contemporary) both *require* and *believe in* concepts of justice, as well as the religious and/or secular ethics they reflect.[68] The social stability and ontological security of any community is partly dependent upon its system of justice and its belief that, in moral terms, it is superior to its competitors and enemies.[69] Appeals to religious morality and secular justice in the conceptualisation and prosecution of war are one proof of this. Thus it is a truism that political communities and combatants believe *their* wars to be just. In the ancient world, theories of just war fulfilled—as they continue to fulfil—an ontological requirement of complex political communities: a need for individuals to believe in the essential virtue of their community and, by extension, of themselves. There is nothing contradictory, therefore, in describing just war thought (ancient or otherwise) as rooted in pragmatism, essentially permissive in character, and yet obsessed with justice and morality.

---

67. Referring to more modern doctrine, this position is also eloquently argued by Chris Brown, 'Just War and Political Judgement', in *Just War: Authority, Tradition, and Practice*, ed. Anthony F. Lang Jr., Cian O'Driscoll, and John Williams (Washington, DC: Georgetown University Press, 2013), 35–48.

68. In seeing an equally important role for the ideational as for the material in understanding the emergence of ancient just war thought and the military activities of ancient states, this study could be understood as contributing to constructivist international relations literature or 'critical international theory in historical mode', as described by Richard Devetak, 'A Rival Enlightenment? Critical International Theory in Historical Mode', *International Theory* 6 (3) (2014): 417–53 at 421; cf. Devetak, *Critical International Theory: An Intellectual History* (Oxford: Oxford University Press, 2018), 158ff. Constructivist international relations theory in the sense described by, for example, Alexander Wendt, 'Anarchy Is What States Make of It', *International Organization* 46 (2) (1992): 391–425; Wendt, *Social Theory of International Relations* (Cambridge: Cambridge University Press, 1999); Christian Reus-Smit, *The Moral Purpose of the State: Culture, Social Identity, and Institutional Rationality in International Relations* (Princeton, NJ: Princeton University Press, 1999).

69. The concept of ontological security, initially developed by the psychoanalyst Robert Laing, was subsequently applied to the identity and actions of states and citizens by the sociologist Anthony Giddens in his *Modernity and Self-Identity: Self and Society in the Late Modern Age* (Stanford, CA: Stanford University Press, 1991). Since then, ontological security has gained increasing traction within International Relations scholarship as a means of explaining elements of state behaviour. See, inter alia: Jennifer Mitzen, 'Ontological Security in World Politics: State Identity and the Security Dilemma', *European Journal of International Relations* 12 (3) (2006): 341–70; Brent J. Steele, *Ontological Security in International Relations: Self-Identity and the IR State* (Abingdon: Routledge, 2008); Bahar Rumelili (ed.), *Conflict Resolution and Ontological Security: Peace Anxieties* (London: Routledge, 2015).

Lessons from the Earliest Just War Traditions

A better understanding of the earliest just war traditions can teach us something about how we approach the ethics of war today. Contemporary scholars of just war can be (very) roughly divided into two camps: the classical (perhaps better referred to as the 'traditionist') and the revisionist. In the second half of the twentieth century, following the interventions of Paul Ramsey, Michael Walzer, and James Turner Johnson, the traditionist camp very much dominated the debate and usually found themselves aligned against proponents of realism and neo-realism. This camp of scholars drew on the so-called 'classical' Western just war corpus, identified with the Christian and later natural law traditions of just war. Central to their conception of just war was the recognition that *ius ad bellum* and *ius in bello* norms were two sides of the same just war coin, existing independently of one another but acting in concert to create a fully articulated and comprehensive just war doctrine.

Over the last two decades, however, an increasingly influential 'revisionist' camp of scholars, consisting principally of analytical philosophers (rather than theologians, International Relations theorists, or historians), began to critique many of the fundamental claims made by the traditionist camp. Revisionist scholars have approached the ethics and laws of war more or less ahistorically, although they have been willing to adopt historical terminology in their arguments. The hallmark of the revisionist approach is an emphasis on the role, obligations, culpabilities, and liabilities of the individual in war, shifting the focus away from the state as the sole locus of authority and culpability. Critically, most revisionists insist that war and military actions should be judged by the same rules as govern harm in everyday life. War, it is argued, does not represent a separate or unique moral category. Philosophers such as Jeff McMahan, David Rodin, Cécile Fabre, Helen Frowe, and Seth Lazar (among others) have sought to emphasise the critical importance of determining who is culpable—and therefore liable to harm—in war.[70] In so doing, they have mounted a significant

---

70. See especially: Rodin, *War and Self-Defense*; David Rodin, 'The Moral Inequality of Soldiers: Why *jus in bello* Asymmetry is Half Right' in *Just and Unjust Warriors: The Moral and Legal Status of Soldiers*, ed. David Rodin and Henry Shue (Oxford: Oxford University Press, 2008), 44–68; Jeff McMahan, 'The Morality of War and the Law of War', in ibid., 19–43; McMahan, *Killing in War*; Cécile Fabre, 'Cosmopolitanism, Just War Theory and Legitimate Authority', *International Affairs* 84 (5) (2008): 963–76; Fabre, *Cosmopolitan War*; Helen Frowe, 'Individualism and Collectivism in the Ethics of War', in *A Companion to Applied Philosophy*, ed. Kimberley Brownlee, David Coady, and Kasper Lippert-Rasmussen (Chichester: Wiley-Blackwell, 2017), 342–55; Frowe, *Defensive Killing*; Frowe, 'The Just War Framework', in *Oxford Handbook of Ethics of War*, ed. Seth Lazar and Helen Frowe (New York: Oxford University Press, 2018), 41–58; Seth Lazar, 'Responsibility'; Lazar, *Sparing Civilians* (Oxford: Oxford University Press, 2015); Lazar, 'Liability and the Ethics of War: A Response', in *The Ethics of Self-Defense*, ed. Christian Coons and Michael Weber (New York: Oxford University Press, 2016), 292–304.

challenge to two key principles of contemporary just war doctrine and the laws of armed combat, commonly referred to as the 'war convention'.

The interrelated principles of the war convention state, firstly, that the validity of *ius ad bellum* claims should remain independent from the observation of *ius in bello* norms; and secondly, that there exists a moral and legal 'equality of combatants', meaning that combatants partaking in an 'unjust' war should enjoy the same *in bello* privileges and protections as those partaking in a 'just' war. By problematising the autonomy of the *ius ad bellum* and *ius in bello* categories (as well as the more recent category of *ius post bellum*), revisionist scholars have questioned assumptions about *who* is deserving of harm or protection during war.[71] In contradistinction to the 'equality of combatants' doctrine, McMahan and others have argued for the moral basis of an 'asymmetry of combatants' (and non-combatants) pertaining to wartime actions. This holds that individuals complicit in unjust wars forfeit *in bello* privileges and are liable to be harmed, not only as active combatants, but even as prisoners of war and non-combatants.[72] As McMahan explains,

> According to the standard view, soldiers fighting in a just cause and those fighting in an unjust cause are both permitted to use violence within the same constraints. [... T]his is a mistake. Soldiers fighting in a just cause are justified in using violence within certain limits. But soldiers fighting in an unjust cause are *not* morally justified in using violence, even against enemy combatants, in the service of their country's war aims. For no one has a right to use violence as a means to the achievement of immoral aims.[73]

It should be stressed that the differing versions of the asymmetry thesis are intended to *limit* the destructiveness of war by deterring unjust aggressors, limiting harm to those who truly 'deserve' punishment, and protecting those who are 'innocent'. Unfortunately, much of the moral asymmetry argument is reliant upon the existence of an unimpeachable and universally recognised arbiter of justice: something the global community has thus far failed to create, and seems unlikely to create any time soon.

---

71. Jeff McMahan, 'The Ethics of Killing in War', *Ethics* 114 (4) (2004): 693–733; McMahan, 'On the Moral Equality of Combatants', *Journal of Political Philosophy* 14 (4) (2006): 377–93; Rodin, *War and Self-Defense*, esp. 70–99, 122–40; Rodin, 'Moral Inequality of Soldiers', 44–68. Arguments both for and against the asymmetry thesis can be found in David Rodin and Henry Shue (eds), *Just and Unjust Warriors: The Moral and Legal Status of Soldiers* (Oxford: Oxford University Press, 2008).

72. McMahan, *Killing in War*, 155–202. Rodin proposes a mitigated version of the asymmetry thesis (he does not endorse attacks on non-combatants, for example), which he terms 'restrictive asymmetry': Rodin, 'Moral Inequality of Soldiers', 55–56.

73. Jeff McMahan, 'War and Peace', in *A Companion to Ethics*, ed. Peter Singer (Oxford: Blackwell, 1991), 384–95 at 388.

While revisionist scholars have produced some of the most sophisticated and persuasive theoretical treatments of just war of the last half-century, the literature has generally underestimated the real-world dangers of some of its more radical claims—and in particular, the impact of creating polarised identities of just/moral and unjust/immoral combatants and non-combatants. These scholars have failed to consider seriously the ways in which moralised identities can affect how individuals are treated during times of violence, whether as combatants, non-combatants, or prisoners of war. McMahan himself imagines a scenario in which 'considerations of justice would permit us to kill' enemy prisoners.[74] And yet perceptions of the enemy during armed conflict have a consistent tendency to veer toward the simplistic and the extreme, or the 'psychological irresistibility of the lower standard', as Shue puts it.[75] In light of such inevitable wartime prejudices, to simply recommend that there probably needs to be a separation between the morality of war and the law of war, as McMahan has done, does not offer a satisfying or practicable solution to such dangers. Divorcing morality from law also creates a host of concomitant problems—not least that of trying to persuade soldiers as to why they should bother to observe amoral or immoral laws.[76]

The confident assertions found in revisionist literature regarding the distinction between justice and injustice in war are based on a belief that morality is fixed and discoverable; that 'the morality of war is not a product of our devising. It is not manipulable; it is what it is.'[77] Such universalising moral claims rely on appeals to moral intuitions as first principles, yet history shows us that moral intuitions do not arise from a metaphysical or material vacuum. As Maja Zehfuss highlights, ethics are 'made, rather than out there, to be discovered: we invent the claims to the good that we apparently merely invoke'.[78] The cultural norms that inform the ethics of war are the product of contingent historical conditions and traditions. Put simply, every philosophical 'first principle' is nothing more than a cultural creation. And, as cultural creations, they are subject to change over time.

To insist that war is an arena in which universal moral truths can be applied is worryingly reminiscent of the types of just war thought we have

---

74. Jeff McMahan, 'Killing in War: A Reply to Walzer', *Philosophia* 34 (1) (2006): 47–51 at 49.

75. Henry Shue, 'Do We Need a "Morality of War"?', in *Just and Unjust Warriors: The Moral and Legal Status of Soldiers* (Oxford: Oxford University Press, 2008), 87–111 at 111. See also Christopher Kutz, 'Fearful Symmetry' in ibid., 69–86.

76. See McMahan, 'Morality of War', 35; McMahan, 'Killing in War', 48–49. See Shue's insightful response and critique: Shue, 'Do We Need a "Morality of War"?', 88–91, 95.

77. McMahan, 'Morality of War', 35. Yet McMahan and Rodin admit that judgements and distinctions concerning the moral and legal culpability of combatants are prone to both epistemic and pragmatic limitations.

78. Zehfuss, *War and Politics of Ethics*, 207.

seen in the ancient Near East: worrying because, as we have seen, absolutist interpretations of moral and legal inequality hampered the development of any meaningful *in bello* norms. The potential for the deliberate or careless slaughter of people branded as unjust and wicked (perhaps even preemptively or preventively) is hardly fantastical, but rather firmly rooted in historical precedent.[79] In a modern context, perhaps the most obvious examples of the potential dangers of such claims can be seen within certain elements of Salafi jihadism. Here, radical *ius ad bellum* claims have resulted in a complete abandonment of *in bello* limitations.[80] For example, the 1998 declaration of jihad issued by Osama Bin Laden's World Islamic Front specifically stated that 'to kill the Americans and their allies—civilians and military—is an individual duty for every Muslim'.[81] This interpretation of just war, based on a stark distinction between good and evil, innocent and guilty, stands in contrast to more nuanced classical literature on jihad or more moderate modern interpretations.[82] Nor are such reactions limited to the extremist fringe. Over the last two decades we have seen at first hand how the strident demonisation of Islamic terrorists since the '9/11' World Trade Center attacks has resulted in significant breaches of international law by Western liberal-democratic states. Specifically, we have witnessed 'non-state combatants' being stripped of legal status and becoming, like ancient Near Eastern prisoners of war, persons without any effective legal status or protections.[83] One consequence of

---

79. See Richard Abels, 'Cultural Representation and the Practice of War in the Middle Ages', *Journal of Medieval Military History* 6 (2008): 1–31; Cox, 'Asymmetric Warfare'.

80. See, inter alia, Kelsay, *Islam and War*, 69–74, 100–110; Michael Bonner, *Jihad in Islamic History: Doctrines and Practice* (Princeton, NJ: Princeton University Press, 2008), 157–65; Nahed Artoul Zehr, 'Legitimate Authority and the War against Al-Qaeda', in *Just War: Authority, Tradition, and Practice*, ed. Anthony F. Lang Jr., Cian O'Driscoll, and John Williams (Washington, DC: Georgetown University Press, 2013), 97–113 at 98.

81. 'Jihad Against Jews and Crusaders ('World Islamic Front Statement, 23 February 1998'), available at http://fas.org/irp/world/para/docs/980223-fatwa.htm (accessed 9 January 2023).

82. See, for example: *Jihad in Medieval and Modern Islam*; Kelsay, 'Al-Shaybani'; Kelsay, 'Islamic Tradition'; *Al-Tabari's 'Book of Jihad': A Translation from the Original Arabic*, with an introduction, commentary, and notes by Y. S. Ibrahim (Lewiston, NY: Edwin Mellen Press, 2007); 'Advice and Guidance to the Fighters on the Battlefields', The Official Website of the Office of His Eminence Sayyid ʿAli al-Sistani, The Holy City of Najaf, February 12, 2015, http://www.sistani.org/english/archive/25036/ (accessed 9 January 2023).

83. On the refusal to grant juridical status to non-state combatants, and the implications for human rights and abuse, see, inter alia: John C. Yoo and James C. Ho, 'The Status of Terrorists', *Virginia Journal of International Law* 44 (2003): 207–28, esp. 209–22; Joshua L. Dratel, 'The Legal Narrative', in *The Torture Papers: The Road to Abu Ghraib*, ed. Karen J. Greenberg and Joshua L. Dratel (Cambridge: Cambridge University Press, 2005), xxi–xxiv at xxi; Seymour M. Hersh, *The Chain of Command: The Road from 9/11 to Abu Ghraib* (New York: Harper, 2005), 1–72; Helen Frowe, *The Ethics of War and Peace: An Introduction*. Abingdon: Routledge, 2016), 205–22.

this has been a move towards the implementation and justification of torture against such persons.[84] There has also been a reliance on claims to military necessity, whereby the incontestable justice of the war is understood to excuse an ever-widening latitude for military violence in the face of non-combatant risks and casualties.[85] A similar logic underpins Walzer's arguments for extreme military violence in the case of 'supreme emergency'.[86]

That even liberal-democratic states may be inclined towards universalising claims to justice, and the negative impact that such claims may have when combined with the application of military force, has been discussed by Nicholas Rengger. Liberal-democratic states, convinced of the moral superiority of their form of political association, have typically identified non-liberal, non-democratic systems as unjust. Alongside this, just war has been viewed as a viable punitive instrument to combat injustice. The problem, remarks Rengger, is that when 'injustice is everywhere, the reasons to use force to oppose it are not hard to find'.[87] Arguably, this is one of the driving forces behind a 'new interventionism' apparent in international relations of the twenty-first century (alternatively labelled as 'liberal imperialism'), which has justified military force beyond redressing violations of territorial sovereignty. Instead, such interventionist force is justified on the basis of instating or reinstating

---

84. See, inter alia: Karen J. Greenberg and Joshua L. Dratel (eds), *The Torture Papers: The Road to Abu Ghraib* (Cambridge: Cambridge University Press, 2005); Ryder McKeown, 'Norm Regress: US Revisionism and the Slow Death of the Torture Norm', *International Relations* 23 (1) (2009): 5–25; Kerstin Fisk and Jennifer Ramos (eds), *Preventive Force: Drones, Targeted Killing, and the Transformation of Contemporary Warfare* (New York: New York University Press, 2016); Jessica Wolfendale, 'The Narrative of Terrorism as an Existential Threat', in *Routledge Handbook of Critical Terrorism Studies*, ed. Richard Jackson (Abingdon: Routledge, 2016), 114–23; Ruth Blakeley and Sam Raphael, 'British Torture in the "War on Terror"', *European Journal of International Relations* 23 (2) (2017): 243–66; Andris Banka and Adam Quinn, 'Killing Norms Softly: US Targeted Killing, Quasi-secrecy, and the Assassination Ban', *Security Studies* 27 (4) (2018): 665–703; Rory Cox, Faye Donnelly, and Anthony F. Lang Jr. (eds), *Contesting Torture: Interdisciplinary Perspectives* (Abingdon: Routledge, 2023). See also the considerable information available from the Costs of War Project website, 'Costs of War', Watson Institute, International & Public Affairs, Brown University, https://watson.brown.edu/costsofwar/costs (accessed 9 January 2023).

85. See Neta C. Crawford, *Accountability for Killing: Moral Responsibility for Collateral Damage in America's Post-9/11 Wars* (New York: Oxford University Press, 2003), 4–12, 160–75; Crawford, 'Bugsplat: US Standing Rules of Engagement, International Humanitarian Law, Military Necessity, and Noncombatant Immunity', in *Just War: Authority, Tradition, and Practice*, ed. Anthony F. Lang Jr., Cian O'Driscoll, and John Williams (Washington, DC: Georgetown University Press, 2013), 231–49 at 235–41, 245.

86. Walzer, *Just and Unjust Wars*, 251–68.

87. Nicholas Rengger, *Just War and International Order: The Uncivil Condition in World Politics* (Cambridge: Cambridge University Press, 2013), 67; cf. ibid., 1–2, 8–9, 31–35, 106, 158–79.

the 'rule of law'.[88] Yet this understanding of 'rule of law' is very much dependent on whatever state is seeking to justify its intervention. In the modern world, this has often been Western liberal-democratic states, and thus a liberal-democratic concept of law. In turn, this is a product of what Kishore Mahbubani has identified as a 'deeply held unconscious assumption that the West remains, in one way or another, a morally superior civilization'.[89]

Once again, the spectres of chauvinism so apparent in the ancient Near East seem to haunt the modern international stage: absolute claims to justice, universalising claims regarding the proper form of political authority and sovereignty, and conscious or subconscious assertions of cultural superiority. The result is a *less* restrictive use of force in international politics. Whether rooted in cosmology, theology, political ideology, or moral philosophy, universalising and absolutist interpretations of moral truth and justice are arguably the most dangerous elements of ethical thought about war.[90]

Just war thought was designed from its inception to legitimise war retrospectively as well as in anticipation of future conflicts. Indeed, I would posit that much of what is discussed today under the term *ius ad bellum* would be better described using the term *ius pro bello*. As for *ius in bello* considerations, these were largely irrelevant to ancient just war traditions. Much historical *ius ad bellum/ius pro bello* thought was wholly antithetical to *in bello* restraints. Ironically, then, the closest modern parallels to ancient just war doctrine are to be found in extremist religious teachings, on the one hand, and revisionist just war literature, on the other. While obviously very different in tone and purpose, both approaches seek to ground warfare in objective moral truths. The result is that *in bello* norms, having developed gradually across the Islamic and Western worlds since c. 1000 CE, are being increasingly eroded.

If we can learn anything about war from ancient just war traditions, it is that political communities and figures of authority within those communities will tend to view war as a viable means to defend their interests and, if feasible, to acquire further resources or to deter potential future threats. In seeking to justify military action, political leaders are likely to continue to adopt the historical languages of just war drawn from a variety of traditions relative to their particular cultural context. They are able to employ this language so effectively

---

88. Jane Stromseth, David Wippman, and Rosa Brooks, *Can Might Make Rights? Building the Rule of Law after Military Interventions* (New York: Cambridge University Press, 2006), 5, 9.

89. Kishore Mahbubani, *The Great Convergence: Asia, the West, and the Logic of One World* (New York: Public Affairs, 2013), cited in Edward Luce, *The Retreat of Western Liberalism* (New York: Grove Press, 2017), 160.

90. As Quincy Wright observed many years ago, '[w]hen war is fought for broad, ideological objectives, such [*ius in bello*] rules have tended to break down because the end is thought to justify all means and war has tended to become absolute'. Wright, *Study of War*, 1:160.

because historical just war traditions provide ready-made conceptual and rhetorical toolkits geared *primarily* towards legitimising and justifying war, not interrogating it or condemning it. One might quip that giving just war doctrines to states with well-stocked militaries is like giving a cookie recipe to a sugar addict with a well-stocked kitchen: it's only going to be a matter of time before you're eating cookies. Virtually all states have the ingredients to make war; all they need is the recipe to make their wars just. So it's only going to be a matter of time before states are fighting justified wars. The problem, as Robert Holmes puts it, is that 'a justified war [. . .] is not necessarily a just war'.[91] The most potent danger arises when leaders or publics become so convinced of the justice of their own cause that they cannot accept the possibility of ambiguities concerning issues such as just cause or enemy culpability. Indeed, the perceived strength of claims to justice seems to be directly proportional to convictions of enemy culpability and immorality. The more one is convinced of one's own morality, the more one is likely to vilify or even dehumanise the enemy. In such wars, restraint is unlikely because it is understood as unnecessary; it may even be considered undesirable or foolhardy. The importance of victory—of 'good' overcoming 'evil'—becomes an ever-greater priority, regardless of the human costs to the enemy, whether intended or unintended.

In the final analysis, does this mean that 'just war' is *just* war? Well, yes and no. The origins of just war thought strongly indicate that just war traditions emerged as a means to enable war, rather than to mitigate it. And yet these traditions were neither nihilistic nor simplistic. Pulling from embedded cultural norms in religion, ethics, law, and politics opened up avenues of action for war leaders. But this came at a cost. When one binds concepts of divine justice, morality, and political authority to warfare, the result is that the consequences of defeat are more substantial. Rather than being solely a material setback, defeat is transformed into a divine judgement on the iniquity and political illegitimacy of a war leader and a people. This has the capacity to undermine severely the political authority of any ruler. Donning the panoply of the just war may be empowering, but it also invites caution. And people still want to believe themselves to be just, which may possibly mitigate degrees of violence. Although international law and military ethics have evolved considerably since the ancient world, when contemporary political leaders and soldiers appeal to the language of law and ethics, certain expectations inevitably follow.[92] To this extent, just war traditions may indeed encourage some restraint, as regards both the decision to go to war and the manner in which war is conducted.

---

91. Robert L. Holmes, 'Can War Be Morally Justified? The Just War Theory', in *Just War Theory*, ed. Jean Bethke Elshtain (Oxford: Basil Blackwell, 1992), 197–233 at 223.

92. Walzer, *Just and Unjust Wars*, xxiii; see also Lang and O'Driscoll, 'Introduction: The Just War Tradition', 13–14.

Throughout this book I have endeavoured to demonstrate that there is much value in looking beyond the standard canon of sources when writing the history of the just war. Doing so has revealed that the first identifiable just war traditions emerged up to five thousand years ago, in the Bronze Age Near East, developing hand in hand with some of the first complex and large-scale political communities. While each society examined in this volume developed its own individual just war tradition, these had many similarities to one another, just as they share many features with later just war thought. Above all, they were grounded in a desire to rationalise, sacralise, and legitimise war for a variety of purposes. They can be characterised as *ius pro bello* traditions, for at their core they were designed to justify and even glorify warfare, not to restrain it. Ancient just war traditions demonstrate how absolute judgements in the realms of morality or justice can intensify the brutality of war—certainly in its conceptualisation, and potentially in its prosecution. The reality, of course, is that in something as complex as war there are very few absolute truths. If we can keep this foremost in our minds, then perhaps as individuals and as political communities we may be more reluctant to go to war in the first place, or a little less vicious when we do.

APPENDIX 1

Periodic Chronology of Ancient Egypt with Primary Centres of Power

Period	Power Centre(s)	Date (BCE)[a]
Pre-dynastic	*Multiple* / Nekhen (Hierakonpolis)	5000–3150
Early Dynastic (Dynasty 0–II)	'White Fort' (Memphis)	3150–2686
Old Kingdom (Dynasty III–VI)	Memphis	2686–2181
First Intermediate Period (Dynasty VII–XI)	Het-Nesut (Herakleopolis) / Thebes	2181–2055
Middle Kingdom (Dynasty XI–XII)	Thebes / Itj-towy	2055–1648
Second Intermediate Period (Dynasty XIV–XVII)	Avaris / Thebes	1648–1550
New Kingdom (Dynasty XVIII–XX)	*Multiple*[b] / Thebes	1550–1069
Third Intermediate Period (Dynasty XXI–XXV)	*Multiple*[c]	1069–664
Late Period (Dynasty XXVI–XXX)	Sais / Satrapy of Persia	664–332

[a] All dates are approximate. The exact dates of specific kings and dynasties continue to be contested among scholars. It is also uncertain at exactly what date certain kings were able to unite the Two Lands (thus founding a so-called 'kingdom period'), or exactly when kings lost centralised control and a so-called 'intermediate period' began.

[b] The official royal capital changed several times during the New Kingdom. Based initially in Thebes, the 'heretic' pharaoh Akhenaten (c. 1364–1247/c. 1352–1336) built a new capital, Amarna/Akhtetaten, between Memphis and Thebes. This was swiftly abandoned after Akhenaten's death and the capital was moved back to Thebes. During the Nineteenth Dynasty, Ramses II constructed a new capital, Pi-Ramses, in the delta region. Again, following Ramses II's death, the capital was moved by his successor Merneptah (c. 1213–c. 1203), this time to Memphis.

[c] Centres of power included Thebes (dominated by Kushite rulers), Hermopolis, Memphis, and the eastern and western delta regions.

APPENDIX 2

Internal Narrative Chronology of the Tanakh[a]

Event	Date (BCE)
Genesis	c. 4000
Birth of Abraham	2216
Abraham's descent into Egypt	2216–2141
Sojourn	1926–1496
Exodus	1496
Conquest of Canaan under Joshua	1456
Period of Judges	1456–1080

[a] For these dates, see Redford, *Egypt, Canaan, and Israel*, 258–59. Note that other versions of the texts, including the Greek Septuagint and the Samaritan Pentateuch, contain variant chronologies.

… REFERENCE BIBLIOGRAPHY

Primary Sources

Die ägyptisch-hethitische Korrespondenz aus Boghazköi, edited by Elmer Edel, 2 vols (Opladen: Westdeutscher, 1994).
Al-Tabari's 'Book of Jihad': A Translation from the Original Arabic, with an introduction, commentary, and notes by Y. S. Ibrahim (Lewiston, NY: Edwin Mellen Press, 2007).
Ancient Egyptian Literature: A Book of Readings, compiled and translated by Miriam Lichtheim, 3 vols (Berkeley: University of California Press, 1973-1980) [AEL].
The Ancient Near East: An Anthology of Texts and Pictures, edited by James B. Pritchard, 2 vols (Princeton, NJ: Princeton University Press, 1958-1975) [ANEA].
The Ancient Near East: Historical Sources in Translation, edited by Mark W. Chavalas (Malden, MA: Blackwell, 2006) [HST].
Ancient Near Eastern Texts relating to the Old Testament, edited by James B. Pritchard, 3rd edn (Princeton, NJ: Princeton University Press, 1969) [ANET].
Ancient Records of Egypt: Historical Documents from the Earliest Times to the Persian Conquest, edited and translated, with commentary, by James Henry Breasted, 5 vols (Chicago: University of Chicago Press, 1906-1907) [ARE].
Aquinas, St Thomas, 'Summa theologiae': Latin Text and English Translation, Introduction, Notes, Appendices and Glossaries, edited by Thomas Gilby O.P. et al., 61 vols (London: Blackfriars; New York: McGraw-Hill, 1964-1981), vol. 35: *Consequences of Charity (2a2ae. 34-46)*, edited and translated by T. R. Heath O.P. (1972).
Aristotle, *Nicomachean Ethics*, translated by Martin Ostwald (Upper Saddle River, NJ: Prentice Hall, 1999).
Aristotle, *The Politics*, translated by Stephen Everson (Cambridge: Cambridge University Press, 1998).
Aristotle, *Problems*, vol. 2: *Books 20-38: Rhetoric to Alexander*, edited and translated by Robert Mayhew and David C. Mirhady (Cambridge, MA: Harvard University Press, 2011).
Augustine: Political Writings, edited by E. M. Atkins and R. J. Dodaro (Cambridge: Cambridge University Press, 2001).
Augustine of Hippo, Saint, *Questions on the Heptateuch*, introduced and annotated by Joseph T. Lienhard, translated by Joseph T. Lienhard and Sean Doyle, in *The Works of Saint Augustine: Writings on the Old Testament*, edited by Boniface Ramsey, with a general introduction by Joseph T. Lienhard (New York: New City Press, 2016), 3-476.
Barton, George A., *Royal Inscriptions of Sumer and Akkad*, (New Haven, CT: Yale University Press, 1929).
Beckman, Gary, *Hittite Diplomatic Texts*, edited by Harry A. Hoffner Jr., 2nd edn (Atlanta, GA: Scholars Press, 1999) [HDT].
Bryce, Trevor, *Letters of the Great Kings of the Ancient Near East: The Royal Correspondence of the Late Bronze Age* (Abingdon: Routledge, 2003) [LettGK].
Cicero, Marcus Tullius, *On Duties (De officiis)*, edited by M. T. Griffin and E. M. Atkins (Cambridge: Cambridge University Press, 1991).
Cicero, Marcus Tullius, *On the Republic; On the Laws*, translated by Clinton W. Keyes (Cambridge, MA: Harvard University Press, 1928).
Clausewitz, Carl von, *On War*, edited and translated by Michael Howard and Peter Paret (1976; repr. New York: Everyman's Library, 1993).

Conciliorum oecumenicorum decreta, edited by Josephus [Giuseppe] Alberigo, Josephus [Giuseppe] A. Dossetti, Périklès-P[ierre] Joannou, Claudio Leonardi, and Paolo Prodi, 3rd edn (Bologna: Istituto per le scienze religiose, 1973).

Decretum magistri Gratiani, in *Corpus iuris canonici: Editio Lipsiensis secunda post Aemilii Ludouici Richteri*, edited by A. Friedberg, 2 vols (Leipzig: Tauchnitz, 1879–1881), vol. 1.

The Duties of the Vizier: Civil Administration in the Early New Kingdom, translated with commentary and analysis by G.P.F. van den Boorn (London: Kegan Paul International, 1988),

The El-Amarna Correspondence: A New Edition of the Cuneiform Letters from the Site of El-Amarna Based on Collations of all Extant Tablets, collated, transcribed, and translated by Anson F. Rainey, edited by William M. Schniedewind and Zipora Cochavi-Rainey, 2 vols (Leiden: Brill, 2015).

The Epic of Gilgamesh, translated, with an introduction and notes, by Maureen Gallery Kovacs (Stanford, CA: Stanford University Press, 1989).

Frood, Elizabeth, *Biographical Texts from Ramesside Egypt*, edited by John Baines (Atlanta, GA: Society of Biblical Literature, 2007).

The Geography of Strabo, translated with an Introduction and Notes by Duane W. Roller (Cambridge: Cambridge University Press, 2014).

Gilgamesh (Translated from the Sîn-leqi-unninnī Version), translated by John Gardiner and John Maier, with the assistance of Richard A. Henshaw (New York: Vintage Books, 1985).

Goedicke, Hans, 'The Thutmosis I Inscription near Tomâs', *Journal of Near Eastern Studies* 55 (3) (1996): 161–77.

Götze, Albrecht, *Die Annalen des Mūršiliš: Mitteilungen der vorderasiatisch-aegyptischen Gesellschaft 38* (Leipzig: Hinrichs, 1933).

Götze, Albrecht, *Hattušiliš: Der Bericht über seine Thronbesteigung nebst den Paralleltexten; Mitteilungen der vorderasiatisch-aegyptischen Gesellschaft 29* (Leipzig: Hinrichs, 1925).

Grotius, Hugo, *The Rights of War and Peace*, edited with an introduction by Richard Tuck, from the edition of Jean Barbeyrac, *Major Legal and Political Works of Hugo Grotius*, 3 vols (Indianapolis: Liberty Fund, 2005).

Gurney, O. R., 'Hittite Prayers of Muršili II', *Annals of Archaeology and Anthropology* 27 (1940): 1–167.

Güterbock, Hans G., 'The Deeds of Šuppiluliuma as Told by His Son, Muršili II', *Journal of Cuneiform Studies* 10 (1956): 41–68, 75–98, 107–19.

Herodotus, *The Histories*, translated by Robin Waterfield, with an introduction and notes by Carolyn Dewald (Oxford: Oxford University Press, 1998).

Hoffner, Harry A., Jr., *Hittite Myths*, edited by Gary M. Beckman (Atlanta, GA: Scholars Press, 1990) [*HitM*].

Hoffner, Harry A. Jr., *Letters from the Hittite Kingdom*, edited by Gary M. Beckman (Atlanta, GA: Society of Biblical Literature, 2009) [*LettH*].

The Holy Bible: King James Version (n.p.: World Bible Publishers, 2005).

The Iliad, translated with an introduction by Richard Lattimore (Chicago: University of Chicago Press, 1961).

The Jewish Study Bible [Tanakh], Jewish Publication Society Tanakh translation of the Masoretic Text, edited by Adele Berlin and Marc Zvi Brettler; consulting editor Michael Fishbane, 2nd edn (New York: Oxford University Press/Jewish Publication Society, 2004) [*JSB*].

Jihad in Medieval and Modern Islam: The Chapter on Jihad from Averroes' Legal Handbook 'Bidāyat al-Mudjtahid' and the Treatise 'Koran and Fighting' by the Late Shaykh-al-Azhar, Mahmūd Shaltūt, translated and annotated Rudolph Peters (Leiden: Brill, 1977).

Josephus, Flavius, *Flavius Josephus: Translation and Commentary*, edited by Steve Mason, 10 vols (Leiden: Brill, 2000-2017), vol. 10: *Against Apion*, translation and commentary by John M. G. Barclay (2007).
Kitchen, Kenneth A., *Ramesside Inscriptions: Historical and Biographical*, 8 vols (Oxford: Blackwell, 1969-1990).
Korošec, Viktor, *Hethitische Staatsverträge: Ein Beitrag zu ihrer juristischen Wertung; Leipziger Rechtswissenschaftliche 60* (Leipzig: Weicher, 1931).
Lacau, Pierre and Henri Chevrier, *Une chapelle de Sésostris Ier à Karnak*, vol. 2: *Planches* (Cairo: Institut français d'archéologie orientale, 1969).
Lambert, W. G., *Babylonian Creation Myths* (Winona Lake, IN: Eisenbrauns, 2013).
Lambert, W. G., A. R. Millard, and M. Civil, *Atra-Hasīs: The Babylonian Story of the Flood, with the Sumerian Flood Story* (Winona Lake, IN: Eisenbrauns, 1999).
Langdon, S. and Alan H. Gardiner, 'The Treaty of Alliance between Ḫattušili, King of the Hittites, and the Pharaoh Ramesses II of Egypt', *The Journal of Egyptian Archaeology* 6 (3) (1920): 179-205.
Law Collections from Mesopotamia and Asia Minor, edited by Martha T. Roth, with a contribution from Harry A. Hoffner Jr. (Atlanta, GA: Scholars Press, 1995) [*LCMAM*].
The Laws of the Hittites: A Critical Edition, edited by Harry A. Hoffner Jr. (Leiden: Brill, 1997) [*LawH*].
Livy, Titus, *Livy in Thirteen Volumes*, vol. 1: *Books 1 and 2*, translated by B. O. Foster, (London: William Heinemann; New York: G. P. Putnam's, 1919).
Luckenbill, Daniel David, *Ancient Records of Assyria and Babylonia*, 2 vols (Chicago: University of Chicago Press, 1926-1927).
The Major Historical Texts of Early Hittite History, edited by Trevor R. Bryce (Brisbane: University of Queensland, 1983) [*MHTH*].
Manetho, *History of Egypt and Other Works*, translated by W. G. Waddell (1940; Cambridge, MA: Harvard University Press, 2014).
Miller, Jared L., *Royal Hittite Instructions and Related Administrative Texts*, edited by Mauro Giorgieri (Atlanta, GA: Society of Biblical Literature, 2013).
Plato, *The Laws*, translated by Trevor J. Saunders (Harmondsworth: Penguin, 1970).
Plato, *The Republic of Plato*, translated by Allan Bloom (New York: Basic Books, 1968).
Quran: The Final Testament, translated by Rashad Khalifa (Tucson, AZ: Islamic Productions, 1989).
Reichberg, Gregory M., Henrik Syse, and Endre Begby (eds), *The Ethics of War: Classic and Contemporary Readings* (Oxford: Blackwell, 2006).
The Royal Inscriptions of Mesopotamia, Assyrian Periods, vol. 2: *Assyrian Rulers of the Early First Millennium BC, I (1114-859 BC)*, edited by A. Kirk Grayson (Toronto: University of Toronto Press, 2002).
Sage, Michael M. (ed.), *Warfare in Ancient Greece: A Sourcebook* (London: Routledge, 1996).
Singer, Itamar, *Hittite Prayers*, edited by Harry A. Hoffner Jr. (Atlanta, GA: Society of Biblical Literature, 2002) [*HitP*].
Strudwick, Nigel C., *Texts from the Pyramid Age*, edited by Ronald J. Leprohon (Atlanta, GA: Society of Biblical Literature, 2005).
Sturtevant, Edgar H. and G. Bechtel, *A Hittite Chrestomatby* (Philadelphia: Linguistic Society of America, 1935).
Sun Tzu and Sun Pin, *The Complete Art of War*, translated with a historical introduction and commentary by Ralph D. Sawyer, with the collaboration of Mei-chün Lee Sawyer (Boulder, CO: Westview Press, 1996).
The Tale of Sinuhe and Other Ancient Egyptian Poems 1940-1640 BC, translated by Robert B. Parkinson (Oxford: Oxford University Press, 2009) [*ToS*].

(The) Tanakh: see *The Jewish Study Bible [JSB]*.
Thucydides, *The Peloponnesian War*, translated by Rex Warner, with an introduction and notes by M. I. Finley (Harmondsworth: Penguin, 1954).
Treaty, Law and Covenant in the Ancient Near East, edited by Kenneth A. Kitchen and Paul J. N. Lawrence, 3 vols (Wiesbaden: Harrossowitz, 2012).
Urkunden des ägyptischen Altertums, Abteilung IV: Urkunden der 18. Dynastie, edited by Kurt Sethe and Wolfgang Helck (Leipzig: Hinrichs; Berlin: Akademie Verlag, 1906–1958).
Xenophon, *Cyropaedia*, vol. 2: *Books 5–8*, translated by Walter Miller (Cambridge, MA: Harvard University Press, 1914).

Secondary Literature

Abbès, Makram, 'Can We Speak of Just War in Islam?', *History of Political Thought* 35 (2) (2014): 234–61.
Abels, Richard, 'Cultural Representation and the Practice of War in the Middle Ages', *Journal of Medieval Military History* 6 (2008): 1–31.
Adams, William Y., 'The Kingdom and Civilization of Kush in Northeast Africa', in *The Civilizations of the Ancient Near East*, edited by Jack M. Sasson, John Baines, Gary Beckman, and Karen S. Rubinson, 4 vols (Peabody, MA: Hendrickson, 2000), 2:775–89.
Ahlström, Gösta W., *Who Were the Israelites?* (Winona Lake, IN: Eisenbrauns, 1986).
Ahmad, Ahmad Atif, 'The Evolution of Just War Theory in Islamic Law: Texts, History, and the Purpose of 'Reading'', *American Foreign Policy Interests* 28 (2) (2006): 107–15.
Aho, James A., *Religious Mythology and the Art of War: Comparative Religious Symbolisms of Military Violence* (Westport, CT: Greenwood Press, 1981).
Akurgal, Ekrem, *The Art of the Hittites*, translated by Constance McNab, photographs by Max Hirmer (New York: Abrams, 1962).
Al-Dawoody, Ahmed, *The Islamic Law of War: Justifications and Regulations* (New York: Palgrave Macmillan, 2011).
Albright, William Foxwell, *The Archaeology of Palestine*, revised edn (Harmondsworth: Penguin, 1960).
Albright, William Foxwell, *From the Stone Age to Christianity: Monotheism and the Historical Process*, 2nd edn (Baltimore: Johns Hopkins University Press, 1957).
Allen, Nick, 'Just War in the *Māhabhārata*', in *The Ethics of War: Shared Problems in Different Traditions*, edited by Richard Sorabji and David Rodin (Aldershot: Ashgate, 2006), 138–49.
Alt, Albrecht, *Essays on Old Testament History and Religion*, translated by R. A. Wilson (Oxford: Basil Blackwell, 1966).
Altman, Amnon, 'Tracing the Earliest Recorded Concepts of International Law: (5) The Near East 1200–330 BCE', *Journal of the History of International Law* 12 (2010): 101–54.
Altman, Amnon, *Tracing the Earliest Recorded Concepts of International Law: The Ancient Near East (2500–330 BCE)* (Leiden: Martinus Nijhoff, 2012) [*ERCIL*].
Ardrey, Robert, *The Hunting Hypothesis: A Personal Conclusion concerning the Evolutionary Nature of Man* (New York: Atheneum, 1976).
Armstrong, Karen, *A History of God: The 4000-Year Quest of Judaism, Christianity and Islam* (New York: Ballantine Books, 1993).
Assmann, Jan, 'Axial "Breakthroughs" and Semantic "Relocations" in Ancient Egypt and Israel', in *Axial Civilizations and World History*, edited by Johann P. Arnason, S. N. Eisenstadt, and Björn Wittrock (Leiden: Brill, 2005), 133–56.
Assmann, Jan, *Cultural Memory and Early Civilization: Writing, Remembrance, and Political Imagination* (New York: Cambridge University Press, 2011).

Assmann, Jan, *Das kulturelle Gedächtnis: Schrift, Erinnerung und politische Identität in frühen Hochkulturen* (Munich: Beck, 1992).
Assmann, Jan, *Ma'at: Gerechtigkeit und Unsterblichkeit im Alten Ägypten* (Munich: Beck, 1990).
Assmann, Jan, *Moses the Egyptian: The Memory of Egypt in Western Monotheism* (Cambridge, MA: Harvard University Press, 1997).
Assmann, Jan, *Of God and Gods: Egypt, Israel, and the Rise of Monotheism* (Madison: University of Wisconsin Press, 2008).
Assmann, Jan, *Politische Theologie zwischen Ägypten und Israel* (Munich: Carl Friedrich von Siemens Stiftung, 1995).
Assmann, Jan, *Religion and Cultural Memory: Ten Studies*, translated by Rodney Livingstone (Stanford, CA: Stanford University Press, 2006).
Avalos, Hector, 'Legal and Social Institutions in Canaan and Ancient Israel', in *The Civilizations of the Ancient Near East*, edited by Jack M. Sasson, John Baines, Gary Beckman, and Karen S. Rubinson, 4 vols (Peabody, MA: Hendrickson, 2000), 2:615-31.
Aymard, André, 'Le Partage des profits de la guerre dans les traités d'alliance antiques', *Revue historique* 217 (1957): 233-45.
Bachvarova, Mary R., *From Hittite to Homer: The Anatolian Background of Ancient Greek Epic* (Cambridge: Cambridge University Press, 2016).
Badawi, Nesrine, and John Kelsay, 'Sunni Islam', in *Religion, War and Ethics: A Sourcebook of Textual Traditions*, edited by Gregory Reichberg and Henrik Syse, with Nicole H. Hartwell (Cambridge: Cambridge University Press, 2014), 301-82.
Baines, John, 'Contextualizing Egyptian Representations of Society and Ethnicity', in *The Study of the Ancient Near East in the Twenty-First Century: The William Foxwell Albright Centennial Conference*, edited by Jerrold S. Cooper and Glenn M. Schwartz (Winona Lake, IN: Eisenbrauns, 1996), 339-84.
Baines, John, 'Kingship, Definition of Culture, and Legitimation', in *Ancient Egyptian Kingship*, edited by David O'Connor and David P. Silverman (Leiden: Brill, 1995), 3-47.
Balkaran, Raj, and A. Walter Dorn, 'Violence in the *Vālmīki Rāmāyaṇa*: Just War Criteria in an Ancient Indian Epic', *Journal of the American Academy of Religion* 80 (3) (2012): 659-90.
Banka, Andris, and Adam Quinn, 'Killing Norms Softly: US Targeted Killing, Quasi-secrecy, and the Assassination Ban', *Security Studies* 27 (4) (2018): 665-703.
Barnes, Jonathan, 'The Just War', in *The Cambridge History of Later Medieval Philosophy: From the Rediscovery of Aristotle to the Disintegration of Scholasticism 1100-1600*, edited by Norman Kretzmann, Anthony Kenny, and Jan Pinborg (Cambridge: Cambridge University Press, 1982), 771-84.
Barrandon, Nathalie, 'La Transgression dans la guerre au temps de Cicéron: Droit et crauté', in *La Transgression en temps de guerre: De l'Antiquité à nos jours*, edited by Nathalie Barrandon and Isabelle Pimouguet-Pedarros (Rennes: Presses Universitaires de Rennes, 2021), 97-123.
Bartor, Assnat, '"When you go forth to war against your enemies . . .": Narrative Reading of Deuteronomic Warfare Legislation', in *The Reception of Biblical War Legislation in Narrative Contexts: Proceedings of the EABS Research Group 'Law and Narrative'*, edited by Christoph Berner and Harald Samuel (Berlin: De Gruyter, 2015), 1-21.
Batiffol, P., P. Monceaux, E. Chénon, A. Vanderpol, L. Rolland, F. Duval, and A. Tanquerey, *L'Église et le droit de guerre* (Paris: Bloud and Gay, 1920).
Beal, Richard H., 'Hittite Military Organization', in *The Civilizations of the Ancient Near East*, edited by Jack M. Sasson, John Baines, Gary Beckman, and Karen S. Rubinson, 4 vols (Peabody, MA: Hendrickson, 2000), 1:545-54.

Beal, Richard H., 'Hittite Military Rituals', in *Ancient Magic and Ritual Power*, edited by Marvin Meyer and Paul Mirecki (Leiden: Brill, 1995), 63–76.

Beal, Richard H., 'Making, Preserving, and Breaking the Peace with the Hittite State', in *War and Peace in the Ancient World*, edited by Kurt A. Raaflaub (Malden, MA: Blackwell, 2007), 81–97.

Beal, Richard H., *The Organisation of the Hittite Military* (Heidelberg: Carl Winter, 1992).

Beal, Richard H., 'The Organization of the Hittite Military' (PhD dissertation, University of Chicago, 1986).

Beard, Mary, *The Roman Triumph* (Cambridge, MA: Harvard University Press, 2007).

Beckman, Gary, 'Foreigners in the Ancient Near East', *Journal of the American Oriental Society* 133 (2) (2013): 203–16.

Beckman, Gary, 'The Religion of the Hittites', *Biblical Archaeologist* 52 (2/3) (1989): 98–108.

Beckman, Gary, 'Royal Ideology and State Administration in Hittite Anatolia', in *The Civilizations of the Ancient Near East*, edited by Jack M. Sasson, John Baines, Gary Beckman, and Karen S. Rubinson, 4 vols (Peabody, MA: Hendrickson, 2000), 1:529–43

Beckman, Gary, 'The Siege of Uršu Text (CTH 7) and Old Hittite Historiography', *Journal of Cuneiform Studies* 47 (1995): 23–34.

Bederman, David J., *International Law in Antiquity* (Cambridge: Cambridge University Press, 2001) [*ILA*].

Bell, Daniel A., 'Just War and Confucianism: Implications for the Contemporary World', in *Confucian Political Ethics*, edited by Daniel A. Bell (Princeton, NJ: Princeton University Press, 2008), 226–56.

Bell, Lanny, 'Conflict and Reconciliation in the Ancient Middle East: The Clash of Egyptian and Hittite Chariots in Syria, and the World's First Peace Treaty between "Superpowers"', in *War and Peace in the Ancient World*, edited by Kurt A. Raaflaub (Malden, MA: Blackwell, 2007), 98–120.

Bellah, Robert N., 'What is Axial about the Axial Age?', *European Journal of Sociology* 46 (1) (2005): 69–89.

Bellamy, Alex, *Just Wars: From Cicero to Iraq* (Cambridge: Polity, 2006).

Berryman, Carrie Anne, 'Captive Sacrifice and Trophy Taking Among the Ancient Maya: An Evaluation of the Bioarchaeological Evidence and Its Sociopolitical Implications', in *The Taking and Displaying of Human Body Parts as Trophies by Amerindians*, edited by Richard J. Chacon and David H. Dye (New York: Springer, 2007), 377–99.

Bittel, Kurt, *Hattusha: The Capital of the Hittites* (New York: Oxford University Press, 1970).

Black, Anthony, *A World History of Ancient Political Thought* (Oxford: Oxford University Press, 2009).

Blakeley, Ruth and Sam Raphael, 'British Torture in the "War on Terror"', *European Journal of International Relations* 23 (2) (2017): 243–66.

Blenkinsopp, Joseph, 'Are there Traces of the Gibeonite Covenant in Deuteronomy?', *Catholic Biblical Quarterly* 28 (2) (1966): 207–19.

Bloch, Marc, 'Toward a Comparative History of European Societies', in *Enterprise and Secular Change: Readings in Economic History*, edited by Frederic C. Lane and Jelle C. Riemersma (Homewood, IL: Richard D. Irwin, 1953), 494–521 [Originally published as 'Pour une histoire comparée es sociétiés européennes', *Revue de synthèse historique* 46 (1928): 15–50].

Bonner, Michael, *Jihad in Islamic History: Doctrines and Practice* (Princeton, NJ: Princeton University Press, 2008).

Boone, Elizabeth H. (ed.), *Ritual Human Sacrifice in Mesoamerica: A Conference at Dumbarton Oaks, October 13th and 14th, 1979* (Washington, DC: Dumbarton Oaks, 1984).

Booth, Ken, 'Ten Flaws of Just Wars', *The International Journal of Human Rights* 4 (3–4) (2000): 314–24.

Boy, John D., and John Torpey, 'Inventing the Axial Age: The Origins and Uses of a Historical Concept', *Theory and Society* 42 (3) (2013): 241–59.
Brahimi, Alia, *Jihad and Just War in the War on Terror* (Oxford: Oxford University Press, 2010).
Braudel, Fernand, *The Mediterranean in the Ancient World*, translated by Siân Reynolds (London: Penguin, 2002).
Breasted, James Henry, *A History of Egypt: From the Earliest Times to the Persian Conquest* (1906; repr. Cambridge: Cambridge University Press, 2015).
Bright, John, *A History of Israel*, 3rd edn (1959; Philadelphia: Westminster Press, 1981).
Brock, Peter, *A Brief History of Pacifism, from Jesus to Tolstoy* (Toronto: Syracuse University Press, 1992).
Brown, Chris, 'Just War and Political Judgement', in *Just War: Authority, Tradition, and Practice*, edited by Anthony F. Lang Jr., Cian O'Driscoll, and John Williams (Washington, DC: Georgetown University Press, 2013), 35–48.
Brown, Peter, *Augustine of Hippo: A Biography* (Berkeley: University of California Press, 1969).
Brown, Warren C., *Violence in Medieval Europe* (New York: Longman, 2011).
Brundage, James A., 'The Hierarchy of Violence in Twelfth- and Thirteenth-Century Canonists', *The International History Review* 17 (4) (1995): 670–92.
Bryan, Betsy, Roxie Walker, Salima Ikram, and Joel Irish, 'Execration and Execution: A Skeleton of a Bound Captive from the Mut Temple Precinct', in *International Congress of Egyptologists XI, Florence (Italy), 23–30 August 2015, Museo Egizio Firenze: Paper and Poster Abstracts* (2015), 22.
Bryce, Trevor, *The Kingdom of the Hittites*, 2nd edn (Oxford: Oxford University Press, 2005).
Budge, Wallis, *Egyptian Religion* (1959; repr. Secaucus, NJ: Citadel Press, 1997).
Burkert, Walter, *Homo necans: The Anthropology of Ancient Greek Sacrificial Ritual and Myth*, translated by Peter Bing (Berkeley: University of California Press, 1983).
Catling, H. W., 'Cyprus in the Middle Bronze Age', in *The Cambridge Ancient History*, vol. 2, Part 1: *History of the Middle East and the Aegean Region, c. 1800–1380 BC*, edited by I.E.S. Edwards, C. J. Gadd, N.G.L. Hammond, and E. Sollberger, 3rd edn (Cambridge: Cambridge University Press, 1973), 165–75.
Chevereau, Pierre-Marie, 'L'Art et la science militaires dans l'Égypte ancienne', *Stratégique* 74–75 (1999) [online publication of the Institut de stratégie comparée (ISC)]; article available at http://www.mafhoum.com/press6/160C31.htm (accessed 9 January 2023)].
Christophe, Louis-A., 'L'Organisation de l'armée égyptienne à l'epoque ramesside', *La Revue de Caire* 207 (1957): 387–405.
Cifola, Barbara, 'Ramses III and the Sea Peoples: A Structural Analysis of the Medinet Habu Inscriptions', *Orientalia* 57 (3) (1988): 275–306.
Cifola, Barbara, 'The Terminology of Ramses III's Historical Records with a Formal Analysis of the War Scenes', *Orientalia* 60 (1991): 9–57.
Cline, Eric H., 'Amenhotep III and the Aegean: A Reassessment of Egypto–Aegean Relations in the 14th Century BC', *Orientalia* 56 (1) (1987): 1–36.
Cline, Eric H., and David O'Connor, 'The Mystery of the "Sea Peoples"', in *Mysterious Lands*, edited by David O'Connor and Stephen Quirke (London: UCL Press, 2003), 107–38.
Clooney, Francis Xavier, 'Pain but not Harm: Some Classical Resources toward a Hindu Just War Theory', in *Just War in Comparative Perspective*, edited by Paul Robinson (Aldershot: Ashgate, 2003), 109–26.
Cogan, Mordechai, '"Ripping Open Pregnant Women" in Light of an Assyrian Analogue', *Journal of the American Oriental Society* 103 (4) (1983), 755–57.
Cohen, Ronald, 'Warfare and State Formation: Wars Make States and States Make Wars', in *Warfare, Culture, and Environment*, edited by R. Brian Ferguson (Orlando, FL: Academic Press, 1984), 329–58.

Collins, Billie Jean, 'Hittite Religion in the West', in *Pax Hethitica: Studies on the Hittites and Their Neighbours in Honour of Itamar Singer*, edited by Yoram Cohen, Amir Gilan, and Jared L. Miller (Wiesbaden: Harrassowitz, 2010), 54–66.

Collins, Billie Jean, *The Hittites and Their World* (Atlanta, GA: Society of Biblical Literature, 2007).

Collins, John J., 'The Mythology of Holy War in Daniel and the Qumran War Scroll: A Point of Transition in Jewish Apocalyptic', *Vetus Testamentum* 25 (3) (1975): 596–612.

Connor, David, *Ancient Nubia: Egypt's Rival in Africa* (Philadelphia: University Museum, 1993).

Contamine, Philippe, *War in the Middle Ages*, translated by Michael Jones (Oxford: Blackwell, 1984).

Corey, David D., and J. Daryl Charles, *The Just War Tradition: An Introduction* (Wilmington, DE: ISI Books, 2012).

Cowley, A. E., *The Hittites: The Schweich Lectures for 1918* (London: Oxford University Press, 1920).

Cox, Rory, 'Approaches to Pre-Modern War and Ethics: Some Comparative and Multi-disciplinary Perspectives', *Global Intellectual History* 6 (5) (2018): 592–613.

Cox, Rory, 'Asymmetric Warfare and Military Conduct in the Middle Ages', *Journal of Medieval History* 38 (1) (2012): 100–125.

Cox, Rory, 'The Ethics of War up to Thomas Aquinas', in *The Oxford Handbook of Ethics of War*, edited by Seth Lazar and Helen Frowe (New York: Oxford University Press, 2018), 99–121.

Cox, Rory, 'Expanding the History of the Just War: The Ethics of War in Ancient Egypt', *International Studies Quarterly* 61 (2) (2017): 371–84.

Cox, Rory, 'A Law of War? English Protection and Destruction of Ecclesiastical Property during the Fourteenth Century', *The English Historical Review* 128 (535) (2013): 1381–417.

Cox, Rory, 'Gratian (circa 12th century)', in *Just War Thinkers: From Cicero to the 21st Century*, edited by Daniel R. Brunstetter and Cian O'Driscoll (Abingdon: Routledge, 2018), 34–49.

Cox, Rory, Faye Donnelly, and Anthony F. Lang Jr. (eds), *Contesting Torture: Interdisciplinary Perspectives* (Abingdon: Routledge, 2023).

Craigie, Peter C., *The Problem of War in the Old Testament* (Eugene, OR: Wipf and Stock, 1978).

Craigie, Peter C., 'Yahweh is a Man of Wars', *Scottish Journal of Theology* 22 (2) (1969): 183–88.

Crawford, Neta C., *Accountability for Killing: Moral Responsibility for Collateral Damage in America's Post-9/11 Wars* (New York: Oxford University Press, 2003).

Crawford, Neta C., 'Bugsplat: US Standing Rules of Engagement, International Humanitarian Law, Military Necessity, and Noncombatant Immunity', in *Just War: Authority, Tradition, and Practice*, edited by Anthony F. Lang Jr., Cian O'Driscoll, and John Williams (Washington, DC: Georgetown University Press, 2013), 231–49.

Cross, Frank Moore, *Canaanite Myth and Hebrew Epic: Essays in the History of the Religion of Israel* (Cambridge, MA: Harvard University Press, 2021).

Crouch, Carly L., *War and Ethics in the Ancient Near East: Military Violence in Light of Cosmology and History* (Berlin: Walter de Gruyter, 2009).

Cryer, Frederick H., *Divination in Ancient Israel and its Near Eastern Environment: A Socio-Historical Investigation* (Sheffield: JSOT Press, 1994).

Curry, Patrick, 'Introduction', in *Astrology, Science and Society: Historical Essays*, edited by Patrick Curry (Woodbridge: Boydell, 1987), 1–4.

Daddi, Franca Pechioli, 'Le cariche d'oro', in *Hittite Studies in Honor of Harry A. Hoffner Jr. on the Occasion of His 65th Birthday*, edited by Gary Beckman, Richard Beal, and Gregory McMahon (Winona Lake, IN: Eisenbrauns, 2003), 83–92.

Darnell, John C. and Colleen Manassa, *Tutankhamun's Armies: Battle and Conquest during Ancient Egypt's Late Eighteenth Dynasty* (Hoboken, NJ: Wiley, 2007).

David, Arlette, 'Devouring the Enemy: Ancient Egyptian Metaphors of Domination', *The Bulletin of the Australian Centre for Egyptology* 22 (2011): 83–100.

David, Arlette, 'The Sound of the Magic Flute in Legal and Religious Registers of the Ramesside Period: Some Common Features of Two 'Ritualistic Languages'', in *Law and Religion in the Eastern Mediterranean: From Late Antiquity to Early Islam*, edited by Anselm C. Hagedorn and Reinhard G. Kratz (Oxford: Oxford University Press, 2013), 13–39.

Davies, Philip R., *In Search of Ancient Israel* (Sheffield: JSOT Press 1992).

Davis, G. Scott, 'Introduction: Comparative Ethics and the Crucible of War', in *The Ethics of War in Asian Civilizations: A Comparative Perspective*, edited by Torkel Brekke (Abingdon: Routledge, 2006), 1–36.

Dawson, Doyne, 'The Origins of War: Biological and Anthropological Theories', *History and Theory* 35 (1) (1996): 1–28.

Day, John, *God's Conflict with the Dragon and the Sea: Echoes of a Canaanite Myth in the Old Testament* (Cambridge: Cambridge University Press, 1985).

De Martino, Stefano, 'The Military Exploits of the Hittite King Hattušili I in Lands Situated between the Upper Euphrates and the Upper Tigris', in *Silva Anatolica: Anatolian Studies Presented to Maciej Popko on the Occasion of His 65th Birthday*, edited by Piotr Taracha (Warsaw: Agade, 2002), 77–85.

De Martino, Stefano, 'Symbols of Power in the Late Hittite Kingdom', in *Pax Hethitica: Studies on the Hittites and Their Neighbours in Honour of Itamar Singer*, edited by Yoram Cohen, Amir Gilan, and Jared L. Miller (Wiesbaden: Harrassowitz, 2010), 87–98.

Devetak, Richard, *Critical International Theory: An Intellectual History* (Oxford: Oxford University Press, 2018).

Devetak, Richard, 'A Rival Enlightenment? Critical International Theory in Historical Mode', *International Theory* 6 (3) (2014): 417–53.

Dewey, John, *The Middle Works, 1899–1924*, edited by Jo Ann Boydston, 15 vols (Carbondale: Southern Illinois University Press, 1976–1983).

Dowden, Ken, *The Uses of Greek Mythology* (London: Routledge, 1992).

Dowden, Ken, and Niall Livingstone, 'Thinking Through Myth, Thinking Myth Through', in *A Companion to Greek Mythology*, edited by Ken Dowden and Niall Livingstone (Malden, MA: Wiley-Blackwell, 2011), 3–23.

Dratel, Joshua L., 'The Legal Narrative', in *The Torture Papers: The Road to Abu Ghraib*, edited by Karen J. Greenberg and Joshua L. Dratel (Cambridge: Cambridge University Press, 2005), xxi–xxiv.

Drower, Margret S., 'Syria c. 1550–1400 BC', in *The Cambridge Ancient History*, vol. 2, Part 1: *History of the Middle East and the Aegean Region, c. 1800–1380 BC*, edited by I.E.S. Edwards, C. J. Gadd, N.G.L. Hammond, and E. Sollberger, 3rd edn (Cambridge: Cambridge University Press, 1973), 417–525.

Ducrey, Pierre, *Guerre et guerriers dans la Grèce antique* (Paris: Payot, 1985).

Ducrey, Pierre, *Le Traitement des prisonniers de guerre dans la Grèce antique: Des origines à la conquête romaine* (Paris: E. de Boccard, 1968).

Duggan, Lawrence G., *Armsbearing and the Clergy in the History and Canon Law of Western Christianity* (Woodbridge: Boydell, 2013).

Dwyer, Philip G., 'Violence and Its Histories: Meanings, Methods, Problems', *History and Theory* 56 (4) (2017): 7–22.

Dwyer, Philip G., and Marc S. Micale (eds), *The Darker Angels of Our Nature: Refuting the Pinker Theory of History and Violence* (London: Bloomsbury, 2021).

Edgerton, William F., 'The Government and the Governed in the Egyptian Empire', *Journal of Near Eastern Studies* 6 (3) (1947): 152–60.
Eisenstadt, S. N. (ed.), *The Origins and Diversity of Axial Age Civilizations* (Albany: State University of New York Press, 1986).
Elias, Norbert, *The Civilising Process: Sociogenetic and Psychogenetic Investigations*, translated by Edmund Jephcott (revised edn), edited by Eric Dunning, Johan Goudsblom, and Stephen Mennell (Malden, MA: Blackwell, 2000).
Elshtain, Jean Bethke, *Just War Against Terror: The Burden of American Power in a Violent World* (New York: Basic Books, 2004).
Elshtain, Jean Bethke, *Women and War* (Chicago: University of Chicago Press, 1995).
Esposito, John, *Unholy War: Terror in the Name of Islam* (Oxford: Oxford University Press, 2002).
Evans, Mark, 'Moral Theory and the Idea of a Just War', in *Just War Theory: A Reappraisal*, edited by Mark Evans (Edinburgh: Edinburgh University Press, 2005), 1–21.
Eynikel, Erik, *The Reforms of King Josiah and the Composition of the Deuteronomistic History* (Leiden: Brill, 1996).
Eyre, Christopher, *The Cannibal Hymn: A Cultural and Literary Study* (Liverpool: Liverpool University Press, 2002).
Eyre, Christopher, 'Crime and Adultery in Ancient Egypt', *The Journal of Egyptian Archaeology* 70 (1) (1984): 92–105.
Fabre, Cécile, *Cosmopolitan War* (Oxford: Oxford University Press, 2011).
Fabre, Cécile, 'Cosmopolitanism, Just War Theory and Legitimate Authority', *International Affairs* 84 (5) (2008): 963–76.
Faghfoory, Mohammad H., 'Shi'ite Islam', in *Religion, War and Ethics: A Sourcebook of Textual Traditions*, edited by Gregory Reichberg and Henrik Syse, with Nicole H. Hartwell (Cambridge: Cambridge University Press, 2014), 389–470.
Fales, Frederick M., *Guerre et paix en Assyrie: Religion et impérialisme* (Paris: Publications de l'École pratique des hautes études, 2010).
Faulkner, Raymond O., 'The Battle of Megiddo', *The Journal of Egyptian Archaeology* 28 (1942): 2–15.
Feder, Yitzhaq, *Blood Expiation in Hittite and Biblical Ritual: Origins, Context, and Meaning* (Atlanta, GA: Society of Biblical Literature, 2011).
Feder, Yitzhaq, 'A Levantine Tradition: The Kizzuwatnean Blood Rite and the Biblical Sin Offering', in *Pax Hethitica: Studies on the Hittites and Their Neighbours in Honour of Itamar Singer*, edited by Yoram Cohen, Amir Gilan, and Jared L. Miller (Wiesbaden: Harrassowitz, 2010), 101–14.
Feldman, Louis H., 'The Command, according to Philo, Pseudo-Philo, and Josephus, to Annihilate the Seven Nations of Canaan', *Andrews University Seminary Series* 41 (1) (2003): 13–29.
Ferguson, R. Brian, 'Explaining War', in *The Anthropology of War*, edited by Jonathan Haas (Cambridge: Cambridge University Press, 1990), 26–55.
Fiala, Andrew, *The Just War Myth: The Moral Illusions of War* (Lanham, MD: Rowman and Littlefield, 2008).
Finer, Samuel E., 'State- and Nation-Building in Europe: The Role of the Military', in *The Formation of National States in Western Europe*, edited by Charles Tilly (Princeton, NJ: Princeton University Press, 1975), 84–163.
Finkelstein, Israel, 'King Solomon's Golden Age: History or Myth?', in Israel Finkelstein and Amihai Mazar, *The Quest for the Historical Israel: Debating Archaeology and the History of Early Israel; Invited Lectures Delivered at the Sixth Biennial Colloquium of the International Institute for Secular Humanistic Judaism, Detroit, October 2015*, edited by Brian B. Schmidt (Atlanta, GA: Society for Biblical Literature, 2007), 107–16.

Finkelstein, Israel, 'Patriarchs, Exodus, Conquest: Fact or Fiction?', in Israel Finkelstein and Amihai Mazar, *The Quest for the Historical Israel: Debating Archaeology and the History of Early Israel; Invited Lectures Delivered at the Sixth Biennial Colloquium of the International Institute for Secular Humanistic Judaism, Detroit, October 2015*, edited by Brian B. Schmidt (Atlanta, GA: Society for Biblical Literature, 2007), 41–55.

Finkelstein, Israel, and Amihai Mazar, *The Quest for the Historical Israel: Debating Archaeology and the History of Early Israel; Invited Lectures Delivered at the Sixth Biennial Colloquium of the International Institute for Secular Humanistic Judaism, Detroit, October 2015*, edited by Brian B. Schmidt (Atlanta, GA: Society for Biblical Literature, 2007).

Finkelstein, Israel, and Neil Asher Silberman, *The Bible Unearthed: Archaeology's New Vision of Ancient Israel and the Origin of Its Sacred Texts* (New York: Simon & Schuster, 2002).

Finley, Moses I., *Ancient History: Evidence and Models* (1985; repr. London: Pimlico, 2000).

Fish, Thomas, 'War and Religion in Ancient Mesopotamia', *Bulletin of the John Rylands Library* 23 (2) (1939): 387–402.

Fishbane, Michael, *Biblical Interpretation in Ancient Israel* (Oxford: Clarendon Press, 1985).

Fisk, Kerstin, and Jennifer Ramos (eds), *Preventive Force: Drones, Targeted Killing, and the Transformation of Contemporary Warfare* (New York: New York University Press, 2016).

Flannery, Frances, '"Go back by the way you came": An Internal Textual Critique of Elijah's Violence in 1 Kings 18–19', in *Writing and Reading War: Rhetoric, Gender, and Ethics in Biblical and Modern Contexts*, edited by Brad E. Kelle and Frank Ritchel Ames (Atlanta, GA: Society of Biblical Literature, 2008), 161–73.

Fleming, Daniel E., 'Yahweh among the Baals: Israel and the Storm Gods', in *Mighty Baal: Essays in Honor of Mark S. Smith*, edited by Stephen C. Russell and Esther J. Hamori (Leiden: Brill, 2020), 160–74.

Flynn, Shawn W., *YHWH is King: The Development of Divine Kingship in Ancient Israel* (Leiden: Brill, 2014).

Focarelli, Carlo, 'The Early Doctrine of International Law as a Bridge from Antiquity to Modernity and Diplomatic Inviolability in 16th- and 17th-Century European Practice', in *The Twelve Years Truce (1609–1621): Peace, Truce, War and Law in the Low Countries at the Turn of the 17th Century*, edited by Randall Lesaffer (Leiden: Brill/Nijhoff, 2014), 210–32.

Forde, Steven, 'Classical Realism', in *Traditions of International Ethics*, edited by Terry Nardin and David R. Mapel (Cambridge: Cambridge University Press, 1992), 62–84.

Foster, Benjamin R., 'Transmission of Knowledge', in *A Companion to the Ancient Near East*, edited by Daniel C. Snell (Malden, MA: Blackwell, 2005), 245–52.

Fotion, Nicholas, *War and Ethics: A New Just War Theory* (London: Continuum, 2007).

Frandsen, Paul John, 'Aspects of Kingship in Ancient Egypt', in *Religion and Power: Divine Kingship in the Ancient World and Beyond*, edited by Nicole Brisch (Chicago: The Oriental Institute of the University of Chicago, 2012), 47–73.

Frankfort, Henri, *Kingship and the Gods: A Study of Ancient Near Eastern Religion as the Integration of Society and Nature* (Chicago: University of Chicago Press, 1948).

Freu, J., 'Les Guerres syriennes de Šuppiluliuma et la fin de l'ere amarnienne', *Hethitica XI*, edited by René Lebrun (Louvain-la-Neuve: Peeters, 1992): 39–101.

Freud, Sigmund, *Moses and Monotheism*, translated by Katherine Jones (London: Hogarth Press and Institute of Psycho-Analysis, 1939).

Freud, Sigmund, 'Thoughts for the Times on War and Death (1915)', in *The Standard Edition of the Complete Psychological Works of Sigmund Freud*, vol. 14: *1914–1916*, translated and edited by James Strachey et al. (London: Hogarth Press and the Institute of Psycho-Analysis, 1957), 273–302.

Fried, Morton H., 'Warfare, Military Organization, and the Evolution of Society', *Anthropologica* 3 (2) (1961): 134–47.

Fritz, Volkmar, 'Conquest or Settlement? The Early Iron Age in Palestine', *The Biblical Archaeologist* 50 (2) (1987): 84–100.

Fritz, Volkmar, *The Emergence of Israel in the 12th and 11th Centuries BCE*, translated by James W. Barker (Atlanta, GA: Society of Biblical Literature, 2012).

Frowe, Helen, *Defensive Killing* (Oxford: Oxford University Press, 2011).

Frowe, Helen, *The Ethics of War and Peace: An Introduction* (Abingdon: Routledge, 2016).

Frowe, Helen, 'Individualism and Collectivism in the Ethics of War', in *A Companion to Applied Philosophy*, edited by Kimberley Brownlee, David Coady, and Kasper Lippert-Rasmussen (Chichester: Wiley-Blackwell, 2017), 342–55.

Frowe, Helen, 'The Just War Framework', in *The Oxford Handbook of Ethics of War*, edited by Seth Lazar and Helen Frowe (New York: Oxford University Press, 2018), 41–58.

Gaballa, G. A., *Narrative in Egyptian Art* (Mainz am Rhein: Von Zabern, 1976).

Gabriel, Richard A., *The Military History of Ancient Israel* (Westport, CT: Praeger, 2003).

Gadd, C. J., 'Assyria and Babylon, c. 1370–1300 BC', in *The Cambridge Ancient History*, vol. 2, Part 2: *History of the Middle East and the Aegean Region, c. 1380–1000 BC*, edited by I.E.S. Edwards, C. J. Gadd, N.G.L. Hammond, and E. Sollberger, 3rd edn (Cambridge: Cambridge University Press, 1975), 21–48.

Gardiner, Alan H., *Egypt of the Pharaohs: An Introduction* (Oxford: Clarendon Press, 1961).

Gaster, Theodor H., *Thespis: Ritual, Myth and Drama in the Ancient Near East* (Bristol, CT: Hildreth Press, 1950).

Geertz, Clifford, *The Interpretation of Cultures: Selected Essays* (New York: Basic Books, 1973).

Gelston, Anthony, 'The Wars of Israel', *Scottish Journal of Theology* 17 (3) (1964): 325–31.

Giddens, Anthony, *Modernity and Self-Identity: Self and Society in the Late Modern Age* (Stanford, CA: Stanford University Press, 1991).

Gilan, Amir, 'Hittite Religious Rituals and the Ideology of Kingship', *Religion Compass* 5 (7) (2011): 276–85.

Ginzburg, Carlo, 'Morelli, Freud and Sherlock Holmes: Clues and Scientific Method', *History Workshop Journal* 9 (1) (1980): 5–36.

Giveon, Raphael, *The Impact of Egypt on Canaan: Iconographical and Related Studies* (Freiburg: Universitätsverlag; Göttingen: Vandenhoeck & Ruprecht, 1978).

Glatz, Claudia, and Roger Matthews, 'Anthropology of a Frontier Zone: Hittite–Kaska Relations in Late Bronze Age North-Central Anatolia', *Bulletin of the American Schools of Oriental Research* 339 (2005): 47–65.

Gnirs, Andrea M., 'Ancient Egypt', in *War and Society in the Ancient and Medieval Worlds: Asia, the Mediterranean, Europe, and Mesoamerica*, edited by Kurt A. Raaflaub and Nathan S. Rosenstein (Cambridge, MA: Harvard University Press, 1999), 71–104.

Gnirs, Andrea M., and Antonio Loprieno, 'Krieg und Literatur', in *Militärgeschichte des pharaonischen Ägypten: Altägypten und seine Nachbarkulturen im Spiegel der aktuellen Forschung*, edited by Rolf Gundlach and Carola Vogel (Paderborn: Schöningh, 2009), 243–308.

Goebs, Katja, 'Kingship', in *The Egyptian World*, edited by Toby Wilkinson (Abingdon: Routledge, 2007), 275–95.

Goedicke, Hans, 'The Alleged Military Campaign in Southern Palestine in the Reign of Pepi I (VI Dynasty)', *Rivista degli studi orientali* 38 (3) (1963): 187–97.

Goedicke, Hans, 'The Rules of Conduct for Egyptian Military', *Wiener Zeitschrift für die Kunde des Morgenlandes* 88 (1998): 109–42.

Goedicke, Hans, 'Sinuhe's Duel', *Journal of the American Research Center in Egypt* 21 (1984): 197–201.

Goedicke, Hans, 'Unity and Diversity in the Oldest Religion of Ancient Egypt', in *Unity and Diversity: Essays in the History, Literature, and Religion of the Ancient Near East*, edited by Hans Goedicke and J.J.M. Roberts (Baltimore: Johns Hopkins University Press, 1975), 201–21.
Goetze [Götze], Albrecht, 'Warfare in Asia Minor', *Iraq* 25 (2) (1963): 124–30.
Good, Edwin M., 'Capital Punishment and Its Alternatives in Ancient Near Eastern Law', *Stanford Law Review* 19 (5) (1967): 947–77.
Good, Robert M., 'The Just War in Ancient Israel', *Journal of Biblical Literature* 104 (3) (1985): 385–400.
Goodman, M. D., and A. J. Holladay, 'Religious Scruples in Ancient Warfare', *The Classical Quarterly* 36 (1) (1986): 151–71.
Gottwald, Norman K., '"Holy War" in Deuteronomy: Analysis and Critique', *Review and Expositor* 61 (4) (1964): 297–310.
Gottwald, Norman K., *The Politics of Ancient Israel* (Louisville, KY: Westminster John Knox Press, 2001).
Gottwald, Norman K., *The Tribes of Yahweh: A Sociology of the Religion of Liberated Israel, 1250–1050 BCE*. (London: SCM Press, 1980).
Goudie, Kenneth A. *Reinventing Jihād: Jihād Ideology from the Conquest of Jerusalem to the End of the Ayyūbids (c. 492/1099–647/1249)* (Leiden: Brill, 2019).
Graff, David A., 'The Chinese Concept of Righteous War', in *The Prism of Just War: Asian and Western Perspectives on the Legitimate Use of Military Force*, edited by Howard M. Hensel (Farnham: Ashgate, 2010), 195–216.
Greenberg, Karen J., and Joshua L. Dratel, *The Torture Papers: The Road to Abu Ghraib* (Cambridge: Cambridge University Press, 2005).
Grossman, Dave, *On Killing: The Psychological Cost of Learning to Kill in War and Society* (Boston, MA: Little, Brown and Company, 1995).
Gunkel, Herman, *Schöpfung und Chaos in Urzeit und Endzeit* (Göttingen: Vandenhoek & Ruprecht, 1895).
Gunnell, John G., *Political Theory: Tradition and Interpretation* (Lanham, MD: University Press of America, 1987).
Gurney, O. R., 'The Hittite Empire', in *Power and Propaganda: A Symposium on Ancient Empires*, edited by Mogens T. Larsen (Copenhagen: Academisk Forlag, 1979), 151–65.
Gurney, O. R., *The Hittites*, revised 2nd edn (Baltimore: Penguin, 1962).
Guthrie, Charles, and Michael Quinlan, *Just War: The Just War Tradition: Ethics in Modern Warfare* (London: Bloomsbury, 2007).
Güterbock, Hans G., 'The Hittite Conquest of Cyprus Reconsidered', *Journal of Near Eastern Studies* 26 (2) (1967): 73–81.
Güterbock, Hans G., 'Hittite Historiography: A Survey', in *History, Historiography and Interpretation: Studies in Biblical and Cuneiform Literatures*, edited by Hayim Tadmor and Moshe Weinfeld (Jerusalem: The Magnes Press, 1983), 21–35.
Haas, Jonathan (ed.), *The Anthropology of War* (Cambridge: Cambridge University Press, 1990).
Hall, Ian, 'The History of International Thought and International Relations Theory: From Context to Interpretation', *International Relations* 31 (3) (2017): 241–60.
Hallo, William W., and K. Lawson Younger (eds), *The Context of Scripture*, 4 vols (Leiden: Brill, 1997).
Hamblin, William J., *Warfare in the Ancient Near East to 1600 BC: Holy Warriors at the Dawn of History* (Abingdon: Routledge, 2006) [*WANE*].
Handy, Lowell K. (ed.), *The Age of Solomon: Scholarship at the Turn of the Millennium* (Leiden: Brill, 1997).
Hannig, Rainer, *Die Sprache der Pharaonen: Grosses Handwörterbuch Ägyptisch-Deutsch (2800–950 v. Chr.)*, 5th edn (Mainz: Philipp von Zabern, 2009).

Hanson, Paul D., 'War, Peace, and Justice in Early Israel', *Bible Review* 3 (3) (1987): 32–45.
Hanson, Victor Davis, *A War Like No Other: How the Athenians and Spartans Fought the Peloponnesian War* (New York: Random House, 2005).
Harbour, Frances V., 'Reasonable Probability of Success as a Moral Criterion in the Western Just War Tradition', *Journal of Military Ethics* 10 (3) (2011): 230–41.
Harle, Vilho, *Ideas of Social Order in the Ancient World* (Westport, CT: Greenwood Press, 1998).
Hasel, Michael G., 'Assyrian Military Practices and Deuteronomy's Laws of Warfare', in *Writing and Reading War: Rhetoric, Gender, and Ethics in Biblical and Modern Contexts*, edited by Brad E. Kelle and Frank Ritchel Ames (Atlanta, GA: Society of Biblical Literature, 2008), 67–81.
Hasel, Michael G., 'The Destruction of Trees in the Moabite Campaign of 2 Kings 3:4–27: A Study in the Laws of Warfare', *Andrews University Seminary Studies* 40 (2) (2002): 197–206.
Hasel, Michael G., *Domination and Resistance: Egyptian Military Activity in the Southern Levant, ca. 1300–1185 BC* (Leiden: Brill, 1998).
Hasel, Michael G., 'Merenptah's Reference to Israel: Critical Issues for the Origin of Israel', in *Critical Issues in Early Israelite History*, edited by Richard S. Hess, Gerald A. Klingbeil, and Paul J. Ray Jr. (Winona Lake, IN: Eisenbrauns, 2008), 47–60.
Hasel, Michael G., *Military Practice and Polemic: Israel's Laws of Warfare in Near Eastern Perspective* (Berrien Springs, MI: Andrews University Press, 2005).
Hashmi, Sohail H., 'Interpreting the Islamic Ethics of War and Peace', in *The Ethics of War and Peace: Religious and Secular Perspectives*, edited by Terry Nardin (Princeton, NJ: Princeton University Press, 1996), 146–68.
Hauser, Alan J., 'Two Songs of Victory: A Comparison of Exodus 15 and Judges 5', in *Directions in Biblical Hebrew Poetry*, edited by Elaine R. Follis (Sheffield: JSOT Press, 1987), 265–84.
Hawk, L. Daniel, 'Conquest Reconfigured: Recasting Warfare in the Redaction of Joshua', in *Writing and Reading War: Rhetoric, Gender, and Ethics in Biblical and Modern Contexts*, edited by Brad E. Kelle and Frank Ritchel Ames (Atlanta, GA: Society of Biblical Literature, 2008), 145–60.
Hayes, William C., 'Egypt: From the Death of Ammenemes III to Seqenenre II', in *The Cambridge Ancient History*, vol. 2, Part 1: *History of the Middle East and the Aegean Region, c. 1800–1380 BC*, edited by I.E.S. Edwards, C. J. Gadd, N.G.L. Hammond, and E. Sollberger, 3rd edn (Cambridge: Cambridge University Press, 1973), 42–76.
Hayes, William C., 'Egypt: Internal Affairs from Tuthmosis I to the Death of Amenophis III', in *The Cambridge Ancient History*, vol 2, Part 1: *History of the Middle East and the Aegean Region, c. 1800–1380 BC*, edited by I.E.S. Edwards, C. J. Gadd, N.G.L. Hammond, and E. Sollberger, 3rd edn (Cambridge: Cambridge University Press, 1973), 313–416.
Heagy, Thomas C., 'Who was Menes?', *Archéo-Nil* 24 (2014): 59–92.
Helck, Wolfgang, Eberhard Otto, and Wolfhart Westendorf (eds), *Lexikon der Ägyptologie*, 7 vols (Wiesbaden: Harrassowitz, 1972–92).
Hersh, Seymour M., *The Chain of Command: The Road from 9/11 to Abu Ghraib* (New York: Harper, 2005).
Herzog, Chaim, and Mordechai Gishon, *Battles of the Bible: A Modern Military Evaluation of the Old Testament* (New York: Random House, 1978).
Heyking, John von, 'Taming Warriors in Classical and Early Medieval Political Theory', in *Ethics, Nationalism, and Just War: Medieval and Contemporary Perspectives*, edited by Henrik Syse and Gregory M. Reichberg (Washington, DC: Catholic University of America Press, 2007), 11–35.

Hindery, Roderick, 'Hindu Ethics in the *Rāmāyana*', *The Journal of Religious Ethics* 4 (2) (1976): 287–322.
Hobbs, T. Raymond, *A Time for War: A Study of Warfare in the Old Testament* (Wilmington, DE: Michael Glazier, 1989).
Hoffman, Michael A., *Egypt before the Pharaohs: The Prehistoric Foundations of Egyptian Civilization* (London: Routledge & Kegan Paul, 1980).
Hoffner, Harry A., Jr., 'Histories and Historians of the Ancient Near East: The Hittites', *Orientalia* n.s. 49 (4) (1980): 283–332.
Hoffner, Harry A., Jr., 'Hittite Mythological Texts: A Survey', in *Unity and Diversity: Essays in the History, Literature, and Religion of the Ancient Near East*, edited by Hans Goedicke and J.J.M. Roberts (Baltimore: Johns Hopkins University Press, 1975), 136–45.
Hoffner, Harry A., Jr., 'Propaganda and Political Justification in Hittite Historiography', in *Unity and Diversity: Essays in the History, Literature, and Religion of the Ancient Near East*, edited by Hans Goedicke and J.J.M. Roberts (Baltimore: Johns Hopkins University Press, 1975), 49–62.
Hoffner, Harry A., Jr., 'The Treatment and Long-Term Use of Persons Captured in Battle according to the Maşat Texts', in *Recent Developments in Hittite Archaeology and History: Papers in Memory of Hans G. Güterbock*, edited by K. Aslihan Yener and Harry A. Hoffner Jr. (Winona Lake, IN: Eisenbrauns, 2002), 61–72.
Holmes, Robert L., 'Can War be Morally Justified? The Just War Theory', in *Just War Theory*, edited by Jean Bethke Elshtain (Oxford: Basil Blackwell, 1992), 197–233.
Holzgrefe, J. L., 'The Origins of Modern International Relations Theory', *Review of International Studies* 15 (1) (1989): 11–26.
Hornung, Erik, *Conceptions of God in Ancient Egypt: The One and the Many*, translated by John Baines (London: Routledge, 1983).
Hornung, Erik, *History of Ancient Egypt*, translated by David Lorton (Edinburgh: Edinburgh University Press, 1999).
Hout, Theo van den, 'A Century of Hittite Text Dating and the Origins of the Hittite Cuneiform Script', *Incontri linguistici* 32 (2009): 11–36.
Hout, Theo van den, 'Institutions, Vernaculars, Publics: The Case of Second-Millennium Anatolia', in *Margins of Writing, Origins of Cultures*, edited by Seth Sanders (Chicago: University of Chicago Press, 2006), 221–60.
Hout, Theo van den, 'Khattushili III, King of the Hittites', in *Civilizations of the Ancient Near East*, edited by Jack M. Sasson, John Baines, Gary Beckman, and Karen S. Rubinson, 4 vols (Peabody, MA: Hendrickson, 2000), 2:1107–20.
Houwink ten Cate, P.H.J., 'The History of Warfare according to Hittite Sources: The Annals of Hattusilis I (Part I)', *Anatolica* 10 (1983): 91–109.
Houwink ten Cate, P.H.J., 'The History of Warfare according to Hittite Sources: The Annals of Hattusilis I (Part II)', *Anatolica* 11 (1984): 47–83. [*AoH*]
Hubrecht, Georges, 'La "Juste Guerre" dans le Décret de Gratien', in *Studia Gratiani, Volume 3*, edited by Jos Forschielli and Alph M. Stickler (Bologna: Institutum Gratianum, 1955), 160–77.
Hume, Robert E., 'Hinduism and War', *The American Journal of Theology* 20 (1) (1916): 31–44.
Hutter-Braunsar, Sylvia, 'Die Terminologie der Zerstörung eroberten Acker- und Siedlungslandes in hethitischen Königsinschriften', in *Der orientalische Mensch und seine Beziehungen zur Umwelt: Beiträge zum 2. Grazer Morgenlandischen Symposium (2.–5. Marz 1989)*, edited by Bernhard Scholz (Graz: Grazer Morgenländische Studien, 1989), 201–18.
Huysmans, Jeff, 'Security! What Do You Mean? From Concept to Thick Signifier', *European Journal of International Relations* 4 (2) (1998): 226–55.

Hyams, Paul R., *Rancor and Reconciliation in Medieval England* (Ithaca, NY: Cornell Press, 2003).
Ishay, Micheline, *The History of Human Rights: From Ancient Times to the Globalization Era* (Berkeley: University of California Press, 2004).
Janzen, Mark D., 'The Iconography of Humiliation: The Depiction and Treatment of Bound Foreigners in New Kingdom Egypt' (PhD dissertation, Memphis University, 2013).
Jasnow, Richard, 'Egypt: Middle Kingdom and Second Intermediate Period', in *A History of Ancient Near Eastern Law*, edited by Raymond Westbrook (Leiden: Brill, 2003), 255–88.
Jasnow, Richard, 'Egypt: New Kingdom', in *A History of Ancient Near Eastern Law*, edited by Raymond Westbrook (Leiden: Brill, 2003), 289–359.
Jasnow, Richard, 'Egypt: Old Kingdom and First Intermediate Period', in *A History of Ancient Near Eastern Law*, edited by Raymond Westbrook (Leiden: Brill, 2003), 93–140.
Jaspers, Karl, *Vom Ursprung und Ziel der Geschichte* (Frankfurt am Main: Fischer Bücherei, 1959).
Johnson, James Turner, 'The Broken Tradition', *The National Interest* 45 (1996): 27–36.
Johnson, James Turner, *Can Modern War be Just?* (New Haven, CT: Yale University Press, 1984).
Johnson, James Turner, *Ethics and the Use of Force: Just War in Historical Perspective* (Farnham: Ashgate, 2011).
Johnson, James Turner, *The Holy War Idea in Western and Islamic Traditions* (University Park: Pennsylvania State University Press, 1997).
Johnson, James Turner, *Ideology, Reason, and the Limitation of War: Religious and Secular Concepts 1200–1740* (Princeton, NJ: Princeton University Press, 1975).
Johnson, James Turner, 'The Just War Idea: The State of the Question', *Social Philosophy and Policy* 23 (1) (2006): 167–95.
Johnson, James Turner, *Just War Tradition and the Restraint of War: A Moral and Historical Inquiry* (Princeton, NJ: Princeton University Press, 1981).
Johnson, James Turner, *Morality and Contemporary Warfare* (New Haven, CT: Yale University Press, 1999).
Johnson, James Turner, *The Quest for Peace: Three Moral Traditions in Western Cultural History* (Princeton, NJ: Princeton University Press, 1987).
Johnson, James Turner, 'St. Augustine (354–430 CE)', in *Just War Thinkers: From Cicero to the 21st Century*, edited by Daniel R. Brunstetter and Cian O'Driscoll (Abingdon: Routledge, 2018), 21–33.
Johnson, James Turner, 'Thinking Morally about War in the Middle Ages and Today', in *Ethics, Nationalism, and Just War: Medieval and Contemporary Perspectives*, edited by Henrik Syse and Gregory M. Reichberg (Washington, DC: Catholic University of America Press, 2007), 3–10.
Johnson, James Turner, and John Kelsay (eds), *Cross, Crescent, and Sword: The Justification and Limitation of War in Western and Islamic Tradition* (New York: Greenwood, 1990).
Jones, Gwilym H., '"Holy War" or "Yahweh War"?', *Vetus Testamentum* 25 (3) (1975): 642–58.
Kákosy, László, 'Egypt in Ancient Greek and Roman Thought', in *Civilizations of the Ancient Near East*, edited by Jack M. Sasson, John Baines, Gary Beckman, and Karen S. Rubinson, 4 vols (Peabody, MA: Hendrickson, 2000), 1:3–14.
Kalmanovitz, Pablo, *The Laws of War in International Thought* (Oxford: Oxford University Press, 2020).
Kalyvas, Stathis N., *The Logic of Violence in Civil War* (New York: Cambridge University Press, 2006).
Kang, Sa-Moon, *Divine War in the Old Testament and in the Ancient Near East* (Berlin: Walter de Gruyter, 1989).

Karenga, Maulana, *Maat, the Moral Ideal in Ancient Egypt: A Study in Classical African Ethics* (New York: Routledge, 2004).
Keefe, Alice A., 'Rapes of Women/Wars of Men', in *Women, War, and Metaphor: Language and Society in the Study of the Hebrew Bible*, edited by Claudia V. Camp and Carole R. Fontaine (Atlanta, GA: Scholars Press, 1993), 79–97.
Keen, Maurice H., *The Laws of War in the Late Middle Ages* (London: Routledge & Kegan Paul; Toronto: University of Toronto Press, 1965).
Kelle, Brad E., *Ancient Israel at War, 853–586 BC* (Oxford: Osprey, 2007).
Kelle, Brad E., 'Wartime Rhetoric: Prophetic Metaphorization of Cities as Female', in *Writing and Reading War: Rhetoric, Gender, and Ethics in Biblical and Modern Contexts*, edited by Brad E. Kelle and Frank Ritchel Ames (Atlanta, GA: Society of Biblical Literature, 2008), 95–111.
Kelle, Brad E., 'What's in a Name?: Neo-Assyrian Designations for the Northern Kingdom and Their Implications for Israelite History and Biblical Interpretation', *Journal of Biblical Literature* 121 (4) (2002): 639–66.
Kellison, Rosemary, *Expanding Responsibility for the Just War: A Feminist Critique* (Cambridge: Cambridge University Press, 2019).
Kelsay, John, 'Al-Shaybani and the Islamic Law of War', *Journal of Military Ethics* 2 (1) (2003): 63–75.
Kelsay, John, *Arguing the Just War in Islam* (Cambridge, MA: Harvard University Press, 2007).
Kelsay, John, *Islam and War: A Study in Comparative Ethics* (Louisville, KT: Westminster John Knox Press, 1993).
Kelsay, John, 'Islamic Tradition and the Justice of War', in *The Ethics of War in Asian Civilizations: A Comparative Perspective*, edited by Torkel Brekke (Abingdon: Routledge, 2006), 81–110.
Kelsay, John, and James Turner Johnson (eds), *Just War and Jihad: Historical and Theoretical Perspectives on War and Peace in Western and Islamic Traditions* (New York: Greenwood, 1991).
Khadduri, Majid, *War and Peace in the Law of Islam* (Baltimore: Johns Hopkins University Press, 1955).
Klengel, Horst, *Geschichte des Hethitischen Reiches* (Leiden: Brill, 1999).
Klengel, Horst, 'Problems in Hittite History, Solved and Unsolved', in *Recent Developments in Hittite Archaeology and History: Papers in Memory of Hans G. Güterbock*, edited by K. Aslihan Yener and Harry A. Hoffner Jr. (Winona Lake, IN: Eisenbrauns, 2002), 101–9.
Kline, Meredith G., *Treaty of the Great King: The Covenant Structure of Deuteronomy; Studies and Commentary* (1963; repub. Eugene, OR: Wipf and Stock, 2012).
Knapp, A. Bernard, 'Island Cultures: Crete, Thera, Cyprus, Rhodes, and Sardinia', in *Civilizations of the Ancient Near East*, edited by Jack M. Sasson, John Baines, Gary Beckman, and Karen S. Rubinson, 4 vols (Peabody, MA, 2000: Hendrickson, 1995), 3:1433–49.
Kolb, Robert, 'Origin of the Twin Terms *jus ad bellum/jus in bello*', *International Review of the Red Cross* 37 (320) (1997): 553–62.
Korošec, Victor, 'The Warfare of the Hittites: From the Legal Point of View', *British Institute for the Study of Iraq* 25 (2) (1963): 159–66.
Koskenniemi, Marti, *The Gentle Civilizer of Nations: The Rise and Fall of International Law, 1870–1960* (Cambridge: Cambridge University Press, 2001).
Kratz, Reinhard G., *The Composition of the Narrative Books of the Old Testament*, translated by John Bowden (London: T&T Clark, 2005).
Krentz, Peter, 'Deception in Archaic and Classical Greek Warfare', in *War and Violence in Ancient Greece*, edited by Hans van Wees (London: Duckworth, 2000), 167–200.

Krentz, Peter, 'Fighting by the Rules: The Invention of the Hoplite Agon', *Hesperia* 71 (1) (2002): 23–39.

Kruchten, J., 'Rétribution de l'armée d'après le décret d'Horemheb', *L'Égyptologie en 1979: Axes prioritaires de recherches* 2 (1982): 143–48.

Krüger, Thomas, '"They Shall Beat Their Swords into Plowshares": A Vision of Peace through Justice and Its Background in the Hebrew Bible', in *War and Peace in the Ancient World*, edited by Kurt A. Raaflaub (Malden, MA: Blackwell, 2007), 161–71.

Kuhrt, Amélie, *The Ancient Near East c. 3000–330 BC*, 2 vols (London: Routledge, 1995) [*KANE*].

Kümmel, Hans Martin, *Ersatzrituale für den hethitischen König* (Wiesbaden: Harrassowitz, 1967).

Kutz, Christopher, 'Fearful Symmetry', in *Just and Unjust Warriors: The Moral and Legal Status of Soldiers*, edited by David Rodin and Henry Shue (Oxford: Oxford University Press, 2008), 69–86.

Kyle, Donald G., *Spectacles of Death in Ancient Rome* (London: Routledge, 1998).

Lackenbacher, Sylvie, 'Nouveaux documents d'Ugarit: I—une lettre royale', *Revue d'assyriologie et d'archéologie orientale* 76 (2) (1982): 141–56.

Lang, Anthony F., Jr., 'The Just War Tradition and the Question of Authority', *Journal of Military Ethics* 8 (3) (2008): 202–16.

Lang, Anthony F., Jr., 'Rules and International Security: Dilemmas of a New World Order', in *War, Torture and Terrorism: Rethinking the Rules of International Security*, edited by Anthony F. Lang Jr. and Amanda Russell Beattie (Abingdon: Routledge, 2009), 1–22.

Lang, Anthony F., Jr., and Cian O'Driscoll, 'Introduction: The Just War Tradition and the Practice of Political Authority', in *Just War: Authority, Tradition, and Practice*, edited by Anthony F. Lang Jr., Cian O'Driscoll, and John Williams (Washington, DC: Georgetown University Press, 2013), 1–16.

Lang, Anthony F., Jr., Cian O'Driscoll, and John Williams (eds), *Just War: Authority, Tradition, and Practice* (Washington, DC: Georgetown University Press, 2013).

Lanni, Adriaan, 'The Laws of War in Ancient Greece', *Law and History Review* 26 (3) (2008): 469–89.

Lawrence, A. W., 'Ancient Egyptian Fortifications', *The Journal of Egyptian Archaeology* 51 (1965): 69–94.

Lazar, Seth, 'Liability and the Ethics of War: A Response', in *The Ethics of Self-Defense*, edited by Christian Coons and Michael Weber (New York: Oxford University Press, 2016), 292–304.

Lazar, Seth, 'Responsibility, Risk, and Killing in Self-Defense', *Ethics* 119 (4) (2009): 699–728.

Lazar, Seth, *Sparing Civilians* (Oxford: Oxford University Press, 2015).

Leahy, Anthony, 'Death by Fire in Ancient Egypt', *Journal of Economic and Social History of the Orient* 27 (2) (1984): 199–206.

Lemche, Niels-Peter, *Ancient Israel: A New History of Israelite Society* (Sheffield: JSOT Press, 1988).

Lemche, Niels Peter, *The Israelites in History and Tradition* (Louisville, KY: Westminster John Knox Press; London: SPCK, 1998).

Lemche, Niels Peter, 'The Old Testament—A Hellenistic Book?', *Scandinavian Journal of the Old Testament* 7 (2) (1993): 163–93.

Lesaffer, Randall, and Janne E. Nijman (eds), *The Cambridge Companion to Hugo Grotius* (Cambridge: Cambridge University Press, 2021).

Lewis, Mark E., 'The Just War in Early China', in *The Ethics of War in Asian Civilizations: A Comparative Perspective*, edited by Torkel Brekke (Abingdon: Routledge, 2006), 185–200.

Lichtheim, Miriam, *Moral Values in Ancient Egypt* (Fribourg: University Press Fribourg; Göttingen: Vandenhoeck & Ruprecht, 1997).
Lightfoot, Kent G., and Antoinette Martinez, 'Frontiers and Boundaries in Archaeological Perspective', *Annual Review of Anthropology* 24 (1995): 471–92.
Lind, Millard C., *Yahweh is a Warrior: The Theology of Warfare in Ancient Israel* (Scottdale, PA; Kitchener, Ontario: Herald, 1980).
Linklater, Andrew, *Violence and Civilization in the Western States Systems* (Cambridge: Cambridge University Press, 2017).
Littauer, M. A., and J. H. Crouwel, 'The Origin of the True Chariot', *Antiquity* 70 (1996): 934–39.
Liver, Jacob (ed.), *The Military History of the Land of Israel in Biblical Times* (Jerusalem: Israel Defence Forces Publishing House, 1964).
Liverani, Mario, 'The Ideology of the Assyrian Empire', in *Power and Propaganda: A Symposium on Ancient Empires*, edited by M. T. Larsen (Copenhagen: Akademisk Forlag, 1979), 297–317.
Liverani, Mario, *International Relations in the Ancient Near East, 1600–1100 BC* (Basingstoke: Palgrave Macmillan, 2001) [*LIR*].
Liverani, Mario, 'The King and His Army', in *At the Dawn of History: Ancient Near Eastern Studies in Honor of J. N. Postgate*, edited by Yağmur Heffron, Adam Stone and Martin Worthington (University Park: Penn State University Press, 2021), 301–12.
Liverani, Mario, 'Storiografia politica hittita—II: Telepinu, ovvero: Della solidarietà', *Oriens Antiquus* 16 (1977): 105–31.
Livingstone, Alasdair, and Birgit Haskamp, 'Near Eastern Mythologies', in *A Companion to Greek Mythology*, edited by Ken Dowden and Niall Livingstone (Malden, MA: Wiley-Blackwell, 2011), 357–82.
Lo, Ping-cheung, 'The *Art of War* Corpus and Chinese Just War Ethics Past and Present', *Journal of Religious Ethics* 40 (3) (2012): 404–46.
Lo, Ping-cheung, 'Varieties of Statecraft and Warfare Ethics in Early China: An Overview', in *Chinese Just War Ethics: Origin, Development, and Dissent*, edited by Ping-cheun Lo and Sumner B. Twiss (Abingdon: Routledge, 2015), 3–25.
Lo, Ping-cheung, and Sumner B. Twiss (eds), *Chinese Just War Ethics: Origin, Development, and Dissent* (Abingdon: Routledge, 2015).
Longman, Tremper, III, and Daniel G. Reid, *God is a Warrior* (Grand Rapids, MI: Zondervan, 1995).
Loprieno, Antonio, 'Defining Egyptian Literature: Ancient Texts and Modern Literary Theory', in *The Study of the Ancient Near East in the 21st Century: The William Foxwell Albright Centennial Conference*, edited by Jerrold S. Cooper and Glenn M. Schwartz (Winona Lake, IN: Eisenbrauns, 1996), 209–32.
Lorton, David, *The Juridical Terminology of International Relations in Egyptian Texts through Dynasty XVIII* (Baltimore: Johns Hopkins University Press, 1974).
Lorton, David, 'The So-Called "Vile" Enemies of the King of Egypt (in the Middle Kingdom and Dyn. XVIII)', *Journal of the American Research Center in Egypt* 10 (1973): 65–70.
Lorton, David, 'Terminology Related to the Laws of Warfare in Dynasty XVIII', *Journal of the American Research Center in Egypt* 11 (1974): 53–68.
Lorton, David, 'The Treatment of Criminals in Ancient Egypt: Through the New Kingdom', *Journal of the Economic and Social History of the Orient* 20 (1) (1977): 2–64.
Luce, Edward, *The Retreat of Western Liberalism* (New York: Grove Press, 2017).
Luiselli, Maria Michela, 'The Ancient Egyptian Scene of "Pharaoh Smiting His Enemies": An Attempt to Visualize Cultural Memory', in *Cultural Memory and Identity in Ancient Societies*, edited by Martin Bommas (London: Continuum, 2011), 10–25.

Lyons, David, 'Ethical Relativism and the Problem of Incoherence', *Ethics* 86 (2) (1976): 107–21.
Macalister, R. A. Stewart, 'Exploration and Excavation', in *The Cambridge Ancient History*, vol. 1: *Egypt and Babylonia to 1580 BC*, edited by J. B. Bury, S. A. Cook, and F. E. Adcock, 2nd edn (Cambridge: Cambridge University Press, 1928), 112–44.
Machinist, Peter, 'Literature as Politics: The Tukulti-Ninurta Epic and the Bible', *The Catholic Biblical Quarterly* 38 (4) (1976): 455–82.
Macqueen, J. G., 'The History of Anatolia and of the Hittite Empire: An Overview', in *Civilizations of the Ancient Near East*, edited by Jack M. Sasson, John Baines, Gary Beckman, and Karen S. Rubinson, 4 vols (Peabody, MA: Hendrickson, 2000), 2:1085–105.
Macqueen, J. G., *The Hittites and Their Contemporaries in Asia Minor*, revised and enlarged edn (London: Thames and Hudson, 1986).
Mahbubani, Kishore, *The Great Convergence: Asia, the West, and the Logic of One World* (New York: Public Affairs, 2013).
Malamat, Abraham, 'Conquest of Canaan: Israelite Conduct of War according to Biblical Tradition', *Revue internationale d'histoire militaire* 42/Édition de la Commission israelienne d'histoire militaire (1979): 25–52.
Malbran-Labat, Florence, *L'Armée et l'organisation militaire de l'Assyrie à l'époque des Sargonides* (Geneva: Droz, 1982).
Mapel, David R., 'Realism, War and Peace', in *The Ethics of War and Peace: Religious and Secular Perspectives*, edited by Terry Nardin (Princeton, NJ: Princeton University Press, 1997), 54–77.
Marcuson, Hannah, and Theo van den Hout, 'Memorization and Hittite Ritual: New Perspectives on the Transmission of Hittite Ritual Texts', *Journal of Ancient Near Eastern Religions* 15 (2015): 143–68.
Marek, Christian, *In the Land of a Thousand Gods: A History of Asia Minor in the Ancient World*, translated by Steven Rendall (Princeton, NJ: Princeton University Press, 2019).
Margalith, Othniel, 'On the Origin and Antiquity of the Name Israel', *Zeitschrift für die Alttestamentliche Wissenschaft* 102 (2) (1990): 225–37.
Matthews, Victor H., and Don C. Benjamin, *Old Testament Parallels: Laws and Stories from the Ancient Near East*, revised 3rd edn (New York: Paulist Press, 2006).
Mattox, John Mark, *Saint Augustine and the Theory of Just War* (London: Continuum, 2006).
Mayes, A.D.H., *Deuteronomy* (London: Oliphants, 1979).
Mayor, Adrienne, *Greek Fire, Poison Arrows, and Scorpion Bombs: Biological and Chemical Warfare in the Ancient World* (Woodstock: Overlook Press, 2004).
Mazar, Amihai, 'The Search for David and Solomon: An Archaeological Perspective', in Israel Finkelstein and Amihai Mazar, *The Quest for the Historical Israel: Debating Archaeology and the History of Early Israel; Invited Lectures Delivered at the Sixth Biennial Colloquium of the International Institute for Secular Humanistic Judaism, Detroit, October 2015*, edited by Brian B. Schmidt (Atlanta, GA: Society for Biblical Literature, 2007), 117–39.
McDermott, Bridget, *Warfare in Ancient Egypt* (Stroud: Sutton Publishing, 2004).
McKeown, Ryder, 'Norm Regress: US Revisionism and the Slow Death of the Torture Norm', *International Relations* 23 (1) (2009): 5–25.
McMahan, Jeff, 'The Ethics of Killing in War', *Ethics* 114 (4) (2004): 693–733.
McMahan, Jeff, *Killing in War* (Oxford: Oxford University Press, 2009).
McMahan, Jeff, 'Killing in War: A Reply to Walzer', *Philosophia* 34 (1) (2006): 47–51.
McMahan, Jeff, 'The Morality of War and the Law of War', in *Just and Unjust Warriors: The Moral and Legal Status of Soldiers*, edited by David Rodin and Henry Shue (Oxford: Oxford University Press, 2008), 19–43.

McMahan, Jeff, 'On the Moral Equality of Combatants', *Journal of Political Philosophy* 14 (4) (2006): 377–93.
McMahan, Jeff, 'War and Peace', in *A Companion to Ethics*, edited by Peter Singer (Oxford: Blackwell, 1991), 384–95.
McMahon, Gregory, 'The History of the Hittites', *The Biblical Archaeologist* 52 (2/3) (1989): 62–77.
Meier, Samuel A., *The Messenger in the Ancient Semitic World* (Atlanta, GA: Scholars Press, 1988).
Mendenhall, George E., 'Ancient Oriental and Biblical Law', *The Biblical Archaeologist* 17 (2) (1954): 25–46.
Mendenhall, George E., 'Covenant Forms in Israelite Tradition', *The Biblical Archaeologist* 17 (3) (1954): 49–76.
Mendenhall, George E., 'The Hebrew Conquest of Palestine', *The Biblical Archaeologist* 25 (1962): 66–87.
Mendenhall, George E., *Law and Covenant in Israel and the Ancient Near East* (Pittsburgh, PA: Biblical Colloquium, 1955).
Mendoza, Rubén G., 'The Divine Gourd Tree: Tzompantli Skull Racks, Decapitation Rituals, and Human Trophies in Ancient Mesoamerica', in *The Taking and Displaying of Human Body Parts as Trophies by Amerindians*, edited by Richard J. Chacon and David H. Dye (New York: Springer, 2007), 400–43.
Menu, Bernadette, 'La Legitimation de la guerre dans l'idéologie pharaonique', *Droit et cultures* 45 (2003): 49–64.
Miller, Jared L., *Studies in the Origins, Development and Interpretation of the Kizzuwatna Rituals* (Wiesbaden: Harrassowitz, 2004).
Miller, J. Maxwell, and John H. Hayes, *A History of Ancient Israel and Judah*, 2nd edn (Louisville, KY: 2006).
Miller, Patrick D., Jr., *The Divine Warrior in Early Israel* (Cambridge, MA: Harvard University Press, 1973).
Mitchell, Martha, 'William L. Marcy', in *Encyclopaedia Brunoniana* (Providence, RI: Brown University Library, 1993), available at https://www.brown.edu/Administration/News_Bureau/Databases/Encyclopedia/search.php?serial=M0120 (accessed 9 January 2023).
Mitzen, Jennifer, 'Ontological Security in World Politics: State Identity and the Security Dilemma', *European Journal of International Relations* 12 (3) (2006): 341–70.
Morenz, Siegfried, *Egyptian Religion*, translated by Anne E. Keep (London: Methuen, 1973).
Morkevičius, Valerie, 'Power and Order: The Shared Logics of Realism and Just War Theory', *International Studies Quarterly* 59 (1) (2015): 11–22.
Morkevičius, Valerie, *Realist Ethics: Just War Traditions as Power Politics* (Cambridge: Cambridge University Press, 2018).
Morkot, Robert G., *The A to Z of Ancient Egyptian Warfare* (Lanham, MD: Scarecrow Press, 2003).
Moser, Christopher L., 'Human Decapitation in Ancient Mesoamerica', *Studies in Pre-columbian Art and Archaeology* 11 (1973): 1–72.
Muchembled, Robert, *A History of Violence: From the End of the Middle Ages to the Present* (Cambridge: Polity, 2012).
Muhlestein, Kerry, 'Royal Executions: Evidence Bearing on the Subject of Sanctioned Killing in the Middle Kingdom', *Journal of Economic and Social History of the Orient* 51 (2) (2008): 181–208
Muhlestein, Kerry, *Violence in the Service of Order: The Religious Framework for Sanctioned Killing in Ancient Egypt* (Oxford: Archaeopress, 2011).

Müller, Reinhard, *Jahwe als Wettergott: Studien zur althebräischen Kultlyrik anhand ausgewählter Psalmen* (Berlin: De Gruyter, 2008).

Müller-Wollermann, Renate, 'Symbolische Gewalt im Alten Ägypten', in *Extreme Formen von Gewalt in Bild und Text des Altertum*, edited by Martin Zimmermann (Munich: Herbert Utz, 2009), 47–64.

Munn-Rankin, J. Margaret, 'Diplomacy in Western Asia in the Early Second Millennium BC', *Iraq* 18 (1) (1956): 68–110.

Murnane, William J., 'The History of Ancient Egypt: An Overview', in *Civilizations of the Ancient Near East*, edited by Jack M. Sasson, John Baines, Gary Beckman, and Karen S. Rubinson, 4 vols (Peabody, MA: Hendrickson, 2000), 2:691–717.

Neff, Stephen, *War and the Law of Nations: A General History* (Cambridge: Cambridge University Press, 2005).

Neumann, Iver B., and Einar Wigen, *The Steppe Tradition in International Relations: Russians, Turks and European State Building 4000 BCE–2018 CE* (Cambridge: Cambridge University Press, 2018).

Ni Lexiong, 'The Implications of Ancient Chinese Military Culture for World Peace', in *Confucian Political Ethics*, edited by Daniel A. Bell (Princeton, NJ: Princeton University Press, 2008), 201–25.

Nibbi, Alessandra, 'Some Remarks on the Merenptah Stela and the So-Called Name of Israel', *Discussions in Egyptology* 36 (1996): 79–102.

Niditch, Susan, 'War and Reconciliation in the Traditions of Ancient Israel: Historical, Literary, and Ideological Considerations', in *War and Peace in the Ancient World*, edited by Kurt A. Raaflaub (Malden, MA: Blackwell, 2007), 141–60.

Niditch, Susan, *War in the Hebrew Bible: A Study in the Ethics of Violence* (New York: Oxford University Press, 1993) [*WHB*].

Niditch, Susan, 'War, Women, and Defilement in Numbers 31', in *Women, War, and Metaphor: Language and Society in the Study of the Hebrew Bible*, edited by Claudia V. Camp and Carole R. Fontaine (Atlanta, GA: Scholars Press, 1993), 39–57.

Noth, Martin, *The Chronicler's History* (Sheffield: JSOT Press, 1987).

Noth, Martin, *The Deuteronomistic History* (Sheffield: JSOT Press, 1981).

Noth, Martin, *The History of Israel*, revised 2nd edn, translated by Peter R. Ackroyd (London: A. & C. Black, 1960).

Nussbaum, Arthur, *A Concise History of the Law of Nations* (New York: Macmillan, 1947).

Nussbaum, Arthur, 'Just War: A Legal Concept?', *Michigan Law Review* 42 (1943) (3): 453–79.

Ober, Josiah, 'Classical Greek Times', in *The Laws of War: Constraints on Warfare in the Western World*, edited by Michael Howard, George J. Andreopoulos, and Mark R. Shulman (New Haven, CT: Yale University Press, 1994), 12–26.

Ober, Josiah, 'The Rules of War in Classical Greece', in Josiah Ober, *The Athenian Revolution: Essays on Ancient Greek Democracy and Political Theory* (Princeton, NJ: Princeton University Press, 1996), 53–71.

Ober, Josiah, and Tomer Perry, 'Thucydides as a Prospect Theorist', *Polis: Journal for Ancient Greek Political Thought* 31 (2014): 206–32.

O'Brien, William V., *The Conduct of Just and Limited War* (New York: Praeger, 1981).

O'Connor, David, 'Egypt's Views of Others', in *Never Had the Like Occurred*, edited by John Tait (London: UCL Press, 2003), 155–85.

Oded, Bustenay, 'Cutting Down Orchards in Assyrian Royal Inscriptions: The Historiographic Aspect', *Journal of Ancient Civilizations* 12 (1997): 93–98.

Oded, Bustenay, *War, Peace and Empire: Justifications for War in Assyrian Royal Inscriptions* (Wiesbaden: Reichert, 1992).

O'Driscoll, Cian, 'Hedgehog or Fox? An Essay on James Turner Johnson's View of History', *Journal of Military Ethics* 8 (3) (2009): 165-78.
O'Driscoll, Cian (ed.), *James Turner Johnson and the Recovery of the Just War Tradition*, special issue of *Journal of Military Ethics* 8 (3) (2008): 163-262.
O'Driscoll, Cian, 'Keeping Tradition Alive: Just War and Historical Imagination', *Journal of Global Security Studies* 3 (2) (2018): 234-47.
O'Driscoll, Cian, 'Rewriting the Just War Tradition: Just War in Classical Greek Political Thought and Practice', *International Studies Quarterly* 59 (1) (2015): 1-10.
O'Driscoll, Cian, *Victory: The Triumph and Tragedy of Just War* (Oxford: Oxford University Press, 2019).
Oller, Gary H., 'Messengers and Ambassadors in Ancient Western Asia', in *Civilizations of the Ancient Near East*, edited by Jack M. Sasson, John Baines, Gary Beckman, and Karen S. Rubinson, 4 vols (Peabody, MA: Hendrickson, 2000), 3:1465-73.
Osiel, Mark J., *Obeying Orders: Atrocity, Military Discipline, and the Law of War* (New Brunswick, NJ: Transaction Publishers, 2002).
Panitschek, Peter, 'Zur Gewalttoleranz in der Kriegsführung des frühen Alten Orients', in *'Böser Krieg': Exzessive Gewalt in der antiken Kriegsführung und Strategien zu deren Vermeidung*, edited by Margit Linder and Sabine Tausend (Graz: Grazer Universitätsverlag, 2011), 9-34.
Partridge, Richard B., *Fighting Pharaohs: Weapons and Warfare in Ancient Egypt* (Manchester: Peartree Publishing, 2002).
Paskins, Barry, 'Realism and the Just War', *Journal of Military Ethics* 6 (2) (2007): 117-30.
Perry, William J., *Children of the Sun: A Study in the Early History of Civilization* (London: Methuen, 1923).
Peters, Rudolph (ed. and trans.), *Jihad in Medieval and Modern Islam* (Leiden: Brill, 1977).
Pierson, Paul, 'Increasing Returns, Path Dependence, and the Study of Politics', *The American Political Science Review* 94 (2) (2000): 251-67.
Pimouguet-Pedarros, Isabelle, 'Guerre, norms et transgressions dans le monde grec', in *La Transgression en temps de guerre: De l'Antiquité à nos jours*, edited by Nathalie Barrandon and Isabelle Pimouguet-Pedarros (Rennes: Presses Universitaires de Rennes, 2021), 65-81.
Pinker, Steven, *The Better Angels of Our Nature: A History of Violence and Humanity* (London: Penguin, 2011).
Polish, Daniel F., 'Just War in Jewish Thought', in *The Concept of Just War in Judaism, Christianity, and Islam*, edited by Georges Tamer and Katja Thörner (Berlin: De Gruyter, 2021), 1-41.
Posener, Georges, *De la divinité du Pharaon* (Paris: Imprimerie nationale, 1960).
Preiser, Wolfgang, 'History of the Law of Nations: Basic Questions and Principles', in *Encyclopedia of Public International Law*, vol. 7: *History of International Law, Foundations of International Law, Sources of International Law, Law of Treaties*, edited by Rudolph Bernhardt (Amsterdam: North Holland Publishing, 1984).
Preß, Richard, 'Das Ordal im Alten Testament', *Zeitschrift für die Alttestamentliche Wissenschaft* 51 (1933): 121-40.
Pury, Albert de, Thomas C. Römer, and Jean-Daniel Macchi (eds), *Israel Constructs Its History: Deuteronomistic History in Recent Research* (Sheffield: JSOT Press, 2000).
Rad, Gerhard von, *Holy War in Ancient Israel*, translated and edited by Marva J. Dawn, introduction by Ben C. Ollenburger, bibliography by Judith E. Sanderson (Grand Rapids, MI: Eerdmans, 1991).
Rahe, Paul A., 'Justice and Necessity: The Conduct of the Spartans and the Athenians in the Peloponnesian War', in *Civilians in the Path of War*, edited by Mark Grimsley and Clifford J. Rogers (Lincoln: University of Nebraska Press, 2002), 1-32.

Rainey, Anson, 'Shasu or Habiru: Who Were the Early Israelites?', *Biblical Archaeological Review* 34 (6) (2008): 51–55.

Ramsey, Paul, *The Just War: Force and Political Responsibility* (1968; repr. Lanham, MD: University Press of America, 1983).

Ramsey, Paul, *War and the Christian Conscience: How Shall Modern War Be Conducted Justly?* (Durham, NC: Duke University Press, 1961).

Ray, John, 'Soldiers to Pharaoh: The Carians of Southwest Anatolia', in *Civilizations of the Ancient Near East*, edited by Jack M. Sasson, John Baines, Gary Beckman, and Karen S. Rubinson, 4 vols (Peabody, MA: Hendrickson, 2000), 2:1185–94.

Raymond, Gregory A., 'The Greco-Roman Roots of the Just War Tradition', in *The Prism of Just War: Asian and Western Perspectives on the Legitimate Use of Military Force*, edited by Howard M. Hensel (Farnham: Ashgate, 2010), 7–28.

Redford, Donald B., 'The Concept of Kingship during the Eighteenth Dynasty', in *Ancient Egyptian Kingship*, edited by David O'Connor and David P. Silverman (Leiden: Brill, 1995), 157–84.

Redford, Donald B., *Egypt, Canaan, and Israel in Ancient Times* (Princeton, NJ: Princeton University Press, 1992).

Redford, Donald B., *Pharaonic King-Lists, Annals and Day-Books: A Contribution to the Study of the Egyptian Sense of History* (Mississauga, Ontario: Benben, 1986).

Redford, Donald B., *The Wars in Syria and Palestine of Thutmose III* (Leiden: Brill, 2003).

Reichberg, Gregory M., 'Jus ad bellum', in *War: Essays in Political Philosophy*, edited by Larry May (New York: Cambridge University Press, 2008), 11–29.

Reichberg, Gregory M., *Thomas Aquinas on War and Peace* (Cambridge: Cambridge University Press, 2017).

Rendtorff, Rolf, 'Between Historical Criticism and Holistic Interpretation: New Trends in Old Testament Exegesis', in *Congress Volume: Jerusalem, 1986*, edited by J. A. Emerton (Leiden: Brill, 1988), 298–303.

Rendtorff, Rolf, *The Problem of the Process of Transmission in the Pentateuch* (Sheffield: JSOT Press, 1990).

Rengger, Nicholas, *Just War and International Order: The Uncivil Condition in World Politics* (Cambridge: Cambridge University Press, 2013).

Rengger, Nicholas, 'On the Just War Tradition in the Twenty-First Century', *International Affairs* 78 (2) (2002): 353–63.

Reus-Smit, Christian, *The Moral Purpose of the State: Culture, Social Identity, and Institutional Rationality in International Relations* (Princeton, NJ: Princeton University Press, 1999).

Ritner, Robert K., *The Mechanics of Ancient Egyptian Magical Practice* (Chicago: The Oriental Institute of the University of Chicago, 1993).

Rodin, David, 'The Moral Inequality of Soldiers: Why *jus in bello* Asymmetry is Half Right', in *Just and Unjust Warriors: The Moral and Legal Status of Soldiers*, edited by David Rodin and Henry Shue (Oxford: Oxford University Press, 2008), 44–68.

Rodin, David, *War and Self-Defense* (Oxford: Oxford University Press, 2002).

Rodin, David, and Henry Shue (eds), *Just and Unjust Warriors: The Moral and Legal Status of Soldiers* (Oxford: Oxford University Press, 2008).

Rosenne, Shabtai, 'The Influence of Judaism on the Development of International Law', *Netherlands International Law Review* 5 (2) (1958): 119–49.

Rostovtseff, Michael I., 'International Relations in the Ancient World', in *The History and Nature of International Relations*, edited by Edmund A. Walsh (New York: Macmillan, 1922; repr. Miami: HardPress Publishing, 2013), 31–65.

Roy, Kaushik, 'Hinduism', in *Religion, War and Ethics: A Sourcebook of Textual Traditions*, edited by Gregory Reichberg and Henrik Syse, with Nicole H. Hartwell (Cambridge: Cambridge University Press, 2014), 471–543.

Rumelili, Bahar (ed.), *Conflict Resolution and Ontological Security: Peace Anxieties* (London: Routledge, 2015).

Russell, Frederick H., *The Just War in the Middle Ages* (Cambridge: Cambridge University Press, 1975).

Sabbahy, Lisa K., *Kingship, Power, and Legitimacy in Ancient Egypt: From the Old Kingdom to the Middle Kingdom* (Cambridge: Cambridge University Press, 2021).

Sabine, Lorenzo, *Notes on Duels and Duelling, Alphabetically Arranged, with a Preliminary Historical Essay*, 3rd edn (Boston, MA: Crosby, Nichols, and Company, 1859).

Saggs, H.W.F., 'Assyrian Warfare in the Sargonid Period', *Iraq* 25 (1963): 145–54.

Santosuosso, Anthony, 'Kadesh Revisited: Reconstructing the Battle between the Egyptians and the Hittites', *The Journal of Military History* 60 (3) (1996): 423–44.

Schachner, Andreas, 'Gedanken zur Datierung, Entwicklung und Funktion der hethitischen Kunst', *Altorientalische Forschungen* 39 (1) (2012): 130–66.

Schachner, Andreas, *Hattuscha: Auf der Suche nach dem sagenhaften Großreich der Hethiter* (Munich: Beck, 2011).

Schneider, Joseph, 'Primitive Warfare: A Methodological Note', *American Sociological Review* 15 (6) (1950): 772–77.

Schneider, Thomas, 'Foreigners in Egypt: Archaeological Evidence and Cultural Context', in *Egyptian Archaeology*, edited by Willeke Wendrich (Malden, MA: Wiley-Blackwell, 2010), 143–63.

Schoske, Sylvia 'Das Erschlagen der Feinde: Ikonographie und Stilistik der Feindvernichtung im alten Ägypten' (Inauguraldissertation zur Erlangung des Doktorgrades [doctoral dissertation], Universität Heidelberg, 1982).

Schulman, Alan R., *Ceremonial Execution and Public Rewards: Some Historical Scenes on New Kingdom Private Stelae* (Freiburg: Universitätsverlag; Göttingen: Vandenhoeck & Ruprecht, 1988).

Schulman, Alan R., *Military Rank, Title, and Organization in the Egyptian New Kingdom* (Berlin: Hessling, 1964).

Schulman, Alan R., 'Some Observations on the Military Background of the Amarna Period', *Journal of the American Research Center in Egypt* 3 (1964): 51–69.

Schwally, Friedrich, *Semitische Kriegsaltertümer, Heft 1: Der heilige Krieg im alten Israel* (Leipzig: Deiterich/Weicher, 1901).

Scurlock, JoAnn, 'Neo-Assyrian Battle Tactics', in *Crossing Boundaries and Linking Horizons: Studies in Honor of Michael C. Astour on His 80th Birthday*, edited by Gordon D. Young, Mark W. Chavalas, and Richard E. Averbeck (Bethesda, MD: CDL, 1998), 491–517.

Seeher, Jürgen, *Gods Carved in Stone: The Hittite Rock Sanctuary of Yazilikaya*, translated by Giles Shepard (Istanbul: Ege Yayinlari, 2011).

Seeher, Jürgen, 'Die Zerstörung der Stadt Hattusa', in *Akten des IV. Internationalen Kongresses für Hethitologie, Würzburg, 4.-8. Oktober 1999*, edited by Gernot Wilhelm (Wiesbaden: Harrossowitz, 2001), 623–34.

Selden, John, *De iure naturae et gentium iuxta disciplinam ebraeorum* (London: Excudebat Richardus Bishopius, 1640).

Seton, D. R., 'The King of Egypt Annihilating His Enemies: A Study of the Symbolism of Ancient Monarchy' (M.A. dissertation, University of Birmingham, 1971).

Sewell, William H., Jr., 'Marc Bloch and the Logic of Comparative History', *History and Theory* 6 (2) (1967): 208–18.

Sharma, Serena K., 'The Legacy of *Jus Contra Bellum*: Echoes of Pacifism in Contemporary Just War Thought', *Journal of Military Ethics* 8 (3) (2009): 217–30.
Shaw, Ian, *Egyptian Warfare and Weapons* (Princes Risborough: Shire, 1991).
Shaw, Ian, 'Egyptians, Hyksos and Military Technology: Causes, Effects or Catalysts?', in *The Social Context of Technological Change: Egypt and the Near East, 1650–1150 BC*, edited by Andrew J. Shortland (Oxford: Oxbow, 2001), 59–71.
Shaw, Ian, 'Socio-economic and Iconographic Contexts for Egyptian Military Technology in the East Mediterranean: The Knowledge Economy and "Technology Transfer" in Late Bronze Age Warfare', in *The Knowledge Economy and Technological Capabilities: Egypt, the Near East and the Mediterranean, 2nd Millennium BC–1st Millennium AD; Proceedings of a Conference Held at the Maison de la Chimie, Paris, France, 9–10 December 2005*, edited by M. Wissa (Barcelona: Aula Orientalis, 2010), 77–85.
Shue, Henry, 'Do We Need a "Morality of War"?', in *Just and Unjust Warriors: The Moral and Legal Status of Soldiers*, edited by David Rodin and Henry Shue (Oxford: Oxford University Press, 2008), 87–111.
Silverman, David P., 'The Nature of Egyptian Kingship', in *Ancient Egyptian Kingship*, edited by David O'Connor and David P. Silverman (Leiden: Brill, 1995), 49–94.
Simpson, Anthony, 'Freud on the State, Violence, and War', *Diacritics* 35 (3) (2005): 78–91.
Singer, Itamar, *The Calm before the Storm: Selected Writings of Itamar Singer on the Late Bronze Age in Anatolia and the Levant* (Atlanta, GA: Society of Biblical Literature, 2011).
Singer, Itamar, 'From Hattuša to Tarhuntašša: Some Thoughts on Muwatalli's Reign', in *Acts of the 3rd International Congress of Hittitology*, edited by Sedat Alp and Aygül Süel (Ankara: Uyum Ajans, 1996), 536–41.
Singer, Itamar, '"Old Country" Ethnonyms in "New Countries" of the "Sea Peoples" Diaspora', in *AMILLA The Quest for Excellence: Studies Presented to Guenter Kopcke in Celebration of His 75th Birthday*, edited by Robert B. Koehl (Philadelphia: Instap Academic Press, 2013), 321–33.
Śliwa, Joachim, 'Some Remarks concerning Victorious Ruler Representations in Egyptian Art', *Forschungen und Berichte* 16 (1974): 97–117.
Smelser, Neil J., *Comparative Methods in the Social Sciences* (Eaglewood Cliffs, NJ: Prentice Hall, 1976).
Smend, Rudolf, *Yahweh War and Tribal Confederation: Reflections upon Israel's Earliest History*, translated by Max G. Rogers (Nashville, TN: Abingdon Press, 1970).
Smith, Grafton Elliot, Bronislaw Malinowski, Herbert J. Spinden, and Alexander Goldenweiser, *Culture: The Diffusionist Controversy* (New York: W. W. Norton, 1927).
Smith-Christopher, Daniel L., 'Gideon at Thermopylae?: On the Militarization of Miracle in Biblical Narrative and "Battle Maps"', in *Writing and Reading War: Rhetoric, Gender, and Ethics in Biblical and Modern Contexts*, edited by Brad E. Kelle and Frank Ritchel Ames (Atlanta: Society of Biblical Literature, 2008), 197–212.
Smoak, Jeremy D., 'Assyrian Siege Warfare Imagery and the Background of a Biblical Curse', in *Writing and Reading War: Rhetoric, Gender, and Ethics in Biblical and Modern Contexts*, edited by Brad E. Kelle and Frank Ritchel Ames (Atlanta, GA: Society of Biblical Literature, 2008), 83–91.
Solomon, Norman, 'The Ethics of War in Judaism', in *The Ethics of War in Asian Civilizations: A Comparative Perspective*, edited by Torkel Brekke (Abingdon: Routledge, 2006), 39–80.
Solomon, Norman, 'Judaism and the Ethics of War', *International Review of the Red Cross* 87 (858) (2005): 295–309.
Somaglino, Claire and Pierre Tallet, 'Gebel Sheikh Suleiman: A First Dynasty Relief After All...', *Archéo-Nil* 25 (2015): 122–34.

Sorabji, Richard, 'Just War from Ancient Origins to the Conquistadors Debate and its Modern Relevance', in *The Ethics of War: Shared Problems in Different Traditions*, edited by Richard Sorabji and David Rodin (Aldershot: Ashgate, 2006), 13–29.
Sorabji, Richard, and David Rodin, 'Introduction', in *The Ethics of War: Shared Problems in Different Traditions*, edited by Richard Sorabji and David Rodin (Aldershot: Ashgate, 2006), 1–10.
Spalinger, Anthony J., 'The Army', in *The Egyptian World*, edited by Toby Wilkinson (Abingdon: Routledge, 2007), 118–30.
Spalinger, Anthony J., *Aspects of the Military Documents of the Ancient Egyptians* (New Haven, CT: Yale University Press, 1982).
Spalinger, Anthony J., 'New Kingdom Triumphs: A First Blush', in *Rituals of Triumph in the Mediterranean World*, edited by Anthony J. Spalinger and Jeremy Armstrong (Leiden: Brill, 2013), 95–122.
Spalinger, Anthony J., *War in Ancient Egypt: The New Kingdom* (Malden, MA: Blackwell, 2005).
Steele, Brent J., *Ontological Security in International Relations: Self-Identity and the IR State* (Abingdon: Routledge, 2008).
Stern, Philip D., *The Biblical Herem: A Window on Israel's Religious Experience* (Atlanta, GA: Scholars Press, 1991).
Stoltz, Fritz, *Jahwes und Israels Kriege: Kriegstheorien und Kriegserfahrungen im Glauben des alten Israel* (Zurich: Theologischer Verlag, 1972).
Stone, Lawson G., 'Ethical and Apologetic Tendencies in the Redaction of the Book of Joshua', *Catholic Biblical Quarterly* 53 (1) (1991): 25–36.
Stromseth, Jane, David Wippman, and Rosa Brooks, *Can Might Make Rights? Building the Rule of Law after Military Interventions* (New York: Cambridge University Press, 2006).
Subedi, Surya P., 'The Concept in Hinduism of "Just War"', *Journal of Conflict and Security Law* 8 (2) (2003): 339–61.
Syse, Henrik, 'The Platonic Roots of Just War Doctrine: A Reading of Plato's *Republic*', *Diametros* 23 (2010): 104–23.
Teichman, Jenny, *Pacifism and the Just War: A Study in Applied Philosophy* (Oxford: Blackwell, 1986).
Théodoridès, Aristide, 'The Concept of Law in Ancient Egypt', in *The Legacy of Egypt*, edited by J. R. Harris, 2nd edn (Oxford: Oxford University Press, 1971), 291–322.
Théodoridès, Aristide, 'Mettres des biens sous les pieds de quelqu'un', *Revue d'égyptologie* 24 (1972): 188–92.
Thistlewaite, Susan Brooks, '"You may enjoy the spoil of your enemies": Rape as a Biblical Metaphor for War', in *Women, War, and Metaphor: Language and Society in the Study of the Hebrew Bible*, edited by Claudia V. Camp and Carole R. Fontaine (Atlanta, GA: Scholars Press, 1993), 59–75.
Throop, Susanna A., and Paul R. Hyams (eds), *Vengeance in the Middle Ages: Emotion, Religion and Feud* (Farnham: Ashgate, 2010).
Tibi, Bassam, 'War and Peace in Islam', in *The Ethics of War and Peace: Religious and Secular Perspectives*, edited by Terry Nardin (Princeton, NJ: Princeton University Press, 1996), 128–45.
Tierney, Brian, *The Idea of Natural Rights. Studies on Natural Rights, Natural Law and Church Law 1150–1625* (Atlanta, GA: Scholars Press, 1997).
Tiesler, Vera, and Andrea Cucina (eds), *New Perspectives on Human Sacrifice and Ritual Body Treatment in Ancient Maya Society* (New York: Springer, 2007).
Tikhonov, Vladimir, 'Chinese and Korean Religious Traditions', in *Religion, War and Ethics: A Sourcebook of Textual Traditions*, edited by Gregory Reichberg and Henrik Syse, with Nicole H. Hartwell (Cambridge: Cambridge University Press, 2014), 597–630.

Tilly, Charles, 'Reflections on the History of European State-Making', in *The Formation of National States in Western Europe*, edited by Charles Tilly (Princeton, NJ: Princeton University Press, 1975), 3–83.

Trigger, Bruce G., *Nubia under the Pharaohs* (London: Thames and Hudson, 1976).

Trigger, Bruce G., Barry J. Kemp, David O'Connor, and Alan B. Lloyd, *Ancient Egypt: A Social History* (Cambridge: Cambridge University Press, 1983).

Trimm, Charlie, *Fighting for the King and the Gods: A Survey of Warfare in the Ancient Near East* (Atlanta, GA: SBL Press, 2017).

Tuten, Belle S., and Tracy L. Billado (eds), *Feud, Violence and Practice: Essays in Medieval Studies in Honor of Stephen D. White* (Farnham: Ashgate, 2010).

Tyldesley, Joyce, *Judgement of the Pharaoh: Crime and Punishment in Ancient Egypt* (London: Weidenfeld & Nicolson, 2000).

Valbelle, Dominique, *Les Neufs Arcs: L'Égyptien et les étrangers de la préhistoire à la conquête d'Alexandre* (Paris: Colin, 1990).

Vanderpol, Alfred, *La Doctrine scolastique du droit de guerre* (Paris: A. Pedone, 1919).

Van Seters, John, *In Search of History: Historiography in the Ancient World and the Origins of Biblical History* (New Haven, CT: Yale University Press, 1983).

Vaux, Roland de, *The Early History of Israel*, translated by David Smith, 2 vols (London: Darton, Longman and Todd, 1978).

Veyne, Paul, *Did the Greeks Believe in their Myths? An Essay on the Constitutive Imagination*, translated by Paula Wissing (Chicago: University of Chicago Press, 1988).

Wachsmann, Shelley, *Aegeans in the Theban Tombs* (Leuven: Uitgeverij Press, 1987).

Walker, Philip L., 'A Bioarchaeological Perspective on the History of Violence', *Annual Review of Anthropology* 30 (2001): 573–96.

Walker, R.B.J., *Inside/Outside: International Relations as Political Theory* (Cambridge: Cambridge University Press, 1993).

Waltz, Kenneth N., *Theory of International Politics* (1979; repr. Long Grove, IL: Waveland Press, 2010).

Walzer, Michael, 'The Ethics of Warfare in the Jewish Tradition', *Philosophia* 40 (2012): 633–41.

Walzer, Michael, 'The Idea of Holy War in Ancient Israel', *The Journal of Religious Ethics* 20 (2) (1992): 215–28.

Walzer, Michael, *Just and Unjust Wars: A Moral Argument with Historical Illustrations*, 4th edn (New York: Basic Books, 2006).

Ward, William A., and Martha S. Joukowsky (eds), *The Crisis Years: The 12th Century BC: From beyond the Danube to the Tigris* (Dubuque, IA: Kendall Hunt, 1992).

Watson, Alan, *International Law in Archaic Rome: War and Religion* (Baltimore: Johns Hopkins University Press, 1993).

Weber, Max, *Ancient Judaism*, translated and edited by Hans H. Gerth and Don Martindale (Glencoe, IL: The Free Press, 1952).

Weber, Max, *The Methodology of the Social Sciences*, translated and edited by Edward A. Shils and Henry A. Finch (New York: The Free Press, 1949).

Webster, David, 'Warfare and the Evolution of the State: A Reconsideration', *American Antiquity* 40 (4) (1975): 464–70.

Weeden, Mark, 'Poetry and War among the Hittites', in *Warfare and Poetry in the Middle East*, edited by Hugh Kennedy (London: I. B. Tauris, 2013), 73–97.

Wees, Hans van, 'Defeat and Destruction: The Ethics of Ancient Greek Warfare', in *'Böser Krieg': Exzessive Gewalt in der antiken Kriegsführung und Strategien zu deren Vermeidung*, edited by Margit Linder and Sabine Tausend (Graz: Grazer Universitätsverlag, 2011), 69–110.

Wees, Hans van, 'Genocide in the Ancient World', in *The Oxford Handbook of Genocide Studies*, edited by Donald Bloxham and A. Dirk Moses (Oxford: Oxford University Press, 2010), 239–58.

Wees, Hans van, *Greek Warfare: Myths and Realities* (London: Duckworth, 2004).

Weinfeld, Moshe, *Deuteronomy and the Deuteronomic School* (Oxford: Clarendon Press, 1972; repr. Winona Lake, IN: Eisenbrauns, 1992).

Weinfeld, Moshe, 'Divine Intervention in War in Ancient Israel, and in the Ancient Near East', in *History, Historiography and Interpretation: Studies in Biblical and Cuneiform Literatures*, edited by Hayim Tadmor and Moshe Weinfeld (Jerusalem: The Magnes Press, 1983), 121–47.

Weippert, Manfred, '"Heiliger Kreig" in Israel und Assyrien: Kritische Anmerkungen zu Gerhard von Rads Konzept des "Heiligen Krieges im alten Israel"', *Zeitschrift für die Alttestamentliche Wissenschaft* 84 (4): 460–93.

Wellhausen, Julius, *Prolegomena to the History of Israel, with a Reprint of the Article 'Israel' from the 'Encyclopaedia Britannica'*, translated by. J. Sutherland Black and Allan Menzies, with a preface by W. Robertson Smith (1885; repr. Charleston, SC: BiblioBazaar, 2006).

Wells, Bruce, 'Law and Practice', in *A Companion to the Ancient Near East*, edited by Daniel C. Snell (Malden, MA: Blackwell, 2005), 183–195.

Wendt, Alexander, 'Anarchy Is What States Make of It', *International Organization* 46 (2) (1992): 391–425.

Wendt, Alexander, *Social Theory of International Relations* (Cambridge: Cambridge University Press, 1999).

West, Stuart A., 'The Habiru and the Hebrews: From a Social Class to an Ethnic Group', *Jewish Bible Quarterly* 7 (3) (1979): 102–7.

Whetham, David, *Just Wars and Moral Victories: Surprise, Deception and the Normative Framework of European War in the Later Middle Ages* (Leiden: Brill, 2009).

Whitehouse, Helen, 'Egypt in European Thought', in *Civilizations of the Ancient Near East*, edited by Jack M. Sasson, John Baines, Gary Beckman, and Karen S. Rubinson, 4 vols (Peabody, MA: Hendrickson, 2000), 1:15–31.

Whitney, K. Williams, *Two Strange Beasts: Leviathan and Behemoth in Second Temple and Early Rabbinic Judaism* (Winona Lake, IN: Eisenbrauns, 2006).

Wickham, Chris, 'Problems in Doing Comparative History', in *Challenging the Boundaries of Medieval History: The Legacy of Timothy Reuter*, edited by Patricia Skinner (Turnhout: Brepols, 2009), 5–28.

Wight, Martin, *Systems of States*, edited with an introduction by Hedley Bull (Leicester: Leicester University Press, 1977).

Wildung, Dieter, 'Erschlagen der Feinde', in *Lexikon der Ägyptologie*, vol. 2: *Erntefest–Hordjedef*, edited by Wolfgang Helck and Wolfhart Westendorf (Wiesbaden: Harrassowitz, 1977), 114–17.

Wilgaux, Jérôme, 'Trangressions et sanctions divines en temps de guerre en Grèce ancienne', in *La Transgression en temps de guerre: De l'Antiquité à nos jours*, edited by Nathalie Barrandon and Isabelle Pimouguet-Pedarros (Rennes: Presses Universitaires de Rennes, 2021), 49–64.

Williams, Bernard, *In the Beginning Was the Deed: Realism and Moralism in Political Argument*, selected, edited, and with an introduction by Geoffrey Hawthorne (Princeton, NJ: Princeton University Press, 2005).

Williams, R. J., '"A People Come Out of Egypt": An Egyptologist Looks at the Old Testament', *Vetus Testamentum Supplements* 28 (1974): 231–52.

Wolf, Herbert M., 'The Historical Reliability of the Hittite Annals', in *Faith, Tradition, and History: Old Testament Historiography in Its Near Eastern Context*, edited by A. R. Millard, J. K. Hoffmeier, and D. W. Baker (Winona Lake, IN: Eisenbrauns, 1994), 159–64.

Wolfendale, Jessica, 'The Narrative of Terrorism as an Existential Threat', in *Routledge Handbook of Critical Terrorism Studies*, edited by Richard Jackson (Abingdon: Routledge, 2016), 114–23.

Wong, Gregory T. K., 'Song of Deborah as Polemic', *Biblica* 88 (1) (2007): 1–22.

Wright, Jacob L., 'Military Valor and Kingship: A Book-Oriented Approach to the Study of a Major War-Theme', in *Writing and Reading War: Rhetoric, Gender, and Ethics in Biblical and Modern Contexts*, edited by Brad E. Kelle and Frank Ritchel Ames (Atlanta, GA: Society of Biblical Literature, 2008), 33–56.

Wright, Jacob L., 'Warfare and Wanton Destruction: A Reexamination of Deuteronomy 20:19–20 in Relation to Ancient Siegecraft', *Journal of Biblical Literature* 127 (3) (2008): 423–58.

Wright, Quincy, *A Study of War*, 2nd edn, 2 vols (1942; repr. Chicago: University of Chicago Press, 1965).

Wright, William, *The Empire of the Hittites* (London: Nisbet, 1884).

Yadin, Yigael, *The Art of Warfare in Biblical Lands in the Light of Archaeological Discovery* (London: Weidenfeld & Nicolson, 1963).

Yadin, Yigael, *Hazor: The Rediscovery of a Great Citadel of the Bible* (London: Weidenfeld & Nicolson, 1975).

Yamada, Masamichi, 'The Second Military Conflict between "Assyria" and "Hatti" in the Reign of Tukulti-Ninurta I', *Revue d'assyriologie et d'archéogie orientale* 105 (2011): 199–220.

Yee, Gale A., 'By the Hand of a Woman: The Metaphor of the Woman Warrior in Judges 4', in *Women, War, and Metaphor: Language and Society in the Study of the Hebrew Bible*, edited by Claudia V. Camp and Carole R. Fontaine (Atlanta, GA: Scholars Press, 1993), 99–132.

Yeivin, Shmuel, *The Israelite Conquest of Canaan* (Istanbul: Nederlands Historisch-Archaeologisch Instituut in het Nabije Oosten, 1971).

Yoo, John C., and James C. Ho, 'The Status of Terrorists', *Virginia Journal of International Law* 44 (2003): 207–28.

Younger, K. Lawson, Jr., *Ancient Conquest Accounts: A Study of Ancient Near Eastern and Biblical History Writing* (Sheffield: Sheffield Academic Press, 1990).

Zampaglione, Gerardo, *The Idea of Peace in Antiquity*, translated by Richard Dunn (Notre Dame, IN: University of Notre Dame Press, 1973).

Zehfuss, Maja, *War and the Politics of Ethics* (Oxford: Oxford University Press, 2018).

Zehr, Nahed Artoul, 'Legitimate Authority and the War against Al-Qaeda', in *Just War: Authority, Tradition, and Practice*, edited by Anthony F. Lang Jr., Cian O'Driscoll, and John Williams (Washington, DC: Georgetown University Press, 2013), 97–113.

Zenger, E., 'Tradition und Interpretation in Exodus XV 1–21', in *Congress Volume Vienne 1980*, edited by J. A. Emerton (Leiden: Brill, 1981), 452–82.

Zimmerman, Martin, *Gewalt: Die dunkle Seite der Antike* (Munich: Deutsche Verlags-Anstalt, 2013).

Ziskind, Jonathan Rosner, 'Aspects of International Law in the Ancient Near East' (PhD dissertation, Columbia University, 1967).

Book Reviews

Morschauser, Scott, 'Review: Michael G. Hasel, *Military Practice and Polemic: Israel's Laws of Warfare in Near Eastern Perspective* (Berrien Springs, MI: Andrews University Press, 2005)', *The Catholic Biblical Quarterly* 68 (4) (2006): 731–32.

Wright, Jacob L., 'Review: Michael G. Hasel, *Military Practice and Polemic: Israel's Laws of Warfare in Near Eastern Perspective* (Berrien Springs, MI: Andrews University Press, 2005)', *Journal of Biblical Literature*, 125 (3) (2006): 577–79.

Online Resources (accessed 9 January 2023)

'Advice and Guidance to the Fighters on the Battlefields', The Official Website of the Office of His Eminence Sayyid ʿAli al-Sistani, The Holy City of Najaf, February 12, 2015, http://www.sistani.org/english/archive/25036/.

'The Challenge of Peace: God's Promise and Our Response' ('A Pastoral Letter on War and Peace by the National Conference of Catholic Bishops, 3 May 1983'), PDF available at https://www.usccb.org/upload/challenge-peace-gods-promise-our-response-1983.pdf.

'Costs of War', Watson Institute, International & Public Affairs, Brown University, https://watson.brown.edu/costsofwar/costs.

'Deuteronomy 20:11', Bible Hub, https://biblehub.com/text/deuteronomy/20-11.htm.

'Devarim—Deuteronomy—Chapter 20', Chabad.org, *The Complete Jewish Bible, with Rashi Commentary*, https://www.chabad.org/library/bible_cdo/aid/9984/jewish/.

'General Montgomery's message, Operation Overlord—Normandy landings' (address to the 21st Army Group, 5 June 1944), D-Day and Battle of Normandy Encyclopedia, https://www.dday-overlord.com/en/d-day/files/montgomery-message.

'Jewish Prayers: Prayer for the Well-Being of the Israel Defense Forces', Jewish Virtual Library, https://www.jewishvirtuallibrary.org/prayer-for-the-well-being-of-the-israel-defense-forces.

'Jihad Against Jews and Crusaders' ('World Islamic Front Statement, 23 February 1998'), available at http://fas.org/irp/world/para/docs/980223-fatwa.htm.

The Latin Vulgate Bible, http://www.latinvulgate.com/.

'Lieutenant Colonel Tim Collins' Eve-of-Battle Speech' (19 March 2003), 'Royal Irish: The Irish Soldier in the British Army' website, https://www.royal-irish.com/stories/lieutenant-colonel-tim-collins-eve-of-battle-speech.

'Military Rabbinate', Israel Defense Forces website, https://www.idf.il/en/minisites/military-rabinate/.

INDEX

Page numbers in italics refer to illustrations

Aaron, 349
Abimelech, 334, 361, 364, 386
Abner, 353, 361, 364, 416
Abraham, 272, 281, 283, 300, 318, 329, 357, 359n66
Absalom, 289
Abu Simbel, *46–47*, 69, *122*, *127–29*, 132, 145
Abydos, 63
acculturation, 68, 71, 77–78, 125n31
Achaea, 187, 200, 322. *See also* Ahhiyawa
Achan, 399
Adad-Nirari I, 203
Adad-Nirari II, 167
'Admonitions of Ipuwer,' 66
Aegyptiaca (History of Egypt) (Manetho), 60–61
Agamemnon, 322
Ahab of Israel, 276, 310, 318–19, 390
Ahhiyawa, 187, 200, 229–30, 260–62. *See also* Achaea
Ahimelech, 406
Ahmose, son of Abana, 107, 111, 128, 135
Ai, 313–14, 328n114, 382, 391
Akhenaten, 70, 74, 136, 210
Akhethhotep Hemi/Nebkauhor, 90n26
Akkadian, 156, 157n144, 168, 174, 244n42
Alaksandu of Wilusa, 220
Alašiya. *See* Cyprus
Aleppo, 214, 231n160
Alexander the Great, 71, 75
Alt, Albrecht, 286
Altman, Amnon, 11, 338–39, 346
Amada stele, 136
Amalek, 331, 332n155, 357
Amaziah, 338, 346, 389, 404
Ambrose of Milan, 439
ambush, 121–22, 239–43, 335n171, 357–59, 410, 416–17
Amenemhet I, 65
Amenhotep II, 105, 109, 112, 124, 132, 136, 140–42, 150, 278

Amenhotep III, 74, 95, 97, 155, 183
Amenhotep IV, 155
Ammuna, 224–25, 230
Amon, 319–24
Amorites, 319–21, 331, 379
Amos (Book of), 374n129, 387
Amose, 69
Amose son of Ebana, 80
amphictyonic theory, 286–87, 297–98, 308, 337n182
Amun-Re, 70, 96–99, 103, 108–9, 150n122, 158n146
Amurru, 214–15, 250
Ancient Egyptian Literature (Lichtheim), 80
'Anitta Chronicle,' 169–70
Anitta Inscription, 38
Anitta of Kuššara, 179–80, 240
Ankhesenamun, 209, 227n150
annals: descriptions of, 37; Hittite, 171–75, 251; of pharaohs, 61, 69, 79–80, 107, *108*, 114; as propaganda, 112; and ravaging, 243
'Annals of Hattušili I,' 172, 211–12, 240–41, 243–44, 246–47
anticipation (of war), 444–45
'Apology of Hattušili III,' 174, 216, *217*, 416
Apophis, 68
appanteš, 254
'Appu and His Two Sons,' 191
Aquinas, Thomas, 429–30
archaeology, 23, 277–78, 285, 287–89, 293, 312n84, 443. *See also* scholarship
archery, 45–46, *48*, 120–21
architecture, 69, 78, 178
Arendt, Hannah, 11
Arinna, 169, 188–91, 195–96, 198–99, 207, 223–25, 231, 247, 423
Aristotle, 26, 432–34
armour, 47
army sizes, 38–42, 314n90

arnuwala, 254
Arnuwanda I, 198–99, 205, 236
Arnuwanda II, 225
Arzawa, 168–69, 208, 222, 235, 239–40
Asahel, 353
Asmunikal, 198–99
assassination, 360–61, 363–64, 394, 407, 410, 415–17. *See also* Jael; Sisera
Assmann, Jan, 66n27, 147, 436n36, 437
Aššurbanipal, 346, 401
Aššurnasirpal II, 348, 375–76
Assyria: army sizes of, 40; and brutality, 256, 258, *355–56*, 374, *375–76*, 377, 381, 384, *387*, 400–401; and communications of war, 345–46; and defeated gods, 401; and the destruction of trees, 369–70; and envoys, 155, 260; and imperialism, 172n32, 272, 284, 314, 365; and Israel, 269, 290, 293, 301, 314; and just causes for war, 316–17; military tactics of, 38, 219; the rise of, 181n74; sources for, 27, 169, 276, 298, 343–44; and treaties, 156; and war with the Hittites, 196–97, 203; weaponry of, 45, 50–51
Aswan Dam, 73
asymmetry thesis, 449
atrocity. *See* brutality; *herem*; massacre; rape
Atum, 96, 133. *See also* Amun-Re
Augustine of Hippo (saint), 13–14, 31, 273, 327–28, 433, 439
'Autobiography of Ahmose, son of Abana,' 107, 111, 128, 135, 138n65
auxiliary units, 41
Axial Age hypothesis, 436n36
Ay, 209–10

Babylon, 27, 231n160, 232, 248, 258, 269, 284, 291, 389–90
Babylonian Talmud, 295
Baines, John, 161n156
Balaam, 350, 406
Balawat, *388*
barbaroi, 104n79
Battlefield Palette, 33, *130*
Beal, Richard, 38, 42n27, 206, 237
Beckman, Gary, 187, 193
Bederman, David, 11, 85–86, 177, 182, 258, 293, 426n4
Benjaminites, 332, 337, 358, 362, 384, 396, 398, 416–17

'Biography of Amenemheb,' 114, 129, 135, 138n65
Bittel, Kurt, 165n3
Black, Anthony, 97, 147n112
'Black Obelisk,' 276
Bloch, Marc, 20–21
blockades, 53
The Book of Lord Shang, 436
'The Book of the Cow of Heaven,' 110n104
Book of the Dead, 93–94
booty. *See* plunder
Breasted, James Henry, 79–80, 91
Bronze Age: battles of the, 39; and brutality, 258; and copper, 74; and the crisis years, 166–67; cultural interactions of the, 18; and international relations, 30, 175; labour in, 250; legal systems of the, 85; and mutilation of the dead, 135; warfare, 32–33, 37, 39, 47; weapons of the, 45, 50
Brown, Chris, 428n6
brutality: background on, 4; and blinding, 256–57, 368, 389; and burning, 140–41; and capital offences, 90; and children, 45, 111, 139–42, 145, 160, 253, 304, 348, 365, 377–80, 382, 384–87, 418; and decapitation, 354–55, *356*, *357*; and defenestration, 394; and Egyptian norms, 88, 128–29, 160; and flaying alive, *376*, 377; and impalement, 136–37, 142, 258, 325, 374, *375*, 382, 389, 392, 418; and individuality, 118; inscriptions of, *108*, 109, 112; and kings, 393–94; and mutilation of the dead, *115*, 134–36, 142, 160, 252, 256, 354–55, 377–78, 388, 392, 427; and plunder, 113–14; and prisoners of war, *126–27*, 139–41, 254, 417–18; and rebellion, 110–11; and reciprocity, 92, 102; and the Tanakh, 373–74; and trampling, 130–31; and vengeance, 207–8; and xenophobia, 123–25. See also *herem*; massacre; rape; reciprocity; torture
Bryce, Trevor, 173n38, 183n83
Buhen, 52, *53*
Burkert, Walter, 24–25, 441n53
burning, 140–41

Canaan, 284–89, 297, 300n27, 306–7, 310, 316–18, 380–81, 385, 392, 402–3
'Cannibal Hymn,' 95, 131

INDEX [495]

'The Capture of Joppa,' 121–22
Carchemish, 182, 186, 209, 248–49
casus belli, 99, 104, 198, 251
Cate, Howink ten, 38
cavalry, 38, 55
challenges to battle, 345–48, 353, 410, 417. *See also* declarations of war
Champollion, Jean-François, 79
Chaoskampf, 292, 317, 421
chariotry, 38–39, 43–46, 50–51, 55, 69, 121, 131, 238–39
Cheops, 95
Chevereau, Pierre-Marie, 119–20
Chief of the Royal Bodyguard, 186
China, 16–17, 435–36, 446
Christianity, 11–19, 71, 103, 270, 272–73, 277, 311n81, 344, 430, 437, 439, 444
Chronicles (Book of), 315, 329, 403
Cicero, 10, 14, 28, 201, 233, 327, 433–35
Clausewitz, Carl von, 445
Coffin Texts, 131
Collins, Tim, 440
combat: and brutality, 251, 376–78, 382, 387–88; and definitions of war, 7n10; and disease, 236; ethics of, 134; and the gods, 109; hand-to-hand, 29, 55, 351–52; and honour, 351–53; and liberal-democratic states, 451–52; and Moses, 406; norms of, 121, 265, 417–18; protections for, 5, 427; and restraint, 252; single, 353; visual scenes of, 78, 81; and the war convention, 449–50. *See also* duels
'Complaints of Khakheperresonb,' 66
'Comprehensive Annals,' 174
Confucius, 16, 436
Covenant Code, 281, 297. *See also* Yahweh
Crouch, Carly, 384–85
cults, 70, 89, 96, 134, 181–82, 187n12, 188, 235–37, 286, 297, 402. *See also* magic; oracles; rituals; Yazilikaya
cuneiform, 76, 168–69, 174n45
Curry, Patrick, 9
'The Curse of Agade,' 101
Cyprus, 74–75, 167
Cyropaedia (Xenophon), 113–14

daggers, 50
Daniel (Book of), 279, 292
Danite tribe, 336–37
Daoism, 16, 436

Darius I, 284
David: the armies of, 44; and brutality, 378n143, 383, 386, 388–89; and destroying religious property, 403, 405; dynasty of, 281, 284, 288, 290, 332; envoys of, 407; and Goliath, 351–54, 400, 416; and honour, 361–62; and Joab, 361, 416; as a model king, 273n11, 300; and oracles, 309–10; and prayer, 304; and ravaging, 337; and Saul, 289, 303n37, 331, 335, 354, 361–62, 377–78, 394, 406–7; and spoils of war, 400; and a united monarchy, 269n1, 275, 284, 288; and Yahweh, 273n11, 325–26
David, Arlette, 130–31
Decalogue, 280, 283, 286, 293, 300, 307, 315
deceit, 359–64, 410, 416
declarations of war, 119–20, 234–35, 265, 345–48, 410, 417. *See also* challenges to battle
Decretum (Gratian), 328
'Deeds of Šuppiluliuma I,' 174, 195, 204, 416
Deir el-Bahri, 146
De officiis (Cicero), 433
'The Destruction of Mankind,' 110
Deuteronomistic historiography, 281n49, 288, 297–99
Deuteronomy (Book of): and the Covenant, 293–94, 310, 333; and the death penalty, 185n2; and the Deuteronomist, 281–82; on enemies, 365–66; and rebellion, 334; and ritual, 308; and scholarship, 371n116; and self-defence, 324; and trees, 370–71, 373; and a united monarchy, 288, 289n72; and war, 282, 297–99, 308, 310, 313, 330–31, 333, 344–48, 357, 364–67, 372–73, 379–81, 410, 416; and women, 141n84, 263n128, 380, 394–97, 418; and Yahweh, 305, 307, 310, 313
diaries, 37
didactic literature, 81
diffusionist theory, 33n3
Dinah, 360, 364, 395–96
diplomacy, 76, 81, 154–9, 175, 182, 215, 218, 259–62, 293, 319–22, 407
divine authority, 4, 94–111, 145, 185–89, 195–97, 212, 251, 264–65, 300–325, 332, 414–15. *See also* Yahweh
divine intervention, 309–13, 315

[496] INDEX

Djoser (king), 64
documentary hypothesis, 281, 283
do ut des, 92
Dowden, Ken, 25–26
duels, 120, 351–54, 362, 410, 437. *See also* combat
'Duties of the Vizier,' 116
dw (evil), 88
Dynasty IV, 88
Dynasty V, 88, 131
Dynasty XII, 92–93, 293
Dynasty XV, 68
Dynasty XVII, 69
Dynasty XVIII, 69, 138
Dynasty XX, 71, 106
Dynasty XXI, 71

Early Dynastic kingdom (Egypt), 63–64, 94
Edom, 284, 289–90, 302, 305, 319, 326–27, 335, 338, 350, 383, 389
Egypt: Archaic Period of, 63; background on, 19; the borders of, 73, 77, 104, 106, 110, 117; capital offences in, 90; and cultural interactions, 437–38; and diplomacy, 76, 81, 85, 155–59, 162; and domestic law, 89–93; and ethics of war, 85–88; the geopolitics of, 73–77; and identity, 77–78; infiltration of, 68–69, 71; and Israel, 292–93; and the 'Memphite Theology,' 90; military conduct of, 118–53; military history of, 37–41, 44–47, 51–52; and natural resources, 74–76; the political-military achievements of, 59, 65–66; propaganda of, 126, 130, 136, 146–47, 157, 161; romanticisations of, 59; the royal ideology of, 87, 89, 94–112, 117, 125, 131–33, 160, 413, 421, 428; source material for, 27, 78–84; unification of, 33, 59, 61–65, 69, 95. *See also* divine authority; Middle Kingdom (Egypt); New Kingdom (Egypt); Old Kingdom (Egypt); pragmatism; treaties; *specific dynasties*
Egyptian Late Period, 75
Egyptology, 60–62, 78–84, 140n79, 141, 146. *See also* scholarship
Ehud, 362–63
Eighteenth Dynasty, 105
El (Elohim), 271, 281–82
El-Amarna letter, 76, 162

Elias, Norbert, 10
Elijah, 336n175
Elisha, 390–91
En-dor, 310
enslavement, 149–53, 199, 253–55, 257, 265, 347, 364–65, 420, 438. *See also* forced labour
envoys, 76, 85, 155–56, 259–61, 319, 407, 411, 416–17
Epic of Gilgamesh, 74, 418
'Epic of Tukulti-Ninurta,' 156
epureššar, 53
erschlagen der Feinde, 142, 143, 144–49, 162
Esther (Book of), 136n61, 279, 325, 374
Euripides, 432
Eurocentrism, 11–14
Eusebius, 60
evil (*dw*), 88
execration texts, 123
Exodus (Book of), 281, 284–85, 292, 303–7, 310–11, 324, 330–31, 349, 379, 386n187, 404

Fabre, Cécile, 448
fetial law, 434
Finkelstein, Israel, 289n72
Finley, Moses, 2n4, 29n86
First Cataract (of the Nile river), 66, 73
First Dynasty, 75–76
First Intermediate Period, 65–66
Fishbane, Michael, 366n96
Flannery, Frances, 405n279
forced labour, 364–65, 425–26. *See also* enslavement
fortifications, 52, 53–54, 55, 66, 104–5, 166, 253, 288–89
fortresses. *See* fortifications
Fourth Cataract (of the Nile River), 107
Freud, Sigmund, 29
Frowe, Helen, 448
Fulgosius, Raphaël, 428

Gebel Sahaba, 45
Gebel Sheik Suleiman, 75
Geertz, Clifford, 3, 24n66
Genesis (Book of), 273n11, 281, 283, 292, 318, 329, 359n66, 360
genocide. *See herem*
Gideon, 40, 392–93
Giveon, Raphael, 293

Glatz, Claudia, 183
Gnirs, Andrea, 80, 86–87
Goedicke, Hans, 87, 153n130, 352n41, 437
Goetze, Albrecht, 33, 43, 254
good (*nfr*), 88
Good, Robert, 296, 323, 341
Gottwald, Norman, 280, 286–87, 289, 294n97, 299, 384
Graf, Karl, 280
Gratian, Master, 273, 328, 433
Great Harris Papyrus, 139
'Great Hymn to Osiris,' 110–11
Greece, 11, 18–19, 26, 75, 177, 430–38
Greek (language), 272–73
Greek Pentateuch, 272, 278, 312n83, 364n93
Greek Septuagint, 14, 280
Grossman, Dave, 151n126
Grotius, Hugo, 31, 429–30
Gunnell, John, 12, 14
Gurney, O. R., 193, 264–65
Güterbock, Hans, 172, 195, 238n20

habiru, 359, 359n66
Hadith, 272
Hall, Ian, 9
Hamath, 168
Hamblin, William, 86
Hammurabi, 90, 94, 188n16, 248, 294
Han Feizi, 436
Hantili, 224–25, 230, 248
Hantili II, 260
Harle, Vilho, 9
Hasel, Michael, 371–72
Hatshepsut, 70, 146
Hattuša, *54*, 165–71, 174–75, 178–83, 210, 240
Hattušili I, 38, 172–73, 180, 190, 210, 238, 249, 255. *See also* 'Annals of Hattušili I'; 'Political Testament of Hattušili I'
Hattušili II, 213–14
Hattušili III, 134, 156–59, 174, 200–201, 203, 229–30, 232, 237–38, 245, 258–62. *See also* 'Apology of Hattušili III'
Hazael of Aram, 275
Hebrew Bible. *See* Tanakh
herem, 251, 282, 311–12, 314, 324, 328n114, 347–48, 366, 378–88, 398–99, 403, 423. *See also* brutality; massacre
Herodotus, 73, 75, 77–79, 437
Hezekiah, 312, 400, 404

Hierakonpolis (Nekhen), 33, 143–44
hieroglyphics, 79, 136, *137*, 168–69, 193
Hindu, 16–17, 446
The Histories (Herodotus), 75
Hittites: and agriculture, 189, 211, 245, 250–51, 255; background on the, 19, 165–69; capital cities of the, 165–66, 179–80; and capital offences, 185; and chief priests, 188; and the chronology of kings, 170–71; the collapse of the, 166–67; and cultural interactions, 438; and declarations of war, 119–20, 234–35, 265; and diplomacy, 182, 215, 221, 235, 259–62, 265–66; and ethnicity, 180–81; historical documents of the, 169–70; and justice, 189–92, 197–98, 424–25, 428–29; and law, 175, 177, 185, 190–93, 202–4, 208, 211, 233, 237, 243, 255–56, 263–65, 294, 397, 424; and making peace, 263–64; and mass deportation, 254; and military expansion, 173–74, 179–80, 201, 210, 219, 230–31; military history of the, 38–39, 41–46, 51–52, 56, 121–22; and military tactics, 238–46, 253; and morality, 196–97, 242–43, 264–65, 425; and propaganda, 171–72, 211, 216–17, 248; and property, 202–4, 211, 246–47, 264; rediscovering the, 168–69; and religious culture, 177–79, 223–24, 227–29, 233, 245–49, 401; the royal ideology of the, 183–200, 413, 428; royal seals of the, 193; the socio-economic system of the, 186; source material for the, 27, 171, 174–79, 182; texts of the, 52–53; and usurpation, 216, 225–26. *See also* divine authority; mythology; pragmatism; prayer; prisoners of war; ravaging; self-aggrandisement; self-defence; self-reflection; sin; treaties; vengeance
Hoffner, Harry A., 231n160, 239n25, 256
Holmes, Robert, 454
holy war, 282, 296–99, 337n182, 378
Homer, 26, 55, 352n40, 438
honour norm (in war), 353–54, 354n49, 360–64
Horemheb, 157n142
Horus, 63, 95–96, 100, 119–20
Hrzony, Bedrich, 169
Hulla, 263

human sacrifice, 122–23, 258, 322–23, 348, 350, 380
Huqqana of Hayasa, 222
Hutter-Braunsar, Sylvia, 245n49
Hyksos, 51n52, 68–69, 105, 124

the *Iliad* (Homer), 26, 55, 352n40, 438
'The Illuyanka Tales,' 241–42
immortality, 224
immunity: and ancient warfare, 419, 426; diplomatic, 154, 259–62, 265–66, 407–8, 417; and elites, 391, 393–94; non-combatant, 141, 145, 154, 160, 265, 385–87; priestly, 405–6; prisoners and, 138; religious, 248–49; and religious property, 404–5; and women, 397, 418. *See also* religious sanctuary
impalement. *See* brutality
Inanna, 188
'Indictment of Mita of Pahhuwa,' 212–13
Ineb Hedj, 52
injustice, 101–2, 225–30, 233n169, 266, 316, 319, 337–41, 424–25
instruction literature, 81, 91–92
'Instruction of King Amenemhet,' 138
'Instruction of Ptahhotep,' 89–91
'Instructions of King Ammenemes I to King Sesostris I,' 110n101
'Instructions to King Merikare,' 90–91, 101, 111, 119, 124, 154
international law, 20n52
Inyotef I, 65
Inyotef II, 65
Iron Age: cultural interactions of the, 18; and international relations, 30; legal systems of the, 85; and mutilation of the dead, 135; warfare of, 32, 47; weapons of, 45, 50
Isaiah, 339, *340*, 341
Isfet, 66, 73, 77, 86–87, 100, 102–3, 124, 145, 162
Ish-bosheth, 353n45, 361, 364, 394
Ishtar, 188, 196n45, 216–17, 348
Islam, 17, 71, 103, 270, 272–73, 277, 438, 446, 451, 453
Israel: and agriculture, 371; alliances of, 328–29; and the Ark, 99n61, 293, 308, 315, 350, 398–99; background on, 19, 269, 271–72, 275; and challenges to battle, 345, 353, 410; creation stories, 292; and cultural transmission, 292–93, 438; and declarations of war, 345, 410; and defence of allies, 328–29; and exile, 269, 272, 284–85, 287, 290–91, 379, 385, 405; and free passage, 326–27; and justice, 341–42; and law, 293–94, 296, 318–23, 333–34, 341–42, 346, 396; and military defeats, 306, 310, 313–15, 443; military history of, 40, 43–44, 51; and military tactics, 343–45, 353, 357–59; and morality, 337, 351, 364, 408; and peace, 341, 346–48, 364; and religious purity, 329; source material for, 27, 269–70, 274–85; and territory, 317–24, 336; in translation, 303; the tribes of, 284, 286, 288, 297, 300, 332, 336–37, 358–59; and tricksterism, 271–72, 328n114, 359, 362; as a United Monarchy, 288–89, 297, 299, 302, 413. *See also* Judah; Samaria; Tanakh; Yahweh
Israel Defense Forces (IDF), 439
Israeli Military Rabbinate, 439
Israel Stele, 274–75
Itjtowy, 65
ius ad bellum, 1–2, 5, 8, 22–23, 88, 160, 296, 301, 413–14, 420–21, 425–26, 436–37, 449–53
ius in bello, 2, 5, 8, 22–23, 88, 118, 125, 160, 265, 371, 409–11, 416, 419–20, 449–53. *See also* limitations
ius pro bello, 2, 445–46, 453, 455
iusta causa, 22–23, 316–17, 326, 339. *See also* just cause

Jacob, 360–61, 398
Jael, 363, 417. *See also* assassination
Janzen, Mark D., 148n115
Jaspers, Karl, 436n36
Jehoahaz, 276, 314, 328
Jehoash of Samaria, 404
Jehoiachin of Judah, 401
Jehoshaphat, 310, 318–19
Jehovah, 270–71
Jehu, 276, 335–36, 363–64, 394, 407
Jephthah, 319–23, 331, 346, 349
Jeremiah (Book of), 332, 362
Jericho, 312–13, 328n114, 349–50, 382
Jeroboam of Samaria, 334
Jerome (saint), 273

Jerusalem, 52, 290, 312–13, 367–68, 404
Jerusalem Talmud, 295
Jerusalem Temple, 269, 284, 398n242, 400–402, 404, 406
Jewish Study Bible, 395
jihad, 103–4, 272, 451
Joab, 353, 361, 416
Joel, 340
Johnson, James Turner, 8–9, 13, 16, 444, 448
Joram, 335
Josephus, 60, 68
Joshua: the authority of, 300; and brutality, 337, 373–75, 379, 381–83, 391–92; the compositional history of, 366–67; and the conquest of Canaan, 277–78, 284–85, 297, 300n27, 306–7, 330, 336, 366–67; and the Covenant, 293, 306; and divine intervention, 297, 311–12, 314, 328; the historical narrative of, 281, 312n84, 316; and impaling, 136n61; and ritual, 349–50; source material for, 279; and spoils of war, 399–400; and the Tanakh, 278; and a united monarchy, 288; and war, 358, 392
Josiah, 282, 289, 298, 300–301, 328, 406
Judah: army size of, 51; battles of, 328, 338; the creation of, 274, 284; the fall of, 269, 272, 280, 284, 315; the geopolitical history of, 290; as a point of reference, 271; and rebellion, 335; and religious reform, 300; in source material, 276–77, 281; as a vassal state, 290, 328–29; and war, 298; weaponry of, 50
Judges (Book of): and army sizes, 40; and assassination, 363, 416–17; and authority, 300; and blinding, 257; and brutality, 379, 381; and the conquest of Canaan, 277, 285, 306, 316, 345n5; and declarations of war, 346; and historical narrative, 278–79, 281, 298n19; and Samson, 332n156; and self-defence, 319, 321–22; and the tribes of Israel, 44, 284, 286–88, 297, 332n159, 336–37; and a united monarchy, 288, 297; and war, 373; and women, 396; and Yahweh, 306, 312, 314, 320n116, 323–24, 349n26
Just and Unjust Wars (Walzer), 2, 13
just cause, 99–112, 198–221, 315–36. See also *iusta causa*

justice. *See* brutality; injustice; instruction literature; *legibus solutus; Ma'at;* prayer; reciprocity; xenophobia
just war thought (discussion of), 7–21, 24, 28–31, 413, 427–55. *See also* revisionist just war theory (discussion of); war (definitions of)

Kadashman-Enlil, 155
Kadashman-Enlil II, 232
Kadesh (battle of), 39, 56, 98, 105, 112, 121, 132–34, 241
'Kadesh Bulletin,' 132
Kadesh Poem (Ramses II), 41, 98, 132–34, 157n144
Kalyvas, Stathis, 7n10
Kamose, 68–69, 96, 105, 114, 124
Kamrusepa, 191
Kang, Sa-Moon, 87, 245, 298n19
Karnak Temple, *50*, 61, 63, 70, 72, *82*, 96–97, 107–10, *126*, 135, *152*, 157, 162
Kaska, 39, 183, 199–200, 203, 208, 238–40, 244, 425
Kaššu, 263
Keilah, 325
Kelle, Brad, 276n22
Kellison, Rosemary, 442–43
Kelsay, John, 17
Khadurri, Majid, 17
khopesh, 50
King James Bible, 372n121
Kings (Book of), 44, 51, 278n31, 281, 315, 318, 329, 333–36, 379, 401, 404. *See also* Second Book of Kings
Kitabl al-Siraj (Maimonides), 295n2
Kizzuwatna, 218–20
Korošec, Victor, 218n117, 219, 230, 246, 264–65
Krüger, Thomas, 339n192
Kuhrt, Amélie, 80, 277, 374n131
Kupanta-Kurunta of Mira-Kuwaliya, 248–49
Kush, 64n22, 76
Kuššara, 170n22, 180

Labarna, 170, 173, 180, 230–31
Lachish, 51, 374–75
Lagash, 33, 94. *See also* Stele of the Vultures
Laing, Robert, 447n69
Laish, 336–37
lament literature. *See* prophetic texts

Laws (Plato), 26
Lazar, Seth, 448
Legalism, 16, 435–36
legibus solutus, 89
Leshem, 336–37
Levi, 281–82, 360–61, 364, 406
Leviticus (Book of), 292, 398
lex talionis, 203, 331
liberal-democracies, 451–53
Libyans, 41, 74, 77, 107, 136
Lichtheim, Miriam, 80, 88–89
limitations: and ancient States, 426; on combat, 111–12, 121–22, 160, 208; and global consensus, 15; and jihadism, 451; and the Legalists, 436; and Plato, 432; and realists, 445; on weapons, 120–21, 160. See also *ius in bello*
literacy, 2–3, 291–92
Liverani, Mario, 11, 29, 106, 113, 121, 159, 179, 321–22
Livingston, Niall, 25–26
Longman, Tremper, 15n39
Loprieno, Antonio, 80, 87
Lorton, David, 125, 138
Lot, 329, 357
Luiselli, Maria, 146

Ma'at, 66–68, 73, 77–78, 86–93, 99–107, 110, 112–13, 117, 137, 145, 160–62, 420–21
Maccabees, 19–20, 439
maces, 47–48
Machtpolitik, 436
magic, 122–23, 131–32, 196, 236–37, 310, 348–51. See also cults; oracles; rituals
Mahbubani, Kishore, 453
Manapa-Tarhunta, 208–9
Manetho, 60–61, 63, 68
Marcy, William L., 117n129
marriage, 209, 227n150, 328, 360, 384n180, 418. See also women
Maşat Höyük, 256
massacre, 297, 315, 317, 326, 332, 334, 368, 374, 377–88, 405, 418, 426. See also brutality; *herem*
Matthews, Roger, 183
Mayes, A.D.H., 299, 372n119, 381n172
McDermott, Bridget, 103, 139n73
McMahan, Jeff, 448–50
Medinet Habu, 44, *115–16*, 144, 166
Mediterranean Sea, 74

Megiddo: battle of, 38, 52, 111–12, 135, 142, 152; city of, 116–17, 335n174; Megiddo Pass, 328; surrender of, 150
Menahem, 276
Mendenhall, George, 286, 293–94, 331
Menes (King), 62–63
Mengzi/Mencius, 436
Mentuhotep, 65
Mentuhotep II, 65
Mentuhotep III, 65
Menu, Bernadette, 86–87, 95
mercenaries, 41, 43, 75; and codes of conduct, 87–88; and enemies, 77; the ethnicity of, 126; and *hapiru*, 254; and the Hittites, 186. See also soldiers
mercy, 150–51, 161, 190, 208–9, 373, 382n163, 383–84, 390–91, 393. See also reciprocity
Merneptah, 70, 96–97, 106–7, 109, 135–36, 142, 274
Mešedi, 42
Mesha, king of Moab, 275, 322n125, 335, 350, 377, 384, 399
Mesha Stele, 275–76. See also Moabite Stone
Meshwesh, 77n55
Mesoamerica, 148
Micah (Book of), 339n192, 341
Micaiah, 310, 318–19
Middle Kingdom (Egypt): background on the, 65; foreigners of the, 125n31; imperialism of, 76; instruction literature of, 104; and integration, 78; and military history, 37, 40, 46; propaganda of the, 66, 131. See also *specific dynasties*
Middle Kingdom (Hittite), 170, 202, 254
Midian, 330–31, 380
milhemet hova, 295n1
milhemet mitzva, 295–96, 347–48
milhemet reshut, 295–96, 347
military intervention, 158, 192, 206, 452–53
military strategy: and pitched battles, 55; textual evidence of, 37–38
Mishnah, 20, 272, 295–96, 439
Moabite Stone, 275–76, 399. See also Mesha Stele
Montgomery, Bernard, 439–40
Morenz, Siegfried, 88, 97
Morkevičius, Valerie, 446n64
Moses: the authority of, 300; and brutality, 379–80, 386, 403; and conquest,

306–7; and the Covenant, 305, 308; the death of, 382; and free passage, 326–27; historical confirmation of, 60; and the historical narrative, 279, 283, 292–93, 300, 311; and magic, 348n20, 349, 350n32; and the Song of the Sea, 303n40, 381; and vengeance, 324, 330; and war, 357, 392; and Yahweh, 298, 300, 303, 305, 307, 311, 313, 324, 330, 386, 402, 406
Mount Sinai, 306–7
Müller-Wollerman, Renate, 148n115
mummification, 136
Muršili I, 172, 195–96, 248
Muršili II, 174–75, 191–92, 200–201, 207–10, 222, 225–27, 229, 234–35, 248–49, 252–53. *See also* 'Ten Year Annals of Muršili II'
mutilation of the dead. *See* brutality
Muwattalli II, 157, 188, 214–15, 220–22, 241
mythology, 25–26, 177–78, 191, 216, 223, 241–42, 292, 351, 357, 418

Narmer (king), 52, 63
Narmer Palette, 33, *34–36*, 63, 79, 95, 138, 144, 355
navy, 44
ne-arim, 44
Nebo, 275–76
Nebuchadnezzar I, 94, 284, 367–68, 401–2
Neferti, 92, 100–101
Nefertiti, 146
Nerik, 169n19
Neša, 180, 240
Neumann, Iver, 11
New Kingdom (Egypt): background on the, 69; capital cities of the, 70–71; changes within the, 70–71; and chariots, 44; and Greece, 437; imperialism of, 59, 69, 74–75, 97, 103, 106–9, 111; and integration, 78; king lists of the, 61–63; military history of, 37, 39–41, 69–70; navy of, 44; propaganda of, 68–70, 106; puppet kings of the, 150–51. *See also specific dynasties*
New Kingdom (Hittite), 170, 173, 188, 218, 223, 264–65
nfr (good), 88
Niditch, Susan, 25, 271, 291, 359, 378, 385n186

night attacks, 119, 170, 238–41, 243, 335n171, 357–59, 410, 416
Nile valley, 73–74
Nine Bows, 77, 97, 100–101, 122–24, 304
Niqmaddu II, 249–50
nomes, 63
non-combatants. *See* brutality; immunity; priests; women
Northern Israel, kingdom of. *See* Samaria
Noth, Martin, 281n49, 286
Nubia, 41, 64n22, 75–76, 124, 128
Numbers (Book of), 40, 284, 311, 312n83, 320n115, 330, 379–80, 391, 400
Nussbaum, Arthur, 433

the occult. *See* magic
O'Connor, David, 77
Oded (prophet), 391
Oded, Bustenay, 316
O'Driscoll, Cian, 15
Old Kingdom (Egypt): background on the, 62–64; and military history, 37, 40; Pyramid Texts, 95–96; splintering of the, 65; tombs of, 45. *See also specific dynasties*
Old Kingdom (Hittite), 38, 170, 173, 188, 190–91, 193, 202, 216–17, 223–25, 231, 247–48, 264–65
Old Testament, 14, 273, 277, 348, 439–40. *See also* Tanakh
Omri, 269n1, 275–76, 290
ontological security, 447
oracles, 236, 309–10, 318, 325, 332, 336, 339n191. *See also* magic; rituals
oral traditions, 2–3
Osama bin Laden, 451
Otter, Jean, 168

pacifism, 7n12
Paddatissu of Kizzuwatna, 260
Palermo Stone, 61
Panku, 185–86, 231
papyri, 79, 112
path dependence, 147
patriarchy, 141, 145, 188, 395. *See also* women
peasant revolution thesis, 286–87
Pepy I, 152–53
Pepy II, 64, 95
Philo of Alexandria, 397

Pinker, Steven, 10
pistols, 352n42
Pithana, 179–80
Piyama-radu, 261–63
Piye, 119–20
'Plague Prayers' (Muršili II), 175, 225–29, 233n169, 237
Plato, 26, 431–33
plunder, 113–17, 127–28, 138–39, 154–55, 204, 230–31, 246–52, 337, 397–400, 418–19
Poem of Miriam, 296
'Poetical Stela of Thutmose III,' 108–9
'Political Testament of Hattušili I,' 231–32
Politics (Aristotle), 26, 432–33
pragmatism: and ancient war, 5, 437, 443, 445–46; and diplomacy, 259; and Egypt, 77, 161–62; and enslavement, 151; and the Hittites, 177, 213, 221–24, 232, 238n21, 255, 264; and Israel, 347, 359, 365, 367, 405, 410, 416–17; and the Legalists, 436; and profit, 150; and restraint, 426; and theological absolutism, 390
prayer, 177, 187–91, 198–99, 207, 223–24, 247, 348–49. *See also* 'Plague Prayers' (Muršili II)
presumption (of war), 444–45
Priestly Code, 282–83
priests, 198, 262, 265, 402, 405, 406, 407
prisoners of war, 137–51, 160, 210, 225, 252–58, 265, 383, 388–91, 394–95, 410, 417–18, 425–26, 450–51. *See also* priests
Pritchard, James B., 141n81, 157n144, 275
'Proclamation of King Telipinu,' 173, 224–25, 230
profit. *See* plunder
property: and crimes against the king, 90, 185n2, 213; destruction of, 111, 127–28, 141, 151–53, 160, 199–200, 245, 330, 332, 368–69, 399, 410–11, 418, 423, 425; of the gods, 233; and immunity, 155; ownership of, 112–14, 137, 140, 189, 252; religious, 246–49, 266, 401–2, 404–5, 418–19; restitution of, 92, 198, 202–5, 211–12, 233, 246, 264, 329, 414; sexual, 396–97; and treaties, 250

'Prophecy of Neferti,' 66
prophetic texts, 92–93, 100–101, 125, 305, 332, 339–41
Prophets (Book of), 315
prospective memory, 147
Proverbs (Book of), 273n11
Psalms (Book of), 305n48, 341n195
Ptah, 99, 145
pyramids, 64

Qarqar (battle of), 40
Questions on Numbers (Augustine), 327–28
Quran, 272

Ra, 100
Ramses II: and battle, *39*, 41, *46*, 56, 106, 112, 121, 132–33, 241; the capital city of, 70; as the defender of Egypt, 105; and diplomacy, 258; and the dissemination of texts, 161n156; and divine intervention, 95–96, 98–99; and enslavement, 150; smiting scenes of, 144–45; treaties of, 69, 134, 156–59
Ramses III, 40, *48*, 106, 139, 144, 166
Ramses IV, 112, 139
Ramses XI, 71
Ramsey, Paul, 12, 448
rape, 262–63, 332, 337, 360, 364, 395–97, 438. *See also* brutality; women
Raubkrieg, 230, 246–47
ravaging, 152–54, 198, 243–45, 248
Rawls, John, 31
Re, 99, 110
realism, 445–47
rebellion, 110–12, 201, 211–16, 261, 333–35, 368, 376–77, 415
reciprocity, 92–93, 101–2, 331–32, 334, 339–41, 392–93, 441. *See also* brutality; *do ut des*; *lex talionis*; mercy
recta intentio, 22–23
Redford, Donald, 118, 277, 279n37
reform, 70, 404, 406
Rehoboam, 289, 334, 401
Reid, Daniel, 15n39
Rekhmire, 91
religious sanctuary, 154–55. *See also* immunity
Rengger, Nicholas, 452
Republic (Plato), 431–32

restraint: and ancient Egypt, 111, 120, 125, 131, 134, 153; and ancient Greece, 430–32; and ancient war, 411, 426, 453; and belligerent equals, 429; and capitulation, 368; and chaos, 421; and combat, 234, 251; and defeat, 149, 197; and defensive war, 435; and Hittite kings, 208–9, 215, 240, 245–46, 248; and massacre, 326, 419, 426; and modern war, 118, 440; and morality, 454; and non-combatants, 252–54; and pragmatism, 150, 162; and scholarship, 8, 371; and the Tanakh, 331, 347, 390–91, 393, 405, 416

revisionist just war theory (discussion of), 13, 448–54. *See also* just war thought (discussion of)

rituals, 235–37, 255–56, 258, 281–82, 308–12, 348–50, 406. *See also* cults; magic; oracles

Rodin, David, 448, 449n72

Rome, 11, 18–19, 148, 177, 327n137, 430, 433–35, 437

Rosenne, Shabtai, 30

Rosetta Stone, 79

Roth, Martha, 189–90

Royal Irish Regiment, 440

rule of law, 453

sacred spaces, 154–55, 199, 245, 247–49, 400–405, 419

Saint Augustine of Hippo. *See* Augustine of Hippo (saint)

Saint Jerome. *See* Jerome (saint)

Saite Dynasty, 75

Samaria, *276*; army size of, 40, 51; battles of, 275–76, 314, 328; the creation of, 274, 284; the fall of, 269, 277, 280, 284, 287, 290, 315; the geopolitical history of, 290; as a point of comparison, 271; in source material, 276–77, 280; and usurpation, 334–35; as a vassal state, 328–29; weaponry of, 50

Samson, 257, 332n156, 349, 389, 403

Samuel: and the Ark, 308n60, 315; background on, 278n31; and brutality, 393–94, 416; and David, 400, 416; and Goliath, 351n36, 352n40, 354n49; and *herem*, 379; the historical narrative of, 281; and holy war, 297; and Ish-bosheth, 353n45; and magic, 349; and oracles, 325; and rebellion, 333; and Saul, 302, 303n37, 310, 331, 335, 354n49, 357n55, 374n131, 399; and the tribes of Israel, 44, 288, 299–300; and Yahweh, 326, 335

Šapinuwa, 257

Sargon II, 376–77

Sargon of Akkad, 233, 243–44, 317

Saul: armies of, 44; and David, 284, 289, 331, 335, 351n38, 353–54, 361–62, 377–78, 394, 406–7; the death of, 389; and impalement, 374; and mercy, 393; and spoils of war, 399–400; and a united monarchy, 275, 284, 288, 299, 302; and war, 297, 302, 331, 332n155, 353, 357n55, 377; and Yahweh, 303, 310, 331, 335, 399

Schneider, Joseph, 6

scholarship: biblical, 27, 277–83, 286, 295–96, 316, 348, 371n116, 379, 410; classical, 448; and the comparative method, 18–25; Greek, 430–31; Hebrew, 301; and historians, 37, 75, 79, 172; and the Hittites, 168–69, 171; and international relations, 29–30; and Israel, 15, 269n1, 270–71, 274, 292, 343; and the New Kingdom (Egypt), 69; and pharaohs, 94–95; revisionist, 448–50; sources for, 79–81, 83–84; and temporality, 24; and this book, 3–6; and war, 6–16, 102, 442. *See also* archaeology; Egyptology

Schoske, Sylvia, 144

Schulman, Alan, 136, 145, 147

Sea Peoples, 71, 157, 166–67, 288

Second Book of Kings, 281, 314, 344, 367, 372, 390, 404, 407n290. *See also* Kings (Book of)

Second Cataract (of the Nile river), 75, 104

Second Intermediate Period, 78, 90, 105, 125n31

Second Temple Period, 280, 284

Sed festival, 97

self-aggrandisement, 230–33, 264–65, 336–38

self-defence, 101–10, 198–205, 211, 217, 264, 302, 317–29, 409, 414–15, 420, 433–34

self-reflection, 224–30, 264, 429

Senakhte, 64

Senusret I, 96, 111
Senusret III, 65–66, 104, 131–32
Seth, 99–100, 158n146
Seti I, *50*, 109–10, *126*, *152*
Setnakht, 112
Seton, D. R., 142
set-piece battles, 119–20
Shalmaneser I, 258
Shalmaneser III, 40, *276*, *388*
Shalmaneser V, 284
Sharri-Kushuh, 249–50
Shattiwaza, 192
Shaw, Ian, 37, 51n52
Sheba, 288n70
Sherden, 41, 139
Sheshonq I, 72, 401
Shishak, 401
Shue, Henry, 450
siege warfare, 52–53, 55, 113, 253, 344, 365–68
Sihon, 327–28, 379
Sima Fa, 436
Simeon, 360–61, 364
sin, 184, 190–91, 193, 196, 225–29, 237, 307, 313–15, 408
Singer, Itamar, 165n3, 190–91, 221n131, 223, 229n154
Sisera, 363–64, 373, 417. *See also* assassination
Six Cataracts of the Nile River, 73
Sixth Dynasty, 88
skr-nh, 138–39
slavery. *See* enslavement
Smend, Rudolf, 298, 308n60
Smith-Christopher, Daniel, 385
smiting scenes, 142, *143*, 144–49, 162
Socrates, 431–32
Sodom, 273n11
soldiers, 81, 83–84, 87–88, 115–16, 246, 419–20, 442. *See also* mercenaries
Solomon, 51, 269n1, 277, 284, 288–90, 328, 371n116, 401, 404
Solomon, Norman, 295
'Song of David,' 304
'Song of Deborah,' 280, 296–97, 363
'Song of Hannah,' 304
'The Song of Kumarbi,' 216
'Song of Moses,' 381
'Song of the god LAMMA,' 223
'The Song of the Sea,' 303

Spalinger, Anthony, 38–39, 87, 112, 142n87
spearmen, 46–47, *49*
Stele of the Vultures, 33, *36*, 94
Stern, Philip, 367n104
Strategems of the Warring States, 436
Strauss, Leo, 11
Sumerian, 89, 104n79, 174n45, 223n140
Sunashshura of Kizzuwatna, 218–19, 250, 258
the supernatural. *See* magic
Šuppiluliuma I: and brutality, 258; and diplomacy, 192–93; and military expansion, 174, 201, 215; and military tactics, 203, 238, 240, 248, 250; and plunder, 204, 250; and prisoners of war, 253; and ravaging, 244; and self-defence, 200; the sins of, 226–28, 230; and treaties, 214, 220, 227, 230; and vengeance, 207–10, 225, 240; and war challenges, 235. *See also* 'Deeds of Šuppiluliuma I'
Šuppiluliuma II, 167

Tabernacle, 406
'Tale of Sinuhe,' 81, 114, 120–21, 129, 136, 160, 292–93, 352, 416
'Tale of the Eloquent Peasant,' 81, 92
Talmud, 20, 272, 295–96, 439
Tanakh, 272; and the Amalekite, 310–11; and assassination, 360–64; authors of the, 344; background on the, 269–72, 278, 291; and brutality, 135, 377–89, 391; and challenges to battle, 346–48; and the Christian Bible, 272; and Christian warfare, 439; and the conquest narrative, 285–87, 297, 307–8, 316, 423; and declarations of war, 346–48; and defending people, 324; and destroying religious property, 402–5, 419; and diplomatic immunity, 407–8, 411, 417; and Egypt, 437; as a historical source, 277, 279–85, 288; the influence of the, 438–39; and instructions on war, 344–47, 364–65, 367; internal narrative chronology of the, 278–85, 300, 411; and Israelite kings, 301; and Israelite warfare, 343; and the just war tradition, 272–74, 291, 315–16, 408–11; and killing priests, 405–7; and law, 175, 296; literary processes of the,

280–83; on magic, 350–51; and the Masoretic text, 278; and mercy, 391; and navies, 44; and non-combatants, 385; and political authority, 301–3, 307, 408–9; and property, 318–19; and rituals, 236n11; and scholarship, 296; and self-defence, 325; and spoils of war, 398; and the Talmud, 295; and weaponry, 351; and women, 124n29; and Yahweh, 187n11, 300–301, 303–4, 306–14, 317, 323, 329, 333, 342–43, 405, 408, 413, 415, 421–23. *See also* Israel; Yahweh; *specific books of the Tanakh*
Tapikka, 236, 256
Tarhuntašša, *176*, 182, 186
Tawananna, 182, 186
Tel Dan, 275, 288
Telipinu, 173, 191
Tell el-Amarna, 168
Temple of Horus, 33
Temple of Medinet Habu, 71
'Ten Year Annals of Muršili II,' 174, 231, 235n1
Teššub, 187–92, 195, 223, 225, 424
'Testament' (of Hattušili I), 172–73
Texier, Charles, 168
Theban Temple of Amun-Re, 37
'The Instructions of Any,' 94n39
Théodoridès, Aristide, 158n146
Third Intermediate Period, 71
Thirteenth Dynasty, 67
Thistlewaite, Susan Brooks, 396–97
Thucydides, 431
Thutmose I, 70, 111, 128
Thutmose III: the annals of, 107, *108*, 109, 111–12, 114; and battle, 38, 52, 98, 116, 121, 129, 152, 278; booty lists of, 135; as the defender of Egypt, 105; and divine intervention, 97–98; instructions of, 91; and mercy, 109, 150; smiting scenes of, *126*
Thutmose IV, 105
Tiglath-Pileser III, 276, 290
Tikulti-Ninurta, 203
Tilly, Charles, 28
Tombos Stele, 128
Torah, 272, 279, 303, 366
torture, 121, *122*, 137, 256, 452. *See also* brutality

treaties: *ade*, 156; and diplomacy, 260–62; and divine authority, 187; Egyptian-Hittite, 69, 81, *82–83*, 156–59, 162, 171, 221, 228–29; Hatti-Kizzuwatna, 256; Hatti-Mitanni, 188, 206, 220; Hatti-Wilusa, 220–21; and the Hittites, 43, 175, *176*, 182, 189–93, 202, 215–22; and plunder, 250, 254; and pragmatism, 222; and prisoners of war, 258; and rebellion, 258; and refugees, 254; *riksu*, 156–59; standardised rules for, 85; and the Tanakh, 289; and vassal states, 189, 191–93, 201, 205, 211–15, 218–22, 248, 258, 293, 390, 415; violations of, 205–7, 212–15, 227, 230, 425; and war declarations, 345
trees (the destruction of), 124, 129, 151–53, 243n39, 368–73, 416
Tudhaliya I, 43, 170, 213, 241n32
Tudhaliya II, 205–6, 218–19, 250, 258, 260
Tudhaliya III, 171, 183, 199
Tudhaliya IV, *176*, 193, *194*, 196–97, 203, 215, 222–23, 232, 235, 263–64
Tudhaliya the Younger, 226–27
Tukulti-Ninurta I, 232
Tuniya of Tikunani, 249
Turin Papyrus, 61, 63, 68
Tushratta, 203
Tutankhamun, 123, 209–10
Twelfth Dynasty, 65, 67
Twenty-Fifth Dynasty, 76

Uhha-ziti, 208
Uni/Weni, 80
unjust war. *See* war guilt
Uraeus, 98n58
Urhi-Teshub, 216–17

Valley of the Kings, 70
Vanderpol, Alfred, 12
van Wees, Hans, 384, 430–31
vassal states. *See* self-defence; treaties; *specific vassal states*
Vattel, Emer de, 428
vengeance, 4, 204–13, 225, 228, 304–5, 310n78, 318, 321n118, 324, 330–32, 393–96, 414–15. See also *herem*
Veyne, Paul, 26
viziers, 65
Voegelin, Eric, 11

von Rad, Gerhard, 282, 296–99, 308, 337n182, 378
Vulgate Old Testament, 14, 365n9, 372n121

Walker, Robert, 14n37
Waltz, Kenneth N., 446
Walzer, Michael, 2, 13, 387, 448, 452
war (definitions of), 6–7. *See also* just war thought (discussion of)
war guilt, 111, 207, 224–30, 321–22, 336–37, 434
War of the Lelantine Plain (Strabo), 120n8
Warring States period, 16
weaponry: history of, 44–51; Hittite, 42–43, 238; and Israel, 44, 351, 410; ranged, 351–52, 416; and status, 351–52. *See also specific weapons*
Weber, Max, 387
webs of significance, 3
Wellhausen, Julius, 270, 280
Wells, Bruce, 177
Weni, 41, 152–53
Wigen, Einar, 11
Williams, Bernard, 442
Winckler, Hugo, 171n26
Wolff, Christian, 428
women, 70, 124n29, 140–42, 146, 160, 182, 255, 363, 380–87, 394–98, 418. *See also* Arinna; marriage; patriarchy; rape; Tawananna
'The Words of Neferti,' 100–101
Wright, Jacob, 333
Wright, Quincy, 23, 454n90
Wright, William, 168
Writings of the Ancient World (Society of Biblical Literature), 80

xenophobia, 78, 86, 102–4, 123–26, 181, 433
Xenophon, 113–14
Xsy, 125

Yadin, Yigael, 51
Yahweh: and assassination, 364; and Babylon, 332; and the Covenant, 283, 293–94, 297, 300–301, 305–6, 310, 313–15, 323–24, 329, 332, 342, 397, 402, 404, 409, 422–23; the creation of, 284, 292; as a cultic shrine, 286; and divine intervention, 309–12, 320, 322–26, 328, 329n145, 343, 422; as impartial, 341; and magic, 349–50, 410; and mercy, 390–91; and monotheism, 291, 402, 405, 423; as a physical manifestation, 309, 409; and punishment, 272–73, 338–39, 341–42, 383–84, 387, 393, 399, 408, 415, 423; and rebellion, 334–36; references to, 276; and Saul, 331; and spoils of war, 398–99; as a storm god, 187n11; as a term, 271; and war, 270, 297–99, 303–12, 320, 322–26, 328, 337–40, 342, 357–59, 373, 378–82, 409, 422; and the Yahwist, 281. *See also* divine authority; *herem*; Israel; Tanakh
Yahwism, 439
Yazilikaya, *178–79*, 181–82, 193, *194*
Younger, Lawson, 87, 102, 172n35, 293n90

Zannanza, 209–10, 225, 227
Zealots, 439
Zedekiah, 257, 368
Zehfuss, Maja, 450
Zubaba, 238n20

A NOTE ON THE TYPE

THIS BOOK has been composed in Miller, a Scotch Roman typeface designed by Matthew Carter and first released by Font Bureau in 1997. It resembles Monticello, the typeface developed for The Papers of Thomas Jefferson in the 1940s by C. H. Griffith and P. J. Conkwright and reinterpreted in digital form by Carter in 2003.

Pleasant Jefferson ("P. J.") Conkwright (1905–1986) was Typographer at Princeton University Press from 1939 to 1970. He was an acclaimed book designer and AIGA Medalist.

The ornament used throughout this book was designed by Pierre Simon Fournier (1712–1768) and was a favorite of Conkwright's, used in his design of the *Princeton University Library Chronicle*.

GPSR Authorized Representative: Easy Access System Europe - Mustamäe tee
50, 10621 Tallinn, Estonia, gpsr.requests@easproject.com